W9-AFN-228

MUSIC OF THE WHOLE EARTH

Long *bhenr*/trumpets, supported by bamboo poles, are played by
Oraon musicians to accompany dancing and singing. Bihar, India.

DAVID RECK

Photographs Selected by Carol Reck

MUSIC OF THE WHOLE EARTH

Charles Scribner's Sons · New York

Library of Congress Cataloging in Publication Data

Reck, David.
     Music of the whole earth.

     Includes bibliographies and index.
     1. Music—Analysis, appreciation. I. Title
MT6.R273   780   76-12493
ISBN 0-684-14631-2
ISBN 0-684-14633-9 pbk.

PHOTOGRAPH CREDITS

While careful attention has been paid to acknowledging each photograph properly, if any source has been inadvertently omitted, it will be included upon notification in any future editions.

	Page
Courtesy Africana Museum	45 (top), 344
Australian Information Service	3 (bottom), 52 (top)
Gregory Bateson, courtesy Dr. Margaret Mead	392
Barbara Benary	160 (top)
Paul F. Berliner	248
Cinerama Releasing	322
CNT/Magnin, courtesy National Council of Tourism in Lebanon	60 (top), 126
Courtesy collection Paul F. Berliner	99 (bottom)
Consultate General of Japan, New York	436
Edward S. Curtis	3 (top)
Courtesy Davison Art Center, Wesleyan University, Middletown, Connecticut	9 (left), 106 (top), 140 (top), 376–77
Herbert A. Feuerlicht	29 (top), 120 (bottom), 163, 267, 486
Courtesy Field Museum of Natural History	263
David Freund	160 (bottom)
Charlotte J. Frisbie, June 1963	505, 509
Courtesy Joseph Green, writer, director, producer of *Yiddle with His Fiddle*	338

Heyn, courtesy Library of Congress	xiii (top right)
Japan Air Lines	296
Japan National Tourist Organization	29 (bottom), 113 (top), 431 (top and bottom)
James Kimball	23, 120 (top), 217, 231, 498
Percival R. Kirby, courtesy Africana Museum	130 (left)
Jean-Jacques LeBlanc	xii (top left), 41 (top left)
Russell Lee, courtesy Library of Congress	238, 365
Library of Congress	31 (bottom), 48 (top), 52 (bottom), 55 (top), 90 (bottom), 191, 201, 348, 399
Alan Lomax, courtesy Library of Congress	354
Courtesy instruments collection, David P. McAllester, photos by Carol Reck	58 (bottom), 60 (bottom), 67 (left), 82 (right), 99 (top), 106 (bottom), 113 (bottom), 127 (left), 138 (bottom), 260
Susan McAllester	37 (top), 407
Dr. Robert MacLennan, formerly Department of Public Health, Papua, New Guinea	12, 86, 96, 181, 303
Colin McPhee	367 and 390, bottom (reprinted from Colin McPhee, *Music in Bali,* © Yale University Press, 1966, by permission), 390 (top, courtesy Dr. Margaret Mead)
Metropolitan Museum of Art	9 (right, Fletcher Fund, 1956), 48 (bottom, Whittelsey Fund, 1949), 73, top, and 82, left (Crosby Brown Collection of Musical Instruments, 1889), 196 (Fletcher Fund, 1917), 275 (Harris Brisbane Dick Fund, 1939)
New Mexico Department of Development	6 (bottom), 404
Bill Pearson	291, 329
Performing Arts Program of the Asia Society	31 (top), 208, 313, 422
Carol S. Reck	ii–iii, xii (top right and bottom), xiii (bottom), 6 (top), 9 (left), 18 (top), 43, 55 (bottom), 58 (top and bottom), 73 (bottom), 90 (top), 99 (bottom), 101 (top), 106 (top), 122 (top), 127 (right), 138 (top), 140 (left), 166, 170, 172, 214, 220, 225, 236, 241, 251, 253, 269, 280, 297, 309, 319, 333, 335, 376–77, 383, 394, 410, 463, 470, 494, 519, 525
David B. Reck	148, 455
Gary M. Rees	326
Research Group Triangle	264, 483 (top and bottom)
Collection Arnold and Barbara Rubin	184
Andrea Samuelson	175
South African Information Service	xiii (top left), 122 (bottom), 359
UNICEF/Massa Diabate	18 (bottom)
United Nations	20 (top and bottom), 37 (botton), 41 (top right and bottom), 101 (bottom), 130 (right), 140 (right), 179, 293
Frances Valesco	345
Courtesy Wesleyan University Music Department, Middletown, Connecticut	73 (bottom), 138 (top)

FRONT COVER, LEFT TO RIGHT

Top row

Kissar/lyre: Metropolitan Museum of Art, Crosby Brown Collection of Musical Instruments, 1889

Fiddler, singer, bagpiper: James Kimball
Masked dancers: Japan National Tourist Organization
Tar/lute player: Performing Arts Program of the Asia Society

Second row
Boy playing musical bow: Courtesy Africana Museum
Tina Turner: Cinerama Releasing
Musicians, Egyptian tomb painting: Library of Congress

Third row
Bluegrass band: Bill Pearson
Polish band: James Kimball
Kissar/lyre player: Percival R. Kirby, courtesy Africana Museum

Bottom row
Man playing horn trumpet: South African Information Service
Street musicians: United Nations
Indian dancers: Carol S. Reck

BACK COVER, LEFT TO RIGHT

Top row
Dervishes: Herbert A. Feuerlicht
Musician on Greek vase: Metropolitan Museum of Art, Fletcher Fund, 1956
Sankyoku ensemble: Carol S. Reck

Second row
Balinese dance-drama scene: Performing Arts Program of the Asia Society
Dragon head on *veena*: Carol S. Reck
Tuba: Courtesy instruments collection, Wayne Forrest, photo by Carol S. Reck

Center
Mouth bow player: Dr. Robert MacLennan, formerly Department of Public Health, Papua, New Guinea
Shaman with hoop drum: Library of Congress

Third row
Shakuhachi/flute player: Carol S. Reck
Woodcut of musicians: Metropolitan Museum of Art, Harris Brisbane Dick Fund, 1888
Brass band: United Nations
Musician with *daiko*/drum: Courtesy Davison Art Center, Wesleyan University, Middletown, Connecticut, photo
　　　by Carol S. Reck

Bottom row
Mance Lipscomb: Bill Pearson
Shadow puppet: Carol S. Reck
Peasant wedding: Herbert A. Feuerlicht

CONTENTS

PREFACE

This book is a description of a journey I have taken—with my ears and eyes and heart and brain—through an exquisitely beautiful and relatively unexplored country: the musical landscape of the whole earth. It is a journey that I began many years ago, one that is still in progress and will continue for the rest of my life. It is a journey that has also been taken by others, but by far too few of us, comfortable as we tend to be under our respective cultural blankets. In one sense, what I have put into words is a kind of journal, a notebook, containing my own perceptions as a performing musician (in Indian music), a composer (in Western music), and a scholar (in ethnomusicology—the bridge between the two). I would hope that in sharing my own ideas and what I have learned from other human beings, from observations of our planet (from stars, trees, grass, mountains, seas, animals, clouds), and from books (for we all owe what we are to a kind of mystical coming together of others and other things into our unique selves), other persons will be motivated to make their own explorations of world music, or at least a part of it. The perceptions and vision—perhaps vastly different—of each of us journeyers would then create a kind of field of flowers of understanding over and around the magically invisible yet real, intangibly tangible (felt) *terra firma* of the earth's music.

On another level this book is meant to be a kind of "Whole Earth Catalog of World Music," full of bits and pieces (and large chunks) of information: about instruments, myths, meanings, concepts, uses, life- and music-ways, thought patterns, bread-and-butter methods of working, sound carpentry (that

is, how music is put together), anecdotes, world concepts of musical architecture, rhythm, melody, harmony, polyphony, as well as ensembles, orchestras, maps, sources, and directions (for such things as building home-grown musical instruments). Special sections interrupt the flow of the text to describe music of a particular area or kind, or to provide a synopsis of what I consider to be a particularly beautiful book or article. In browsing through this information—culled from the remarkable knowledge of the people listed in the bibliographies—the reader should do well to remember that man's (and woman's) thinking is continually in process: ideas and perceptions change, sometimes with lightninglike quickness. To give only one example, scholars-musicians such as Sumarsam and his students are beginning to approach Javanese *gamelan* music in a fresh and exciting new way, one that directly challenges many of the older academic systems and viewpoints about the *gamelan* presented in these pages. We should thus remain undogmatic and remember that our "facts" and "information" are really only temporary stopping points in a field of change, and that music—living, sounding, feeling *music* (not words)—is at the center.

In the building of this book, or the watching of it grow, I have had to make many difficult decisions. A true book on *Music of the Whole Earth* would consist of thousands of volumes filling a huge library; one on the music of only a single area could be of encyclopedic proportions. Therefore, I have had to pick and to choose, to emphasize certain cultures or musics, and to omit or pass over others. These choices, of course, are personal and in no way reflect the worth or quality of a given musical culture. It should be noted also that those musics which have been described in some detail in the text are far more complex and subtle and rich than the few pages I have allotted to them would indicate. To get a fuller picture of each music the reader should go to the works of scholars who are specialists in these areas and, if possible, to the musicians themselves (preferably in their own countries). I have also had to make bold generalizations, almost all of which might be tempered with an endless list of exceptions. In talking about music in general, on the average, in the whole, we are often forced to pass over music in the small, the rich and varied tapestry of musics that underlies our concepts. There is not, for example, really *a* musical culture of sub-Saharan Africa (there are hundreds, perhaps thousands), any more than there is *a* musical culture of Europe or Asia or India or the United States, yet I am constantly forced for the sake of brevity to use phrases like "in Africa," "in the Americas," or "in the Far East." Perhaps the most difficult decision was on spelling. What does one do with words from hundreds of languages spelled and misspelled differently in dozens of sources and often embroidered with a maze of diacritical marks? My solution was a rather pragmatic one. For the sake of readability I have decided to present each word in one of its possible spellings and to omit most of the diacritical markings. Thus again the reader is cautioned to remain undogmatic: what he finds on these pages may elsewhere be spelled differently, and what appears in print in the English alphabet may have little or no relationship to what is spoken (that is, its sound), say, in Tibetan or Voltaic.

A major problem in any book on non-Western music is what to do about musical examples. How can one reduce a multitude of foreign musical systems with subtle intonations and inflections, slides and ornaments, or intricate rhythms into a European notation that is really wedded to only *one* of the world's traditions and is (now, in the twentieth century) proving increasingly inadequate even for music within our own culture? And what about the reader who does not read music, or who lacks the time or desire to sit down at a piano and hack out

the examples note by note? To solve this dilemma, I have put musical concepts and examples into a kind of graphic notation that varies from the precise to the imprecise, from notes and pitches and rhythms per se to drawings and graphic representations, as the occasion seemed to demand. I hope that these notational devices will represent to the mind's eye of the reader (at a glance, immediately) the concepts and techniques written about in the accompanying text. The musician or music student who wishes to go into matters further may sit down and "read" those examples with accompanying staves, or refer to the books listed in the bibliographies, almost all of which have examples in conventional European notation.

A note concerning the photograph captions: Although a great deal of effort has been made to give local names of instruments and data as to where and by whom they are used, in some cases this has not been possible. In these instances, I have cited commonly used English designations for the instruments and indicated the closest general geographical and/or ethnic sources.

For their help, encouragement, friendship, and teaching I would like to thank in particular three extraordinary ethnomusicologists: David McAllester, Mark Slobin, and Gen'ichi Tsuge. Much of what has found its way into this volume—in information, attitudes, and (most of all) a sense of awe at the beauty and wonders of world music—has come from them. Much has also been indirectly contributed by my teachers in India—notably Veena Thirugokarnam Ramachandra Iyer and B. Rajam Iyer—and by some of the very special master musicians who have come together under one roof at Wesleyan University in Connecticut: A. Adzenyah, Sumarsam, R. Raghavan, Namino Torii, and Douglas Mitchell. My special thanks also go to dozens of other indirect contributors to this book, friends and colleagues, who have helped me in many areas: Ralph Samuelson (Japan), James Kimball (fiddling and banjo, Appalachia and eastern Europe), Alvin Lucier and Tom Johnson (modern and electronic music), Wayne Forrest and Sam Quigley (Java), Charlotte Frisbie (Native American), Paul Berliner (Africa), Shitalakshmi Prawirohardjo (Java), Gordon Spearritt (New Guinea), and Barbara Benary (India).

I would also like to express my appreciation to others who have helped and encouraged me in my musical journey (often appearing at the right moment like angelic guides): Peter Phillips, Robert Brown, Paul Pisk, Richard Winslow, and Oliver Daniel. I thank also my brother, anthropologist Gregory Reck, for many helpful suggestions; Patricia Cristol, my editor; and pupils over the years at the New School for Social Research, at Wesleyan University, at the National Humanities Faculty summer workshop in Moraga, California, and at Amherst College for teaching me more than I would care to admit. Appreciation is due to my respected colleagues at Amherst College, who have watched this project grow and offered encouragement and helpful suggestions and from whom I have also learned much. Finally—though the list is far from complete—recognition is due to the Rockefeller Foundation and the Guggenheim Foundation whose generous support allowed me almost four years of study in India, and to my talented and remarkable wife, Carol S. Reck, whose research and skills as a photographer and photo editor have enhanced the beauty of this volume as words could not.

David Reck

For their help in obtaining photographs, we extend warm thanks to the following: Dr. K. T. Wu, Robert Dunn, and Jerry Kearns of the Library of Congress; Anthony Hughes and Nancy McKeon of *Africa Report*; Tom Prendergast of the United Nations; Russell Sanjec of Broadcast Music, Inc.; Wyman Parker and Richard S. Field of Wesleyan University; Pat Murai of Japan Air Lines; Mrs. Nan Parnell, Johannesburg; Mrs. L. J. de Wet of the Africana Museum; the South African Information Service; Dr. Margaret Mead and Shari Segel of the Institute for Intercultural Studies, Inc.; New Mexico Department of Development; Field Museum of Natural History; Australian Information Service; National Council of Tourism of Lebanon; Consulate General of Japan; Japan National Tourist Organization; and Yale University Press.

For supplying photographs and background material we thank Mrs. Beate Gordon, Director, Performing Arts Program of the Asia Society, which sponsored the tours of P'ansori (1972), Tōpèng Dance Theater of Bali and Music of Iran ensemble (1973). For material on Macedonian music, dance, weddings, and customs, thanks are due to Herbert A. Feuerlicht and Roberta Strauss Feuerlicht. Dr. Gordon Spearritt and Dr. Robert MacLennan generously shared their research and photographs on music and customs in New Guinea.

For their generosity in providing photographs we gratefully acknowledge Dr. Charlotte Frisbie, David Freund, Bill Pearson, Jean-Jacques LeBlanc, Barbara Benary, James Kimball, Gary M. Rees, Frances Valesco, Andrea Samuelson, and Research Group Triangle.

For their encouragement and sharing of photographs, musical instrument collection, and background materials, we also thank David and Susan McAllester. Ann Novotny and Mary O'Grady gave valuable advice and guidance. Others whose assistance is greatly appreciated are Alvin Lucier, Ralph Samuelson, Dr. Gen'ichi Tsuge, Namino Torii, Abraham Adzenyah, Wayne Forrest, Arnold and Barbara Rubin, Paul Berliner, and Harvey Horowitz.

Carol S. Reck

Opposite: (*Top left*) Japanese musician, Tokyo.

(*Top right*) Banjara woman, Maharashtra, India.

(*Bottom*) Rattan craftsman, Madras.

This page: (*Above left*) Ndebele woman, southern Africa.

(*Above right*) Native American, Sioux tribe (Broken Arm).

(*Left*) Classical dancer, Java (Martati).

"One fire burns in many forms."
Rig-Veda (India, ca. 3000–2000 B.C.)

PART ONE:

Beginnings/Patterns

1

THE UNIVERSAL HOROSCOPE

The earth is full. Of peoples of all shapes and sizes, of a variety of skin colors, of different ideas and attitudes and life-styles, who live in different geographies, on islands, mountains, and plains, in varying climates, surrounded by vegetation of every imaginable sort. Whether we are aware of them or not, our own lives are full of influences from these people. The coffee we drink was first brought to London by a Persian merchant in 1650. The sugar we put in it is a gift from the people of south India dating back at least twenty-five hundred years to the days when heavy seagoing traffic plied the Arabian Sea. (Our word for sugar comes from *sarkkarai*, a word in Tamil, the principal south Indian language.) According to tradition, the Chinese invented paper around 200 A.D., and to the Chinese we also owe explosives, silk, the idea of the clock, the compass (it was used in divining), the ancestor of reed organ pipes, and a host of other major inventions and discoveries. Our numbers and mathematics come from the Arabic cultures of the Middle East; chess came to us from India; many of our medicines—quinine, for example—were discovered by so-called primitive jungle peoples with their encyclopedic knowledge of the plants in their environment. Without the Eskimo we would be cold indeed in the winter, for they have given us mittens and the parka; without the American Indians our dinner tables would be almost empty, lacking squash, corn, tomatoes, beans, peanuts, potatoes, and pumpkins—and without tobacco we would be devoid of our after-dinner smoke.

The earth is also full of a variety of musics, musics that can be as different as men are from men, or societies from societies, or the frozen ice lands of the north from the steaming tropical jungles, yet that are somehow tied together by that wonderful common denominator, the human being. Men and women everywhere have eyes, noses, ears, voices, and hands, inventive and inquisitive brains, and (perhaps most important) a capacity for feeling. For art, and music is an art, concerns a depth of expression which somehow reaches beneath the surface of our being and touches on mysteries that seem to us very, very important, one might even say essential, to the core of what we are; and all the scientific inquiry and philosophizing of recent and distant centuries (even the superrationalism of our computers) has not been able to put "that," the feeling, its mysteries and importance, into words or equations.

It is perhaps a little deflating to think that we, in our comfortable homes filled with gadgets and books, with the farthest corners of the globe just a plane flight away, share a capacity for art,

1

for creation, imagination, and expression, no greater (or less) than that of a near-naked tribal whose chief tools and possessions may be stone axes and digging sticks. There are great poets in languages we have never heard about. Eighteen hundred years ago Allur Nanmullaiyar wrote in the Tamil language:

> If one can tell morning
> From noon from listless evening,
> Townslept night from dawn, then one's love
> Is a lie.

An anonymous poet sang in the Navaho language of the American Southwest:

> With beauty may I walk.
> With beauty before me, may I walk.
> With beauty behind me, may I walk.
> With beauty above me, may I walk.
> With beauty below me, may I walk.
> With beauty all around me, may I walk.
> In old age, wandering on a trail of beauty, lively, may I walk.
> In old age, wandering on a trail of beauty, living again, may I walk.
> It is finished in beauty.
> It is finished in beauty.

An Australian aborigine sang in the Djanggawul dialect:

> Lightning flashes through the clouds,
> The flash of the Lightning Snake!
> In a blinding flash lights up the palm's foliage,
> Glistening on the wet palms,
> Glistening on the shining leaves.

And the great twelfth-century mystic and poet Milarepa wrote in the Tibetan language:

> Accustomed long to meditating
> On the whispered chosen Truths,
> I have forgotten all that is said
> In written and printed books.
>
> Accustomed long to know
> The meaning of the wordless,
> I have forgot the way to trace
> The source of words and the roots of verbs.
>
> Accustomed long to the application
> Of each new experience to my own growth,
> I have forgot
> All creeds and dogmas.

Great composers and musicians, also, have created in musical idioms that are stranger to us, now, than the far side of the moon. But while the expressive core remains (and as human beings on this earth we all share it), an elaborate system of cultural conditioning forms our expressive out-bursts of poetry, art, and music into different molds. We all have tongues and vocal cords, and we say (more or less) the same things, but we speak in different languages. Almost from the moment

(*Above*) Navaho riders in Cañon de Chelly, Arizona.

(*Left*) Aborigine musician, Australia.

of birth, in the attitudes of our parents, in our immediate environment, in the sounds our ears hear, the shaping and conditioning process begins. And what we call music—the way we make it, the way we listen to it, what we expect of it—is shaped, too: by our relationships, attitudes, value systems, religions, languages, ways of counting and categorizing, even philosophical abstractions, as well as by our inheritance of particular musical languages (scales, instruments, forms, etc.).

Just as people live in houses built in different shapes and of varying materials—mud or straw or brick or snow—so people live in different musical worlds. And just as we, who live for the most part in squares and box-rooms, might feel uncomfortable in a conical tepee or a circular hut, so we may also at first feel disoriented hearing the music of a Navaho ceremonial, or of a New Guinean men's house, or of a Javanese court *gamelan*. Yet we as men and women (and man is an amazingly adaptable animal) can and do adjust to different environments, perhaps never fully erasing from our memories the comforts and familiarity of our philosophical or material "home," but nevertheless moving into the unfamiliar, the unexplored. This restlessness, this impulse for the unexpected, the new, a kind of endless search for new sources of energy and ornamentation of our lives, is counterbalanced by a strong instinct for the familiar, the safe, the comfortable. We tend to accept the way we think and are, the ways of our society (the one we grew up in), and our art and music as "normal." But across the seas, in mountain valleys, even in our own backyards, are different groups of people with their own ideas, just as fixed as ours, about what is "normal." Each group believes its attitudes, aspirations, and music to be the natural state of affairs in the world, and for each group it is.

We are going to try to bridge the gap between what for us is the normal way music is, between our Western/European/American musical culture and that of other peoples. In some instances the leap is a very easy one. Instruments and musical ideas have traveled around the world since before the very beginnings of recorded history, large-scale migrations have occurred, individuals like Marco Polo have traveled on fabulous voyages, musical influences and counterinfluences have made world music into a complex spiderweb of relationships. But here and there pockets remain, points relatively untouched by outside influence. We can more easily enjoy African drumming, for example, because of its ties to our popular music and jazz (by way of the Caribbean and Latin America) than the music of the Sioux Indians of the northern Great Plains, which, although geographically in our own country, has remained isolated from the mainstream of our musical experience. But the situation is a complex one. Even in the case of close political or economic ties between nations or peoples, culture, especially musical culture, can be resistant to genuine understanding. We can "understand," accept, a Japanese television set almost without a second thought, but to understand and enjoy a concert of traditional Japanese music requires a great deal of effort on our part.

Bridges to other musical cultures, though, are facilitated by some very basic characteristics of our own civilization, reflected in our jazz, rock, and avant-garde music—namely, our urge to innovate, to explore creatively new worlds of sound and experience. Because ours is a tradition of change, we are amenable to the "new," whether it is a bar of soap or a bar of music. Many of the sounds and structures of our new music find echoes in the far corners of the world, and while these ties may be accidental or coincidental, they at least provide us with musical toeholds in doors that otherwise might be difficult to open.

As we approach an understanding of various musics of the whole earth, both through the study of the structure and raw materials of the music itself and through a study of the social and cultural fabric that produces it, we will find, I hope, certain musics to which we respond directly, emotionally, experientially, rather than rationally. To me, at the very least, that is what music is all about. Reading about it, understanding how it works or how it fits into a time or a space on our planet, may expand our mental horizons or insights or understandings (perhaps even of ourselves and our culture). But ultimately music is *making* music, and *hearing* it, in a primal and and mysterious response that we feel and enjoy in the depths of our being.

Basham, A. L. *The Wonder That Was India*. New York: Grove Press, 1954.
Cronyn, George W., ed. *American Indian Poetry*. New York: Ballantine Books, 1972.

Edwardes, Michael. *East-West Passage: The Travel of Ideas, Arts, and Inventions between Asia and the Western World*. New York: Taplinger Publishing Co., 1971.

Evans-Wentz, W. Y., ed. *Tibet's Great Yogi Milarepa*. London: Oxford University Press, 1928.

Rothenberg, Jerome. *Technicians of the Sacred*. Garden City, New York: Doubleday and Company, 1968.

Underhill, Ruth M. *Red Man's America*. Chicago: The University of Chicago Press, 1953.

(*Above*) Sage Narada singing with *tamburā*.
Fresco in Mattancherry Palace, Cochin,
India.

(*Left*) Navaho chief blanket. Native American.

2

THE LADDER
OF ORPHEUS

In India, it is said, the universe hangs on sound. Not ordinary sound, but a cosmic vibration so massive and subtle and all-encompassing that everything seen and unseen (including man) is filled with it. The ancient *rishis*, the seers, practiced yoga and austerities to tune themselves to this cosmic sound, to make it vibrate in their spinal columns, hearts, and brains. From this sound the great god Siva created music and dance and taught it to his wife, the goddess Sri. The art of music passed on to other heavenly beings, to the celestial entertainers, the *gandharas* and *kinnaras*, to the goddess of learning and language, Saraswati, to the monkey-god Hanuman, to the immortal sage Narada. In time the Himalayas, the abode of the gods, were filled with joyful music-making, drama, and dance. But on earth civilization was in utter and hopeless decline. People, bogged down in earthly desires, sickness, and death, bored with the four *vedas*, the holy scriptures of Hinduism, begged the gods for something to relieve them of their sorrows and hardships, something to ornament their lives and turn their hearts toward the sweet nectar of the gods. The god Brahma meditated for a hundred thousand years and then decided to give them music as a fifth *veda*, equal to the scriptures, a divine gift that contained the seeds of both happiness on earth and the path to *moksha*—ultimate release, supreme salvation. Bharata, a great sage, wrote it all down in a gigantic manual, the classic *Natyasastra*, and music has filled the Indian subcontinent ever since.

The Chinese, however, are more precise. Around 2697 B.C. a certain Ling Lun was sent by the emperor, Huang-ti, to the west to cut bamboo pipes from which the fundamental pitches of sound could be produced. The lengths of these pitch pipes, carefully calculated by musicians and astrologers working together, were of great importance, not only because they put music from its very beginning in tune with the harmonic relationships of the universe, with the great metaphysical clockwork, but because they assured the emperor himself that his reign would likewise harmonize with all the elements of nature and the supernatural. The acoustically perfect pitches of the twelve *lü*, the imperial panpipes, were divided into two groups of six, reflecting the eternal push-pull of *yin* and *yang* (the controlling forces of the universe) and represented by the male and female phoenix. The pitches and their mathematically perfect relationships were used as a basis for weights, measures, and architecture; each tone formed the basis of the correct musical cosmological scale for each of the twelve months and twelve hours. Further divisions were connected with the five directions and five elements, with man's very nature, everything in harmony with everything else. So

7

music in China evolved from the twelve pipes of *lü*, moved into the quietude of Confucian ceremonies and finally into the great orchestras in the opulent courts of the emperors.

To the Navaho in the American Southwest, music also has been an expression of harmony between man the forces of nature. The Holy People who travel on sunbeams, lightning, and rainbows developed, in their long and turbulent mythological history, a way of life and worship that kept the world in balance. They discovered how to build houses, to farm, to marry, and to trade; and they discovered in songs and ceremonials a way to control what they feared: disease, storms, drought, wind, and various wild and domestic animals. Then, still long before time began, the Holy People— the Sun, Changing Woman, the Hero Twins, and others—decided to move far away to new homes, and they held a great ceremony at which they created the Earth Surface People, the ancestors of the Navaho, and taught them all that they knew: their crafts, their way of life, and their music and ceremonies. This sacred music, of great supernatural power and potential, is sung today for enjoyment and to establish power over a world that is difficult and full of danger.

In the beginning, before the lush island of Java was populated by human beings, Sang Hjang Batara Guru, the king of the gods, fashioned a giant gong. Different strokes on the gong were signals to lesser gods living on the island, a kind of primordial telegraph; but as the messages and strokes became more and more complex, the signals confused all who heard them. So the king made a second gong tuned to a different pitch and struck the two gongs in alternation or in different patterns and combinations. But as the musical language again outgrew its resources, a third gong was made, and the set was called *gamelan Munggang*. Many centuries later, after Java was populated by human beings, Sang Hjang Batara Guru was reborn as the god-king Sri Panduka Maharadja Dewabuddha. He remembered the three gongs of his previous birth and for sacred occasions he created the *Mandalasana*, a special place where performances of singing and dance, accompanied by the three gongs of *gamelan Munggang*, could entertain both men and gods. Although the *gamelan* orchestra expanded in later times, the music remained "mysterious as moonlight, pure and changing like flowing water," a bridge from men to the gods.

The Asaba people of Nigeria received their music from a hunter of the Ibuzo tribe named Orgardié. One day, deep in the forest in search of big game, he lost his way. Hearing the first music that anyone had ever heard, he hid in a clump of underbrush and discovered that the sound was coming from a group of forest spirits approaching on a path. Orgardié stayed in his hiding place long enough to memorize the music of all the songs he heard and the steps to the dances that went with them. He found his way back to the village and taught the songs, called *egu olo*, and dances to his fellow men. From the Ibuzo, music traveled to Asaba land. And even today every fresh dance and song is believed to have been first heard by hunters in the jungle, created by forest spirits.

The earliest native literary works in Japan, the *Kojiki* (714 A.D.) and the *Nihon Shoki* (720 A.D.), describe how long ago the Sun Goddess was insulted by her brother who had just been appointed Guardian of Hell. Furious, the Sun Goddess disappeared into a cave, and the world darkened into an eternal twilight. Crops stopped growing, animals howled, and all the people of the world became afraid. The other gods gathered at the mouth of the cave, but neither begging nor tears could entice the Sun Goddess out of the darkness. Finally a feminine deity, Ame no Uzume, stepped forward and began a humorous and obscene dance, and the music, dancing, and laughter of the gods aroused the Sun Goddess's curiosity so much that she came out of hiding. All was once more put right in the world. And Ame no Uzume's invention, the arts of music and dance, have remained in Japan, like the sun, ever since.

Music, most people of the world say, originated somewhere other than in man. It came some time far in the past from gods or other supernatural beings who, perhaps when man needed it or asked for it, perhaps even at the moment of man's creation, gave music as a gift. But the process did not stop there; the relationship is an ongoing one. Men have kept the gods' gift of music as correctly and purely as they could, a continuous thread from the mythological past; but at the same time new pieces of music are continually being given to man. The Plains Indians (such as the Sioux, Cheyenne, Blackfoot, Pawnee) received new songs in visions, or from birds, bears, and other animals. Black Elk, an Oglala Sioux medical practitioner, describes how birds and animals would talk to him

(*Left*) Japanese musicians, print by Toyokuni (1769-1825).

(*Below*) Musician playing lyre (*kithara*), detail of Greek vase, ca. 490 B.C.

when he was a boy, teaching him phrases of songs and bits of melody. Later on, during a severe illness, he had a complex Jungian vision in which wise old men, great horses of the sky, wind, lightning, and the four directions taught him the songs that would give him power and sustain him in life. An Apache driving home from a peyote ceremony said that he learned a new song from the humming motor of his pickup truck!

If men are credited in a society with the ability to create music, this ability itself is considered to be the result of a divine gift, a concept not unknown to us in the West. Tirugnana Sambandar, for instance, was a great composer of religious music in eighth-century India. Once as a child he was left alone and, becoming hungry, he cried for milk. A radiant woman appeared and fed him milk from her breasts. As she left, Sambandar recognized her as Parvati, consort of the god Siva, and immediately burst into song, his talent received from the mother's milk of the goddess.

While it is our tendency, perhaps, to scoff at musical origin myths because they are not "true" in the historical sense, we should remember that our civilization, its philosophers, scientists, psychologists, and theorists have not come up with any solid answers either, though theories abound. Perhaps we should reexamine the myths and seek out a meaningful interpretation of them.

Music was taught to man, or stolen, or gotten by accident, just as were other earthshaking inventions, such as fire and language. Somehow, and we cannot explain why, it turns us on. It is both a pleasure to our lives and a connection to the spiritual. Those of us who are composers and performers may have experienced the feeling that our music is coming to us from a source outside, or from parts of ourselves so deep and inexplicable and wonderful that it seems out of our normal day-to-day existence of thought patterns and responses. Whether we call this flooding from "outside" our conscious minds a god, a supernatural animal, or the human subconscious or unconscious really does not matter. While the labels differ, the contents of the bottle are the same. In listening to music, also, we experience things that seem to transcend casual enjoyment and time-passing. What these experiences really are, whether we connect them to *moksha*, with the Holy People of the Sky or other deities, with an ethical harmony of relationships between ourselves and the entire natural world, or with the inner workings of the human psyche, we all know that something inexplicable happens in our consciousness; we feel it, it is intangible, perhaps irrational, but it is there.

Long ago, Greek poets and chroniclers sang the legend of Orpheus, son of Apollo and the Muse Calliope. Presented with a lyre and taught to play it by his father, Orpheus was a born musician, and soon he made music of such beauty and power and perfection that not only humans but also wild animals gathered around him, their hearts touched, captivated, calmed. Even the trees growing in the warm sun of Mother Earth bent their branches and flowers toward him. And brittle and craggy rocks (forgetting their natural hardness) became as soft as damp clay.

In time the great musician Orpheus wed the beautiful Eurydice, but the nuptial ceremonies were marred by foreboding omens. Within months Eurydice stepped on a poisonous snake in the grass, was bitten in the foot, and died. The heartbroken Orpheus, alone with his music and his lyre, sang out his loneliness and grief. But his powers failed him. Nothing changed, nothing happened—not in his heart, nor in the cold existential inevitability of the world. He resolved, then, to go where living men and gods had never been—to the regions of the dead—to seek out his beloved wife.

Entering a cave, Orpheus descended into the Stygian realm, protected, guided, and comforted at every turn by the magical power of his music. Eventually he stood before Pluto himself, his queen, and the innumerable dreadful and tortured creatures of darkness. In the deathly cold and silence, he, Orpheus, lifted his lyre and began to sing—of the world of sunlight and flowers, of happiness and life, but most of all of love, of his love for the exquisite Eurydice. It is written that the pale ghosts shed tears, that Ixion's wheel stood still, and that Sisyphus rested from his labors and sat on his stone to listen. Even the Furies were overcome by the beauty of the song, tears of compassion uncharacteristically streaming down their terrible cheeks. Pluto relented. Eurydice was brought out, still limping from her wounded foot. She would be allowed to follow Orpheus into the upper air, but on one condition: that he not turn around and look at her until they had both again reached the world of the living. Slowly, in complete silence, they ascended the dark and steep passageways. But near the end of their journey, on the very brink of the sunlight, Orpheus forgot himself and turned to see if his wife was following him. Within an instant she was borne away. Having done the impossible once, Orpheus was not allowed again to enter the realm of the dead. Once again he sang his sorrow, melting the cruel hearts of tigers, causing great oaks to move their massive trunks and limbs and walk about like animals.

Orpheus, obsessed by the memory of his twice-dead Eurydice, scorned the advances of other women. Again and again he returned in his thoughts and songs to her beauty and his love for her, and to their tragic fate. One day a group of Thracian maidens attempted to seduce the great musician. Ignored and repulsed, they threw javelins at him, and stones; all fell harmless at his feet when they came within the range of the sound of his music. But, finally, the maidens raised their voices in a communal scream, drowning out the sound (and power) of his voice and lyre; and in anger and frustration they tore the great musician limb from limb. The Muses gathered up the fragments of his body and buried them at Liberthra, where even today the nightingales sing more sweetly than in any other place in Greece. Orpheus's shade traveled a second time into the land of the dead, where he found his beloved Eurydice and embraced her with loving arms. For eternity they walk together, the master poet/musician and his inspiration. And to this day the music of Orpheus is remembered on earth and on the mountains of the gods. And on clear crystal nights, his lyre may still be seen high up in the heavens, placed by Jupiter among the stars.

Bulfinch, Thomas. *The Age of Fable or Beauties of Mythology.* Edited by J. Loughran Scott. Philadelphia: David McKay, 1898.

Hood, Mantle, and Susilo, Hardja. *Music of the Venerable Dark Cloud.* Los Angeles: Institute of Ethnomusicology, UCLA, 1967.

Kluckhohn, Clyde, and Leighton, Dorothea. *The Navaho.* Garden City, New York: Doubleday and Company, 1962. (The Natural History Library, Anchor Books)

Malm, William P. *Japanese Music and Musical Instruments.* Rutland, Vermont, and Tokyo: Charles E. Tuttle, 1959.

Malm, William P. *Music Cultures of the Pacific, the Near East, and Asia.* Englewood Cliffs, New Jersey: Prentice-Hall, 1967.

McAllester, David P. Conversation, 1972.

Merriam, Alan P. *The Anthropology of Music.* Evanston, Illinois: Northwestern University Press, 1964.

Neihardt, John G. *Black Elk Speaks.* Lincoln: University of Nebraska Press, 1961. (A Bison Book)

Piggot, Juliet. *Japanese Mythology.* London: Paul Hamlyn, 1969.

Sarabhai, Mrinalini. *Understanding Bharata Natyam.* Baroda, India: The Maharaja Sayajirao, University of Baroda, 1965.

Varadachari, K. C. *Alvars of South India.* Bombay: Bharatiya Vidya Bhavan, 1970.

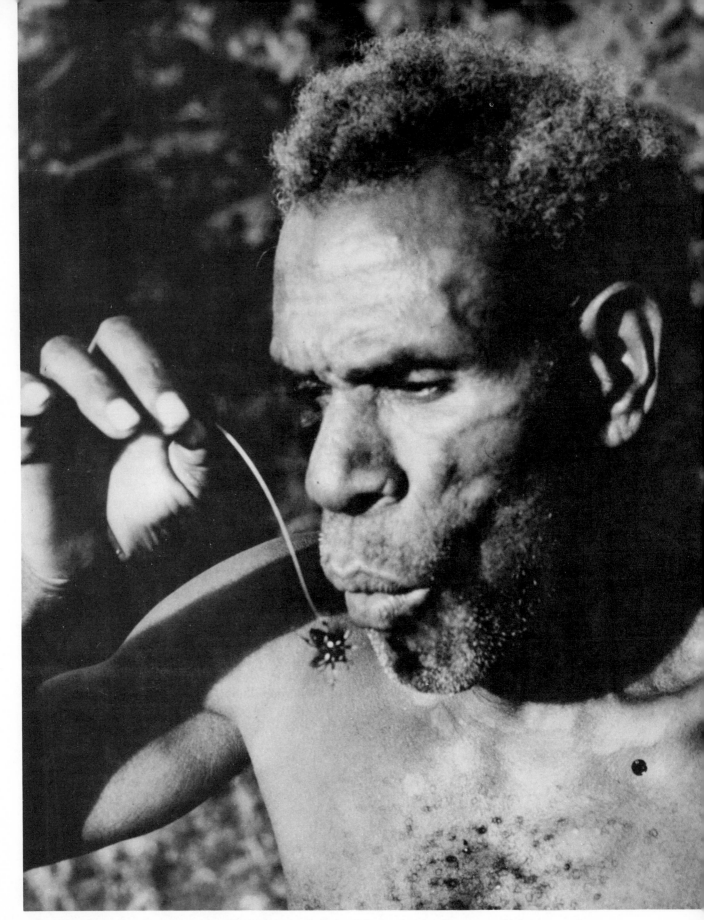

Man with live sago beetle. Overtones of the fundamental pitch of the beetle wings' buzzing, which acts as a drone, are produced by varying the shape of lips and mouth cavity. Mahisu, Wam chief, Sepik district, New Guinea.

3

THE GLOBAL ORCHESTRA

In the polyglot of musics on the planet—from the gentle buzzing of a New Guinean jew's-harp made from a live insect to the blasting sound of twenty-foot-long trumpets in a Tibetan temple orchestra, from the polyphonic singing of the folk choruses of the Ukraine to the polyphonic singing of the pygmies in central Africa, from the angular plucked melodies of the Japanese *koto* or the Chinese *ch'in* to the swoops and curves of a Webern symphony, from the happy and complex xylophone and flute orchestras of Africa to a jazz band in New Orleans, from the nasal twang and banjo picking of an Appalachian farmer to the nasal tone color and vocal subtleties of an Egyptian pop singer, from an Eskimo shaman's ecstatic chant to the hair-raising beauty of a Plains Indian Sun Dance, and so on (indefinitely)—we must ask a particularly vexing and problematic question: Do the earth's thousands of musical styles—ways of making music, looking at music, instruments, instrumental ensembles, compositional and improvisational techniques, forms and structures—fall into larger groupings? Are there distinct, or at the very least recognizable, areas in world music? Are there sections in the global orchestra?

If we conclude yes, then the problems multiply. Instruments are objects and ensembles can be seen, but music itself is like smoke held in the palm of the hand: elusive, disappearing. And what we can say about it (despite our pretensions) is at best unscientific and subjective. Over a hundred years ago, Henry David Thoreau, sitting in his cabin by the woods near tranquil Walden Pond, contemplated a similar confused and chaotic situation. He wrote, "If a person lost" (physically or intellectually) "would conclude that after all he is not lost, he is not beside himself, but standing in his own old shoes on the spot where he is . . . how much anxiety and danger would vanish. I am not alone if I stand by myself. Who knows where in space this globe is rolling? Yet we will not give ourselves up for lost, let it go where it will." So (taking a deep breath) we will begin.

Music all over the world has a common denominator: man himself/herself. We are all, every one of us, standing with our comprehending, curious, and feeling minds "in our own old shoes on the spot where we are." Besides our universal humanness—or perhaps we should say "animalness" (in the gentle sense)—we share with those persons standing or living around us certain more specific things: maybe an environment, religious beliefs, a life-style, or ways of working or building houses. We also share definitions; we mark the limits of our box, of what is or is not in our world view. One of these definitions is, if we have bothered to think about the subject at all,

WHAT IS MUSIC?

The Greeks were quite specific and defined music (along with poetry) as any art over which the Muses presided. Noah Webster, carrying several thousand additional years of Western civilization on his back and in his head, thought that music was "the science or art of pleasing, expressive, or intelligible combination of tones; the art of making such combinations, especially into compositions of definite structure and significance; the art of invention or writing, or rendering such compositions." This definition is not bad, but we must—if we are to approach the music of the *whole* earth (not just that of Europe and the Americas) wisely and intelligently—make several important clarifications. Concepts about whether or not something is a "science" or an "art," or whether or not something (like music) is "pleasing," "expressive," or "intelligible," differ radically from culture to culture and even within the same culture. An Ituri forest pygmy's answers would differ radically from those of a Javanese *gamelan* musician or a Navaho medical practitioner/singer. Even in the same room a European symphonic conductor, a jazz saxophonist, a rock star, and a middle-class American Archie Bunker type from the Bronx might come to blows about the meaning of the same words and about the definition of music itself. And what is a "composition" (improvisation?) of "definite structure" (to whom?) and "significance" (to whom, and why, and must it be?); what in a certain society in its place and time on the planet is "inventing" or "writing" (how about playing "by ear"?), or "rendering" such "compositions"?

In the early twentieth century the composer Edgard Varèse dropped off all the subjective adjectives, nouns, and picturesque similes that had been cluttering definitions of music until his time and stated purely and simply: *"Music is organized sound."* But even this definition, good as it is, has run into problems in recent years. For example, John Cage (b. 1912) wrote a piano piece which the pianist does not play; the performer sits at the keyboard for a designated length of time, *in silence.* (Music can be organized silence.) La Monte Young (b. 1935) wrote a piece which is basically the watching of a butterfly flying around a room. (Music can be a watching of something.) Composers like Dick Higgins (b. 1938) and Nam June Paik (b. 1932) have written pieces that are entirely or in part actions, (physical) movement, ideas (nonsound), or concepts. (Music can be anything set in motion and done.) And recently, marvelous recordings have been released of the singing and "music" of dolphins, whales, and Canadian wolves, and of the sound of natural environments—a forest, a jungle, birds, the seashore. (Music can be whatever we comprehend.)

Perhaps the best solution is to our problem of definition is a catholic one:

> *Music is whatever we ourselves, or any other individuals, or groups of people, or societies, or cultures, on planet earth (and perhaps elsewhere) comprehend as being music.*

To this definition we might add that music is *mostly* (but not entirely) sound, that it is organized in some way, that it may be intimately and inseparably though loosely connected with what we in the West consider separate phenomena (namely, dance, body movement, visual arts, religion, mysticism, power, medicine, astronomy, mathematics, architecture, group interaction, social structure, language, cooking, sex, walking, magic, psychology, being, thinking, or any other of a perhaps infinite number of possibilities), and, finally, that although all the peoples of the world have music in one form or another, many of them do not have even a roughly equivalent word for it!

Once we have decided what music is, or can be, we face another problem: while there are some small tribal groups that have a rather unified musical style—something comparatively intellectually compact and comprehensively pocket-sized—other cultures are excruciatingly varied and complex. The United States is an excellent example. When we talk about music here do we mean European classical music, the avant garde, older or less radical contemporary styles, pop (the Andrews Sisters? Frank Sinatra? Irving Berlin?), rock (early black? the Beatles? acid? folk? metal? theatrical?), jazz (New Orleans style? Chicago? swing? bebop? cool? the new thing?), soul, gospel, Latin, blues and other black folk forms, hymns, white spirituals, country and western, white folk music (from Appalachia? Texas? the South? New England?), commercial folk music (performed by aficionados and city "folk"), or the music of ethnic minorities (Irish, Spanish, Latvian, Ukrainian, Polish, Greek, American Indian, Caribbean, Mexican, Italian, Chinese, Japanese, Filipino, Armenian, and so on)? Or (take a breath) do we include Muzak, TV music, movie background music, jukeboxes, records, transistor radios, transcendental be-ins, accordionists' conventions, marching bands, barbershop quartets, penny whistles, rhythm bands, and one-armed street-corner harmonica players? Music in the United States, like music everywhere else, exists at various social levels. There is classical or art or "good" music for the rich and the intellectual elite, middle-of-the-middle-of-the-road easy-listening music for the middlebrows, rock and rock/pop for the rebellious/youth subculture, the avant garde for the avant-garde and art people, folk and labor songs for New Left liberals, country music for the farmers and common man, and a variety of black musics for the ghettos. But what happens when (America being a democratic place) a nice Jewish boy from the Bronx is crying his heart out over Chicago black ghetto blues, or the graduate of Harvard with a blueblood genealogy going back to the *Mayflower* twangs his banjo, or the Mississippi sharecropper's daughter appears in a starring role at the Metropolitan Opera in Mozart's *Marriage of Figaro*? It is all quite complex.

Other societies may have what we might call a dominant musical culture, but there might also be numerous pockets of people who live differently and who make music differently. The gypsies in Europe, American Indians and ethnic groups in the United States, or tribal peoples in southeast and south Asia are obvious examples.

Like world historians and philosophers and scholars in comparative religions, we must make choices, sweeping and sometimes atrocious generalizations (remembering all the while the infinite exceptions and their musical uniqueness and beauty). And we shall have to determine averages, noting the old Yankee cracker-barrel philosopher's admonition that "averaging is when you sit with one foot in a bucket of boiling water and the other foot encased in a block of ice and say that you are comfortable!"

DIVISIONS

Geographers see the world as a series of zones, marked by certain climates, landscapes, and ways of life that reflect how human beings have dealt with existence in these environments. There are the world's deserts, for example, with their desert people; there is the polar zone with its harsh winds and blizzards and Laplanders and Eskimos; there are rugged mountains and mountain people; the lush or fetid tropics, jungles, savannas, steppes, plains, islands—each with peoples working out their destinies in different or similar ways. There are also temperate zones, sometimes encompassing people—like the populations of Japan, China, France, England, Germany, and Argentina—of vastly different cultural worlds or life-styles. Environment can be important musically. In the building of instruments, for example, the availability of bamboo, gourds, wood, horn, skin, or metal—at least in the old days—greatly influenced what was done and how.

Life-styles are also a factor in music. Nomads could scarcely be expected to carry around grand pianos and pipe organs, while the transport of instruments is of no concern at all to agricultural villagers rooted to ancestral homes and fields. Stratified societies may have craftsmen who make instruments or musicians who specialize in performance, while democratic tribes and villages may have total participation in their music-making. Dwellers in the megalithic cities that have sprung up all over the earth may have certain things in common with each other, with other dwellers, as do farmers, shopkeepers, craftsmen, and (yes) musicians. Technology is still another important factor: there is no doubt that life (and music) are approached very differently in Europe and America than in an isolated village in India where all or almost all that is used is made by the hands (and locally) and time floats by, day following night, as it has for ages.

Two geographers, Richard Joel Russell and Fred Bowerman Kniffen, have divided the world, culturally, into the following areas:

1. Polar (northern Europe, Asia, and America)
2. European (western, eastern, Mediterranean sectors)
3. Dry World (north Africa, the Middle East, and a Turko-Mongolian realm
    stretching to China)

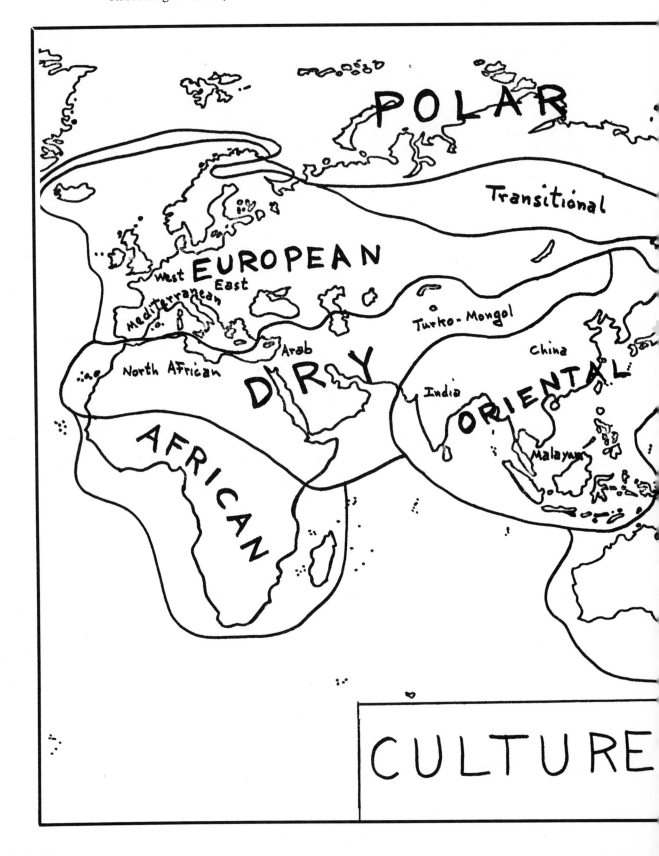

4. African (south of the Sahara)
5. Oriental (India, China, and Malayan spheres of influence)
6. Pacific (islands)
7. American (American Indian, Anglo, and Latin)

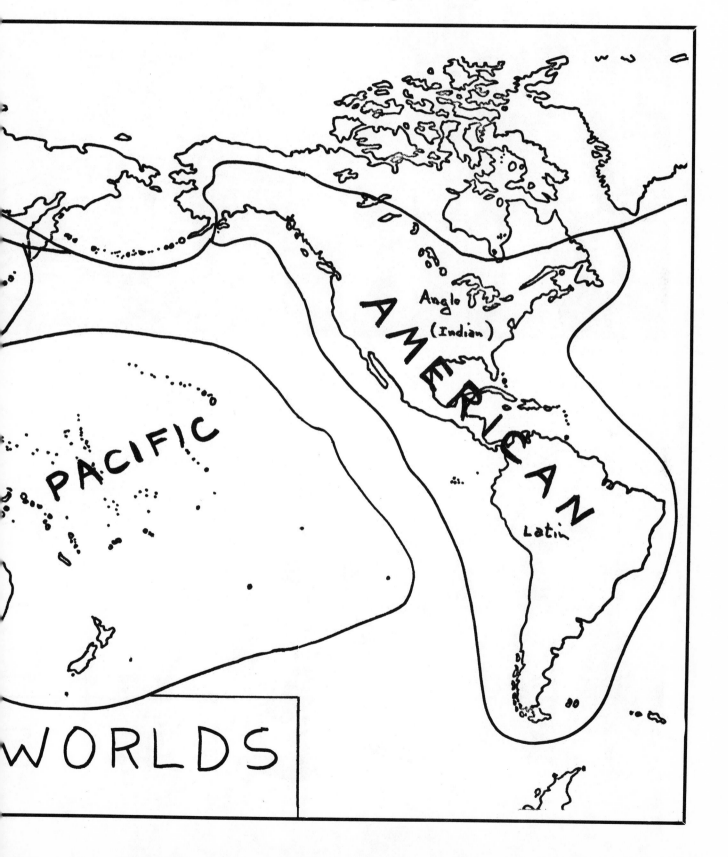

Landscape, south India.

Landscape, Mauritania.

Several interesting patterns emerge from this format. One is the split that separates the cultural world of dry, Moslem, caucasoid northern Africa from that of predominantly negroid, savanna/forest, Sudanese-Bantu southern Africa.

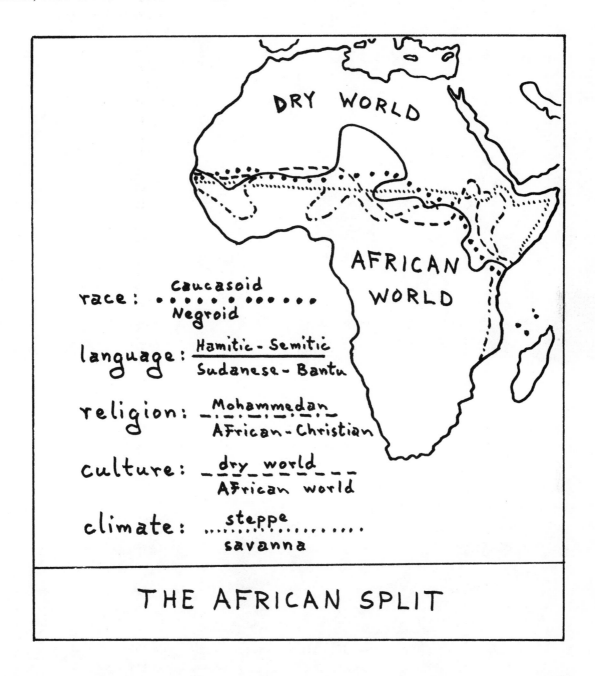

race: Caucasoid
······ ·· ·· ···
Negroid

language: Hamitic - Semitic
—————————————
Sudanese - Bantu

religion: Mohammedan
- - - - - - - - - -
African - Christian

culture: dry world
- - - - - - - - - -
African world

climate: steppe
··················
savanna

THE AFRICAN SPLIT

This split, with all kinds of transitions and overlappings, of course, is also reflected in the musical styles of these regions: northern African music connects with the music of the Middle East, that is, with other Islamic/Arabic/Turkish cultures in the "Dry World"; southern African music, on the other hand, does its own thing in a multitude of indigenous styles marked by (careful—here is the first of our necessary but dangerous generalizations) a strong affirmation of rhythm, a magnificent variety of instruments and ensembles, solo and choral song, harmonization, and polyphony. In recent years there has also (as we shall see later) been a strong influence from European and American musical sources.

Scholars have divided Africa into a number of large cultural areas. A variety of musical styles

Street musicians, Tunis, north Africa.

Dancers in Senegal, sub-Saharan Africa.

exists in each of them; in a sense, each tribal group has its own music (or even several musics) although there may be considerable cross-influences between neighbors. At least one ethnomusicologist
has scoffed at the idea of talking about "African music" as a unit at all; there is as much variety in
Africa, he has noted, as in Europe and Asia combined. And although we shall use the term "African
music" in this book as another of our necessary oversimplifications, we shall do well to remember
its qualifications.

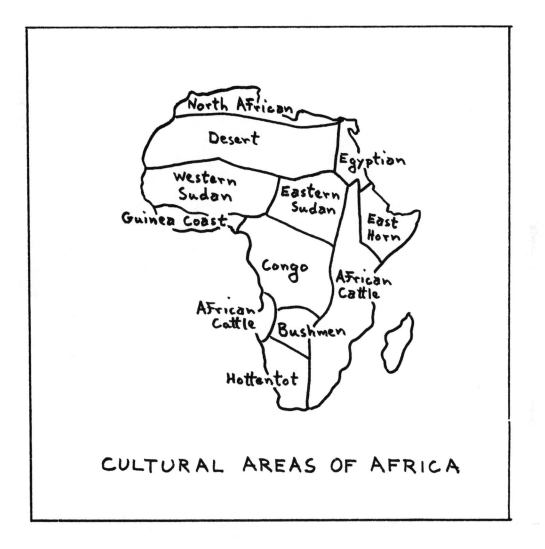

CULTURAL AREAS OF AFRICA

AFRICAN LANGUAGES

▦ **AFROASIATIC**
- A. Semitic
- B. Berber
- C. Cushitic
- D. Chad
- E. Ancient Egyptian (Coptic)

▤ **SUDANIC**
- F. Chari-Nile
  1. Central
  2. Eastern
     a) Nilotic
     b) Nubian and others
- G. Central Saharan
- H. Maban
- I. Furian
- J. Songhai
- K. Koman

▥ **NIGER-CONGO AND KORDOFANIAN**
- L. Atlantic
- M. Mandingo
- N. Voltaic
- O. Kwa
- P. Lio
- Q. Adamawa and Eastern Niger-Congo
- R. Benue-Niger (including Bantu)
- S. Kordofanian

▤ **CLICK**
- T. Koisan
  1. Northern
  2. Central
  3. Southern
- U. Sandawe
- V. Hatsa

Detail of a wedding picture, 1907, Wielkopolska region of western Poland.

Another interarea cultural break occurs in Europe. The west—Nordic, Germanic, English—contrasts with the very different east, made up of highly divergent cultures and subject from the earliest times to influences and peoples moving across the continent from Asia. Much of what we traditionally call "eastern Europe" is called by geographers a "shatter belt," that is, a cultural area absorbing influences from both sides. This shatter belt begins in Finland and runs south through the Baltic area, Poland, Czechoslovakia, Hungary, Romania, Yugoslavia, Bulgaria, and parts of Greece. Influences, especially musical influences, have also moved up from the south, notably during the conquests of the Turkish Empire in the sixteenth, seventeenth, and eighteenth centuries. We might note, for example, in the Balkans the use of complicated dance meters, highly diverse scales, "nontempered" intonation, and elaborately ornamented vocal melodies, sometimes with sections in free rhythm.

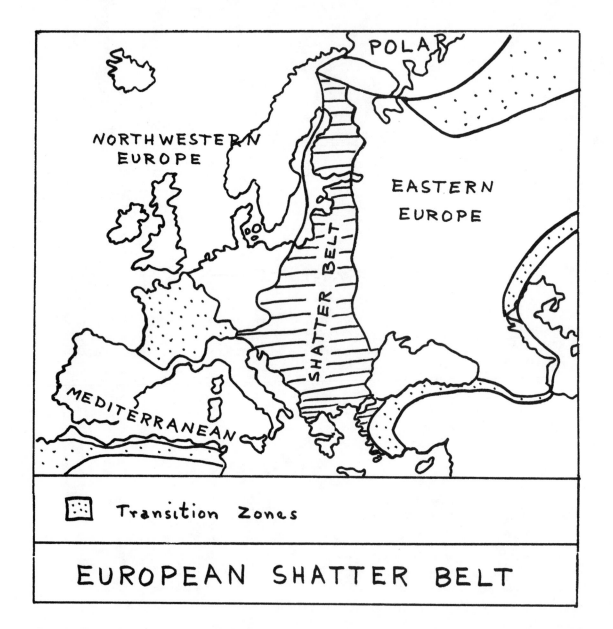

Linguistically also there is a division of Europe into east and west, with the Germanic (north) and Romanic (south/Mediterranean) languages dominant in the west and the Balto-Slavic and Finno-Ugrian languages dominant in the east. Today, the political barriers, systems, and alliances (capitalistic and communistic) reemphasize this traditional split. See map on page 25 and key on page 26.

LANGUAGES OF EUROPE

I. INDO-EUROPEAN

⬚ Germanic	⬚ Romanic	⬚ Balto-Slavic
1. Icelandic	11. French	20. Great Russian
2. Swedish	12. Walloon	21. Little Russian
3. Danish	13. Catalan	22. White Russian
4. Norwegian	14. Spanish	23. Bulgarian
5. German	15. Gallegan	24. Serbo-Croatian
6. Low German	16. Portuguese	25. Slovenian
7. Dutch	17. Italian	26. Checho-Moravian
8. Flemish	18. Sardinian	27. Slovakian
9. Frisian	19. Rumanian	28. Sorbian
10. English	(+ others)	29. Polish
		30. Lithuanian
		31. Lettish

⬚ Hellenic	⬚ Celtic	⬚ Aryan	⬚ Anatolic
32. Greek	33. Breton	38. Iranic	40. Armenian
	34. Welsh	39. Ossetic	
	35. Irish		
	36. Gaelic		
	37. Manx		

⬚ Thraco-Illyrian	
41. Albanian	

II. URAL-ALTAIC

⬚ Finno-Ugrian		⬚ Samoyedic
42. Finnish	49. Votiak	54. Samoyedic
43. Karelian	50. Cheremissian	
44. Estonian	51. Mordvinian	
45. Magyar	52. Vogulic	
46. Lappish	53. Ostiak	
47. Syryenian		
48. Permian		

⬚ Turkish-Tataric	
55. Turkish	59. Kirghizic and Turkomanic
56. Tataric	60. Kalmuckian
57. Bashkirian	61. Nogaic
58. Chuvashian	

III. SEMITIC	IV. HAMITIC
⬚	⬚
62. Maltese	64. Berber
63. Arabic	

V. CAUCASIC	IV. BASQUE
⬚	⬚
65. Caucasic	66. Basque

Europe may also be looked upon as having a Mediterranean zone, characterized not only by climate and a very old history of civilization, but also by commerce and occasional intellectual or political closeness to north Africa and the Middle East. Spain, Sicily, Greece, Albania, Bulgaria, and parts of Yugoslavia, Romania, and Hungary were all dominated by Islamic conquerers at one time or another, sometimes for extended periods. Musically this is an important factor to remember. And in many of these countries folk epic singers and puppeteers still portray the great battles and the heroes of the fight for Christianity and nationalistic self-rule.

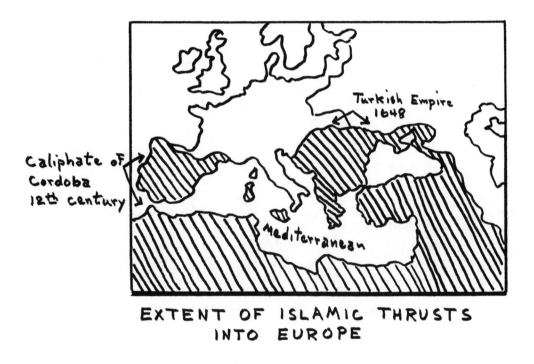

EXTENT OF ISLAMIC THRUSTS INTO EUROPE

The Dry World, stretching in a belt from north Africa to China, is marked by two sectors: the Arab-Berber realm and the Turko-Mongolian realm.

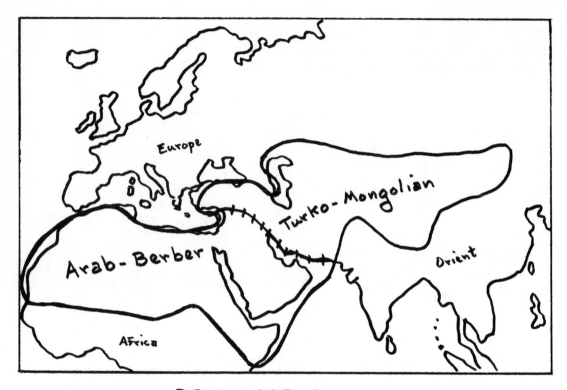

DRY WORLD

This extensive area coincides in many ways with the spread of Islam, but influences have moved back and forth in all directions through trade, pilgrimages, and conquests. From time to time cultural centers like that of the Abbasids at Baghdad, of the Hamdanids at Aleppo, or of the Amirate of Cordova (in Spain) have burst into flower, pulled scholars and musicians into their vortex, effected the flow of culture outward into a wide area, and then disappeared. Musically, despite the many regional styles, there are numerous similarities: in instruments (plucked lutes like the *dotar* or *'ūd*, drums like the tambourine, goblet-shaped *darabuka*, or the pair of *naqqāra*), ensembles (like the double-reed pipe—in Turkey called *zurnā*—with drums), the use of numerous scales, and, in classical idioms, elaborate ornamentation, similar forms, and development of the modal/expressive/melodic ideas of the *maqam*.

The Oriental world, indeed all of Asia, is a complex lacing of interacting cultures. Besides the Arctic and forested areas of Siberia with their amazingly sparse population of tribal peoples and European inroads, the steppes and plains of central Asia with Turkish-speaking and Mongol peoples, and the "dry" areas of Iran and Afghanistan, there are three areas that might be looked upon as cultural clusters, or spokes in a wheel. One of these is the subcontinent of India (itself influenced by Islamic invaders from the west) which exported Buddhism to China, Korea, Japan, and southeast Asia. Along with religion came many other cultural elements, among them instruments, chant, and music. Hindu culture—religion, mythology, and architecture (not to mention Sanskrit words)— also filtered into southeast Asia, particularly Java and Bali, where it has been adapted into musical art forms such as the *wayang kulit* classical shadow puppet play accompanied by the *gamelan* orchestra. Indian classical music, with its *raga*/modes and *tala*/time cycles relates in many ways to the classical systems found in the Persian/Islamic/Dry World to the west. There are similar relationships in folk music, such as the double-reed pipe and drum combination connected with weddings and cele-

(*Above*) Orchestra accompanying Mevlevi
dervish dances, Konya, Turkey.

(*Left*) Masked dancers/musicians at Hanamaki
Festival, Morioka prefecture, Japan.

brations. Other idioms, like the large percussion orchestras of Kerala, the numerous theatrical and dance forms, or the polyphonic singing styles of tribal peoples, are more unique. And even the absorbed outside musical forms have been, in a sense, "Indianized."

China has been also, from the earliest times, a large and influential cultural center. Musical styles and instruments—like the large ceremonial orchestras or ch'in-type board zithers and a variety of lutes—along with language, alphabet, literature, crafts, religion, and culture in general, moved out from China in the early part of this era into Tibet, Korea, and Japan, and down into southeast Asia. But the influence may have also from time to time been a two-way affair, and each of these smaller Asian countries—Japan, Korea, Vietnam, Cambodia, Tibet, Laos, Thailand, Burma—has certainly developed musical forms and styles and instruments and idioms that are beautifully unique. Mongolia has also in the past been an important carrier of musical traditions and instruments into China, both through its trade routes connecting to the Middle East and its periodic extensive conquests.

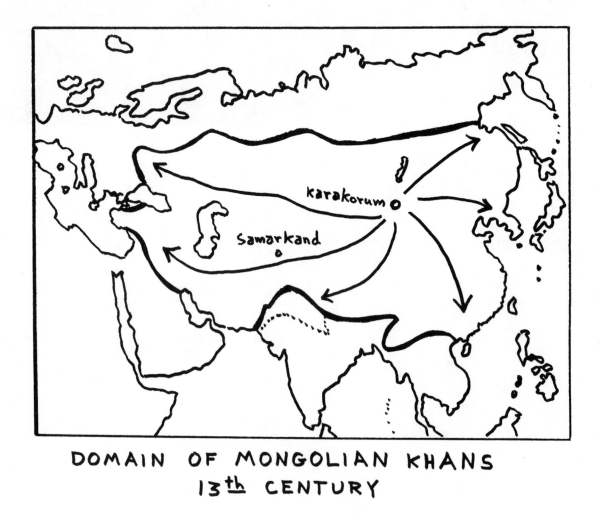

DOMAIN OF MONGOLIAN KHANS
13th CENTURY

The Malayan area is the third large cluster in the Orient; it includes Indonesia (Java and Bali are especially noted for their music), Malaysia, and southeast Asia. Here ensembles are made up of marvelous collections of tuned gongs, chimes, xylophones, and metallophones. In the old days lavish courts supported large troupes of musicians and dancers, and in many areas these arts are still flourishing. The Malayan group also spreads out into the Pacific islands, with which it has linguistic ties (the Pacific is believed to have been colonized thousands of years ago by Malayan peoples); but the most curious connection is with the Malagasy Republic—the island of Madagascar—off the coast of Africa. Besides language, many musical similarities exist, among them instruments like the tube zither and xylophones.

Scene from Balinese Tōpèng dance-drama, *The End of King Bungkut.*

Native American life and ritual, from an engraving by Robert Vaughan in Smith's *Generall Historie*, 1624.

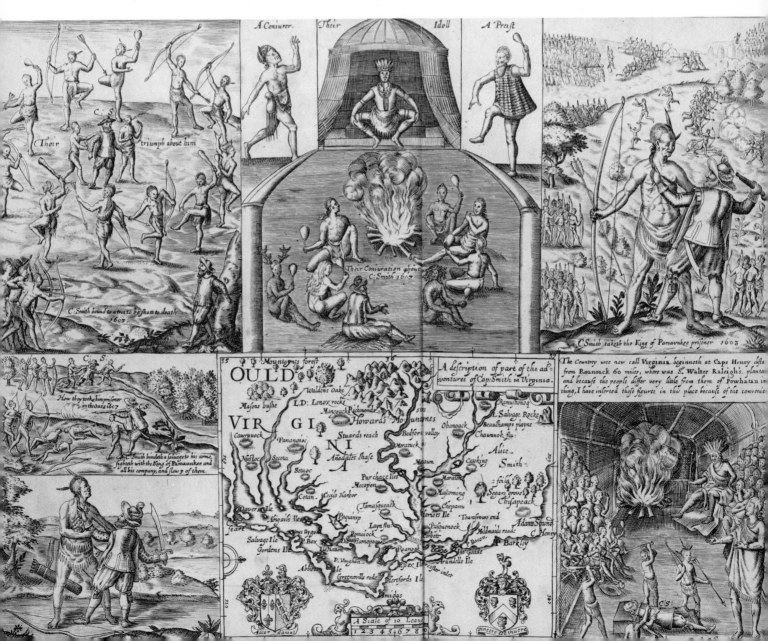

A rough mapping of the Oriental world and its movements and influences over the past several thousand years of history would then be:

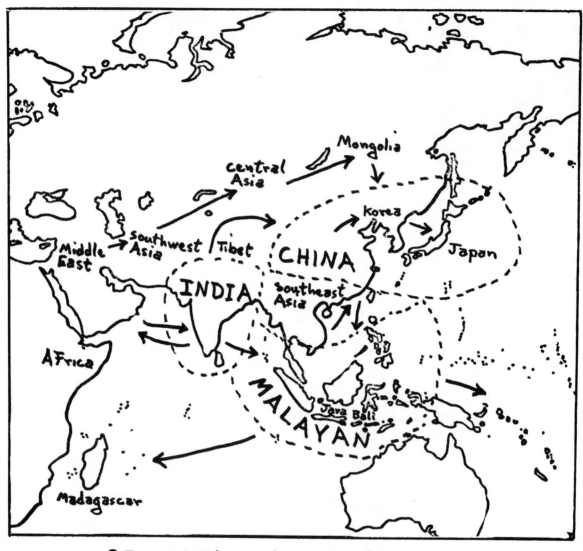

ORIENTAL WORLD

A final factor to take into consideration, particularly in terms of Asian music, is the great divergence among "high" culture classical forms connected with the courts and cities, the whole central span which encompasses the folk culture of villages and rural areas, and the music of tribal peoples who live in the more isolated areas in the hills and jungles. There is also the whole spectrum of religious music and chant—Hindu, Buddhist, Confucian, Shinto, Islamic—as opposed to folk or classical music, and on top of this the overlay of Western-influenced pop idioms.

The Pacific has also been divided into several zones. The continent of Australia with its native aborigine culture forms one area; then there is Melanesia, which includes the amazingly diverse and musically unexplored island of New Guinea; Micronesia, with its thousands of mini-islands to the north; and the vast and beautiful South Pacific realm of Polynesia to the east.

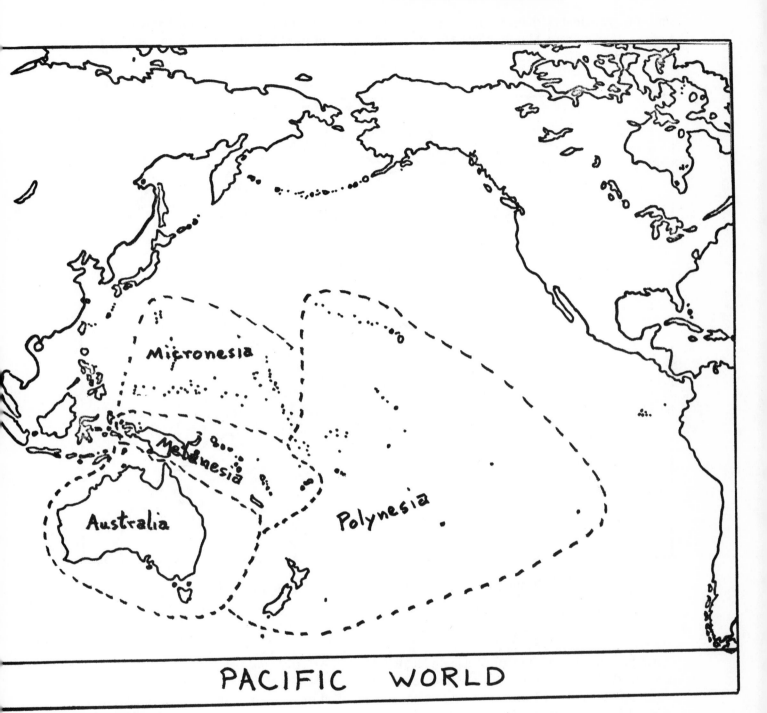

PACIFIC WORLD

Each of these areas contains polyglot musical styles, but if we may again generalize: there is a love of polyphonic and harmonic singing; there are also numerous chants with an emphasis on their words (genealogies, histories, myths, poems); and instruments are simpler to the east (small drums, shakers, a few tube zithers) and more complex and ornate in the west. New Guineans in the Sepik River region, for example, make gigantic flutes and log drums.

The Native Americans, from the snows of the Arctic down through the forests, plains, deserts, mountains, and tropical jungles of the Americas, are also a culturally diverse people. Or, rather, *were—*

since the genocidal skirmishes and colonization of the continent have left only cultural remnants of a once dominant race. Our mapping of American Indian cultural areas, therefore, is in a sense historical, a picture of the past.

NATIVE AMERICAN CULTURAL AREAS

Urban high cultures existed, of course, in Mexico, Central America, and the Andes, and much evidence of their music remains in rock carvings and instruments. Large pockets of Indian people remain, particularly in Latin America. In what is now called the United States anthropologists have grouped Native Americans into several cultural areas; and musically, we too can mark highly distinctive styles, for instance that of the eastern Woodlands, the Southeast, the Great Plains, the Southwest, the Great Basin, or the Northwest. The musics of tribal groups even in the same area may differ from one another, like that of the Navaho and Pueblo peoples, both in the Southwest. In very recent years there has been an attempt at renewal of Indian language and culture; there has been renewed interest in indigenous musical styles and performance, and also an interchange of songs and music (and costume) through intertribal celebrations, powwows, or politics. Much recent Indian music cuts across tribal lines in what David McAllester has called a "pan-Indian stye." At the same time there are Native American rock bands and country and western groups, some of them excellent!

What is happening and what has happened in the electric utopia of America since colonization is of interest not only in terms of this one area, but also, as we shall see, in terms of the music of the entire world. The primary movement was originally from northern Europe—the British Isles,

France, Germany—to the northern part of the New World, and from Spain and Portugal to the central and southern parts. But to these cultural ingredients was added a third: the catalyst of hundreds of thousands of black slaves brought from Africa to work clearing the virgin land and farming the plantations.

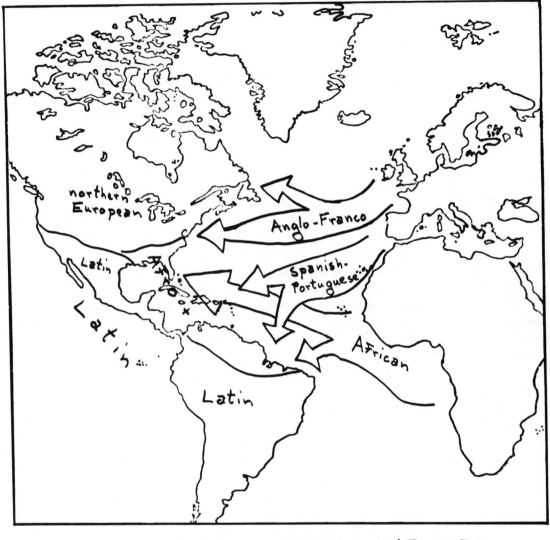

EARLY MAJOR CULTURAL INFLUXES
IN THE NEW WORLD

While the Franco-Anglo tradition, enriched by waves of successive immigration, has continued and evolved to this day—note New England fiddling contests or the folk and professional music of Appalachia (to give only two examples)—and the Spanish/Portuguese tradition flourishes from the southwestern United States through Mexico and southward, a major synthesis occurred in the music of the new black Americans. Stripped of most of their African ways of life, environment, religion, law, and arts, they developed what was in essence a new and totally unique culture, a synthesis of what they could keep from Africa with the imposed ways of their European masters. Musically we could mark as "African" the extensive use of call-and-response form, the great variety of instrumental and vocal timbre (like guttural noises and rasps), "bluesy" intonation and bending of pitch, loose but happy ensemble togetherness, strong rhythmic elements (drumming and melodic accenting), and improvisation; the "European" elements are most of the instruments played (trumpets, piano, guitar, etc.), song and hymn repertoire, the (European) system of harmony, some scales, and many of the forms. What has happened is that this hybrid style, evolved from the plantations, the little frame churches, the southern city slums, and the Caribbean, now dominates or at least permeates most of the music we hear in the United States. And the idiom of American-born pop, rock, jazz, soul, ragtime, blues—whatever one wants to list—has been exported and accepted enthusiastically in almost every nook and cranny of this earth of ours. At least in the cities of the world, if the present tendencies continue, this will be the dominant earth music everywhere in the near future.

BALANCES AND DISAPPEARANCES

This world of ours, as everybody knows, is changing rapidly. It has always changed, gone from one thing to the next, with sudden dead ends and beginnings anew or gradual permutation. Great cities and civilizations, peoples and kingdoms, are like so many ocean waves, like plants and species living out their cycles in the seasons. But it is also a truism that the planet is now changing faster than even before. An entire "Third World" of "developing countries" is attempting to evolve patterns of life based on Western (European/Soviet/American) models. It matters little (in our study of the earth's music) whether these revolutionary changes are brought about by capitalism, socialism, Marxism, or benevolent or repressive despotism. Or by war or by science or by hunger. They are happening; that is what is important. The world is changing, the cultural makeup and world views and religions and professions and life-styles of people are changing, and music—as one of the interlocking pieces in the puzzling and amazing pattern of existence—is also changing.

Today one can see businessmen in suits and neckties carrying their gray/black briefcases to work in Tehran, Cairo, Kyoto, or Bombay. One can hear transistor radios blaring from ancient Buddhist *stupas* in southeast Asia or pre-Columbian pyramids in Mexico. Tibetan monks chew Doublemint gum and sport Swiss wristwatches; lithesome Javanese maidens pore over the pages of *Vogue* or *Harper's Bazaar* to check out the latest fashions. Imported plastic buckets, cheap toys, and gadgets flood the most remote jungle marketplaces in Africa and Asia. The dizzying smell of carbon monoxide and the honking of cars, buses, taxis, and trucks seem to have penetrated almost everywhere; and tribal or national disputes are settled in once quiet environments by a deadly shining arsenal of weapons supplied by the factories of "developed countries."

Along with this flood of things have come a flood of means and a flood of ways. Agricultural experts bring miracle crops, new fertilizers, and advanced techniques and replace water buffaloes with (gasoline-dependent) tractors and farm machinery; nutrition experts attempt to change thousand-year-old eating habits and tastes; medical advisers preach cleanliness and hygiene; military advisers teach advanced ways of death; and educators attempt to imbue "backward" tribal and rural peoples with foreign languages, mathematics, economics, history—or whatever else we consider to be knowledge—in order that they may march into the twentieth century and join the rest of the human race. There is no doubt that people inside and outside of the "advanced" or "developed" countries consider these countries (or at least some of them, depending on one's ideological view) to be utopian: to be good and therefore worthy of imitation.

In music, as in movies or modern painting or in any of the other arts and sciences, the West has been extolled, copied, imitated, reproduced, and absorbed. Japanese music, for example, since the days of the Meiji Restoration (begun in 1868)—a conscious national policy of Westernization and industrialization—has gradually moved into the orbit of European/American tradition. Japanese orchestras, string quartets, conductors, and composers (not to mention violinists trained in the revolutionary Suzuki method) are among the best in the world; and there are also Japanese rock bands, jazz combos, cocktail pianists, and country and western groups! Other industrializing countries have absorbed Western music along with their machines and assembly lines: one can hear pianists playing Brahms and Chopin in Peking and Djakarta, symphony orchestras in Baghdad or Calcutta, and German folk songs or Stephen Foster or Protestant hymns in the highlands of New Guinea, the islands of the Pacific, or the forests of central Africa. Rock bands plug into local and sometimes undependable electrical outlets in Katmandu, Budapest, Beirut, Lagos, Mombasa, Pôrto Alegre, Bangkok, Seoul, and Bangalore. And American back-basin river-bottom Mississippi Delta blues is sung in

James Bond peeps over the wall at the Sultan's palace parade ground, Solo, Java.

The Tokyo-Osaka "bullet train" crossing a bridge below sacred Mount Fujiyama.

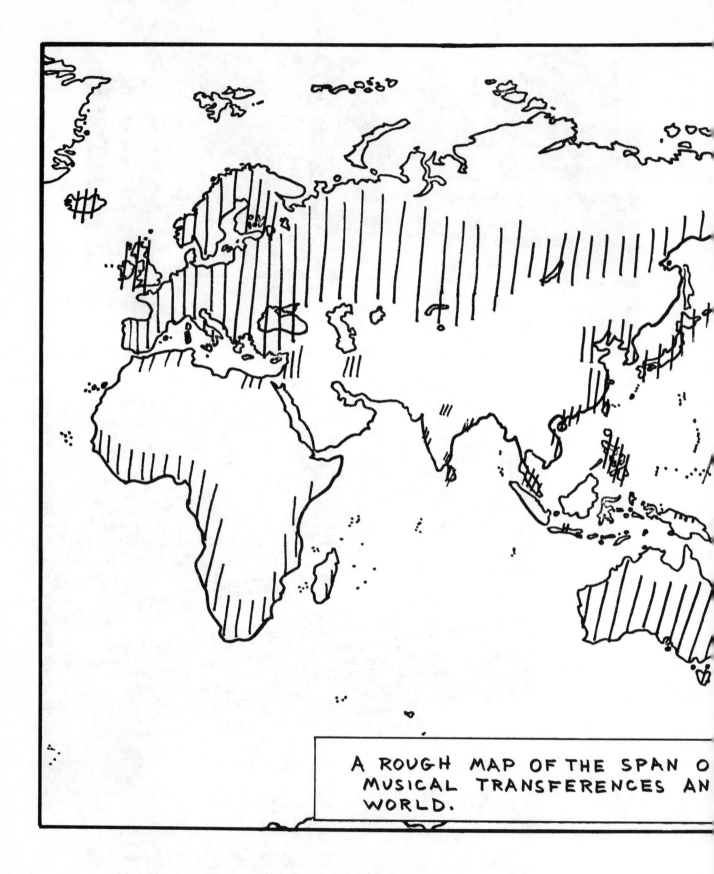

A ROUGH MAP OF THE SPAN O
MUSICAL TRANSFERENCES AN
WORLD.

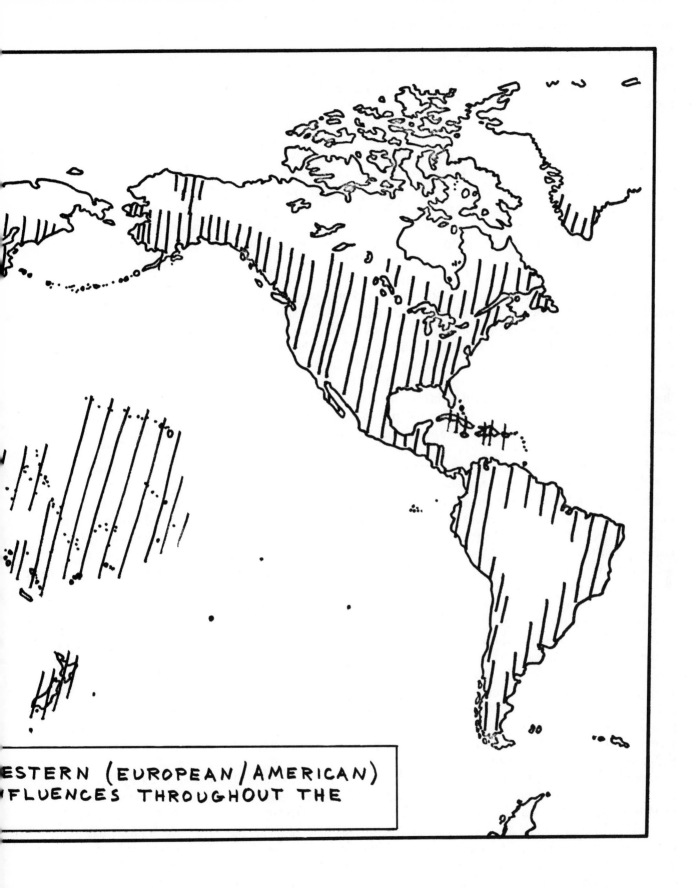

ESTERN (EUROPEAN/AMERICAN)
FLUENCES THROUGHOUT THE

Norwegian, Slovakian, Serbian, German, Portuguese, Mandarin, Turkish, Siamese, Hindi, Italian, Greek, Japanese, and a host of other tongues. To understand fully this amazing and confusing state of affairs, we must step back a little into the history of Europe and its relationship with the rest of the world.

Our two geographers have stated the situation quite clearly and bluntly:

> European culture (and we should include the United States) is noted for its aggressiveness. Europeans, since the dawn of history, have gone to distant lands as tradesmen, soldiers, and colonizers. With them has gone the notion that their own culture traits are "right," all departures being "wrong," barbaric, or of low order. Many Europeans have felt the duty, at times with missionary zeal, of spreading European culture and "enlightenment" among foreign and "less fortunate" peoples. Rarely does the European question the superiority of his own culture traits.

To be sure, other high and powerful civilizations had conquered, destroyed, dominated, and colonized—one thinks of the great thrusts of the Mongols, the Turks, and the Assyrians, for example, or Japan, or of the lesser but no less imposing domains of the Incas and Aztecs in the Americas, or the various empires of China. The pattern is a familiar one in the history of the world. But the cultural waves that moved out of Europe from the beginning of the sixteenth century were on a scale larger than anything the world had previously experienced. Exploitation and trade and power were only three factors: there was also the self-righteous need to spread religion (in this instance, Christianity) and "superior" cultural patterns. The European plan during the whole colonial era was, despite all the excitement and romanticism that it generated, nothing less than an attempt to dominate the earth.

With the whole idea of colonization, with the complex movement of raw materials taken from underdeveloped countries and sent back as factory-finished products to world markets, with the adminstrators and settlers and missionaries, came condescending attitudes toward native cultural traditions, many of them thousands of years old. Local culture was to be ignored and tolerated at best, or destroyed—as it was in the Americas—at worst. Many of the colonies became transpositions, European cultural islands stuck onto remote areas of the poor earth's geography like so many postage stamps. We might note Canada, New Zealand, the United States, Russia (in central and east Asia—now absorbed into the Soviet Union), Australia, South Africa, much of Latin America, the Hawaiian and many other islands in Polynesia and the Pacific. Other places had the overlay of the European elite; and even educated natives were expected to display the veneer of European languages, mannerisms, affectations, and tastes. Today, though the world is changing radically, many of the old attitudes remain. Nationalistic "revolutionary" governments are among the worst offenders, often trying to enforce cultural change and "advancement" upon their own "backward" peoples. Many of the world's magnificent musical traditions are connected in people's minds with old and corrupt regimes, with "old-fashioned" ways of life, or with religious practices now viewed as superstitious and absurd. And the neon electric glow of Western musical forms, styles, and instruments, blared out by the ever expanding popular media and connected with the relative prosperity and humbling technology of the West, is too novel, too exciting and attractive to resist.

Perhaps now, in the late twentieth century, it is time for us to think about what Peter Phillips has called "endangered musics," to be concerned about disappearing musical styles and forms and techniques in the same way that we have become concerned with "endangered species" of birds and animals, or the unthinking disruption and destruction of the ecology of our earth. Much music has disappeared already; much of what we talk about in this book should properly be spoken of in the past tense. During our lifetimes much more will disappear—or maybe not. Music, we know, is one of the most fragile things on earth; an entire tradition going back thousands of years can (if it relies on oral transmission) disappear in a single generation. One broken link can end the chain. At the same time music has a resilience and a conservatism that makes it hold on, even when other cultural patterns in a society change. We perform and enjoy the music of J. S. Bach (1685-1750) or Wolfgang

(*Above left*) McDonald's hamburger chain, Tokyo branch.

(*Above right*) Woman at the state library, Accra, Ghana.

(*Below*) Brass band, Accra, Ghana.

Amadeus Mozart (1756-91) even though the world that gave birth to their art has long since disappeared. The Navaho people in the American Southwest still sing the old and powerful songs, though they now may work in lumber mills or power plants, drive pickup trucks, and wear blue jeans and cowboy shirts. And in Japan the old traditional forms of music are preserved, like rare and ancient and beautiful flowers kept under glass, even though the everyday environment around them is filled with factories, pollution, television soap operas, and subway rush hours.

It is a curious irony that two powerful factors in the destruction of indigenous cultures and their musics—the European colonial empires and the modern age of advanced communications and technology—have also given us hope for their preservation. It was through the hundreds of thousands of European adventurers, administrators, and missionaries who fanned out around the globe (and wrote about what they saw and experienced) that we in the West first became aware of other cultures. And here and there exceptional individuals—like the Englishman Sir Thomas Stamford Raffles in Java, or A. H. Fox Strangways in India—became entranced by what they saw and heard and attempted to understand foreign and seemingly strange musical systems with appropriate humility and respect. More recently, radio, recordings, television, and the cinema have seduced millions away from age-old traditional musical forms; but at the same time the tape machine has made it possible to record and preserve and transport music over thousands of miles so that we may—more than was ever dreamed possible before—listen to much of our earth's music on the spot where we stand, in our own two shoes. And the cinema and the camera allow us to see other cultural worlds as we never have before.

Music has always changed and evolved. Singers and orchestras and their instruments have faded into time only to be preserved in stone or memory. Influences have come and gone, moved across continents or oceans, been assimilated, given birth to new forms and hybrids. Many, many times on this earth of ours musics have seemed to die, only to burst out again, phoenixlike, and to flourish. Let us hope that the diverse sections of the global orchestra will sound together (and apart) for years to come. They must.

Hammond, Peter B. *An Introduction to Cultural and Social Anthropology*. New York: Macmillan, 1971.

Jones, LeRoi. *Blues People*. New York: William Morrow and Company, 1963.

Khan, Sufi Inayat. *Music*. New Delhi: The Sufi Publishing Company, 1962.

McAllester, David P., ed. *Readings in Ethnomusicology*. New York: Johnson Reprint Corporation, 1971.

McAllester, David P. Lectures at Wesleyan University, Middletown, Connecticut, 1971-72.

Morgan, Kenneth W., ed. *Islam—The Straight Path*. New York: The Ronald Press, 1958.

Nettl, Bruno. *Folk and Traditional Music of the Western Continents*. Englewood Cliffs, New Jersey: Prentice-Hall, 1965.

Nettl, Bruno. *Theory and Method in Ethnomusicology*. Glencoe, Illinois: The Free Press, 1964.

Nketia, J. H. Kwabena. *The Music of Africa*. New York: W. W. Norton, 1974.

Phillips, Peter. Conversation, 1973.

Russell, Richard Joel, and Kniffen, Fred Bowerman. *Culture Worlds*. New York: Macmillan, 1951.

Taylor, Robert B. *Introduction to Cultural Anthropology*. Boston: Allyn and Bacon, 1973.

Thoreau, Henry David. *A Week on the Concord and Merrimack Rivers*. New York: The New American Library of World Literature, 1961. (A Signet Classic)

Webster's New Collegiate Dictionary. Springfield, Massachussetts: G. & C. Merriam, 1956.

Kombu/trumpet players in *panchavadyam* orchestra during a ritual temple procession, Kerala, India.

4

MACHINATIONS
OF SOUND

THE MAGICAL EXTENSIONS

Man, with his brain, arms, legs, muscles, eyes, ears, mouth, fingers, and toes, has been called the most sophisticated and complicated machine in existence, indeed the origin of and model for the (externalized) tools and machines that he has been so busy inventing for the past thousands of years. After all, it was man's imagination, his brain, that conceived of tools and machines, or took advantage of accidental discoveries, extending and restructuring them; and even the simplest of tools are really extensions of the body: the stone club and metal hammer are modeled after the arm and fist, the rake is an exaggeration of the claw-shaped fingers and hand, the bicycle (or, more correctly, the wheel) extends the efficiency of the legs, and telescopes and microscopes (and television) are eyes that move through the air or probe inner and outer distances, touching mysteries that boggle the imagination. *Homo sapiens*—man the animal—is equally distinguished as *homo fabricans*—man the maker, the inventor of objects—and for most of us all over the world in the twentieth century, existence is inconceivable (perhaps impossible) without the whole complex of inventions, tools, and gadgets with which we surround ourselves.

Man, with his lungs, mouth, tongue, vocal cords, throat, chest, and body, is also a musical instrument, a natural one. And this sound-making capacity, shared, incidentally, with insects, birds, and other mammals, as well as with the natural world and elements—water, rocks, the sky (thunder), wind, earth, trees—is universal. Every human being on earth is (potentially, at least) a walking, living, breathing machination of sound.

Musical instruments, like tools and machines, are extensions of man's body: they expand, extend, broaden his music-making potential, increase (but not always) his range or forms of expression, delight his ears with new timbres and sounds, make possible technical feats (lightning-fast notes or thunderous earthshaking loudness, for example) that seem to free him from his bodily limits like the wings of a bird lifting it from the everyday confines and dangers of the earth. It is no accident, then, that musical instruments from their very earliest days have been connected with magic and supernatural power.

In the caves of Les Trois Frères, dating from the Upper Paleolithic (ca. 15,000 B.C.), among the hunt-magic paintings of bison, elk, horses, and other animals there is the figure of the "Great Sorcerer," believed by many scholars to be a representation of a dancing shaman, or religious practi-

44

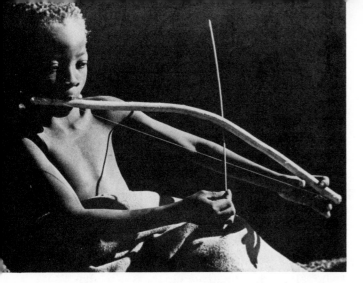

Pondo boy playing *umqunge*/musical bow, south Africa.

Shaman (?) with Musical Bow (?)
from Les Trois Frères
(after drawing by Breuil)

"The Great Sorcerer"
from Les Trois Frères
(after drawing by Breuil)

tioner, in a ritual costume of skins, bear's paws, deer horns, and an owl-like mask, a costume strikingly similar to that worn by Siberian shamans right up into modern times; and chant, songs, and instruments are a necessary part of shamanistic practice. Another painting in the same caves shows a bison-man (or a shaman dressed as or transformed into a bison) apparently playing a musical bow and using his mouth as a resonator! The musical bow, which is similar to but sometimes larger and more complex than the hunting bow, is found all over the world. The Maidu Indians of California used it to contact the spirits, the Bushmen of the Kalahari Desert in southern Africa play it for enjoyment as well as for rain-magic, and the Kamba people of Kenya use it to induce religious trance, while in Greek mythology it is connected with the god Apollo.

The hoop drum made from a hoop covered with stretched skin (and sometimes with a handle) is indispensable to shamanistic ritual and practice all through central Asia from Tibet to northern Siberia and among the Eskimos and American Indians (who, after all, came from northeastern Siberia). In Tibet, for example, the shaman plays and thus "rides" his drum—which becomes something like a sacred celestial horse—on his "flights" to other worlds and during the subsequent communication with spirits and other supernatural creatures. Whether these shamanistic mystical "flights" are actual or an ecstatic inner religious experience is a matter of belief; but what is important to us here is that the hoop drum both as a ritual object and as an instrument beaten during the ceremony (that is, itself, its sound, and the action of making its sound) is essential for the successful execution of the ritual.

Similarly (but not identically) in the ceremonial life of the Shona people of east Africa the sound and music of the metallic-keyed *mbira*, plucked with the fingers, forms a mystical "bridge" between the earth world of the humans and the supernatural world of the spirits, so that the spirits can travel down to "visit" and possess the bodies of devotees. The drums played in Haitian voodoo ceremonies are also used to invoke the gods and to generate possession, and, in fact, specific drumming patterns (as well as characteristic dance movements) are connected with specific gods. In Africa—the source of so many Caribbean/American practices, instruments, and beliefs—not only drumming patterns but also the drums themselves may be associated with certain gods. For example, among the Yoruba people the *iqbin* (an upright drum set on small wooden legs) is sacred to Orishamla, the "Great Deity," and his cult, which includes among others albinos, hunchbacks, and cripples; the *bata* (a double-headed, truncated, cone-shaped drum) is sacred to the thunder god Shango, his wife, Ova, and other deities; while the *dundun* (small bowl-shaped drums) belong to the cult of Egungen, the younger brother of Shango.

The bull-roarer, a flat piece of wood or other material whirled over the head at the end of a piece of string, makes an eerie roaring sound believed by the Australian aborigines to represent the voices of the supernatural Eternal People of the Dream. The American Indians connected this instrument—found, incidentally, made of bone at a number of Paleolithic sites—with magic and the windlike voices of spirits.

Spirits are believed to dwell within many of the world's musical instruments. The Kamaiura Indians of the Amazon jungles of Brazil keep their massive (three- to four-foot-long!) flutes in a special house, a shrine, where they are worshiped before being brought outside for festival occasions. The drums and flutes of many of the native peoples of New Guinea are similarly housed and worshiped. The *atumpan*, a drum shaped like a large, elongated wooden bowl resting on an elephant's foot played (usually in pairs) by the Ashanti people of Ghana, is believed to hold (or symbolize) the souls of ancestor drummers as well as the soul of the tree from which it was made. A special ceremony marks the choice of the tree nearly a year before it is cut down, and other ceremonies mark important stages of its manufacture. In Java the gongs and other instruments of the *gamelan* orchestra are thought to contain spirits with an almost human familiarity and presence. The reverence and respect shown to these instruments (and to their spiritual essence)—they are not stepped over, shoes are removed before playing them, ceremonies are held with them especially before performances—is a characteristic reflected in other parts of Asia as well. In India on Saraswati Puja Day, the day of worship of the goddess of music, musicians also worship their *sitārs* and *veenas* and *tamburās* and drums with flowers and incense in an elaborate ritual as sincere and deeply felt as that offered to any of the other gods.

The trumpet made from the conch shell with its acoustically rich cutting blast (and natural origins: it is a gift from the sea) is considered to have a supremely significant and auspicious sound, not only on the islands of Oceania, but in the Hindu and Buddhist ceremonials of Tibet, India, China, Japan, and southeast Asia. In ancient China large bells rung with the appropriate prayers were believed to attract rain and ensure a good harvest; the temple block *mu yü*, carved from wood in the shape of a fish—the symbol of wakeful attention and (naturally) associated with water—was also used with prayers to induce rain. The Maori islanders of New Zealand, as well as their neighbors in Australia and the South Pacific, attributed a similar rain-making capacity to the *pakuru*, two sticks which were hit together, one stick representing clouds and the other lightning. In the Malay archipelago, gongs avert natural catastrophe, heal disease, and aid human activity.

In Tibet instruments made from human bones, especially those of criminals or persons who have met a violent death, are considered to have particularly strong occult powers and are used in magic, exorcism, and sorcery. The *rkan-dung* is a short trumpet made from the human thighbone covered with human or yak skin and ornamented with brass, coral, and turquoise. It is said to conjure up (or dispel) demons by its sound. The similarly powerful *rnga-ch'un* is an hourglass-shaped drum made of two human skullcaps stuck top to top, with two skin drumheads that are struck by little balls at the ends of strings when the drum is twisted!

Of course, many societies throughout the world do not assign any particular supernatural significance to their instruments, which are treated rather as tools, admired perhaps for their quality or the beauty of their design but regarded ultimately as functional objects for use—that is, simply to make music with. A French-Canadian fiddler once chided me for photographing his beautiful old violin as it lay in its case on the grass: "Why take a picture of *that* piece of wood? Without me it's only a chunk of wood." Such a comment, even taken tongue-in-cheek, would be unheard of in many parts of Asia, Africa, and South America. As an object, as a sound, a simple bamboo flute in the Mato Grosso jungles of Brazil enjoys greater power, veneration, and prestige than even a Stradivarius violin in Europe! But instruments can and do become associated in the minds of people with certain functions within a given culture. For instance, the pipe organ in Europe and the Americas is connected with church worship and religious ceremonies, a function that in India (in temples, weddings, and rites of passage) is served by the double-reed pipes, the *shehnai* or *nagaswaram* and drums. Among the Basongye of Kasai the two-note *epudi* (ocarina) is associated with hunting; it is played to accompany hunters' songs before and after the hunt, for signaling, and for reproducing tonal language. In west Africa certain drums and trumpets are connected with the office of the king or tribal chieftains, and their usage is strictly controlled by law. The kettledrum *kurga*, often mounted on the back of an animal, was the symbol of power for Mongol chieftains and was also used as a signal drum in warfare. The Moghul rulers of medieval India also used similar kettledrums mounted on the backs of elephants, horses, and camels as symbols of the regal authority of the palace. In Gabon the eight-stringed *valiha* zither, made from a tube of bamboo with a palm leaf hood, is played to accompany epic songs about eight great heroes. Each string represents one of the warriors and is given his name.

Sexual symbolism is also attached to musical instruments. The panpipes of ancient China were divided into a male and female side reflecting the eternally balanced opposition of the life principles, *yin* and *yang*. The designation of pairs of instruments as male and female (whether merely for convenience, or as part of a larger symbolism) is common throughout the world. In west Africa the high-pitched drum of a pair is "male" and the larger, deeper-pitched drum is "female"; among the Luba people of the south Congo pairs of the *malimbe* wood xylophone are designated as *malume*, the male, with fifteen wood bars, and *makaji*, the female, with nine wood bars. On the island of Bali the metal-keyed xylophones *gender* and *gangsa* are built in pairs or quartets in each octave size. Half of the instruments are "female" and are tuned a fraction lower than their "male" companions. When the instruments of a set are played together this minute tuning difference creates the shimmering, waterlike effect so characteristic of Balinese *gamelan* music. Male/female concepts also find their

een Schaman ofte Duyvel-priester.
in 't Tungoesen Lant

Siberian shaman with hoop drum, from N. C. Witsen: *Noord en Oost Tartaryen*, 1785.

The lute was important in six-teenth- and seventeenth-century European courtship ritual. Print by Crispin van de Passe (1564–1637 [?]).

way into world thought about musical modes and scales and seemingly abstract structural concepts. Indonesian *patets* and Indian *ragas*, for example, can be divided by gender, and in European classical music theory there are "male" and "female" chord sequences in cadential endings.

Flutes and drumsticks, as almost archetypal phallic symbols, are often associated with love-magic. The flute, the universal pastoral pipe of the shepherd, was used exclusively as a serenade instrument by young American Indian men in the Central Woodlands and Great Plains areas, a function shared in European folklore. In India the flute is the instrument of Krishna, the divine lover, whose legendary affairs of the heart engendered some of the world's most beautiful erotic poetry and songs. In New Guinea flutes and flute music are connected with certain rites (such as the deflowering of virgins) that may be explicitly sexual in nature. The jew's-harp also has romantic connotations, particularly in southeastern Asia. Among the Naga and Kachin tribal people it is used almost exclusively for serenades and is considered so irresistible that playing it is forbidden during harvest time when people's minds must not be distracted from their work. In Formosa among certain tribes the jew's-harp functions as a kind of love letter and proposal rolled into one. A youth plays the instrument in front of a girl's house and leaves it there; if the girl accepts the gift of the jew's-harp, she has symbolically accepted the marriage proposal of her suitor. In Austria at the beginning of the nineteenth century, jew's-harps of silver (called *maultrommel*) were also used for serenading. So popular was the custom and so persuasive the sound that female virtue was considered endangered, and the authorities repeatedly banned the instruments. The lute and the mandolin had a particularly romantic history in European courtship ritual, while in Mexico today the guitar (built in many shapes and sizes) upholds its reputation as the instrument par excellence for serenades and seductions (with a little help, of course, from the voice of the serenader and the poetry of his songs).

Even the most democratic society has its classes, its social strata, or at the very least its more powerful and less powerful individuals and groups. Instruments, too, both in themselves and in their association with certain types of individuals or functions within a culture, have social status. And there can be considerable social mobility (up or down) for instruments as time passes. For example, the bagpipe enjoyed several periods of fashion among continental European nobility during the fifteenth and sixteenth centuries, only to return to its lowly peasant status thereafter. In India instruments were associated with the social level of the castes who played them: stringed instruments like the *veena* with the high-caste Brahmins, reed pipes (less "clean" because they are played with the mouth) with lower-caste Hindu Pillais and Muslims, and folk instruments—"nonclassical" drums and village pipes like the *bahudari*—with outcasts and tribals. Instruments associated with the court and with court ("classical") music usually enjoy a high status, as do those, such as the ritual hourglass-shaped dance drums and large flutes of New Guinea, which play an essential part in the ceremonial and religious life of the community. From the eighth century A.D. on, the drums, pipes, lutes, flutes, and zithers of the Japanese *gagaku* orchestra were part of the personal property (and music) of the emperor and thus part of the aura that surrounded this descendant of the sun. On the other hand, many of the percussion instruments now used in the European symphony orchestra (excluding the kettledrums with their long kingly associations) began their social ascendancy as lowly folk instruments played only by jugglers, street entertainers, and exotic foreign ensembles.

Curiously, some instruments cut across social barriers, and vastly different musical worlds are created upon what for all practical purposes is the same instrument. In Western musical culture instruments like the piano and guitar have this chameleonlike, multifaceted identity, depending upon who is playing them and how. A piano played in the studied classical style of a conservatory-trained pianist, in the hands of a barrelhouse boogie-woogie artist, in the musical lunges and darts and chording of a jazz musician, or in the explosive free-for-all attitude of an avant-garde composer is in a way four almost schizophrenically different instruments, each with its own personality and the subsequent associations and status. Many "high" instruments have filtered down virtually unchanged to become bona fide "folk" instruments in folk traditions, perhaps most notably the violin and clarinet, which are common in village and rural musical styles throughout eastern Europe, the Balkans, and the Middle East, indeed throughout the world. Where store-bought models of these instruments are unavailable, local craftsmen imitate them as best they can. In southern Mexico and Guatemala, for example, delicate violins are crafted, often out of a single piece of wood (the European violin is a composite of as many as seventy pieces of wood glued together). "High" and city-culture instruments which become extinct in the ever changing styles and fads of civilization may be preserved in the more conservative soil of rural culture. The courtly medieval psaltery and dulcimer, for example, exist to this day in European folk traditions. Finally, an instrument may be extremely highly regarded within one culture or subculture—like the bagpipe in Scotland and Ireland—with all the trappings of a prestigious high art form, while in neighboring cultures the same instrument may remain a relatively underdeveloped part of "lowly" folk forms.

Here we should perhaps utter a word of caution: the status of instruments, the divisions into "high" and "low," folk or classical, although real in a sociological sense, is in actuality unreal in terms of the nature of the instruments themselves and the skill with which they are played. Talented and deeply feeling musicians all over the world make highly creative and expressive music no matter what they find in their hands. One famous African musician was described by an admirer: "He could make beautiful music with anything. If all he had in his hands was two rocks . . . he would make them sing."

The musician's relationship with his instrument is an intimate one. Like (or unlike) a wife it is an inseparable companion, a constant friend, with him perhaps for his entire life, connected not only with his livelihood or moments of relaxation, but (as an extension of himself) with his deepest thoughts and feelings as well. The musician's fingers are like nerve endings, tentacles, drawing from his inner self an expression that is transferred through an otherwise inert object (his instrument) into sound and the hearts of others. Through the years the really creative musician will explore every nook and cranny of this instrument, discovering its strengths and weaknesses, its limitations as well as its possibilities. He will become familiar with its "voice," its subtle timbres and hidden sounds, and he may develop astounding virtuosity. The *didjeridoo* played by the Australian aborigines is a hollow eucalyptus branch one end of which may be placed in a large shell or can to increase its resonance. It is stored in a stream or in damp mud when not in use to preserve it and keep it soft-toned. It is blown and sung through (sometimes simultaneously) and basically produces only two pitches a tenth apart (although there is a strong coloring of overtones). Yet it is extremely difficult to play really well, and a skilled performer may be able to produce as many as fifty or sixty tone colors and sonic/rhythmic pattern combinations!

The apparent simplicity or complexity of an instrument, in fact, can be deceptive. Few of the world's instruments are as simple in construction as the bamboo flute, a length of bamboo with holes bored or burned into it and perhaps with a notched mouth hole. But in Japan and in India a music of unparalleled virtuosity, of subtle inflection and timbre in an almost endless catalog of scales, is played on this instrument. And in countries influenced by Arabic culture, the reed *nāy*, a simple, long, end-blown tube with finger holes, produces a similarly complex music. By contrast the music produced on a four-thousand-dollar modern electronic organ with its space-age circuitry and dozens of gadgets and buttons may be of the one-finger-at-a-time variety. We might make note of an unwritten law: simplicity of construction in a musical instrument does *not* equal simplicity of the music played upon it. Nor does structural complexity automatically equal sound complexity. The potential of an instrument is what is important, and the use that the musician's imagination will put it to. Even with the horn trumpets and clay ocarinas of Africa with their two or three notes, or the similarly "limited" flutes and panpipes of Peruvian Indians, a rich and complicated music is made by combining a number of these instruments (each with its different pitches) into ensembles, with each player fitting in his part like the pieces of a jigsaw puzzle. Each instrument then becomes in reality a fragment of a larger "instrument"—the ensemble.

We who have grown up in heavily industrialized countries might have difficulty understanding the true significance of our unwritten law: *simplicity does not equal simplicity, complexity does not equal complexity*. We tend to think in simplistic terms of "progress" from the "primitive" to the "sophisticated"; we tacitly accept the primacy of the machine over the hand, or, on another level, the electrical over the mechanical. And, finally, we may equate technological complexity with value judgments like "good" or "civilized." But when applied to art, and certainly to music, such assumptions break down. If they were true, then an electronic music synthesizer would be a better, more sophisticated instrument than the Stradivarius violin (which it is not) and Karlheinz Stockhausen would automatically be a greater composer than Wolfgang Amadeus Mozart (which he probably is not). And our bamboo flute would be left entirely out of the running! We must then remember a supplement to our unwritten law: simplicity or complexity in music and musical instruments, in construction and in sound (and we might as well jump in with both feet and say *in all art*), really has little or no relationship to the ultimate value, the beauty or power, or the music (or art). Other (invisible) factors are involved. And perhaps in the final analysis they are intangible, indefinable— felt rather than spoken. A five-note tune played in the mountains by a Balkan shepherd on his reed pipe with only his flock as an audience may ultimately be more beautiful, more important (if we may use such words), than the intensity of a second-rate rock band playing to a hundred thousand people and backed by a mountain of electronic equipment. In a sense, music is the great equalizer: at the precise moment he begins to play, every musician, and every instrument, is born equal.

★★★★★★★★★★★★★★★★★★ **THE WAY OF THE** *CH'IN* ★★★★★★★★★★★★★★★★★★

According to legend, the *ch'in*, a Chinese zither with seven strings, was invented by Fu-hsi in 2900 B.C. From time immemorial until the very recent past it has been associated with the life of the literati, with those extraordinary scholars/public servants (perhaps the most famous of whom was K'ung-fu-tzu, or Confucius, traditionally considered to have lived from 551 to 479 B.C.), who spent most of their lives studying, reading, thinking, teaching, philosophizing. For these scholars there was perhaps nothing in the world outside that was not described and analyzed in their books, if interpreted and thought about correctly. The verse from the *Tao-tê-ching* might well have been applied to them: "Without going outdoors I know the world, without looking out the window I see the way of heaven."

The *ch'in* was the very symbol of the literary life, enhancing and ornamenting by its presence—along with books, desk, inkstand, scrolls, chessboard, flowers, antique vessels, and incense burner—the sanctum of the scholar's library. Its shape, lacquering, and ornaments were not only pleasing to the eye; its venerable age and appearance also suggested the wisdom of the sages of bygone ages.

Not all scholars could play the *ch'in*—to own it was enough—but for those who did, its serene sound and the discipline of its playing technique were, to those who understood its inner significance, *ch'in tao*, a Way to the ultimate enlightenment. Playing the *ch'in* was meditation, a direct communication with *tao*, a return to original purity and harmony with all things, to a regulated, fully virtuous, transcendent nature, to utmost simplicity, introspection, primordial serenity.

The sounds of the *ch'in* were the "sounds of emptiness" which could set the heart of the player in tune with the universe, in harmony with the all-pervading mysteries of *tao*. And as a symbol of these mysteries the *ch'in* could, if contemplated upon, lead to a realization of eternal truths and cosmic harmony. The music of the *ch'in* was not, then, a fine art, but rather a path of wisdom.

Along with elements like jade and cowrie shells, the *ch'in* was believed to be imbued with the powers of the *yang* principle, the essence of light and vitality (opposing decay); hence it had the power to purify the body and to increase the life-span. To play the *ch'in* was no casual matter. It was to be approached humbly, with cleanliness of body and mind and in fresh clothes, as if standing before a superior. To play was in a sense a magical act, a ritual for communication with mysterious powers. The times and places to play were carefully prescribed; for example:

Aboriginal dancers with *didjeridoo* and stick clappers, northern Australia.

Scholar playing the *ch'in* in an idyllic setting. Print, Ming dynasty, sixteenth to seventeenth century, China.

Upon meeting someone who understands music.
In a storied pavilion.
Sitting on a stone.
Having climbed a mountain.
Resting in a valley.
In a cool breeze when there is a bright moon.

The tones of the *ch'in* were connected with communing with the essence of flowing streams, rugged rocks, mist-enshrouded mountains, and forests; and even when sitting in his room the scholar-musician was to think of forests, mountains, streams.

As an object the structure of the *ch'in* is replete with symbolism. Its length is 3 *sh'ih*, 6 *ts'un*, 5 *fen* (about 126.5 cm) which corresponds to the 360 degrees of the celestial sphere. Its breadth of 6 *ts'un* (about 20.5 cm) is equivalent to the "six harmonies" of heaven, earth, and the four cardinal points. On its underside a sound hole called the "dragon pond" measures 8 *ts'un* to let pass the winds of the eight directions; another sound hole called the "phoenix pool" measures 4 *ts'un* and "unites the four seasons." The original five strings (two were added later) represent the five tones of music as well as the five elements. The thick strings are like a prince (slow, harmonious, unobstrusive) and the thin strings are like statesmen (pure, unselfish, obedient); and all the strings together symbolize the Right, like a well-regulated, harmonious, peaceful kingdom.

Other parts of the *ch'in* are named after two of the most important imaginary animals of Chinese mythology: the dragon, lofty and awe-inspiring, and the phoenix, with its regenerative potential. Both animals are connected with vitality and fertility.

Each *ch'in* is inscribed with laudatory phrases, quotations from antiquity, or poems, as well as its own name. Among the names given to various *ch'ins* are Spring Thunder, Great Elegance, Bells on a Snowy Night, Floating Sonorous Stone, A Crane Crying in the High Air, and Immortal of the Pine Forest.

The technique for playing the *ch'in* is extremely complicated, and this, together with the cost of an instrument, its own special musical notation, and the secrets of style that had to be learned directly from a master, made it an instrument for the elite. There are all kinds of touches, plucks, and ornaments applied to pieces learned from the repertoire. For example, an explanation of the "clear touch" includes the following directions:

The movement of the fingers should be like striking bronze bells or sonorous stones. Slow or quick, no secondary sounds shall be produced, so that when hearing these tones one obtains an impression of purity—as of a pool in Autumn; of brilliancy—as of the shining moon; of dim resonance—as of a resounding valley; as of the babbling water in mountain gorges; of profundity—as of a resounding valley. These tones shall in truth freeze alike heart and bones, and it shall be as if one were going to be bodily transformed into an Immortal.

A description of another touch explains how a thin vibrato like "confidential whispering" or "fallen blossoms floating down a stream" can be achieved not by any movement of the fingers, but through the pulsation of blood in the fingertip! The descriptions of finger technique are often shown symbolically or metaphorically, or are compared with movements of nature or of birds. The poetical and philosophical beauty of the *ch'in-pu*, or handbooks for the study of the *ch'in*, make them much more than mere technical manuals or collections of songs; they are, in fact, a guide to the scholar-musician on his mystical journey of *ch'in-tao*.

The *ch'in*, connected with the dragon and phoenix, also has associations with the crane, the plum tree, the pine tree, and the sword:

the crane: graceful, dignified, a flier, symbol of longevity.

the plum tree: with blossoms that delight the eye with their colors, symbol of creative power and female beauty.

the pine tree: whose gnarled trunk teaches perception of antique beauty.

the sword: symbol of straightness and the purity of the superior man.

Two anecdotes:

Ch'en Chih loved to play the lute, which he did almost continuously day and night. After twenty-eight years of music and meditation a purple flower suddenly blossomed out of his *ch'in*. He ate it, and immediately disappeared as an Immortal.

In the beginning of the Shao-hsing period (1131–62) Sheng Hsun was prefect of Hsiang-yang. He had built for himself a beautiful pavilion over a stream, and he played his *ch'in* there daily. One day a storm wind arose and the rain poured down in torrents. His *ch'in* changed into a huge red carp and, riding it, he disappeared into the sky.

★★★★★★★★★★★★★★★★★★★★★★★★★★★★

Musical instruments, no matter what culture on earth they are found in, often represent the most complex development of the technology of that culture. For example, the brass and wood-wind instruments of twentieth-century Europe-Japan-America are mass-produced by machines in factories, with scientific measuring devices to ensure uniformity and acoustical correctness. And the "systems" for electric guitars or music synthesizers or electronic organs reflect directly the space-age circuitry of lunar landing vehicles, satellites, and computers. But even in so-called primitive societies, instruments touch the limits of technical skill and thought. For building an instrument, even if it is of "found" materials like gourds, sticks, bamboo, cans, or pots, is no simple matter. First, there must be an awareness or a discovery of the laws of acoustics, of the way sound and different pitches can be made and modified. Then there must be the solution of all kinds of technical problems, like increasing sound through resonators, methods of attaching strings or drumheads, tuning, bridges, frets, sound holes, handles, mouthpieces, bows, or boring finger holes. The maker must have a knowledge of the materials used—metal, wood, plastic, bamboo, clay, skins, horn—and the technology and tools to work with them, to shape them to the desired end. Finally, the instrument must fit into the cultural mold expected of it in the larger spectrum of society: it must be able to serve its musical and nonmusical (ritual or sociological) functions; it must be fabricated in an acceptable shape and decorated with traditional patterns; and it must be able to produce music that is considered by its society to *be* music.

There is a tremendous conservatism in the shaping of musical instruments, a conservatism that is at times counteracted by brilliant experimentation and innovation. This approach is made necessary in part by the very nature and limits of sound-producing mechanisms—vibrating string lengths, skins, tubes, reeds, sized lengths of wooden slabs—as well as by the purely physical characteristics (fingers, hands, mouth, lips, arms, lungs, legs, body) of the human beings who must play them. But this is not all. For there has always been another push-pull in the design elements of musical instruments: between the *necessary*, the purely functional (and all the problems that this involves), and the *aesthetic*, the crafting into shapes that somehow seem meaningful and beautiful. Once a shape has gained acceptance, it is fantastically resistant to change; it becomes "normal," the way things are done, like the shape of a house or the food one eats. Just as the earliest automobiles were modeled after carriages (and even today the motors generally are put—like a horse—in front of the driver, where, as one manufacturer has stated, "it belongs") the shape or elements tend to retain the old, the familiar, perhaps for thousands of years, even when they are no longer functionally necessary. The electronic music synthesizer is fitted with an "archaic" piano keyboard, and the gadgetry-modified electric guitar, which is not really a guitar at all in the old sense, still is built to look like a guitar. There might be also (and this is highly conjectural—no studies have yet been made) a deeply human unconscious musical memory preference, in the Jungian sense, for certain archetypal images.

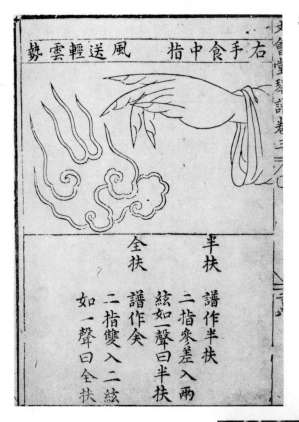

Symbolic image showing expressive plucking technique for playing the *ch'in*: "Wind blowing the clouds," from *W'en hui t'ang ch'in pu*.

Circuitry in electronic music synthesizer.

Is it, for example, just an amazing coincidence that the acoustically complex shape of the European violin is a shadow image of the mother-goddesses hewn out of marble in Mesopotamia and the Cyclades from around 2500 B.C.?

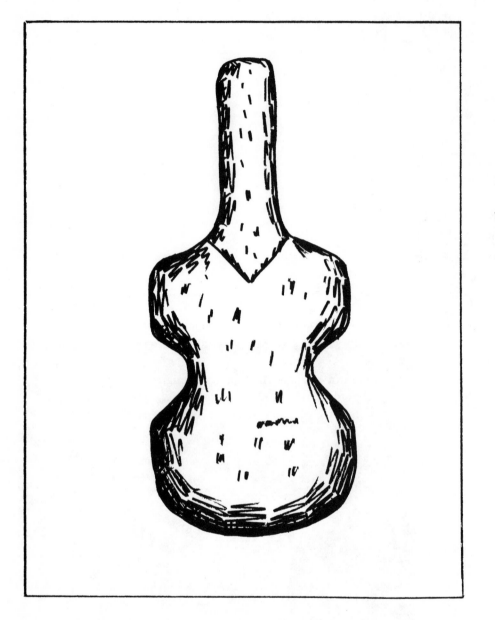

Violin-Shaped Female Idol
from Amoyos (Cyclades)
(ca. 2500 B.C.)

But beyond function, instruments are among the most beautiful art objects that man has ever crafted. Shapes are extended, exaggerated into arabesques, flowers, or animal shapes: the open ends of drums in New Guinea, for example, are carved to form open-mouthed birds and crocodiles, the bowed *mayurī* of south India is shaped like a peacock (and even has peacock feathers), while the scraped *yü* used in Chinese Confucian ceremonial music has bamboo teeth set comblike in the back of a carved crouching tiger. In Burma the plucked zither *migyaun* is a wooden stumpy crocodile, the *kudyapi* of the Philippines (also a plucked zither) is shaped like a miniature boat, and in Russia, as well as all through eastern Europe and Indian Latin America, clay and wood whistles are shaped like birds (especially) and frogs, as well as people and other animals. Fish-shaped instruments are found all over the world from the slit wood blocks (*mu yü*) played in Taoist and Buddhist temple ceremonies of China and Japan to the stringed *pochette* of sixteenth-century Italy. The tip of bowed and plucked string instruments above the peg box (where the ornamental "scroll" is on the violin) has always been a special place for carved faces and heads, almost like the figureheads of ships. European *chitarrones, lira da gambi,* citterns, lutes, and violins often culminated in the grimacing or singing heads of people, animals, or gnomelike creatures, while in the Orient dragon heads (complete with ivory teeth and eyes) or animals (cranes, elephants, peacocks, or tigers) predominate. Especially interesting is the use of carved horse heads on fiddles all through central Asia, an area where among (until recently) a primarily nomadic people horses are highly valued. Since horsehair is often also used for the strings and bowstring of the fiddle, the instrument—from the Yugoslav *gusle* to the Mongol *khil-khuur*—in effect becomes a symbolic representation of the horse. Such symbolism, fortified by design elements, is (as we have seen in the Chinese *ch'in*) common in the Orient. The Japanese *koto* (a plucked zither similar to the *ch'in*) is connected with the dragon, and the parts of the instrument are named for parts of this mythical animal. Similarly, the Indian plucked *veena* is thought of as a representation of the body of Saraswati, the goddess of music, with the frets being her ribs, the resonator her hips, and so forth. The bridge of many plucked and bowed instruments in the Far East is called the "horse."

We often think of European instruments as being straightforward and strictly down-to-business, with valves and keys and shapes governed by practicality and acoustics. But as any visit to a museum will show, from the Renaissance right up into the nineteenth century European craftsmen displayed the highest level of their skills and imagination in the decoration and ornamentation of musical instruments. The wood of instruments of every type was carved into figurative or floral designs, or inlaid with ivory, mother-of-pearl, or different colors of wood. The legs and bodies of spinets and pianos and harpsichords were similarly carved, inlaid, gold-plated, or painted with pastoral scenes. The pipes of organs in the great cathedrals were literally immersed in heavenly congregations of angels and celestial trumpeters, harpists, and choirs. The necessarily long tubes of brass instruments (horns, trumpets, trombones) were bent in a variety of ways: into concentric spirals, loops, hoops, *S* shapes, and half-moons—and as if this were not enough, the metal was engraved with ornamental arabesques and ornamental patterns. Woodwinds were also decorated, particularly the porcelain flutes and horns which were painted and glazed like fine china. Today we tend to connect extravagant ornamentation with instruments from the Mediterranean, the Middle East, and the Orient— with the inlay and carved floral sound hold of the *'ūd* lute, for example, or the ivory inlay on the *sitār*, or the carved and lacquered racks for the metal slabs and gongs of the Indonesian *gamelan*. But the instinct for instrument ornamentation is, like the human instinct for bodily decoration, a worldwide phenomenon. The Plains Indians of the United States ornamented drums with feathers, beads, rawhide strands, and painted designs, for example, while the Hopi of the Southwest painted symbolic colors and designs on their bull-roarers. Clay and wood rattles shaped like animals or people were and are common throughout the Americas. In the Amazon wings of phosphorescent insects and butterflies are attached to instruments (and, made into necklaces, worn as jewelry). In Africa burned or incised repetitive designs and reliefs and carvings of people, spirits, and animals cover instruments, while beads, cowrie shells, cloth, ribbons, tassels, buttons, thread, snakeskin bands, leather coverings, fur, cord, macrame, feathers, hair, teeth, rings, jangles, bits of metal, basketry, wickerwork, and painted designs—in short, almost everything imaginable, or possible—are also used.

Decorative elements may also be more subtle, more integrated into the design of the whole instrument: for instance, in the length and shape of the neck of a fiddle or plucked lute, in the size and shape of tuning pegs (those of the violin are unobtrusive in contrast to the magnificent turned pegs of the Indonesian *rebab*), in the curves and angles of its resonating sounding box, or in the design of its bridge, or the cutting and ornamentation of sound holes. Many of these elements we shall examine later when we look at the construction of musical instruments. In drums not only the overall shape of the instrument is important, but also the functional/ornamental way the skin drumhead is attached and the visual arrangement of the laced thongs or strings that hold it in place.

The decoration or nondecoration of musical instruments is, of course, directly related to the attitudes and preferences and conventions of the society that makes it. The functional and simple pragmatism of design seen in most Western instruments can also be seen in the tools, lamps, weapons,

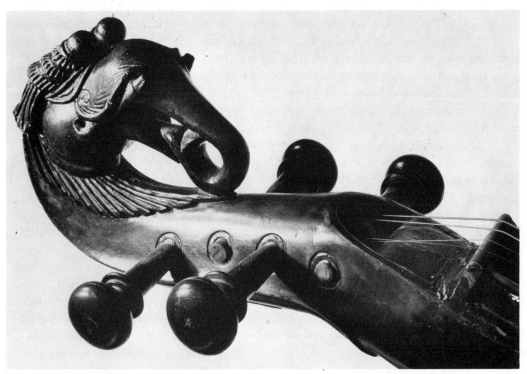

Yali or dragon head above peg box on south Indian *veena*.

Native American Plains-style ceremonial peyote rattle with gourd, horsehair tuft, and beadwork.

computers, and architecture of the "advanced" nations (although this is certainly an oversimplification: the frivolous and nonessential gadgetry, dashboards, fins, lights, and chrome of automobile design directly contradicts our assumption). Ornamentation may be entirely decorative, or it may serve a mystic or supernatural purpose such as the totemic animals carved on drums and zithers in Melanesia, or the powerful symbols (often derived from visionary experiences) painted on drumheads by American Plains Indians. An interesting use of design is found in the Japanese *koto* zither: special patterns called *ayasugi* are carved on the *inside* of the instrument where, although unseen, they are said to be essential to the tone of the instrument! A people's and consequently a maker's relationship to the raw materials of the instrument is also a factor. In Japan, for example, for hundreds of years there has been a love and an appreciation of the natural shape of things—a stone formed by the elements, the sea, wind, or rain, over many centuries; or the twists and bends of a branch or a piece of driftwood. Traditional craftsmen try to work around the beauty of these ingrown natural elements—in a sense the raw material remains itself, becomes itself. There is no attempt to disguise its shape or force it to conform to a totally preconceived idea. This attitude is reflected in the concern for the beauty of the grain of the wood and its preservation as a "natural" part of the instrument—on the *koto*, parabolic swirling designs created by the rings of the tree cut at a certain angle. The *shakuhachi* flute is perhaps the example par excellence; a high classical instrument that preserved completely the natural joints and asymmetrical bends of a chunk of bamboo!

In the countries influenced by Arabic culture, religion has played a direct role in the decoration of instruments. Islam forbade the use of figurative designs in art and architecture, and the result was the development of the profuse abstract designs, the swirls and arabesques and plantlike patterns or the stylized calligraphy, which we find inlaid and modeled on walls, windows, and ceilings of mosques and palaces throughout north Africa and southwest Asia, or carved into wooden or stone screens, or woven into rugs, or decorating musical instruments from Tangier to Calcutta.

In fact, geography (as well as the available technology) may greatly influence the shape and type of musical instruments within a given culture. Instruments are made from the materials at hand. Thus shark skins, seashells, and bones from fish are extensively used in the South Pacific. Coconuts, gourds, and bamboo are used in the tropical regions where this type of vegetation grows. Goat skin is extensively used (for bagpipes and drums) in the Mediterranean and eastern Europe, while cattle skins or skins from wild animals are more common in sub-Saharan Africa where such animals abound. Pottery and metal instruments are made where crafts using these materials are highly developed, as in Africa and in east and southeast Asia (which has been called the "gong-chime" cultural area). In highly industrialized countries, synthetic materials like plastic and nylon, sophisticated alloys, and electronic circuitry influence the shape and sound of instruments. The very nature of these raw materials, their pliancy, strengths, and weaknesses, determines the final shape of the instruments made from them. For example, plastic may be cast in almost any shape, wood can be carved or laminated, to an extent, and metal can be cast or hammered within limitations; but bamboo, which is a very hard substance to work with (or, rather, against), tends to retain its natural shape. Thus bamboo instruments as a rule retain the essential character and undisguised shape of bamboo.

We have noted how musical instruments as "machinations of sound" are extensions of the human body and how they not only carry out the musical thought of the persons who play them, but in some instances expand and modify these ideas or give birth to entirely new concepts. Instruments are also to a great extent wedded to the sound and style of the musical culture in which they are found. Frets, finger holes, and tunings are set to fit specific scales or melodies; tone colors match the preferred cultural standard of what is beautiful; specific details of construction may nurture special effects or a certain style of ornamentation. Many instruments are capable of a dual musical function, such as a melody accompanied by a drone (with specific melody strings or pipes and specific drone strings or pipes), a characteristic found in the string instruments of India, central Asia, and folk and medieval Europe, as well as in the bagpipe and the numerous "double" clarinets and oboes of the Mediterranean area and eastern Europe. Similarly, some instruments seem to have a "harmonic"

Collection of instruments from
Lebanon displaying Arabic/
Islamic design motifs. Top:
kanun/zither; right: *'ūd*/lute;
bottom right: *duff*/tambourine;
bottom left: *nai*/end-blown
flute; left: *buaoc*/long-necked
lute.

Reeds of different lengths blown
across the top produce different notes of the scale.
Panpipes from Peru.

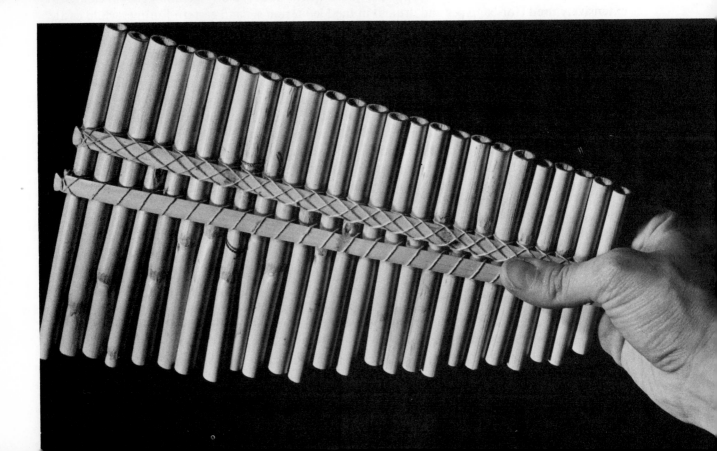

nature, or at least the capability of playing both melody and chords, sometimes simultaneously (like the guitar, piano, organ, accordion, and southeast Asian *khaen* mouth organ).

In fact, the musical style of a particular culture may be virtually inseparable from the instruments on which it is played. It is hard to imagine the music of the African *mbira* or east African *malimbe* xylophone on any other instruments. How could the translucent brilliance of the Balinese *gamelan* be achieved on anything other than this particular combination of gongs and chimes? Or can, or should, we expect a piano to be capable of reproducing the subtle intonations and ornaments of Turkish classical music, or a *sitār* to play a Bach fugue? Music removed from the sound/timbre/ style/intonation of the instruments for which it was intended can sound inanely oversimplified at best and absurd at worst. And this is an extremely important point, one that we in the West who tend to think of music (in theory, at least) as an abstraction of melodic, rhythmic, and harmonic elements all too easily ignore or forget. Scholars of world music are acutely aware of the problems of putting a music into Western musical notation (a distortion to begin with, but one that is necessary for the communication of ideas) which will then be played on the piano (a further and sometimes hideous distortion). Luckily today we have tape and gramophone recordings so that we can hear an authentic performance (often in its native surroundings), and ethnographic films give us a visual record of the performance situation and environment.

Musical instruments, then, fit the specific characteristics of their musical cultures like a glove on the hand—but (as in all gross generalizations or simplifications) there is a fly in the ointment. Or rather several flies. The first is that we must not forget the musician, his techniques, and the skills of his performance. While we can examine an instrument and postulate its potential, we cannot really imagine the actual music played on it within a musical culture. For example, if we take the Egyptian *nāy* flute or the Persian *surnāy* double-reed pipe and move our fingers across the finger holes we will find that each plays only one scale. But in actuality each of these Middle Eastern instruments (through the musician's use of special fingering and lip techniques) has the capability to play an almost infinite variety of scales, colored by subtle shades of intonation, ornaments, glissandos, and other special effects. Similarly, we may write off the two- or three-note South American ocarinas as simpleton's toys, while in actual musical practice these deceptively simple instruments are combined into ensembles which through special performance techniques (like hocketing, the playing of different notes of a melody on different instruments) create a delightful music full of melodic, harmonic, and rhythmic life.

The other fly buzzing around our generalities is that instruments, like people, migrate. And instruments as mechanical objects move from culture to culture much more easily (and quickly) than musical ideas, philosophies, and abstract concepts. Once within a foreign culture or subculture, they are likely to be adapted (through modification of playing technique) to the musical style of the new culture. Both the European violin and clarinet, for example, have been adopted by musicians from the Near East to India—and, in fact, by folk musicians playing in a variety of styles all through Europe and the Americas. An equally striking example (and one that is all too easily forgotten, because of its familiarity) is the adaptation of European symphonic instruments to jazz. Classical musicians could not at first believe (they were, in fact, horrified) that the same instruments they used to play Berlioz or Mozart could make the sounds—the bends, shudders, glissandos, colors, and range—played by the predominantly black early jazz musicians. The instruments were and are the same, of course, but the playing techniques and their uses are vastly different.

SOUND WORKINGS AND REFLECTIONS. I.

Sound, as almost everybody knows, is a disturbance in the air. It begins in a sound source and spreads out in waves, much like the expanding circle of ripples created by a pebble thrown into a quiet pond. There are a limited number of ways that sound can be produced, and it is unmute testimony to the imagination of man that he has discovered most of them and has used them with astounding variety. To begin with, something must be made to vibrate. A solid object may be hit (like a log drum), scraped (like a comb), whirled through the air (like a bull-roarer), shaken (like a rattle), plucked (like the metal prongs of an *mbira*), or rubbed (like the glass harmonica, invented by Benjamin Franklin, consisting of tuned glass bowls rotating out of a trough filled with water which are rubbed by the fingertips). A stretched skin may be beaten, rubbed, or scraped (as in the drums of the world); or stretched strings may be made to vibrate by plucking them (like the guitar), by the friction of a bow or stick rubbed across them (like a fiddle), or by striking them (like a hammer dulcimer). Reeds set in an enclosed chamber with air forced across or through them (by breath, bellows, or bag) will vibrate into sound (like a harmonica, oboe, or bagpipe), as will breath (or air) split across the edge of a hole and into an enclosed space (like blowing across the top of a bottle or a flute). Air buzzed through the tightened lips into a tube also causes sound vibrations (like trumpets, horns, trombones). And, finally, sound can be produced by electronic means.

Once a sound has been created—and this is the primeval function of the machines we call musical instruments (and the one thing they all have in common)—a number of things can be done. One thing is to do nothing further: to let the instrument remain basically as a one-sound, and perhaps one-note, music-maker (like the Indian *ektār*, which is a one-stringed plucked drone, the European ratchet noise-maker, or the Chinese wood-block *mu yü*). In truth even this is not as simple as it may at first appear to be: for example, instruments with acoustically rich sounds like bells and gongs can make an almost infinite variety of sounds depending upon how they are played (struck, rubbed, scraped, bowed), with what (rubber- or cloth-tipped or wood or metal beaters), in what manner (with full force or softly), and where (at the edge, in the center, to one side). The south African musical bow and the worldwide-distributed jew's-harp are made to produce a variety of different notes and sounds by changing the size and shape of the mouth (which is used as a resonating chamber). Even two sticks hit together in different places, like the *pakuru* of Oceania, can produce different sounds.

The next step is to increase the instrument's potential, to make it capable of producing a number of different sounds and/or pitches. This can be done many ways; before going into them, we might coin (without going into the acoustical reasons) another of our convenient rules-of-thumb:

What is:		What is:
longer		shorter
bigger		smaller
thicker	will make	thinner
more dense	a lower, deeper	less dense
heavier	sound	lighter
more relaxed	than	more tense
looser		tighter
softer		harder
slower		faster

We must remember that in any given instrument (or part of an instrument) several of these principles will be working together, interrelating, and that always in the background is the performer and his skills at modifying what may already be there. For instances, the pitch of a string will be influenced by

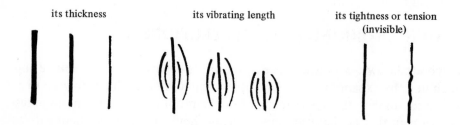

its thickness   its vibrating length   its tightness or tension (invisible)

and possibly also (as we have noted in the case of the musical bow) by the shape and size of its resonator. A variance in any one of these factors will produce a different pitch. Similarly, a drum can produce different pitches according to

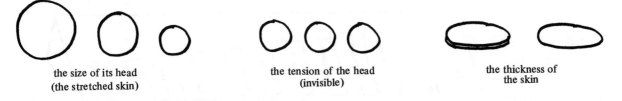

the size of its head
(the stretched skin)

the tension of the head
(invisible)

the thickness of
the skin

or how it is played, as well as by special details of construction like an overlay of multiple heads or the addition of tuning paste. The tuned gongs found in southeast Asia and the Far East get their pitch characteristics not only by their size and thickness but by the acoustical properties of their shape, notably by curved and bent edges and by centrally placed "knobs" or "bubbles."

With these factors in mind—the complex interrelationship of elements more or less following the principles of our rule-of-thumb—we might now examine in greater detail how multipitched instruments are put together.

An amazing number of the earth's musical instruments are really combinations of single sound-producing agents that are duplicated in different sizes and thicknesses and strung together like beads on a chain. It is almost like those family portraits so popular about fifty years ago with the mother and father at one end and the children lined up, oldest to youngest, tallest to smallest, on one side.

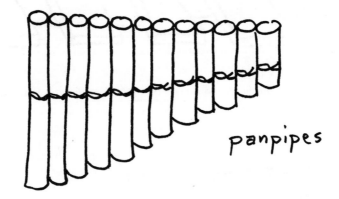

panpipes

Different lengths of tubing blown across (panpipes: highly developed in performance among the Indians of the Andes; also found in Africa, Europe, and China. Same principle: the pipe organ).

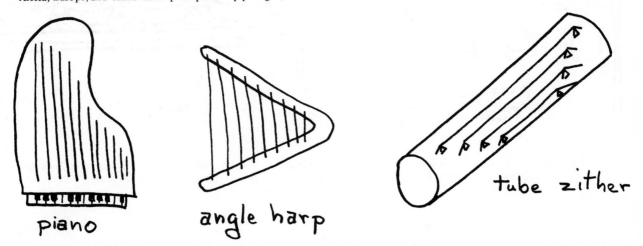

piano

angle harp

tube zither

Different lengths of vibrating strings (harps, zithers, pianolike instruments: Africa, the Middle East, Europe/America, east and southeast Asia. Many varieties highly developed).

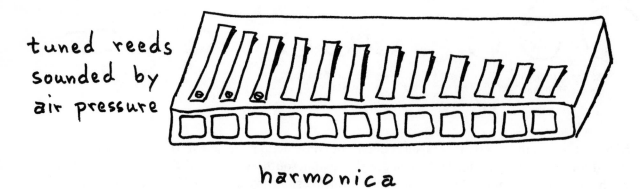

harmonica

Different sizes of vibrating "free" reeds (east Asian *sheng* mouth organ, harmonica, accordionlike instruments: originally in the Far East, since the early 1800s in Europe and subsequently worldwide).

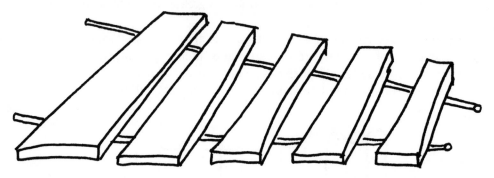

Different sizes of wood or metal slabs usually in a horizontal rack (xylophones, *marimbas*, Javanese *saron*-like instruments: southeast Asia, Africa, to Latin America).

pien chung
(China)

bonang
(Java)

Sets of tuned bells, chimes, gongs, or hung slabs usually of metal (in China also of stone, notably jade). Predominant from China to southeast Asia and Indonesia. They may be hung vertically or set in a rack. Also found in European church bell towers.

tuned drums in set   **naqqāra (Arabia)**

Sets of tuned drums. Burma—the *saing waing* with twenty-one drums placed in a circular stand—and in Africa: in Uganda a set of fifteen drums may be played by four to five players. A pair of drums tuned precisely or relatively (high and low) common in Africa and in Arabic-influenced areas. (Example: the *naqqāra*.)

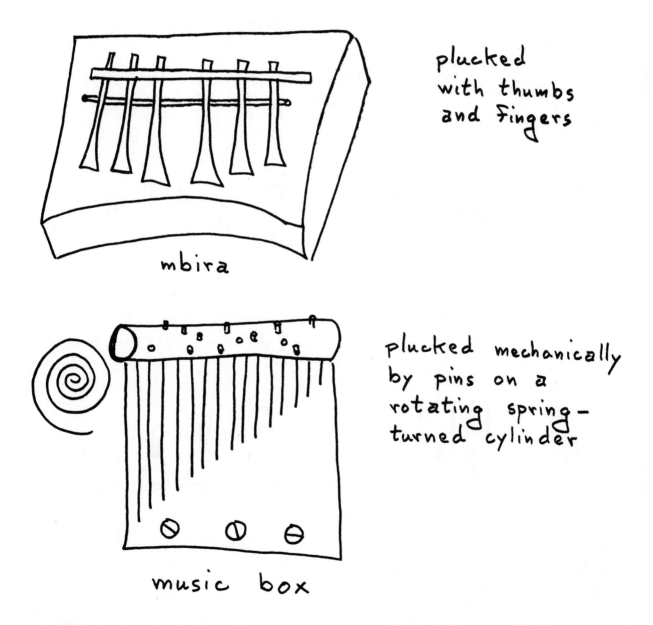

plucked
with thumbs
and fingers

mbira

plucked mechanically
by pins on a
rotating spring-
turned cylinder

music box

Different sizes of flexible plucked metal or bamboo tongues (the African *mbira*, also the European music box).

In the same category we might place those ensembles comprised of a number of musicians playing different sizes of the same "limited" one- or two- or three-note instrument (which go together in a set), like the panpipe and ocarina groups of Peru and South America, the natural trumpet bands of West Africa, the groups of Swiss hand-bell ringers, the *skuduchiav* flute ensembles of Lithuania, or in Indonesia the *gamelan angklung* orchestra, each instrument of which is made up of one or more bamboo tubes set loosely in a frame and tuned in octaves which rattle melodiously when shaken. In Estonia sets of five *ragas* shepherds' horns, played by five performers, are tuned whole tones apart.

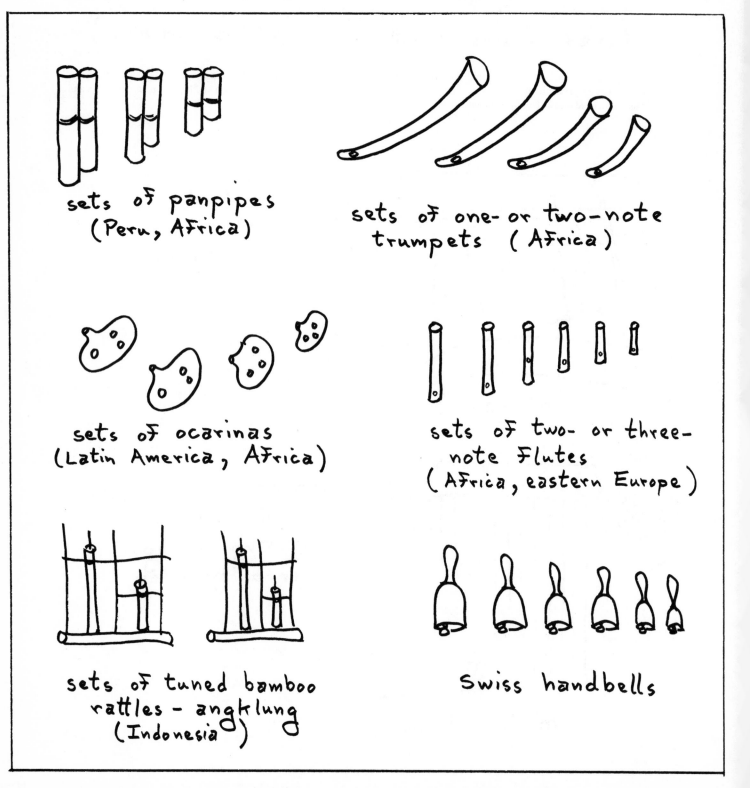

sets of panpipes
(Peru, Africa)

sets of one- or two-note
trumpets (Africa)

sets of ocarinas
(Latin America, Africa)

sets of two- or three-
note flutes
(Africa, eastern Europe)

sets of tuned bamboo
rattles - angklung
(Indonesia)

Swiss handbells

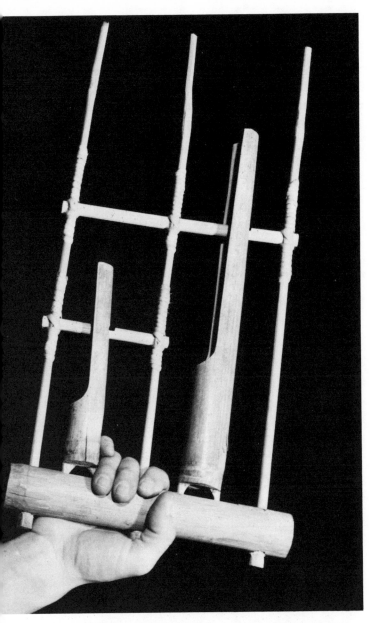

Angklung/tuned bamboo tube rattle, Bali. Different sizes tuned to different pitches are played in an ensemble, the *gamelan angklung*.

Valves and tubing of the modern tuba, with American musician Wayne Forrest.

Wind instruments, especially flutes and horn- or trumpetlike instruments, all have a further potential for producing different notes, a potential that is inherent in the very nature of sound being produced by forcing air through a tube. When the lips of the player (the blower) are progressively tightened and/or the pressure of air is increased (by "overblowing"), an acoustically natural series of notes occurs: the "overtone" or "harmonic" series. The longer the tubing, the easier it is to produce these notes. The length and the bore (the internal size) of the tube give the tuning of the lowest note of the series, and consequently of each of the higher pitches which proceed "up" according to strict mathematical and acoustical proportions.

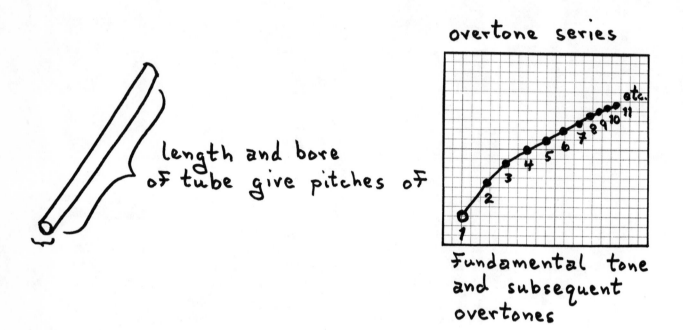

Every trumpet or horn on earth can produce at least a few of these overtones (from 1 to 6 on our graph), familiar as the notes of fanfares, horn and bugle calls, and the brass parts of classical symphonies. But the problem for musicians and inventors was to fill in the gaps between the notes of the series so that trumpeters and horn players could play scales and melodies possible on violins and flutes and other instruments. One possibility was to play the upper "partials" in the series (from our number 7 up), but these notes, while possible, are difficult to control and to keep in tune. The simplest solution (and a uniquely European one) was to change the length of the tube, so that different fundamentals and different overtones could be played. The trombone, which dates from the fifteenth century, utilizes a telescoping movable slide which can almost instantaneously change the length of its tubing (and open up a new series of possibilities of notes). Horns used "crooks," or removable pieces of tubing in different lengths, to achieve the same result (but not nearly as instantaneously). It was not until the invention of valves by Stoetzel and Bluehmel in Germany about 1815 that European brass instruments reached the potential that they have today. Basically, a modern "valve" trumpet, horn, or tuba is a tube with alternating channels of different length. The valves,

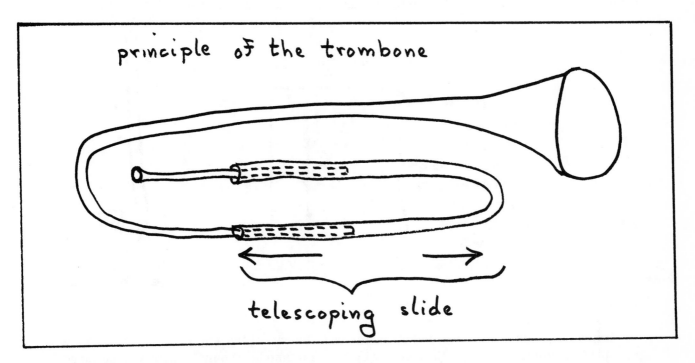

singly or in combination with one another, guide the flow of air into the desired channel or channels, each of which, through tightening the lips or increasing the air pressure, can produce its own overtone series. The changes can be instantaneous, as fast as the fingers or lips can move. It is this quality that distinguishes these instruments from the horns and trumpets of Africa, Asia, Oceania, and the European folk tradition: the valve instruments are constantly (unseen externally) changing in length.

Simplified Diagram of Valve System on Horns/Trumpets/European Brass Instruments

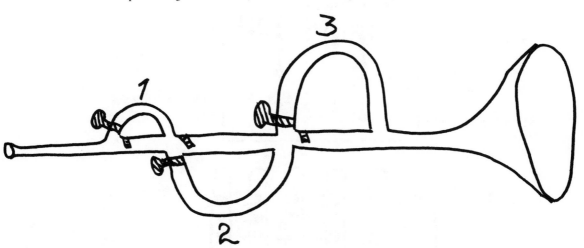

The airflow can be channeled through the tubing of 1, or 2, or 3; or in any possible combination: like 1 plus 2, 1 plus 3, 2 plus 3, or 1 plus 2 plus 3. The valves open or close the "gates" to the respective channels. A different-length tube results from each combination.

The Polish *fujarka wielkopostna* and the Slovak *konkovka* are long end-blown flutes which play entirely in overtones. By opening or closing one hole near the bottom of the instrument (increasing or decreasing the length of the vibrating air column), two overtone series a step apart can be achieved, making possible scales and melodies. In this instance the finger functions somewhat like the valve.

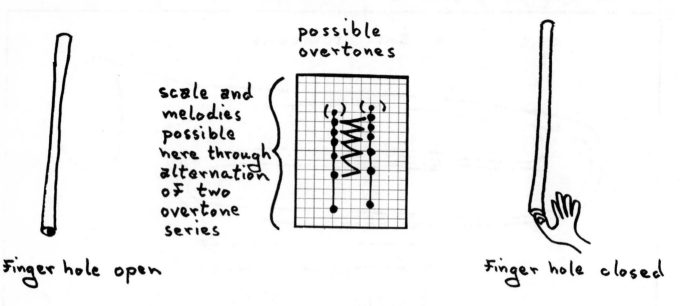

possible overtones

scale and melodies possible here through alternation of two overtone series

Finger hole open

Finger hole closed

Most flutes, double-reed pipes, and clarinetlike instruments of the world use the overblowing principle (sometimes aided as on the recorder by a little thumb hole) only to increase their range: the same series of notes fingered over the holes of the flute, for example, can be overblown to produce parallel series an octave, an octave and a fifth, and with more difficulty two octaves or (occasionally) two octaves and a third, or more.

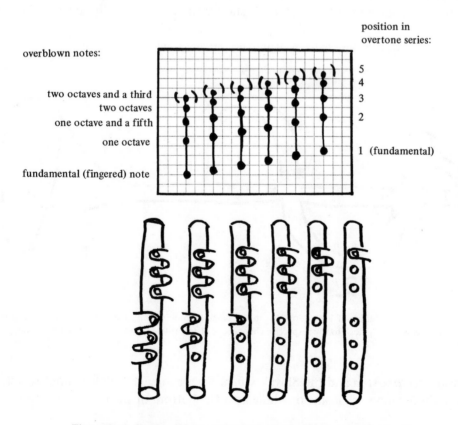

position in overtone series:

overblown notes:

two octaves and a third
two octaves
one octave and a fifth
one octave

fundamental (fingered) note

5
4
3
2

1 (fundamental)

Thus only six finger positions over the holes (in the above example) can give
—through overblowing to notes of the overtone series—twenty or more notes.

The common way that many different notes can be produced on a single musical instrument is through the lengthening and shortening of a vibrating string or an air column (we have already seen how this is done on the trombone and on European valved brass instruments). On instruments whose sound source is a stretched string (such as the plucked *dotar* or *ch'in* or the bowed *rabāb* or violin) the string can be pressed or touched (usually by the fingers but also by a sliding object like a stone or bottle-neck) at different places, instantaneously changing the vibrating length of the string.

Remember our rule-of-thumb— the *longer* the vibrating string is, the lower the pitch will be; the *shorter* the vibrating string is, the higher the pitch will be.

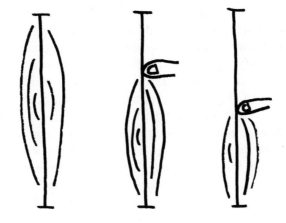

On some instruments like the hurdy-gurdy, popular in France in the eighteenth century, and the Swedish bowed *nyckelharpa*, the string is touched, or "stopped," mechanically: the player's fingers press down little keys or levers which in turn stop the string(s) at predetermined points. This use of finger-extension mechanisms, while unusual on stringed instruments, is common on European wood-wind instruments—flutes, oboes, bassoons, clarinets, saxophones—of the past several hundred years. We shall shortly see why.

On wind instruments, such as the Arabic *nāy* or Balkan *kaval* flutes, the Chinese *sona* or Mediterranean *gaita* reed pipes, or the European Renaissance *cornetto* with its trumpetlike mouthpiece, holes are drilled or burned into the sides of the cylindrical or conical tubing. By opening or closing these holes with the fingers the length of the vibrating air column inside the tube can be changed to achieve notes of different pitches.

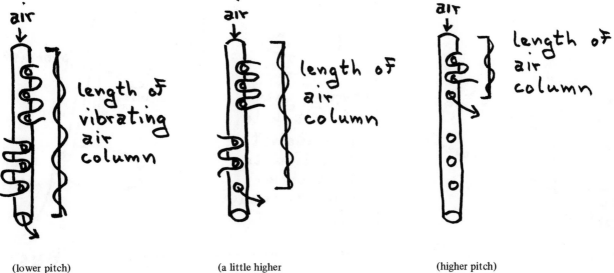

(lower pitch)
longer air column

(a little higher pitch)
slightly shorter air column

(higher pitch)
shorter air column

In actuality the acoustical process is much more complicated than this. The flutists and pipists of the world have discovered many ways to alter and expand this very basic pitch process; for example, by tightening or loosening or refocusing their embouchure (shape of their lips), by "half-holing" (covering only part of a hole with the fingers), by "cross-fingering" (leaving open holes between those stopped by the fingers), or by overblowing. In fact, as we have mentioned, there is very little that an extraordinary musician cannot do on an ordinary pipe or flute with finger holes.

The limitations of fingered string and woodwind instruments lie rather in the size and shape of the human fingers and hand, in its reach and spread. Five holes spaced three inches apart on a three-foot-long flute, for example, could not be played by anyone except perhaps a giant or a gorilla. To overcome these physical limitations, and to achieve a more acoustically "correct" positioning of holes, as well as perhaps to satisfy that peculiar fascination of Western man for the mechanical (as opposed to the natural), European inventors have covered their woodwind instruments—with the happy acquiescence of European musicians—with a miniaturized plumbing of little keys and springs and hinges and levers and pads. With these mechanized extensions of their fingertips, musicians can play much more, and much more easily (according to the necessities and preferences of Euro-American music) and on much longer pieces of tubing, like the bassoon or the tenor saxophone, than would otherwise be possible. On the other hand, these "improvements," like so many of those of industrialized societies, have removed the musician one giant step from the ecologically natural *feel* of the instruments: mechanical pads cover the holes, not the tips of the fingers, which can, like sensual perceptive antennas, feel the intimate touch of the finger holes and the flow of breath vibrating (magically) into music.

A fourth way a variety of different pitches can be produced on an instrument is by increasing or decreasing the tension of a flexible sound producer, what we might call the "Law of the Rubber Band." An instrument called the "mosquito drum" in Haiti, the "ground bow" or "pit harp" in Africa, and the *kudam*, or "clay pot," in India—along with its cousin, the "washtub" or "gut-bucket bass" of the United States—is built by stretching a wire or gut string from a resonator (a leather-covered pit in the ground or an overturned washtub) to a fairly vertical stick, bow, or pole. By manipulating the stick (or the resonator) the musician can increase or decrease the tightness of the string and thus get different notes.

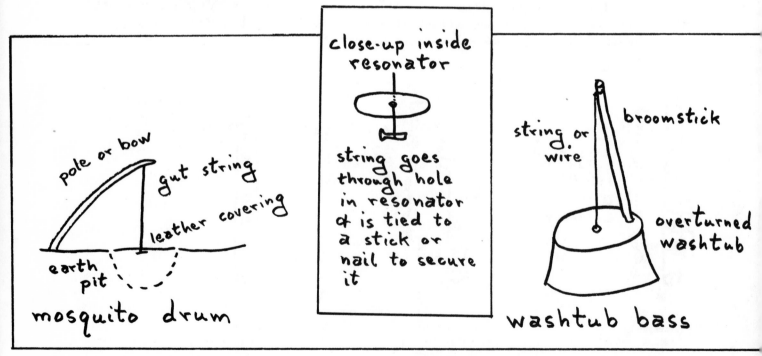

On the lyre, so prevalent in the ancient Near East and Mediterranean and now common in many forms and varieties in Africa, as well as on many of the world's other stringed instruments, strings of

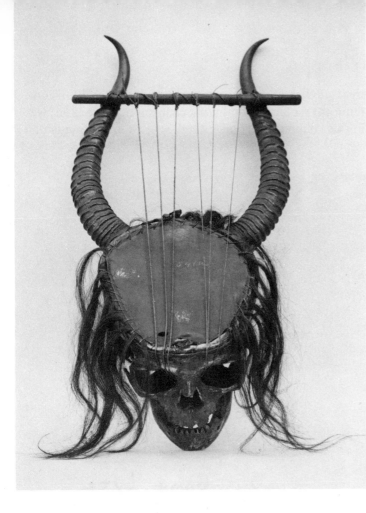

Kissar/lyre made from human
skull and gazelle horns,
central Africa.

Chang go/hourglass-shaped drum from Korea.

more or less equal length are tuned to different pitches through an increase or decrease of tension. This procedure (unless the notes are to be random) requires a tuning mechanism of some kind; we shall discuss some of the possibilities later in this chapter. Of course, thicker or thinner strands of

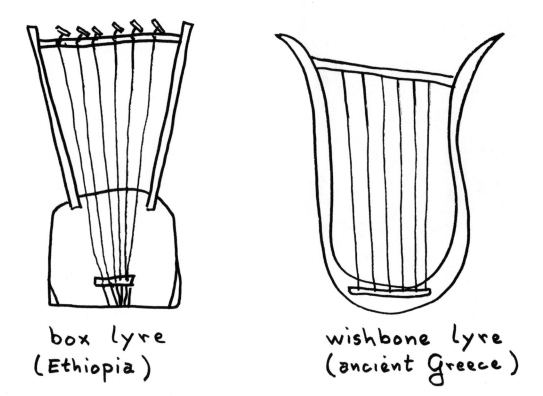

box lyre
(Ethiopia)

wishbone lyre
(ancient Greece)

wire or gut (or nylon) string can also be used to achieve respectively lower- or higher-pitched strings (other things, like tension and length, being equal).

The stretched skins of drumheads can also be tuned by increased or decreased tension, and it is common practice for percussionists throughout the world to tune their drums to precise or relative pitches by hammering in pegs or rims, tightening screw mechanisms (like on the European kettle-drum or the modern version of the goblet-shaped *dunbak* of Iran), or by tightening the lacing holding the head, by dampening the drumhead with water (the skin stretches, thus giving a lower pitch), or by heating the head over a fire (the skin gets drier/tighter/lower). But a drummer may also be able to get a variety of notes, some of them quite precise, out of his drums in performance. This may come as something of a surprise to those of us in the West (the European/American tradition) who think of drums primarily as noise-makers, and whose ears are not attuned to the subtle varieties in pitch and tone color that an African or an Indian (East or West) might hear.

Many of the earth's drums, from the *tapone* of Thailand to the *dhol* of Bastar or the *kihembe ngoma* of east Africa, have two drumheads (at either end of a barrel-, conical-, or truncated cone-shaped body) tuned to precise pitches or relative high and low pitches and played respectively by the right and left hands (sometimes holding sticks) of the player. Other drums, with single heads,

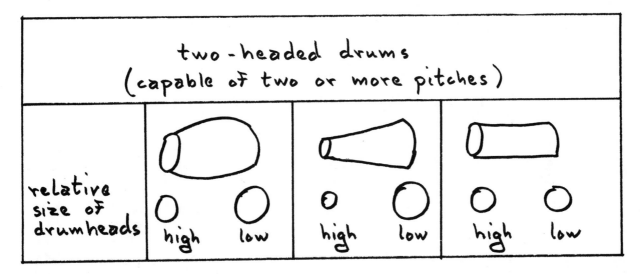

may be combined into pairs (a larger, lower-pitched one with a smaller, higher-pitched one) like the kettle-shaped *naqqāra* of Turkey, the *tabla* of India, or the *agbadga* "talking drums" of Ghana.

We have mentioned the limited-note trumpets, panpipes, bells, and flutes which, combined into ensembles, function as a larger "instrument." Drum ensembles, particularly those in Africa, may be thought of in the same way, like the royal drum ensembles of Uganda with up to fifteen tuned drums played by four to six players. The many different timbres and pitches of the drums thus combined create a "melody" as real and as wonderful (if not more so) as notes and chords picked out on a one-piece, one-person instrument like the piano or guitar.

But even with a single- or double-headed instrument, drummers can make a variety of sounds and pitches: the head or body of the drum can be hit in different places or with different strokes (or beaters), part of the head can be damped with one finger or hand to pick up overtones, or the skin may be pressed with the heel of the hand (as on the Indian *tabla*) or foot (as on the large frame drums played by the Ga people of Ghana) or the fingers (as on the Iraqi *bendir* tambourine) to increase the tension and the pitch. In India on both the *tabla* and the barrel-shaped *mridangam* each drumhead is actually made up of three layers of leather (some of them with the center cut out). In addition a hard black spot of iron filings and rice flour is centered on one head, while a damp dab of rice paste is put on the other before each performance. Each drum is then quite an acoustically sophisticated instrument capable of making many different sounds and pitches under the capable hands and fingers of the performer.

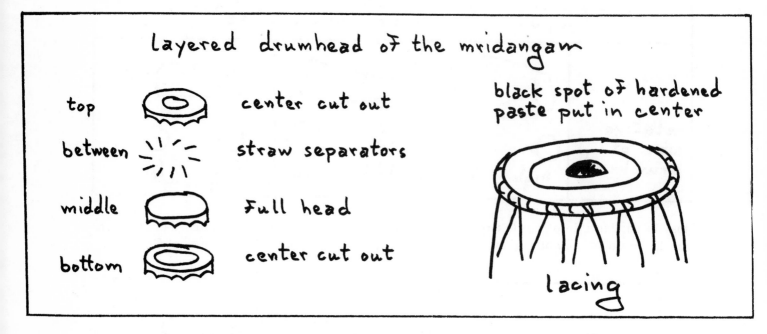

Another type of drum, found from Latin America through Africa and India to China and Japan, can produce melodies of up to seven or more tones—a full octave—as well as glissandos and other special effects on a single drumhead! This is always an hourglass-shaped drum with strings or leather thongs stretched from the rim of one drumhead to the other. By squeezing the strings or thongs with his hands or between one arm and the body, the performer can instantaneously increase or decrease the tension of the head. The exact shape of the hourglass body of the drum may vary—from the *dundun* and *gangan* of Ghana to the *udukkai* of Kerala in India or the *chang go* which is virtually the national drum of Korea—but the basic principle of playing it remains the same.

We should remember, then (and we cannot emphasize this enough), that drums in many parts of the world, far from being simple noise-makers, are extremely sophisticated instruments which in the hands of virtuoso musicians are capable of producing not only breathtaking rhythms, but also an amazing variety of pitches and timbres.

II.

Once sound has been produced on a musical instrument in one or more of the many ways we have seen so far, it may be amplified and reflected—increased in volume and/or projected in a certain direction.

Sound increasers are called *resonators*. One of the acoustical characteristics of sound is that when it passes into a partially or fully enclosed air space it bounces around like a ping-pong ball in a jar, building up energy and getting considerably louder in the process. It also gets richer by picking

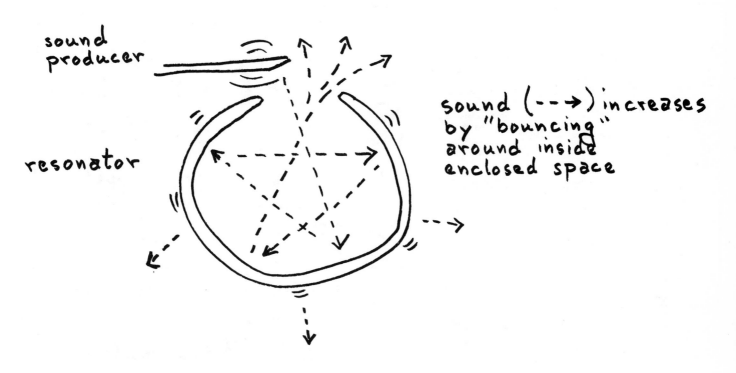

up something of the timbral quality of the container. Water amplifies sound—which combined with the reflecting quality of tiles and porcelain and the small size of the room is why people love to hear themselves sing in the bathtub! Stretched skin also amplifies sound (all drums are therefore amplifiers as well as sound producers), as do multiple stretched strings or wires tuned to the same pitch. And, finally, in the latter half of the twentieth century electronic amplifiers have become the sound increasers and enrichers par excellence capable of modifying and projecting the barely audible sound of a whisper or a jew's-harp or a plastic guitar to the ears of one hundred thousand or more listeners sitting in the open air. We shall now examine some of these sound increasers in greater detail.

Many of the resonators used by man for his musical instruments are more or less "found" or natural objects which except for a little hollowing out and trimming and fitting are kept in their original recognizable shape. Among these we might include Mother Nature's gifts, such as gourds and calabashes and hollow pods, bamboo tubes, turtle and armadillo shells, animal bladders, hollowed-out logs, or the human mouth and chest cavities, and manufactured items, such as clay pots and jars, barrels, balloons, skin bags, tin cans and containers, or metal or plastic or ceramic tubing. Other resonators may be subtly constructed by craftsmen: carved out of single blocks of wood like the Bulgarian *gadulka* or the south Indian *veena*, capped with stretched skin like the Arabic *rabāb*, built, boxlike, like the Japanese *koto*, or shaped carefully out of many pieces and glued together like the European violin or the Mediterranean *'ūd*.

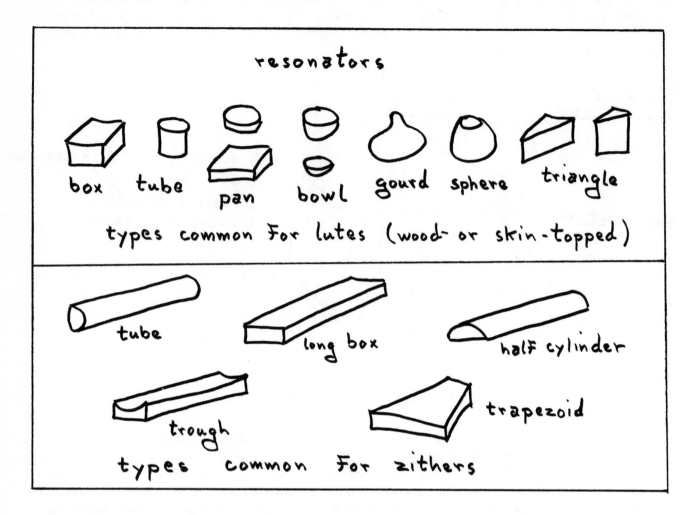

The resonator may be attached or held close (unattached) to an instrument; it may form an integral part of the instrument's construction; or it may be the entire body of the instrument.

The search by craftsmen for the shape of a "perfect" resonator for a particular instrument may cover centuries; the evolution of the final shape of the violin, for example, makes fascinating history. But the shapes and sizes of resonators may also be determined by the materials and technology at hand, by acoustical experimentation, or by standards of beauty or the habits of tradition. We must remember also that the entire instrument, every bit and piece of it, vibrates when music is made with it. The sound-carrying qualities of the materials from which the instrument is made—types of wood, metal, or skins, or their combination—and their shape and internal relationships and finishes (lacquers, varnishes, oils) are all important factors. The addition or subtraction of a little detail like the sound post of a violin (a little post inside the body of the instrument that carries the sound from the top to the bottom) can make all the difference in the world. A similar important sound-increasing detail in the guitar that few people know about is the addition of little strips of wood glued in a fan-shaped pattern under the "belly."

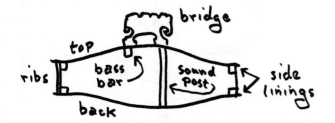

cross section of European violin body (resonator)

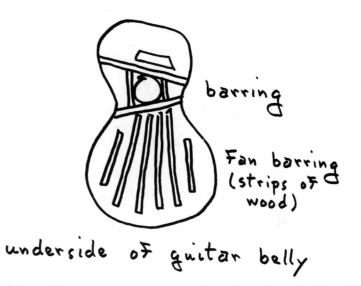

underside of guitar belly

The size and placement of holes in a resonator (out of which the richocheting sound can emerge) are also important and can vary from the single circular hole of the guitar or Russian *balalaika*, the slits of the *valiha* tube zither from Madagascar, or the *F-* and flame-shaped holes of European bowed instruments, to the ornate circular "flowers" of the *'ūd* and the lute, or the tiny circular pinpricks of the Indian *veena*.

Reflectors amplify sound by focusing it, bouncing it off in a specific direction much as a tennis ball can be bounced off a concrete wall. Indeed, walls and bandshells in parks as well as concrete and fiber glass "clouds" in concert halls are all sound reflectors, although they are not attached to instruments. Reflectors are usually shaped like a seashell, a cupped hand, a half-circle, a hood or umbrella; and they may be made from palm leaves, half-gourds, split coconut shells, or even saucers and tin pans. The body of a grand piano with its contoured wood box and raisable lid is both resonator and reflector. Sound may also be given direction by guiding it through a tube, a bell shape, or a conical megaphone. The flaring bells at the ends of trumpets and reed pipes all over the world serve this function, although they also enrich the timbre of the sound.

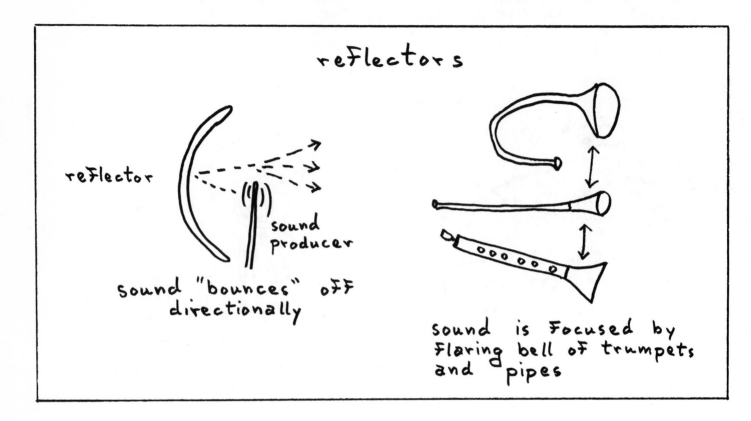

reflectors

reflector

sound producer

sound "bounces" off directionally

sound is focused by flaring bell of trumpets and pipes

Increasers—resonators and reflectors—are most necessary for stringed instruments as well as for plucked idiophones like the African *mbira* because of the sometimes inaudible quietness of the vibrating plucked or bowed string or metal (or bamboo) tongue. Wind instruments as a rule do not need resonators (except for their flaring bells) because of their natural cutting loudness—although the *didjeridoo* eucalyptus tube of the Australian aborigines is sometimes focused into a bucket or large can to increase and enrich its sound. But many percussion instruments, despite their original loudness, use this acoustical principle. We have noted that all drums—with skins (or more recently plastic) stretched over a frame or hollowed-out form—are resonators as well as sound producers. The idea of the drum as a resonator attached to bowed or plucked string/metal/bamboo instruments is found especially in Africa, the Middle East, and in central and east Asia. The skin may be stretched on one or both sides of a frame (as on the Japanese *shamisen* or the American banjo, the latter a derivative of African prototypes), it may cap a small cylinder (the Chinese bowed *erh hu*) or half-sphere (the Indian coconut fiddle *ravanastram*), or it may be stretched across all or part of the top of a shaped resonator (the Arabic *rabāb*, the Yugoslav *gusle*—both fiddles—or innumerable harps, lutes, and lyres from the African continent).

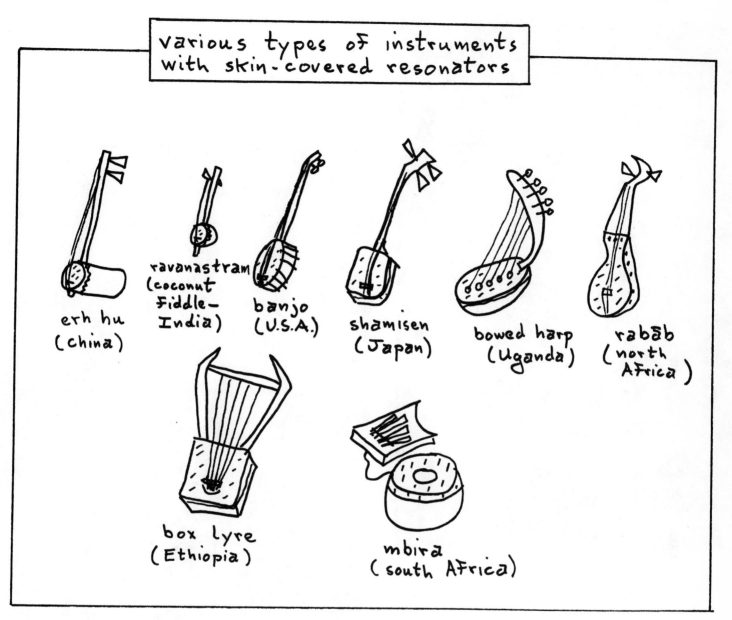

various types of instruments with skin-covered resonators

erh hu (china)

ravanastram (coconut fiddle—India)

banjo (U.S.A.)

shamisen (Japan)

bowed harp (Uganda)

rabāb (north Africa)

box lyre (Ethiopia)

mbira (south Africa)

The type of skin used to cover the resonator varies immensely (ox, goat, sheep, buffalo, lizard, game animals, etc.) but it may be governed by tradition: as, for instance, in the use of snake skin for the Chinese *erh hu* or female (!) cat skin for the Japanese *shamisen*.

In many cases the bridge (which raises the string) is placed right on the surface of the stretched leather so that the vibrations of the string carry through directly. Leather-topped string instruments have a particularly brilliant and rich tone quality that in some cases may even be mistaken for the penetrating nasal sound of double-reed pipes.

Thus far we have looked at instruments that have a single resonator/reflector to increase all the many sounds that may be made upon it. But, in fact, every enclosed space as well as every object from pencils to stones to jars or cans (and even buildings and rooms) has its own "tuning," a specific pitch or sound vibration to which it responds. As an experiment, try singing (loudly) a gradual rise from low notes to high in a small room, or into a can or metal wastebasket. Certain pitches will resound—these are the pitches sympathetic to the tunings of the room or the can resonator. Once for a period of several weeks whenever I practiced on my instrument, the south Indian plucked *veena*, I was

Sesando/tube zither with cane body and palm-leaf sound reflector, Timor, Indonesia.

Folk *sheng*/mouth organ from western China. One of the bamboo pipes has been pulled out of the wind chest to show the free reeds which vibrate (like those of a harmonica or organ) to produce tones.

bothered by a slight buzz or rattle that occurred every time I sounded a particular note. Careful examination of the instrument revealed nothing wrong and I was perplexed—until one day when I noticed the loosened lid on a tiny jar on my desk bouncing around just as I played the troublesome note. The rattle was simply the sympathetic response of a tuned resonator (the jar) to the sounding of its fundamental pitch!

The different notes of the *khaen* mouth organ found in classical and folk forms all through southeast Asia (it is known as the *sheng* in China and the *sho* in Japan) are sounded by channeling air across little tuned metal reeds which then vibrate into sound, the same sound-producing method as that of the European harmonica. But to increase and enrich the sound of the *khaen* each reed is set in a bamboo pipe, which is, in turn, tuned to the precise pitch of the reed. Thus if an instrument has, say, ten reeds and ten different pitches, it will also have ten tuned tubular resonators.

This principle of having a tuned resonator for every available pitch on an instrument is especially common on melodic percussion instruments like xylophones and *marimbas* which are made up of tuned blocks of wood or metallic slabs cut or forged to different sizes. In Africa many of the wood xylophones have gourds carefully chosen to match the pitch and size of each slab. These gourds are attached under their respective slabs, and, as an added refinement, a strong membrane woven by spiders to protect their eggs may be glued over the opening in each gourd. The result is not only increased sound, but a richer tone quality and a somewhat "buzzing" timbre. In Java the *gender* has bamboo or metal tubes of different lengths under its metallic keys, while the popular Central American instrument the *marimba* uses squarish tubes. Fine tuning to a higher pitch may be achieved not only by cutting the length of the resonator, but also by decreasing its internal space (remembering our rule-of-thumb) by filling it with wax, sand, or even water.

Finally, we might take a look at two of the most "natural" yet unusual of all sound increasers: the human body and old Mother Earth herself! Among the acoustical discoveries of early "primitive" man must have been the resonating quality of hollow trees and half-shell rock formations, of natural amphitheaters, and the magical (unexplainable) echo effects of valleys and mountain walls. It is probably not entirely conjectural to believe that his choice of deep caves, such as Les Trois Frères, for what are believed to be ceremonial centers for hunting or seasonable or human rites was guided in part by the mystical acoustical transformation of sound—of singing, instruments, and the human voice—in the dark resonance of these underground sanctums. The earth (above ground) has been used as a sound producer for countless centuries: in the sometimes earthshaking stamping of feet in dances or the beating of rhythm sticks and poles or bamboo tubes on the ground. It was only one small step to hollowing out the earth into a small pit or trench and making a resonator out of it, or, rather, into it.

The Yoruba of west Africa and the Alur north of Lake Albert, to mention only two examples, play xylophones mounted over a pit in the ground, an extension of the similarly placed log drums found in many other places in the world. In Ethiopia a narrow, tapering, trumpetlike hole is made in the ground and howled into; this ecological instrument is called "the lion's roar." More commonly, the pit is capped or topped with a "lid" of stone, bark, hide, or planks; thus made, it can be stamped or danced upon or extended to function as a resonator for an earth-based string or percussion instrument. On certain ceremonial occasions the Uitoto Indians of Colombia dig a pit and cover it with boards. Over it they place a large hollowed-out tree trunk on four posts, close to the boards. The men of the tribe stamp on the hollow tree trunk until it begins to swing, hitting the boards and creating resonant tones. In Uganda children make a zither out of sticks, a string, and a central post resting on a stone slab over the resonating chamber hollowed in the ground.

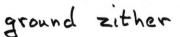

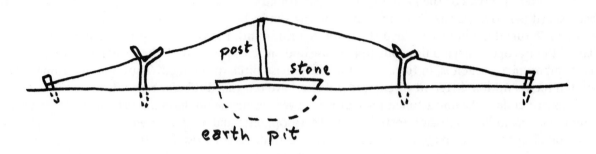

We have mentioned earlier the plucked ground bow common in many parts of Africa (known as the "mosquito drum" in the Caribbean). Not only can different pitches be produced by increasing and decreasing the tension of the string—the tip of the flexible stick is held by the player—but the string can be stopped in various places by pinching it lightly between the forefinger and thumb. The pygmies of the Congo often utilize a second player who drums with sticks on the cover of the pit.

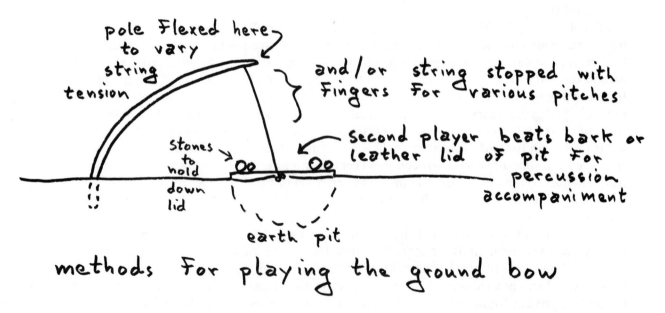

The use of the earth as an essential component of a musical instrument is, in fact, quite a beautiful concept. It points to a time when there was a mystical connection between man and the ground he walked and slept on, which gave him, through the natural magical growth of plants, food for his stomach, and which, through these connections, nurtured his brain in a never-ending search for the meaning of life itself.

But there are also practical reasons for the use of the musical earth. Acoustically it is a wonderful resonator: the rough chunks of soil or smooth edges of mud in a pit give a rich, mellow tone color to sound. Some of the great old concert halls in Europe and the Americas were built with earth pits under the planking of their stages (a refinement lost to recent architects who have designed the many glass and concrete acoustical nightmares that fill our civic and cultural centers). The stage for the *noh* theater form of Japan uses large earthen pots buried in soil under its stage as sound increasers and enrichers, and some of the old masters of the Chinese *ch'in* did the same in their music rooms and studies.

But the earth, too, is free, easy to work with, and readily available everywhere—at least in the tropical and semitropical regions where it is used for musical instruments. Those of us who are surrounded by the paraphernalia of "civilization"—gadgets, objects, books, tools, and the like—and thus in a sense are immobilized, imprisoned by our objects, tend to forget that for many of the world's peoples (although their number grows less every day) mobility was an absolute necessity. Slash-and-burn agriculturalists, hunters, foragers and gatherers, and nomadic herders were constantly or seasonally on the move; what they owned or used had to be carried with them or constructed anew wherever they went. The American Indian tepee and the central Asian yurt, for example, were easily transported (if one had horses or oxen), while the Eskimo igloo or the Australian aborigine brush shelter could be built from the available materials of the land wherever one found oneself at the end of the day. Tools and objects that could not be carried could similarly be "found"; and anthropologists have marveled at the ability of "primitive" peoples to see "instant tools"—stones or branches or gourds or leaves of the right shape—almost everywhere. The same ingenuity has been applied to musical instruments: everyday objects (pots, hunting bows, boomerangs, leather aprons, hoe handles) are transformed into sound-makers, or the readily available materials of Mother Nature—branches, vines, reeds, fibers, logs, animal bones, gourds, bamboo, and earth—can be crafted into jew's-harps, flutes, rattles, drums, pipes, or stringed instruments in a matter of minutes or hours. Such instruments, because they are so easy to make, are, in a sense, disposable. They are by no means limited to tribal peoples: a pair of spoons clacked together is used as accompaniment in Turkey and in the fiddling traditions of New England and Appalachia (and elsewhere); rural southern Americans, black and white, make rhythms on the common washboard; and in the same region blacks too poor to own an instrument used to make wall harps. A string or wire was stretched between two nails hammered into the wall of a house. A stone was jammed under the string for increased tension and tuning and a bottle-neck slid up and down the string to achieve the subtle whines and glissandos of blues accompaniment. The house was the resonator. And the music was wonderful.

wall

nail

stone

string

nail

bottle-neck used to
stop string

wall harp

The human body, as we have mentioned, is also a musical instrument, an eminently portable one. There is the human voice, of course, and all the clicks and tricks that the mouth and vocal cords can do; there are the feet, which can stamp out rhythms; and there are the hands, which can clap together or slap various parts of the body-drum (for different timbres), an art delightfully developed in Africa and in the Americas. But two parts of the human body are also utilized to

Man playing jew's-harp by hitting it with contracted palm muscles. Larger than others commonly found in New Guinea, this jew's-harp is played seriously and only by men, never by women. Tekim Valley, New Guinea.

function as resonators: the chest cavity (and lungs) and the mouth cavity. A half-gourd resonator is often attached to the African musical bow and its cousin, the bar zither. The open end of this gourd is then cupped against the chest of the player, making in effect a double sound increaser, half-gourd, half-human. In south India the *ghatam*, a large clay pot played like a drum with the fingers and capable of all the complicated rhythms of Indian classical drumming, is held in the lap of the musician. By constantly changing the angle of the opening of the pot in relation to his bare chest, sometimes pressing it against his body, the performer gets a kaleidoscopic variety of tones and timbres, which duplicate those of the *mridangam* drum.

The mouth is perhaps the most amazing resonator of all. Through movement of the cheeks, lips, and tongue the player can change the size and shape of his resonating cavity at will, instantaneously, with complete freedom. Each shaping of the mouth results in a kind of "tuning," with its own special acoustical resonance characteristics. Using the vibrations from a single sound source—notably the single vibrating string of the musical bow or the flexible blade of the jew's-harp—the player need only move his mouth, as if to form words, to cause different overtones to sound. (This is the same natural acoustical series of pitches we examined in relation to trumpets and flutes.) Complete "natural" melodies and a variety of tone colors can thus be played, entirely through the skilled movement of the flexible mouth cavity resonator! And, as if this were not enough, the breath (inhaling and exhaling through the mouth) can be used as an additional sound increaser.

GROUPINGS

There is a little bit of the librarian in everybody, a love of putting things on shelves, arranging them neatly in niches, systematizing and classifying them. Life and nature, as we all know, is sometimes chaotic, a happy or horrifying conglomeration seemingly moving in all directions at once without shape or reason, far removed from the neat theories of historians or the symmetrical arrangement of butterflies. In music, too, the spontaneous and unconscious expression and organization of sound is offset by what for many may be every bit as instinctive: the need for rational structuring and explaining, for a comprehensible *gestalt*. Like the grandeur of a great oak tree split in an naturalist/ scientist's mind into a crisscross grid of categories and functions, man's structuring of music (what is essential is invisible, must be felt by the heart deeply) is in a sense a forcing of magnificently twisted branches and wind- and sun-shaped leaves into geometric slots and boxes. But this attitude, this way of seeing, of simplifying and making understandable, and of needing the mental security understanding affords, is a basic characteristic of man as man, as much a part of him as his fingers and toes. It influences what he sees, how he sees (and feels and thinks), and what he does; it influences how he comprehends music (and feels and thinks about it), and it influences how he makes it.

The classification of musical instruments is like the scientist's grid over the oak tree: somehow it seems necessary (at least in the rationalism of "high" cultures), yet no system fits perfectly without all kinds of loose ends and leaking corners. Instruments could be classified according to how they are made, according to size (from the acorn rattles to walk-in pipe organ housings), how they are played or held (sitting, standing, walking, over the shoulder, around the neck, set on the ground, with the fingers, fists, hands, mouth, feet, eyelashes), according to their function and status in society (religious, secular, folk, courtly, middlebrow), or by their historical age (from the fifteen-thousand-plus-year-old musical bow to the four-thousand-nine-hundred-year-old [according to Chinese tradition] *ch'in*, to the twenty-year-old electronic music synthesizer). Instruments could be categorized according to the kind of music that is played upon them: instruments for Confucian or Buddhist ceremonial music in China, for example, for jazz and blues in the United States, for classical traditions in Europe or India, or for village and folk music in the same areas. They could also be classified by their distribution or predominance in certain areas of the globe, as, for instance, the gongs and chimes found from China to Indonesia; the *rabābs, zurnās, nāys, dümbeks, tabalas*, tambourines, and lutes of Arabic-influenced cultures spreading from north Africa into the Balkans, central Asia, and Indonesia; or the dispersion of European/American instruments through colonialism or the more recent economic and cultural exploitation. The list is, perhaps, endless.

In China during the fifty-fourth year of Emperor K'ang-hsi (reign 1661-1722) of the Ch'ing dynasty the instruments used in *Ya* music when it was performed for Confucian ceremonies were divided into eight categories according to the material from which they were made and sounded. There were the instruments of:

1. metal (like bells, gongs, or sets of tuned bells or metal slabs hung in racks)
2. stone (like the *t'e ch'ing*, a large, single, sonorous stone gong, or the *pien ch'ing*, a set of tuned stone chimes hung from a rack)
3. silk (like the *ch'in* or *shē* zithers whose strings were made of silk)
4. bamboo (like the *ch'ih* or *ti* flutes, the *kuan* reed pipe, or the *p'ai hsiao* pan-pipes)
5. gourd (the *sheng* reed mouth organ, whose wind chamber was originally made from a gourd)
6. earth (like the *hsüan*, an ocarina of baked clay or porcelain, described as being "the size of a peach")
7. skin (all drums, like the *chien ku, t'ao ku*, and *po fu*)
8. wood (like the *chu* box, which was struck, or the *yü*, shaped like a crouching tiger, which was scraped).

The scholars of ancient India devised a classification based on the acoustical properties or nature of the sound-producing part of the instrument. Thus all *vadya*, or instruments, fit into four broad categories, strikingly similar to those in use today:

1. *tata*: sound produced by stretched strings, bowed, hit, or plucked (like the *veena* lute or the *ravanastram* coconut fiddle)
2. *sushira*: sound produced by wind or breath (like the *sangu* conch shell trumpet or the *venu* bamboo flute)
3. *avanaddha*: sound produced on stretched skin, that is, on drums (like the tiny hourglass-shaped *damaru* or the giant-sized earth drum *bhumi-dundhubi*)
4. *ghana*: sound produced by striking solid objects (like the finger cymbals, *talam*, or the *ghatam* clay musical pot).

In the oral and written traditions of European classical music, instruments were and are usually thought of in terms of their functions as sections of the orchestra. There are the *strings* (violins, violas, cellos, basses), the *woodwinds* (flutes, oboes, clarinets, bassoons), the *brasses* (trumpets, trombones, horns), and the *percussion* (a potpourri of everything the percussionist plays from timpani and bass drum to triangle, glockenspiel, and perhaps even the piano). But in the early twentieth century Erich M. von Hornbostel and Curt Sachs invented a comprehensive system based on the same four broad acoustical categories as those of ancient India, but greatly expanded (with subgroupings) to include the subtle variances and details of construction of instruments under each general heading. A numerical cataloging system similar to the Dewey Decimal System was also devised. The Sachs-Hornbostel classification, despite some flaws and inconsistencies, is what is used almost universally by scholars and ethnomusicologists today. The four broad categories are:

1. *idiophones*: sound produced by the vibration of a (solid) material, free of any kind of applied tension (rattles, scrapers, wood blocks, cymbals, bells, gongs)
2. *membranophones*: sound produced by the vibration of stretched skin or membrane (including plastic) (drums)
3. *aerophones*: sound produced by the vibration of an air column, that is, by wind or breath in a tube or across a reed (pipes, flutes, horns, trumpets, clarinets)
4. *chordophones*: sound produced by the vibration of stretched strings (fiddles, lutes, zithers, harps).

Mantle Hood has attempted a further refinement of this system by incorporating into a symbolized and numerical representation (which could be fed into a computer) almost everything that could be said about an instrument from the details of its construction and the way it is played to its place in society and mythic or religious associations. For instance, he represents the *ntumpan*, one of a pair of master drums (together called *atumpan*) played by the Ashanti and other Akan peoples of Ghana, in this way:

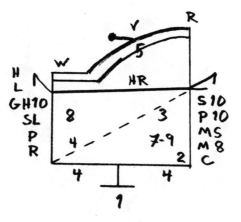

Reading the symbols from the top, left to right, we can see that the instrument is tuned by W (wetting the head) and by ⟋ (tuning pegs) supporting V lacing to R (relative pitch) of H and L (high and low). The ⟋ outer shape is given (top line) paralleled by its inner shape, and it is made of 5 (wood). It is played by ⟍ and ⟋ (two crooked sticks, left hand and right hand). It has an HR ("hardness ratio," an arbitrary and somewhat subjunctive 1-to-10 scale of values, pitch, density, etc.) of 8 in loudness, 3 in pitch, 4 in quality, 7-9 in density, and—beneath the rectangle—4 in technique, 1 in finish, and 4 in motif. The ▭ rectangular box indicates the family (membranophones) and the dotted line ⟋⟋ , that the drums are played in a slanting position. They are held by ⊥ (a stand). Going to the left of the rectangle we can see that the *atumpan* are associated with GH (a group of high social status) and that they are 10 (highly valued). They are S (symbolize the soul of ancestor drummers and a tree), are honored with L (libations), and have P (magic power). R (ritual) is associated with their manufacture. Going to the right of the rectangle we read: S10 (society values them at 10, highly), P10 (so does the player), MS (the maker of the drum has special status), M8 (their monetary value is 8), and C (they are indispensable to the life cycle of man)!

While such a detailed coded description may be of use to the expert or museum archivist, for the average music lover or scholar a series of photographic musical instrument "mug shots" and closeups, photos of the instrument being played, or a detailed line drawing, along with a short verbal description, would probably be sufficient. We shall now look at a few instruments under each category, examine some details of their construction, and attempt to define terms (like lute, zither, horn, or clarinet) that will be (and have been) used to describe seemingly quite different types of instruments in this book.

Idiophones

Idiophones—instruments made from an inherently resonant material that is made to vibrate—have an extremely long history. Jingles of rattling substances strung on cords are found in many European Paleolithic sites; a stone xylophone (technically a lithophone) was dug up from a burial site in Vietnam dating from the Neolithic period; and bronze cymbals, shell clappers, bells, and rattles were common in Mesopotamia and China from the third millennium B.C. Of course, the musical leavings of history are deceptive: instruments of stone, bone, clay, or metal remain to be found, while perhaps the majority—made of wood, gourds, bamboo, leather, or other perishable materials—disappear in the decay of the ages.

Calabash rattle with outside beadwork, Ghana.

Pien ch'ing/suspended stone chimes. Print
from a Confucian music handbook,
P'an-kung li-yüeh ch'üan-shu.

In construction, idiophones cover the full spectrum of technological complexity from a pair of polished stones hit together (the *kajrak* of Uzbekistan) or the hollowed-out log drum (found in Africa, south Asia, Oceania, and South America) to the elaborately cast bronze Shan drum of Burma, the plucked *mbira* of Africa, or the many-tuned metal slabs of the Javanese *saron* set in an ornately carved wood frame. They may be extremely easy to play or fiendishly difficult. They may be built to produce only one or two notes (or sounds), or they may span several octaves, in a variety of tunings. And, finally, they may be constructed to produce sound by striking, stamping, rattling, scraping, plucking, friction (bowing, rubbing), or wind.

Similar or duplicate instruments—musical "identical twins"—which are struck together are among the simplest and most common of the idiophones. There are the Spanish castanets, the wood or metal spoons (Greece, Hungary, Turkey, central Asia, United States), clicking pairs of stones or pebbles (like the Uzbek *kajrak* or the Hawaiian *ili ili*), or rhythm sticks (like the Latin American *claves* or the *pakuru* of Oceania). In ancient Egypt precisely carved ivory or wood clappers were made in the shape of a pair of hands, perhaps pointing to an anthropomorphic origin for this musical concept. Pairs of cymbals also fall into this category: from the tiny tinkling *talam* of Indian dance music to the crashing cymbals of China, Turkish military music, or European/American orchestral and band music.

By far the largest family of idiophones is that made up of instruments that are hit with a stick or beater. The simplest are "found" or utilitarian objects—logs, shields, pots—that are picked up on the spur of the moment and beat upon; the most complex are those made up of a set of tuned bars or slabs (from largest to smallest according to our rule-of-thumb). If the bars are made of wood the instrument is a *xylophone*, if of metal a *metallophone*, if of stone a *lithophone*. They may or may not have (tuned) gourd or tubular resonators. We have already noted the popularity of xylophones in Africa, although they are also common in Latin America and in southeast Asia, and in Indonesia, where metallophones form the basis of a unique orchestral tradition. Lithophones are mainly a Chinese phenomenon, except for oddities like the lithophone with crudely cut stone bars set on a tablelike rack invented by a local clergyman in Cumberland, north England, which enjoyed a brief (and very local) vogue in the nineteenth century.

One of the problems in the construction of all these instruments is how to keep the objects (the slabs or bars) in place, since they vibrate—and can rattle and bounce—when struck. If they are secured too tightly their vibrations will be inhibited and their potentially resounding, bright sounds will be muffled to dull thuds. Somehow a balance must be found (as for the human condition!) between freedom and restraint. The simplest solution is to drill little holes in the objects and to suspend them from a frame, as is done with the *L*-shaped stone slabs of the Chinese *pien ch'ing* or with the *kempul* tuned gongs of the Javanese *gamelan*.

pien ch'ing
suspended stone
slabs (China)

kempul
suspended gongs
(Java)

pien chung
suspended bells
(China)

Little handles or loops may be built into the sound producer itself through which the cord or string may be threaded, such as in the *pien chung* set of suspended tuned bells from China. We are a little ahead of ourselves here in that sets of tuned bells or gongs form a different subfamily from sets of tuned wood, metal, or stone slabs in the standard Sachs-Hornbostel system; but the problems of mounting them are similar.

If the slabs or gongs are placed vertically, as in the African *malimbe* xylophone or the Javanese *saron* metallophone, the problems are a little greater. One solution—that of the *saron*—is to drill little holes near either end of each slab and to fit them loosely over vertical rods, cushioning the base on which the slabs sit with little pieces of felt, cloth, rubber, or a similar nonsounding material.

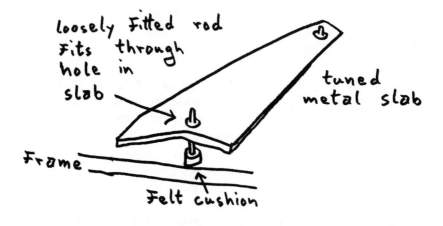

Another method, the one preferred by the makers of African and Central American xylophones, is to suspend the bars in string or fiber lacings, which, in turn, are strung across a wooden rack. The tuned bars may be plain, notched, or with holes to help keep the string in place.

ways of stringing slabs on xylophones

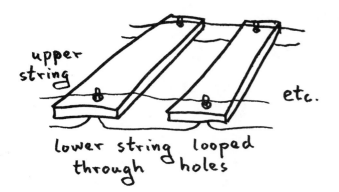

upper
string

lower string looped
through holes

etc.

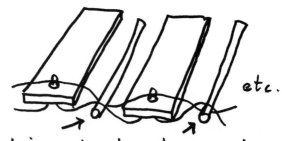

etc.

string also laced around small
sticks to help separate
musical slabs

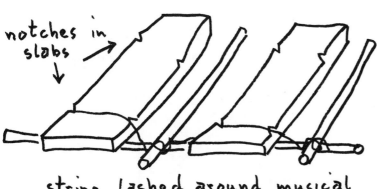

notches in
slabs

string lashed around musical
bars and support sticks
mounted on a frame

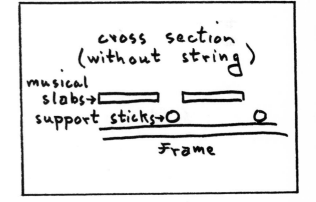

cross section
(without string)

musical
slabs→

support sticks→

frame

strung double holes
ranat/xylophone
(Thailand)

etc.

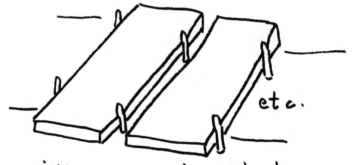

little separators between
slabs on a padded or stretched
string rack
gambang/xylophone (Java)

etc.

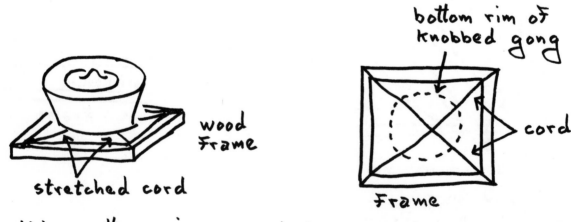

bottom rim of
knobbed gong

cord

Frame

wood
Frame

stretched cord

this pattern is repeated for each gong in the set
and combined into a single rack

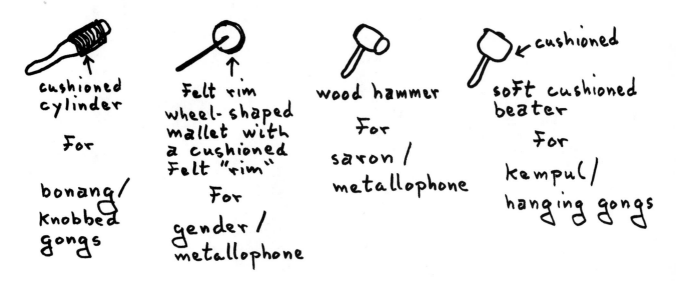

some Javanese mallets and beaters

cushioned cylinder

For

bonang/ knobbed gongs

Felt rim wheel-shaped mallet with a cushioned Felt "rim" For gender/ metallophone

wood hammer For saron/ metallophone

cushioned soft cushioned beater For kempul/ hanging gongs

Gongs—large circular sheets of metal—are another important family of idiophones. They may be flat, bulging, with a central "knob," tuned or untuned; they usually have a bent rim that can be of considerable depth. The bronze drum valued in the Shan states of Burma is unusual in that it is a highly ornamented gong cast in the shape of a drum. The owner of one of these "drums"—which can propitiate demons and avert evil—is said to have a social status higher than a man possessing seven elephants. Gongs can come in tuned sets, like the *bonang* of Java or the *cheng lo* of China. The steel drums of Trinidad and other Caribbean islands are an ingenious application of the tuned gong principle: different sections of the top (or bottom) of a large oil drum are hammered out into tuned bulges or indentations to give full notes of the scale. Instruments of treble and bass pitch range are then played together in a "steel band."

Bells are perhaps the only instruments in the world regularly played by animals. Made of wood or metal and with an attached inside clapper, they are strung around the necks of sheep, goats, and cattle almost everywhere. As the animals bend their heads to graze or sway in walking these bells ring gently in a quiet pastoral orchestration that magnificently combines the functional with the (musically) beautiful. Because of their great resonance and carrying power, bells (along with trumpets) have long been used for signaling. Even today there are bells on fire engines, bicycles, and steam locomotives, in church steeples and on the walls of schools. But bells have also commonly been used in a religious context. In China there was the large *po chung*—50 cm in height, hung from a rack, and played like gongs in Confucian and temple ceremonies—as well as the set of sixteen suspended tuned bells, the *pien chung*, dating from the Chou dynasty. Both types of bell instruments were struck (from the outside) with beaters. The Ghanaian *gankogui* is made up of two connected bells (with a high and low pitch) held in one hand and played with a stick held in the other; its rhythms are an essential component of every percussion ensemble. The "rings," or sets, of tuned bells with a freely swinging clapper inside in European and American church belfries may include massive giants of two thousand or more pounds. Each bell is mounted on a frame attached to a large wheel, which, in turn, is connected to a rope. (The large wheel has the effect of a gear which reduces the amount of muscle needed to swing the bell.) The bell ringers (one man to a rope) ring not tunes, but mathematical sequences of tones (with permutations and variations) called "changes." Smaller hand bells with attached handles and inside clappers, like the Tibetan *dril-bu* played in religious ceremonies, are also common throughout the world.

Iatmul men playing paired *garamut*/slit drums, before skin-cutting initiation ceremony. The end of each drum is a carved crocodile head, and the drum sound is the crocodile's voice which "produces" the cuts in the skin. Middle Sepik region, New Guinea.

Log drums—also idiophones and not really "drums" since they have no stretched skins—qualify among the earth's largest and heaviest instruments. In the rain forests of Assam, in India near the Burmese border, the Naga people make beautifully carved and ornamented log drums thirty to forty feet long. They are raised on a stand and roofed over in their own special house, as befits an instrument so important in the ceremonial and social life of its people. Log drums, which are found also in the Pacific, southeast Asia, Africa, and tribal South America, have a long slit made the length of the log, through which it is hollowed out. Usually the opposite sides of the lip of the slit have a different thickness, giving at least two possible pitches. Slit drums can be made from logs of any size, and, in fact, in Indonesia they are relatively tiny and hollowed out of bamboo.

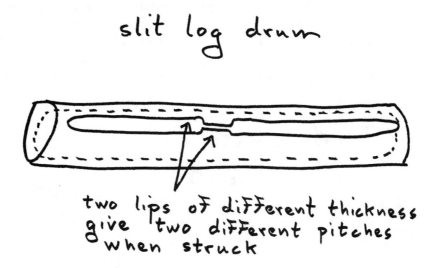

slit log drum

two lips of different thickness give two different pitches when struck

Tubes or gourds beat against the ground or against the body are found in the same areas as the log drum, and they are interesting in that quite often they are played by women in connection with fertility rites.

Instruments that rattle when shaken make up another important subgroup in the family of idiophones. Usually they include a container-resonator filled with pellets or some other rattling substance; they can have a handle (for the hands) or they may be attached to a belt (shaken when the wearer is dancing) or even to another instrument like a drum or harp. Rattles can be amazingly subtle instruments: often they are the only instruments used by the American Indians of the Southwest to accompany their songs. The rattles set a background pulse and create a variety of moods and expression through different sound qualities and performance techniques. Rattles throughout the world are made from every imaginable material: deer hooves, shells, gourds, pods, hard leather pouches, basketry, tin cans, gold and silver, plastic, pottery. Among the American Indians of the Eastern Woodlands, rattles are made of the shells of turtles. Furthermore, the head of the unfortunate (or fortunate—not everyone after his demise is made into a musical instrument) animal is stretched grotesquely over a stick of wood to become the handle. The sound of the rattles can vary tremendously according to the size of the container/resonator (it can be lower/louder if the container is larger) or the nature of its material. The rattling substance is also important; it can be sand, beans, pebbles, twigs, dried seeds, beads, metal or clay pellets of different sizes and textures. In African instruments such as the Nigerian *shekere* or the gigantic *agbé* the rattling pellets—beads or cowrie shells or short lengths of bamboo—are woven into a macrame netting put around the *outside* of the gourd or calabash.

Little *bell rattles* and *jingles,* often strung on cords or a belt sewed into clothing and worn every day or for dancing, date from ancient times and are common throughout the world. Pellet bells (little tinkling bells enclosing a "trapped" pellet that bounces around freely inside) made of silver, gold, and bronze were common in pre-Columbian Latin America, China, and the ancient Near East. By their very nature they exist in a delightfully ambiguous never-never land somewhere between jewelry and music; in India today they are strung around ankles or waists or attached to rings and worn by both housewives and dancers, and even in England they were perhaps once more common than they are today, as the old rhyme attests: "Rings on her fingers, and bells on her toes; she shall have music wherever she goes." Little objects fastened or strung close together that rattle or jingle against one another when shaken make up another subfamily of idiophones. The Plains Indians of North America attached strings of deer hooves or cartridge casings to their leather dance belts; nut shells, cowrie shells, and pieces of bone are strung together in South America and Africa; and in the Balkans strings of coins are popular.

Jingles and jangles (or jangling jingles) can also be attached to sticks which are thumped against the ground; they can be tied to the wrists of drummers, or fastened to the bows of fiddles or onto other types of melody instruments (*mbiras*, lyres, harps) where they rattle or ring along with the melody—a sound particularly loved in Africa. They can also be put on metal rods or frames: the ancient Egyptian and biblical *sistrum* (it dates from at least 2500 B.C.) is used to this day by the congregation and priests of the Ethiopian Coptic Christian Church to praise the Lord in services and sound. The Indonesian *angklung* with its rattling tuned bamboo tubes is a related instrument.

rattling metal
disks strung
on wire rods

pellet
"trapped"
inside

pellet bell, or
bell rattle

Ethiopian brass and wood
sistrum

Scrapers are also extremely ancient instruments and have been found in Paleolithic sites together with bull-roarers and bone flutes. In Mexico and among the Indians of North America bones and sticks were notched in a crisscross pattern and then scraped rhythmically with another stick. In Central America and the Caribbean gourds are similarly notched: the *güiro* of Latin American dance bands is an example. In the rural southern United States a notched mule's jawbone was often used, as well as the "found" instrument, the washboard, scraped with a metal rod or a spoon. A more unusual (and mechanical) scraper is the ratchet, which has a long European history. Its loud and distinctive sound functions not only as part of an orchestra percussionist's bag of tricks, but also as a toy (popular at Easter time), a noise-maker at football matches, and as an attention-getting signal for peddlers and, in Amsterdam, garbage collectors!

Plucked idiophones create sound by the flexing and releasing of flexible materials, or tongues; hence their name, *linguaphones*. Jew's-harps with their single plucked tongue belong to this group, although they are actually hybrids using the air of the mouth cavity to get different tones. (Incidentally, the jew's-harp has never in its long and distinguished history had anything to do with the Jewish people. The name is more likely a corruption of "*jaw's* harp," although one scholar has suggested it may also have come from the French *jouer*, "to play.") In Oceania and Asia the jew's-harp—both the vibrating tongue and its frame—is whittled out of a single piece of bamboo; but in its present form and shape, found all over the world, it is commonly made from a forged iron frame

Belt of deer-hoof rattles, Yaqui
Native Americans.

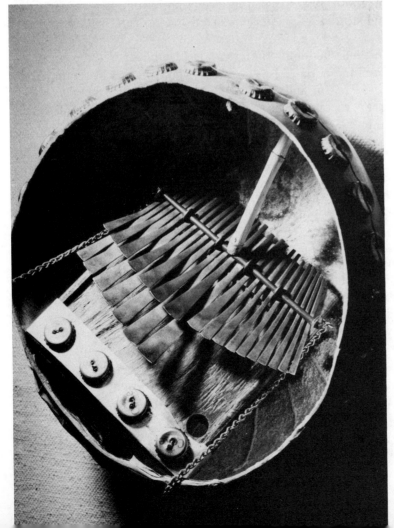

Mbira dzavadzimu propped inside
its gourd resonator. The bottle
caps add a soft buzzing to the
gentle sound of the metal keys,
which are plucked with thumbs
and forefingers. Made by black-
smith John Kunaka Maridzambira.
Shona people, Rhodesia.

fitted with a steel tongue. We have noted, and should perhaps reemphasize here, its amazing reputation as a sexy instrument!

The African *mbira* with its multiple plucked metal or bamboo tongues is also a linguaphone. Each tongue can be tuned by moving it in or out (making the vibrating area longer or shorter); in addition, little jangles or rings are added above the bridge or in other places on the instrument to give it a buzzing or jangling timbre.

A small number of idiophones also produce sound by friction. There was Benjamin Franklin's glass harmonica, for example, and in Europe and America the musical saw which is an ordinary carpenter's saw bowed with a violin bow. By bending the saw the musician can get all the notes of a melody as well as a lovely vibrato. A similar instrument is the nail violin made of different sizes and lengths of nails driven into a resonator. A single note comes from each nail as it is bowed.

We have looked into the family of idiophones in great detail, not only because they form a very interesting and very important family of instruments in world music, but because they are sometimes looked down upon as "primitive" country cousins to the more "advanced" string and wind instruments of "high" city culture. In actuality some of the most beautiful and distinguished instruments of the world belong to this family, and the music made upon them can be equal technically and expressively to any, anywhere.

Membranophones

Membranophones are instruments whose sound source is a vibrating skin or membrane. All drums are membranophones (except log "drums" and Burmese metal Shan "drums" which are idiophones since neither has a skin), but not all membranophones are drums, since stretched skins can be made to sound not only by striking them with hands or sticks but by friction and air as well. The perishable nature of membranes, like that of wood, makes it impossible to gauge their history, but Mesopotamian vases and artwork dating from about 3000 B.C. picture drums and drum playing; and several small Babylonian statuettes dated around 2000 B.C. are of men and women holding small frame drums in their hands.

Drums and drumming seem to have flourished and proliferated in certain parts of the earth more than in others, notably in Africa and India, but this is not to say that they are not important elsewhere. They function, for example, as exciting and essential accompaniment to "melody" instruments in the Islamic world from north Africa to Iran, and in the Balkans. In China drums are traditionally said to have been invented in 2579 B.C., and many types, shapes, and sizes exist here and in Korea and Japan functioning (importantly) in classical, religious, and folk genres. Throughout the world the fact that there may be only one or two types of drums in a cultural area, or that the music played upon them is relatively "simple," actually can be quite deceptive. We have noted, for example, the importance of the shaman's drum for magic and mystical "flights" in Siberia and the Arctic; the same holds true in the music of the Native Americans, the Indians, where the drum was and is highly valued in society and looms (impressive as a proud black thundercloud over the high plains) as *the* all-powerful and essential instrument for and in much of their music. Only in Europe/America have drums (and drumming) remained relatively subsidiary, undernourished, under-developed, under-everything, and connected more with folk and military traditions than with "high" culture. But even this is a simplification. African-derived drumming traditions have flourished in Latin America and the Caribbean; and the great synthetic forms developed by Afro-Americans— jazz, blues, gospel, rock, and others—with their emphasis on complex rhythmic impulse and percussion backgrounds have brought about a creative musical revolution at least in popular musical genres.

Like their neighbors in the family of musical instruments, the idiophones, drums and other membranophones suffer from ethnocentric prejudices, and not only in Europe and America. High-culture string and wind instruments and the human voice are considered to "make music," while drums and other sound-producing instruments (of orchestral percussion sections) are considered to "make noise." This amazing distinction and the hierarchical relationship it implies is, of course, on

Drummer with *dappu*/hoop drum, Andhra Pradesh, India.

Drum-makers in Dakar, Senegal.

the abstract musical level completely erroneous. But cultures, and the individual people in them, are free to order the world and the musical world in any way they see fit; when gentle people in Des Moines (or New York, or London, or Paris) get severe headaches from jazz or rock with its often volcanic percussion, they are, in a sense, expressing traditional value judgments within the confines of their own culture. But when we look into and hear the music of other areas, we must try to overcome the limits of our own experiences and prejudices, including the bias (for most of us) that separates "melody" and "percussion" instruments. We should perhaps reemphasize the point made earlier that drums and idiophones are instruments of great subtlety and variety both in themselves and in ensembles, and that their music (once we hear it) is in a sense as "melodic," or, at least, as musical, as that of any other type of instruments.

It is perhaps the impressive sound of drums that has connected them in the minds of people with power, supernatural and temporal. In seventeenth-century Denmark and Germany no one below the rank of baron was allowed to own a kettledrum unless he had taken it into battle. Until the more noisy and lethal weapons of the twentieth century made them obsolete, drums were an inseparable part of warfare the world over: for signals, to frighten the enemy, to boost the morale and fighting spirit of one's own soldiers, and, just as important, as a part of the paraphernalia of the military tradition.

We noted earlier how drums as sound and as objects may be essential to religious practices and ritual (such as the shaman's drum of Siberia); how they can, in association with ceremonies or spells, have magical power (to cure disease, bring rain, control storms, placate demons, or assure a good life or harvest); and, finally, how they themselves are often believed to contain spirits. For example, in Africa among the Banyankole people, drums are kept in their own hut, a special shrine, and offerings of milk are given to them daily. They are cared for by special guardians, whose functions are almost like those of priests. In addition, the drums themselves actually *own* a large herd of cattle, an accumulation of offerings given to them and protected by the king. Cattle from this herd are killed only on special occasions; only the guardians may eat their flesh, and skins from only these cattle are kept for making new drums or repairing old ones.

The basic working mechanism of drums is pretty simple: they have only three parts, namely, a skin, a shell or frame over part of which the skin can be stretched, and a connector to attach one to the other. A drum can have one head (or stretched skin), two, always on opposite ends of the shell, or, extremely rarely, more; the *panchamukha vadyam* of ancient India had five heads—but it was a very freakish instrument! Usually there is one skin to a head, but in India (as we have seen) on instruments like the *tabla* and *mridangam* each head may have up to three layers of leather, with additional "spots" of rice paste or other substances added to the surface. A drum's skin can be made from any available membrane depending on the ecology of the area and the size of the drum; animals who have donated (always involuntarily) the skins off their backs (literally) to the music of drums include lizards, sharks, cattle, buffalo, deer, pigs, goats, sheep, snakes, walruses, monkeys, and a host of game animals. In the industrialized West, drumheads—like so much else in life—are made from artificial substances, usually plastics. An anonymous ruler of the pre-Columbian Incas gets the prize for the most unusual (and frightening) drumheads: after an unsuccessful insurrection he had the captured rebel chiefs flayed alive and their complete skins inflated and made into drums to be played in a concert of victory music!

With only a few exceptions, the playing surface of drumheads in every nook and cranny of the world is round. Why? Could it be that in the dark mists of the past someone discovered that the tension of the leather could be more evenly stretched if it were on a round shell or frame, and that this invention spread throughout the world as the way (simply, purely) that drums were made, as a convention, an unquestioned tradition? Or could there be other reasons? The symbolism of the circle, the ring without beginning and end, is an old one. It is an image etched on man's consciousness from the first time his (then animal) eyes perceived the sun and the full moon. To Coptic Christians the circle became eternity, a snake biting its own tail; in Egypt it was the powerful sun disk; in India it expanded into the *chakra*, a great mystic wheel of the gods and representation of the cycles of existence; in China it enclosed the symbols for *yin* and *yang*, the opposing harmonic principles of the universe. Black Elk, a holy man of the Sioux of the American Great Plains, has described how everything an Indian does is "in a circle" because the Power of the World works in circles; and everything in his environment from the circular dome of the sky to the circular floor of his home, the tepee, parallels this sacred shape. But there could be more pragmatic reasons as well: the hollowed-out log and the clay pot with its circular mouth are archetypal drum shapes; both, capped with stretched leather, are used as drums to this day. The clay pot relates to the hemispherical shape of the family of kettledrums from the small *tabala* of Senegal to the *naqqāra* of Turkey or the timpani of Europe. The hollowed-out log remains the basic raw material of many of the world's drums—in Africa, south Asia, Oceania, and the Americas—even though it may be carved and modified into a variety of shapes. And the cylindrical shape of a log stubbornly remains like the face of an ancestor even when drums are assembled (barrel-like) or made from nonwood materials like metal or fiber glass; behind every snare drum, military field drum, or bass drum in Europe and America (or anywhere) is the shadow memory of a log.

Drums are classified into three types, according to the shape of their shell, or body. The first group has some kind of a tube (or log-related shape) for its body. The second family has a kettle (or pot-related) shape that may be made of metal, clay, or less commonly of wood or half-gourds and calabashes. The final group is made of skin stretched on a frame that is usually circular (a hoop), but can be square or, rarely, triangular.

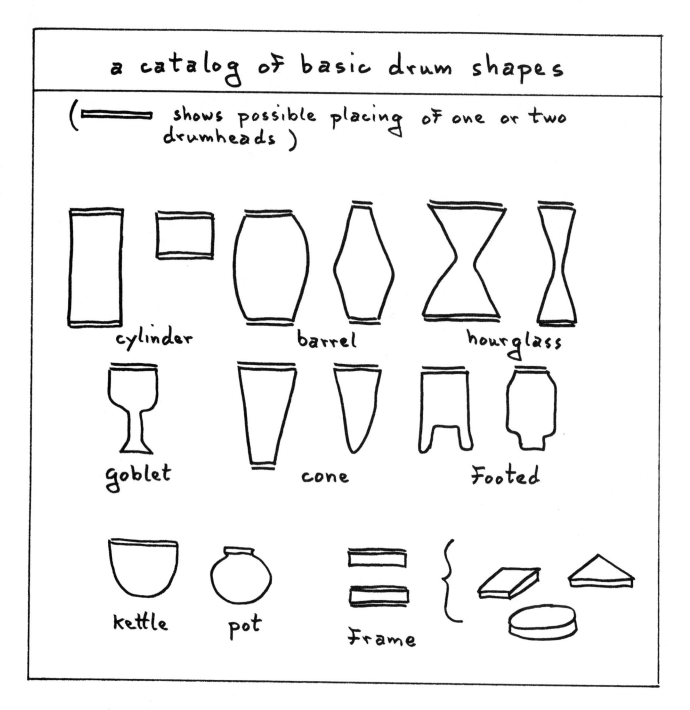

These basic shapes are, of course, modified in numerous ways according to traditional design patterns, and they come in all sizes. The hourglass shape, for example, varies from drums three or four feet long in New Guinea to tiny rattle drums in India that measure barely three inches. A preference for certain shapes can also be seen in certain areas of world music. Footed drums are found in Africa and Oceania. Goblet-shaped drums (like the Arabic *darabuka* span the entire area of the Islamic and Islamic-influenced world. The kettledrum is found in central Asia (where it might have originated), India, Iran, Turkey, the Middle East, north Africa, and finally in Europe. Barrel- and cone-shaped drums are abundant in Africa and Asia, but not in Europe, where cylinders are preferred. The American Indians built and played both cylindrical and frame drums; in the Southwest they also used pot drums.

The family of frame drums is amazing not only because of its distribution—which is almost worldwide—but because of its antiquity. Small pottery statuettes of women playing round frame drums with their hands have been dug up from the ruins of Ur (2000 B.C.); similar drums, often with rattling jangles attached, are played to this day in the Middle East, where they are still associated with the singing and dancing of women. Known as the *duff, tār,* or *doira* south and east of the Mediterranean, this instrument migrated to Europe (along with so many others from the (Middle East) where it became known as the tambourine, and where—nearly four thousand years after Ur—it is played by the *women* of gypsy ensembles and Salvation Army bands! We have noted the importance of the frame drum (without jangles) as the principal instrument of central and north Asian shamanism; in the Arctic it becomes the principal instrument of the Eskimos and measures as much as several feet across; it is found in India as both a folk and a classical percussion instrument as well as in other regions of south Asia; and, finally, it is found among the Indian peoples of North and Central America. Square frame drums, some of them quite large, are played in Ghana; and frame drums of the circular variety—with hoops made of bent wood or clay—are also found in sub-Saharan Africa.

The technology of drum-making centers around two procedures: the attaching of the skin to the body or frame of the drum, and the tuning, the increasing or decreasing of the tension of the membrane once it is attached. The skin can be glued or tacked to the drum's body, or it may be jammed between a tightly fitting hoop and the body of the drum. If, instead of a hoop, string or tongs are wrapped around the neck of the drum binding the skin to it, the drum is said to be *neck-laced.*

attachment of drumheads

glued · tacked · jammed between hoop and body · neck-laced (cord wrapped around neck)

Lacing moving away from the drumhead and parallel to the drum's body is another important method of attachment. If the lacing is strung through holes punched directly in the skin of the drumhead, the drum is *directly laced* (not to be confused with "straight-laced"). A further elaboration—and an important one—is to take the skin of the drumhead and lace, stitch, or wrap its edges around a hoop which is more or less movable. This hoop is then kept in place by lacing (*indirect lacing* is the technical term) or by a screw mechanism, both of which can easily control the tension of the drumhead.

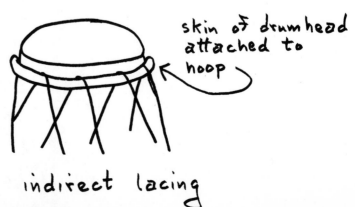

skin of drumhead attached to hoop

direct lacing · indirect lacing

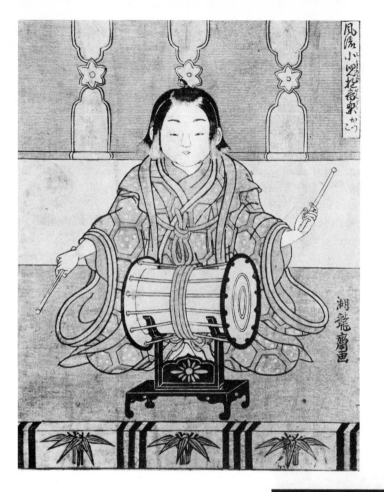

Musician with *daiko*/drum. Print by Koriusai
(1710–80), Japan.

Detail of Native American drum of aspen
log and deer hide, Taos Pueblo.

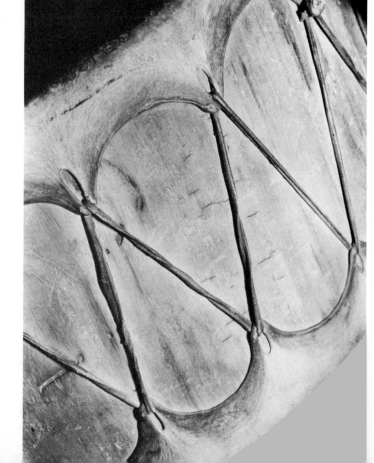

The lacing itself may be attached to an opposite drumhead (if there is one) in a kind of mirror duplication, or—in the case of single-headed instruments—laced around the drum shell or connected to pegs, holes, or nails.

Tuning (to precise or relative pitch) may be done by wetting the drumhead—which makes the leather softer, looser, hence lower-pitched; by holding it over a fire—making the head drier, tighter, higher-pitched; by tightening or loosening the lacing; or by moving the hoop (by hammering manipulation of attached indirect lacing, or a screw mechanism). Four common ways of working with lacing (other than restringing or retying it) are to stretch it by jamming wedges under it, to string it through movable tuning rings which can easily be shifted, to hammer in pegs to which it is attached, and—in hourglass-shaped drums—to squeeze the lacing with the hands or arms or tighten it with a "waist" belt. As we have noted earlier the pitch of a drumhead can also be changed by directly pressing it, by damping it with the hand or foot (to pick up different overtones), or, in the case of some drums, by hitting it in different places.

People generally do not think much about the position of instruments in relation to the player. There are, for example, instruments that are set on the ground or floor in front of the sitting or standing performer (like the piano or the gong). There are instruments that are held in the hands (like the flute or ocarina), pressed against the body (like the European violin), propped on the knees (like the Bulgarian bowed *gadulka*) or held on the lap (like the Russian *gusli* zither). There are instruments wrapped completely around the body of the player (like the American Sousaphone), or hung from the neck or waist (like some African *malimbe* xylophones). There are instruments that virtually or literally surround a player (like the console of a large European pipe organ or the Thai *khong vong yai* knobbed gongs), and others so small (like the harmonica or jew's-harp) as to be almost invisible when they are played. Drums, too, are held and played in a variety of ways.

The drum's physical relationship to the player can tell us a great deal about how it is played. Drums played on only one head are usually placed upright or propped at an angle (like the Latin American *conga* or the African *agbadga*), the most notable exceptions being the drums hung horizontally like gongs found in many places in the Orient (for example, the massive Japanese *da daiko* of the *gagaku* orchestra). If both heads of a drum are to be played, it must be held or placed sideways, horizontally (like the Indian *dhol* or the Javanese *batangan* dance drum), unless it is small enough (like the Indian and Tibetan hourglass-shaped *damaru*) to be swung around in one hand.

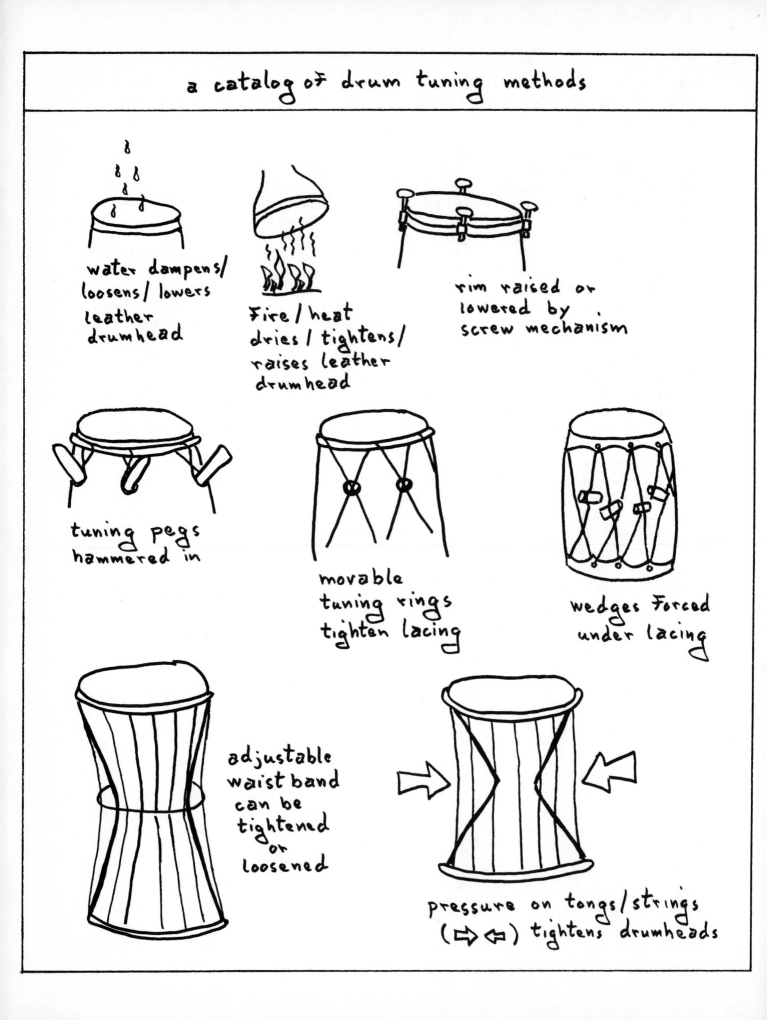

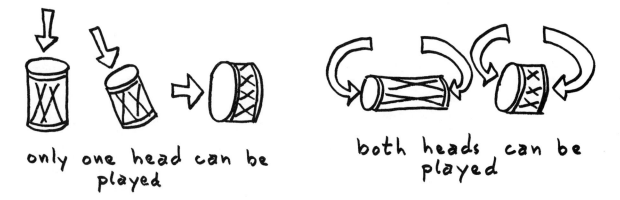

only one head can be
played

both heads can be
played

Many of the earth's drums come in (sometimes inseparable) pairs—like the Turkish *naqqāra*, the *tabla* of India, or the Ghanaian *atumpan*—giving them the same pitch and sound potential as a two-headed, horizontally played drum.

tabla

naqqāra

atumpan

Drums can be set on the floor or ground in front of the player or propped against his body, held in place by his feet, legs, or knees. They can also be carried, giving the drummer the freedom and mobility to dance, as he often does in Africa and south Asia, to move around, or otherwise to participate in the musical or ritual action. Frame drums (like the *duff* or tambourine) are almost always light enough to be held in one hand—a characteristic shared with some hourglass-shaped drums—and they may be provided with a handle for this purpose.

Frame drums with
handles (Eskimo, Tibetan)

hourglass-shaped
drum with handle
(New Guinea)

Larger drums are often suspended from the musician's body, around his neck, waist, or shoulder, leaving both his hands free for playing. Drums may also be held in a rack or stand. In Africa and in the Euro-American tradition these racks, like those used for the Ewe master drum of Ghana or the snare drum in the United States, are relatively simple and purely functional. But in east and southeastern Asia racks and stands, like those of the Javanese *tjiblon* dance drum or the *bedug*, or the suspended Japanese *da daiko*, are beautiful objects in themselves and may be ornately carved, painted, and lacquered.

Drums make their music by being struck, and the most flexible and amazing of all beaters are the human hands. With his hands and the ten drumsticks called fingers, a drummer can coax a seemingly endless variety of sounds from a single drumhead: tapping with the fingertips, with the fingers flat; slapping with four or five fingers together as a unit (stiff or relaxed), or with different parts of the palm; or grazing the drumhead with the side of the hand like a slanted musical karate chop. The force of the hitting can be precisely controlled (a fact often forgotten by young drummers, and their critics, both of whom seem to equate the skills necessary for drumming with those of boxing!), from a rhythmic whispering to exuberant outbursts. A variety of sticks, mallets, and beaters can also be used. And just as for idiophones the type of stick or mallet or beater, its weight and size, its material (wood, dried wound leather, etc.), and the nature of its tip so much determine the characteristic sound of a drum that they must really be considered a part of the instrument. In Africa sticks are often bent, or crooked, a simple bit of mechanical engineering that gives them extra leverage and force. The weighted ends of mallets perform a similar function. In India in the drum traditions of the *tavil* (played for religious purposes) and the *suddha maddalam* (associated with the *kathakali* dance form) players combine the best of two worlds: in one hand they play with a stick, with the other they play with their fingers, each of which is wrapped in strips of cloth soaked in a mixture of rice paste and calcinated lime shell which is allowed to harden. The fingers are then a set of brittle little drumsticks, which can balance in volume the wooden stick of the other hand and also achieve the ringing, cutting timbre associated with these drums.

When we mentioned earlier that all drums were membranophones, but not all membranophones were drums, we were referring to a minority which (like all minorities, human or otherwise) is often forgotten in the noise and numbers of the crowd. Drums are made to sound by striking, but stretched skins may also be set into vibration (and sound) by friction. Instruments of this type are called friction drums. The skin is stretched over a shell or resonator (an earth pit, a pot, a barrel, or drum shape) and pierced by a stick or cord which is then rubbed or twirled between the palms of the hands to begin the vibration. Friction drums in Africa and in some other parts of the world are connected with fertility and/or puberty initiation rites. They are found also in Europe where they function as festival noise-makers and children's toys. Friction and the sound can also be created by whirling the cord—and the attached "drum"—around the head.

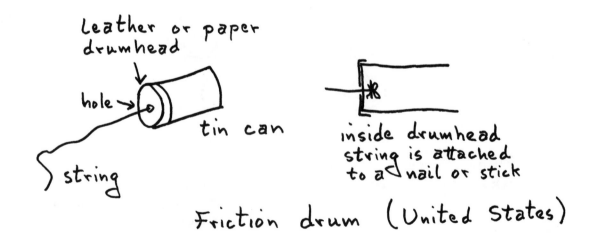

Friction drum (United States)

Membranes can also be set into vibration by the voice or by other musical sounds. Here the sound and all the pitches are created by other means, the membrane mainly amplifying the sound and changing its timbre. Megaphones with attached membranes (of spider's egg coverings) are made of gourds and animal horns in Africa, where they function as voice disguisers. The Euro-American kazoo, which when sung or hummed into sounds like a muted trumpet or saxophone, is a similar instrument. Since this use of a tiny stretched membrane, also found in African gourd xylophone resonators and in Chinese and Korean flutes, is mainly a tone-coloring device, we shall discuss it more fully in the section on timbre.

Aerophones

Aerophones are instruments through, in, or around which air is made to vibrate. They are classed in four families according to the way sound is made upon them: air is blown across a sharp edge in a pipe or tube (flutes), air is forced through or over reeds (oboes, accordions), air is forced between the tightened lips of the player (trumpets, horns), or the instruments act directly on the outer air (bull-roarers).

Bone flutes have been found (together with bull-roarers) at many Paleolithic sites, and conch shell trumpets appear in Neolithic times; instruments of wood or bamboo or reed would, of course, have long since disappeared. By the time of the ancient urban civilizations in Babylonia, Sumer, Persia, Egypt, China, and Greece aerophones of every major type were in use (wall carvings and murals and vases tell us that), but the worldwide distribution of these instruments suggests that their migrations and/or concurrent invention happened much earlier, and not necessarily in the Near or Far East.

Flutes

Flutes are usually tubular, but they can also be globular (ocarinas), or conical (in Africa made from animal horn). Their playing position may be vertical, horizontal, or oblique, and they achieve different pitches by the use of finger holes. They are grouped according to their type of sound hole.

End-blown flutes produce sound when air is blown across the upper opening of the tube itself. The edge opposite the player's lips may be sharpened to produce a clearer, more reliable tone. Simple end-blown flutes without finger holes are found in Africa (among the Majo people of Ethiopia) and in New Guinea, where different sizes, some up to four feet long, are combined in ensembles. The panpipe, a set of end-blown flutes of different lengths and without finger holes, is found all over the earth; it was and is a particularly important instrument in the native music of Peru, but it has also had its day as a popular folk instrument in southern Europe and Greece (it was, after all, the instrument of Pan), in Africa, and in ancient China. End-blown flutes may also have finger holes, usually from one to six, and are found in this form in the Americas, in Africa, and perhaps most notably in the Middle East (the *nāy*) and the Balkans (the *kaval*) where its beautiful breathy sound and its virtuosity make it a popular instrument.

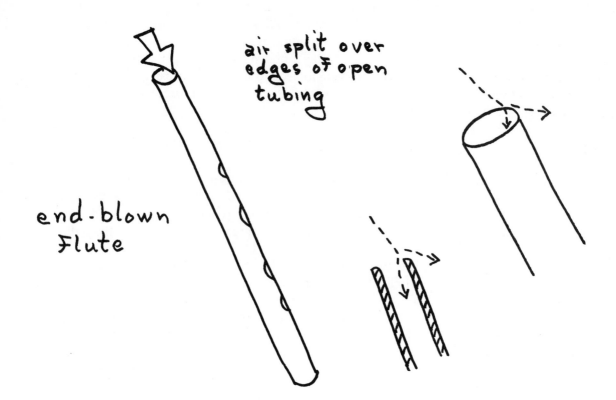

The *notched flute*, in which a small *V*- or *U*-shaped notch is cut into the edge blown across, is a technical "improvement" of the end-blown flute: it makes it easier to play. It is found in South America where it is made of bone, wood, clay, gourd, metal, or soft stone; throughout Africa; and across Asia to Japan (the bamboo *shakuhachi*) and Indonesia (the *suling* of Java).

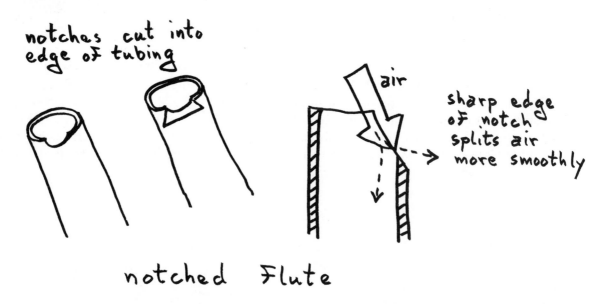

In *block flutes* (also called *duct flutes*) and whistles the air is guided through a tiny passageway to the sharp edge of an opening cut into the tube. This duct can be built in a number of ways and, except for the key mechanisms of European instruments, represents the most complicated technology of flute-making. Amazingly, bone flutes of this type but without finger holes are found in Pale-

Flutists at festive Deer Dance in Iwate prefecture, Japan.

Native American block flutes. Left (with leather thongs), Taos Pueblo. Right (with fur band), Iroquois.

olithic deposits. Block flutes are found throughout the world (the European recorder is one)—though rarely in the Orient—but they were particularly well developed among the Indians of the Americas who used tubes made of wood, bird bones, or black shale. Globular flutes and whistles made of pottery and often shaped like birds, animals, or humans were and are made all through Central and South America; similar instruments are popular as folk instruments, such as bird whistles in Russia and eastern Europe. In the Balkans, double flutes—like the Yugoslav *dvoynice*—have the capability for playing both melody and accompaniment or drone. The Maori of New Zealand make a particularly beautiful incised wood globular flute with two finger holes. In Africa similar instruments are made from gourds and globular-shaped seed shells. We have used the Italian name *ocarina* to designate globular flutes.

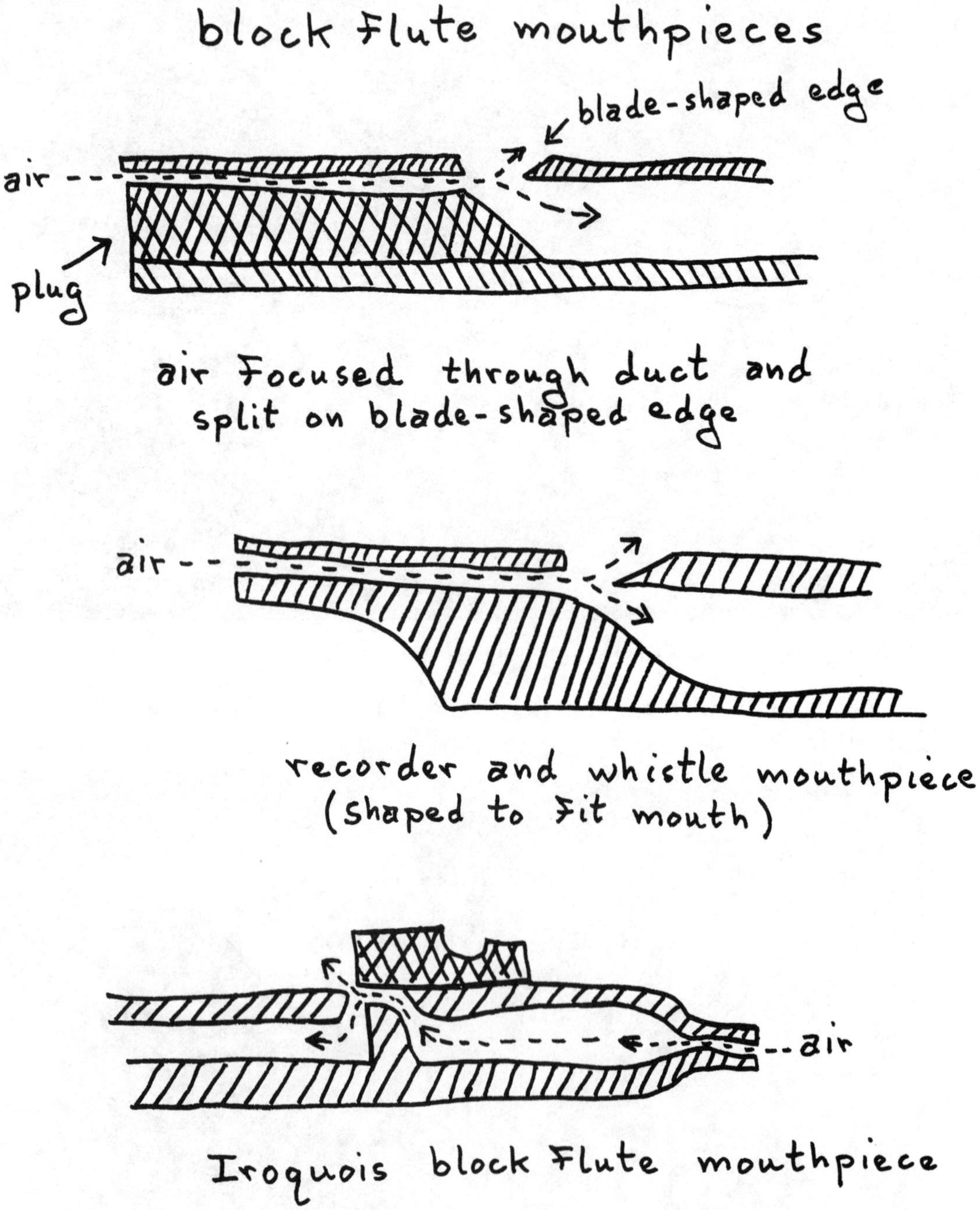

block flute mouthpieces

blade-shaped edge

air

plug

air focused through duct and
split on blade-shaped edge

air

recorder and whistle mouthpiece
(shaped to fit mouth)

air

Iroquois block flute mouthpiece

Transverse flutes are played and held horizontally; the upper end of the tube is blocked and a mouth hole (which is blown across) is cut into the side of the tubing. It can have six or more finger holes. Surprisingly, this instrument, the common flute and fife of Europe and the United States, appears much later than other types of flutes in the annals of flute history and is also much less widespread. While it is found in South America (a silver and copper Peruvian flute dating from about 800 A.D. has been found) and Africa, one must travel to China, Korea, and Japan—where many varieties are made—or India—where it is commonly made of bamboo—to find the transverse flute in the mainstream of popular and classical non-European music-making.

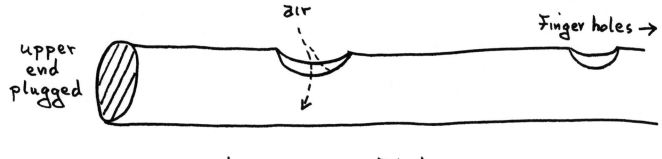

transverse Flute

We usually think of the finger holes on flutes (as well as on other wind instruments) as being evenly spaced and acoustically placed so that they can produce a continuous stepwise scale. But this need not necessarily be so. For example the *nyere*, a transverse flute played by the Korakora people of Rhodesia, has three closely spaced finger holes for the right hand and one in the middle of the flute for the left hand.

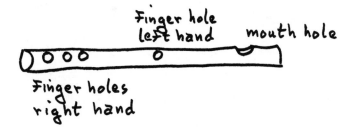

Many two- and three-note flutes and ocarinas have their finger holes tuned to play melodic chords, or skips; or the finger holes may be bored not according to any acoustical scheme whatsoever but according to traditional proportions or the stretch of a player's fingers. There may be variance also in the placement of the mouth hole. The *piibar* bark flute from Estonia, for example, puts it in the middle, with three finger holes on either side!

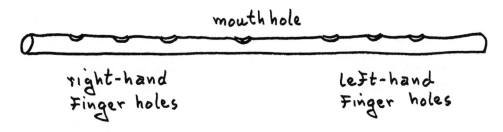

Reed Instruments

Reed instruments are of two major types: vibrating *beating reeds,* in which one or more reeds are attached to the end of a tube and a variation of the length of the tube (through the fingering of finger holes) produces notes of different pitch; and vibrating *free reeds,* in which the size of the reed itself (placed in a tube or chamber) produces the pitch, and thus a separate tuned reed is needed for every note of the instrument. Beating reeds are made in two varieties: *single-reed* instruments, which we shall call by the generic name *clarinet* (though they may differ considerably from the familiar European clarinet); and *double-reed* instruments, which are called by the generic name *oboe* or *pipe.* A few multiple-reed pipes have more than two reeds, notably the *pi nai* of Thailand which has four. But this is certainly an exception.

The prototype of the sound-producing equipment of the *single-reed clarinet* is a tongue (the vibrating reed) cut directly into a piece of cane or bamboo so that it partially covers a small breath hole (which is blown into).

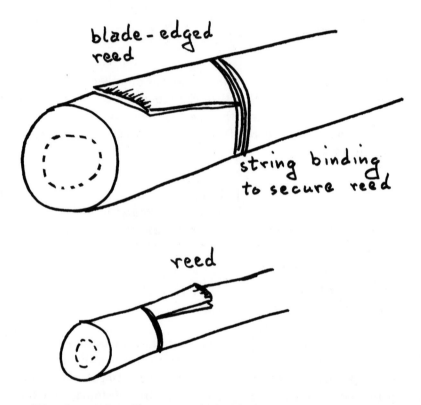

In later instruments (like the modern European clarinet) the reed may be a separate piece, the tubing may be shaped to fit better in the mouth, and the binding may be a clasp of metal; but the basic relationship between these parts remains the same. The simple one-piece sliced cane and reed, attached as a unit to the end of tubing with finger holes, forms the mouthpiece of many of the world's clarinets. The player may press this mouthpiece (including the reed) between his lips, or he may insert it so that it vibrates more or less freely in the cavity of his mouth, a practice more common in the countries bordering on the Mediterranean and in Asia.

An amazing feature of clarinets is that they—like flutes and double-reed pipes—are often combined into double and triple instruments. The multiple tubes, each with its own set of finger holes and reed or sharing a common reed, may be hollowed out of a single piece of wood or fastened together in a variety of ways. Each pipe of a double or triple clarinet has its musical function: for example, the Egyptian *argūl* has one melody and one drone pipe, the Uzbek *kūshnāy* has two melody pipes, and the *launeddas* from Sardinia has three pipes which play the melody, the accompanying polyphony, and a drone. Double (and triple) wind instruments of any kind, of course, have their limitations—the musician has, after all, only one mouth and one pair of hands. But the music made upon them can be quite complex and startlingly beautiful.

   If the reed mouthpiece of the clarinet is inserted into a cow horn it becomes a hornpipe; or the horn may be placed on the lower end of a regular single clarinet. The mouthpiece (or mouthpieces, if it is a double clarinet) may also be attached inside a horn, which is then pressed cuplike against the face of the musician, covering his mouth. The Welsh *pibcorn* has cow horns at either end of its tube. Often this cupped mouthpiece is made of wood, as in the *diplye* of Yugoslavia, a double clarinet with six finger holes in one pipe and two in the other. The *pūngī* of India, used by snake charmers to charm cobras, uses a gourd which is blown into as an air chamber, the reeds and the double pipes (one melody and one drone) coming out the other side.

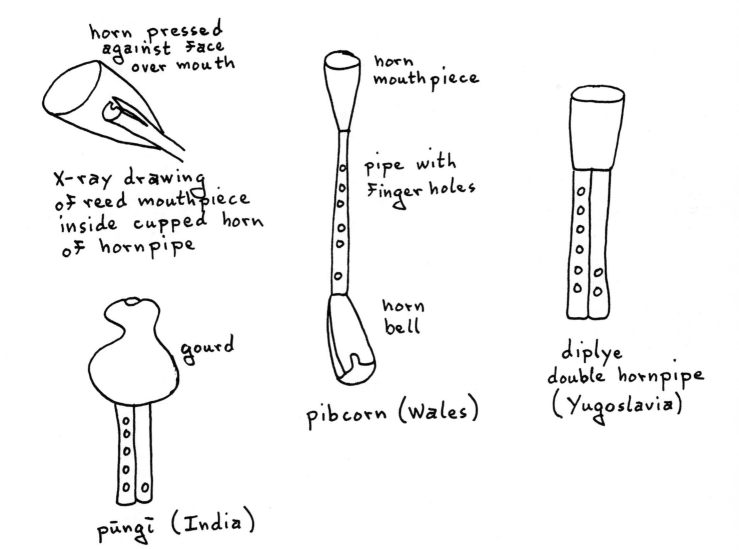

horn pressed against face over mouth

X-ray drawing of reed mouthpiece inside cupped horn of hornpipe

gourd

pūngī (India)

horn mouthpiece

pipe with finger holes

horn bell

pibcorn (Wales)

diplye double hornpipe (Yugoslavia)

   The bagpipe is an extension of the gourd or cupped air chamber idea but with one advantage: the bagpiper can stop blowing once he has filled the bag (a one-way valve prevents the air from escaping) and take a breath, rest his lungs, or even sing along with his own playing! Pressure on the bag keeps the air flowing into the attached pipes. The bag itself, at least in the Middle East, the Balkans, and in eastern Europe, is made from part of all of a goat skin. The hair of the goat may be retained as a decorative element and sometimes even the (stuffed) head, or a wooden facsimile of it. Instruments like the *zūkra* of Tripoli and Tunisia, as well as similar instruments in Greece and the Mediterranean, are basically hornpipes with an attached bag; but the pipes can also be double-reed, and as such belong in the next section.

Double-reed pipes are widely used all over the world except in the Americas and tropical Africa. Their history stretches back in time at least to Sumer, Babylonia, and the great civilizations in Egypt and Greece. The sound-producing reed mouthpiece is similar to that of clarinets except that the air is blown through the liplike opening between a pair of vibrating reeds. The simplest way to make a double reed is to pinch an ordinary reed (found in a marsh or near a river) flat, clamp it, bind it around a tiny tube, and then insert this rudimentary mouthpiece into the pipe of the instrument. In fact, there is no basic difference in the mouthpieces of modern Euro-American oboe and bassoon players (who may spend hours each week making their own reeds), except that they may start with two separate reeds which are then pinched together.

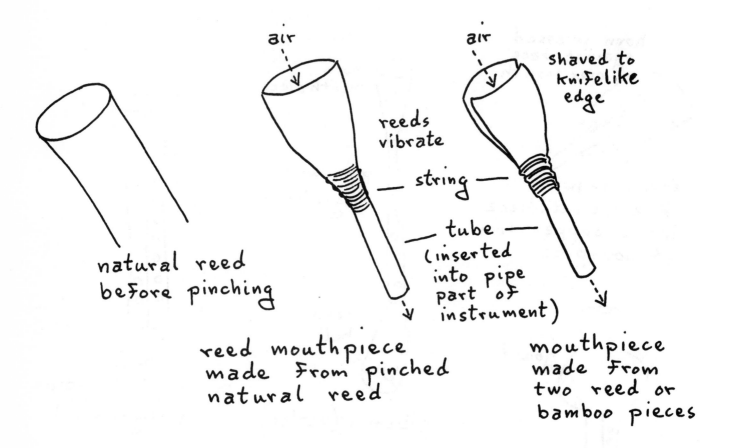

The pipe part of double-reed instruments—and of clarinets, flutes, trumpets, horns, in fact, any wind instrument—is usually made to be cylindrical or conical (although other shapes have been experimented with, or are—like the globular flutes—widely in use). The outside shape of the instrument can sometimes be highly deceptive; what is important is what is on the *inside*—this is where the sound bounces around and the pitches are made. Cylindrical-bore tubes and conical-bore tubes have different acoustical properties, and either type may be fitted with a flaring bell.

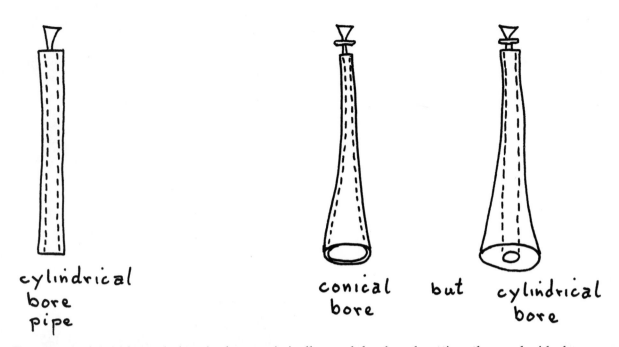

cylindrical
bore
pipe

conical
bore

but   cylindrical
bore

The sound of double-reed pipes is characteristically nasal, loud, and cutting; they make ideal instruments for outdoor performances, processions, and dances. The conical *zurnā* of Turkey, and its musical brothers (sisters) and cousins in north Africa, the Middle East, and Asia, is indispensable for weddings, funerals, special family events, festivals, and celebrations. In Tibet it becomes the *rgya-glin* of Tantric Buddhist temple ceremonies, in China the *sona*. Cylindrical bore pipes are also common, like the *hichiriki* of Japan, which though made of a little bamboo tube barely eight inches long has a sound that rings above the entire *gagaku* orchestra. Like clarinets, pipes can be made into double and triple instruments, such as the *aulos* made of two unattached pipes pictured so often on Greek vases.

Bagpipes are also made with double-reed sound producers. The *gaida* of Bulgaria, and similar folk instruments from Yugoslavia, Greece, and Spain, has a chanter (the pipe with finger holes on which the melody is played) and one drone pipe. The French *cornemuse* has a chanter and two drones, while the highland pipes of Scotland have a chanter and three drones (two tenors and a bass). Usually the drone pipes are equipped with single reeds so that the drone accompaniment is a little softer and of a slightly different timbre than the melody played on the chanter. The Italian *zampogna*, however, is an all double-reed instrument and has two chanters as well! Another family of bagpipes, found in northern Europe and the British Isles, is much softer, quieter, and sweeter in tone and can be played indoors with vocal music or guitar accompaniment. These get their air not from a bag (and lung power) but from a bellows. The Irish Union-pipe has a chanter, three single-reed drones, and regulators which allow chords to be played.

Free-reed instruments (with their tuned reeds, one for each note) date from the earliest times in the Orient—the Chinese *sheng* mouth organ is first mentioned around 1100 B.C.—where, like the *khaen* of Cambodia or the *sho* of Japan, they are still played. While the Eastern instruments all include gourd or gourdlike wind chambers and tuned bamboo pipes, the European versions (the idea emigrated, as we have noted, around the 1820s) took two main forms, both of which have become highly popular and much maligned folk machinations of sound. One is the mouth organ or harmonica; the other is the accordion and all its variants. Both make ideal folk instruments: they are portable, fairly easy to play, and capable of making both melody and harmonic accompaniment. In Russia there are many types of accordion, from the *livenskaya*, which produces different diatonic notes depending upon whether the bellows are squeezed in or pulled out, to the *bayan*, which has fifty-two keys for the right hand (melody) and one hundred for the left hand (bass notes and

Polish musician with *dudy*/bagpipes. The bag is made of goatskin turned inside out; the pipes are decorated with metal and horn bands. Jan Greń from Sopotnia Mała, in the Żywiec region of Poland.

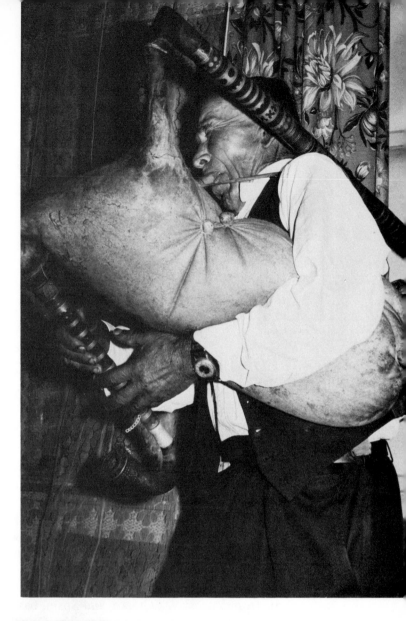

Peasant wedding party in Macedonia, Yugoslavia. The musicians play accordion, clarinet, and goblet-shaped relative of the *darabuka*.

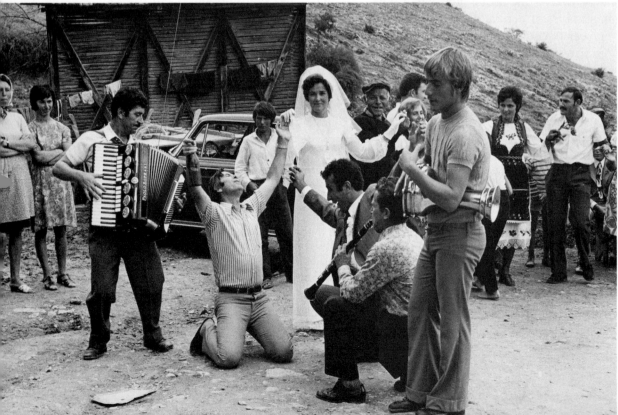

chords). In England the concertina, invented in 1844, is a popular instrument. The harmonica, too, exists in a number of forms, most them developed by the firm of Matthias Hohner, established in 1857. In its simplest form, sucking in and blowing out produce two different series of notes which combine to form a major scale (with several breaks). Chords can be played by cupping the mouth over several holes simultaneously, single notes by blocking all except one opening with the tongue.

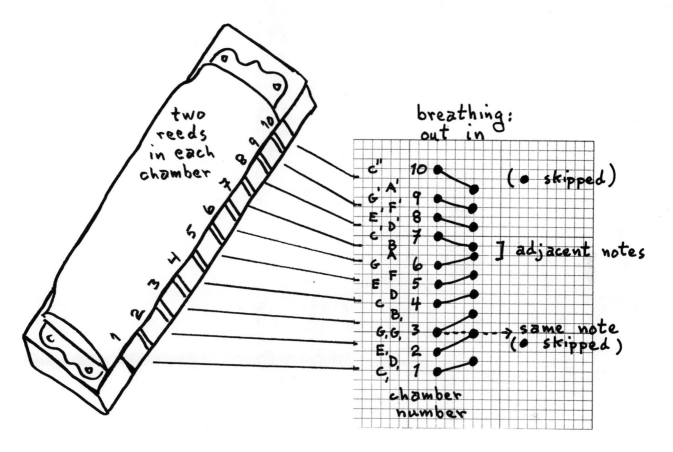

sound mechanics of the harmonica

Different sound characteristics can be achieved by manipulation of the mouth cavity and tongue just as in playing the musical bow or the jew's-harp. In the United States a unique style of play was developed by black musicians: reeds are "bent," or flattened in pitch, by a tightening of the lips and mouth, and sound is further changed by a fluttering of the right hand cupped over the outside of the instrument; and instead of playing in the key the harmonica is tuned in (the mouth holes 1-4-7-10 give the tonic, or first note of the major scale—see the section on melody), different notes are chosen as tonal centers in a technique called "cross-harping." The result is a wonderful example of what we described earlier: the expansion of the limited mechanics of an instrument by the incredible skill and imagination of the performer!

Horns and Trumpets

Sound is produced on horns and trumpets by air forced between the compressed lips of the player. Technically, *horns* are made of a curved tubing with a conical bore (like the horns of animals), and *trumpets* are made from straight tubes with a cylindrical bore (like a length of bamboo), but commonly these terms are used interchangeably. Horns and/or trumpets may also be globular, like the conch shell and gourds.

Trumpet players with drummer in a religious street procession, Madras, India.

Musician with trumpet made of animal horn, south Africa.

The lips of the player may simply be pressed against a hole in the end or (common in Africa) side of the trumpet, or, as in the brass and metal instruments of Europe and Asia, against a special cup-shaped mouthpiece. We have already examined in detail how musicians play different notes by utilizing Mother Nature's musical gift, the overtone series, and by a further extension of this principle in the European invention of valves. Trumpets/horns can also produce notes of different pitches in the same way that flutes, double-reed pipes, and clarinets do: by finger holes in the tubing. African horns commonly have a single finger hole which gives them the capability of two fundamental pitches. The *cornetto* which flourished in Europe during the Renaissance and for which composers like Monteverdi, Schuetz, and the Gabrielis wrote their trumpet parts was perhaps the highest development of this type of instrument. A slightly curved tubing about two feet long of a hard, close-grained wood such as pear was sliced in half lengthwise and gouged out to form a conical bore. The two halves were glued and bound back together and a further covering of leather glued on to seal any possible air leaks. Normally there were six finger holes and a thumb hole. A similar but less classical instrument— it was popular in military bands—was the serpent, so named because its eight feet of conical tubing (wood covered with canvas and leather) were folded in serpentine form. It is one of the quirks of fate that this principle—combining the mouthpiece sound producer of brass instruments with the fingering facility of woodwinds—was abandoned by later European instrument-makers. Perhaps in the future there will be a rediscovery of *cornetto*-type instruments with their beautiful vocal-like sound. It certainly ought to happen.

Horns and trumpets are found almost everywhere on earth. Besides the only slightly modified natural instruments like conch shells and animal horns (both of which have been found in Neolithic excavations), elephant tusks and bamboo, or bamboo-gourd combinations (like the *asukusuk* of Uganda), metal trumpets have been made since the Bronze Age. The tubing of metal horns and trumpets can be straight or bent in a variety of patterns—*S* shapes, *U* shapes, spirals, loops—to facilitate handling (and save space) or because of design traditions. In South America bark trumpets of different lengths are bound together and played like a giant-sized set of panpipes. In the mountains of Tibet, the *rag-dung*, a telescopic ceremonial trumpet from five to twenty feet long, is played at the monasteries and temples on festive occasions. I have been told that to increase their breath and skills young monks jog from the top of a short hill into a glen and to the top of the opposite hill, all the while playing a single long tone on this trumpet! The *alphorn*, made of wood, from four to twelve feet long, and used for signaling, calling cattle, and for music, is a similar instrument and is found not only in Switzerland but also in Estonia, Poland, and Romania. It would be an amazing connection to tie in the long horn/trumpet, its sound echoing across valleys and snowy peaks, with the unique musical perception of mountain peoples thousands of miles apart. Unfortunately for our theories, instruments like the *rag-dung* and *alphorn* are found in China, in Euro-America (the tuba), and in the pancake flatness of Holland and the steppes of central Asia.

Outer Air Instruments

A final class of wind instruments are those that create sound by acting directly on the outer air, sometimes called *free aerophones*. The principal instrument of this group is the bull-roarer, which when whirled over the head at the end of a piece of string gives a roaring sound connected by many peoples with the voices of supernatural beings or the magical qualities of the wind. George Antheil, an early twentieth-century American composer, borrowed a similar though non-"musical" aerophone of the industrial age—the airplane propeller—for one of his pieces. Unfortunately, at the first performance when the propeller roared up to full speed it blew over music stands and sent the paper pages of the new composition flying over the heads of the astonished audience.

Chordophones

Chordophones are instruments that have strings held at tension as sound producers; they may be sounded by plucking (with fingers or plectrums), bowing, striking, friction, or, rarely, by wind.

Resonators—sound increasers and reflectors—which we discussed earlier in detail, are an important element in the construction of chordophones, which by their nature have a softer, gentler tone than other instruments. Chordophones are divided into four subgroups: musical bows/harps, lyres, lutes, and zithers.

Musical Bows and Harps

The great antiquity of the *musical bow*, from its possible depiction on the walls of the cave of Les Trois Frères to its use in the present (Africa, Asia, the Americas), is well established. As an instrument it has appeared again and again in this chapter, connected with myths and the gods in ancient Japan and Greece and in Africa; with magic, trance, and ceremonials in Africa and among some North American Indian peoples; and with the resonators of attached gourds or the human chest or mouth cavity, or pits in the ground. It is usually sounded by plucking or by tapping the string with a light stick. Musical bows can be classed according to their resonator, for instance, as *gourd bows*, *mouth bows*, or *ground bows*. Their pitch may be changed not only by the fluctuation of the mouth cavity, but also by stopping the string with the fingers (and in Africa occasionally with the chin of the player), or by the addition of a noose which divides the string into two unequal vibrating sections giving two possible notes. If several strings are added to an instrument it becomes a *compound musical bow*, which in Africa is built in two ways: a number of bows, each with its own string, are attached and flexed from a resonator, usually a wood box; or a rigid bow-shaped piece of wood is fitted with several strings which end at different places along its neck.

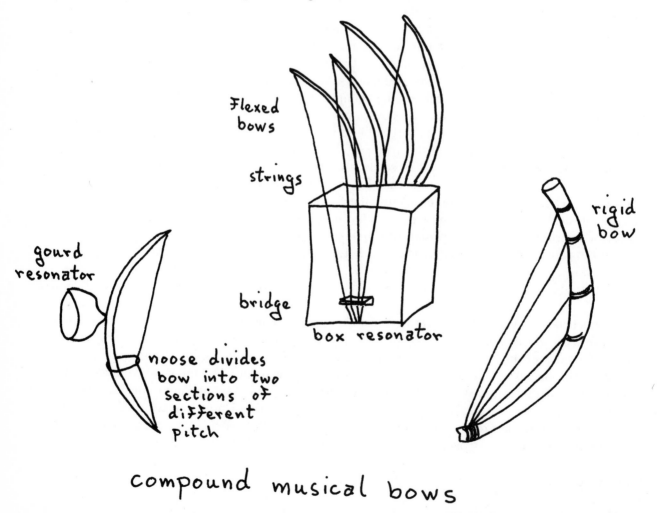

compound musical bows

It is but a small step from the construction of the rigid bow with several strings to the *bow harp*, one end of which is inserted into a boxlike resonator, often skin-topped, its strings tuned with either pegs or a knotted string mechanism. Bow harps appeared in Egypt and Sumer at least five thousand years ago, and they are found today in forms that vary from the very simple and pragmatic (common in Africa) to the highly ornamented and beautifully built, like the *saung kauk* of Burma.

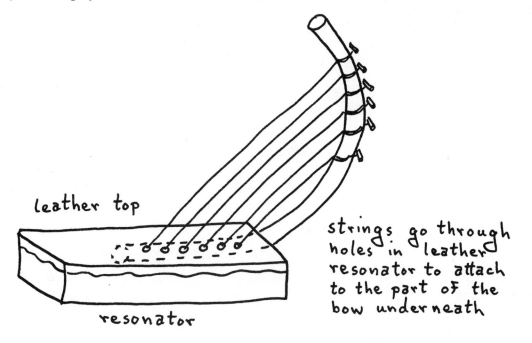

leather top

resonator

strings go through holes in leather resonator to attach to the part of the bow underneath

★★★★★★★★★★★★★★★★★ THE MECHANICS OF TUNING ★★★★★★★★★★★★★★★★★

Tuning is the largest technical problem in making stringed instruments, not only in harps, but in lyres, zithers, and lutes as well. We might as well examine this problem now as we begin to approach more complicated instruments. First of all, strings must be tight. But then their pitches must be made to conform to musical concepts of the culture in which they are used, or to a relationship with each other. Remembering our acoustical rule-of-thumb, a string (once it is strung) can be made to sound higher or lower in two ways: by tightening or loosening it, or by making its vibrating length shorter or longer.

The invention of tuning pegs by one or more anonymous geniuses perhaps on several continents sometime back in the shadows of the past was as important in the history of stringed instruments as the invention of the wheel in the history of transportation. Pegs are used to adjust the tension of strings in the most "primitive" of instruments and in contemporary violins and pianos, and the basic principle—almost classical in its simplicity—remains the same: a tapered circular peg is twisted into a tapered circular hole; the friction (going around and in, pressing it down further into the hole) holds it in place, yet it can easily be moved by a twist of the hand. The peg may be fitted with a shaped and sometimes ornamental "handle" or knob making it easier to grip, and adding leverage, or it may be turned with a key which fits over its tip (as in the autoharp, piano, and on many European and Middle Eastern zithers).

Instrument maker tunes his '*ūd*, Beirut, Lebanon.

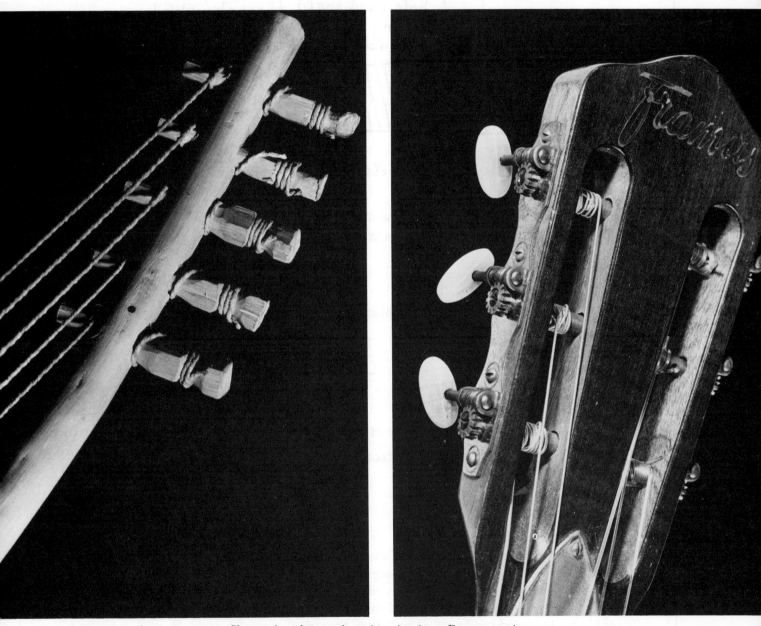

Tuning mechanisms: pegs on Kenyan bow harp and machine heads on European guitar.

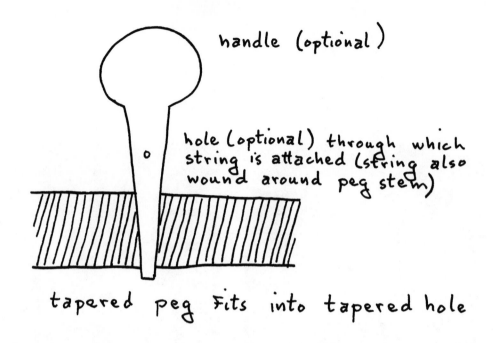

handle (optional)

hole (optional) through which
string is attached (string also
wound around peg stem)

tapered peg fits into tapered hole

Tuning nooses or rings that can easily be slid along the string to shorten it and/or adjust its tension are also commonly used, sometimes in combination with pegs, both in Africa and in Asia.

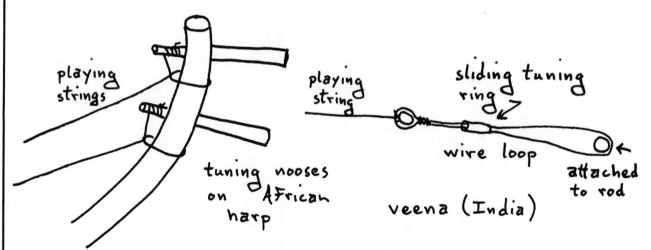

playing strings

tuning nooses on African harp

playing string

sliding tuning ring

wire loop

attached to rod

veena (India)

Knotted or wound string or hide strips wrapped around the neck of an instrument also function as tuning devices, provided there is enough friction to hold them in place and keep them from slipping. The Burmese *saung kauk* bowed harp uses this principle (also common in Africa): its strings are attached to silk cords which are then wrapped around the neck; the end of each silk cord hangs loose and can be pulled to tighten the string.

Finally, there is the European invention of the tuning "machine," a tiny gear mechanism that connects a metal peglike screw turned by the fingers with a rotating bar to which the strings are attached. Almost all modern European plucked instruments—like the guitar and mandolin—use this device, although bowed instruments, with the exception of the string bass, have resisted it.

The most common way of varying the vibrating length of strings is found on the major zithers of the Orient—the *ch'in* of China, the *kaya kum* of Korea, and the *koto* of Japan—as well as on various tube zithers from the islands off southeast Asia and in Malagasy (Africa).

Here each string is fitted with its own movable bridge which can be adjusted until the length of the string and its tuning are correct. In the case of some tube zithers there may be little adjustable bridges at both ends of the string.

★★★★★★★★★★★★★★★★★★★★★★★★★★★★★

Angle harps are distinguished from bow harps in that they form a sharp, elbowlike angle rather than a gently curved bow, and they generally have more strings. Like bow harps they have a long history, at least four thousand years, and are found in wall reliefs dating from ancient Egypt and Assyria. Today they are found in Africa and in central Asia from Iran up into Russia, and as far east as China. They may or may not have a resonator.

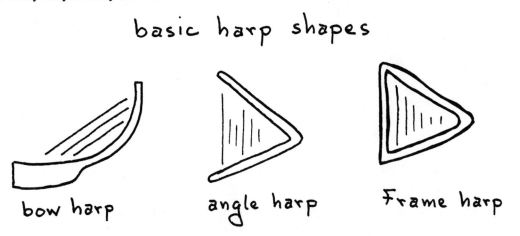

basic harp shapes

bow harp   angle harp   frame harp

Frame harps apparently originated in Europe in the Middle Ages. The addition of a pillar between the neck and the resonator gives the frame a triangular shape, and the subsequent added strength makes possible the stringing of numerous strings at comparatively high tension. Early frame harps were fairly small and easy to carry around—medieval manuscripts abound with pictures of them—but they gradually increased in size and complexity to the large symphonic harp familiar to classical music and Harpo Marx enthusiasts today. From the twelfth or thirteenth century on, the frame harp was exceedingly popular in both Ireland and Britain as demonstrated by *The Laws of Wales* which stated that three things were necessary for a man in his home: a virtuous wife, a cushion on his chair, and a well-tuned harp! The Irish harp remained a popular instrument up to the end of the last century.

Lyres

Lyres are built from a box or bowl resonator with two arms that zoom out parallel to its top. The arms are connected near their tips by a crossbar from which strings are strung to run across a bridge on the resonator. Lyres are classified according to their construction.

Box lyres, like early harps, date back at least five thousand years, and examples encrusted with gold or silver and precious stones have been found in the diggings at the royal cemetery at Ur. They spread throughout the Middle East, up into ancient Phoenicia and Greece and south into Ethiopia, the only place where they remain, virtually unchanged, as part of modern musical culture. The *kithara* of ancient Greece was used to accompany epic songs about heroes and the gods; a similar box lyre was the "harp" of the biblical King David; and the *bagana* of Ethiopia is similarly—two thousand five hundred years later—an instrument of the royal family, nobility, and the priestly class.

In contrast the *bowl lyre*, with a skin-topped shallow turtle shell, bowl, or pot as a resonator, has always been a people's instrument. The Greek *lyra* was played by amateurs and commoners, and the similar *kerar* of Ethiopia remains a popular folk instrument. Bowl lyres are extremely common today in the Congo, Central African Republic, Gabon, Uganda, Kenya, Tanzania, and southern Sudan as well as in Ethiopia, and they are played with great skill to accompany songs.

Musician with *kissar*/lyre, found in east and north Africa. The instrument is ornamented with cloth, mirrors, metalwork, twine, and bells.

Bassari musician with spike fiddle, Dakar, Senegal.

The *Celtic* or *Nordic lyre* was played from as early as 700 A.D. in many of the countries of northern Europe and is distinguished by the fact that it was carved from a single piece of wood. It was both plucked and (more commonly) bowed. Several versions, like the Welsh bowed *crwth* with four melody and two drone strings or the Finnish and Estonian *talharpa*, survived as a living tradition into the eighteenth and nineteenth centuries.

Lutes

Lutes consist of two parts: a neck (or fingerboard) and a body (the sound box, or resonator). The string or strings are attached at one end of the body and run across a bridge up to the end of the neck where they connect to pegs or some other tuning device. At the minimum there may be one string, but more commonly there are two, three, or more, often divided into melody and drone functions. Melody strings are fingered along the neck either by touching them (common in bowed instruments) or by pressing them (common in plucked instruments). Lutes may be bowed, plucked with the fingers or a variety of picks and plectrums, or (rarely) tapped.

We must remember that the word *lute* when used in the context of world music is a generic term describing a class of widely varying instruments. The European violin, for example, is a "bowed lute," as is the Arabic *kāmanja*; the guitar, along with the Indian *sitār* and the popular Middle Eastern–Mediterranean *'ūd*, is a "plucked lute." It is simply easier to use the single name of a familiar instrument to describe other like (although perhaps exotic) instruments, rather than to go through an entire rigmarole of technical terms. For example, the term *clarinet*, once we have defined it, is easier to use and to understand than "single-reed sound producer on a tube of conical or cylindrical bore with finger holes"! With this in mind, we shall proceed with the very, very large family of instruments classed under the generic term *lute*.

Long lutes have extremely long necks and proportionally small resonating sound boxes, or bodies. They are plucked. Seals and statuettes tell us that long lutes existed in the third millennium B.C. in Mesopotamia, during the Eighteenth Dynasty in Egypt, and in ancient Greece and Rome. Today they are common in Africa, and in central, south, and east Asia, but not in the Euro-American cultural complex where the *banjo*, an African-derived instrument, is the only common example.

The easiest way to build a long lute—and this may also have been its historical origin, although we have no way of knowing for sure—is to puncture the resonator (which can be a leather-topped coconut, frame, or hollowed-out bowl, or a gourd) with a long stick or bamboo rod: the neck. The stick or bamboo may go to the middle of the resonator, or it may puncture it completely, coming out the other side; in either case, the stick gives the instrument its structural strength (the resonator can be quite flimsy) and the strings may be fastened to both ends of it.

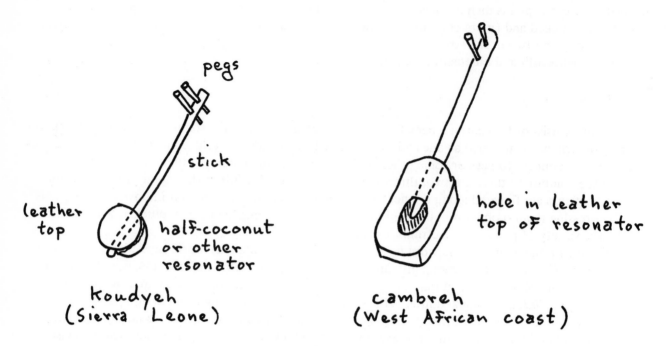

This structural principle is also used for shorter-necked plucked instrument and bowed lutes; bowed instruments with the stick going completely through the resonator are so common, especially in the Middle East, Africa, and Asia, that they have their own generic name: *spike fiddles.*

The other two ways of making lutes are to attach the neck and body at the point where they meet, usually bolstered with additional support (as in the violin and guitar), or to carve the entire instrument—neck and sound box—from a single piece of wood (such as in the Indian *veena* or the Turkish *saz*).

Typical long lutes include the central Asian *tār* with a figure-eight-shaped sound box top, or "face," covered with leather (in Azerbaijan with the heart membrane of a bull!), the Indian *sitār* and drone *tamburā*, the Turkish *saz*, the Japanese *shamisen*, the Chinese *san hsien*, the Afghani *tanbūr*, and the African *khalam* (Senegal) and *icbacarre* (Mozambique)—but these are only random items in a list that potentially is almost endless.

Short lutes have necks that are shorter than their sound boxes. In some cases this is compensated for by running the fingerboard onto or over the body of the instrument, as on the guitar or violin. Short lutes seem to have originated in central Asia—small clay figurines found near Samarkand dating from as early as or earlier than the eighth century B.C. show musicians playing this type of lute. The *'ūd*, which originated in the Middle East around the seventh century A.D., remains to this day throughout the Mediterranean not only as an important instrument of a living musical tradition, but, historically, as a prototype which generated the invention of many (if not all) of the European plucked instruments. *El'ūd*—the Arabic name—became the European lute, one of the classic instruments of the fifteenth and sixteenth centuries. Its Spanish name, *qitara*, became the guitar which over several centuries has assumed its present shape. Many folk instruments, like the Romanian *kobza*, also relate to the shape and sound of the *'ūd*.

In the Ukraine of Russia the large *bandoura* with its almost circular face and as many as thirty strings (combining a zither function with fingered lute technique) is a popular short-necked lute, while the *balalaika* with a triangular-shaped body and (usually) three strings is almost—with the accordion—the Russian national instrument. The *p'i p'a* with its moonlike round face from China and the Japanese pear-shaped *biwa* are other instruments of this family.

Bowed lutes, which we shall call by the generic name *fiddle*, come in as perplexing a variety of shapes and sizes as the long- and short-necked plucked lutes. Sound is produced by the friction of drawing a bow across the stretched strings of the instrument. Strands of horsehair make an ideal material for the bowstrings (and sometimes also for the playing strings), but plant fibers, thread, and gut are also used. Resin or chalk rubbed on the strings helps to increase the friction. While related in shape to plucked lutes, many fiddles have developed certain special structural characteristics related to the mechanics of playing them. The strings may be stretched over an arched bridge so that they can be sounded one or two at a time (as on the violin), for example, or they may be placed one above the other with the strands of the bow in between them (as on the Chinese *erh hu*).

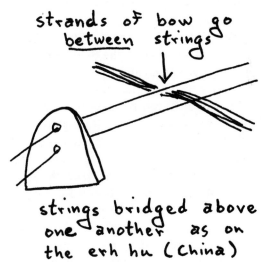

The sound box may be "waisted" with a built-in indentation to leave room for free movement of the bow (as on the European violin family, or the Indian *sarinda* and *sarangi*).

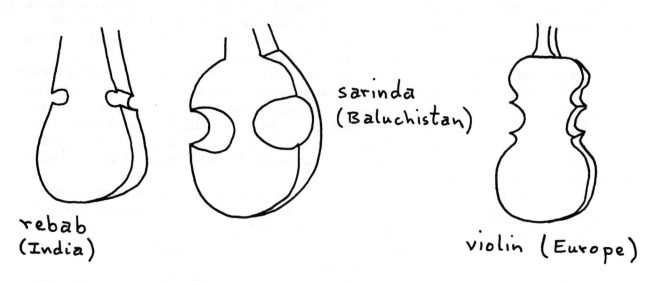

rebab
(India)

sarinda
(Baluchistan)

violin (Europe)

The precise origin of bowed instruments is one of music's most intriguing mysteries. Al Farabi, an Arabic scholar who died around 950 A.D., mentions the *rabāb,* and books dating from about the same time in China and Spain describe similar instruments. Before the ninth century there is no indication on stone or clay or page anywhere in the world of bowing, yet by the tenth century fiddles were in common use from the Atlantic shores of Europe and north Africa across Asia to the Pacific. How, where, or when—beyond the preceding facts—nobody knows!

Long-necked fiddles, invariably spike fiddles of the kind already described, are found in a belt representing the limits of Arabic-Islamic influence and/or trade (through the great caravan routes of central Asia). Certain instruments like the *rabāb* and the *kāmanja* have migrated not only in structure and shape but in name as well as far as Indonesia and Iran respectively. The Yugoslav one-stringed *gusle* (used to accompany epic singing), the Afghani *ritchak* (its sound box made of a rectangular discarded oil tin), the Philippine *git-git,* the Mongol *khil-khuur* (with its carved horse head at the end of the neck), the Burmese *sa dueng,* and the African Taureg *amz'ad* (played to accompany sensuous love songs) all belong to this amazingly prolific family.

Short-necked fiddles apparently also came from the Middle East, but, unlike the spike fiddles, they migrated up into central and northern Europe and as far east as India. They also may have partially skin-covered sound boxes, although tops made entirely of wood are more common as one travels north. Quite often they are carved and hollowed out of a single piece of wood. Typical short fiddles are the north African *rabāb* (different in structure if not in name from the spike fiddle *rebab*), the Greek *lyra,* the Bulgarian *gadulka,* the Apache fiddle of the American Southwest, the European violin family (and all its ancestors and folk versions, such as in Poland and Norway), and in a slightly different line of development the instruments of south and central Asia like the Kazakh *kobuz,* or the *sarangi* and *sarinda* of India. We should remember also that harps, zithers, and lyres have also been played with bows from time to time. More mechanical instruments like the medieval European hurdy-gurdy, with the strings sounded by a revolving resined wheel turned by a crank, and the Swedish *nyckelharpa,* which is bowed but has the strings stopped by little keys pressed by the fingers, are also members of this family.

★★★★ TYING IT TOGETHER: A MISCELLANY OF THE CONSTRUCTION OF ★★★★ LUTES AND OTHER STRINGED INSTRUMENTS

STRINGS AS SOUND INCREASERS

Each playing string of an instrument can be doubled with one or more strings tuned to its (same) pitch. This is called stringing in *double* or *triple courses*. The result is a brighter, louder sound. The Turkish-Arabic *qānūn* zither uses triple courses (three strings for each pitch); the lutes *'ūd*, mandolin, and twelve-string guitar use double courses, as do the *tambur*, *saz*, and *tār* of Iran and Turkey. The piano is strung in single (for low notes), double (for medium-low notes), and triple (for medium to high notes) courses.

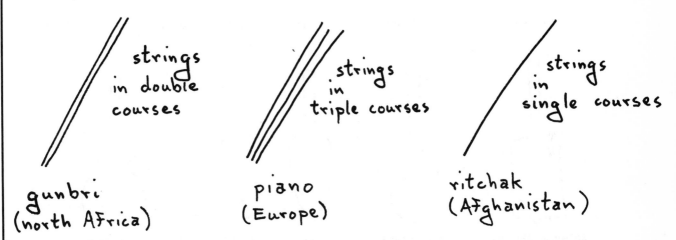

strings in double courses — gunbri (north Africa)

strings in triple courses — piano (Europe)

strings in single courses — ritchak (Afghanistan)

Sympathetic strings are extra strings that are tuned in relation to the playing strings to important pitches (like the tonic and dominant) or to a specific scale, *raga*, or mode. They are not played, but vibrate and sound in sympathy with the notes sounded on the playing strings, increasing the volume and enriching the tone color. The European *viola d'amore* (written for by Bach and earlier composers) has sympathetic strings, and the *Hardanger fele* (or fiddle) of Norway has four to five sympathetic strings under its four playing strings, but this acoustical principle has been most highly developed in instruments in India: on the plucked *sarod*, the bowed *sarangi*, and the *sitār* (which may have up to thirteen sympathetic strings, besides five melody and two drone playing strings).

SHAPES

The shape of the sound box of a lute can vary almost to the extent of one's imagination. Part or all of the face can be covered with leather. Besides the "waisted" fiddle shapes, a few possibilities, reduced to basic shapes (without their ornamental figureheads or pegs), are given on the next page.

FRETS

On many of the earth's bowed instruments (like the *rabāb* and *sarangi*) the strings are stopped merely by touching them with the fingertips or fingernails. On other bowed and on many plucked lutes and zithers the strings are pressed against the fingerboard with the fingers. The fingerboard may be *unfretted* or *fretted*. The unfretted fingerboard is a smooth surface (like that on the European violin, the Arabic *'ūd*, or the Indian *sarod*) that may be completely plain, or marked with little indicators like the inlaid dots on the Chinese *ch'in*. Fretted fingerboards have a series of raised crosspieces made of metal, wood, or string upon or between which

A Catalog of Some Lute Shapes

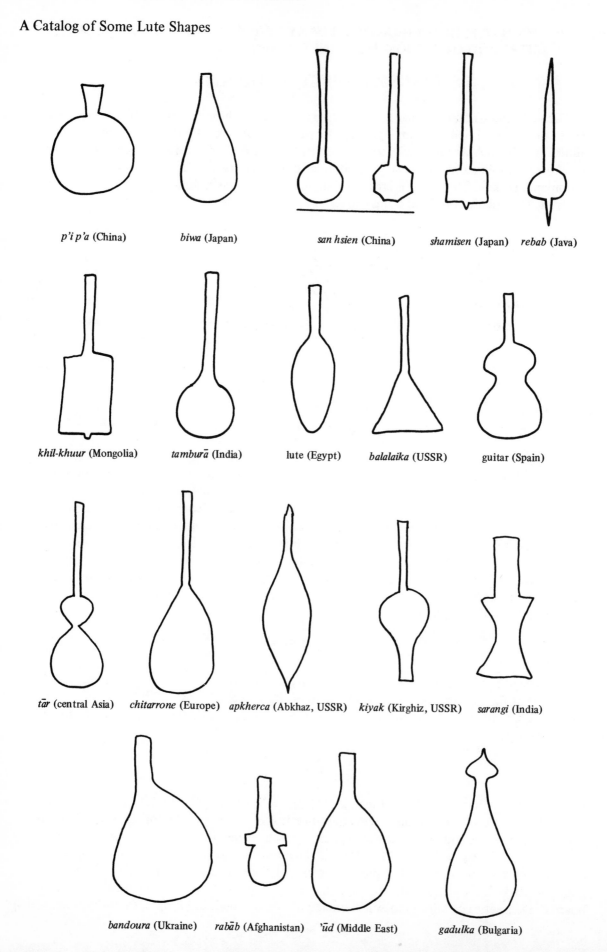

p'i p'a (China)   biwa (Japan)   san hsien (China)   shamisen (Japan)   rebab (Java)

khil-khuur (Mongolia)   tamburā (India)   lute (Egypt)   balalaika (USSR)   guitar (Spain)

tār (central Asia)   chitarrone (Europe)   apkherca (Abkhaz, USSR)   kiyak (Kirghiz, USSR)   sarangi (India)

bandoura (Ukraine)   rabāb (Afghanistan)   'ūd (Middle East)   gadulka (Bulgaria)

the fingers are pressed. They are spaced musically, that is, according to the scales or musical principles of their culture.

The Persian *tār* and many of the plucked lutes of central Asia have frets made of gut strings wrapped around the neck of the instrument. These frets are movable and can be adjusted according to the scale the musician is to play in. The Indian *sitār* has similarly adjustable arched metal frets attached to gut strings. Other Indian classical and folk instruments have their frets set semipermanently in wax (they can be adjusted by softening the wax). On most Euro-American instruments (like the guitar, banjo, or dulcimer) the metal frets are inlaid permanently into the wood of the fingerboard. The Chinese *p'i p'a* has wood frets that are glued onto the face. Many African, Indian, and southeast Asian instruments (like the Thai *chakhe*, the Indian *bīn*, or the Ugandan bar zither) have frets that are raised high off the neck or body; central Asian and European lutes and zithers, among others, tend to have frets set a mere fraction of an inch above their bases.

STRINGS AND BRIDGES

The strings that are stretched to produce sound on lutes and zithers are made in any culture from the strongest or best available material, according to tradition, or preferences for sound color/timbre. Strings are made from the raised skin of bamboo (Malagasy, southeast Asia), bark, fiber, or twine (Africa), silk (China, Japan, Korea), gut (Europe, Africa, Asia), and more recently wire and nylon, which, exported from industrialized countries, have replaced older, more traditional materials.

The *bridge* raises the string above the face of the instrument. (We have noted that in many Asian languages what we call the bridge is called the "horse," which is in a sense more accurate, for the string[s] does "ride" across its back.) Like frets, bridges come in all types and shapes and sizes: they can be mere rough wedges, bars, stones, or chips of wood, or they can be carved in intricate patterns; they can be thin and bladelike or bulky; the string(s) may be set across notches in them (or behind them) or through holes in them; bridges may be glued in place or movable; there may be one bridge for all the strings (common in lutes and lyres) or a separate bridge for each string (common in Asian and some African zithers).

There is, in fact, a whole fascinating technology of bridge-making. For example, on the south Indian *veena* the carved bridge (called *kudarai*, or "horse") is fairly thick-legged and is topped by an almost flat, slightly curving brass plate cushioned on a layer of resin. This curved bridge surface, common on many of India's classical instruments, causes a slight nasal buzz as the strings vibrate against it from their initial point of contact, a sound we associate with Indian music. On the *tamburā*, little cotton or silk threads called *jivam* (or "life") are added at a precise point between the bridge surface and the playing strings to increase this buzz and enrich the timbre with a stronger mixture of audible overtones. Strings are held in place by a notched raised portion behind the flat bridge face. On the *veena* there is another metal plate curving off to one side which functions as an additional bridge for the three drone strings.

The bridges (called *ji*) of the Japanese *koto* are made of wood, ivory, or (recently) plastic. They are unornamented—though their shape in itself is extremely beautiful in the simplicity and functionality of its design—and movable (to adjust the tuning). There is one bridge for each of the thirteen strings. In Africa on a hybrid type of instrument called the "harp" lute (or *kora* in Guinea and Senegambia), since it combines the structure of a lute (neck and body) with the playing technique of a harp (strumming open strings), the bridge is high and notched something like a Christmas tree to hold from five to twenty-one strings. Just as in the violin, the tension of the strings holds the bridge upright in place.

The *gadulka* of Bulgaria and a number of other eastern European fiddles have bridges with a short leg and a long one: the long leg is fitted through a hole on the top board of the sound box and reaches through to the bottom side. It combines the functions of a bridge with those

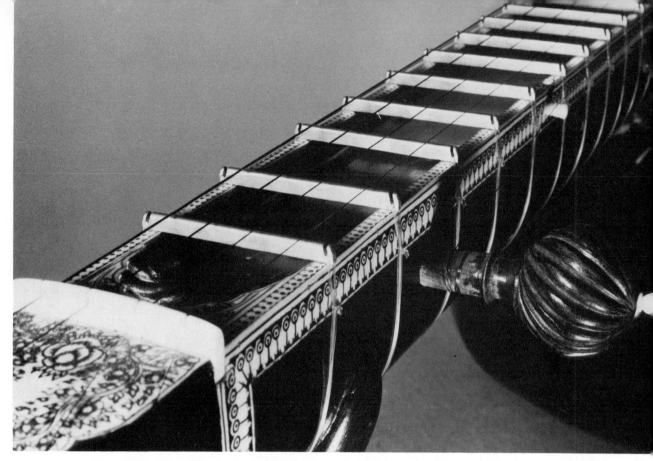

Frets on a *bīn*, north India. The frets are movable and held in place with gut or plastic string. They are relatively high over the concave troughlike neck.

The bridge and resonator face of a box lyre from Uganda. The belly is cowhide, and the strings are cow sinew.

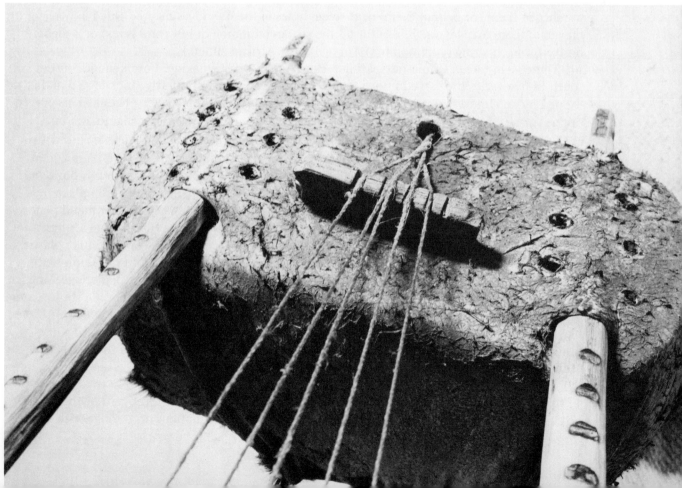

of the sound post of the European violin, carrying the vibration of the strings through the resonator to the wood on the bottom!

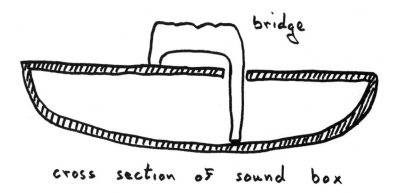

cross section of sound box

On instruments with many sympathetic strings under the regular playing strings, such as the Indian bowed *sarangi* or the plucked *sitār*, there may be holes in the lower part of the bridge or an additional lower bridge to hold these extra strings. The bridges of many guitars and of the Japanese *biwa*, to name only two examples, may also have a mechanism by which the strings may be secured.

PICKS AND PLECTRUMS

Just as in the case of drumsticks in relation to drums, picks or plectrums can greatly influence the sound of a plucked instrument and consequently the nature of the music that it makes. The human fingers are (with the hands) an incredibly sophisticated mechanism: they are flexible, minutely controllable, and can be used singly, in combination, or as a unit. They can pluck the strings with their fleshy tip, with the inside of the fingernail, with a combination of both, or with an outward stroke brushing (away from the palm) with the outside of the nail. But the fingers and nails make a relatively quiet (though beautiful) sound. Picks and plectrums increase the sound considerably and make it stronger.

Finger picks are extensions of the fingernails (one fits over each finger) made from plastic, bone, wire, metal, ivory, bamboo, or some similar material. The Japanese *koto* player, for example, wears ivory finger picks on the thumb, index, and middle fingers of his right hand. *Plectrums* are held in the fingers and vary from the small blades of plastic or bone the size of a coin to quills to the hand-sized, weighted plectrums in a variety of fascinating shapes used with the Japanese *biwa* and *shamisen*. The advantages of plectrums are that a stronger stroke can be used (using the wrist, hands, and forearm) and that great musical speed can be developed by plucking the string both downward and upward with a quick flick of the wrist.

BOWS

Bows have only two essential parts: the stretched cluster of horsehair or fiber that is drawn across the string of a fiddle to make the sound, and the wooden bow which holds it. In its simplest form, the flexing of the bow itself holds the hair part tight, but often the player grips the bow (and the hair strands) in a manner that allows him to control the tension with his hand as he plays. Bows like those of the classical European string instruments (and their folk variants) have a screw mechanism for tightening or loosening the tension of the horsehair.

A large, heavy plectrum is used with the *shamisen*, Japan. Print by
Toyokuni (1769-1825).

Bassari musicians/dancers with tube zithers,
Senegal.

Catalog of Some Bow Shapes

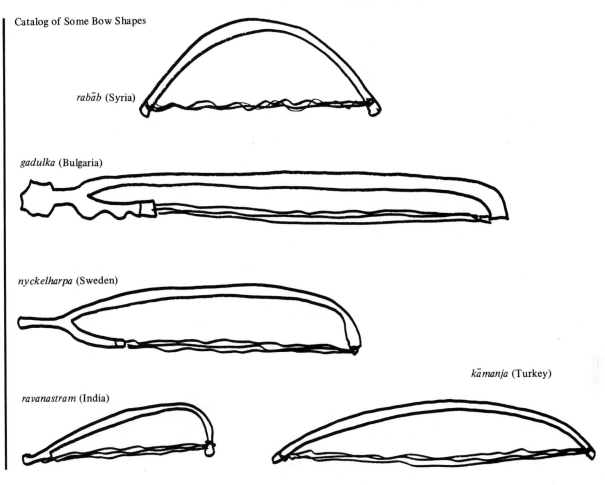

rabāb (Syria)

gadulka (Bulgaria)

nyckelharpa (Sweden)

kāmanja (Turkey)

ravanastram (India)

★★★★★★★★★★★★★★★★★★★★★★★★

Zithers

The strings of *zithers* are stretched across and parallel to the body which is one continuous shape. Separate resonators may be added, but more commonly the entire body itself serves as a resonator. The strings may be plucked or struck. Zithers are classified according to the shape of their body: stick or bar, tube, raft, trough, and board.

In their simplest form, *stick* or *bar zithers* (such as the single-stringed *enzenze* of Uganda) are similar to musical bows with three or four frets added. The stick may be straight or bent and the gourd resonator may be held against the resonating chest of the player. The north Indian *veena*, or *bīn*, represents a slightly more complicated development of this type of zither: the bamboo tube is polished and ornamented, as are its two (or sometimes three!) gourd resonators; there can be a peacock or bird figurehead and numerous playing and drone strings which are stopped either by fretting with the fingers or by sliding a polished stone or metal tube along the strings (much as in the steel, or Hawaiian, guitar).

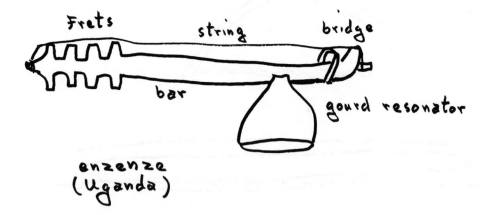

enzenze
(Uganda)

Tube zithers are made entirely from a tube, usually of bamboo. The strings were formerly the sliced skin of the bamboo itself, but today metal strings are attached. This type of zither is found in the southeast Asian mainland and islands and in Africa. The *valiha* (Malagasy) is a typical example and may include refinements such as tuning pegs, metal strings, movable bridges, or a palm-hood resonator/reflector.

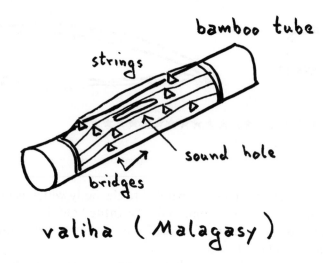

valiha (Malagasy)

Raft zithers, which are made and played in central Africa, are made by binding together a series of thin tubes (much as a raft is made by binding parallel logs together). A string is usually cut from the skin of each tube, a gourd resonator may be added, or nut shells may be put inside the tubes for an added rattling effect.

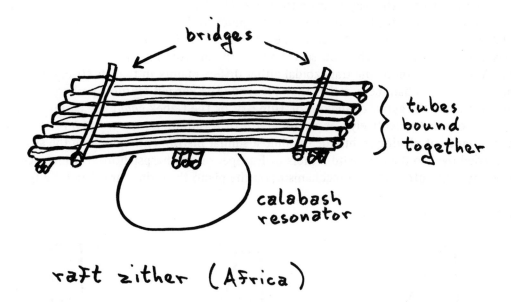

raft zither (Africa)

Trough zithers, such as the *lulanga* of the Bashi people of the Lake Kivu area, Congo, have a hollowed-out, troughlike part on the body of the instrument under the strings. They are found in east and central Africa.

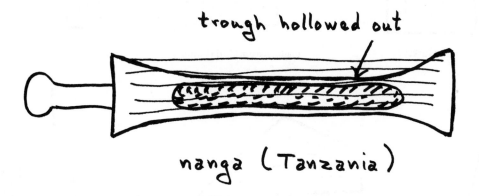

nanga (Tanzania)

Board zithers represent the largest and most complex family of zither types. They have a fairly flat or slightly arched surface over which the strings are stretched, and the body itself (often a hollow, boxlike structure) is usually also a resonator/reflector. We might further subdivide board zithers into four main types: the long, surfboard-sized instruments of the Far East; the trapezoidal-shaped sound boxes found in Arabic/Islamic countries (and consequently up into eastern Europe, Russia, north India, and China and in fact western Europe and the Americas); rectangular and lute-like zithers (Europe and Asia); and the more mechanical keyboard zithers like the piano, harpsichord, and clavichord of the European tradition.

The long zithers, as we have seen in our section on the Chinese *ch'in*, are among the oldest and most important high classical instruments of the Far East. Many of them have high movable bridges, and their playing technique and repertoire are complex and immense (similar perhaps to that of the piano in the West). Besides the seven-stringed *ch'in*, there are the twenty-five-stringed *shē* and the fourteen-stringed *cheng* of China, the twelve-stringed *kaya kum* of Korea, and the thirteen-stringed *koto* of Japan. In southeast Asia there are the zoomorphic crocodile-shaped *mi gyaun* of the Bon people of Burma, the *kachapi* of Java, besides various tube and trapezoidal zithers.

Trapezoidal zithers, the earliest evidence of which dates from the tenth-century Middle East, are smaller, like flattish boxes; they may be fashioned with legs like a small delicate table, or set on a tabletop, on the knees of the player, or on the floor. The Turkish *qānūn* has up to seventy-two strings, twenty-four pitches set in triple courses, which are plucked. It is found in various versions throughout the Islamic world from north Africa to the Far East. The *tjelempung* of Java, for instance, with twenty-six strings (thirteen double courses) is one of the improvising instruments in the *gamelan* orchestra. Another version of the trapezoidal zither differs mainly in that its strings are struck with little knobbed sticks or hammers, rather than plucked. The Persian *santūr* is perhaps the prototype, and instruments like the gypsy *cimbalom* of Hungary or the Uzbek *chang* are eastern European and central Asian cousins (respectively), as are the *santir* of Kashmir and the *yang ch'in* of China. Amazingly, this variance of playing technique on almost similar instruments (plucking the strings or hitting them) is carried over to the keyboard zithers of Europe: on the harpsichord, for instance, the strings are plucked by quills attached to a mechanism; on the piano the strings are struck by felt hammers.

Catalog of Some Board Zither Shapes

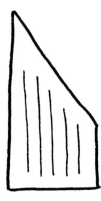

qānūn (Turkey)   piano, harpsichord (Europe)   *koto* (Japan)

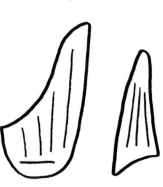

autoharp (United States)   *gusli* (USSR)

kantele (Finland)

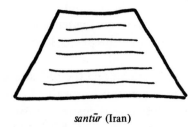

The shapes of zithers may be determined either by the progressive length of the strings (long to short) or by an averaging of the length of the longest string.

santūr (Iran)

Hand-struck and hand-plucked zithers were popular in Europe before they were submerged from the sixteenth century on in the general popularity of keyboard instruments. The psaltery (held against the chest of the player) was played by minstrels and amateurs (like the clerk of Chaucer's *Canterbury Tales*) until the Renaissance. The gentle *kantele* of Finland accompanied the epics and tales of the bards, and the *gusli* of the Volga region in Russia ornamented the songs of ballad singers; both of these zithers are still played on a small scale today. Zithers are sometimes also called "dulcimers" or (if they are struck) "hammer dulcimers."

Another group of board zithers bears some resemblance to members of the lute family. Their shape may be lutelike, but they are usually played flat in front of the player rather than held; they may have tuning pegs and even a short neck and ornamental scroll. Among these instruments we might include the Thai *chakhe*, and many Euro-American zithers like the thirteen-stringed Swedish *hummel* ("bumble bee") with its pearlike shape, the eight-stringed Norwegian *langleik*, the Appalachian dulcimer, the autoharp, and the electric ("Hawaiian") steel guitar, the latter a recent instrument—developed since the 1930s—which is popular in American "country and western" music and may include (besides electronic amplification and modification) several keyboards and numerous pedal attachments.

HOME-GROWN MUSICAL INSTRUMENTS

For those of us who have grown up in industrialized "advanced" countries, acquiring a musical instrument is only a little more complicated than going to a supermarket for a package of tomatoes or a loaf of bread. Just as bread is baked in a mechanized bakery or tomatoes are grown (scientifically) on multiacre corporation farms, instruments are made by men and machines in factories and assembled on assembly lines; and they are readily available and relatively inexpensive. But in recent years a great many people have discovered a very basic joy, one that Henry David Thoreau wrote about over a hundred years ago: what you do or make or create yourself can give you several thousand times the satisfaction of something bought in a store, for it becomes (as a product of your own mind and hands) something more than a mere object—it becomes a part of yourself.

There is today a happy subculture of people enjoying their own home-grown tomatoes (and carrots, parsley, onions, potatoes, peas, cucumbers, corn, and pumpkins!) or slicing into freshly baked loaves of bread warm enough to melt butter at the touch. It seems to me that there is also the creative potential for a subculture making their own machinations of sound.

The first step is to forget, at least for a while, the more complicated instruments of a technological society. It is possible, of course, to craft a guitar or a violin or a harpsichord from plans or a kit, but this takes a great deal of skill and perhaps months of time; worse, the mental effort involved—aside from an inordinate amount of patience—is mainly the concentration of following directions, like painting an imitation "Rembrandt masterwork" by numbers. The instrument-makers and musicians of the earth have constructed an amazing variety of instruments, and they have solved technical problems—such as tuning, reeds, bridges, shapes, materials—in a number of pragmatic and imaginative ways. Some of their instruments are practically "instant," requiring only a few minutes to make; others may require several hours of work, others days. If we take advantage of the experience and knowledge of these musical master craftsmen, of the many details of construction already described in this chapter, we (meaning you, meaning anybody) can build simple prototypes of the world's instruments in a matter of hours. These prototypes could be expanded, or complicated, or decorated according to the skills and imagination of each individual. Better yet, they could be played with music of one's own making!

We have seen how people all over the world make use of their environment, the materials that it provides, as raw materials for the construction of their musical instruments. We, in Europe or the United States, are not surrounded by gourds and vines and bamboo groves, but we do have a veritable jungle of discarded tin cans, plastic containers, bottles, piping, scrap metal, and junk, much of which could be recycled to make music with. Our resources also include lumberyards and hardware stores and many easy-to-use materials such as plastic putty and fiber glass. Our workshop will need only a collection of basic tools (hammer, saw, nails, hand or electric drill, pliers, matt knife, files or rasp) plus several specialized tools described later.

The plans for instruments are for the roughest, easiest-to-make prototypes. Corners could be carved or molded, for example, or intricate shapes could be cut with a jigsaw. Found objects—like chairs or teapots or auto parts—could also be utilized. The world instruments described in this chapter or seen in museums could further extend your range of possibilities, hence your imagination.

★★★★★★★★★★ A PRIMER OF MUSICAL INSTRUMENT CONSTRUCTION ★★★★★★★

1. BULL-ROARER

Materials: a flat, rulerlike piece of wood, not too long
a length of string (2 to 3 feet); nylon fishing wire is strong and good
Tools: a saw (if necessary)
a drill

Tie string through
hole drilled in wood.

Decorate wood with felt-tip pen, watercolors, or
incised designs.

Directions for playing: Swing bull-roarer at end of string over head until it spins, creating roaring sound. Speed of swinging controls pitch. Several bull-roarers built to different sizes can produce different pitches according to our rule-of-thumb.

2. RECYCLED RATTLES

Materials: thrown-away soft drink, beer, or juice cans
dried beans, pebbles, sand, twigs, etc.
masking tape or plastic putty
optional: a dowel or stick for a handle (8 to
10 inches)
Tools: saw, for the handle (if necessary)

Put rattling materials (beans, etc.) into cans. Seal with
masking tape or putty. For handle, jam stick through
(drinking) hole as far as possible into can.

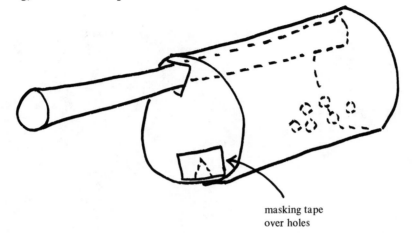

masking tape
over holes

Directions for playing: Shake.

3. SCRAPER

Materials: two pieces of wood (one smaller and flat)
Tools: rasp (or wood files)

Notch larger piece of wood periodically, or in designs.

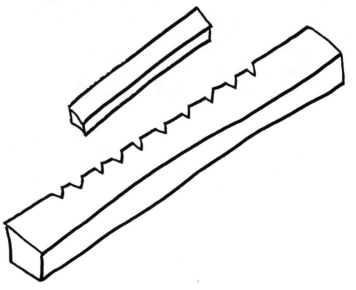

Directions for playing: Scrape in various rhythmic patterns.

Students in the World Music Program at Amherst College with their homemade instruments. Among those constructed by students were *mbiras* based on African designs, zithers (tube and long Far Eastern types), *tamburās* (Indian), double-reed *zurnā*-like double pipes, drums, harps, and plucked and bowed lutes. Among the innovations was the substitution of an old piece of blue jean material for the skin cover of a lute's resonator.

4. FRAME DRUMS (DOLDRUMS)

Materials: wood (1 × 2, or 1 × 3, plus a small dowel or
            1 × 1)
        skin (see your local tannery, or ask at a leather-
          craft shop or shoemaker; as a last resort buy
          a drumhead from a music store)
        upholstery tacks, or large-headed nails
Tools: hammer
        saw

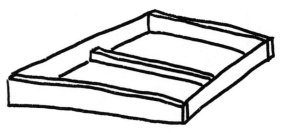

Make a squarish frame at least 1½ inches smaller on
all sides than your piece of leather. The central piece
(or dowel) is for added support and should be at
least 1 inch below the top of the frame. A triangular
or circular hoop frame could also be made.

Soak the leather in water (to stretch it), then tack
it—stretching it across the frame—as tightly as
possible.

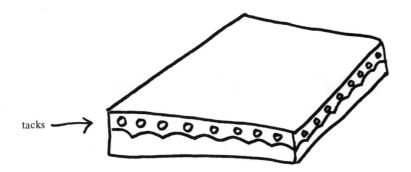

tacks ⟶

Optional: add jangles (like bottle caps loosely strung
on a wire) to rim.

Attention potters: You can make a clay circular frame
dotted with holes through which the skin can be
bound with string or leather lacing.

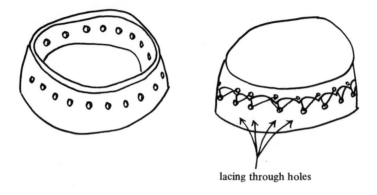

lacing through holes

Or: Mark hoop with an indentation and fasten skin with strands of hide or string wound
around hoop and in groove.

5. FLUTES

Materials: plastic (easiest) or metal tubing (such as electrical tubing), or bamboo—from 1 inch
          to 1½ inches in diameter
          workable putty (like plastic wood or plumbing sealers)—it must harden after applica-
          tion
Tools: tube cutter (for metal)
          saw (for wood or plastic)
          drill (electric or hand "egg-beater" type) with drill bits ¼ inch or larger
          vise, or an extra pair of hands to hold flute while drilling
          dowel, several feet long and small enough in diameter to insert into tubing
          "rattail" file (for bamboo flutes only) mounted on doweling

mouth hole

block with putty or sealer

finger holes

this end open

Plan to make several flutes at one time;
experiment with length and finger hole
placement

Transverse Flute
1. Cut tube to size (1 to 2 feet).
2. Block one end with putty—it must be completely
   sealed against air leaks—press on inside with dowel.
3. Drill a blow hole near the blocked end; experiment with size until you (or a flutist) can get a
   sound.
4. Drill finger holes; start with one or two, testing
   each for sound—make sure they fit your hands
   and fingertips. Thumb(s) can have their hole(s)
   on the underside of the flute.

For end-blown and notched flutes omit the mouth
hole and sealer (leave both ends open).

For bamboo flutes: Bamboo is hollow except for
the joints which have thin inside walls; drill through
and clean these walls with the rattail file mounted
on a stick or doweling. Cut the bamboo so that one
of these walls, left intact, forms the blocked end
near the mouth hole.

Directions for playing: Blow across mouth hole (or end) for sound, finger finger holes for different notes.

6. MBIRA AMERIKANA

Materials: wood tongue depressors (from drugstore), heavy plastic spoons (supermarket), or heavy steel wire (like coat hangers or thicker) beaten flat with hammer and cut to size

tin can or plastic bottle (for resonator)
small piece of wood (paperback book size)
wood or metal stripping
wire (optional)
nails or screws

Tools: saw
hammer
pliers or wire cutters
tin snips (if can is attached)

Place any number of keys (tongue depressors, plastic spoons, steel) on wood base and over wire (dowel) so that they come out to different vibrating lengths—test by sound. Secure them in place with stripping.

Attach tin can resonator with string or wire, or cut and nail to bottom of wood (a plastic bottle can be cut to shape with a matt knife).

underside
cut and bend
tin and nail
in place

any number
of
keys
(tongue depressors,
plastic spoons,
flattened
steel)

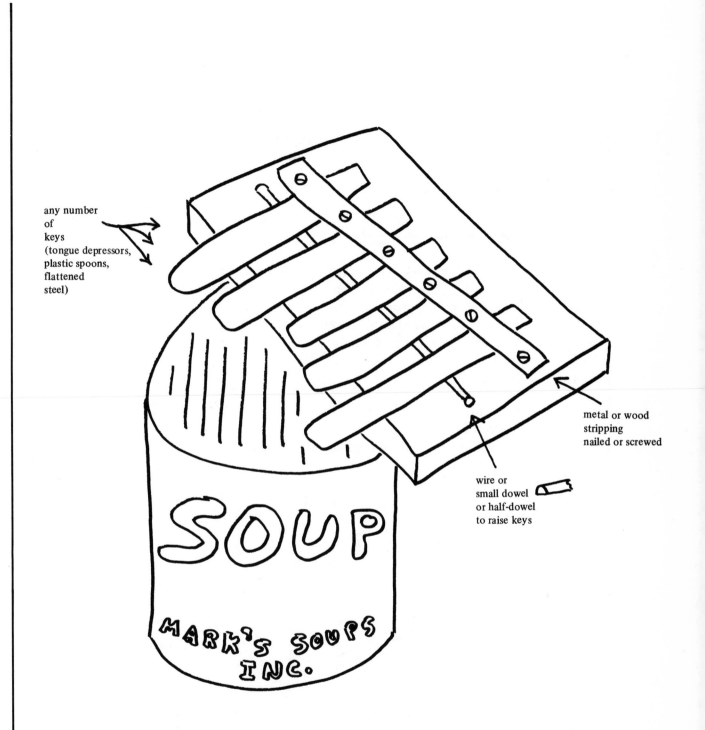

metal or wood
stripping
nailed or screwed

wire or
small dowel
or half-dowel
to raise keys

Directions for playing: Pluck the keys with the thumbs of both hands.

7. KOUNTER-KULTURE *KOTO* (BOARD ZITHER)

Materials: one nice large plank, 12 to 18 inches wide, and from 2 to 4 feet long (several nar-
    rower boards could also be nailed together, raftlike, with several supporting
    crosspieces underneath)

"modern corner bead" molding—it looks like this:

 —about 1 or 2 feet,

or triangle blocks sawed out of a 1 X 3:

string: various sizes of nylon fishing line (cheapest), "music" wire or piano wire
    (sizes .013, .015, and .018 [thickest] can be bought by packet or pound at wire
    dealers or from piano tuners), or nylon or steel guitar strings (get a full set of six,
    plus extras later as needed) available at music stores
washers (metal, fairly large)
nails

Tools: hammer
    saw
    wire cutters, or scissors
    knife or file

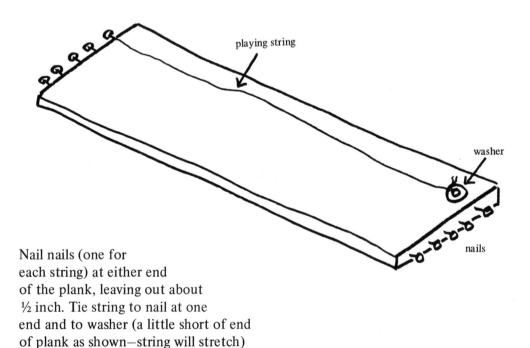

Nail nails (one for
each string) at either end
of the plank, leaving out about
½ inch. Tie string to nail at one
end and to washer (a little short of end
of plank as shown—string will stretch)
at other. Stretch string and pop washer over nail at
its end of plank. Repeat for each string.

Cut bridges from molding or plank—one or two for each string. Notch top of each bridge with knife or file to hold string.

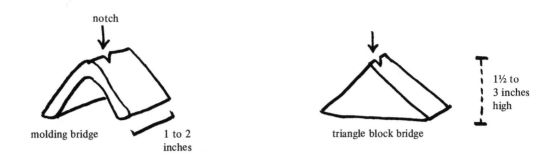

Place bridges under each string, tuning (by ear) by shortening or lengthening playing area or by increasing tension of string. If playing string is too loose, retie it, or increase the height of its bridge(s).

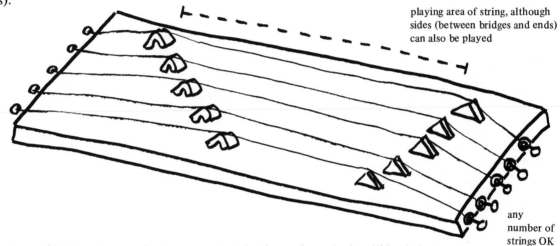

Use one type of bridge in your instrument (not both, as shown)—it will look better.

Decorate plank (with paints), or oil, polish, or stain it.

Directions for playing: Pluck the strings. Vibrato and slides up to several notes higher can be achieved by pressing on the string (with the nonplucking hand) between the bridge and end of the plank.

8. DESOLATION ROW BANJO (STICK LUTE)

Materials: a board (1 X 2, 1 X 3, or 1 X 4) from 2 to 3½ feet long
    a resonator: large plastic bottles like for Clorox, apple juice, milk, or mineral water
      (2- to 4-quart size) or a large tin can (cafeterias and restaurants throw them out)
    strings (possibilities described in directions for *koto*)
    molding, or small piece of wood for bridge, small half-round molding for frets and
      other refinements
    Elmer's glue
    metal washers
    nails
    dowels (circular sticks) in several sizes for pegs, or guitar "machine," usually comes
      in a set of three (for tuning and holding three strings), available for a little over
      three dollars at guitar and music shops.

Tools: hammer
        saw
        matt knife (or sharp pocket knife)
        tin snips (only if tin can resonator is used)
        drill (electric or hand)
        wire cutters or pliers or scissors (depending on type of strings)
        a reamer (for shaping peg holes, if pegs are used)

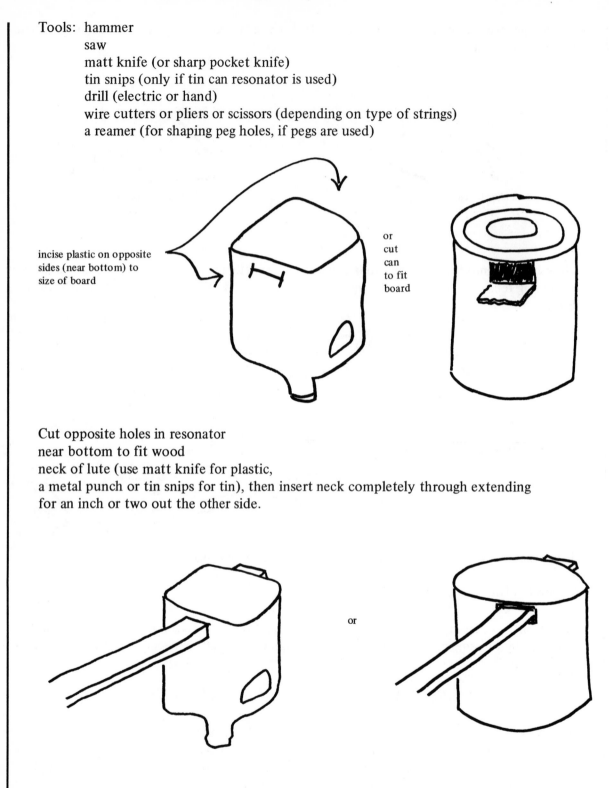

incise plastic on opposite
sides (near bottom) to
size of board

or
cut
can
to fit
board

Cut opposite holes in resonator
near bottom to fit wood
neck of lute (use matt knife for plastic,
a metal punch or tin snips for tin), then insert neck completely through extending
for an inch or two out the other side.

or

Nail resonator flaps to wood neck, if necessary to hold them in place.

At this end of the instrument:
1. hammer in nails at the end of the stick to hold the strings, and
2. fashion a bridge
(may be glued or anchored in place)
with notches—one for
each string.

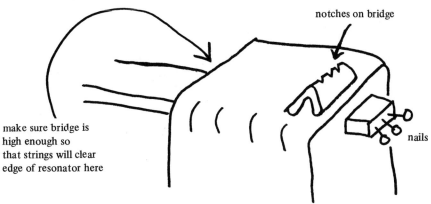

notches on bridge

make sure bridge is
high enough so
that strings will clear
edge of resonator here

nails

At the other end of stick (a) install guitar machine (look at a cheap guitar to see how it is done),

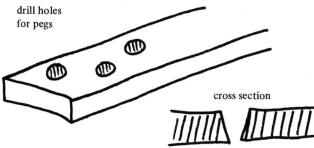

drill holes
for pegs

cross section

taper with reamer

or (b) drill holes, one for each peg, and
shape them—tapering to the underside
of the neck—with a reamer. Be careful
not to make the hole too large—it must
be smaller than your dowel peg (which
you will whittle down to size).

Fashion pegs. Whittle (with the matt
or pocket knife) and shape further with
rasp or files to taper toward the end.
Keep testing them in peg holes for a
snug fit.

It might be well to practice making
several pegs and holes on an old board,
just to get the craft down and feel
more at home with your home-grown
Stradivarius!

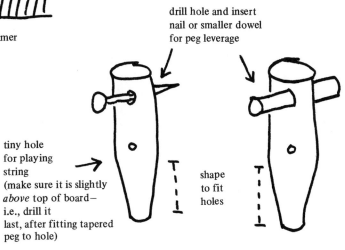

drill hole and insert
nail or smaller dowel
for peg leverage

tiny hole
for playing
string
(make sure it is slightly
above top of board—
i.e., drill it
last, after fitting tapered
peg to hole)

shape
to fit
holes

Fit strings to nails (you can use our metal washer method) at one end and to pegs (through tiny holes) at the other. Tighten, wrapping strings around pegs until strings ring. Tune them any way you like.

You now have a fretless banjo!

By stopping the string along the board neck with your fingers or with a glass bottle cap (or a tiny spice or pill bottle) you can play almost any scale or melody.

Now, for some added refinements:

Add a second smaller bridge (called a "nut" on the violin) near the pegs. This bridge need not be very high— from ¼ to ½ inch is plenty. A small piece of molding will do. Notch it for the strings and glue it (Elmer's) in place.

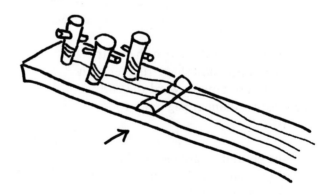

And finally, using your ear, make dots or lines to show where you put your fingers, or make frets (half-round molding is fine), testing all the frets and marking their placement before gluing them.

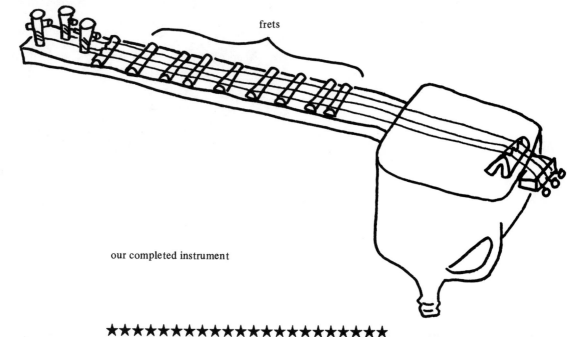

frets

our completed instrument

★★★★★★★★★★★★★★★★★★★★★★★★

In a sense, many of the pages of this chapter which explain in detail how instruments work and are put together can be viewed as a manual for the construction of musical instruments. If you can build a flute from plastic tubing or a Clorox-bottle banjo, you can (using a little imagination) build a prototype of almost any instrument of the family groupings of idiophones, membranophones, aerophones, and chordophones. Objects found in junkyards, chosen carefully for their pitch and sonic capabilities, can be transformed: automobile hubcaps can be hung to become gentle ringing tuned gongs (like the Javanese *kempul*), brakeshoes or other pieces of steel or iron can be hung from racks like the ancient Chinese *fang hsiang.*

Xylophones and metallophones can be constructed by cutting hardwood slabs or metal electrical piping, or iron and steel bars (you need a friendly metal shop for the latter), and assembling them according to the traditional methods shown on pages 91–95. The problems of making drums are only those of finding skins and drum shells (try plastic sewer tubing, large cardboard tubes thrown away by rug dealers, cut to size, small wood barrels, cooking pots, plant pots, plastic or tin garbage cans and waste buckets—anything barrel- or pot- or frame-shaped). Methods of attaching drumheads to the shells are shown on page 105. Potters can utilize their craft (as they have for several thousand years) to make flutes, ocarinas, and whistles—and even for clay xylophonelike instruments, bells, and hung chimes. Once the basic flute tubing with finger holes has been made, the tube can be fitted with any of the reed mouthpieces (pages 116–18). For the less adventurous a trumpet, oboe, or clarinet mouthpiece (with reeds) can be purchased from a music shop; this mouthpiece can then be fitted on the end of your homemade tube (use wax, putty, modeling clay, or cloth wrapping to seal it for air leaks) to transform it into a folk trumpet, oboe, or clarinet! Harps are as easy to make—three pieces of wood nailed triangularly for a frame—and so are lyres, fiddles, musical bows, tube and raft and stick zithers, ground harps, and any imaginable type of lute. Reflectors/resonators are to be found everywhere (see pages 77–87). Materials like papier-maché (fortified by wire or fiber glass tape) are almost free and can be molded to any shape. Finally, your instrument, if the sound is too small for your liking, can be wired for sound: purchase a cheap contact microphone (harmonica contact mikes begin at under $2.50) with the appropriate adapter plug and fasten it

Gender, built by Barbara Benary and her students at Livingston College as part of a small *gamelan* orchestra (using plans devised by Dennis Murphy). The tuned resonators are built from stacked coffee cans. This *gamelan* beautifully duplicates the instruments and sound of the Javanese original.

Harry Partch with cloud chamber bowls, one of many homemade instruments made by the iconoclastic American composer/craftsman.

against the surface of your instrument with masking or electrical tape. Plugged into the amplifier of a hi-fi system, your home-grown instrument can fill your house (if not your neighborhood—not recommended) with music.

Why make an instrument? We in the so-called civilized, advanced, industrialized nations live in a world of objects which we use but rarely understand. We drive cars but we cannot fix them, we watch television or listen to records without knowing how they work, we purchase pancake and cake mixes without thinking that we are paying double the price for simple, basic ingredients that it would take three minutes (yes, *three minutes*) to put together ourselves. We tacitly assume that experts *know* about such things, and in this maze of specialization, we (poor dummies) are totally dependent on others. I happen to believe that quite often our hands can tell us things that our minds, boxed in by all the preconceptions of our culture, may not be able to conceive. Which is another way of saying that what we *do* can be much, much more humanly valuable than what we *buy*.

John Blacking, in his beautiful comparison of his own (European) culture with that of the Venda people of south Africa, notes that while the Africans take for granted that every human being, because he is a human being, is quite naturally a musician, capable of all the intricacies of composition and performance, we in the Euro-American cultural complex assign musical ability to a talented few, to a specialized elite. The experts perform and compose (and make instruments), and the rest of us merely listen, passively or actively, intelligently or stupidly, whatever the case may be. We do not *make* music, we *buy* it. And something very human and personal is lost in the process.

Earlier we noted a typical Beckettian misconception of the modern world, and in particular of the industrialized "advanced" countries: that what is more complex is more advanced (or more intelligent, civilized, beautiful, good, cultured, artistic, and so on); and that what is simple is presumably less intelligent, civilized, beautiful, good. But if we are to come to terms, really and deeply, with the world's music and peoples (and with our own music and with ourselves) we must try to break out of this mental straight-jacket. The simple Japanese *shakuhachi*, a bamboo flute with five finger holes, is one of the most difficult instruments on earth to master, for example. Similarly, an African ensemble of one- and two-note gourd ocarinas may play a music that is more touching, more meaningful, more humanly expressive than all the bombast of a second-rate romantic symphony played by one hundred virtuosos in a symphony hall.

Several summers ago I participated in a project conceived by the composer Peter Phillips, and this extraordinary experience, a very personal one, helped me to escape (at least partially) my own cultural conditioning and tacitly accepted values. It also proved that the Venda people of Africa as described by Professor Blacking know a great deal more about human musicality than we do. In the summer project Mr. Phillips and I worked with fifteen adult individuals, only a few of whom had ever touched a musical instrument. We talked about and worked with sound, we listened to a great deal of music, both in the European classical tradition and from the far corners of the world. The students (who were actually our "teachers," since they never ceased to amaze us) began to dig into themselves, to find their own inner song. They invented and built musical instruments, which they then taught themselves to play. They began to "hear" melodies, for which they developed their own notations or memory devices. And finally, they joined together into ensembles to make music together, for which they composed extended musical structures. The music which these "unmusical" people had created by the end of the three-week project was like a garden of truly rare and beautiful flowers. It was largely outside the Western musical tradition in which we had all grown up, and it was different from any other music on earth. It was, in fact, a new tradition, one that grew from each individual and from the combined efforts of the group. And it was a music that was at once powerful, imaginative, and (above all) humanly expressive. It taught us all that music is inherent in man (and woman), that an instrument (one's own) is an extension of the human being, and that if the heart sings, the instrument sings.

Baines, Anthony. *Bagpipes.* Occasional Papers on Technology, No. 9. Oxford: The University Press, 1960.

Baines, Anthony, ed. *Musical Instruments Through the Ages.* London: Penguin Books, 1973.

Buchner, Alexander. *Folk Music Instruments of the World.* New York: Crown Publishers, 1972.

Dietz, Betty Warner, and Olantunji, Babatunde. *Musical Instruments of Africa.* New York: The John Day Company, 1965.

Grame, Theodore C. "Bamboo and Music: A New Approach to Organology." In McAllester, David P., ed. *Readings in Ethnomusicology.* New York: Johnson Reprint Corporation, 1971.

Grame, Theodore C., and Tsuge, Gen'ichi. "Steed Symbolism in Eurasian String Instruments," *The Musical Quarterly*, vol. 58, no. 1 (January 1972), pp. 57–66.

Hood, Mantle. *The Ethnomusicologist.* New York: McGraw-Hill Book Company, 1971.

Hood, Mantle, and Susilo, Hardja. *Music of the Venerable Dark Cloud.* Los Angeles: Institute of Ethnomusicology, UCLA, 1967.

Jenkins, Jean L. *Musical Instruments.* London: The Horniman Museum, 1970.

Keynton, Tom. *Homemade Musical Instruments.* New York: Drake Publishers, 1975.

Kirby, Percival R. *The Musical Instruments of the Native Races of South Africa.* Johannesburg: Witwatersrand University Press, 1965.

Kothari, K. S. *Indian Folk Musical Instruments.* New Delhi: Sangeet Natak Akademi, 1968.

Krishnaswamy, S. *Musical Instruments of India.* Boston: Crescendo Publishing Company, 1971.

Liang, Tsai-Ping. *Chinese Musical Instruments and Pictures.* Taipei, Taiwan: Chinese Classical Music Association, 1970.

Malm, William P. *Japanese Music and Musical Instruments.* Rutland, Vermont: Charles E. Tuttle, 1959.

Malm, William P. *Music Cultures of the Pacific, the Near East, and Asia.* Englewood Cliffs, New Jersey: Prentice-Hall, 1967.

Marcuse, Sibyl. *Musical Instruments: A Comprehensive Dictionary.* New York: W. W. Norton, 1975.

Morton, David. *The Traditional Music of Thailand.* Los Angeles: Institute of Ethnomusicology, UCLA, 1968.

Nettl, Bruno. *Folk and Traditional Music of the Western Continents.* Englewood Cliffs, New Jersey: Prentice-Hall, 1965.

Nketia, J. H. Kwabena. *The Music of Africa.* New York: W. W. Norton, 1974.

Sachs, Curt. *The History of Musical Instruments.* New York: W. W. Norton, 1940.

Sachs, Curt. *The Wellsprings of Music.* New York: McGraw-Hill Book Company, 1965.

Tsuge, Gen'ichi. Classroom lectures and conversations, Wesleyan University, Middletown, Connecticut, 1971–74.

Van Gulik, R. H. *The Lore of the Chinese Lute.* A Monumenta Nipponica Monograph. Tokyo: Sophia University, in cooperation with Rutland, Vermont: Charles E. Tuttle, 1968.

Winternitz, Emmanuel. *Musical Instruments of the Western World.* New York: McGraw-Hill Book Company, n.d.

Wu, K. T. "Illustrations in Sung Painting," *The Quarterly Journal of the Library of Congress*, vol. 28, no. 3 (July 1971), pp. 173–95.

Whirling dervishes, Konya, Turkey.

PART TWO:

The Workings of Earth Music

5

TIME AND THE RIVER OF RHYTHM

We, in the culture world of Western music—in Europe or the United States—tend to look at music, all music, in a certain way. We think of it as being divided into elements like melody, rhythm, harmony, timbre, ensembles, counterpoint and polyphony, orchestrations, or form much in the same way that medieval philosphers divided the substance of the natural world into the five elements of earth, fire, water, air, and ether. Such a way of looking at music is by no means universal; it is *ethnocentric,* that is, it is *our* way, the way of our culture. In exploring the music of the earth's peoples through our peculiarly Western conceptual gridwork (as we do in the following chapters), I do not mean to imply that this is the only approach: there are many other possibilities. Other peoples think about their musics, perceive their musics (and ours), in different ways, and we shall touch upon some of these ways. At the same time, I hope that our method will better enable us to see and hear, understand and appreciate—and respect—the intricate and varied workings of earth music.

Everything in life and music moves through time. But exactly what time *is* has been a matter for great speculation not only in our own culture, but also among peoples throughout the world and in the past. To most of us time is a measurement of the seconds, minutes, and hours of our clocks, or of the days, months, and years of our calendars. We think of time as progressing—we stand on the edge of the present, a present of successive moments moving like the steps on an escalator into the future, into hopes, dreams, expectations, and at the same time receding into the past, into memories cherished or forgotten. In the larger web of history we are but tiny specks floating somewhere between the turbulent upheavals of the geological ages of the past—the fossils, ruins, and monuments of earlier life—and the hazy vision of a future that holds us at once in awe and terror.

Basically, we as products of Western civilization view this progression of time optimistically— "higher" civilization, we believe, comes from progress: inventions, discoveries, economic growth, pursuit of knowledge, power over nature and environment. Change and newness equal goodness and happiness. We do not really stop to question whether it is ultimately more "civilized" to wage war with rockets and hydrogen bombs than with stone clubs and poisoned arrows, or to make music on electronic synthesizers and eight-track quadraphonic sound systems rather than to improvise on bamboo flutes or drums of buffalo hide and jackwood. Our optimism is unflappable.

But time can also be viewed cyclically. Each day the sun rises and sets, the phases of the moon, like the tides, come and go, the seasons repeat year after year, crops are planted and harvested, individuals move through the stages of life—birth, childhood, marriage, parenthood, death—and the pattern repeats generation after generation. We mark time by these cycles also: "in the spring," "at sunset," or "when we were children." Perhaps we in the great cities of the West have lost much of our feeling for (and perception of) cyclic time, of the gentle rhythms of the earth felt by the Mexican peasant as he hoes his corn day by day and watches it grow, or of the rhythms of life felt in the closely knit communal families of China where generations coexist under one roof, where a person may live his entire life—being born, growing old, watching grandchildren being born—in the same house or village. But year after year we celebrate our "Christmas season"; and even jaded New Yorkers are irresistibly drawn to the parks for a stroll in a kind of unconscious ritual of the first warm sunny day of spring.

Time may also be marked by events. A Navaho will speak of "the winter thirty sheep were killed in a blizzard," an African will remember "the year of the locusts," and a Polynesian will think of the "days of sharks and hurricanes." We as human beings remember, that is we experience past time, in terms of extraordinary events: traumatic experiences, disasters, deaths, perhaps even in the bittersweet flavor of a childhood romance, or an exciting sports event.

Time can move internally, too, within the impulses and vibrations of our bodies, psychologically and physically. Half an hour of waiting (in clock time) at a bus stop or in a dentist's waiting room can seem like an eternity; the same half-hour at a circus or beach in the Caribbean might fly by at the apparent speed of light. Our hearts, our pulses, thump their quiet rhythms like internal clockwork within our bodies. Each day we alternate wakefulness and sleep, we breathe minute by minute to the rhythm of our lungs, and women's bodies (like the moon) mark monthly phases.

Music all over the earth is shaped by the complex of ideas, feelings, and intuitions concerning time; and while these complexes will crop up again and again, we will focus for the moment on the aspect of *rhythm.* Rhythm might be defined as the way sound shapes move in or through time, that is, how music marks time, or how music *makes* time. Two underlying concepts dominate the way most cultures think about music happening in time. The first of these is the *beat,* or rhythmic pulse. Perhaps at one time in the distant past, men first noticed their heartbeats and decided to duplicate this regular thumping with sticks or (later) with drums or hollow logs (which, after all, are duplications of our chest cavities). Or the original impetus might have been footsteps, or dance steps, or the recurrence of patterns of work: hammering, chipping away with stones, grinding or pounding corn. Nobody knows—and it really doesn't matter—but the discovery was an important one, for it remains with us to this day in the claphammer drumming of electric rock groups, in the intense, rapid shaking of rattles in American Indian peyote ceremonies, in the hand motions of symphony orchestra conductors, in the gentle lullabies of Penihing women of Borneo, or underlying the complex rhythms of African drum ensembles.

The beat or pulse, which we can map out (reading from left to right) as

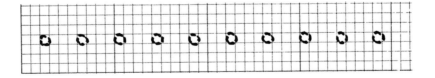

is usually regular. It can be slow (admittedly a subjective term), as in the pulse of the Japanese *gagaku* court music which may move at two- or three-second intervals; medium, as in Mississippi Delta blues; or fast, as in an Irish jig or an Appalachian fiddler's tune. The beat can remain pretty much the same throughout an entire piece, as in jazz, Bach, or an Australian aborigine ritual song, or it may fluctu-

Stick dance, in which the drum rhythms are accentuated by the dancers' clacking sticks. Northwest India.

ate—accelerate or gradually slow down—as in the music of the Javanese *gamelan* orchestras or of Tchaikovsky.

While most of us may think of a beat as being fairly regular, something we can tap our foot to, many musical cultures think of beats in terms of uneven collections of thumps, with a skip or stumble here and there, which are then repeated as a unit. For instance, folk music in India regularly uses the following patterns:

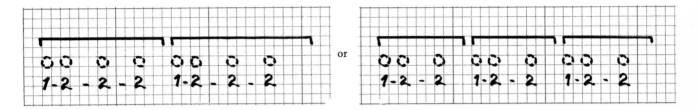

The numbers equal the proportional length of each beat; these patterns are equivalent to fast 7/8 and 5/8 meters respectively in Western music. In the Balkan countries, Turkey, and Greece, even more complicated groups of uneven beats are played and danced to:

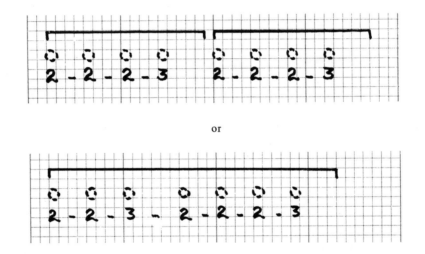

These beat groupings have no real equivalents in the meters of Western music (except perhaps in the music of Bartok and of other composers influenced by him) but might be notated as 9/8 (2 + 2 + 2 + 3) and 16/8 (2 + 2 + 3 + 2 + 2 + 2 + 3) respectively.

Along with music based on beat or beat collections (and often within the same culture) is music that flows like water in a lazy stream, or like the wind—freely and smoothly, expansively. The solo music of the *shakuhachi,* a Japanese bamboo flute, moves in long-held bending tones and sudden darts and spurts, guided by what might be called the "breath rhythm" of the performer. Similarly, the slowly unraveling, improvised *alapana* of India's classical music or the mournful verses of an unaccompanied Welsh ballad flow through time as pure melody shaped by breath and intuition, without a regular underlying pulse. We might map out this melodic progression (again reading from left to right, with relative low and high pitches spaced from the bottom to the top of the graph) as follows:

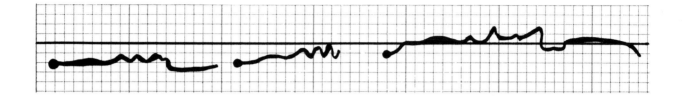

While most of the world's music has a background of a simple beat, man's desire for ornamentation often leads him to more complicated concepts. Among the Oglala Sioux Indians of the northern Great Plains (and other Indian groups), heroic songs, war dances, or ceremonial songs are accompanied by what seems at first to be a straightforward, regular, booming pulse on the large drum. But careful listening reveals that the beat of the drum anticipates by a microsecond the implied beat of the singers, making for an unwavering and tense rhythmic push-pull:

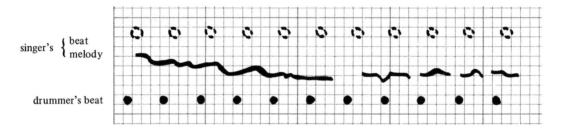

Great skill is required for the correct placement of the drum beat, which must be felt rather than rationalized. Attempts by white musicians to imitate Plains Indian music (in Hollywood films, for example) usually fall flat because the beat accents of voice and drum are placed together, simultaneously, instead of performed with the subtle variance.

Another technique for ornamenting the beat (and a basic element of music) is to fill the spaces between each beat with real or implied (audible or inaudible) regular subbeats. Here, in the concept of subdivision of the main beat, we approach the idea of rhythmic patterns superimposed on beats and of larger rhythmic shapes and structures. For instance, in some American Indian music, gourd or deer hoof rattles are shaken at two or four times the speed of the drum:

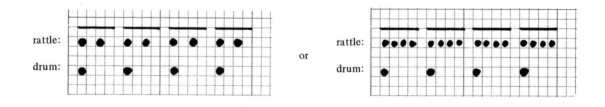

Similarly, in the *gamelan* orchestras of Indonesia the keyed gongs of the *saron* family of instruments (similar to our glockenspiel or celeste) play on and around a skeleton melody, but with the notes repeated or ornamented at double and quadruple speed:

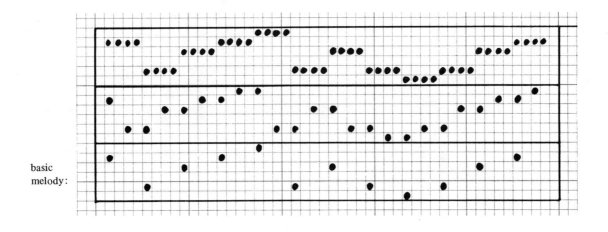

The result is a shimmering, translucent sound, a musical texture that has been compared to the ripples and flashes of running water in the moonlight.

Most musical cultures (our own included) fill the spaces between beats with multiples of two or three:

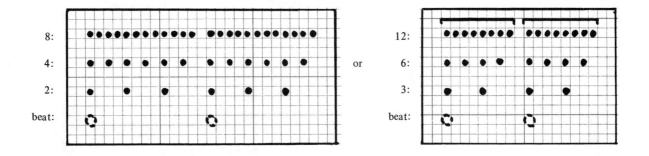

or, as in the more complicated beat groupings (*meters*) of the Mediterranean and the Balkans, with a combination thereof:

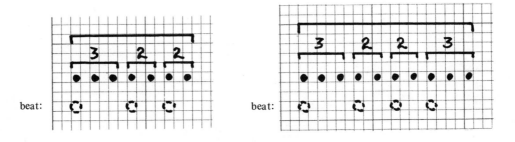

But there are also other possibilities. In south India, particularly among the hereditary temple drummers of the Kerala region, the beat may be subdivided into fives, sevens, and nines.

Timila players, part of the twenty- to thirty-member *panchavadyam* ensemble. Kerala, southwestern India.

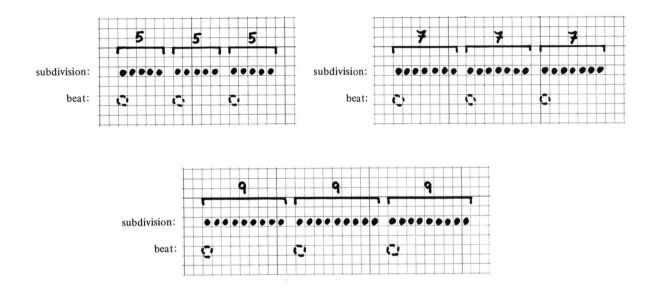

A great deal of tension and excitement is built up in performance by the large percussion ensembles, the *melam* and *panchavadyam,* as the drummers shift from one beat subdivision to the next, something like a Grand Prix race driver shifting gears in his accelerating Ferrari.

On the next level all music—melodic or percussive, with or without a beat—is made up of rhythms, that is, larger patterns, groups, and musical events that occur over time. The combinations of notes that make up melodies and accompaniments, harmonies and counterpoints, all utilize rhythm; we shall examine some of these functions in later chapters. But now we shall focus on some of the techniques used by players of drums, gongs, and other noise-making, "nonmelodic" instruments.

The percussionists of the world live in an almost schizophrenic double role. On one hand they are extroverted soloists or percussion ensemble players; on the other they are accompanists, supporting players of melodic instruments. In east Africa, India, Sri Lanka, and the Caribbean large percussion orchestras—groups of drums, rattles, cymbals, bells, and gongs (sometimes with shell trumpets or horns adding rhythmic punctuation)—create a music of startling rhythmic intensity and precision, often with the sounds of different types of drums adding subtle changes in timbral color. Occasionally drum orchestras even move into the realm of melody and harmony, like the steel bands of the Caribbean and the tuned drum ensembles of the royal courts of Uganda. Or the percussion ensemble may be absorbed as a unit into a larger group of melodic instruments, providing a solid bedrock for, say, the bands and orchestras of Latin American and African popular music. But by and large, percussionists of the world are accompanists, providing underlying rhythmic scaffolding for voice, instrumental soloists, or ensembles. In Turkey, for instance, the goblet-shaped *darabuka* drum accompanies the nasal wailing of the *zurnā* pipe; in India the two-drum set of *tabla* accompanies the multistringed *sitār;* and in Japan the three drums of the *hayashi* ensemble accompany the chanting of actors and chorus in *noh* theater. This is not to imply that percussion plays a subsidiary role in most of the world's music. A Sanskrit proverb states:

Melody is the mother,   श्रुतिर्माता   Srutirmātā
Rhythm is the father.   लय: पिता   layah pitā

Young drummers learning to play *mridangam* at Sri Jayaganesh Talavadya Vidyalayam, Madras.

Very often the drummer functions on an equal footing with melodic instruments, sometimes (as in jazz or Indian music) emerging to be featured alone in solo passages. And even the most simple accompaniment is essential to the total sound and texture of the music.

Drummers make use of stereotyped patterns which, on the simplest level, are short and are repeated as a kind of ostinato under the (often) freer melodies of the soloists. Throughout south central Asia, for example, the barrel-shaped *dholak* drum accompanies the double-reed pipe *bahudari* with two-beat patterns similar to the following (different positioning of the notes indicates different drum sounds):

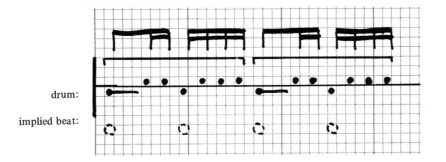

While occasionally the drummer will add special flourishes and accents, usually he sticks to the same time-marking pattern repeated over and over again.

In the classical music of India, the stereotyped patterns become longer, more complex, and much more numerous—perhaps running into the thousands. Young drummers, studying with a master drummer through years of musical apprenticeship, memorize all these patterns, the drum strokes that go with them, and their possible combinations. The drummer's brain becomes something like the memory bank of a computer, and in the heat of performance the patterns emerge instantaneously, effortlessly, arranged to suit the expressive purpose of the moment. The drummer's imagination, then, is highly conditioned by the limits of his resources, as well as by various rules of procedure and this musical tradition. Indian drumming patterns may also be spoken, through a system of mnemonics, or vocal syllables, which duplicate the rhythms and imitate the various sounds made on the drum. The following short rhythmic motifs are taken from one of the beginning lessons in the Tanjore style of south Indian drumming:

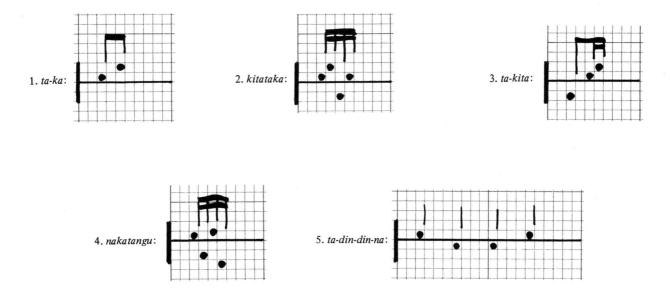

One of an almost infinite number of ways they could be combined is shown in this eight-beat pattern:

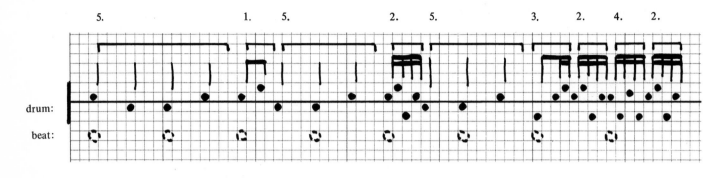

which could be spoken:

> ta—-din—-din—-na—-ta-ka-din—-din—-na—-
> kitataka din—-din—-na—-ta-kitakitataka nakatangukitataka(!)

   Drummers in India think in terms of mathematical proportions, of rhythmic patterns of various length that may be combined to fill a certain amount of space (just as in the preceding example the little motifs were combined to fill eight beats). Suppose a drummer had thirty-two beats to fill with music; he might think in terms of two sixteen-beat patterns (16 + 16 = 32) or any other combination he could think of. For example:

$$
\left.\begin{array}{l}
15 + 17 \\
14 + 18 \\
11 + 7 + 7 + 7 \\
13 + 7\tfrac{1}{2} + 5\tfrac{1}{2} + 3\tfrac{3}{4} + 2\tfrac{1}{4}
\end{array}\right\} \text{all} = 32 \text{ beats}
$$

In addition, he might fill any of the units in a variety of ways. For instance, the fifteen-beat unit in the above example (15 + 17 = 32) could be made up of subunits of 7 + 8, 5 + 5 + 5, 6 + 5 + 4, etc. And to complicate matters further, there are dozens of ways—different strokes and rhythms—in which each small subunit might be filled!

   Classical music in India (both melody and rhythm) happens within recurring cycles of beats called *tala.* Each *tala* has points of emphasis that divide it into sections, or *angas* (literally, "limbs"). While we in Western music tend to think in relatively simple and short beat cycles (most of our music is in 2/4, 3/4, 4/4, or 6/8 meters), the Indian musician prefers longer cycles made up of *angas* of unequal length. In the thirty-five-*tala* system of Karnatic (south Indian) music there are three types of *angas*:

> U = 1 beat (counted by a clap of the hands)
> O = 2 beats (counted by a clap and a wave)
> / = either 3, 4, 5, 7, or 9 beats (counted by a clap and a finger count)

The last type (/) is variable in the number of beats it can include, so any given arrangement of *angas* can produce five different *tala* cycles:

> $/^3$ U O = 6 beats (divided 3 + 1 + 2)
> $/^4$ U O = 7 beats (divided 4 + 1 + 2)
> $/^5$ U O = 8 beats (divided 5 + 1 + 2)
>   etc.

Bugaku performance with *gagaku* musicians in the background. The stage is flanked by the giant *da daiko*/drums. Japan.

Some of the common *talas* (with their constituent *angas*) are:

adi: $/^4$ O O (4 + 2 + 2 = 8 beats)
rupaka: O $/^4$ (2 + 4 = 6 beats)
ata: $/^5$ $/^5$ O O (5 + 5 + 2 + 2 = 14 beats)
jhampa: $/^7$ U O (7 + 1 + 2 = 10 beats)

Recently musicians such as Ravi Shankar have utilized unusual *talas* of eleven and a half, thirteen, or seventeen beats, although the more common Hindustani (north Indian) *talas* such as *teental* (4 + 4 + 4 + 4 = 16) or *jhaptal* (2 + 3 + 2 + 3 = 10) are simpler. But the possibilities are almost infinite.

    In the music of the large *gamelan* orchestras of Indonesia, beat cycles can also be quite long, varying from 16, to 64, and even to 128 beats. These cycles are marked by set patterns in the drums and gongs, a repeating rhythmic structure that underpins the melodic and harmonic happenings of the orchestra something like the movement of a giant Swiss clockwork. Each structure (and each type of beat cycle) is repeated for the duration of the section or composition. The end of each beat cycle is marked by the massive resonating sound of the large gong. One such pattern moves in sixteen-beat cycles:

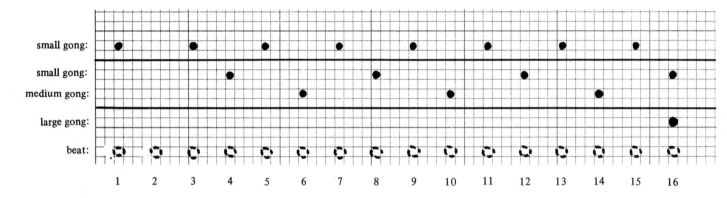

As seen in our example, there are four levels of gong rhythm: the smallest gong (the *ketuk*) plays most frequently (eight notes), the other small gong (the *kenong*) is next with four notes, the medium-sized hanging gong (*kempul*) has only three notes, and the large gong (the *gong*—an Indonesian word!) is struck only once, on the final (sixteenth) beat of the cycle. Similar rhythm structures are also used in the music of the traditional court orchestras of Japan and Korea: *gagaku* and *hyang-ak*.

    In Africa stereotyped rhythmic patterns are also used, notably in the music of the large drum and percussion ensembles. Each player beats out a relatively simple pattern which he repeats (with occasional variation). As more and more patterns are stacked up in simultaneous layers—something like geological strata cutting across cliffs and mesas—the rhythmic texture becomes incredibly complex. One piece called *Siki* (pronounced "sichi") belonging to the "high-life" type of dance music from Ghana uses the following patterns:

The *gankogui,* a resonant double cowbell:

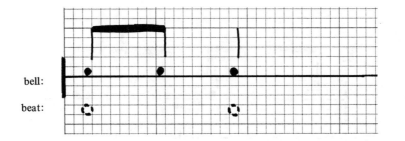

The *apentemma,* a high-pitched, brittle-sounding, cylinder-shaped drum:

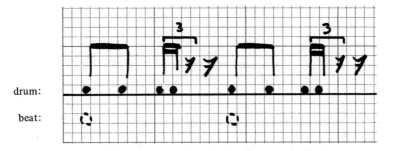

The *donno,* an hourglass-shaped drum which can be squeezed to produce high and low pitches:

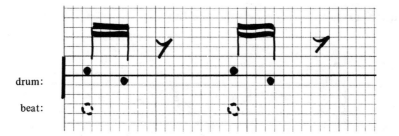

The *tamalenes,* a square drum something like a skin stretched over a small window frame:

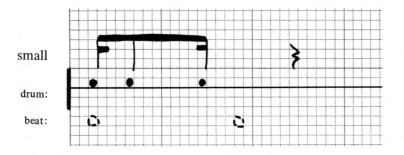

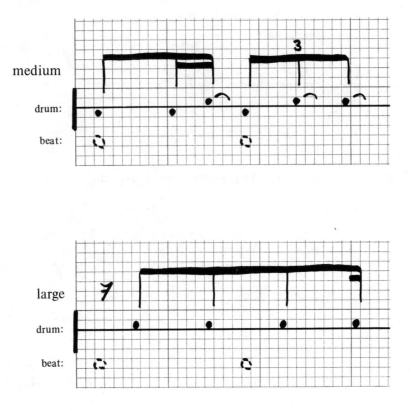

The resultant musical texture looks something like this:

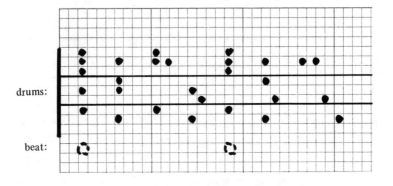

But this is not all! Each performer can ornament his rhythm with variations, and on top of the whole throbbing texture the master drummer plays even more complex patterns (choosing from a network of possibilities, much as the Indian drummer does) on the large, barrel-shaped *atsimevu* drum. Young drummers learn patterns not only through assimilation but through proverbs and riddles, the inflections of which fit various rhythms. There is some controversy among scholars whether African drummers "feel the beat" as we conceive it; indeed, in the more complicated rhythmic compositions (our example is a simple one!) the individual parts seem to be moving on different tracks—in different meters and with different points of emphasis. But there is no doubt that the African musician's perception of rhythmic subtlety is sophisticated, and in most cases notation (even in graph form) is only an approximation.

Dancers performing traditional dance, Senegal.

The stunning virtuosity of African drumming has overshadowed the many other types of music and variety of instruments on that continent—the beautiful songs of the Shona people accompanied by the *mbira,* the haunting choral polyphony of the pygmies of the Ituri forest, the ancient Coptic chants of Ethiopia, or the rollicking *marimba* bands of Senuflo. A strong rhythmic sense characterizes much of Africa's music, and even zithers, trumpets, and lyres are played as if they were tuned drums.

Time in traditional African thought is a two-dimensional phenomenon with a long past, a present, but with virtually no future. And this brings us back to our discussion of time at the beginning of this section. African music does not have beginnings, developments, climaxes, and endings like most Western music (and life!); it simply begins, it sets up levels and continues, and then it stops. African musical time proceeds in what we might call "accumulative but nondirectional" time: rhythmic and melodic textures happen in a kaleidoscopic, circular way, repeating, shifting to different patterns perhaps, but not moving toward an inevitable denouement. Performers may stop when they get tired, when they feel "the time is right," when they run out of words or ideas, or in time to catch a late bus home; the same piece could last several minutes or several hours, depending on the situation. The extent to which the concept of time in a given culture influences its music (and we must remember that Africa has many cultures and many musics—our generalizations will out of necessity have encyclopedic exceptions) is perhaps open to question. But time and rhythm are certainly interrelated threads in the complex tapestry of human civilization.

Adzenyah, Abraham K. Classes and conversations, Wesleyan University, Middletown, Connecticut, 1970–73.

Densmore, Frances. *The American Indians and Their Music.* New York: The Womans Press. Reprinted New York: Johnson Reprint Corporation, 1971.

Hood, Mantle, and Susilo, Hardja. *Music of the Venerable Dark Cloud.* Los Angeles: Institute of Ethnomusicology, UCLA, 1967.

Kimball, James. Conversations, 1972–75.

Kinney, Sylvia. "Drummers in Dagbon: The Role of the Drummer in the Damba Festival." *Ethnomusicology,* vol. 14, no. 2 (May 1970).

Kodaly, Zoltan. *Folk Music of Hungary.* New York: Praeger Publishers, 1971.

Malm, William P. *Japanese Music and Musical Instruments.* Rutland, Vermont, and Tokyo: Charles E. Tuttle, 1959.

Malm, William P. *Music Cultures of the Pacific, the Near East, and Asia.* Englewood Cliffs, New Jersey: Prentice-Hall, 1967.

Mbiti, John S. *African Religions and Philosophy.* New York: Praeger Publishers, 1969.

McAllester, David P. Classes and conversations, Wesleyan University, Middletown, Connecticut, 1971–74.

Merriam, Alan P. "African Music." In Bascom, William R., and Herskovits, Melville J., eds. *Continuity and Change in African Cultures.* Chicago: The University of Chicago Press, 1959.

Nettl, Bruno. *Folk and Traditional Music of the Western Continents.* Englewood Cliffs, New Jersey: Prentice-Hall, 1965.

Nketia, J. H. Kwabena. *The Music of Africa.* New York: W. W. Norton, 1974.

Raghavan, Ramnad V. Classes, Wesleyan University, Middletown, Connecticut, 1971–74.

Reck, David. "The Music of Matha Chhau." *Asian Music,* vol. 3, no. 2 (1972).

Sachs, Curt. *The Rise of Music in the Ancient World.* New York: W. W. Norton, 1943.

Sachs, Curt. *The Wellsprings of Music.* New York: McGraw-Hill Book Company, 1965.

Sambamoorthy, P. *South Indian Music,* vols. 1–7. Madras: The Indian Music Publishing House.

Singer, Alice. "The Metrical Structure of Macedonian Dance." *Ethnomusicology,* vol. 18, no. 3 (September 1974).

Tsuge, Gen'ichi. "Rhythmic Aspects of the *Avaz* in Persian Music." *Ethnomusicology,* vol. 14, no. 2 (May 1970).

Mouth bow played for self-amusement, upper Tekim Valley, New Guinea.

6

FROM BIRDS
TO MELODY BANDS

In the beginning were the birds. At least that is what a significant number of the people of the world who have thought about such things say about the origins of melody. The melodious repertoire and infinite rainbow multicolored plumages of these feathered creatures have ornamented the world for as long as man's ears and eyes can remember. And more than their song, birds, as carriers of visions and dreams, singing in treetops and soaring among clouds and the blue sky, have signified man's greatest hopes and aspirations: for his inner self, outer self, for his earthbound body to put on wings, to defy gravity (with the aid of devices and machines), and to fly through the air!

Bird symbols and voices (real or imaginary) have inspired men to imitate them: in the eagle dance of the American Indians, for example, or the feathery hopping of Australian aborigine ritual, or the magnificent flight of the great mythical bird Garuda in Indian and Indonesian dance drama. "Primitive" hunters early learned the calls of birds (and of other animals as well), both as a lure and as a part of the complex magic of the hunt. The Kayabi people in the lush foliage of the South American Mato Grosso jungle imitate dozens of birds (as well as otters, monkeys, and jaguars), and the Eskimo's remarkable vocal renditions of the cries of geese and swans (and walruses) fool not only the animals themselves but other hunters as well. Whistles and caller gadgets made from bone or leaf or reed serve not only as rudimentary musical instruments, but also, like bows and arrows, harpoons and guns, as functional tools for the hunt. At some point the bird and animal calls (vocal and mechanical) move from their purely functional purpose and begin to serve memory, description, and amusement; that is, they become aesthetic and are woven into more sophisticated musics. The melodies of birds, for example, permeate the songs and flute tunes of New Guinea Papua tribals, they have found their way into the programmatic compositions of high Chinese classical culture (one popular piece for the double-reed oboelike *sona*, titled "The Court of the Phoenix," describes all the sounds of an imaginary palace of birds), and bird calls form the basis for the avant-garde style of the contemporary French composer Olivier Messiaen (b. 1908).

But man himself—physical, mental, emotional man—is perhaps the primal source for melody. After all, it was man who comprehended the songs of the birds, was moved by them, imitated them,

182

and utilized them. The word *melody* itself is derived from Greek words intimately connected with the human voice and the act of singing: *melos* ("song"), *aoidos* ("singer"), *melōidos* ("melodious"), *melōidia* ("a singing," "choral song"). The human body, with its vocal cords, lungs, mouth, and tongue, makes a magnificent musical instrument (and one that is *born*, not made); and when precisely in the primeval past it was first used and developed by man for song—or for language—must forever remain one of the great question marks of time.

We do know that what we call melody touches us deeply, like breath. It somehow reaches the roots of our feelings, mystically transforming the mundane into the extraordinary. On this (internal) level we cannot really begin to explain its meaning; it is as elusive as mist. For melody makes the profane become sacred. Words, ordinary or insignificant when spoken, take on enormous power when chanted or sung; the magical occurs, the plain becomes beautiful.

But melody, all melody, has a structure, and its own, sometimes unique, characteristics. We can examine the mechanics of melody, that is, increase our understanding of world concepts and shaping of melody; but all the time we must remember that melody's essential mystical core, its life-breath, must of necessity—like that of music itself—elude us. How could it be otherwise?

Our first problem is to define melody. To many it is "a sweet and pleasing succession of tones preferably arranged in an order that can be easily remembered, whistled, and hummed." But this definition immediately runs into trouble, even in our European/American culture. Critics and concert-goers (past and present) have complained of "a lack of melody" not only in the music of twentieth-century composers like Boulez and Schoenberg, but in the earlier music of Schubert, Mendelssohn, Bach, Wagner, Verdi, and Beethoven as well (not to mention in rock and roll)! Clearly we must somehow reconcile the seemingly endless melodic sawing away of baroque fiddling with the complex orchestral motivic developments of the romantic era and the cool, mathematically spun-out note sequences of the twentieth century. And to this we must add the deep, masculine, guttural monotones of Siberian Khakass singing, the sliding microtones of Yugoslavian epic *guslari* tale-tellers, the exuberant, lung-bursting vocal lines of the Plains Indians, the wailing "Oriental" scales of the Middle East, the half-spoken, half-sung dialogues and sudden falsettos of Japanese *kabuki* theater, and the seemingly "out-of-tune" gong tonalities of southeast Asia.

Aesthetic criteria such as "sweet," "pleasing," or "beautiful" cause similar rhetorical difficulties. Music is *not* a universal language even within one country: the antagonism shown in the United States by groups of nonadmiring music lovers toward popular legitimate (well loved by *other* people) genres like jazz, rock, or "hillbilly" (a derogatory term for "country music") certainly proves that one man's chocolate chip cookies are another man's stomach ache. Each society has its own aesthetic criteria, its own accepted norms of what is beautiful in music, art, or life, and the criteria can be as different as the facial scarring and tattooing of Africa are from the lipstick and eyeshadow of Europe or New York. Beauty may not even be a factor in many societies' judgments of melody and songs: the Navaho (and other American Indian groups) may be more concerned with a song's power, its metaphysical, supernatural, and curative strength. An Eskimo or Siberian shaman would have the same attitude. A song's usefulness or function in a work or ritual situation can also be a factor, which is why the Roman Catholic Church, for example, prefers the unobtrusive music of Palestrina (sixteenth century), Gregorian chant (collected in the eighth or ninth centuries), and innumerable minor composers to the noisy Masses of Mozart or Beethoven or Stravinsky. Words and the conveyance of understandable language may also be the prime concern, with melody in and for itself relegated to the background, such as in the story-telling of Balkan and central Asian epic singers, the magic and philosophical rhetoric of Hindu *Vedic* chant, or the lengthy sung histories and genealogies of Polynesia and the Pacific. Finally, other elements (musical or otherwise) such as timbre, setting, instrumentation, and performance style—in fact, a whole spectrum of interrelated functions and procedures—color our perception of what we call melody.

For our purposes, then, we shall define melody as "one or more single pitches (or notes) happening one after another (that is, moving sequentially through time) and arranged in a particular order to make a whole (or a part of a whole)." Each society hears and feels its melodies as touchstones of

Many African fabrics use repetition of motifs as in music to form a larger design. Men's weave, Jukun, Nigeria.

deep human or supernatural expressiveness or of power. Each society, too, hears, understands, and appreciates the peculiar intricacies of its own melodies as well as the inherent logic of their structure. It is this aspect, the workings of earth melodies, that we shall now examine.

Shape and Contour

Euro-American musical culture thinks of music (and pitches and notes) as moving in a continuous sweep of "highs" (like the sound of the piccolo) and "lows" (like the sound of the tuba). Actually the terms are somewhat arbitrary: "high" pitches are, in reality, notes that vibrate faster, at greater frequency, than the slower vibrations of "lower" pitches. In India the word *tara,* or "star," is used for the faster-vibrating notes of the upper octave, and the word *mandra,* or "deep, grave, rumbling," for the slower-vibrating notes of the lower octave. The ancient Greeks also categorized notes as "high" and "low," but with meanings diametrically opposite to those of today: to the Greeks low notes were those of the treble strings of the lyre which were closest to the ground, while high notes were those of the bass strings which were closest to the sky (or the player). Other cultures, deriving their terminology from the structure or playing technique of their musical instruments, have thought of notes as being "bigger and smaller," "near and far," or "left-er and right-er" (a terminology that would fit the arrangement of pitches on the piano!). But for the sake of simplicity we shall be completely ethnocentric and graph our melodies as moving through time from left to right (on the page) with the slower vibrations, or "lower" notes, at the bottom and the faster-vibrating pitches, or "higher" notes, moving progressively to the top. All melodies, then, will have a shape or contour of some kind.

Perhaps the simplest shape is a *straight line,* the more or less constant repetition of a single note which has been compared to the reiterative zigzags, dots, and slashes found in folk and so-called primitive art all over the world. Often this contour is slightly modified by occasional auxiliary and neighboring notes, such as in the magic incantations of the Serbs, where fluttering microtones and sighing endings surround the main note; or in Hawaiian chant, where musical phrases end (cadence) on a lower pitch.

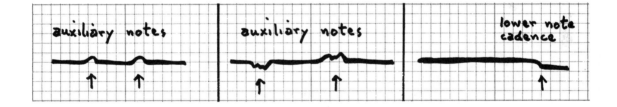

The liturgical recitations, psalms, prayers, and lessons of the Roman Catholic Church surround the main reciting tone with slightly more complex units: initial and final melody formulas that give the illusion of a more elaborate shape (or ornamentation) of the basic one-note melody.

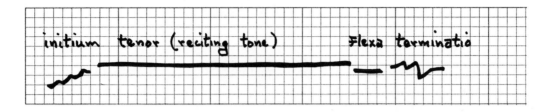

Another basic melody shape is the undulating, or *pendulum movement*: a melody that zigzags up and down, back and forth, covering (more or less) the same ground.

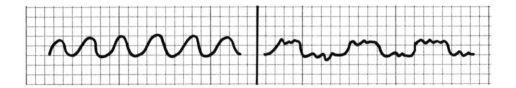

This type of melody is very common in Africa (it is found, for example, in the tunes of the Balwa pygmies and in several traditions in Ruanda and central Africa) but it also exists in Europe and the Americas (as in jazz improvisations and in the music of Vivaldi and Stravinsky) in a more complex form.

Many of the world's peoples seem to prefer what Curt Sachs has called the *"tumbling strain,"* a melodic shape that begins high (often at the extreme top of human vocal range) and then "tumbles" down like a cascading mountain stream into the lower register.

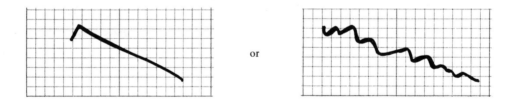

or

Nowhere is this shape more common (and electrifying) than in the music of the American Indians, particularly of the Southwest and Great Plains—the Sioux, Blackfoot, Arapahoe, Flatfoot, Navaho, Zuni, Apache, and others—where the high beginnings of the melodies (or phrases) sung full force (without falsetto!) explode with charged tension before gradually making their descent to the relative relaxation of the lower vocal range. In fact, a (natural) decrescendo often accompanies the descent, and among the Bellacoola (of the Pacific Northwest) one word means both high (pitch) and loud, and another word means both low (pitch) and soft. The descent can be sudden, irregular, or moving down in a kind of terrace effect. After settling down in the lower register, the tumbling strain (in its repetitions of phrase or tune) must "recapture" the tense, high notes of its beginning with a tremendous leap, usually of an octave or even more; the Zuni, for example, skip up almost two full octaves! Often the descending shape is paired with our straight line (repeated note) shape, a melodic structuring that accentuates the psychological and musical characteristics of this form.

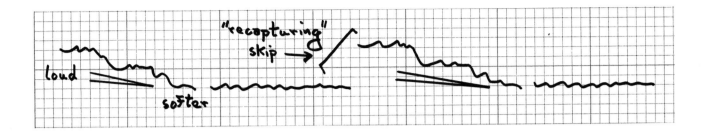

The *arc,* a lopsided mountain shape that begins low, works its way up to its highest pitch (and climax), and then returns (somewhat more swiftly), is the accepted norm for most of the melodies in the European/American musical tradition.

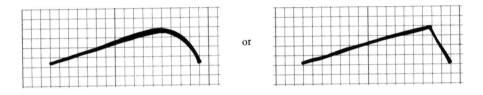

This pattern follows the common archetypal shape of exposition–development (complication)–climax (denouement)–relaxation (ending, summing-up) which seems to underlie much of Western art and thought. It implies a directional movement toward something (a buildup) and a definite conclusion.

Other possibilities of melodic contour, of course, exist—perhaps the most common being the *zigzag,* an alternation of two or three notes.

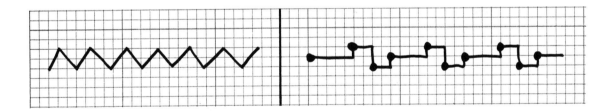

But there are also melodies (less common) and phrases (common) that begin low and end high, or swoop down instead of up.

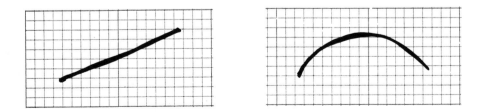

The shape of a melody is rarely a simple up-and-down affair. Usually it is a combination of smaller units of assorted shapes and sizes, which when considered together add up to a total melodic effect, or contour.

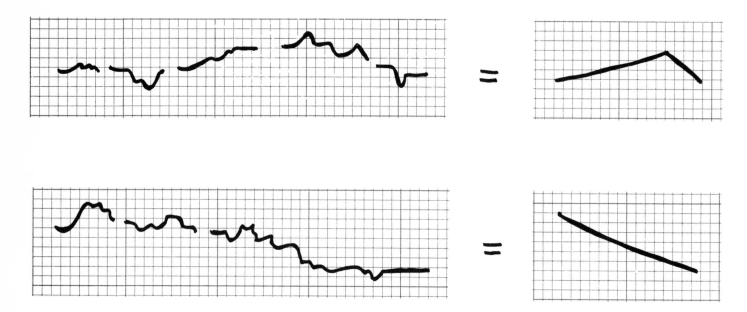

Pitches and Scales

The craftsmen of melody, whether lonely minstrels on the high steppes of central Asia, professional court composers in Java, or blues singers in the rural southern United States, work within a maze of musical elements, intimately connected to the culture in which they live, which predetermine to an extraordinarily large degree the style and form their music will take. In many cultures these elements are taken for granted: music is simply supposed to happen and be made (and performed) in a certain way. It is all the music one hears in a lifetime; if one whistles a tune it will come out (naturally) fitting the (assumed) style of the musical environment. Other cultures—Iran, India, Turkey, Japan, and Europe, for example—have built up elaborate musical systems, with theory, rules, regulations, and procedures that must consciously be learned and followed even by persons who grow up in that environment. In either case music is made within fixed limitations from sets of "building blocks" that must be put together in a certain (expressive) way.

One of these basic building blocks is *pitch*. We have remarked how notes seem "high" or "low," depending on the speed of the vibrations that make them sound in acoustical space. The average human ear can perceive as musical tones vibrations from a low of about twenty (pulses) per second to a high of about twenty thousand cycles per second. A single point (one of an almost infinite number of possibilities) taken anywhere along this sweeping scale of vibrations is what we call pitch.

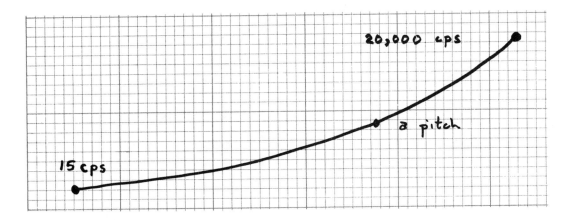

Melodies, when composed and sung, almost always make use of only a portion of the available pitches on this sliding scale. This portion, between the upper and lower limitations, including all the notes in between, is called the *range* of the melody. We might think of the melodic range as something like a fenced enclosure containing not sheep or cattle but a "flock" of notes. Many beautiful melodies (such as those in the Balkans) fall within a comparatively small range (a fifth), while others (like those of the Zuni Indians) push almost to the extremities (upper and lower) of the human voice (two octaves or more).

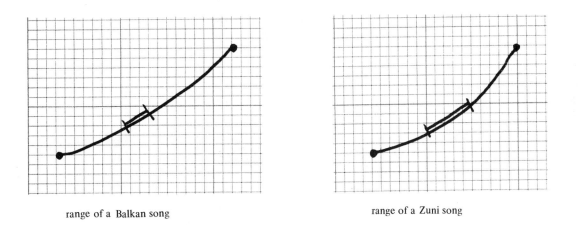

range of a Balkan song   range of a Zuni song

Although musical instruments greatly expand the possible range (the piano spans eight octaves, the Indian *sitār* almost three and a half, and the Japanese *koto* over two), it is interesting to note that the shadow of the human voice remains even in instrumental melody: the additional range is used for accompaniment, as a subsidiary extension (for variety and for "big" moments), or as a different tone color for basically vocal melodies transposed to a different octave.

Melody may slip and slide and waver within the limits of its range in a seemingly indefinite way around a tonal center (as in Yugoslavian epic singing), or it may be arranged in definite steps (as in European classical music), into pitches that fall into a more or less precise location and into a hierarchy of interrelated functions. Many of the world's tonal systems, as, for example, in the Arabic countries or in black American music, are based on a combination of steps and fluctuating areas.

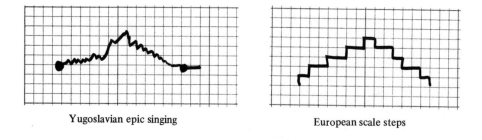

Yugoslavian epic singing   European scale steps

This arrangement of building blocks is called a *scale*. It is important to remember that (except in "high" classical musical cultures) the music precedes the scale: that is, the living, seemingly breathing mystical organism we call melody came from the hearts and minds of composers long before the inquisitive, analytical mind of man reduced it to the theory of its component parts.

Scale types, or *modes,* or even the individual tones that make them up, have often been connected with a complex system of (supposedly) extramusical elements. Aristotle described how specific Greek modes made men sad and grave, relaxed and settled, or agitated (but these modes may also have been connected with specific rhythms and poetic forms). Plato outlawed some of the modes in his ideal state. The *maqam* of the Arabic world and the *raga* of India—which are, more than mere scales, complex systems—are intimately connected in the minds of listeners, performers, and theorists with moods, times of day, seasons, colors, gods, good or bad fortune, and even animals. The five tones of Chinese traditional music are tied to the five directions and the five basic elements of the natural world. In Indonesia, the *patets,* or modes, of the music of the *gamelan* orchestra can convey to an audience times of day or types of action (and feeling), especially when used at theatrical performances. Such connections are not so farfetched as they may at first seem: persons within a given culture acquire them in the same way that they learn language (spoken or musical) or cooking or housebuilding. What is *believed* to be true in a musical culture *is* true. Extramusical connections and associations in the Western world tend to be shaped by compositions or types of music rather than by modes.

The distances between the notes of a scale (or a melody)—the *intervals*—that is, the sizes of the various steps of our musical staircase, are what give scales their particular color.

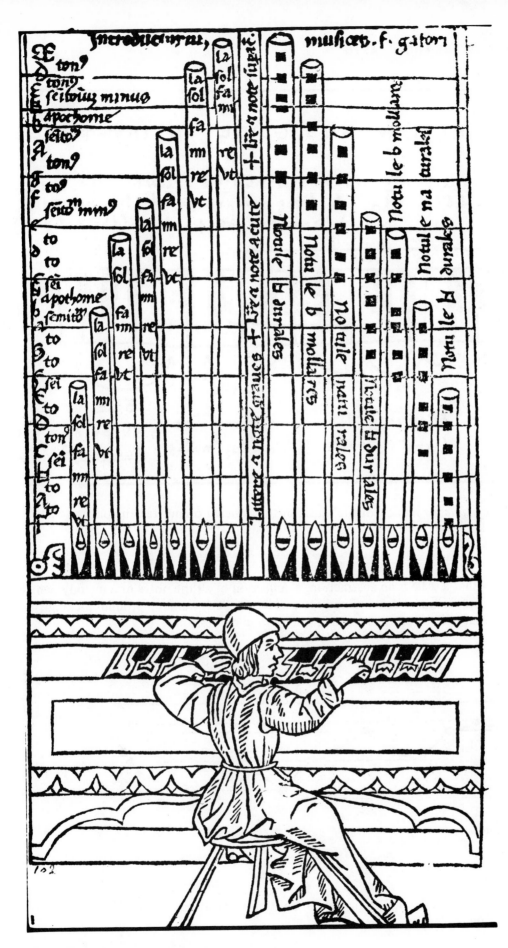

Organ. Woodcut from F. Gafori, *Theorica Naples*, 1480.

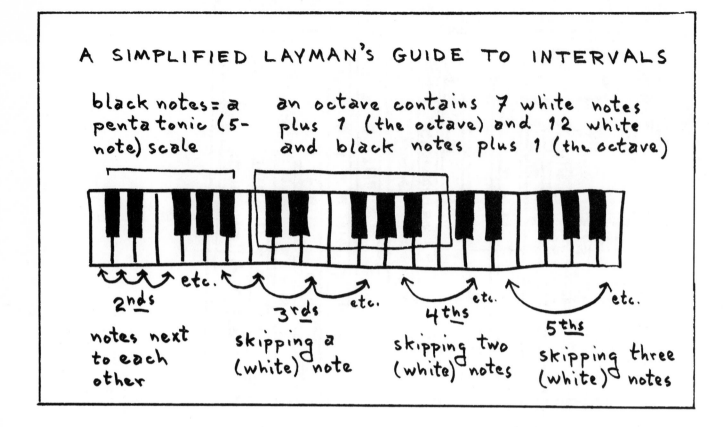

We should remember that a scale is an abstraction, a collection of all the notes of a melody, which are then arranged in an ascending and descending order, while a melody can hop around, picking whatever notes are necessary for its particular musical shape and expression.

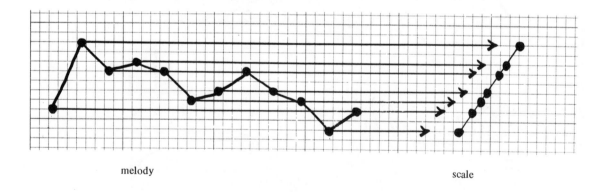

melody   scale

Scales (and the melodies they are derived from) can be built up from strings of seconds (close steps) or from chains of larger intervals.

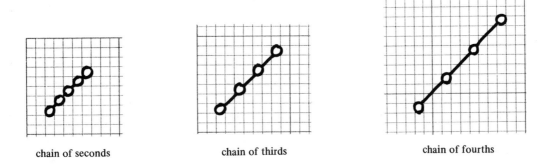

chain of seconds   chain of thirds   chain of fourths

Chains of thirds (which make up much of the music of Polynesia, Oceania, and Africa) and chains of fourths (which characterize much of the music of the American Indians, as well as that of pockets of tribal peoples in south Asia) are often tempered by the addition of subsidiary smaller intervals (seconds) which extend or fill in the notes of the chain.

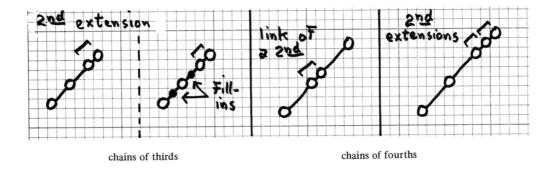

chains of thirds   chains of fourths

The question of measurement of intervals and of pitch has always been a thorny one for scholars: people of one musical culture tend to dismiss the tonal system of another as being simply "out of tune." While certain intervals that bear basic mathematical relationships like the octave (2:1), the perfect fifth (3:2), and the perfect fourth (4:3) occur more or less universally, the tuning of the other pitches and intervals fluctuates widely. To deal with these notes, sometimes jokingly referred to as occurring "between the cracks of the piano keys," Alexander Ellis (1814–90) devised a system of measurement which, though ethnocentric, is the best we have. He assigned each interval of the chromatic scale (from one note on the piano to its nearest neighboring note, white or black) a value of 100 *cents*. An octave would thus have an intervalic value of 1,200 cents.

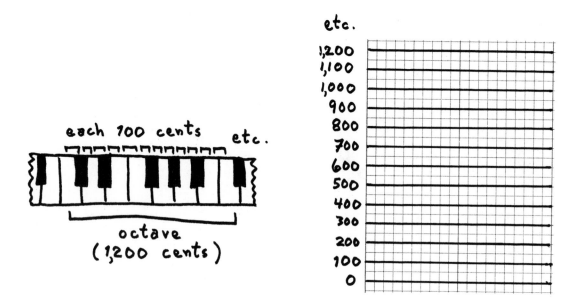

Intervals in world music smaller or larger than those of the classical Euro-American musical system such as the *microtone* (any interval smaller than 100 cents) or the *"neutral" third* (which floats somewhere between the 300 cents and 400 cents respectively of the minor and major third) can be measured accurately by machine and notated in graph form.

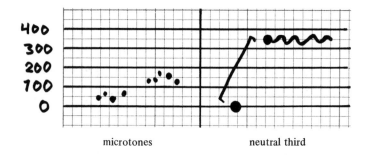

microtones   neutral third

The tiny microtonic intervals are consistently found in the music of the Near East (in Turkish, Arabic, and Persian cultures), in the *ragas* of India, in central Asia, and in the countries of eastern Europe and the Mediterranean (almost certainly the result of Arabic and Turkish influence). The neutral third occurs all over the world, in Africa and south Asia, central Asia and Europe, but perhaps most notably in the United States. Here, in the music of (and influenced by) black Americans, the neutral third, coupled with the neutral sixth and a host of other swooping and sliding microtonally flatted "blue notes," gives a special sound and character to the melodic movement of jazz, blues, gospel, soul, and rock.

Expanded intervals—notes slightly larger or "sharper" than the median of pitch intervals on the piano keyboard—are common, too, especially in the belt stretching from north Africa to Indonesia (and up into eastern Europe), influenced by Arabic musical culture. But many tuning systems, such as those found in the southeast Asian countries of Laos, Cambodia, and Thailand, in Java or in Africa (in harp and xylophone tunings), simply defy any comparison whatsoever with those of the West.

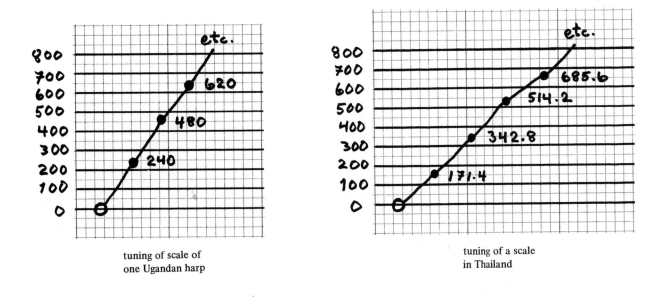

tuning of scale of
one Ugandan harp

tuning of a scale
in Thailand

In Bali and Java the tuning of each collection of gongs, knobbed gongs, and slab metallophones that make up the instruments of a specific *gamelan* orchestra is slightly different than that of any other. Thus while musicians may be interchangeable (from *gamelan* to *gamelan*) the instruments are not!

The notes that make up melodies—whether in the simple three-note tunes of Ceylon's Vedda tribals or the complex twists of the *gusheh* (modes) of Iran—seldom occur on an equal footing. Invariably a hierarchy of interrelated notes develops, similar to the relative weight and importance of pieces on a chessboard (from king to pawns). If a single tone predominates, it becomes a *tonal center,* a center of gravity that exerts a musical "pull" on the other notes of the melody much like a planet or star attracts the satellites revolving around it.

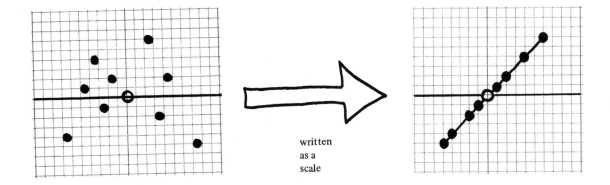

written
as a
scale

Subsidiary tonal centers (like the knights, bishops, and rooks of chess) perform different functions, as, for instance, in the *maqam* modes of Arabic musical culture and the related *ragas* of India, where they establish contrasting tone levels, varying axes, around which a performer may improvise his melody in different parts of a performance.

Bagpiper fingering the chanter, or melody pipe. Two drone pipes can be seen over the musician's right shoulder. Print by Albrecht Dürer, 1514.

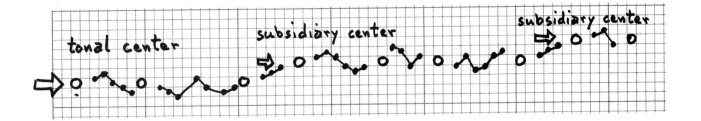

The tonal center is established (and fortified!) by a drone in many parts of the world, by chords (as in Europe and America), or simply through melodic function and/or dominance—a kind of musical survival of the fittest. The tonal center is usually (but not always) given as the lowest, the beginning note of scales; and perhaps here we should emphasize a very important (and often confused) point: the tonal center with its scale—and all the intervals (calculated in cents) that go with it—are *not* fixed at a specific point in our curve of musical vibrations. A tonal center and scale can be shifted in toto to any pitch, much like an elevator as a unit shifts from floor to floor of a skyscraper while it retains its identity.

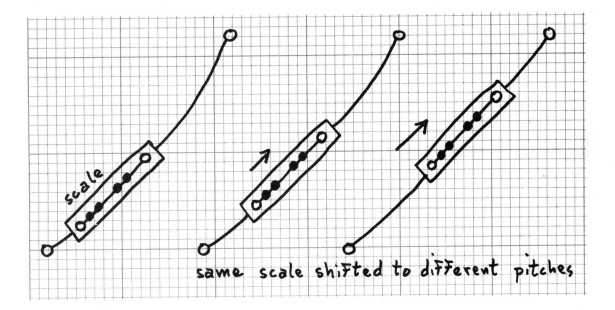

same scale shifted to different pitches

Precisely where, at what pitch, a scale is put may depend on any number of factors: chance, the relatively unchangeable tuning of a specific instrument (like a bamboo flute or a *zurnā* double-reed pipe) or group of instruments (the Javanese *gamelan*), the range of a singer's voice, or a deliberate tuning to a specific pitch. In Euro-American musical culture the transposition of scales has become a regular feature of our musical structure, and *modulation* (the same scales and melodies and chords shifted to a new tonal center) within a single composition (like a symphony or pop tune) is heard as a way to achieve freshness and variety.

Modulation Scheme in Haydn's Symphony
No. 102 in B Flat, First Movement

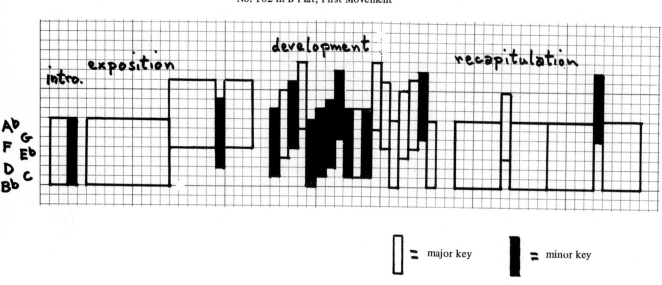

☐ = major key   ■ = minor key

Precise measurement of pitch is so standardized in the West—through pitch pipes, instruments, and notation—that compositions become fixed, frozen indelibly in a certain *key*. Notes, likewise, are thought of as precise facts: "A" above "middle C" is always 440 vibrations per second, "middle C" is always 256 vibrations per second, and so on. We must be extremely careful, therefore, in dealing with other musical systems throughout the world, *not* to assign fixed, static values to notes where such values do not apply. It is important to remember that scales and melodies are built from relationships within a movable tonal unit (like our elevator) and not from absolutes.

Melodies can be built (as we have seen) with very few notes and within an extremely limited range. Many beautiful songs—for example, in Romania, Bulgaria, Hawaii (the *hula*), Borneo, and among the Indians of North and South America, not to mention a world-full of mothers' quiet lullabies and children's songs—use three-, four-, and five-note melodies within the interval of a third, fourth, fifth, or sixth.

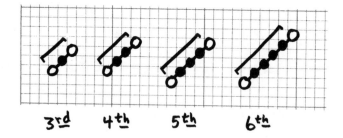

3rd   4th   5th   6th

When melodies span an octave or more, they tend to repeat the same notes of the same scale (although there are exceptions, of course). The human ear and musical mind tend to think of notes an octave apart (that is, at a vibration ratio of 2:1) as being the same note. Thus a man's low voice and a woman's high voice singing the same melody in octaves sound to us like *one* melody. In India the names of the seven notes of the scale—*sa, ri, ga, ma, pa, da, ni*—repeat themselves in higher or lower octaves just as the names of the pitches in the European tradition—A, B, C, D, E, F, G—are repeated over and over again in octave relationships on the keyboard.

In reducing a melody to a scale, then, we can think of the octave as the scaffolding, the outer limits, within which the various notes of an almost infinite number of scales can be put, just as a porcelain bowl can be filled with a variety of soups and puddings of every imaginable flavor. The octave can be filled with a scale of notes separated by equal intervals: some Ugandan harp tunings have a four-note scale (each step is 300 cents) or a five-note scale (240 cents each step), Euro-American music has the twelve-note chromatic scale (100 cents each step) and the six-note "whole-tone" scale (200-cent steps), while Thai court music uses an evenly spaced seven-note scale (approximately 171.4-cent steps).

evenly spaced fillings of octave

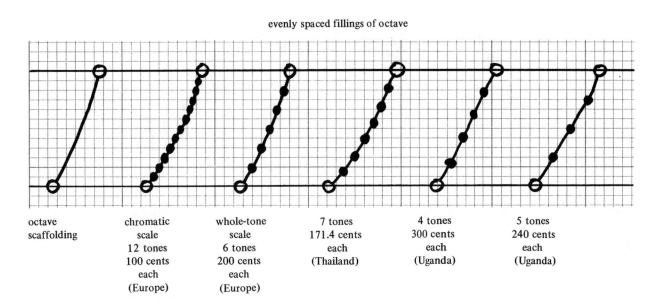

octave scaffolding	chromatic scale 12 tones 100 cents each (Europe)	whole-tone scale 6 tones 200 cents each (Europe)	7 tones 171.4 cents each (Thailand)	4 tones 300 cents each (Uganda)	5 tones 240 cents each (Uganda)

But it is far more common for the octave to be filled with scale notes spaced in an uneven way.

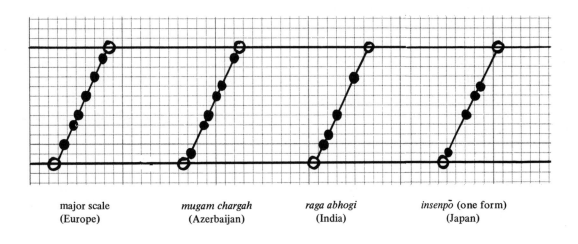

major scale (Europe)	*mugam chargah* (Azerbaijan)	*raga abhogi* (India)	*insenpō* (one form) (Japan)

Perhaps the most universal scale of all is the five-tone pentatonic scale, composed of whole steps and skips of a minor third (the black keys on the piano starting from F sharp give the most common form); it is found in China (where it is the principal scale), Tibet, Mongolia, Oceania, India, Russia, Africa, among American Indians, and in the folk songs and hymns of Europe and the United States. If the world has *a* scale, this is it!

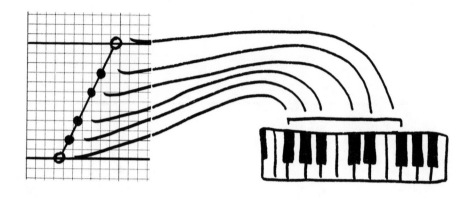

Many varieties of five-tone scales exist (we shall examine some in our specific studies of scale systems). Melodies using six-tone scales of every shape and variety are also common (in central Africa, India, and southeast Asia, for example), but scales using seven (unevenly spaced) tones to the octave are perhaps the world's most important family of melody building blocks.

★★★★★★★★★★★ TONAL SYSTEMS OF THE WHOLE EARTH ★★★★★★★★★★★

CHINA

The Chinese acoustical system, derived from a cycle of overblown fifths, is a perfect (pure) one: its tones were generated by blowing across the tops of a set of bamboo tubes, carefully tuned and arranged by length in mathematical proportion (like blowing across the tops of a set of different-sized soft-drink bottles). The resultant twelve pitches (called the twelve *lüs*) had specific names (like "yellow bell," "forest bell," and the like) and, arranged into panpipes and chimes in two groups of six tones each, represented the opposing principles of male-female or the metaphysical push-pull of the concepts of *yin* and *yang*. The first five notes of the twelve *lü* became the basic pentatonic scale, the *wu sheng*, of traditional Chinese music, while the next two—the sixth and seventh notes derived from the *lü*—became subsidiary changing and passing notes, the *pien*.

詩餘畫譜　明萬曆刻本

圖版六八二

Flutist alone in landscape. Chinese print, Ming dynasty, sixteenth to seventeenth century.

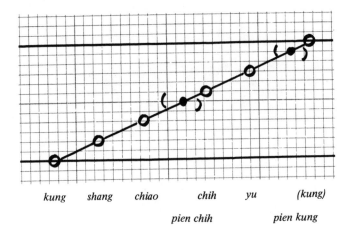

kung   shang   chiao   chih   yu   (kung)

pien chih   pien kung

Music in China from the time of Confucius has been intimately connected with ethical and metaphysical principles, and it is important to remember that the mechanics of music do not (like the "pure" abstractions of mathematics or science in the West) exist in a vacuum. Cultural and philosophical threads, whether from Confucius or Chairman Mao, touch every note with the intimacy and directness of the fingers of a musician on his *ch'in* zither or *p'i p'a* lute.

ANCIENT GREECE

Considerable controversy exists about ancient Greek music, primarily because while we have considerable information about its philosophical and theoretical basis, we have no real idea what the music actually sounded like. The Greeks built their scales on tetrachords, or four-note groupings. The outer notes of each tetrachord were fixed at the interval of a perfect fourth (4:3 ratio). According to the *Harmonics,* a book written by Aristoxenus around 330 B.C., two inner notes could be placed within the tetrachord in a variety of different ways, called "shades." He lists five "shades" but admits that the possible number of "fillings" for the tetrachord is theoretically infinite.

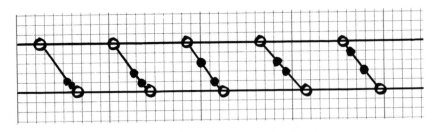

tetrachords with different fillings of "shades"

Two tetrachords could be combined either by overlapping one note (*conjunct*) or by stacking them at the interval of a whole tone (*disjunct*).

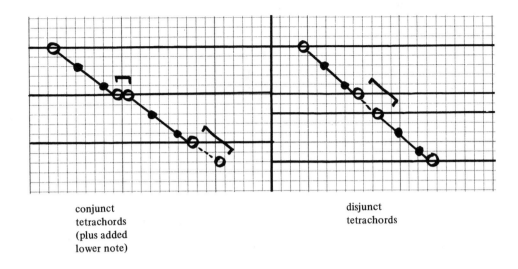

conjunct
tetrachords
(plus added
lower note)

disjunct
tetrachords

Eventually the system was expanded to include a full two-octave scale (the "Greater Perfect System").

The precise nature of the Greek *modes* is a matter of some controversy. Ptolemy (second century A.D.) has given us a list of the scales of the seven modes, but how can one explain the *ethos,* the evocative emotional power and mood, associated with each mode described by thinkers such as Plato and Aristotle? Donald Grout has suggested that the modes might have been more than mere scales: each might have been a collection of melody types, phrases, rhythms, and even poetic forms which, taken together, could express a specific emotional quality.

Such a concept—a musical/expressive area that boxes in many elements, a kind of "musical personality" that is more than a scale and something less than a composition—is common all through the Near East and the Orient. We find it in the eight *echoi* of the Byzantine *kanones* hymns, each *echos* being a repertoire of melodic motifs and ornaments connected with feelings, liturgical occasions or texts, seasons, and hours of the day. And we find it in the Arabic *maqam* (and its cousins throughout the Islamic world), the Hindu *raga,* and the Indonesian *patet.*

The Greek system of music is important also for its investigations into acoustics and the nature of sound. Pythagoras (ca. 500 B.C.) discovered that by dividing a vibrating string in certain mathematically proportional ways the basic intervals could be evolved. For instance, when a string is touched in its exact middle, an octave will sound; when two-thirds of a string is allowed to vibrate, a perfect fifth will sound.

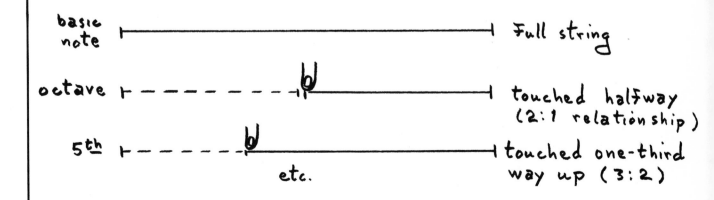

basic note ———————————————— Full string

octave ———————————— touched halfway (2:1 relationship)

5th —————— etc. touched one-third way up (3:2)

Anyone who plays the guitar or violin (or any other similar instrument) unconsciously follows these acoustical principles.

The influence of Greek theory on the music of the European Middle Ages was tremendous, and it continues to this day in concepts, in the way we think and philosophize about music, and even in the musical vocabulary of this book.

JAPAN

The ancient ceremonial *gagaku* court orchestra, which dates from the Nara (710–84) and Heian (794–1191) periods, derives its scales and many of its melodies from the flourishing musical culture of the Chinese T'ang dynasty (618–907). *Gagaku,* which literally means "elegant music," uses two basic seven-tone scales: the *ryo* (male) and the *ritsu* (female), each of which occurs in three transpositions.

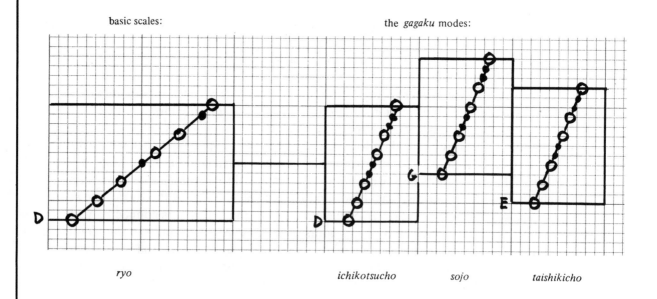

basic scales:

the *gagaku* modes:

ryo   ichikotsucho   sojo   taishikicho

basic scales: the *gagaku* modes:

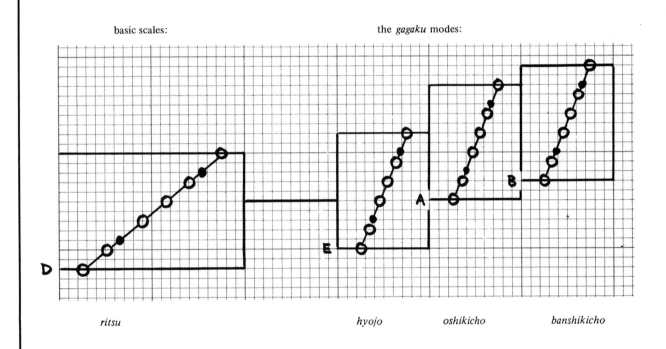

ritsu   hyojo   oshikicho   banshikicho

In actual performance, however, many of the pitches of these scales are sharped and flatted. They are therefore much more complex than they appear to be on paper.

The highly stylized *noh* theater, which originated in the fourteenth century during the Muromachi period, is a synthesis of literature, drama, dancing, and music. The primary purpose of the singing (by solo actors and a male chorus) is to convey the meaning of the words to the audience, so the melodies are often quite austere, broken only by an occasional melisma. The tonal system of *noh* is based on three *nuclear tones*—high, middle, and low—spaced at intervals of a fourth. Either the lowest or the highest of these nuclear tones can function as an ending note. Two other tones are important: one a fifth above the top nuclear tone and another a fourth (or a fifth) below the lowest nuclear tone. The other notes of the scale are subsidiary.

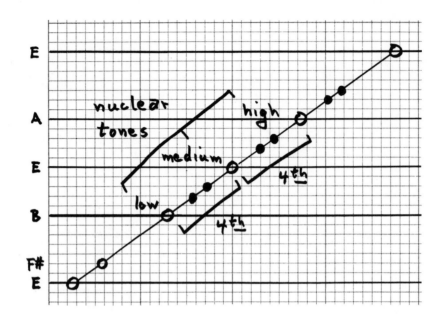

There is a prescribed order for the use of the notes of the *noh* scale in melodies, a complex set of rules and procedures. In addition there are two styles of singing: the "soft" style uses the above tonal system, while the "loud" style uses a compressed system with only two nuclear tones.

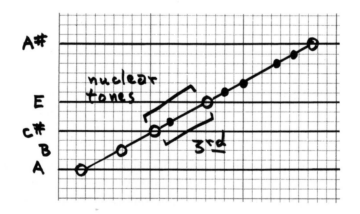

According to Kishibe Shigeo, more recent traditional Japanese music, particularly that written for the *koto* zither, *shamisen* lute, and *shakuhachi* bamboo flute, which has flourished since the Edo period (1603–1867), tends to use two five-note scales, the *insenpō* and the *yosenpō*.

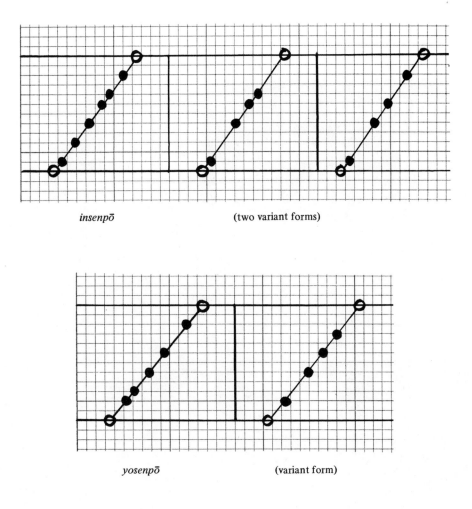

insenpō (two variant forms)

yosenpō (variant form)

IRAN

The Arabic concept of the *maqam* (plural, *maqamat*), a musical mode with a distinct "personality," has spread wherever Islamic conquest has spread—into central Asia and India, throughout north Africa, and into the fringes of Europe bordering on the Mediterranean. Where the conquerors were finally pushed back, in Greece, Bulgaria, and Spain, for example, the musical imprint remains: in "Oriental" scales, in a tense, nasal voice quality singing long, slow, meterless melodies colored by ornate melisma and quick microtonal shakes and mordents, or in instruments like the tambourine or the double-reed pipe. The Arabic *maqam* system is characterized also by a profusion of principal and derivative scales which fill the octave span with ornamentation as elaborate as the calligraphic and flowery arabesques on the walls of ancient mosques. In one survey the north African countries were found to have eighteen *basic* (!) scales, while Iraq had thirty-seven, and Egypt and Syria each had fifty-two!

In Iran, that is, in the Persian classical music system, there are seven basic modal structures (called *dastgah*) and five related scales (*avaz*). The scales of the *dastgah,* made of seven notes and often different in ascent and descent, are built up from fifteen intervals, including steps of 100 cents, 200 cents, "in-between" (to European ears) steps of 150 and 255 cents, and the "neutral third" of about 355 cents. Like the *maqam,* the *dastgah* includes special phrases, ca-

Left to right: *santūr*/zither, singer (Khatereh Parvaneh), *tār*/lute, *kamanchay*/spike fiddle, *dombak*/goblet-shaped drum. Music from Iran ensemble.

dence formulas, and aesthetic characteristics beyond the idea of a mere scale. In fact, the twelve *dastgah,* although all quite different from one another, are based on only nine scales.

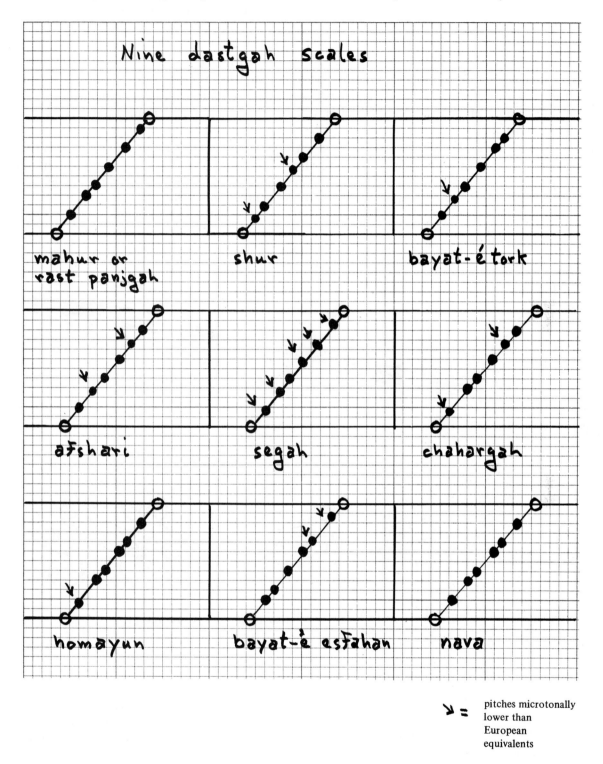

$ \searrow = $ pitches microtonally lower than European equivalents

Below the *dastgah* are a collection of approximately 250 *gusheh,* skeletal melodies and phrases each of which is related to one or more *dastgah* which a performer uses as a basis for improvisation. These *gusheh* are preserved in a large collection known as the *radif.*

INDIA

Melody in Indian classical music is based on the *raga* (literally, "that which colors the mind"), which like the *maqam* is an extremely complex expressive territory connected with colors, seasons, times of day, and moods as well as with purely technical musical elements. Classical Sanskrit theory divided *ragas* into families, each with a "father" (the dominant male *raga*), his "wives" (feminine *ragas*), and "children" (subordinate *ragas*). Present-day north Indian music uses a classification in which all *ragas* are based on twelve *thats,* or major modes. But we shall examine only the south Indian system, developed by Venkatamakhi in his *Sangeetha Makaranda* (ca. 1620).

The octave is divided into twelve steps with the tonal center (called *sa*) and the fifth (*pa*) as stable, unchanging notes. The remaining notes are then shuffled around in a gradually mutating way to form seventy-two basic seven-note generative scales, or *melakartas.* We can map out the channels of possibilities (reading from left to right) using "C" as a tonic.

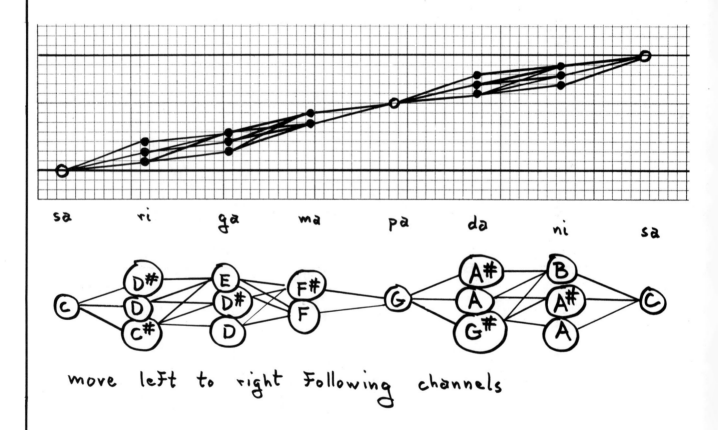

Each *melakarta* scale theoretically can have any number of *ragas* derived from it, although in practice some *melakartas* are extremely popular (with fifty or more "children") while others are almost completely neglected. *Ragas* express their individuality in a number of ways:

> Through the number of notes in their scale—four, five, six, seven, or any combination thereof (for instance, five notes going up and seven notes coming down, or six notes up and four notes down):

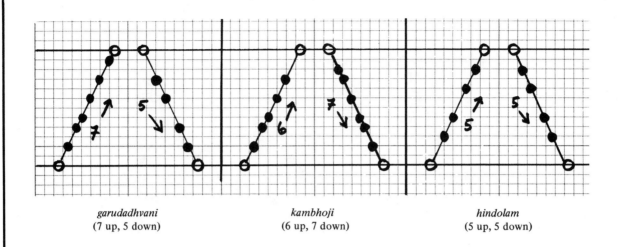

garudadhvani
(7 up, 5 down)

kambhoji
(6 up, 7 down)

hindolam
(5 up, 5 down)

By zigzagging (*vakra*) in the ascent or descent (or in both):

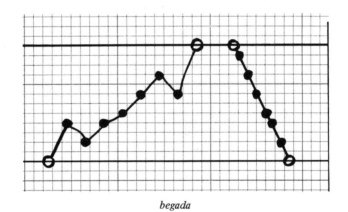

begada

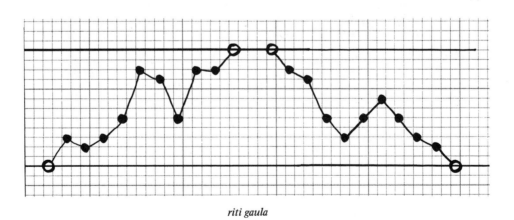

riti gaula

In a special class of *bhashanga ragas*, "visiting notes" not found in the basic scale, which are used judiciously as a kind of musical relish or spice:

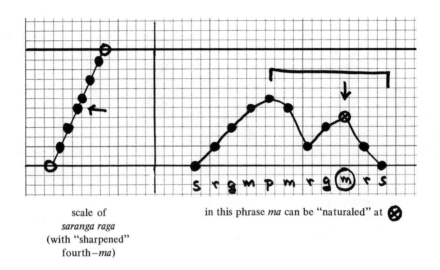

scale of
saranga raga
(with "sharpened"
fourth—*ma*)

in this phrase *ma* can be "naturaled" at ⊗

By special ornaments (*gamaka*) on certain notes:

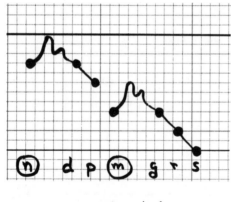

ornaments on *ni* and
ma (*begada raga*)

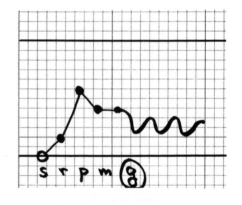

ornament on *ga*
(*kanada raga*)

By a whole vocabulary of emphasized (and deemphasized) tones, inflections, and characteristic musical phrases (*ranjaka prayogas,* literally, "sweet phrases") which are as recognizable to an Indian musician as the facial features of one human being are to another:

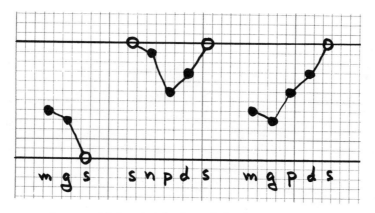

special characteristic phrases in *kambhoji raga*

By special microtonal intonation on certain notes.

The basic *melakarta* system is really an averaging out of the many subtle pitches of Indian music (twenty-two to the octave according to traditional theory!). We should note that these microtones are not used indiscriminately or all together; rather they are used to color the pitches of *ragas* that are built basically on seven-note (or less) scales.

Finally, by mood or other characteristics such as auspiciousness or supernatural power, sweetness, gravity (some *ragas* are deep, profound, others are "light"), and potential (a major *raga* can be explored musically for hours or even days, a minor *raga* may be "found out" in several minutes). In south India about 350 *ragas* are in common use, with perhaps about 60 predominating in concert performances and in musical compositions.

The dizzying technical complexity of the *raga* concept is tempered by the Indian musician's approach: *ragas* are not memorized and hammered out like the scales and exercises of Western music; they are, rather, assimilated, gradually, through hearing and practice, over a period of many years. A musician gets to "know" a *raga* much as we get to know the personality of a friend. The real essence of a *raga* is intangible; it must be felt, experienced, rather than rationalized, thought about. The *raga,* its many facets shining like jewels in a misty tropical moonlight, waiting to be discovered, to touch the emotions, combines the heard and unheard in a mystical union—it is a musical "being," invisible, but as real as breath.

JAVA

The gongs and chimes of each *gamelan* orchestra in Java, as we have mentioned, form a set which has its own unique sound characteristics, a timbral color so individualistic that it can immediately be recognized and perhaps even given a name, such as "The Venerable Dark Cloud," "Splashing Water," or "Eternal as the Sea." One reason for the unique sound of each *gamelan* is that no two are tuned exactly alike: the tunings follow the outlines of the five-tone *slendro* scale (dating from the eighth century) and the seven-tone *pelog* scale (realized by the fifteenth century) but subtle differences exist from one *gamelan* to the next, and perhaps even within the same *gamelan*!

Each scale, more correctly called a *tuning system,* has three modes which are called *patet.* Each *patet,* in turn, is characterized by a set of principal tones that receive special emphasis in the melodies that are built from them. Although *pelog* is technically a seven-tone scale system,

Performance of all-night *wayang kulit*/shadow puppet play. The *dalang*/puppeteer manipulates the puppets so that their shadows are cast on the cloth screen. Extra puppets are lined up on either side of the screen. The audience may view the play from either the shadow side of the screen or the *dalang*'s side, where the *gamelan* orchestra plays directly behind him. Performance by Javanese *dalang* Oemartopo, Wesleyan University, Middletown, Connecticut.

in each of its *patets* two different notes are treated as subsidiary to a basic pentatonic core (a principle we also noted in Chinese music!).

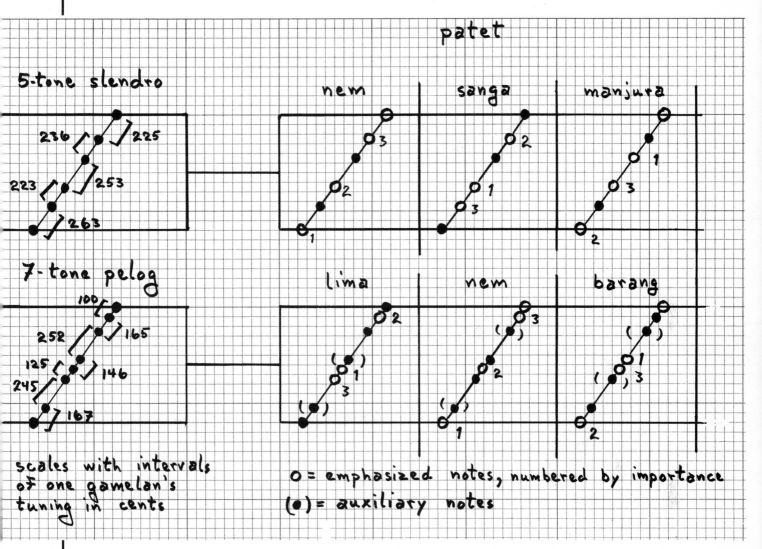

The *Slendro/Pelog* Systems in the Tuning of One *Gamelan*

Again we run into the dichotomy between the idea of a scale system as a cold, scientific, purely technical collection of notes (the West, at least in the twentieth century) and as a warm, humanly expressive musical being, full of so-called extramusical implications (the Middle East, India, Indonesia). If the first approach may be compared to considering a scale as a pile of bricks, of raw materials, the second approach makes each scale system a completed castle, with its own architecture of towers and great halls, hidden rooms and secret passageways.

In Java the nature of the scale system is perhaps best seen in its connections with the *wayang kulit* all-night shadow puppet plays. Each *gamelan* orchestra has in effect two sets of instruments: one set is tuned to the (male) five-tone *slendro* scale, and the other set is tuned to the (female) seven-tone *pelog*. If the story of a particular shadow puppet play is taken from the originally Indian epics, the *Mahabharata* and *Ramayana, slendro* is used; if the story is from the indigenous heroic *Pandji* cycle, *pelog* is used.

The night—and the action of the puppet play—is divided into three sections. The first period, lasting from around 8 o'clock until midnight, uses the first *patet* mode (for instance, *nem* in the *slendro* system). Typical melodic and cadential formulas and compositions based on them reflect the relative calm of this first expository section of the drama. The second time period, from midnight to 3 A.M., uses the second mode of the tonal system (for instance, *sanga* in the *slendro* system). Melodies are then more agitated and dense, reflecting the complications of the plot, the battles, and the ribald humor of the clowns associated with the central section of the shadow puppet play. The final time period, beginning at 3 and ending at dawn, portrays complicated intrigue, the final decisive battles (with the forces of good overcoming evil), and the celebration of the victors. The third mode (in the *slendro* system, *manjura*) is used with melodies that show the greatest amount of activity and bold disjunct motion.

Each of the three *patet* modes, then, accumulates certain types of melodic movement and cadential formulas connected with the moods, times, and actions of the *wayang kulit* plays. Even when played in abstract "purely musical" situations, the *patet* modes retain the aura of these connections in the minds of performers and listeners alike.

EUROPE/AMERICA

The predominant tonal system of Europe and the Americas (and all other areas of the world where Western musical forms have been imitated or adapted) is that of the *major* and *minor scales*. Asian musicians have frequently joked about the paucity of "only two" scales in the European tradition, but this system is deceptively simple. Melody-making is only one of its functions; the others are harmony and contrapuntal combination. In addition, there are the other parameters considered important in the West: orchestration, for example, or musical structure. One is almost tempted to make a Darwinian analogy: melody, scales, and rhythm proliferated in north Africa and south Asia because the full energies of musicians focused on these aspects, while in Europe melody, scales, and rhythm remained relatively simple because they were only part of a larger panorama; the energies of composers and performers were spread equally among problems of harmony, counterpoint, notation, timbre, orchestration, structure, and the working together of large ensembles.

Both seven-tone scales are built on four-note tetrachords (the Greek model!). The major scale uses two tetrachords of identical intervals, while the minor scale superimposes three different upper tetrachords (which can be used interchangeably in a composition) on an unchanging lower tetrachord.

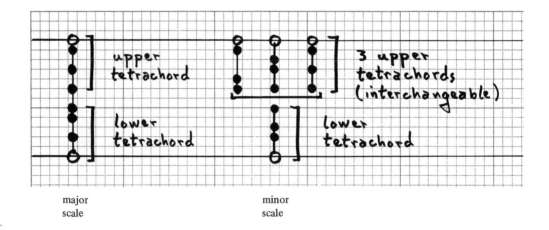

major
scale

minor
scale

In building melodies (and harmonies) the relative simplicity of both scales is complicated by two factors: the first is the shifting of a scale (or a melody) to a new tonal center, or *modulation* (our "elevator" effect), which is heard as being "different" enough to add variety and

Band with fiddle, clarinet, tambourine, and accordion accompanies singers, from Nowe Miasto, central Poland.

freshness to a piece of music or performance. A Western musician thinks of each *transposition* of the same scale as being, in effect, a new scale: C major is different from D major is different from F sharp major, and so on. The second complicating factor is the use of subsidiary tones. We have seen how seven-tone scales in China, southeast Asia, and Indonesia are often made up of a five-tone pentatonic core, the two extra tones functioning as minor subsidiary notes. Similarly, the seven-tone core of Euro-American music is amplified with five extra subsidiary notes, which can occur in music as "accidentals." For the major scale the design of the keys on a piano (if we take C as the tonal center) graphically illustrates this point:

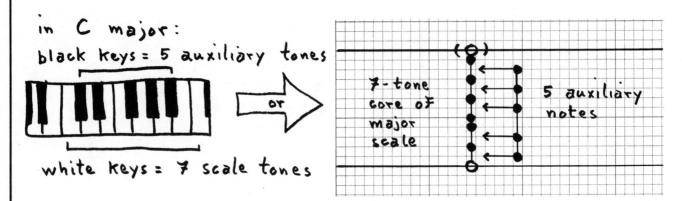

Finally, a whole galaxy of gravitational pulls exists among the tones of the scale, and these pulls are strongly reinforced through the simultaneous use of harmonies.

While the major and minor scales are generally looked upon as being an abstract "building block" system, there is an undercurrent of popular thought which assigns moods and feelings to them and to their transpositions. The major scale has been described as "bright" and "happy," while the minor scale is "dark," "moody," or "sad," and composers, particularly of opera, oratorio, musical theater, or background music, where words or dramatic situations clarify moods and feelings, have to an amazing degree reflected these sentiments—though, of course, exceptions abound. Nineteenth-century critics and composers, like the Russian Alexander Scriabin (1875–1915), assigned moods and colors to different transpositions of the scales, even in purely instrumental music!

Underlying the major-minor diatonic tone system of Europe and America is the older *modal system,* which was first categorized in the eleventh century and exists today in performances of pre-sixteenth-century music, late medieval and Renaissance music, folk music, and the Gregorian chant of the Roman Catholic Church. Many of the fiddling tunes and ballads of the Appalachians in the United States (and in the British Isles) are based on these diatonic (seven-tone) modes, as well as on a variety of pentatonic (five-tone) scales.

Some of the Diatonic Modes

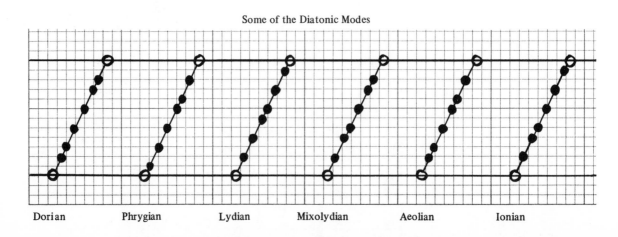

Dorian   Phrygian   Lydian   Mixolydian   Aeolian   Ionian

In the twentieth century composers and musicians have greatly expanded the diatonic system through sometimes startlingly innovative approaches. Bela Bartok (1881–1945), who was a pioneering ethnomusicologist, based his style on elements he had found in the folk music of his native Hungary and in other eastern European countries. The Russian Igor Stravinsky (1882–1971) and the American Charles Ives (1874–1954) also evolved personal styles and techniques related to folk and popular music in their native countries. Perhaps the most radical approach was taken by Arnold Schoenberg (1874–1951), an Austrian composer, who built up a tonal system based on all twelve notes of the chromatic scale. Before composing a piece he would create an arrangement of the twelve tones which he called the *twelve-tone row*. This musical "cell" of tones in a specific ordering, much like the zigzag *ragas* of India, would then be used to generate all the melodies and harmonies in a composition. Schoenberg attempted to avoid the gravitational pulls of tonal centers by giving every tone equal weight in what he called a *pantonal* approach. Unlike most of the scales and modes in the world, the twelve-tone row was an arrangement of absolute pitches:

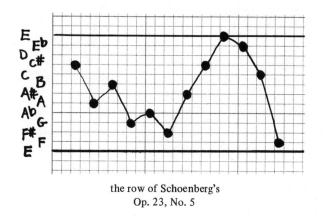

the row of Schoenberg's
Op. 23, No. 5

Schoenberg's *serial* technique, further expanded by his great disciples Alban Berg (1885–1935) and Anton Webern (1883–1945), has been extremely influential in the classical music of the post–World War II years. Its sound, if not its highly rationalized technique, has also filtered into avant-garde jazz.

Besides the dominant tonal systems in Euro-America there is what we might call a "subculture" of scales and systems. Some of these exist in the countries on the southern and eastern periphery of Europe, or among subcultural groups (like the gypsies of Spain and Romania), where the influence of Arabic and Turkish music has been particularly strong. More problematical—both in terms of its importance to Western musical culture as a whole and in terms of its analytical evasiveness—is the music evolved by black Americans. A form called the *"blues"* lies at the root of much black music—jazz, soul, rock—and we shall look at it as an archetypal example.

The blues tonal system is a mixture of diverse melodic and timbral elements built on the European diatonic system. An underlying scaffolding of chord progressions backs up the melodic gravitational pulls of relatively stable tonal centers, notably the first scale degree (the tonic), the fourth, and the fifth.

Black American street singer playing guitar. Note slide in left hand permitting musician to slide up and down strings and play notes between frets. Metalwork on the instrument increases resonance. Flora Molton, Washington, D.C.

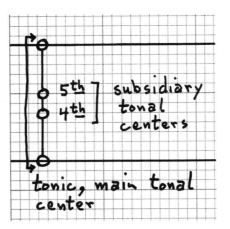

But between these poles, a tremendous tonal fluidity exists. Notes are treated not as steps, but as points in a continuous fluctuation of sweeps, curves, and vibrations. Subtle microtonal slips and slides of pitch and wide vibratos, colored by expressive use of vocal timbre and range, further add to this ambiguity.

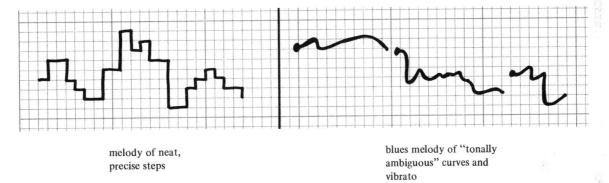

melody of neat,
precise steps

blues melody of "tonally
ambiguous" curves and
vibrato

The use of the "neutral third" (between the major and minor third, or alternating between the two), the "neutral sixth," the flatted fifth and seventh, and a deemphasis of the high seventh—the "leading tone" so important in European music—are also characteristic.

But far beyond its technical externals, the blues is an emotional expression, with a musical "personality" similar to that of the *raga, patet,* and *maqam.* The feeling for and of the blues is essential: mood is its heart and soul.

★★★★★★★★★★★★★★★★★★★★★★★★★★

Tone Building

While many of the melodies of the world have notes of more or less equal status, perhaps the majority move around one or more *tonal centers*. These are established in various ways: by emphasis or repetition, by harmonies (in Western music), or by drones. On the simplest level—the *centric melodies* found in New Guinea, among Great Basin Indians, or in Jewish and liturgical Christian and Maori chants, for example—the satellite subsidiary tones of the melody circle around the tonal nucleus (as Curt Sachs has put it) "like butterflies around a flower."

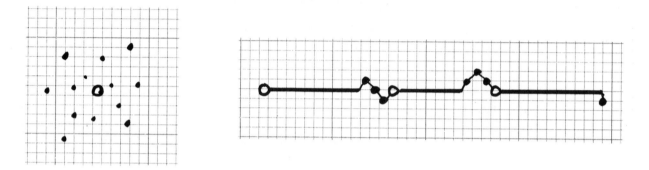

The reinforcement of tonal centers by one or more notes of a continuous drone is found in Euro-America (bagpipes, banjos, country fiddling), Africa, eastern Europe, central Asia, the Arabic-influenced belt from north Africa to Malaysia, and in the pockets of tribal culture in southeast Asia. Elements of the drone perhaps can be found in every musical culture of the world. The drone may be a single pitch like the rhythms of the one-stringed *ektār* which accompanies wandering minstrels in Bengal, or it may be a scaffolding of pitches (often enriched by overtone vibrations) like the *tambūrā* of Indian classical music.

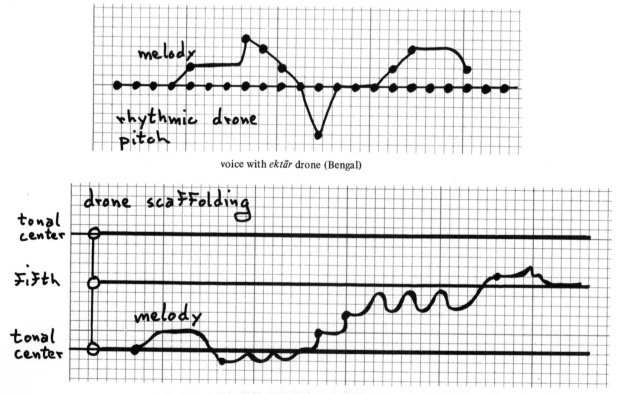

voice with *ektār* drone (Bengal)

voice with *tambūrā* drone (India)

The notes that occur in melodies (and abstracted into their scales) usually exist in a hierarchy of relationships and of greater or lesser importance, or "weight," much like big and little (and medium-sized) fishes in an aquarium.

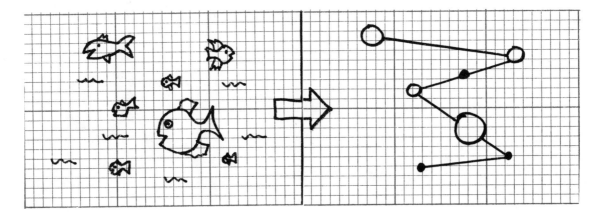

In southeast Asia, India, and many of the countries of the Islamic world these important notes are systematized into melodically consonant *pillar tones*, stable "islands" on which composed or improvised melodies can come to rest. They may even be formalized in a certain order. For example, in Azerbaijan (USSR) the *mugam bayati-shiraz* has a sequence of nine characteristic tone levels (covering an octave and a fifth) around which the improvisation moves as the music progresses.

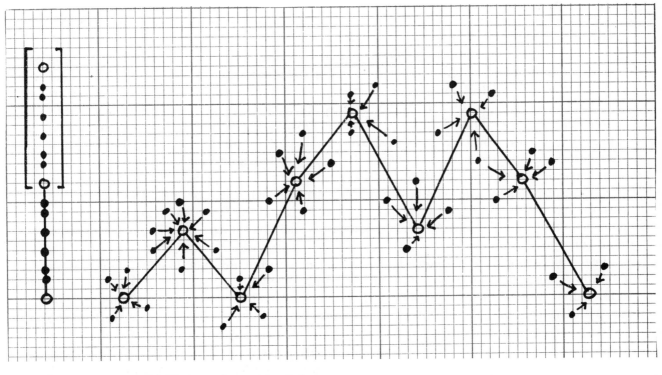

scale   sequential pillar tones of *mugam bayati-shiraz*

A collection of "resting tones," "tiny (unemphasized) tones," "beginning" and "ending tones," as well as "shadow tones" (which show the heart of the mode) are found in each *raga* in India. The weight of certain notes in melodies is achieved in many ways: they may occur more often, they may be emphasized through accents or long duration (resting notes, called "agogic accent"), or they may appear at key points, the extremities of melodies, like musical fingertips, toes, and elbows.

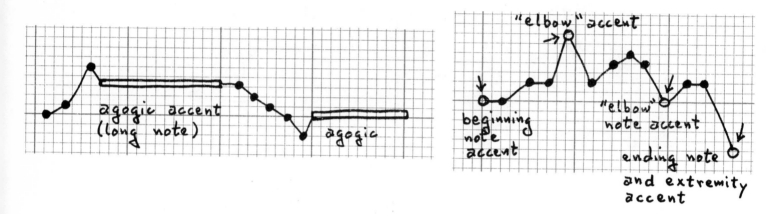

The stringing together of individual notes to make melodies out of expressively dead raw materials seems to many persons to require the magical skill of a medieval alchemist, who with his philosopher's stone turned mercury into gold. But it is really more of a craft, like that of a potter, carpenter, or weaver. And the rules about how a melody is made, whether written or unwritten, whether the composer is even aware of them or not, are no more mysterious than architectural drawings or a recipe for soup.

We have seen how many tonal systems are much, much more than empty scales and note series. The Turkish *maqam,* the Persian *gusheh,* and the Indian *raga,* and perhaps also the American blues all include characteristic note groupings, musical phrases connected with the expressive purposes of a particular mood. The musician assimilates all these melodic patterns, stores them in his brain, and then uses them (calculatedly or spontaneously) in performance. In Japan and China melodies are built by making ample use of stereotyped patterns which are arranged collagelike, or combined with more intuitive phrases. In the Peking opera and the Japanese *kabuki* theater form, catalogs of stereotyped phrases and full melodies connected with certain emotional or dramatic situations are drawn from as the occasion demands. In America's Tin Pan Alley the innumerable composers of popular song also make use of time-worn formulas. In fact, to an extent everyone does. The difference between an exceptionally gifted composer or improviser and a hack lies not in the fact that he uses the patterns and formulas of his culture, but in the way he uses them, to what extent his creativity gives them an extra (sometimes indefinable) spark, and perhaps to what extent his originality extends previous concepts.

Beginnings and endings (*cadential patterns*) are particularly important, like first impressions and last impressions. For instance, in Poland melodies often end with the last note held and then trailing off in a downward glissando. In Java the ending of one musical thought (and the beginning of the next) is signaled in the *gongan,* with the massive reverberations of the large gong. In the United States melodies tend to end on the tonal center and are strongly reinforced by harmonic formulas; in south India little improvised phrases and standard drum patterns signal the end of melodic sections. While the techniques vary from country to country, the basic feeling is there (recognized by those within a culture), as clear as the closing of a door.

Singer, backed by the constant drone of *tamburās*, bringing out the expressive qualities of a *raga*. M. S. Subbalakshmi, Madras.

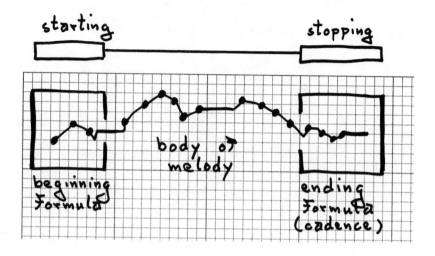

Melody, like rhythm, can float freely without a pulse, like the alternate gliding and sudden darts of a sparrow high in the sky. Or it may be wedded to the chugging rhythms of beat and meter (beat groupings), or even a combination of the two.

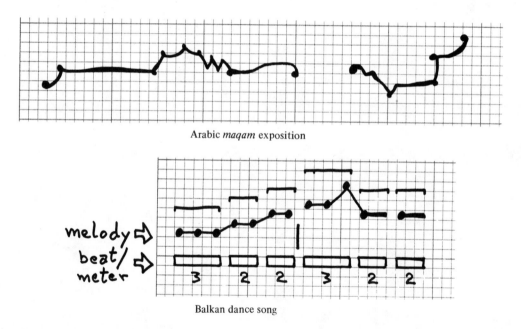

Arabic *maqam* exposition

Balkan dance song

The traditional melodies for the Japanese *shakuhachi* bamboo flute flow without pulse, like slowly moving water, with "breath rhythms" that seem intimately tied, *zen*-like, to deep mystical, mental, and physical impulses of the player. Similarly, the slow, introductory, improvisatory *taqsim* of Arabic music sets the mood and introduces the notes and characteristic phrases of the *maqam* mode (as in India the *alapana* introduces the *raga*) before the performance of set pieces (or improvisations) accompanied by drum (and with beat and meter). A similar "timeless" modal introduction is found in *flamenco* music in Spain. Words (if used) may shape phrases by their poetry, although conversational prose with its pauses and asymmetrical sentences fits the feeling of this type of melody far better. The free, fluid rhythmic movement allows ample time for long, drawn-out notes, sudden twists, or highly ornamented melismatic passages.

The more rhythmic type of melodies, such as the dance pieces of Greece and the Balkans, or many of the folk melodies in the Euro-American tradition often make use of changing melody notes fitted into repeated rhythmic patterns (similar to the repeated rhythm patterns of drummers throughout the world). In medieval Europe long rhythmic formulas (with changing notes happening over them), called *isorhythm,* formed the hidden, internal structure of much of the choral music of the Church. But in folk and popular music, these patterns are brief and easily heard.

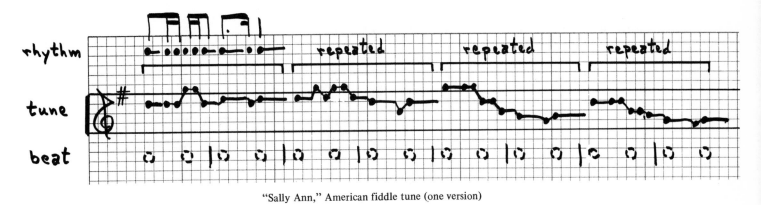

"Sally Ann," American fiddle tune (one version)

Such set, boxlike, recurring rhythmic patterns (with their variants) correspond to the set stanzas of European poetry with its regular rhyme schemes and meter. Of course the rhythmic patterns of melody become much more complicated and full of variants, even in the simplest example, but as often as not a preponderance of one pattern in a melody can be heard.

Another type of melody-rhythm relationship found all over the world (but notable in Africa, the Arabic-influenced cultural belt, and in jazz and other black-derived American musical genres) is *syncopation,* where the intense accents and rhythms of the melody contradict and pull against the rhythms and feeling of the underlying beat.

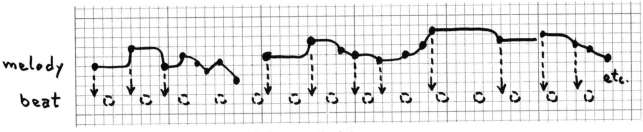

melodic syncopation in jazz

The stringing together of the beads of notes into melodies reflects very basic human impulses: the love of familiar faces and surroundings (or words and ideas), or *repetition*; and the need for the unfamiliar, the unexplored, the "new," or *contrast.* In the early days of European exploration of the rest of the world, when *conquistadores* and missionaries and brave sea captains pushed into uncharted lands and jungles and deserts and seas, the universal assessment of the music of the strange people they met was that it was repetitious and boring. We must today, of course, be extremely careful about using subjective words like "boring": a chess game or a soccer match that may have one group of people gritting their teeth and sitting on the edge of their seats might incite others to uncontrollable yawns! We can add that nothing, *nothing* in music is pure, unabated repetition. Minute variations occur, sometimes quite subtly; and the very fact that music happens in time, moves along the edge of time (with memory and accumulation), indicates change, even if this change is merely in the psychological perspective of the listener.

We have noted the similarity of music made of single repeated notes (or of endlessly repeated short phrases) with the serial recurring zigzags and images of "primitive" and modern "minimal" art. In Hawaii native singers point out distinctions where we hear sameness. The Indians of the Great Basin and west coast areas of the United States have many songs based on repetitions of single phrases; but at a key point in the song the melody is pushed up (in pitch) ever so slightly in what they themselves call "the rise." This subtle "rise," which passed completely unnoticed by white listeners and scholars until fairly recently, is one of the important parts of the structure of these Indian performances and for knowledgeable Indian ears is as exciting a moment as the unsubtle cymbal crashes in a Tchaikovsky symphony are for philharmonic patrons.

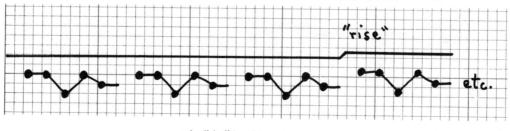

the "rise" in a Yuma song

The tendency toward *variation* operates in a number of ways. On the simplest level the changes are very slight, perhaps accidental. Many cultures do not have the penchant for precision which we in the West have. A song composed of a repeated short phrase (say, in central Africa) may have a thematic cell idea that is extremely loose: any number of variations can be considered (within the culture) as actually "repetitions" of the same recognizable song phrase. In Hungarian folk music, a common variation and extension technique is to transpose short bits of melody up or down at the interval of a fifth.

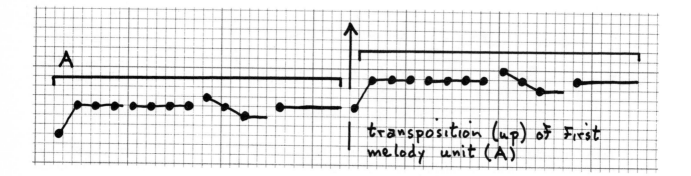

transposition (up) of first melody unit (A)

Similarly, in popular and classical music—in fact in all genres—in the European/American tradition melody is commonly transposed (in whole or in part) to different tone levels (within the key or by the "elevator" process of modulation to different keys). In India a more organic type of variation, the *sangati,* gradually spins out more and more complex variations on one phrase of the melody. These variations are often offset by retaining a nonvarying segment, a beautiful balance of repetition and contrast.

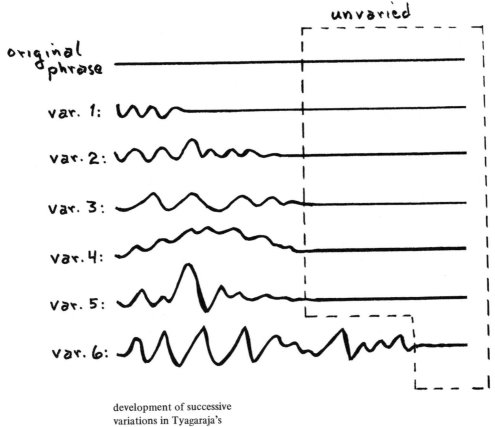

development of successive
variations in Tyagaraja's
Vatapi

Opposed to the more static process of repetition and/or variation is the organic development of melodic ideas from an original cell, much like a tree grows from a single seed. Here each idea, each string of melodic fragments, leads to another in a gradually expanding chain. Repetitions there are, of course, like memories and recurrences; but at the same time there is a searching, a probing, for the new. The feeling is much more plantlike, less that of contained units, boxes. Many of the beautiful melodies of Japanese music seem to fall into this category, as do the slow Arabic introductions to the *maqam,* the Indian *alapana,* the Persian *daramad,* and the classical compositions of Europe (with their motivic and structural developments).

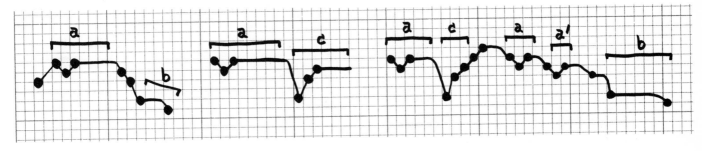

organic growth of melodic cells
(bracketed)

Much of the character of a melody comes from its use of intervals. Larger intervals, *skips,* tend to have (for Western ears, at least) a pull of tension, something like the stretching of a rubber band; while smaller intervals, *steps,* are heard as comparatively relaxed. This tension and relaxation is reflected in the human throat, in the vocal cords, and to a lesser extent in instruments, where fingers may have to spread and strain to reach larger intervals. Angular, athletic melodies full of skips of a fourth or more are found among American Indians, in the tribal pockets of Asia, and in much twentieth-century Euro-American classical music. Stepwise melodies are common all over the world. But perhaps most common (even among the American Indians) are tunes that have skips *balanced* by stepwise motion, an interplay that affords the ear (and voice) contrast and variety.

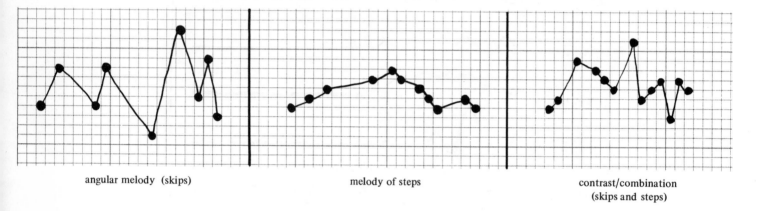

angular melody (skips)   melody of steps   contrast/combination
                                                                          (skips and steps)

Of course, the difference between a step and a skip may blur, or not even be thought about, in a musical culture—so many things depend upon one's perspective.

Melodies may also be characterized as "plain" or "fancy," that is, by the degree of elaborateness of their ornamentation or the lack of it. Like the straightforward simple brown cloth and leather jacket of a Welsh farmer, the tones of a melody may be functional, unornamented, basic, simple. Tunes of this type are prevalent in the folk and classical music of Europe and the Americas (though they are also found in the music of Asia, Africa, and Oceania); one might even say that this approach to melody and tones is basic to the West.

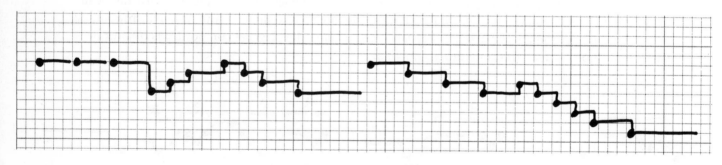

Ein Feste Burg (German chorale tune)

Fiddler, singer, and bagpiper performing together. Feliks Chudy, Maria Majchrzak, Szczepan Sadowski, from Skoraszewice, Poland. The bagpipe is the bellows-operated *dudy* typical of the Wielkopolska region.

But curious exceptions exist: for example, in the highly ornamented bagpipe melodies of Ireland and Scotland, in the graces, turns, and colorings of American Appalachian and country music, or in the virtuosic slides, vibratos, and bending intonations in the black-derived genres of blues, gospel, and jazz. The music of the Balkans, particularly Bulgaria and Greece, is also filled with ornaments, trills, turns, grace notes, and glottal stops that cover the basic skeleton of the melody like the colorful embroidery, braids, laces, ribbons, silver coins, sequins, and pearl-like beads on a Macedonian wedding dress.

A love of intense melodic ornamentation is found throughout the Middle East and north Africa, up into Spain (in gypsy *flamenco* singing), and across Asia into India and Indonesia. Whether there is a connection between this opulent approach to melody and the incredibly elaborate abstract designs of the rugs, mosaics, inlay, and Koranic calligraphy of Islamic and Islamic-influenced cultures is a matter of conjecture. But ornamentation here is considerably more than nonessential decoration; it lies at the core of what the music is.

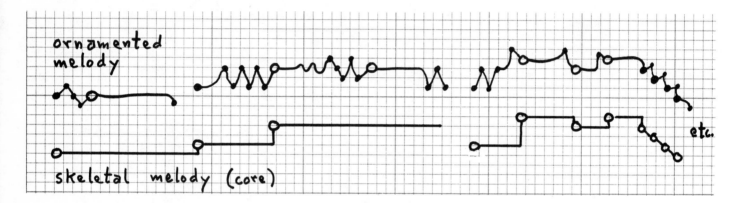

While there may be an unornamented skeleton of relatively stable clean plain tones under the firefly-like movements of the melody, it is the ornamentation itself that brings the melody to life, like the opening and flickering of the eyes of a beautiful woman.

A variety of ornaments is also used in the musics of China and Japan, according to some scholars an influence from ancient India. In the playing of the Chinese *ch'in* zither there are said to be twenty-six varieties of ornament, while traditional Indian music theory lists fifteen types.

Quite often throughout the world highly ornamented melodies are coupled with a free, almost pulseless rhythmic background, the floating, cloudlike setting described earlier. The profusely ornamented keyboard fantasias and preludes of sixteenth- and seventeenth-century European composers like John Bull (ca. 1562–1628), Giles Farnaby (ca. 1560–1640), and William Byrd (1543–1623) were played in a free rhythm similar to that of the equally ornamented *raga alapana* of India. Occasionally they were even notated without bar lines or time signatures! The floating background which is characteristic of genres or sections of pieces in Arabic-influenced areas, without the compulsive thrust of drums and strongly accented rhythms, allows for full concentration on the quiet subtleties of melody, on intonation, timbre—and above all on ornament.

Voices/Instruments

The voice (with the birds) was the mother of melody, and it is impossible to ignore this natural "instrument" that everybody in the world—all three billion of the earth's inhabitants—owns, in fact is born with, and to some degree knows how to use. There are, of course, those rare individuals who are "tone-deaf," in whom nature or their own psychology has short-circuited the connections among ears, brain, and vocal cords. General, and later President, Ulysses S. Grant complained that he could recognize only two tunes: one was "Yankee Doodle Dandy" and the other one wasn't! But for the rest of us the very nature of the human voice—its character, capabilities, range, and tone color—defines the limits of what we call melody.

The comfortable range of the voice, for example, varies from about one and one-half to two and one-half octaves; for many persons it is even less. Melodies, even when written for instruments or orchestras capable of much greater ranges, tend to fall within these vocal limits. In India one of the greatest compliments a musician can get is that his instrument sounds like the voice. Classical, jazz, and pop instrumentalists in Europe and America strive for an almost human "vocal tone." And a large part of the repertoire of world music, perhaps as much as 85 percent, is based on songs, written with words and meant originally for the voice.

We must remember that a melody is seldom an abstraction of pitches, scales, and rhythms. Invariably its quality depends on the way it sounds, on the characteristics of the agent that produces it, and on what we can only call performance style. For example, African singing uses yodeling, growling, raucous, and tense tone qualities, as well as a relaxed style that can approach a near-whisper. Women in Uganda sometimes tap their throats while singing. Tibetan religious chant is done in an extraordinarily low register that seems to fortify the electrifying religious power of the texts. A deep, well-like masculine tone quality is also highly regarded all through central Asia and Siberia. On the other hand, the Indians of the American Great Plains stretch their melodies to the screaming upper (nonfalsetto) limits of the male vocal range (far above that of an Irish tenor!), achieving a hair-raising, tense quality in the vocal line. The relative position of a melody within the range of voice or instrument—called *tessitura*—whether it is at the bottom, in the "relaxed" middle, or at the shrill top, is an important characteristic of a sound.

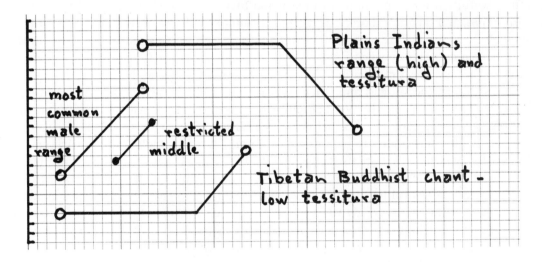

Specific vocal techniques also influence the shaping of melody. In Korea singers use an intense, almost jazzlike, "hot," wide vibrato, while in Japanese *noh* and *kabuki* long notes with almost no vibrato are broken by sudden spasmlike jerks and leaps. The Navaho use falsetto, shouts, and hisses as well as the overaccentuation, staccato, and inner pulsation of longer notes which characterize much American Indian singing. All these elements are really essential, inseparable parts of melody itself. And this is an extremely important realization!

Melody, too, is shaped by "extramusical" elements, such as its performance situation and social setting. Classical musicians in south India, for example, can stop in the middle of a performance to retune their instruments or make comments to their cronies in the audience. There is a constant and sometimes noisy interplay between musicians and the audience, which is expected to react vocally much like a crowd at a rock or informal jazz concert. On the other hand, the strict formality of Japanese classical music is mirrored in the formality of its performance: careful attention is given to the stage, to the arrangement of screens and flowers, and the musicians keep their eyes lowered and sit almost completely immobile.

is like viewing a painting of different shades of red cut with a band of phosphorescent blue—the reds would look different!

To what extent instruments themselves reflect the demands of a music that already exists or shape music in new and expanded ways is similar to the rhetorical question of what comes first: the chicken or the egg. Instruments are invented, of course, to fit preconceived musical ideas—the accordion with its keys for melody notes and buttons for chordal accompaniment is a good example—but it is also entirely possible that instruments were discovered (like the uncharted land of America or penicillin) quite by accident. Once made, an instrument is modified or improved upon and in a very curious way can generate music that is unique to itself. For instance, the finger holes of bagpipes, flutes, and pipes are often drilled *not* to fit the notes of a scale (aural), but to fit the fingers and hands of the players (tactile) or nonacoustical measurements (visual). The notes of the scale (and melodies) then played on the instrument are determined to a large extent by the structure of the instrument itself rather than the ear. In many of the musical cultures of Africa instruments built in this way operate in an entirely different tonal system—scales, tuning, melodies—than the vocal music sung within the same culture!

World musicians, no matter who or where they are, spending perhaps as much time with their instruments as with their husbands or wives, tend to explore creatively the melodic and sound possibilities of their instruments. Often this is done by doodling, by the agile movement of hands and fingers, at random or in a conscious direction. If something useful is discovered, it is followed, extended, explored, remembered. Music and melodies for specific instruments then take on the sometimes very special characteristics of the instrument. For instance, the solo literature for the Japanese *shakuhachi* bamboo flute so fully utilizes the sound of breath and breathing, the delicate changes of intonation, overblown pitches, and unique timbral effects that it cannot really be performed on any other instrument. The melody in its every aspect, in its bones and in its soul, is wedded to the bamboo flute. The Yugoslavian bowed *gusle* fiddle when fingered with the hands in normal playing position produces the microtones that have become characteristic of its melodic style. The Turkish oboelike *zurnā* (and its cousins all over the Mideast and Orient) is capable of "bending" pitches and producing quite subtle changes of intonation simply by a tightening or loosening of the player's lips on the double-reed mouthpiece—a characteristic of its melodies. In addition, the player, by filling his cheeks with air and blowing while simultaneously breathing in, can play nonstop melodic lines without the customary breaks for breathing that are usually necessary in vocal and wind instrument music.

Breath-oriented melodies are strung together in sections, or phrases, like a series of differently shaped and colored boxcars rolling along in a moving freight train. These phrases are separated by holds (long resting notes), pauses, cadential configurations, or pockets of silence during which the singer or performer can take a breath; and each phrase tends to be a microcosm in itself, an idea unit much like the phrase, sentence, or paragraph in language. Once this format for melody-making is accepted (as it is, for example, in India or in the United States and Europe), all music tends to follow it, even when nonbreath instruments (like the piano or violin) make it unnecessary.

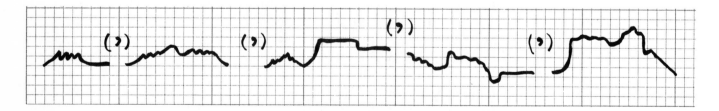

melody divided into phrases

On the other hand, breath-*less* nonstop melodies with notes strung out one after another like links in a speeding chain of objects in a factory assembly line are found all through central Asia and the Far East (played on instruments like the Kazakh *dombra* lute or the Nivkh *tyngryn* fiddle), in the Middle East, and in southeast Asia (fortified by the circular breathing technique of the *khaen* bamboo mouth organ). There are breaks, of course, but the breaks are farther apart and they may be more abrupt, and the melody in between is less apt to fall into the neat, sentencelike phrases of breath-oriented melodies. The effect is of a continuous zigzag of notes happening in (usually) quick succession.

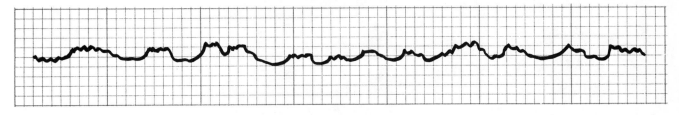

continuous nonstop melody on *tyngryn* fiddle of Nivkhs (USSR)

Bowed and wind instruments—like the pipe, the fiddle, bagpipe, but especially the flute—with this possibility of quick, birdlike fingering and instant tonal response, generate melodies that flutter with fast passages and ornaments like sparrows in a barn. When vocal pieces are performed on these instruments, the basic tunes are decorated with a rich ornamentation that reflects the greater fluency of the instruments and their fingering. In many cultural areas—in European/American popular music, in India, or in eastern Europe, for example—instruments and voice may share the same repertoire. On the other hand, instruments (or rather, the players and composers who use them) may develop their own body of music, with melodies specially fitted to the characteristics of the instruments, their sound, and the techniques of playing them. Thus the forms of Scottish and Irish piping, such as the *pibroch* theme and variations, are special in themselves and unrelated to vocal forms. French Canadian, Irish, and southern American fiddlers have their own special repertoire of fiddling tunes. And Western classical music is largely an instrumental music with many subdivisions (piano literature, string quartets, orchestral music, etc.) depending on the characteristics of the instruments or particular ensembles. Instruments, then, in all their world-full variety—like tools and other inventions—are extensions of man himself. And they have generated, through breath, fingers, and (recently) electricity, extended concepts of music and of melody.

Settings

We have touched upon a kind of unwritten Darwinian law of balances which states that melodies surrounded by all sorts of musical happenings—elaborate accompaniments, countermelodies, orchestrations, and the like—tend toward greater simplicity than melodies allowed to develop in and for themselves. In actuality, of course, nothing is quite so clear-cut: the world is full of too many beautiful simple tunes performed with no distractions save the bending of flowers in the wind. But melodies (and our perception of them) *are* greatly influenced by their setting.

A tune performed alone, whether an Amish hymn, a Hungarian lullaby, or an American Indian love song played on the flute, exists as an entity. Like a leaf or a stone or a *haiku* it simply *is*. But with the addition of a drone, whether the constant single notes of the European hurdy-gurdy, bagpipes, or dulcimer or the open chords of the Indian *tamburā,* a new element immediately enters the picture: the constant relationship between the notes of the melody and the note(s) of the drone. It

Ghanaian singers. Note utilization of guitar.

Rhythmic accompaniments also "color" melody, adding a rhythmic thrust and encouraging stronger accents and perhaps a more percussive quality in the melody itself. Many African melodies, even when sung *a capella,* have a strong rhythmic bias, shadowing the rhythmic complexity of differently pitched drums, rattles, and bells (which make in themselves a kind of "melody"). If a melody floats seemingly unconcerned above the heavy pulsation of drums, that contrast—like a gull gliding above a raging sea—will shape our perception of the melody and ultimately must be regarded as an underlying current in its shape and structure.

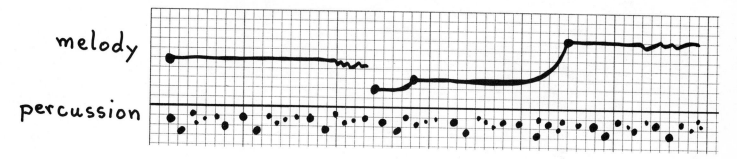

Even more pervasive are the thicker textures that support and surround melodies such as the vocal polyphonies (many-layered melodies) of Polynesia, New Guinea, and Africa or the harmonies of European and American music. The main melody may occur at the top (above the harmonic setting as in hymns and many pop songs), in the middle (within the harmonies as in the Sacred Harp and bluegrass singing styles found in the southern United States), or even at the bottom (beneath the harmony as in the music of the *khaen* mouth organ of Cambodia and Laos.

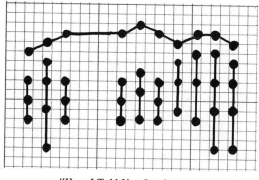

"Have I Told You Lately
That I Love You?"—pop
song (U.S.)
melody above harmony

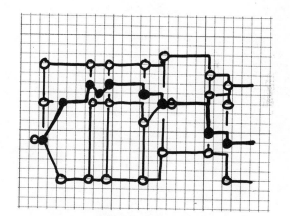

"Amazing Grace" by Isaac
Watts—in Sacred Harp hymn
singing melody is set
within harmony

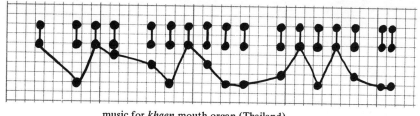

music for *khaen* mouth organ (Thailand)
melody on bottom

Revivalists rally and sing together, Oklahoma.

In many-voiced polyphonic settings the mass of melodic happenings in the texture might be so inter-related that it is impossible to pick out a single tune (or melodic fragment) and say, *This* is the melody.

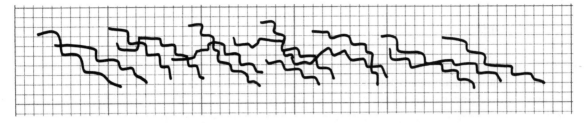

polyphonic choral texture (Ituri forest pygmies)

In Europe and the Americas harmony functions as such a strong musical element that melodies stripped of their harmonic backdrop seem absurd (at worst) or embarrassingly naked (at best). Some melodies, like that of "That's What I Like about the South" as sung by Tommy Duncan of the Texas Playboys, are really nothing more than one- or two- or three-note tunes which draw their vitality from the chords changing and moving behind them. The "talking blues" and square-dance calls (also of the southwestern United States) function in a similar fashion. Euro-American melodies (classical and popular) even on those rare occasions when they happen alone—the solo unaccompanied violin and cello sonatas of J. S. Bach are excellent examples—tend to move in verticalized outlines of (horizontal) chords, and, more subtly, to *imply* invisible inaural harmonies.

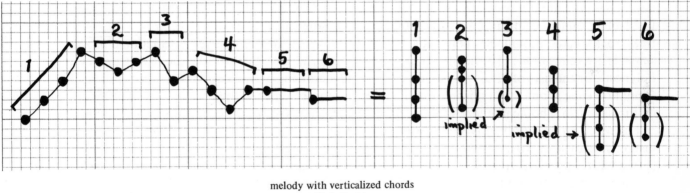

melody with verticalized chords
(J. S. Bach)

In fact, the ears of many Western musicians are so conditioned by a strongly ethnocentric harmonic response that they find "pure" melodies—such as those of the Arabic world—to be dizzying, illogical, and perhaps just a little bit terrifying.

The orchestral (or ensemble) setting may also influence the way a melody sounds. For example, many tunes originally performed in the 1960s rock vocal and guitar style of the Beatles have reap-peared in the lush strings of semisymphonic arrangements piped over the canned Muzak systems of supermarkets and department stores. The striking melodies and attention-demanding words have been transformed by their setting into hardly noticeable background music, as unobtrusive as wall-paper. In fact, melodies removed from their natural habitat often seem, like caged animals in a zoo, mere shadows of their original selves. It is hard to imagine the expansive vocal melodies of Java with-out their setting, floating among the ringing gong tones of the *gamelan* orchestra. Similarly, the po-etic melodies of the Japanese *sankyoku* ensemble seem immovably welded to the tone qualities and working-together of voice, *koto,* zither, *shamisen* lute, and *shakuhachi* flute. Melody, then, while we can isolate it in the laboratory conditions of our mind's eye, is actually so thoroughly interrelated with other musical and nonmusical elements that it can only be characterized and perceived (and loved) as part of the total spectrum of that thing we call music.

Words and Music

We have noticed how words, sometimes quite ordinary words, can take on (magically) deeper and (seemingly) profound meanings when sung. Melody tends to sanctify the profane, to extraordinize the ordinary, and to poetize the prosaic. Even a grocery list or names from a telephone book can seem to have grave, metaphorical, or humorous hidden meanings if chanted or sung, and the most banal thoughts and lyrics (particularly when connected with *affaires du coeur*) cause hearts to flutter, brows to furrow, tears to sparkle on eyelashes like early-morning dew on a forest flower, and innumerable pores on innumerable bodies to tingle electrically.

Songs, words and melodies, have been composed about almost everything man has ever been involved in, or felt, or thought about—although most societies at a given point in history follow styles of what is acceptable subject matter and what is not. For example, a traditional Hawaiian song entitled "The Green Parrot" affectionately describes the attributes of the penis of one of the popular old kings! Such sexually liberated lyrics, though quite common and ordinary on the islands of the Pacific, would horrify singers and listeners of other cultures where, musically at least, anything but the most veiled and metaphorical references to sex are taboo. In the United States love, and all the ramifications of the male-female relationship, is the preferred topic, but work songs—a common genre in many other parts of the world—are proportionately practically nonexistent; who has heard of songs sung at work by accountants, doctors, electricians, auto workers, or aerospace engineers? In the classical music of India almost all the words to classical songs are religious, and even love songs have religious and philosophical undertones; while in traditional Japanese music human love, sensitive feeling, and an acute awareness of nature—rain, seasons, mist, trees, flowers, birds, times of day, trees, rocks, lakes, mountains—permeates the poetry of songs. In many societies functional prosaic subjects are sung about: like the litigation songs of western Zaire, the histories and genealogies of Polynesia, or the lists of birds, rivers, mountains, and stars sung by west coast American Indians. Information sung about, in fact, is information more easily remembered, particularly in nonliterate cultures, and so schoolchildren sing about numbers, alphabets, geography, cultural heros, and modes of behavior. An extraordinarily sophisticated, psychologically therapeutic function is found in the insult songs of west Africa where in a strictly controlled contest opposing groups and individuals (often with suppressed grievances) sing verbal brickbats back and forth. Winners are judged not on vehemence alone, but on the cleverness and humor of their retorts!

No-meaning words and syllables are also found set to melodies in many parts of the world. In the Kentucky folk song "Springfield Mountain," as sung by country lawyer-musician Bascom Lamar Lunsford, meaningful verse lines (about a man bitten by a snake) alternate with a "nonsense" phrase:

> On a summer's day, a man did go
> Way down in the meadow for to mow.
> Come-a toodi darido, toodi daray
> Toodi darido ray.

The songs of the American Indians include so many no-meaning phrases or vocables (sometimes interspersed with "real" words and phrases) that we must count this as one of the most significant characteristics of the style. Here we must be particularly careful about labeling these nonwords as "nonsense syllables," because as vocal (musical) sounds and expressive carriers of the melody they are integral segments (with drums, rattles, notes, words, rhythms, and melodies) of the total picture of the music. A Navaho night chant (it should be read out loud) goes:

Story and songs for musical shadow puppet play in Telugu language, Andhra Pradesh, southern India.

Ohohoho hehehe heya heya
Ohohoho hehehe heya heya
Eo lado eo lado eo lado nase
Howani how owow owe
Eo lado eo lado eo lado nase
Howani how oeoe owe
Howani howani how heyeyeye yeyeyahi
Howowow heya heya heya heya
Howa hehehe heya heya heya
Ohohoho howe heya heya
Ohohoho hehehe heya heya
Habi niye habi niye
Ha'huizanaha sihiwanaha
Ha'haya eaheoo eaheoo
Sihiwanaha ha'huizanaha
Ha'haya eaheoo eaheoo eaheoo eaheoo eaheoo eaheoo

Many societies differ in their classifications of their own songs (and song texts) and we can give only a partial listing here, drawn from sources all over the world. Formerly, for example, Hawaiians classified their *meles,* or songs, into many categories, such as *mele kaua* (war songs), *koihonua* (celebrating the genealogies of chiefs), *ku'o* ("singing" *meles* with protracted musical sounds), *olioli* (songs on joyful subjects), *kanikau* (elegies), *paeaea* (a class of "low" *meles*), *ipos* (love songs), and *inoas* (composed at the birth of a chief and recited at his funeral). *Meles* were further classified according to the complexity of their structure and the highness or lowness of their sentiments.

We might superimpose on this list three broad (and overlapping) categories: songs of power (religious, magical, curative), songs of amusement (social, entertainment), and songs of function (accompanying work, teaching, remembering).

A Partial Listing of Song Types

narrative	learning	no-meaning words
ballad	agriculture	lists
epic	work	history
love	political	genealogy
ceremonial	mythology	event
religious		

classical poetry	exotic	vision	magic
dance	insult	torture	game
humor	litigation	social	lullaby
accumulative	contest	criticism	war
entertainment	dream	curative	secret

Of course such a list is theoretically endless, as are the ways of classification: some societies categorize by the words, others by song origins, others by purpose, and still others by style or by a mixture of diverse elements (such as the number of people in an ensemble, or the social class or caste of the musicians singing the songs!).

We are particularly interested in words and language for their influence on the shaping of melody: through stress patterns, intonation, and poetic structure. Where words are particularly important, where they must be clearly understood—such as in epic narratives, histories, European operatic recitatives, spells, or ritual (but not always)—melodies tend to be simple and subordinate to the no-longer-spoken texts. In the *haka* music for dances of the Maori people of New Zealand the melodies follow a pattern that can only be called heightened speech, similar in some ways to the half-sung, half-spoken *sprechstimme* of twentieth-century music (notably in the opera *Wozzeck* by Alban Berg). The ancient chanted liturgical hymns of the *Rig Veda* (India) follow in their three-note syllabic melodies and simple rhythms the natural accents of the Vedic language; while the later *Sama Veda* chants (also of India) follow word accents less closely and add melismatic touches.

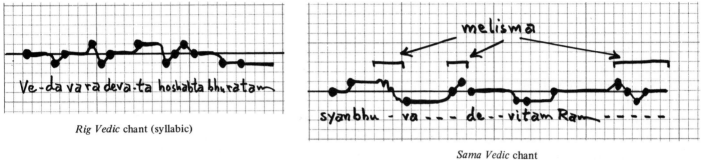

Rig Vedic chant (syllabic)

Sama Vedic chant
(with melismatic touches)

Words and melodies seem always to have been in conflict with each other. Words, if they are to be fully understood, tangle melodic expansion and development; melodies, fully developed, break up words and make them unintelligible. It is as if man were faced with an eternal conflict within himself: on one hand the conservative need to preserve the old (the sacred word) and to communicate in the specifics of language, and on the other the opposing expressive necessity, a creative urge to burst out in the mystical language of song.

Syllabic melodies, with their one-to-one music-to-word ratios, tend to be more word-oriented, while florid *melismatic* melodies, which stretch single words or syllables over (or rather, under) a many-note ornamentation, tend to explore the melodic impulse. A happy balance and a solution to this problem is found in many world musics by ingenious combinations of the two. For instance, Balkan epic tale singers start out their verses with the clarity of the syllabic style; but at the end of certain phrases and key words or ideas (and within strict poetic meter) break into ornate melisma.

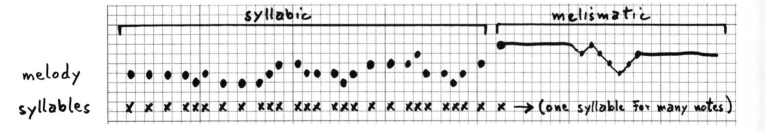

A similar use of occasional melisma within a framework of speech-oriented song is found in the singing of soloists in Japanese *noh* theater. The *mohlan* "courts of love" singers in Laos (with *khaen* mouth organ accompaniment) sing wordy, seemingly endless, nonstop melodies which suddenly break into melisma at cadential points and before interludes. In this case the melismatic phrases function as signals in the structure of the songs.

A richer use of melisma characterizes the melody-making of much of the Arabic and Islamic world, of Mongolia, and of India. Curiously, where the music is predominantly syllabic (as in our earlier examples) the text or poetry underlying the melody must be considerable, and it is run through at considerable speed. But in melismatic melody a few lines of poetry will do, and an hour's performance or more may be based on only a few verses of text. The great national epics with their rich lore of heroic tales combining history and mythology with ethnic and regional pride—found from the Balkans to Mongolia, in India and Indonesia, and formerly throughout northern Europe—are (and were) sung in performances lasting from several hours to all night, and sometimes in cycles extending for a week or more of nightly performances. Here the words, the embroidery of the poetry, the imaginative spinning of the story by the epic singer, dominate. The melodies function purely as a vehicle; by necessity they must be kept simple, out of the way. Yet it is the melodic element that adds to the epic proportions: the larger-than-life heroic grandiosity, the great battles, are somehow magnified, given weight and solemnity by the fact that they are sung and (when compared to other tunes in the musical culture) by the extraordinary nature of their melodies.

The influence of language—its structure, patterns, stresses, and rhythms—on melody is undoubtedly of great importance. Unfortunately extensive study has not yet been made of this subject, and we must depend largely upon hunches and somewhat random and instinctive observations. A noted ethnomusicologist, Bruno Nettl, has compared the rhythmic structure of German and Czech folk songs and found distinctive parallels with their respective languages. For instance, German songs often have an unaccented pickup (or upbeat) while Czech songs do only rarely. In addition, the German melodies flow along smoothly in performance, while the Czech tunes are more frequently chopped with sudden accents. These characteristics parallel the spoken language: in spoken German there is a flow and variety of relatively gentle accents which can come on any syllable of a word, and unstressed articles separate the "heavier" nouns. But in spoken Czech an accent comes automatically on the first syllable of every word, and speakers tend to accent their stressed syllables heavily. In addition there are no articles (like "a" and "the" in English) to precede the initial accents of the nouns.

A similar parallel can be seen in the differences in spoken English between black southern (and ghetto) Americans and the white (northern) mainstream. White persons tend to speak rather quickly, in a relatively flat voice, within a consistently thin tonal band with no sharp ups or downs or sudden changes in volume, and in a word rhythm that is proselike and without strong accents. Clipped precision and clarity of pronunciation, particularly of beginning and ending consonants, are highly valued. Black spoken English, on the other hand, is full of poetical, almost musical, rhythm. There is great emphasis on vowel sounds, and consonants are often blurred in the sharp rises and falls of speech tones, sudden changes in volume (which sound "noisy" to whites), and strongly contrasting accented and unaccented syllables, which can be belted out, lingered on lovingly, or "swallowed" to the point of inaudibility. In music the flexibility and variety of this approach to spoken language is utilized 101 percent in black (and black-influenced) songs with words; but the influence is also carried over into instrumental melody (such as jazz) where saxophones, trumpets, clarinets, and trombones echo the multifaceted sounds of the human voice. By contrast, white popular and classical music (its melody and delivery) tends to be restrained, unraucous, and proper, with milder accents, less use of the full potential of the human voice (from shouts to rasping whispers), and a strong emphasis on rhythmical and structural simplicity and precision.

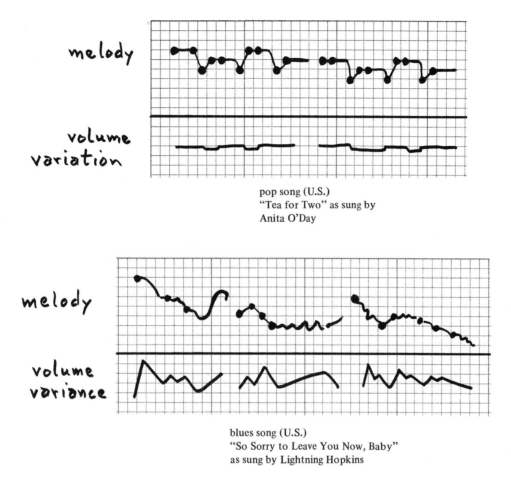

melody

volume
variation

pop song (U.S.)
"Tea for Two" as sung by
Anita O'Day

melody

volume
variance

blues song (U.S.)
"So Sorry to Leave You Now, Baby"
as sung by Lightning Hopkins

Certain languages, those with a lot of vowel sounds (especially *a's* and *o's*), have a reputation for being particularly "musical" languages, that is, the sounds of the words seem to harmonize with the mechanics of singing. Italian is one such language; Sanskrit (the classical language of India) is another. In fact, in Sanskrit, and in many other Indian languages, the vowel *a* is so common that it usually is not written: it is simply assumed that *a* follows every consonant unless special signs for the other vowels indicate otherwise. Thus *malawala-kalajala* would be written (in the native alphabet, of course) as *mlwl-kljl*!

But, in truth, mankind has managed to put languages into song no matter what their sound quality or grammatical makeup. There is really no such thing as an unmusical language. Human beings, too, prefer to sing in more or less the same language in which they speak or write—excluding the naturally conservative ritual and mystical connotations of liturgical music (which tends to use archaic languages)—although sometimes songs too (like many of the ballads of Appalachia) can preserve to a remarkable degree older speech patterns and vocabulary.

One of the most fascinating aspects of speech and melody deals with the relationship between sung words and the tonal languages found, for example, in China, southeast Asia, and Africa. In tonal languages the relative pitch (the highness or lowness) at which a syllable is spoken can determine its meaning. In Jabo, a language spoken in Liberia, for example, there are four different pitch tones; a word like *ba* can thus have four different meanings depending upon the pitch at which it is spoken: *ba(1)* means "namesake," *ba(2)* means "to be broad," *ba(3)* means "tail," and *ba(4)* is a particle that expresses a command. Presumably when such a word is set to a melody, its intended meaning will influence its pitch placement in relation to the other notes (and words) in a melody.

Obviously some accommodation is necessary, because a dogmatic adherence to the "rules" of tonal language would make melody writing a nightmarishly complicated process. Each musical culture must solve the problem in a different way. In Nigeria, the Ibo, for instance, use two tones in their speech: a high and a low. A random sampling of their songs has shown that sometimes the highs and lows of melody and speech tones coincide, sometimes the melody tones remain the same while the speech tones change, but almost never does the movement of the melody move in opposition to the normal tendencies of the speech tones.

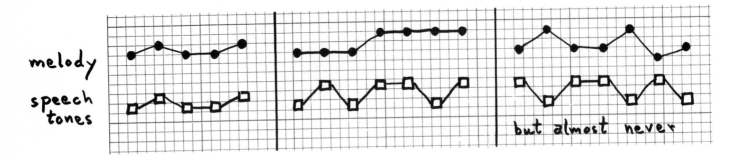

Perhaps another important factor is that the meaning of the words—if there is some doubt about their setting in the tonal fluctuations of melody—is usually made clear by their context, in the poetry, verbal images, and ideas of the songs.

An offshoot of the tonal character of African languages has been the startlingly effective use of the west African "talking drums"—slit logs or drums tuned to two pitches, a high and a low—which can convey sayings, parables, or even stories to listeners familiar with the repertoire of patterns. They can also be used to transmit messages over great distances, functioning like a utilitarian non-electric musical telegraph!

Melodies and tones, particularly in European/American classical music and in China and Japan, can also attempt to paint a musical picture of phrases or ideas of their lyrics. Bell-like tones and tolling patterns echo references to bells, fast-flitting melodies describe the flight or songs of birds, rising notes parallel descriptions of the rising sun, falling passages or deep, dismal low notes picture death. In Western music the cantatas of J. S. Bach or the songs of Charles Ives are full of such melodic (and musical) tone painting.

Perhaps at the opposite extreme of the spectrum is the often ignored possibility that melody and words can have little or no relationship whatsoever. In many of the great European choral works of the Middle Ages (and continuing through the eighteenth-century baroque era) melodies are strung out almost like abstractions, with a full life of their own, the words either moving on an independent track or spaced almost at random in the melodic texture, like pebbles thrown into a stream. In many of the classical songs of south India the words of the poetry are broken up syllable by syllable and are similarly stretched across the ornamented, exquisite musical phrases with little concern for the spoken accents or rhythm of language. This approach to setting words to melody is, of course, entirely legitimate, and quite often the interplay between words and melody (the accents and phrasing of each) makes for a music much more interesting than if the relationship were on a one-to-one basis.

Language, then, can and does affect the way a people will create their melodies. When words are set to music this influence naturally tends to be stronger, but exactly what the relationship will be, how words and notes are balanced, varies from culture to culture (and even within a culture). A curious aspect of melodies, and a sign of the compulsive power of words, can be seen in what I call the *word shadow.* Most of the melodies of the world, the set, composed melodies anyway, have words; but they may also be performed as purely instrumental numbers, as abstract tunes. Now when a melody with words is performed without the words (on an instrument or hummed, for example) it still retains an afterimage of the words! The evocative lyrics of a pop love song remain in the background, for instance, even when the love song is performed on the clarinet or violin. These connections, the word shadows, exist not in the abstract collection of notes that make up the melody, of course, but in the minds of the listeners and musicians (who are familiar with both lyrics and melody). But as such they must be considered as a real factor in the total makeup of the melody that cannot be ignored.

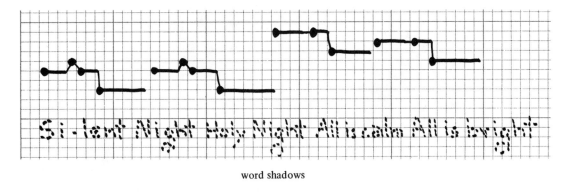

word shadows

On a less basic (and perhaps more artificial) level are the forms and structures of poetry found in the many languages of the world. In Europe poetry tends to move in the regular rhythms of "poetic meter," with various rhyme schemes occurring at the ends of lines (often on the last syllable). Stanzas of two or more lines form units whose internal structure is repeated, boxlike, while the ideas or narrative of the poem move along progressively.

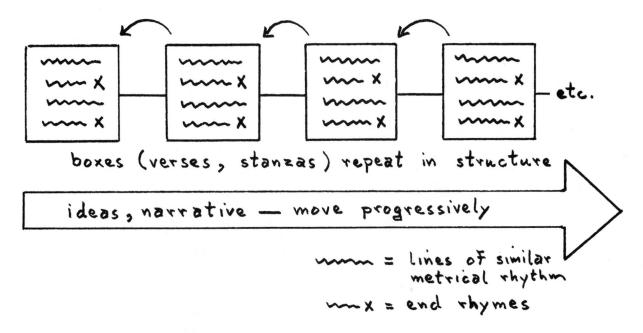

Usually in European music, but especially in folk song, the structure of the words (the poem) and the structure of the melody coincide: verses and stanzas fit glovelike with the beginnings, middles, and endings of phrases of the melody. The emphasis on end rhymes is reflected in the attention given in Europe to musical phrase endings and cadences. Poetic meter often filters into the regular rhythmic patterns of the melody. Even if the music (and the melody) moves progressively and changes (like the narrative of the words), its underlying structure tends to fall into the boxlike strophic patterns of the poetry.

Strophic song structure is also common in Africa, which (as we have seen) shares so many similarities with musical Europe that some scholars consider both to be one huge musical cultural area.

Shona musician accompanying himself on the type of *mbira* called *njari*, which is nestled inside its gourd resonator suspended from a chain around his neck. Simon Mashoko Gwenyambira, Rhodesia.

In eastern Europe, and in many other places throughout the world, poetry is structured not by the recurring rhythms of accented syllables but by a count of the total number of syllables per line. End rhymes are often not a factor, especially in many of the poetic language forms of the Orient—Sanskrit, for example, where internal rhyme, alliteration, puns, or double meanings may be more highly prized. In the classical music of south India song texts are actually structured in prose phrases and sentences. Here melodies follow much less dogmatically than in Europe the form of their words. In the Greek heroic *klephtic* songs both poetry and melody fall into strophic patterns, but (unlike the dominant trend in Europe) they do not coincide. Many of the classical melodies of China do not coincide in structure with their words. In Japan poetry commonly falls into seven- and five-syllable lines, which in the music of *noh* theater are set in an eight-beat framework. Japanese music and poetry both follow the general aesthetic structural principle of *jo* (introduction), *ha* (scattering), and *kyu* (rushing to the end).

We must remember that throughout the earth poetry and song have been interrelated, if not identical. All the "poetry" of the American Indian, for example, until very recently was actually the texts of songs and ritual. And it is extremely likely that great epics like the Greek *Iliad* and *Odyssey,* the Finnish *Kalevala,* or the Indian *Mahabharata* and *Ramayana* were originally not told but sung. Poetry without music is, in fact, unknown, inconceivable, in many parts of the world. There is, too, that nether region that exists somewhere between melody and speech, a part of each, perhaps, but belonging purely, in actuality, to neither: the singing of tales and epics, the speechlike chanting of ritual or spell formulas, or the virtuosic, almost melodic dramatic renderings of poets like the Russian Andrei Andreevich Voznesenski (b. 1933) or the American Allen Ginsberg. Classification in the face of such expressive force seems rhetorical and perhaps ultimately unnecessary.

Coda

We have explored the idea of melody from many different angles, with something of the restless wanderings described for legendary folk heroes on seemingly impossible quests. Melody, we have found, no matter where it exists on this old earth in the hearts and throats and instruments of man, has an inner logic, a sense and structure to its workings. But at the same time we must recognize the limitations of our search: we can analyze the anatomy of melody, we can circle around it, but we cannot touch its expressive essence. Our position is similar to that of a doctor or scientist who can describe in great detail the bones and joints and muscles and organs of the human body and their functions but who is at a loss to explain a single human personality. Melody, in its many varied and sometimes contradictory expressive manifestations throughout the earth, centers around an intangible, almost mystical core. As we stated at the beginning of this section, ultimately it must elude us. Our minds, our understanding, can lead us up to a point, in the right direction, toward appreciation perhaps—but beyond this we must feel.

Bartok, Bela, and Lord, Albert B. *Serbo-Croatian Folk Songs.* Number 7 in the Columbia University Studies in Musicology. New York: Columbia University Press, 1951.

Bebey, Francis. *African Music: A People's Art.* Translated by Josephine Bennett. New York: Lawrence Hill and Company, 1975.

Berry, Wallace. *Form in Music.* Englewood Cliffs, New Jersey: Prentice-Hall, 1966.

Heilbut, Tony. *The Gospel Sound: Good News and Bad Times.* New York: Simon and Schuster, 1971.

Hodier, André. *Jazz, Its Evolution and Essence.* New York: Grove Press, 1956.

Hood, Mantle, and Susilo, Hardja. *Music of the Venerable Dark Cloud.* Los Angeles: Institute of Ethnomusicology, UCLA, 1967.

Isaac, L. *Theory of Indian Music.* Madras: Shyam Printers, 1967.

Jones, A. M. *Studies in African Music.* London: Oxford University Press, 1959.

Kishibe, Shigeo. *The Traditional Music of Japan.* Tokyo: Kokusai Bunka Shinkokai, 1969.

Kunst, J. *Music in Java,* 3rd ed. Edited by E. L. Heins. The Hague: Martinus Nijhoff, 1973.

Malm, William P. *Japanese Music and Musical Instruments.* Rutland, Vermont: Charles E. Tuttle, 1959.

Malm, William P. *Music Cultures of the Pacific, the Near East, and Asia.* Englewood Cliffs, New Jersey: Prentice-Hall, 1967.

McAllester, David P. *Music of the Native North Americans.* Unpublished manuscript.

Morton, David. *The Traditional Music of Thailand.* Los Angeles: Institute of Ethnomusicology, UCLA, 1968.

Nettl, Bruno. *Folk and Traditional Music of the Western Continents.* Englewood Cliffs, New Jersey: Prentice-Hall, 1965.

Nketia, J. H. Kwabena. *The Music of Africa.* New York: W. W. Norton, 1974.

Roberts, Helen H. *Ancient Hawaiian Music.* New York: Dover Publications, 1967.

Rufer, Josef. *Composition with Twelve Notes.* Translated by Humphrey Searle. New York: Macmillan, 1954.

Sachs, Curt. *The Rise of Music in the Ancient World East and West.* New York: W. W. Norton, 1943.

Sachs, Curt. *The Wellsprings of Music.* New York: McGraw-Hill Book Company, 1965.

Sambamoorthy, P. *South Indian Music,* 7 vols. Madras: The Indian Music Publishing House, n.d.

Samuelson, Ralph. Conversations, 1974–75.

Southern, Eileen. *The Music of Black Americans.* New York: W. W. Norton, 1971.

Touma, Habib H. Commentary to phonograph recording: *The Music of Azerbaijan.* Kassel: Barenreiter-Musicaphon, n.d. Volume 24 in UNESCO Collection, *A Musical Anthology of the Orient.*

Tschopik, Harry. Notes to *Music from Mato Grosso Brazil.* New York: Folkways Records and Service Corp., 1955. (This is a recording with extensive notes: Ethnic Folkways Library FE 4446.)

Van Gulik, R. H. *The Lore of the Chinese Lute.* Rutland, Vermont: Charles E. Tuttle, 1968.

Wellesz, Egon, ed. *The New Oxford History of Music. I. Ancient and Oriental Music.* London: Oxford University Press, 1969.

Zonis, Ella. *Classical Persian Music.* Cambridge, Mass.: Harvard University Press, 1973.

Many areas of the Far East are characterized by love of the timbre of gongs. *Kempul*/gongs played by Javanese artist Sumarsam. Other hanging gongs are large *gong ageng* and *si jem*.

7

TIMBRE
AND TIMBER

"Every sound is a Buddha." Cho Chae-son, an extraordinary Korean musician on the *taekeum* flute who was studying piano in the United States, was sitting with me over coffee and attempting to verbalize the musical differences between the East and the West. He pulled out a napkin and drew a series of lines—each with its own shape of curves, bends, and squiggles—matched with cursive phrases like "clear," "wide vibrato," or "end falls into silence." "This list of ways of playing one note is incomplete because at some time in our lifetime we must get up and leave this coffeehouse," he said and laughed. "When I told you that each sound is a Buddha, what I meant was that there is an infinity in each sound, and an infinite number of ways of playing it. If you meditate on it and concentrate, you can touch it." Later he wrote about how he had suggested to his pupils that they practice by putting down their instruments and going outside to "notice how one tree has a different shape from another, and to hear how the wind blows."

In China, too, in the special philosophy surrounding the music of the *ch'in,* each separate note is thought of as complete in itself, a tiny universe. A special mood or atmosphere evoking a reaction in the lettered musician-scholar or listener can be created by subtle nuances, by the many ways of "coloring" a single note. For example, the same note will sound slightly different played on different strings, with the index finger instead of the middle finger, or with any of the twenty-six varieties of vibrato. Music becomes, then, in a sense, a series of "Buddhas," of sound objects in space and time.

Traditional Chinese musical theorists furthermore characterize each of the five notes of the scale with a complex of colors, elements, planets, and directions. Each basic note, before it is even played, then has (at least in theory) its own unique personality:

Note:	*kung*	*shang*	*chiao*	*chih*	*yü*
Direction:	north	east	center	west	south
Planet:	Mercury	Jupiter	Saturn	Venus	Mars
Element:	wood	water	earth	metal	fire
Color:	black	violet	yellow	white	red

252

Timbre is often described metaphorically as visual or tactile textures.

The kaleidoscope of sounds, put together to make music, is more than a mere abstraction of pitches and durations. Music is—like light and dark, sunsets and green forests and azure skies—an ever changing, mind-blowing collection of subtle or brazen "colors" and a constant and ready delight for the ears. The *sound* of sound, that is, the difference between the same note played on the Japanese *koto,* the Cambodian *khaen,* the Bulgarian *gusle,* the English concertina, or a German harmonica, or sung in a rasping, gravel-like, or bell-like voice, is called *timbre.* This quality of sound, although it can easily be heard by (almost) everyone, becomes singularly mysterious and elusive when we attempt to describe it in words. It is no wonder, then, that some of the most poetic and imaginative writing by the world's master musicians, theorists, and musicians-philosophers has centered around timbre. They have described it with a variety of metaphors: nasal, rough, harsh, satin- or silklike, buzzing, sandpapery, dewlike, transcendent, transparent, clear, muffled, mysterious, triumphant, oceanlike, smooth, birdlike, nightlike, rich, pure, vocal, chocolate, sugary, sweet, natural, moonlike, brilliant, emaciated, ebony, oaken, spiderweblike, brittle, steely, liquid, resounding, thin, buttery, dark, earthy, and so on. The timbre of the jew's-harp, we have seen, is considered to be "sexy" in places as diverse as Assam and Austria. The most common metaphor, however, one that is found in many places of the world, is color. In Persia the strings of the *setār* lute are named in colors: white, yellow, and black. In the English language a common synonym for timbre, in fact, is tone color; and in German the word is *Klangfarbe* (literally, "sound-color").

Nineteenth-century European classical composers and musicians were fascinated by the connections between music and color: the symphony orchestra, sometimes augmented with choruses and small groups of instruments offstage or in balconies, was looked upon as a gigantic musical palette with the various instruments functioning like blobs of paint that could be mixed in a seemingly endless variety of ways. Orchestration was (and still is) like painting a picture, using instruments and combinations of instruments instead of colors. Nicolai Rimsky-Korsakov (1844–1908) and Alexander Scriabin (1872–1915) even went so far as to make up lists of colors evoked by various major and minor keys, and the latter incorporated color projections into actual musical performance. In the twentieth century Arnold Schoenberg developed what he called the concept of *Klangfarbenmelodie* through which melodies were created by a succession of different tone colors (rather than through a succession of different pitches and rhythms). Later Anton Webern brilliantly used this concept—series of timbres something like carefully placed patterns of beads on a string—as one of the many cryptic (and overlapping) structural elements in his compositions. In the post–World War II era composers have worked with "constellations," islands of musical activity, or "sound objects," in which timbre is an important element, which float or "happen" in a space/time continuum.

But the color-music connection in Europe is really quite an old and established one. Patricia Cristol has noted that Wagenseil in his 1617 book on the Meistersingers talks about their knowing certain stereotyped melodies as the "Evening Red Tune," the "Blue Corn Flower Tune," the "Black Amber Tune," the "Yellow Lion Skin Tune," and so on. Mozart, Bach, and Monteverdi were masters of the expressive use of timbre, even if they did not verbalize and expound their craft and knowledge as later composers did. And artists have built instruments that played not musical notes but colors, or, in some cases, both! Louis Bertand Castel (1688–1757) invented a *Clavecin Oculaire* ("harpsichord for the eyes") which had an arrangement of colored tapes, one for each finger key, through which light passed; Erasmus Darwin suggested in 1789 that the newly invented Argand oil lamps could be used to send strong light beams through "colored glasses" onto "movable blinds" communicating with the keys of a harpsichord, thus producing "visible music." A. Wallace Rimington (1854–1918) and Thomas Wilfrid (1889–1968) built color organs which could be played on a keyboard or operated automatically. And more recently, Walt Disney (in his film *Fantasia*) and other cinematographic artists have reflected music through visual images on the movie screen. The burst of total experience, multimedia, psychedelic light show/acid rock concerts in the United States in the 1960s was another manifestation of the mystical wedding of light, color, energy, and sound.

In India, according to traditional theory, each of the seven notes of the scale has its own presiding deity (*svaranam devata*) and interpretive seer, sage, or expounder (*rishi*). In addition, each note is connected with the timbre of the call of a certain animal, as well as with a particular mood, or "flavor" (*rasa*):

	1	2	3	4	5	6	7
Note:	*sa*	*ri*	*ga*	*ma*	*pa*	*da*	*ni*
Timbre:	cry of peacock at highest rapture	cow calling her calf	bleat of goat	cry of heron and tonic of Nature (falling water, roar of the forest)	call of night-ingale	neigh of horse	trumpeting of elephant
Mood:	heroism, wonder, resent-ment	sorrow		humor, love		disgust, terror	sorrow

At first glance, these designations seem somewhat fanciful, since in actual musical practice only the first and fifth (*sa* and *pa*) are constant; the other notes fluctuate in pitch and with expressive ornamentation according to the *raga*. But in these concepts there may be an underlying thread of truth that cuts deeper than a strictly scientific rationale, that hints at a basic relationship of the notes with the drone background (*sa* and *pa*) and with each other, and that touches at the heart of the Indian musician's intuitive feeling toward music and sound.

The word *raga* derives from the Sanskrit root *ranja*, "to color, to tinge." And we have seen that while a *raga* is a technical complex of scale, characteristic musical phrases and gestures, ornaments, emphasized notes, deemphasized notes, and so on, it is also—and perhaps more importantly—a musical personality that expresses emotion(s) and mood(s). A fifth-century scholar, Matanga, stated that *raga* "has the effect of *coloring* the hearts of men." Fifteen centuries later the great sitarist Ravi Shankar (b. 1920) has written, "*Raga* is that which *colors* the mind."

Although a *raga* is a musical phenomenon, the great emphasis on its purely expressive values has given birth to the tradition in India describing *ragas* in poetry and, more amazing, to visualize them in images and colors in a painting. For example, in the *Raga-Sagara* the *raga Bhairava* is described as follows: ". . . The sea of notes and microtones, with the nectar of all varieties of rhythms and time measures, the fulfillment of the worship of Siva, with his body always besmeared with ashes, his hair in matted locks, with the shining crescent of the new moon on his head, with [a necklace of] skulls as decorations, I adore Bhairava, the skillful dancer." The allusion to the (musical) sea and nectar may just be a powerful image, or it may refer to the primordial ocean which eons ago, according to Indian mythology, the gods churned in creative energy to produce (among other things) the nectar of eternal life. The great god Siva is described according to traditional iconography in this form as Maha-yogi, the great ascetic, and his dance is nothing less than the dance of the destruction and creation of the world! Altogether the image implies a deep, serious, and powerful *raga*, connected with one of the greatest of gods and with the forces that underlie the universe.

By contrast, the great poet Deo-Kavi (1730–1802?), in a series of poems describing *ragas* called the *Rag-ratnakar*, has pictured *Lalita raga* as a beautiful woman:

> . . . Lalita is of a delicate frame of golden complexion,
>   She wears ornaments and robes made of gold;
> Coming out of her chamber in a spring morning,
>   She waits, her mind full of the expectation of her lover.
>
> Dressed in yellow, she carries a garland of fresh campaka flower,
>   Mingled with blossoms of Asoka and mango;
> She has decked her complexion of gold with ornaments of gold;
>   Her voice is mistaken for the song of the cuckoo in spring mornings.

Painting illustrating Raga Bhairava, Malwa school, ca. 1680, northern India.

The moon leaving the celestial abode (and becoming her face)
　　Has secured the rare fragrance of her sweet and juicy lips.
Lalita is seeking union with her beloved
　　[or: the melody seeks out the notes *da, ni, sa, ga,* and *ma*—a pun or play on
　　words]
　　And coming out of her palace is looking for him.

The rich interplay of color (particularly gold) and images (a beautiful woman, the moon, blossoms, spring, the cuckoo) conveys an expressive whole that could easily be painted and perhaps also, in the sensitive mind of a musician, be transferred into the sounds of the *sitār, sarod, sarangi,* or voice.

Our interpretation of timbre, or tone color, has so far been quite a broad one. On one level, timbre is the coloring of a single sound or note; on another, it is the sound of a particular instrument (say, the clarinet, oboe, or violin) or a vocal style, which actually is a collection of many different timbral possibilities combining somehow into a larger (yet recognizable) identity, much as a unique individual has many facets to his or her personality. Timbre may also refer to the sound of a group of instruments, an ensemble, or an orchestra; or to the voicing of a chord, or (as believed by Scriabin, Rimsky-Korsakov, and other romantic era composers) to *a* chord or to keys, particularly as they sound on the piano. Finally, timbre has been applied mystically (in China, India, and elsewhere) to the characteristic sound of each of the notes of the scale; and, going one step further, we have suggested that *ragas* (and perhaps also the *maqams* of the Persian, Turkish, and Arabic classical musical worlds) might also be thought of as having their own unique (heard, but descriptively intangible) tone colors.

What we hear as timbre actually comes from a variety of elements. First, each sound, each single tone (like a note sung with our voice or played on a flute), is really a conglomerate of many tones, related to the sequence of the overtone series described in the section on instruments (pages 68–70). The relative strength and complexity of these sounding overtones greatly influence the timbre that we hear. For instance, the sound of a high note on the flute or penny whistle, which we might describe as being "icy, pure, clear," is very strong on the fundamental with the higher overtones sounding very weakly; while a low note on the cello, oboe or *zurnā,* clarinet, or Indian *tamburā* has a richer mix of higher overtones, resulting in a timbre that we might characterize as "rich, velvety, or soft." Once, many years ago, I asked a group of my students who were young children to write the colors that popped into their minds when they heard various instruments. Overwhelmingly, they wrote "blue" or "white" for the sound of a flute, and "purple" or "red" for the sound of an oboe! While the timbral mix of overtones on a flute or an oboe is relatively simple, that of bells and gongs is extraordinarily complex, a mishmash of interlocking and overlapping sonic series that clash or melt into each other in a beautifully resounding way. We should remember, also, that each different note on an instrument has a slightly different timbre, and that musicians can vary considerably the tone color of the same pitch by varying their methods of blowing, fingering, hitting, plucking, or whatever. The beauty of music played on an instrument or sung by the voice is in part carried by the nonstop minute variation and fluctuation of timbre. One of the problems of electronic music, by contrast, is the *sameness* of tones generated by electronic means even when pitches and rhythms change.

A second element in the making of timbre is the shape that each note takes as it is sounded. This shape is called the *envelope* and is usually divided into three parts: a beginning (or *attack*), a middle (or *constant state*), and an end (or *decay*). Almost everyone has at one time or another participated in the fun of playing a tape backwards on a tape machine: the notes of a piano, for instance, begin inaudibly and then increase in a quick crescendo (like a thousand-mile-an-hour jet plane approaching from a distance) only to be snipped off suddenly. What we hear is the envelope of a piano sound, but in reverse.

Almost all plucked and struck instruments (like the piano, the African *malimbe* xylophone, the Japanese *shamisen,* or the Persian *santūr* hammer dulcimer) have a sharp attack followed by an almost immediate decay. In instruments with a "brittle" sound (the wood blocks, for example) the decay may be almost immediate or very quick, while on others (like the *santūr* or piano) the decay is gradual, the sound taking many seconds to die away.

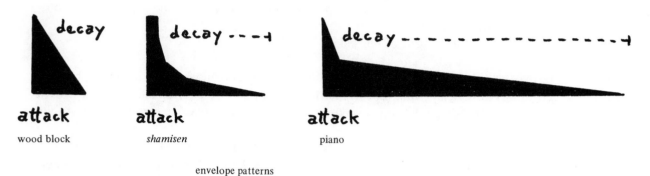

envelope patterns

Bowed and wind instruments (whether the Bulgarian *gusle,* the Chinese *erh hu,* the Tibetan *rgya-glin* trumpet, the pipe organ, or the Cambodian *khaen*) have a much softer attack, followed by a more or less constant steady state, and a decay that can be controlled by the performer (when he stops blowing or bowing, or goes on to the next note).

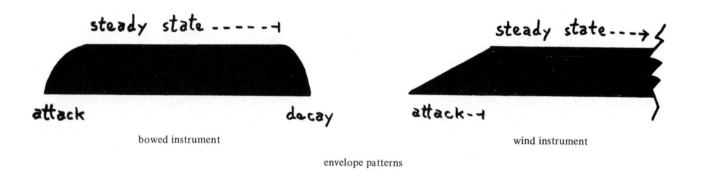

envelope patterns

Of course, the envelope of a note played on an instrument can be altered to a great extent by the technique of the performer as well as by the music he plays—a trumpeter can tongue a sharper attack, for example, or a pianist can play staccato or "with the pedal down"—but still a basic identity remains.

Gongs and cymbals (the latter especially when played with a roll) have unusual envelope characteristics. After an initial bump, the sound decreases but then builds up again, something like water building up behind a dam, only to peak again and then, finally, decay.

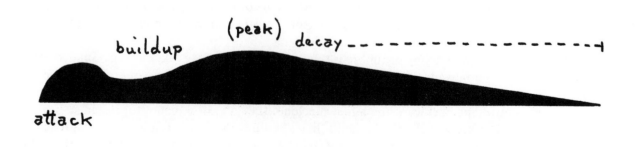

envelope of gong sound

The envelope shape is a lot more important in defining tone color than most of us, musicians and nonmusicians alike, realize. Several years ago as an experiment, acoustical engineers recorded individual tones played on most of the common Western classical musical instruments. They then chopped off (on the taped sound) the attacks and the characteristic decays, leaving only the center portion of each sound. They played the resulting sounds and asked a group of subjects to identify the instruments playing the sounds. Amazingly, the musical guinea pigs were almost totally stymied; they ended up making random guesses and confused the "timbre" of such diverse-sounding instruments as piano, bagpipe, voice, flute, trumpet, trombone, clarinet, banjo, and harp!

A third factor in the making of timbre is the resonating quality of the person or instrument making a tone: if one sings through the nose, or with a "head tone," he will produce quite a different tonal quality than if he were to sing (gutturally) from the back of the throat, or (fully) from the bottom of the chest. And in musical instruments, the construction, design, and materials used, as well as the way sound is produced upon them, greatly influence their tone color. Quite literally timber creates timbre. Suppose we were to construct a series of instruments—say, plucked lutes—that were exact duplicates of each other, down to 1/500 of an inch, down to the tiniest details, except that they were made of different materials: wood, glass, tin, steel, plastic, stone, brass, fiber glass, clay, porcelain, papier-mâché, iron, or bamboo. *Each* would have a different timbre. Even if our imaginary instruments were all made out of different types of wood—pine, ebony, teak, oak, redwood, cedar, birch, spruce—each wood would have a slightly different timbre; and, if the grain were cut to run different ways, or if tiny details varied, like the shape of the bridge, these, too, would influence the resulting sound. And there may be still other factors: in India, for example, it is said that the best *veenas* come from trees cut from groves near temples: as the trees grow over the years from tiny seedlings to saplings to mighty "oaks" (in actuality jackwood), their wood absorbs the beautiful ringing sounds of the temple's bells, and when they are carved into instruments they retain a particularly rich and melodious timbre.

Many of the world's musical instruments have special features which modify their tone quality and give them their own special sound. Africans love extra jangling and rattling effects: pebbles are put inside the body of drums where they can rattle around, and the *mbira,* whose beautiful melodies are played by the thumbs, often has little rings of metal attached to each key which give a kind of a jangling buzz to each tone. In Manipur in eastern India the *pena,* a one-stringed coconut-shell fiddle, is played with an arched bow covered with little bells that jingle as the music is played; and in Tamilnadu in southern India the *villadi vadyam,* a six- to eight-foot-long musical bow over a pot resonator which is hit with sticks to accompany song, is also strung with bells. The *yüeh ch'in* lute of Peking opera has a thin metal plate suspended inside its body to increase resonance and produce its timbre; and the northern Chinese form of the *san hsien* has a metal strip suspended inside its neck for a similar function. In the United States the Dobro, a slide guitar played in mountain and bluegrass music, has a metal resonator mounted in its guitar-shaped body, giving it an appropriately metallic/nasal timbre.

The lowly Euro-American kazoo, which changes the sound of the human singing voice to the timbre of a muted jazz trumpet or saxophone, makes use of a marvelous timbral device found also in Africa and the Far East: a thin membrane, glued over a small hole, vibrates with a nasal buzz when it is set in motion by air or sound. In Africa megaphones which function as voice disguisers are made from gourds or animal horns; the membrane used is spun by spiders to cover their eggs. The same type of membrane is used to cover tiny holes in the gourd resonators of xylophones. On the Korean *ti* flute a tiny hole just below the mouth hole is covered with thin rice paper to produce a "strong" buzzing timbre similar in some respects to a soprano saxophone. Other Oriental flutes use onionskin as a membrane. The *khlui* block flute of the *mahori* orchestras of Thailand also uses this principle.

Special playing techniques are important everywhere on earth to create timbral variety. For example, performers on the Korean *kaya kum* twelve-stringed zither often snap the strings to produce a percussive effect similar to the "slap bass" technique of American string bass playing in early jazz. Much of traditional Japanese classical music also makes use of percussive or "noise" elements—the snapping of strings, the sound of a heavy plectrum hitting the strings, or, on the *shakuhachi* bamboo

Thin paper membranes are pasted over a small hole in the gourd resonators of the xylophone to create a characteristic "buzzing" timbre. Nigeria.

flute, the sound of breath or the sudden subtle squeaks of overtones. This characteristic also carries over into the vocal traditions, particularly of *kabuki* and *noh* theater, with the use of sudden (almost percussive) spasmodic leaps to different registers and a guttural or rasping timbre (sometimes mislabeled "impure") in the lower range of the voice. (We use the word *noise* here in a strictly acoustical sense. It does *not* imply anything derogatory or unmusical, but is, on the contrary, an essential feature of the music and its timbre.) In Arabia different beats on the drum give tone colors, or sounds, that are thought of as muffled (*dum*), less muffled (*dim*), less clear (*tik*), and clear (*tak*). Similar mnemonics describe sounds in the classical and folk drumming traditions of India. And in northern Uganda, women make music in a marvelously varied vocal style in which (besides yodeling, ululating, and glissandoing) they use the incredible technique of tapping their throats with their fingertips while singing!

When it comes to tonal coloring, the human voice is the craziest and most flexible of all the world's instruments. In Cantonese opera a rather low, open-throated timbre is the norm, while in the Peking style singers prefer a high, nasal falsetto. In Peking opera the voice quality (and range) show the character of the part played by the actor/singer: for instance, heroes sing in what William P. Malm has described as a "throat-ripping rasp," while heroines (played by female impersonators, at least in the old days) have a "high, thin tone." The vocal style, as in Western operatic and classical music, is highly artificial, the result of deliberate training. In the Korean *japka* ballads the female singer covers an immense range of vocal timbre varying from what Malm has described as "intense and throaty" to a quality like the "scat singing" of jazz. "Steely-edged tone" may metamorphose into "violent vibrato," and sung nasal held notes into sudden slides or heightened speech. In such an intensely virtuosic style it is difficult to demarcate the dividing line between tonal coloring and melody (and perhaps other musical elements as well): everything is merged in a powerfully expressive *gestalt*.

In sub-Saharan Africa, among the many different ethnic groups and musical cultures and styles, almost everything that the human voice can do is done. Even within a single performance there may be a beautiful balance of different timbral qualities. Singers yodel, croon, sing through the teeth, whistle, growl, sing from the nose, head, chest, belly; they hum, cry, shout, sing with electric tension or in a quiet relaxed way; they make raucous tones, whispers, cries, or animal imitations. (All these terms are, we must stress, subjective and poetic; they are attempts to describe purely musical phenomena.) Africa is, after all, a singer's continent.

This great variety in vocal timbre and the constant expressive coloring of melody has carried over into the black music of the Americas, into the great forms synthesized by black musicians in the United States—the blues, spirituals, gospel, jazz, soul, rock—and thence into the popular music mainstream. An interesting contrast has been noted by Alan Lomax between the timbre and singing styles of white and black American southerners: black musicians tend to sing in a relaxed, open-throated manner in a comfortable range, broken by sudden "raucous, harsh," or swallowed or whispered tones; white folk musicians tend toward an extremely high tessitura, with a resulting "tense, restrained, nasal" timbre, with far less variety of sound and a generally "loud" intensity. Even today, professional Nashville or "country and western" singers are described as having a "nasal twang" in their voices. Curiously, when Yankee pop coffeehouse "folk" singers began to pick up on this tradition, they took the tunes, but they left the timbre back in the southern mountains. Somehow the grits and hog's eyes and blackstrap molasses of the southern style did not fit in with the dainty biscuits, the artificially quaint decor, and the intellectual conversation of the coffeehouse.

Among many of the musical styles of the American Indians, there is a great love for virtuosic singing. Perhaps the most spectacular of these traditions is that of the peoples of the Great Plains—the Flathead, the Cheyenne, the Sioux, the Arikara, the Ojibwa, the Crow, the Blackfoot, and others—where an open-throated (fortissimo) timbre in an extremely high tessitura (at least at the beginning of phrases) colors terse "tumbling" melodies ornamented by wide vibratos, glissandos, swoops and turns, glottal catches, rhythmic chest accents, and shouts. In the Southwest, the Pueblo Indians tend to prefer a deep, low pitch, at times almost a growl, together with great vocal control and choral precision. The Apache and Navaho peoples in their social and dance songs sing in a style characterized by David McAllester as "high, tense and nasal with subtle inflections" ornamenting the "bold" and (sometimes) "acrobatic" melodic line. In the Navaho religious song cycle of the *Yeibetchai*, or "Night Chant," hair-raisingly beautiful, shimmering cascades of falsetto singing break out from the norm of middle-range timbre and texture. Similarly, among the Apache the fantastically costumed masked dancers representing the Gan, or Mountain Spirits, emit shrill falsetto tremolos as they dance in their angular, lightninglike movements.

In general the people of the Eastern Woodlands prefer a quieter, more relaxed vocal timbre, a characteristic found (although the song style and forms are quite different) across the continent in the Great Basin and Pacific Northwest. In the twentieth century intertribal gatherings have resulted in an exchange of songs and musical styles. Religion, too, has been a factor: the messianic Ghost Dance religion which sprang up toward the end of the last century (until it was suppressed by the United States government) brought the relaxed singing style of the Great Basin (specifically, Nevada) to the Great Plains, and in recent years the Native American Church, with members from a wide variety of regions and tribal groups, with its all-night worship, ritual eating of the peyote button, prayer, visions, and singing, has nurtured its own musical style and a quieter, almost hymnlike singing voice.

★★★★★★★★★"TO BURN LIKE FIRE, TO FLOW LIKE WATER" ★★★★★★★★★★★★★

The geography of Tibet is one of the fiercest in the world. The Himalayas, land of eternal snows, their craggy peaks clothed in cyclonic winds or unearthly calm, seem to scrape the roof of the sky. Jagged valleys cut between cliffs and rocky slopes like gashes and broaden into mystical crystal lakes or dry wastelands. Even the plains seem to be just squeezed under the clouds. In this harsh landscape nature seems to do a wild dance: clear sunlight may suddenly be blotted out by dark, blue, boiling clouds carrying torrential rain, blizzards, or hailstones. Just as suddenly and inexplicably come landslides, flash floods, and sickness or drought. It is no wonder, then, that when the gentle message of Gautama Buddha was brought to Tibet from the eighth to the eleventh centuries, it took on a particularly terrifying cast, as if in reflection of the environment and the states of mind it nourished. The psychologically profound and esoteric practices of Tibetan Tantric Buddhism were colored by a kind of spiritual tension, a tightrope balance between fear and awe, with an undercurrent of the ominous, the dangerous, the magical. This substratum is accurately described in sacred texts, such as *The Book of the Dead,* or in the mind-numbing iconography, the visualizations of gods, demons, demigods, and the great saints in sacred paintings and religious sculpture (an iconography of terror, incidentally, characteristic also of Himalayan Hinduism): deities are often portrayed in their ferocious aspect, with fangs, flaming eyebrows, bloodshot eyes, streaming hair, with multi-arms and swollen bellies, and surrounded by skeletons, corpses, or dismembered limbs and heads of less fortunate beings. Or a great *bodhisattva* may be portrayed sitting in complete peace and nonattachment in the middle of such teeming demonic (visual and actual) activity.

The everyday world is but a sliver of a much greater, deeper, and more meaningful world, according to Tibetan Buddhist belief, and to touch, to explore, to experience this Unseen World, this Ultimate Reality, is the aim of all existence. The journey is a difficult one, it is awesome, and it can be (for the psychologically or spiritually unprepared) dangerous.

In the monasteries established in the mountains and valleys of this region, the monks developed a style of chanting, and a *sound* of chanting, that reflected this extranormal world, this Ultimate Reality. The chants, through their sound and method, seem to fragment existence, to move beyond concepts and words and against the normal currents of the mind to a "preverbal" source and essence, to a primordial utterance. On one level chanting is a path, a direct aid to spiritual enlightenment, to the transcendent; but on another, normal distinctions disappear: the singing monks, the sacred words, the sounds, and above all the timbre of their voices *becomes the Ultimate Experience itself!*

Tibetan *thangka*, late eighteenth century. Central figure: legendary jovial monk Ho Shang, who loves children; lower left: Virudhaka, Guardian of the South and King of Khumbanda; lower right: Dhrtarashstra, Guardian of the East and Ruler of the Ghandarvas, playing a lute.

Tibetan Buddhist monks of Thuten Choling monastery chanting during a religious ceremony. The bells are rung at various points in the chanting. Solu Khumbu district, Nepal.

The extraordinary nature of Tibetan chanting comes from a complex of interrelated forces, of ways of dealing with musical time and pitch, and of structure. But it is its extranormal sound and timbre that concern us here. First of all, the pitch level of the chanting is suprahumanly low, well below the voice range of the average male and at the rock-bottom notes of a *basso profundo,* that is around "low C"—two full octaves below middle C—and even "low B." But these low chanted notes were not the exclusive property of a few extraordinarily gifted individuals; in the old days, as many as eighty monks chanted resonantly together in this range. And at certain key moments in a ritual, occurring about every hour and a half or so, each monk splits the tone he is singing so that his voice alone produces a chord of two pitches! The lower bass note is the fundamental and the higher tone ringing clearly above it may be either the fifth harmonic—two octaves and a major third above the fundamental—or the sixth harmonic—two octaves and a fifth higher.

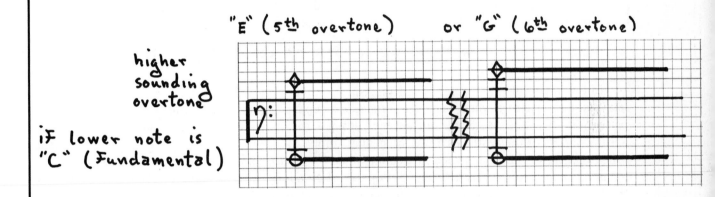

It is said that the chanting of the monks of the Gyuto monastery (who tend to sound the fifth harmonic) "burns like fire," while that of the monks of the Gyume monastery (who tend to sound the sixth harmonic) "flows like water."

Alternating with these chorded tones which span more than two octaves, the monks sweep up from the fundamental in gigantic skips to "normal" sung tones (lying in the "normal" middle range of the male voice)—an effect almost like the collapsing of an enormous, fantastic, mystical balloon—only to drop down again to the same or a different low fundamental sounding along with its "fluted" harmonic.

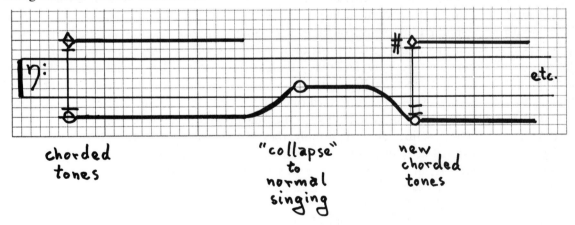

How do the Tibetan monks achieve this extraordinary musical and timbral feat? Acousticians have found that in addition to the resounding deep bass tone, the fluted harmonic, and the usual mix of relatively weak overtones, *there is a third tone sounding in the chord*: the tenth harmonic sounding an octave above the fluted harmonic! In addition, examination of the waveforms suggests that there are two pulses of air coming from the vocal cords rather than the one which is normal in singing. The exact nature of this oscillation is not known, but it may come from the two vocal cords being made to vibrate symmetrically in some way, from the two vocal cords having two natural modes of oscillation, or from a strong interaction between vocal cords and the resonance of the throat cavities. And evidently the fluted harmonics are made to sound by a skilled adjustment of the most remarkable of resonators, the vocal cavities, both in relation to the resonant frequencies of each other and to those of the vocal cord vibration. Only one thing is really certain: great skills and careful motor control are required.

More important than the question of *how* is the fact of *is*. The sound and timbre of Tibetan chanting, "said to burn like fire" or "to flow like water," reflecting the unearthly quality of a profound and esoteric belief, pleasing and suitable for the deities (who encompass certain subterranean aspects of human consciousness), and affecting the mind of the singer, tune the very core of his being to a greater Vibration, felt but inexplicable.

★★★★★★★★★★★★★★★★★★★★★★★★

Among many of the peoples of central Asia and Siberia there is a preference for an extremely low, resonant, guttural vocal timbre and range. The epic singers of the Gorno-Altai and the Yakut perform in this style. More amazing—in fact, along with Tibetan chant, one of the musical/timbral/vocal wonders of the world—is a way of singing among the Tuvin people in the USSR and Mongolia called *sygt* style: the (male) vocalist, accompanied by his *doshpular* plucked lute, sings each musical phrase at the bottom of his register, coming to rest on a long, deep, resonant note. Then, as he holds this tone, he produces a whole series of piccololike fluted harmonics over it, an entire eerie, clear, birdlike melody over the bedrock of this drone! Exactly how this is done, whether with the mouth cavity, vocal cords, or a combination of these, is not known. But the Tuvin *sygt* style is unique, it is extraordinary, and, most important, it is exquisitely beautiful.

In certain areas of the earth there seems to be a preference for a certain type of tone color. Frederic Lieberman, for instance, has suggested that there is a "gong-chime area" stretching from the islands of Indonesia up into Japan, Korea, and China where gongs and chimes, many of them in tuned sets, are important instruments in ensembles (sometimes the only instruments) and where musicians and listeners alike have a great feeling and love for their sound. In India (excluding tribal cultures) both singers and instruments in pop, folk, and classical music tend to favor what we might characterize as a "high, strained, nasal sound."

In southeast Asia the reedy sound of the *khaen* bamboo mouth organ is a characteristic timbre in folk music, and it carries also into the music of ensembles in China and Japan that use its cousins, the *sheng* and the *sho,* respectively. In Turkey there is the *santūr* zither, which has no damping device so its tones mesh in a beautifully liquid aural "cloud," and the "wailing, nasal" double-reed pipe, the *zurnā.* Both instruments, or related ones, are found throughout the Near East and the sound, particularly of the *zurnā,* is reflected in the full-throated, "nasal, intense, strained" vocal style of the area. Singers of traditional music in Bulgaria and Yugoslavia (with their trills, graces, turns, and glottal catches) and in Spain, particularly among gypsy performers in *flamenco* style, also tend to prefer this timbre. In much of the popular music of the United States and Europe the tone color of the electric guitar (and bass and organ), saxophones, and brass are also important.

A particular ensemble of instruments in toto may also be thought of as having its own tone color. In the court music of Thailand the principal ensembles are so divided: the *pi phat* orchestra is characterized by the timbre of xylophones, tuned gong circles, the *pi nai* oboe, and large drums; the *mahori* orchestra emphasizes the sound of stringed instruments—fiddles and zithers—combined with smaller sizes of melodic percussion instruments, flutes, and lighter, smaller drums; the *khruang sai* ensemble uses only strings, flute, and rhythmic percussion. In Korea the traditional court orchestras for Confucian ritual music (*aak*), Chinese T'ang and Sung dynasty compositions (*tang-ak*), and Ko-

The sound of the double-reed pipe and drum is popular from north Africa and Europe to the Far East. Two *zurlas* (right) and *tupan* accompany festival dancing in Skopje, Macedonia, Yugoslavia.

rean music (*hyang-ak*) each have their own special instrumentation and particular sound; while in Japan ensembles like the *gagaku* ceremonial court orchestra, the *hayashi* ensemble of *noh* theater, or the *sankyoku* chamber group each have an unmistakable timbre. In the West the various conglomerations of instruments also have their special "color": a bluegrass band differs in sound from a jug band, a jazz band from a jazz combo, a string trio from a symphony orchestra from a military band from a string quartet. In the baroque era the *concerto grosso* form alternated and contrasted the color and sound of the full orchestra (*tutti* or *ripieno*) with that of the solo group (the *concertino*, or "little consort"), both of which were set against the main mass of orchestral sound. Similarly, during the *wayang kulit* shadow puppet plays of Java, which are backed by the large *gamelan* orchestra, there are times when the *dalang* (who is a puppet master, story-teller, epic singer, entertainer, and philosopher all wrapped up in one) calls for a more quiet, gentler musical accompaniment for his narrative, a chamber color, and only a few musicians (rather than the twenty or more of the full ensemble) improvise behind him.

Music, we noted near the beginning of this section, is a kaleidoscope of sound, a collection of ever changing tonal color and timbral relationships that is like a magic light show for the ears. This quality is easily heard and enjoyed, yet to describe it is like trying to grasp sunlight reflected in water, or to put smoke in one's pocket. But timbre is extremely important: it is—musically—everywhere, in every sound, in voices, instruments, combinations, chords, harmony, melodies, tonal systems. It is an important element of what we call "style." At the same time it is a barrier, one of the first we must cross, to come to an understanding and appreciation of the nonuniversal languages of the earth's musics. If we can shake off our prejudices and learn to enjoy the "nasal twang" of the Appalachian mountaineer, the "tense, nasal, wailing" quality of the Middle Eastern singer, the "spasmodic jerks, low gutturals, and swallowed tones" of Japanese classical music, or the "full-throated, tense falsetto" of American Plains Indian singing; if we immerse ourselves (delightfully) in the *sound* of the gongs and chimes of the Indonesian *gamelan* orchestra, the full-bodied rhythmic darting of west African xylophone ensembles, the subtle breathiness and hidden overtones of the Japanese *shakuhachi* bamboo flute, or the transcendent resonant bass tones and chording of Tibetan chant; if we begin to view timbre—like the many, many sounds of the earth's languages—as an infinitely complex range of aural possibilities, of colors on an enormous palette: then we have taken a gigantic step away from the narrow limits of our "cultural village" toward a real global understanding of man's musical world. The black-and-white screen of our aural perception will burst into a technicolor rainbow.

Cho Chae-son. Conversation, 1972.
Gangoli, O. C. *Ragas and Raginis.* Delhi: Munshi Ram Lal, 1948.
Grout, Donald J. *A History of Western Music.* New York: W. W. Norton, 1960.
Jenkins, Jean L. *Musical Instruments.* London: Horniman Museum and Library, 1970.
Kothari, K. S. *Indian Folk Musical Instruments.* New Delhi: Sangeet Natak Akademi, 1968.
Malm, William P. *Japanese Music.* Rutland, Vermont: Charles E. Tuttle, 1959.
McAllester, David P. Conversations and lectures, 1972–74.
Morton, David: *The Traditional Music of Thailand.* Los Angeles: Institute of Ethnomusicology, UCLA, 1968.
Popely, H. A. *The Music of India.* Boston: Crescendo Publishers, 1966.
Sachs, Curt. *The Rise of Music in the Ancient World East and West.* New York: W. W. Norton, 1943.
Shankar, Ravi. *My Music, My Life.* New York: Simon and Schuster, 1968.
Smith, Huston; Crossley-Holland, Peter; Stevens, Kenneth N.; Cutillo, Brian; and Nga Wang Lek Den. Notes to phonograph recording: *The Music of Tibet: The Tantric Rituals.* New York: Anthology Record and Tape Corporation, 1970 (from the series An Anthology of the World's Music, No. 6).

Quilting party provides diversion during the North Carolina Bluegrass Music Festival, Spruce Pine, N.C.

8

THE QUILT
OF SOUND

The musicologists of the late nineteenth and early twentieth centuries had it all figured out: following Darwin, they inferred an evolutionary history of music, a series of technical innovations and developments that mirrored the inventions and changes of man himself. It all began, they thought, in the *ursatz,* the primal matter, of the grunts and squeals and wails and animalistic cries of cavemen. Gradually these wild and barbaric musical utterances (often "with magical or erotic connotations") took shape, first as one- or two-note chants, then as simplistic and childlike three- and four- and five-note repetitious melodies, or as the screaming emotional outbursts of "tumbling strains." This was the Melodic Age of music, and some cultures—such as those in India or in the various countries of the Middle East—never went beyond it, although they did develop melody alone (or monophony), like some exotic bird, into a fine art. In the West this Golden Age of Melody reached its cloud-covered peaks in the austere unaccompanied beauty of Gregorian chant. There was also an earlier Rhythmic Age which, after its Stone Age beginnings, centered, of course, in Africa. Harmony started because men, women, and children (the scholars surmised) have different vocal ranges, and thus they began (naïvely unaware) to sing their melodies in octaves or in parallel fourths or fifths—a technique frozen in the music of some primitive societies, but adapted and formalized and written down in the organum of the great Church composers of medieval Europe, notably in the Notre Dame School of Leonin and Perotin (late twelfth and early thirteenth centuries). Gradually—like a salamander evolving legs and learning to breathe out of water—polyphony (simultaneous yet independent melodies) was discovered and worked out, again mainly in the Church. There was Giovanni Pierluigi Palestrina (ca. 1525–94), Don Carlo Gesualdo (1560–1613), the Gabrielis (Andrea, ca. 1520–86, and Giovanni, 1554/57–1612), and finally J. S. Bach; and this was the Age of Polyphony. At the same time in this primeval musical jungle there appeared the multicolored magical dinosaur of harmony (simultaneous sounds or pitches worked into chords and sequences of chords), and the Age of Homophony (melody with harmony) began. The entire evolution —paralleling the development of man from slimy, squirming creatures in the water, things that go "bump" in the night, and "the apes"—culminated in the full flowering of high European art, in the sublime musical thought and expression of Mozart, Ludwig van Beethoven (1770–1847), Johannes

Brahms (1833–97), and Richard Wagner (1813–83): a master race of geniuses capering in the Elysian Fields of European melody, harmony, forms, and idioms.

the culmination:
complex texture of
European art music

disorganized
primeval "ooze"
of grunts and
wails

harmony

organum

melody
(monody)

polyphony

melody/polyphony/
the symphony and
sonata, etc.

The only problem with such a neat and logical structure is that it is not true. We know with absolute certainty, for example, that man of twenty or thirty thousand years ago had the same brain and capability for thought as man of today (evolutionary changes take not thousands of years, but *hundreds of thousands* and *millions* of years). And study of contemporary hunters and gatherers has shown that "primitive" man, far from being a "grunter" or a "wailer," uses (and used) his brain (knowledge, thought, logic, invention) in his struggles for survival as much as or more than a "modern" city dweller, say a computer analyst, who is a specialist and whose needs are catered to by other un-self-sufficient specialists from grocers to television repairmen, and who *can* survive without ever really thinking or inventing or discovering at all! There were Galileos and Mozarts in prehistory, but, unlike the extraordinary and sophisticated paintings of the caves in southern France and northern Spain, their traces, their intellectual or musical footprints, have disappeared with rain, wind, and time.

Then there is a second problem: that of the explorers and missionaries who, beginning in the sixteenth century, sailed halfway around the globe, anchored at isolated islands, or trekked into the uncharted jungles or barren deserts of so-called dark continents only to discover that the "savages" there sang in complex polyphony and with harmonies and melodies that sounded beautiful (and strangely familiar) even to European ears. How could these "simple" and "childlike" and "naïve" (not to mention "barbaric" and "heathen") people create a music that rightly belonged on the later and higher evolutionary plane of Eruopean art? There could only be one answer: thousands of miles away from Europe and without the (much later) inventions of radio or the phonograph or television, somehow they had heard European music and imitated it!

Ludicrous and unintelligent as such attitudes appear, these ideas are unfortunately still common today. But anthropologists have shown us that people in non-machine-technology societies lead far from simple lives and that their systems of law, religion, myth, kinship, and art may, in fact, be far more complicated than ours. Furthermore, much indigenous music of many of the world's peoples ("primitive" or otherwise) is technically more complex than that of Europe and America (particularly if one takes popular music into consideration); and much of it is based on harmonic and polyphonic concepts and systems. On top of this is the riddle that one finds in many south Asian countries, in India for example. Tribal people who live in isolated pockets in the hills, deserts, and forests and who must have been related to the original inhabitants of the various regions make music that fully uses harmony and polyphony, while people of the later, more modern, dominant "high" culture prefer a music that is primarily monophonic. The historical movement would appear, then, to have been *away* from the earlier harmonic/melodic style of the tribal people to a later monophonic/melody-oriented music developed and synthesized in "higher" city and palace cultures—in other words, the exact opposite of the evolutionary projection drawn up by our nineteenth-century musicologists!

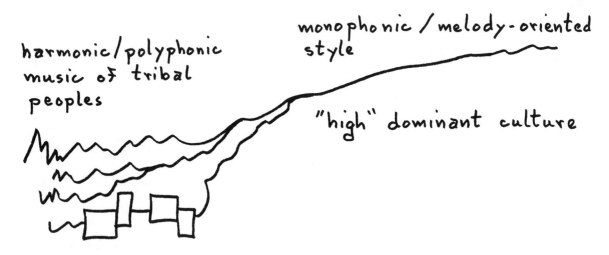

Finally, there is the case of Europe itself: again and again a complex *stile antico* has been abandoned for a more simple *stile moderno*. J. S. Bach's own sons replaced, in a single generation, the father's many-layered baroque polyphony and complex web of harmony with the lucid, transparent textures and simple harmonies and melodies of the classic era; the bombast and gigantic orchestras and tone poems of the late nineteenth century were met head on by the eccentric wit of Satie and the jewel-like compositions of Anton Webern (some of which last for fewer than sixty seconds). And more recently the avant garde has reacted to the dense and complex and mathematical "Dionysian" structures of the post-1950 "international style" (Stockhausen, for example) with "Apollonian" conceptual compositions that reduce music to a minimum, to minute, barely perceived permutations of a single sound, or chord, or texture, or rhythm. This pendulum movement is also reflected in other areas of Western life. In the art world of the 1920s, for example, the theoretical complexities of cubism (and other "isms") were met with the Dadaist objects of Marcel Duchamp, Man Ray, and others (a snow shovel, or a flatiron with a row of thumb tacks attached to its bottom); and in the 1950s and 1960s the complex and emotional outburst of abstract expressionism (Hans Hofmann, Jackson Pollock, and others) gave way to the familiar banal imagery of pop art or the cool austerity of minimal art. In music, then, even limiting ourselves to the accepted traditions of European art music (music historians usually do not consider the popular and folk traditions worthy of their study), a more correct historical mapping would be a sawtoothlike alternation of the "romantic"/ technically complex/(polyphonic) with the "classical"/technically simpler/(homophonic/monophonic):

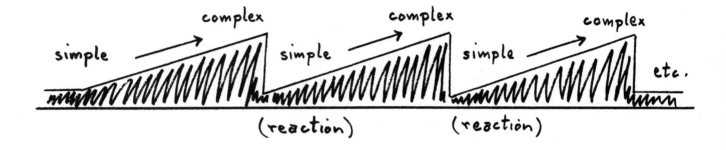

Rather than to build imaginary histories and structures in the sky, it is probably far more useful to look at the music that exists in the world today or in the fresh memory of the recent past. Several facts emerge, and they pop the balloons of a number of popular misconceptions. Harmony, although a complicated and significant development in the music of Europe, is found all over the world; it is not unique to the West. Far from there being one system of harmony (ours) mystically connected with the laws of acoustics and the universe, there are perhaps dozens, each with their own "rules" (often intuitive "ear rules") and methods of procedure. Furthermore, much if not most of the harmonic music-making in the world is by ear, making questionable the assumption that musical notation is a prerequisite for the "higher" and more complex technologies of musical structure. Polyphony is also found in many other places on earth (besides the European tradition), and often it also is performed by ear. Heterophony (simultaneous variation of the same melody in various parts), long connected with the music of exotic cultures—southeast Asia, for example—also exists in the music of the West, not in the classical tradition but in many idioms of ear music including jazz, rock, and bluegrass. And, finally, our terms—harmony, polyphony, heterophony, etc.—are European inventions. They are convenient labels, but they are not mutually exclusive; and taken out of the context of the music of the West (which they were originally meant to describe) they may actually be interchangeable. Still we shall try to use them as intelligently as we can, hoping that perhaps some day scholars will come up with a new (precise and universally understood) vocabulary for the description of the earth's music.

Harmony

Harmony—derived from the Greek *harmonia* ("joint, proportion, concord")—is defined by Webster as a "musical consonance; tuneful sound; concord"; as an "adaption of parts to each other; agreement between the parts of a design or composition giving unity of effect or an aesthetically pleasing whole." For our purposes this is a good definition. But we can amend it for our "theory of world music" with two clarifications: what is aesthetically pleasing, tuneful, in agreement, or concord will vary (like jewelry or hair styles) from culture to culture; and *harmony is the simultaneous happening of pitches.* If melody can be visualized as moving through space and time horizontally, harmony can be thought of as occurring vertically, and, indeed, Western musical notations follow this conceptual picturization:

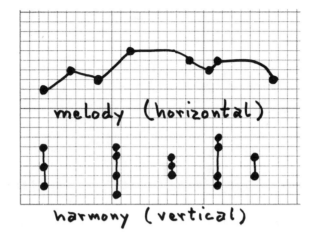

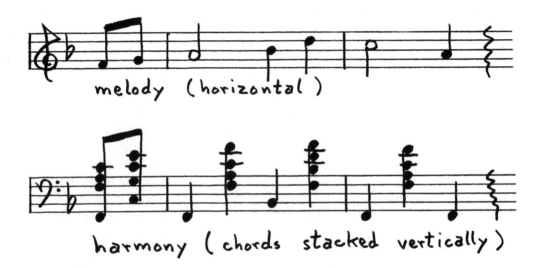

Harmony can happen with its components in absolute simultaneity, in blocks of tones, or *chords,* or it can happen from aggregates of notes that occur sequentially (like *arpeggios*—"broken chords"— or Alberti bass figurations) but which the ear, shaped by cultural conditioning, hears as a single *gestalt,* much as many trees together are viewed as a unit—as a woods or forest.

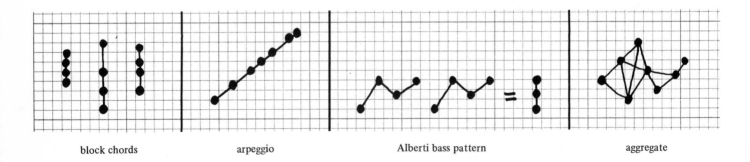

block chords   arpeggio   Alberti bass pattern   aggregate

Woodcut by German artist Hans Burgkmair, from *Der Weisskönig,* ca. 1514–16.

The various parts that occur together to make harmony may be strictly controlled and planned (part of a rational or intuitive system) like the various hedges, flower beds, bird baths, walkways, and fountains in a formal garden; or harmony may be merely what is happening at a given musical moment, or point in time, like a photograph of a street corner which freezes standing or walking people, buses, cars, and objects in a seemingly random simultaneous relationship (although each component is actually going somewhere).

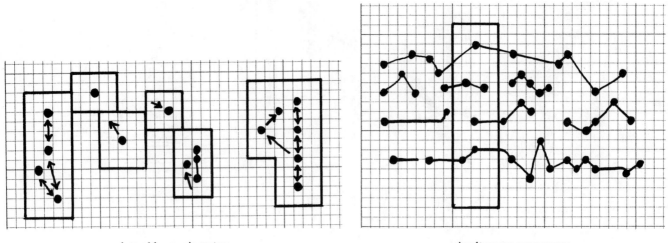

planned harmonic system   simultaneous occurrences

In the real music of the world (or the music of the real world)—as opposed to theoretical analysis, which by its very nature must be a simplification—there is no dichotomy between a harmony of simultaneous occurrences and one of a planned system: even a straightforward harmonic/melodic music like that of the classic era of Haydn and Mozart is full of surprises, or satellite pitches, that move through and against the pure logic and transparency of the harmonies; and there is a system (and a very good one) underlying the sometimes clashing vertical happenings in the music of the Javanese or Balinese *gamelan* orchestras.

Several of the concepts that we have investigated earlier (in the "Machinations of Sound," "From Birds to Melody Bands," and "Timbre and Timber" sections) recur here in connection with harmony; that is, they *seem* to apply to a sizable segment of the earth's music, yet we must remember that they are by no means universal: man's musical imagination here and there and everywhere is subtle, unpredictable, and startlingly elusive. The natural law of the overtone series is a case in point: the pure relationships of the sequences of the harmonics (or partials or overtones—they all mean the same thing) are reflected in harmony all over the world. People sing and play in octaves (the first interval of the series), in fifths (the next) and fourths (etc.), in thirds, and (more rarely) in seconds. They find these intervals, sounded together, pleasant and harmonious; they build them into two- and three- and four-note chords, and from the mountains of Kentucky to the steppes of central Asia or the rice paddies of Tanjore they retain some of them—especially the octave and fifth—as a background drone to their melodies. But musical man also builds chords and harmonies—also considered enjoyable and beautiful—from stackings of pitches *outside* the natural overtone series: the minor chord, for example, so common in Euro-American music, is outside the acoustical ecosystem; and what about the harmonies of Charles Ives or Edgard Varèse? (To explain or justify these harmonies as occurring higher in the upper partials of the overtone series is incorrect because these partials are "out of tune" with the tempered tuning of Western music.) Sequences of harmonies are frequently constructed following the basic "law" of the overtone series—like the chord movement in fifths so basic to much of Western music, classical and popular—but sequences can also follow the logic of a rational system (like Arnold Schoenberg's twelve-tone technique or the chords of the *sho* in Japanese *gagaku*) or the ear.

Harmony can also use the melodic concept of the tonal center. Drone notes establish a strong gravitational pull, a point of reference, for and against the notes of melodies. And in the harmonic system of the West—in classical music from the Renaissance to the early twentieth century and in the popular and folk arts up to the present moment—certain sequences of chords (harmonies) are heard as establishing a tonal center, with the "tonic chord" heard as a definite point of rest. In the West, harmonic movement to more "distant" chords or to temporary other tonal centers functions to establish musical "tension" which is resolved by a return to the familiar territory of the tonic, its chord and satellite chords.

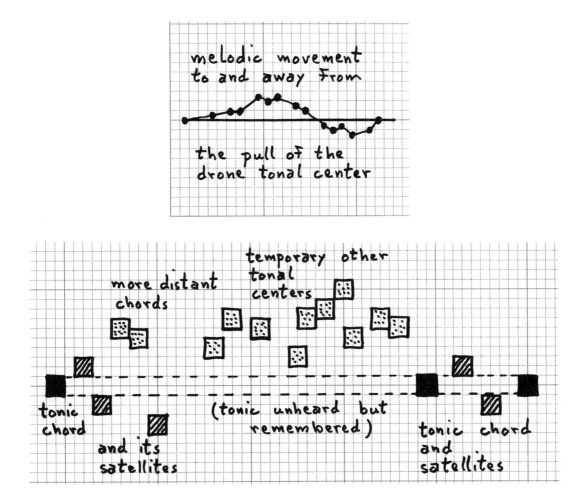

Much of the traditional music in the West, we have noted, is directional—it seems to be going somewhere through time—and this going with its seeming inevitability, its expectations and surprises, is reflected in the harmonic structure: if a piece does not, for example, end on the tonic chord, it sounds to us "incomplete."

The push and pull of tension and relaxation is also a basic theoretical idea in the internal makeup of chords. In the classical music of India, where the melodic notes of the *ragas* form "harmonies" against the static, always-sounding notes of the drone, this relationship is termed *vivadi/samvadi* (it is also applied, as we have seen, melodically, between consecutive notes in a *raga* scale). *Samvadi* notes are those that blend in consonance with the drone or melt into its sound; they are resting places, lovingly lingered on by musicians in performance. *Vivadi* notes create a tension against the drone chord and must (eventually) be resolved. In the music of the West tension/relaxation is connected not only with harmonic movement to and from a tonic, or tonal center, but also with the "dissonance" or "consonance" within the chords themselves. Like so much in life and thought, these terms are completely relative, a matter of personal opinion or taste or education, and although they are used irrationally and arbitrarily by musician and music lover alike, they are assumed to be—like God, or heaven and hell—dogmatically absolute. I have seen astute music lovers hold their ears and scream (unliterally) in agony at "dissonant" chords—the word *dissonant* to them being synonymous with "ugly," "painful," "horrendous," and "unbearable" (and perhaps also "barbaric" and "degenerate")! Surprisingly, these terms (*precisely* the same ones) were used by critics and audiences to describe the harmonies of the gentle Felix Mendelssohn (1809–47) at the premiere of his *Reformation Symphony* well over 150 years ago! Dissonant chords are generally thought to be those with a more complex makeup, or with "clashing" intervals such as seconds (adjacent notes on a piano) or sevenths. By contrast, consonant chords are thought to be those based on thirds, notably major and minor triads, and are considered to be "pleasant," "restful," and "harmonious." But what is not realized is that what is really important—and we are talking about music here in the Euro-American tradition— is not so much the chords (and their harmony) themselves as their context: the dissonances of Bach or Mozart or Tchaikovsky resolve (to us today) in an expected way, while the complex harmonies of Edgard Varèse (1883–1965) or Igor Stravinsky do not—they simply hang there, or they may move and resolve according to different procedures, according to the rules of a different and more unfamiliar game—and we must adjust to their vocabulary to be able to enjoy them. Much of this adjustment is done by history: the harmonies of Debussy or of a cocktail pianist seem comfortable and consonant to most of us today; and I shall forget my shock several years ago, when attending a Saturday afternoon matinee performance by the Philadelphia Orchestra of Charles Ives's *Three Places in New England*, at seeing the good ladies of Philadelphia thoroughly (and genuinely, I believe) enjoy a work whose alleged "dissonances" and harmonic complexity had set audiences howling and booing only thirty years before.

In looking at the musical simultaneous togethèrs of harmony in various places in the world, we can, of course, apply the European criterion of tension/relaxation. Certainly the push/pull of these opposites is a characteristic of our lives (at least in the West) and of the physical machinery of our minds and bodies. But there are other and perhaps equally valid possibilities. Chordal structures, their makeup and sequence, can be looked upon as existing *for* and *in* themselves, as *non*directional objects that happen to be placed in a sequence by a rational system or by tradition, by accident or chance. Where do the (a) mathematically derived simultaneities of a serial work by, say, Webern, or the (b) mysterious vocal chording of Tibetan monks really go? (Some possible answers: [a] to the next mathematically derived sonority, or [b] into the "void of infinity.") On the other hand, certain harmonies may be used in a music simply because people like their sound, or because an instrument is tuned or built in that way. And why not? Are we, sitting among our machines and gadgets in the second half of the twentieth century, so prone to rational systems and scientific explanations that we cannot accept the idea of aesthetic pleasure—perhaps as basic and irrational and human as love— or even accident as determining factors in musical structure? Finally, we must, wherever possible, try to find out how various peoples in the world think about and describe their own music (it may be in terms of light, or of flowers, or the sea, or stars, or the balance of the universe, or the human body, or the movement of animals) and compare it with our own perceptions and analyses. Underneath it all (somewhere) the real music lies.

Drones

A *drone* is a continuous or incessant pitch or group of pitches which occurs more or less constantly and unchangingly behind the developing melody and (sometimes) harmony of a segment of music.

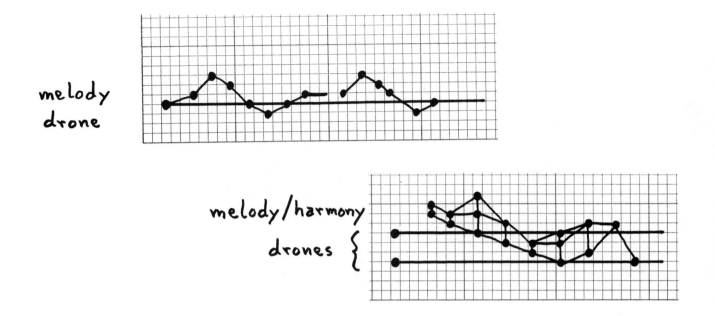

Like the insect drones of a beehive (which are male, have no sting, and are forbidden by instinct to taste the communal honey), musical drones, humble and unexciting in themselves, are extremely important, even essential, in the musical textures where they are used. Without drone notes, for example, the bagpipe would cease to sound like a bagpipe, Indian classical music would cease to sound Indian, the five-string banjo would lose its character, and fiddling from Poland to Sweden to Nova Scotia to Oklahoma would begin to sound like "mere" violin playing.

Psychologically, drones function much like the stable and familiar ground of the solid earth over which we move, walk, and live out our lives, in which we grow our flowers and our food. Everything happens over and in relationship to them, and they are often called, in fact, "grounds."

Commonly, drones happen on the pitches of a tonal center—on the tonic and its octave, or combined with the (acoustically and musically) closely related fifth. But they may also happen on any other note: in the music of the Australian aborigines the rhythmic drone figurations of the eucalyptus tube *didjeridoo* fall a tenth apart (on the tonal center and its third an octave above); in north India one string of the *tamburā* drone instrument is often tuned to the leading-tone seventh (about a half-step below the tonal center!), blending in a rich timbral mixture with the tonic-fifth tuning of the other strings. In a few cases a drone may have no apparent relationship to the tones of a melody; it can seem to our (Western) ears strangely polytonal and dissonant and functioning more like a sound enricher in the musical texture, or like percussive nonpitch drums and idiophones.

Drones can be single-note affairs (like on the single-stringed plucked *ektār*) or they can be a rich, full, open-fifth chord (like on the Scottish highland pipes).

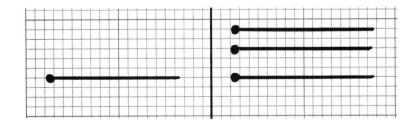

The south Indian *veena* includes four plucked melody strings (top) and three strummed drone strings (bottom).
Veena made by Narayanachary, Tanjore, India.

On the *khaen* mouth organ of Thailand, with its long bamboo pipes and free reeds, the drone
notes (tonic with its fifth below it) form the upper part, often duplicating in rhythmic unison the
melody moving below. In the classical music of south India the (tonic-fifth) chord of the drone functions like a scaffolding, with the developing melodies pulling toward these poles like musical gymnasts.

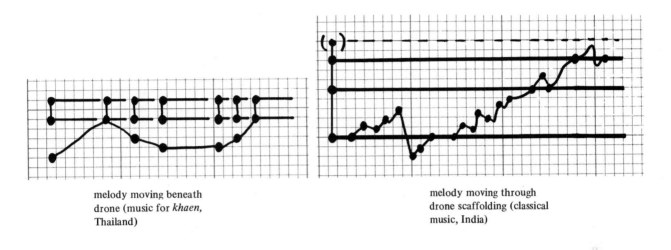

melody moving beneath
drone (music for *khaen,*
Thailand)

melody moving through
drone scaffolding (classical
music, India)

While we usually connect the idea of drones with an incessant sound (like that of the bagpipe),
they can also be played in rhythm (such as on the *khaen*), or alternated with melody notes. Hunters
in Borneo, for example, sing to the beat (and tonic drone) of a gently tapped string. The drone notes
on a banjo (the fifth and other strings) or on a fiddle (the open strings), though not absolutely constant, are emphasized by the frequency, accents, and pitch constancy of their occurrence.

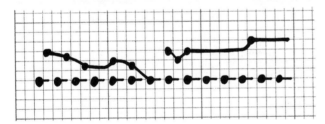

tapped rhythmic drone (Borneo)

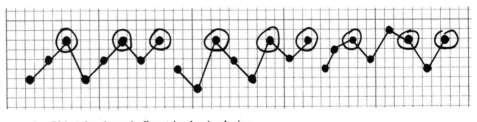

recurring fifth string drone in five-string banjo playing

Drones of this static, unchanging variety are one of those things in life or in nature—like certain types
and shapes of clouds—that are found in startlingly different cultures and environments almost all over
the world. And they are often built into instruments. Bagpipes from Greece and Bulgaria, into north
Africa and central Asia, in eastern Europe, France, Spain, Italy, and Ireland and Scotland invariably
have their drone pipes (along with the "chanter" for the melody). The Mediterranean countries and
the Balkans also abound with double clarinets, oboes, and flutes, one of the tubes of which may

function as a drone. The numerous double and triple clay flutes found in pre-Columbian remains in Central America and South America indicate a music that might have used drone notes. The playing technique on bowed fiddles of every shape and variety from the *lyra* on the Mediterranean islands to the *kpelle* of Liberia to the violins of European and American folk traditions include the touching of open drone strings. Many European folk zithers include drone (as well as fingered playing) strings, as did formerly popular mechanical instruments like the hurdy-gurdy and Scandinavian *nyckelharpa*. In fact, one ethnomusicologist, Bruno Nettl, has found so much use of the drone in European folk music that he marks it as one of the outstanding characteristics of the European tradition! In central Asia many of the plucked lutes, such as the *saz, dotar,* and *tambur,* are played with melodies fingered on one string against the drone sound of open strings; and in India not only are there innumerable special drone instruments (like the *tambūrā* or *sruti-box*), but bowed fiddles (like the *sarangi*) and hybrid plucked lutes (like the *sitār* and *veena*) that include, besides three or four playing strings, a full set of drone strings. Nonnotated vocal ensemble music (from duets and trios to large choruses) all over the world includes drone notes, though usually as part of a more complex musical texture and in conjunction with other techniques which we shall examine later. A random sampling of such sung droning might include the music of a women's three-part Ituri forest pygmy lullaby, a Polynesian choral chant, a Balkan duet for female voices, an Italian dockworkers' polyphonic chorus, a Ukrainian village group, a pair of minstrels accompanied by plucked lyre in Kenya, and a Papago men's religious song in the American Southwest. The two-part singing of the Papago, in fact, points to some of the ways the drone idea is expanded in the ear music of the world, for the drone part in Papago singing occasionally slips down (intentionally) to a lower auxiliary note:

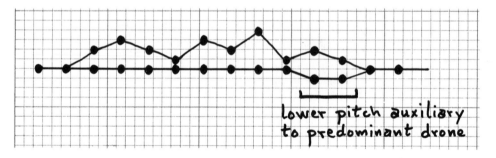

Papago song (male chorus)

Drones can further be expanded by spreading them among the parts in alternation—a kind of antiphonal effect—or by having each voice come to rest on drone notes only to spin off on its own melody, like a ribbon or a bird fluttering off momentarily from and returning to a merry-go-round.

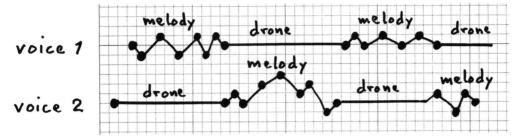

voices alternate antiphonally between the melody and drone notes

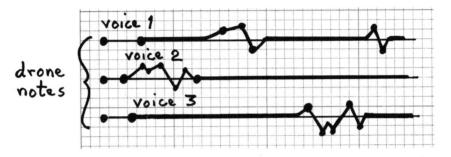

voices rest on acceptable drone notes and then flutter off on musical excursions

Both techniques are common in vocal and instrumental drone-based polyphony—such as in central Africa or in the Ukraine—as well as in much of the melody-based classical music styles of south Asia and the Middle East. The potential for increased musical complication is considerable, and the increased independence of each part results in a texture perhaps more correctly called polyphonic.

Droning notes can also be chanted within a given composition or performance. Long-held notes in much of the world's choral ear polyphony function as temporary drones, at the same time outlining a rudimentary chord structure or bass root movement. The long unmeasured notes of the cantus firmus in the early vocal polyphony of the Church in medieval Europe might be looked upon as static drone poles against which the dozens of notes of the other part (or parts) moved:

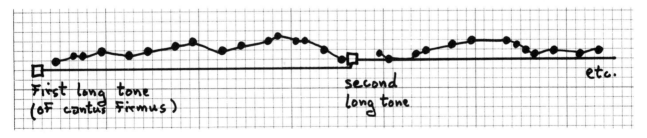

Leonin: *Haec dies* (twelfth century)

In European classical music drone notes became a rather subsidiary compositional technique. There are the long-held bass "pedal points" in the organ music of Bach, for example, over which cascades of chords and melodic passages flow before the music resumes its normal baroque harmonic movement. Both Mozart and Haydn used drone effects when they were imitating village folk music in contredanses or minuets, as did later composers. The recent (post-1960) avant garde, particularly in "live" electronic music, has also developed an interest in the static quality of drones and the effects of subtly moving against them.

Ostinatos

Repeated figurations are called *ostinatos,* and they are among the most important building-block elements in world music. So take notice! An ostinato can be a series of notes, a short melodic fragment, or a bass line; it can be a brief chord sequence, or harmonies, or a combination of melody and harmony; it can also be a rhythm, or a distinctive rhythm combined with melodic and harmonic elements:

SOME OSTINATO PATTERNS

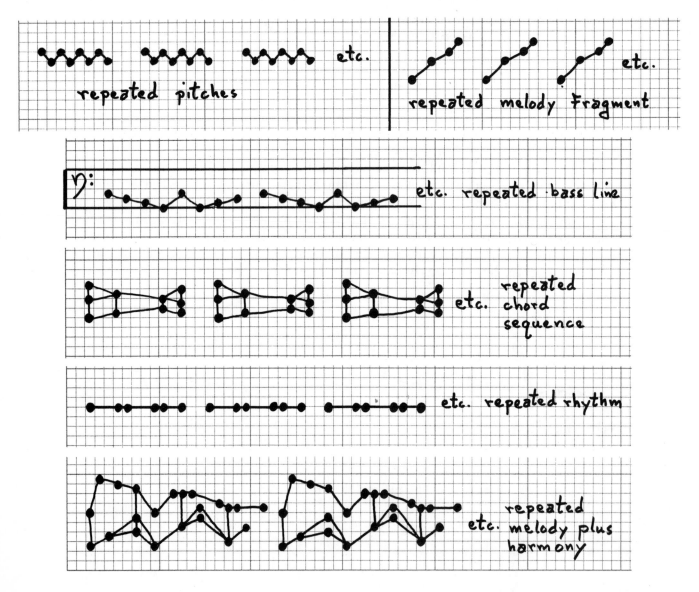

The important factors are that the unit of the ostinato is fairly short (it must be heard) and that it is repeated over and over again, although sometimes with subtle variations. Like the drone, the ostinato satisfies a human liking (and perhaps a basic animal liking also) for a bedrock of the familiar, a solid ground—indeed it is also called a "ground"—which can underlie the flights of creative melodic or harmonic or rhythmic fancy. But unlike the drone, it also provides scope for another basic if not universal human need: that of variety. For an ostinato is not just one sound that is held or repeated, but a little box—like the tent of a miniature circus—that is full of sonic activity. This wonderful repetition/familiarity/variety characteristic of the ostinato unit literally explodes with latent possibilities for its use in musical structures. Its internal workings can be changed kaleidoscopically according to the imagination and invention of the musician; it may provide the accompaniment for a song; it can be combined with other ostinato patterns which are built up like the scraps of cloth in a patchwork quilt, or combined with other elements (and techniques) in a larger and more complex texture. It is, in short, one of the most flexible musical/structural tools that man has ever invented.

On its simplest level, an ostinato may be a more or less regular—and dronelike—alternation of two pitches, a technique found in such diverse sources as Bantu singing (Africa), aborigine *didjeridoo* accompaniments (Australia), and the symphonies of Gustav Mahler (1860–1911) (Europe).

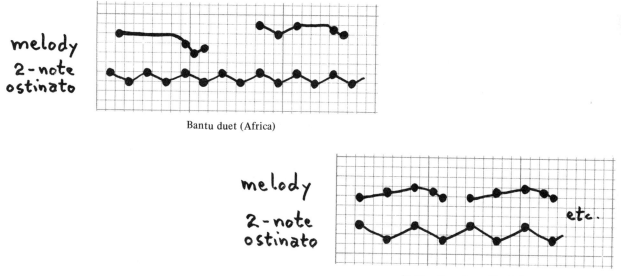

melody
2-note
ostinato

Bantu duet (Africa)

melody
2-note
ostinato

etc.

Mahler: Symphony No. 1 (Europe)

This regular alternation can also be expanded into an alternation of two-, three-, and more-part chords, forming a shifting, moving, yet essentially static background for melodies and (sometimes) harmonies developing over it. The Naga tribal people in Burma do it; it is a popular time-marking and textural technique both in sub-Saharan Africa and in many Arabic musical cultures; and it happens in jazz. John Coltrane (1926–67), for example, often wove his bursting, soaring, explosive improvisations over a rhythmically hypnotic two-chord background.

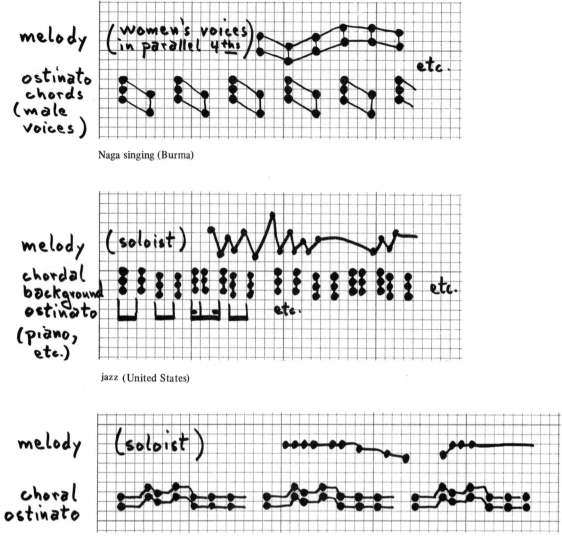

Naga singing (Burma)

jazz (United States)

Bantu singing (central Africa)

Ostinato figurations, often of a longer and more complex type, are extremely important in the music of sub-Saharan Africa. Minstrels and village singers frequently accompany their songs with absolutely stunning (and beautiful) repeated patterns on their plucked lyres and bow harps, bowed fiddles, or plucked *mbiras*. In call-and-response choral singing—with a chorus answering the improvised or stereotyped melodic phrases of a soloist—the choral part is often based upon an ostinato-like phrase that is repeated with variations. The large ensembles of xylophones, flutes, and other instruments build up massive and complex musical textures through the simultaneous overlapping of numerous ostinato layers, a technique also used (as we have seen in the section on rhythm) in drumming.

In Europe and the United States ostinatos have had a checkered history, yet they have been (and are) a common technique in nonnotated "ear" music. In jazz distinctive melodic and chordal "riffs" are coupled with chord changes: short, distinctive melodic/chordal/rhythmic phrases are repeated, their precise notes changing to fit chordal changes but their characteristic melodic contour and rhythm remaining the same.

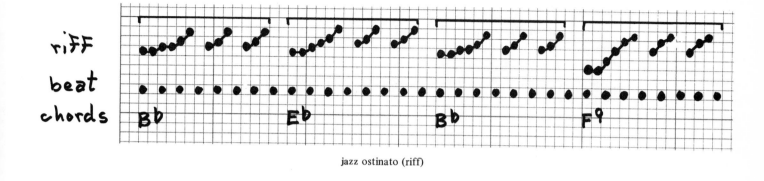

jazz ostinato (riff)

Jazz-influenced popular music of every shape and variety from the country clubs of Long Island to
the ghettos of Detroit (and including soul music and rock) bursts with similar modified ostinato patterns; in fact, the booming bass guitar lines of rock make heavy if not predominant use of the ostinato idea, as do the chordal accompaniments and drumming.

In the European classical music tradition the ostinato concept culminated in one of the great
forms of the baroque period: the stately *passacaglia* or *chaconne*. Originating perhaps, like so many
early forms, from blueprints for keyboard improvisation (organ, harpsichord, clavier, virginal, etc.),
the passacaglia was built on a simple four- to eight-bar harmonic pattern and/or bass melody (called
a "ground bass") repeated throughout the composition. Over this "obstinate" chordal/bass line
ostinato increasingly complex variations were woven; J. S. Bach's Passacaglia in C Minor, written
around 1717 (?), is an excellent example:

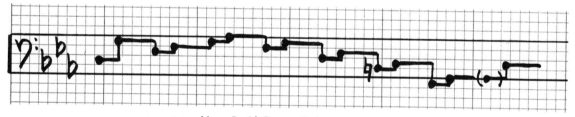

ground bass: Bach's Passacaglia in C Minor

The ostinato has remained (in the West) since Bach's time as one of the many tools of the trade
available to the composer. Accompanimental figurations like the Alberti bass are in a sense a type of
ostinato; and classic and romantic composers frequently used ostinatolike repetitions as a tension-
building device. In the twentieth century composers like Bartok and Stravinsky (especially) were
masters of the ostinato; their music is permeated with striking passages (like the opening and ending
of Stravinsky's *Orpheus* ballet); and more recently the technique is common in electronic music: in
tape loops, or recording tape spliced to form a continuous circle so that the recorded sound repeats
again and again, and through the mechanics of synthesizers and other electronic machinery.

The longer cycles of repeated sequences of notes or harmonies or rhythms, so important and
universal in the structures in the earth's music—like the chords/melodies of the Shona *mbira* musical
style, or the obstinate repeating chords of the black American blues form—are perhaps nothing more
than an expansion in time scale and size of the ostinato idea.

Homophony/Chords

Harmony, we have noted, is the simultaneous sounding of different pitches; it is heard "vertically" in time and space rather than "horizontally" or consecutively. For our purposes we may make a further (and fully arbitrary) distinction: the individual notes in a predominantly harmonic texture have no individuality, they blend in a "harmonic sound," in chords or chord constellations; and frequently they blend rhythmically as well—that is, we hear the rhythm of the mass of the harmony or the chord as a whole rather than the rhythms of its individual parts. This kind of musical texture, called *homophony* or *homophonic* (from the Greek *homo*, "the same," plus *phonos*, "sound, tone"), might be thought of as a series of vertical boxlike units as opposed to the horizontal twisting melodic strands of *polyphony* (*poly*, "many") or *heterophony* (*hetero*, "different"):

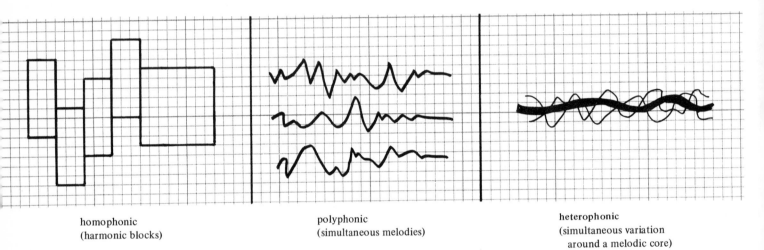

homophonic
(harmonic blocks)

polyphonic
(simultaneous melodies)

heterophonic
(simultaneous variation
around a melodic core)

One of the basic ways the world's peoples make harmony, besides through drones and repeated ostinatos, is through *parallel motion*: another voice or instrument doubles a melody at a certain interval, more or less paralleling exactly its ups and downs.

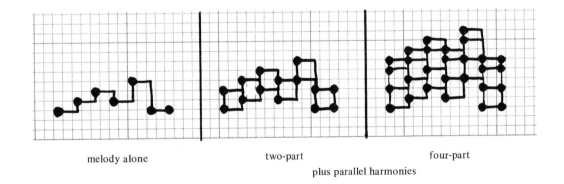

melody alone   two-part   four-part

plus parallel harmonies

Two-part parallel harmony is very common, with one of the voices often doubled at the octave to add a third part, although three real parts (singing *triads*—three-note chords) are also found, especially in Europe. We should note before going on that in many of the world's musical cultures (our own included) the musical texture and the techniques used to create it fluctuate tremendously and with incredible variety. A choral group in the Ukraine, for example, may begin with unison singing, add occasional harmonic notes, then break into a passage of parallel harmonies, going to a melodic bit sung against held drones and fluctuating all the time from one (unison) part to a texture of two, three, or four or more parts. So when we say that a certain culture sings or plays in parallel harmonies we should remember that this is not all they do; it may even be just a fraction of a complex repertoire of musical tools.

The intervals—the musical distance—between the parts in parallel harmonies seem to follow not only regional preferences and traditions (the ear) but acoustics as well. Besides singing or playing at

★★★★★★★ **A LAYMAN'S GUIDE TO PARALLEL HARMONY-MAKING** ★★★★★★★★

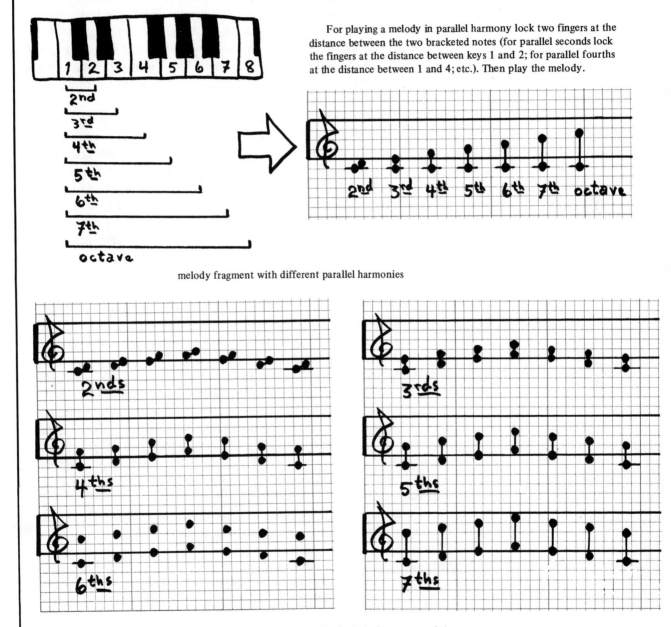

For playing a melody in parallel harmony lock two fingers at the distance between the two bracketed notes (for parallel seconds lock the fingers at the distance between keys 1 and 2; for parallel fourths at the distance between 1 and 4; etc.). Then play the melody.

melody fragment with different parallel harmonies

For most of us parallel harmony in thirds or sixths may sound the most familiar—they are common in two-part harmony in the West; but the other parallel harmonies also occur (Stravinsky's *Le Sacre du printemps*; or interspersed in thicker chordal structures, such as in jazz or pop music).

Parallel harmony may be exact—the interval may always remain exactly the same; or it may be adjusted (as in our examples) slightly to fit the notes of a particular scale (such as the white notes on the piano).

★★★★★★★★★★★★★★★★★★★★★★★★★★★★★★

a unison or an octave—which we, and many other cultures, hear as a doubling, a sameness—there is harmonizing in parallel fifths, fourths, thirds, seconds, sixths, and (occasionally) sevenths or, in thicker textures, in any combination of them.

Parallel fourths and fifths, known as *organum*, were part of the bread and butter of medieval European Church music composers, but whether they were also common in folk music of the period is not known. However, in Iceland there is a style of folk singing in curious archaic parallel fifths. Elsewhere in the world parallel fourth and/or fifth singing is found among the Nagas in Assam and Burma, in some forms of Japanese Buddhist chant, in the polyphonic singing of Oceania and Micronesia, and in the thicker chords and textures of eastern and Mediterranean European folk choral polyphony. In the plucked lute styles of central Asia (such as on the Uzbek *dotar*) parallel fourth and fifth movement is also common—the strings are tuned in fourths or fifths and simply stopped at the same frets or places on the neck of the instrument by the same finger as it plays the melody. In the rock-and-roll style of the United States in the 1950s, Chuck Berry often did the same thing on his electric guitar!

Parallel thirds are so common, so loved, and so appreciated as inherently and unabashedly beautiful in the harmonic music-making of Europe and the Americas that it is hard to imagine that they have not always been there. How long or how distantly in the past they existed in folk traditions we do not know, but we do know that in medieval times there was a sudden and tremendous fad for the parallel third style of *gymel*, or *cantus gemellus* ("twin songs"), possibly originating in England and spreading throughout every notated style in almost every region of Europe. This preference for parallel thirds (and harmonizing and chording in thirds) is one of the innumerable curious and as yet inexplicable ties between the music of Europe and that of sub-Saharan Africa. Besides permeating (to list only a few examples) countless duets in Italian opera (from Mozart to Verdi), symphonic textures, oratorios, folk choruses or instrumental ensembles, piano music (who could forget *Humoresque*?), pop, rock, soul, swing, jazz, fiddling, barbershop quartet singing, bluegrass, old time, Latin or Spanish pop and folk idioms (two voices, two trumpets in harmony), parallel third harmonies are found all through the harmonic and polyphonic styles of Africa—for example, in Bantu singing or in the ostinatos of the *valiha* zither of Madagascar—in pockets of people and music cultures in Asia, and in the singing of Oceania and Micronesia. It exists today also wherever elements of Western musical culture have spread: for example, in the singing of Christians in the former Portuguese colony of Goa in India, in the Philippines (the Spanish colonial influence), or in Japan (Tokyo has been humorously dubbed "Nashville East") where local musicians twang their guitars in hillbilly style and sing close nasal harmonies in perfect replicas of the American country sound.

Parallel singing in seconds is less common in the world, although it is found in the polyphonic singing of the islands of the Pacific, to a smaller extent in Africa, and in eastern Europe, notably in some of the canons of Lithuanian folk song and in the striking vocal and instrumental duet and trio traditions of the Balkan countries.

In the lush tropical state of Kerala in south India there is a unique style of singing choral religious songs or ritualistic dance music in a complete texture of parallel harmonies. The chorus usually does the "answering" part in a call-and-response format, answering or imitating each phrase of a leader/soloist singer's part. But each singer in the chorus, and there may be up to a dozen or more, finds his own pitch at which he sings the melody, blending in a chordal texture that may include any combination of seconds, fourths, fifths, and even sevenths. The chord itself, once estab-

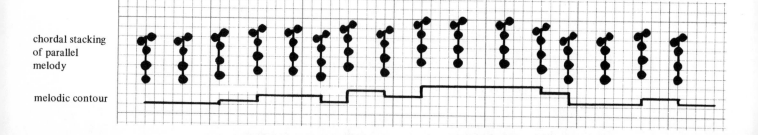

chordal stacking of parallel melody

melodic contour

Close nasal harmonies in thirds characterize much of the bluegrass style of the United States.

lished (in its internal relationships), never changes; it simply slides up and down following the outline of the melody like a chord on a phonograph record changing speeds. This strangely beautiful and "dissonant" chordal melody is also in effect—like similar stackings in Stravinsky's *Le Sacre du printemps*—polytonal, since each and every singer is singing in his own (different) key. Yet there is also a harmonic "blend," and singers make an effort to achieve it.

Blocklike parallel movement in three-note or more-note chords is, in fact, one way that musicians in the world deal with harmonic movement. Parallel triads abound, for instance, in Italy and in the chordal part singing of Germany and the Alps, as they do in other European "ear-born" choral and instrumental traditions. European classical music also has parallel chordal movement, though before Debussy and Ravel (who basked in "impressionistic," smokelike sequences of parallel harmonies) such harmonic sequences were worked out through and around the complex of curious and inexplicable taboos (born in musical practice, but then made into irrefutable dogma by theorists and teachers)—such as the ban on the parallel fifth. One of the innumerable in-jokes among music students is the image of the birdlike theory professor who scans harmony exercises with his eagle eye, zeroing in on parallel fifths and other "infractions," his red pencil flying into action excitedly with every new discovery.

In homophony—a music of a harmonic bed supporting a predominant melody (perhaps over 90 percent of the music, popular and classical, that we in the West make and hear)—the basic building bricks are *chords*. Like clusters of grapes on a vine, chords are groups of notes that happen together (simultaneously, actually) or belong together (conceptually). Chords can be built by stackings of any interval (seconds, thirds, fourths, etc.) or by any combination of them. In the European tradition chords are built on thirds:

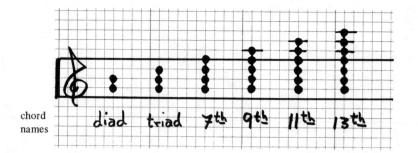

The triad (three-note chord) is the predominant chord in traditional classical, folk, and older popular music. The seventh chord ornaments the triad usage. In jazz and recent pop music sevenths, ninths, and elevenths are common; if triads are used they are "colored" by added notes. (The names of seventh, ninth, and eleventh chords come from the intervalic distance from the bottom note to the top.)

In African harmony there is also a preference for chords built on thirds, although African musicians—being ear musicians rather than paper musicians—are not quite so dogmatic about their makeup. Diads (two-note chords) are common, as are triads. As in the harmonic/polyphonic music of other areas—say New Guinea or Polynesia—the vertical texture can change instantaneously: from unison, to two-part harmony in thirds, to thick chords, and back again. A common chord-building technique is to take a two-pitch chord and double one of its voices at the octave, for example, a third plus an octave or an open fifth (chord) plus an octave.

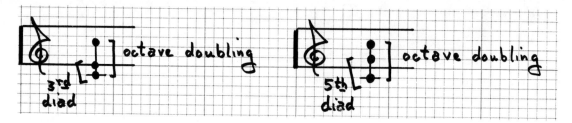

Harmonic and polyphonic singing occurs in many parts of Africa. Women singing high-life music for the installation ceremony of a tribal chief, Accra, Ghana.

Theorists in the West do not regard octave doubling of one or more of the voices in a chord as a separate entity; nor do they regard a rearrangement of the ordering of a chord's pitches as changing its essential unity (though it may change its sound and function). For example, in Western musical theory all the arrangements of notes below are considered to be one and the same three-pitch chord, or triad (shown at either end of the diagram).

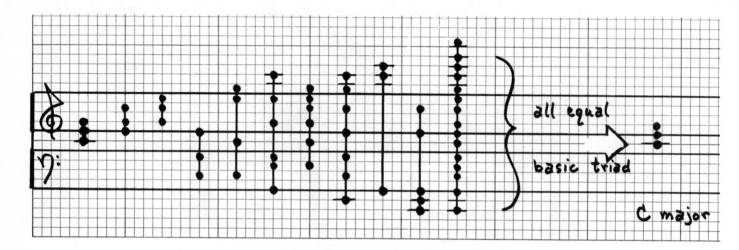

It seems to me, however, that it may be time to reexamine this basic tenet (called octave equivalence), particularly when dealing with the many harmonic systems and practices found in world music (and in the contemporary music of the West). Maybe the octave should be regarded as just another interval—though a very special one—in making up chords (rather than as a duplication or repetition); maybe factors like vertical spacing, the density or opacity of a chord, its highness or lowness, or its timbre should also be taken into consideration. Musical theory is, after all, like the theories of science, merely a description of what seems to be happening; and it should not be confused with the thing itself: in this case, music.

Chords can also be built on intervals other than third stackings, or fifths or fourths plus the octave. The early twentieth century brought a rash of experimentation in Europe and the Americas: Paul Hindemith (1895–1963) built harmonies in stacks of fourths, Arnold Schoenberg derived chords from the note series of his basic twelve-tone set, Charles Ives composed dense tonal masses, or "tone clusters," made up of every note that could be played between the elbows and fingertips of a player's forearm crashed down on a piano keyboard. Since then these chord-building techniques and their sounds have been absorbed into the common musical vocabulary of the West: anyone who has ever gone to a movie or watched television has heard them, although perhaps unconsciously. It is probably a moot point to note that many of these harmonic innovations, revolutionary as they were in Europe and the Americas, were duplications, or reinventions, of harmonic practices that had existed for centuries in other parts of the world.

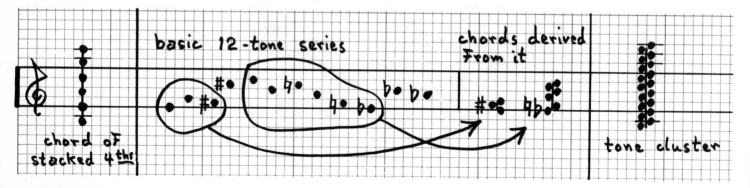

The mouth organ of the Far East—with its free-reed sound producers, tiny teapotlike air chamber, and long, exquisitely arranged bamboo pipes—is probably one of the oldest harmonic instruments in the world. In its southeast Asian form, such as the *khaen* of Cambodia, musicians accompany melodies (played on the lower notes) with chordal drones; and in interludes and cadences (endings) they draw out long, breathlike chordal sonorities. The tones in these chords are drawn from the tonal possibilities of the pipes and reed, and from the scale. The ear of the player and his musical tradition undoubtedly play an important part in the choice of pitches, but we cannot discount another possibility: the nature of the instrument itself, the arrangement of its finger holes.

In Japan the cousin of the *khaen* is the classical *sho* mouth organ, which plays an important role in the layers and sound of the ancient *gagaku* ceremonial court orchestra. The *sho* in the *gagaku* texture is a purely chordal instrument: from a total of fifteen possible notes it has a repertoire of eleven chords. Which chords are chosen and their sequence depends upon the mode (scale) and melody of a particular composition.

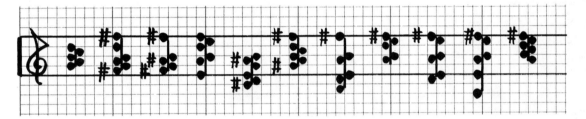

chords of the *sho* in Japanese *gagaku* (accidentals apply only to the chords they precede)

In performance the *sho* player changes his chords in the middle of each bar, beginning very softly and building up in a crescendo that ends just before the next chord. Sound can be produced by both exhaling and inhaling through the instrument. The progression of *sho* chords in *gagaku* is not a "progression" in the sense of European harmonies—that is, they are not moving in inevitable and predictable directions or being pulled by the magnetism of tonal poles, with all the relationships that this involves. Rather they are an *arranged* sequence; or as William P. Malm has so beautifully put it: the chords "freeze" and "solidify" the melody; they enclose it like a solid transparent block of "amber in which a butterfly has been preserved."

Another way of making harmony (which I learned in music school as having been invented by Stravinsky) is used by musicians in Bali and Java, throughout Africa, and in the folk traditions of Europe. If one takes the collection of notes that make up scales and melodies—particularly if they are diatonic (seven notes to the octave) or built of combinations of whole steps and skips (like the pentatonic [five notes to the octave])—and play them simultaneously in almost any combination, they seem to harmonize automatically, through a magic all their own. This "automatic" harmony can happen almost at random, the result of simultaneous melodic occurrences, or it can be planned—composed—or the result of a musician following traditional improvisatory procedures. In central west Africa many of the scales used for melodies have gaps of the interval of a third—sometimes in the "chains of thirds" described earlier in the section on melody—which make them particularly well suited for the harmonic togethers preferred by African musicians' ears.

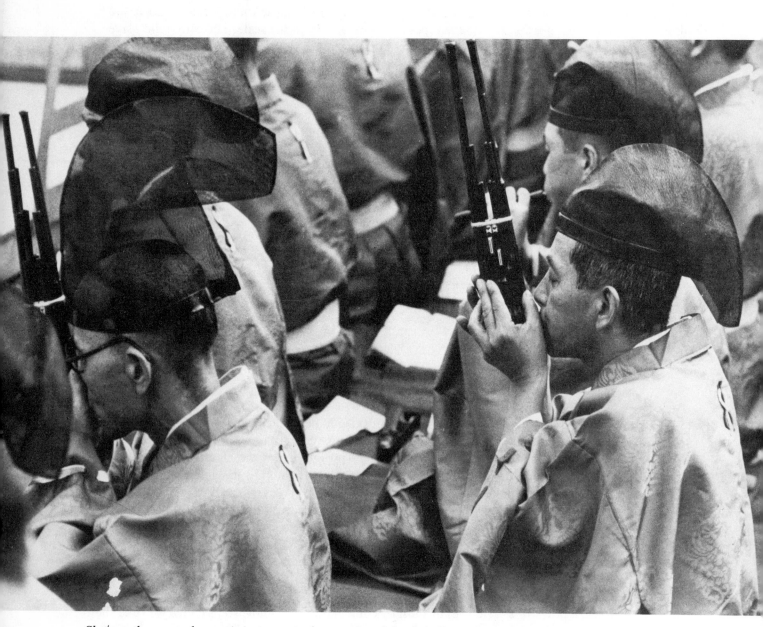

Sho/mouth organ, a harmonic instrument, plays a series of chords in Japanese *gagaku* music.

The music of the Javanese *gamelan* orchestra may be thought of as functioning with many strata. Foreground, *bonang;* background right, *sarons*; background left, *kempul* and *gong ageng*/hanging gongs. Wesleyan University *gamelan* ensemble.

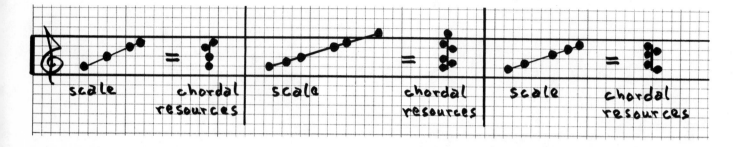

We do not mean to imply that this way of working with harmony is simple. On the contrary, in Africa it is immensely complex and is often combined with other procedures like polyrhythmic phrasings, parallel third movement, dronelike chording, or the alteration of harmonic constellations.

In the *gamelan* music of Java and Bali, many of the harmonic simultaneities are also of this variety. In the interlocking figurations among several instruments or in the two-hand, two-part playing on instruments like the *gender*, adjacent notes may be sounded together or intermediate notes may be skipped to form Indonesian (remember: the tuning is different from ours) thirds, fourths, fifths, and so on. Yet, perhaps because of the dominant thread of the melody to which all instruments and their figurations relate, or because of the ringing timbre or an "inner ear" of the tradition that somehow invisibly guides the choice of pitches happening together, everything blends. The harmonic workings make sense. Better yet, they "work" in the context!

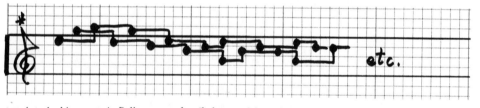

two interlocking parts in Balinese *gamelan* (*kebyar* style) music

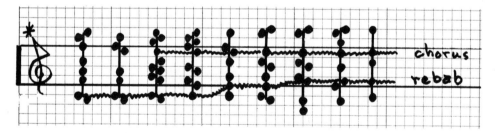

simultaneous pitch occurrences of all melodic parts and ornamenting parts in fragment of Javanese *gamelan*; two melodic strands are shown: a male chorus melody and the *rebab* fiddle melody

*pitches approximate

But while we can freeze the simultaneities in a *gamelan* texture—like a snapshot—it is incorrect to think of the music as a series of vertical blocks. What we actually hear, what we perceive—and what the musicians play (mostly)—are vertical strands. A more correct picture of the Javanese *gamelan* happenings in the preceding example would be:

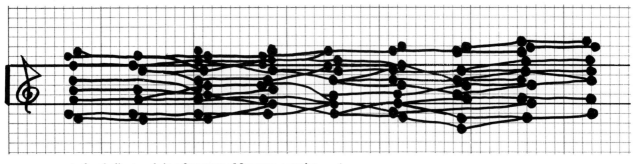

movement of melodic strands in a fragment of Javanese *gamelan* music

And on top of this we would have to add the characteristic rhythms and speeds of the various instruments (and their melodies and figurations in each layer) as well as their tone color—both factors that give the instruments and their parts individuality and help us to hear them as separate parts in the mosaic of the whole.

In the *kebyar gamelan* style of Bali—a modern style with its sudden explosive attacks (described by one musician as being like the sudden "bursting open of a flower"), extraordinarily lavish orchestral textures and effects, bold syncopations, and intricate passagework—block chords are used. These chords with a ringing, brassy sound are built from a clusterlike, simultaneous striking of four of the scale tones, and sometimes they are spaced across the many-octave range of the full orchestra. They may be used as a dramatic beginning for a piece or in a section of a piece:

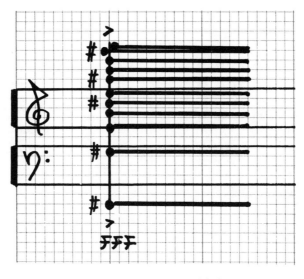

(pitches approximate)

Or they may form rhythmic accompaniments, often ostinatolike, that work underneath the more melodic configurations:

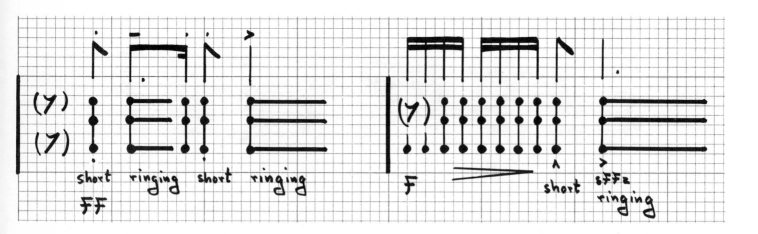

Often these chordal rhythms are fast repeated notes leading to sudden pauses or surprising (to the listener) syncopated accents. By hitting the instruments in different places a variety of timbre is achieved; and the chords may be allowed to ring or they may be damped to create a hollow, metallic clank.

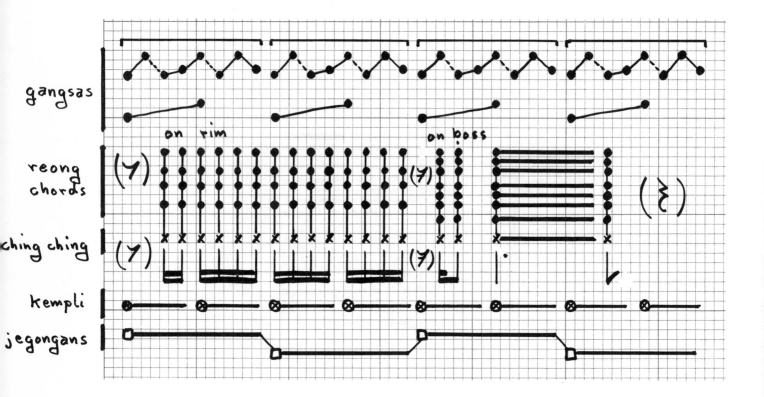

Traditional harmony in the West, whether in folk, popular, or classical music, is based on the root movement of chords. The *root* is the bottom note in a chord stacking of thirds:

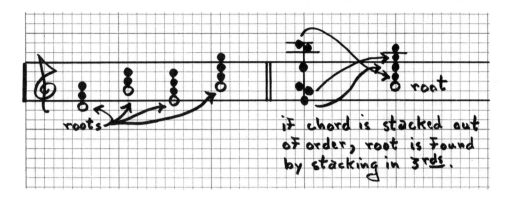

A progression of chords is actually a progression of roots. The "strongest" progression is regarded to be the root movement at the interval of a perfect fourth or fifth, although chords commonly "progress" through intervals of thirds and seconds (and every other possible interval) as well. For example, the following progression—familiar to almost everybody because it forms a harmonic ostinato repeated over and over again in ten to fifty thousand popular, near-popular, unpopular, and never-to-be-popular songs in the United States—uses a root progression by third, third, second, and fourth in one version, and by third, fourth, fifth, and fourth in the other:

the chords that launched ten thousand (plus) tunes

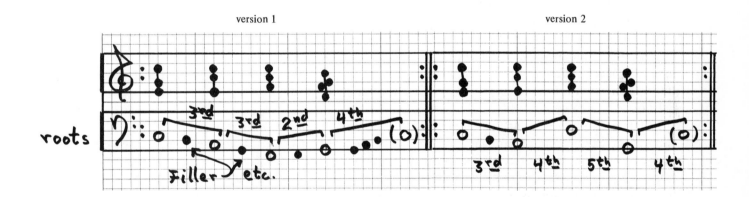

Harmony in the West (and the chords and progressions that make it up) is the most important single element in the entire complex of tonality: chords and progression formulas affirm tonal centers and themselves exist in an entire hierarchy of relationships (something like the gravitational poles and pulls and rotational orbits of planets in the solar system). Harmony reinforces both the macrocosm and the microcosm of musical structure; it colors melody (melody without harmony is considered "naked" or "incomplete"); it provides variety—usually balanced by the familiar and expected; and it can be in itself expressive through its timbre, movement, or sound. While it is impossible for us here to do more than skim across the surface of harmony and its workings in the music of every stratum, of every shape and variety in the West—literally thousands of books have been written about the subject—we can make several additional observations. In the West:

1. Harmony is extremely important, even essential, to the idea of music (as a concept, as a tool) from the Middle Ages to the present day.

2. There is great variance in the use of harmony and chords. Folk music often gets along with

two or three chords without ever changing tonal centers. In classical music, composers in many of the historical periods have expanded the harmonic language of or previous to their time. Thus harmony in the West has seemed to "progress" from the relatively simple to the relatively complex. Pop music as a whole remains rather conservative harmonically (and melodically), lagging behind the innovations and changes of classical music by as much as several hundred years! The harmonic language of jazz is eclectic, depending upon the style of individual performers, and may vary from chording derived from Debussy to that of the avant garde. The twentieth century has, in fact, seen a great deal of innovation, particularly in classical music—many composers and musicians leaving traditional harmony and tonality behind.

3. The harmonic systems of the West—with some exceptions—are not "systems" at all: they are rather observations that theorists have made after the fact, after musicians following their ears and the musical habits and language of their time or style have created their music. Finally, we should note that harmony in the West does not follow some inexorable natural law connected with physics, acoustics, or the movement of stars. It is simply—like the way we dress, or shape our houses, or order the words in our sentences—the way we, in one place, at one time on the planet, do things. Enough said.

Polyphony

Polyphony, remember, is the simultaneous occurrence of two or more relatively independent melodies. Perhaps more correctly we might think of polyphony as the simultaneity of music layers—primarily melodic, but also harmonic or rhythmic—each of which displays enough rambunctiousness to make itself noticeable (in itself) rather than disappearing into the conformist blend of the musical whole. Actually there is no sharp dividing line between what we have chosen to call "homophony," "polyphony," or "heterophony": there is enough overlapping among them to ruin the neatest theoretical blueprint, and some scholars (like Bruno Nettl) prefer to put at least several of these musical happenings in the same basket. If we remember that the differences are just a matter of degree—the independence or standoutishness of voices, parts, or layers (or their homogeneity) might be heard differently by different persons—and that our own choices are more or less arbitrary, then we can proceed (with our qualifications and exceptions tied to our legs like the jangling bells of an Indian dancer)!

The peaceful coexistence of simultaneous melodies can come about in a number of ways. First, there is the expansion of the drone idea: the parts (singers or instrumentalists) may alternate between melody and drone or fly away from (and back to) static drone notes. Or the drone itself (in the spirit of '76) may begin to assert its independence with occasional other auxiliary pitches and perhaps also little melodic figures.

Wanyil/bamboo trumpets, accompanied by drumming, singing, and dancing. Northern Abelam people, near Maprik, New Guinea.

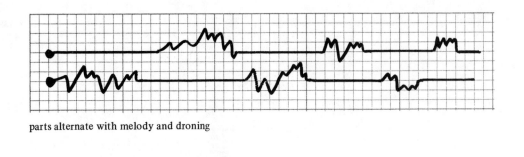

parts alternate with melody and droning

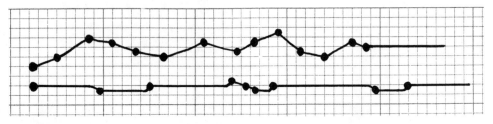

the drone (lower) begins to assert its independence with auxiliary notes (pygmy—Ituri forest)

Second, when a number of people sing or play together, even if they are all following the same melodic strand, there may be anticipations by some voices of where the melody is going, as well as a lagging behind, or a holding of previous notes. While this can be "accidental" in the sense that people in a certain culture may not be concerned with a machinelike precision, it can also be noticed, enjoyed, and used intentionally as part of the musical texture.

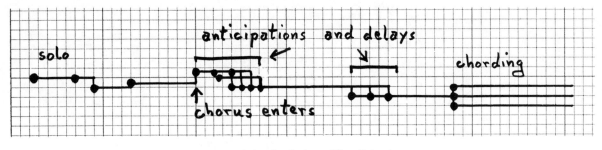

segment of choral polyphony (New Guinea)

A third kind of marginal polyphony occurs in a call-and-response performance (a soloist with an answering chorus) or in an antiphonal format (two soloists or two choruses alternating) when there is an overlapping around the edges—that is, the beginning of one part happens over and simultaneous with the ending of the other, and vice versa.

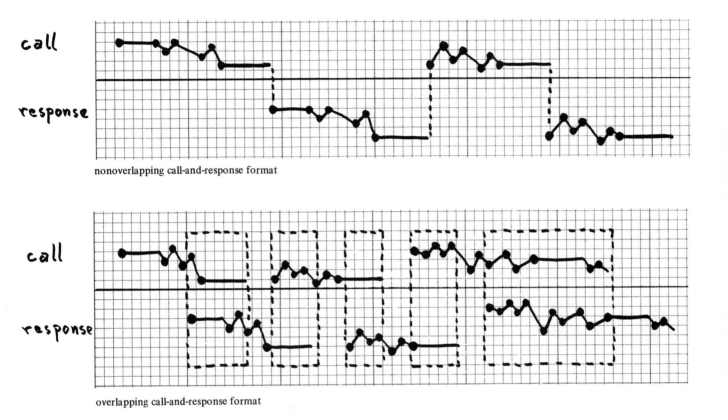

nonoverlapping call-and-response format

overlapping call-and-response format

Related to the overlapping call-and-response idea is the *canon* or *round*. Here each part works through the same melodic material or tune but begins at a different time. Once thought to be strictly a European phenomenon, the round is found among people as diverse as the Ituri forest pygmies, the Bushmen of the Kalahari, the Shona of Rhodesia, and the Jabo of Liberia in Africa and the Nage tribals in the West Flores in Indonesia.

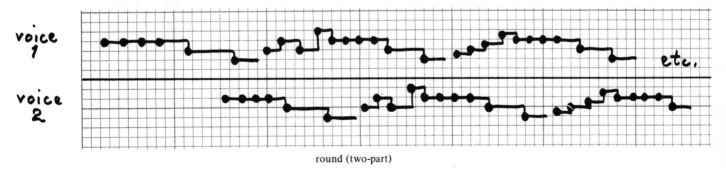

round (two-part)

Rounds can be performed in any number of parts; imitation—as for many of the techniques of nonnotated ear music—is "imperfect," that is, it does not have the rigidity and inflexibility of textbook imitation. Incidentally, the technique of imitation—expanded and conceptualized—is an important one in European art music, and it is used not only in "polyphonic forms" like fugues and concerti grossi, but also as a compositional tool in symphonies, sonatas, tone poems, movie scores, in fact, virtually in everything.

A fifth way of generating polyphony in a complex and many-voiced musical texture is used in the choral singing of the Bushmen and pygmies in Africa. A basic phrase design, a rough melodic plan, and a scale form the raw materials on which each singer may then elaborate in his own way. Extra notes are stuck in, notes are omitted, certain pitches may be lengthened (or shortened), inner motifs may be repeated, and so on. It is almost like twenty to thirty people being given the dimensions and shape of a house and the freedom to elaborate or emphasize (simultaneously) the details of construction that please them or excite their respective creative imaginations. In Bushman and pygmy polyphony there is, then, an intricate balance between individual creativity and the limits and controls of their sonic materials—all meshed in the extraordinary beauty (of sound, of structure) of a recognizable larger design.

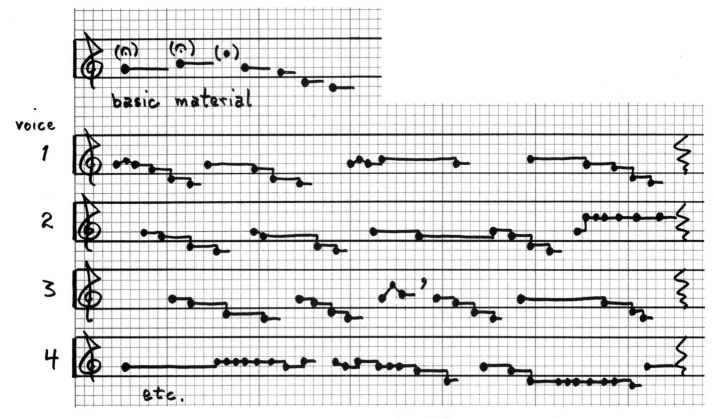

some possible realizations (sung simultaneously)

Another technique—also a product of the African creative imagination—is the use of intricate melodic/rhythmic interlocking patterns, each segment fitting into the next like a wonderful invisible (but heard) jigsaw puzzle, such as in the Malinke xylophone music.

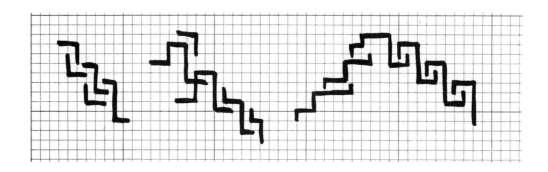

There may also be a superimposition of melodic ostinatos, which work together to build an active, complex, and kaleidoscopically changing musical texture much in the same way as is done in African drumming.

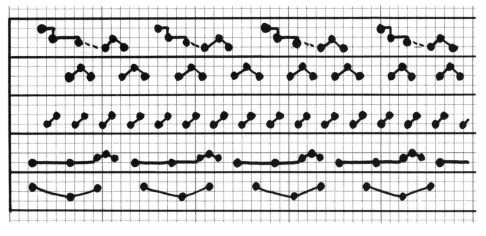

stacking of melodic ostinatos

Music may also be stacked in polyphonic layers moving against or independently of each other. Each layer *in itself* may be a complex texture made up of many elements. For example, each of the three polyphonic techniques given before—the pygmies' motivic working out, the interlocking xylophone parts, or the stacked ostinatos—may function as only one of several layers, say, as an accompaniment texture under a soloist's melody and over a drumming background.

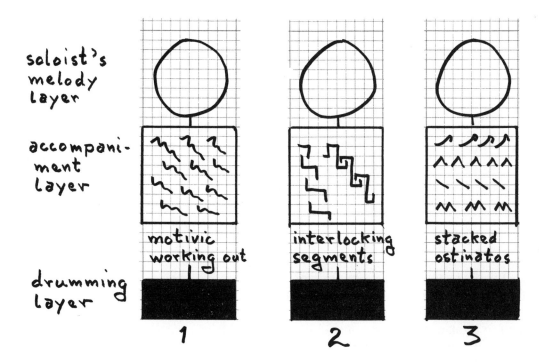

Among the Masai people of Africa there can be as many as three vocal layers (accompanied by percussion): the lead singer's melody, a choral response, and an underlying ostinato pattern.

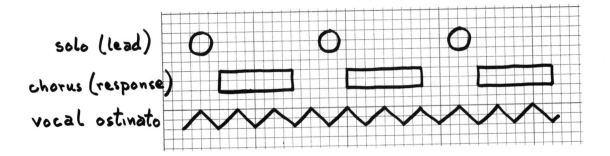

There can also be a stacking of primarily homophonic layers, for example, parallel two-note or three-note chords which then move more or less independently of each other.

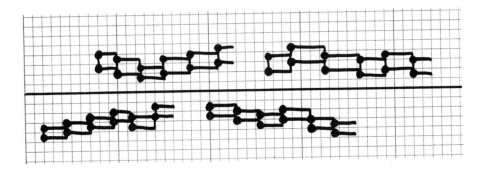

Individual melodic parts are often throught of as moving against each other in one of three possible ways:

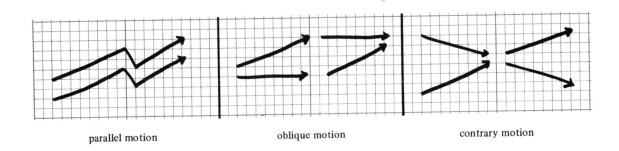

parallel motion   oblique motion   contrary motion

Usually in polyphonic music there is a mixture of these types of movement. Another important characteristic in world polyphony both in Africa and in eastern Europe is the constant fluctuation in the density of its parts. We—versed in European four-part harmony writing and techniques and concepts—tend to think of musical simultaneities as happening in a fairly stable and constant density. Other types of polyphony may, however, begin or end with unisons, expand into occasional harmonies or parallel movement, burst into independent lines, or break into chording seemingly at a moment's notice.

Molokan Russian-American women, part of a choral group, weave shimmering polyphony over the men's parts in traditional religious music.

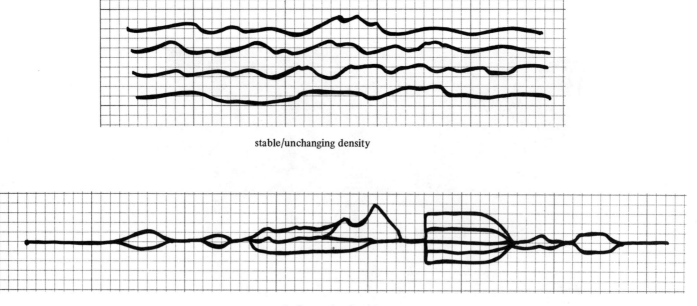

stable/unchanging density

constantly fluctuating density

Such fluctuating polyphonic/harmonic densities are common in the choral music of the Caucasus, Ukraine, and Russia. Songs often begin with a single voice joined by others in unison and then expanding into parts. There may be no more than two or three real parts (omitting doublings at the unison or octave); held dronelike notes and parallel harmonies fill out the texture in the middle around the core of the melody, while a bass line provides a strong bottom. Another characteristic is the cadencing (ending places of phrases or songs) to "open" chords (of octave and fifth, octaves, or unisons).

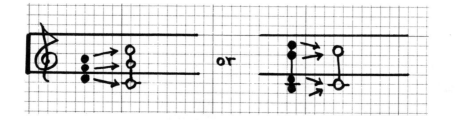

Polyphony in Europe (except in early and late music) is usually chord-based; that is, no matter how many parts are rolling along simultaneously, they all fit into a framework of chord progressions. In the music of J. S. Bach and other composers of the baroque period these chords were plunked out on a keyboard instrument (like the organ or harpsichord) while the polyphony—each part independent yet harmonizing in the general scheme—developed in and through them.

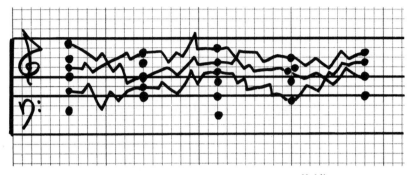

melodic polyphony moving through harmonic scaffolding

The melodic movements of the parts between the blocklike chord changes—like an acrobat swinging through a scaffolding—illustrate another way polyphony is made: the melodies weave their way through, in a sense filling in the space between the poles. What happens in between can be incredibly dissonant as long as there is a resolution on the communal harmonic meeting place of the poles.

This type of many-voiced music-making is also found in early jazz (from the 1920s) where the "front-line" melody instruments (usually cornet or trumpet, clarinet, trombone, and, later, saxophone) weave their group improvisation in a rambunctious texture—brilliant and lively and jumbled like technicolor steel wool—around a base melody and its chord progressions. As also in Bach (and much melodic writing in the West) many of the improvised simultaneous melodies are based on horizontal chordal outlines, arpeggio movement, and semiharmonic figurations that imply the underlying chords.

Recent "new thing" jazz builds polyphony in a different way. Most of the polyphonic textures we have examined so far are based on several principles:

1. Use of the same melodic material in all parts (imitation, "pygmy" tonal working out, etc.)
2. Stacking of ostinatos
3. Functioning musical layers
4. Expanding drones
5. Threading through chord progressions

But polyphony can also happen through the simultaneous occurrence of completely independent and unrelated melodies. Such complex textures, where each musician apparently "does his own thing," are not limited to new jazz or the Westernized avant garde: they are found, for example, in certain musical styles in Malaysia and Korea. In the classical music of Japan—generally not at all of the polyphonic variety—two extremely unusual and interesting compositional processes are used. Both are found in music for the thirteen-stringed *koto* long zither. In the style called *danawase* the original melody of the basic *koto* part (*houte*) is combined with a completely different melody (*kaede*) from a different composition played by the second *koto*. The second melody may have to be changed in its details to fit the first, but its basic and recognizable shape remains the same. In the compositional process called *dangaeshi* different sections, or *dan*, of the same melody are superimposed. Although the melodic materials for each of the two *kotos* comes from the same source, the same composition, the structure is not like the audible working out of the same theme as in rounds or fugues, but rather a blocklike superimposition—like precast concrete blocks—of extended melodic units. Both processes are common also in the classical music tradition of the West: the

American Charles Ives threw together familiar melodies (odd bedfellows) as diverse as "Rock of Ages," "Camptown Races," and "America the Beautiful." A particularly striking example is found in Alban Berg's opera, *Wozzeck*, where at the moment of the heroine's death all the melodies associated with her in previous scenes are played together in an instant, a musical reflection (Berg has told us) of the commonly held folk belief that one's entire life passes before his mind's (and memory's) screen in an instant at the moment of death.

Our scanning of some of the techniques of polyphony in the earth's music has omitted many of the more unusual processes—for instance, those that have grown in recent years in the exciting and highly imaginative field of electronic music. We might mention, however, a music made by the Takasago people of Formosa: with a tone quality of an "organlike hum," two voices begin a long and slow climb, rising from a pitch in the lowest range in a higher and higher chain of notes. The second part, however, rises at a slightly slower rate, slightly out of phase, and the intervals between the two ascending parts widen gradually from tiny microtones (at first) to increasingly larger harmonic spaces (later). The purpose of this extraordinary music is not aesthetic, nor is it meant merely for enjoyment: on the contrary, it is a musical charm to help the millet grow!

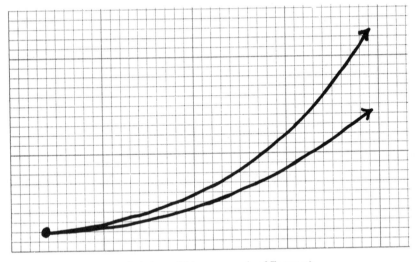

musical charm (Takasago people of Formosa)

Heterophony

Heterophony is a terrible word. In the imagination it seems to have a Mephistophelean tinge, connected maybe with the forbidden and the occult, or conjuring up shadowy practices from the underground: like sadism, incest, necromancy, matricide, zoophilia, or kleptomania. Actually heterophony is nothing to be afraid of; it is quite harmless. Like so many of the words we use in music, it has its meanings (inadequate though they may be), it is used, and it is here to stay (at least for the present). Furthermore, it describes a musical technique that is used in some of the most beautiful music in the word, and it is more common in more diverse musics on our earth than familiar (for us) concepts like harmony or counterpoint. Heterophony—if we may redefine it—is the weaving of melodic strands around a central core of a melody; it is melody-based (rather than harmony-based) and its strands, happening simultaneously, all relate to the central melody in some way: they may be variations of it, they may ornament it, they may scan or punctuate its important notes. The scholar Curt Sachs has described heterophony as being like a group of very different people (in looks, in dress, in characteristics) massed together—as in crossing the street—and walking in the same direction. It is a good image.

Much of the ensemble music of the Orient is heterophonic in nature. Korean ensemble playing chamber music.
Left to right: Sung Keum-yun, *kaya kum*; Chi Young-hee, *hae kum*; Kim So-hee, *yang gum*; Kim Yoon-duk,
komung go.

Heterophony happens to an extent everywhere, wherever musicians play or sing a melody together and they are not in precise unison or octaves or their rhythms are not quite together. This "accidental" heterophony occurs no farther from us (in the United States) than our beginners' junior high school band, the hymn singing of our churches, the woozy sing-alongs at the local bar, or the performance of the national anthem before a basketball game. Culturally we tend to regard heterophonic performance as a defect; it opposes our ideal of preciseness and blend; and furthermore it is not (and this is important) part of our musical language: it is generally not conceived by composers and written into their music. Yet in unwritten "ear" idioms, particularly those deriving from Afro-American sources, it happens perhaps much more than we are aware of: in a harmonica and guitar lead, for example, interpreting the same blues tune simultaneously, or in similar doublings (or triplings) in rock or jazz, or in (white) country forms like bluegrass, or country and western, or western swing.

A working heterophonic texture can be very "slight," that is, with very little fluctuation and departure from the main thread of the melody; it can be "moderate," still retaining the outline of the tune; it may be "dense" or "complex," with the additional part(s) displaying a great deal of individuality and seeming to become, in fact, independent melodies in a contrapuntal (or polyphonic) texture; or it can be anything in between or in combination—the Indonesian *gamelan* orchestra, for example, in the music and instruments of its many layers combines almost every imaginable heterophonic relationship.

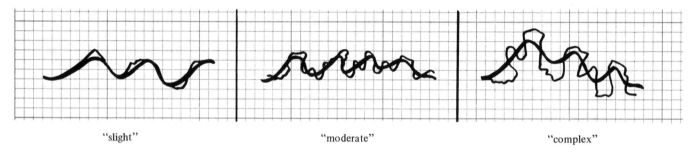

       "slight"   "moderate"   "complex"

(all relative terms)

On one level a heterophonic texture can reflect a society's attitudes toward the togethers of performance. In the singing of the American Indians of the Great Plains, for example, although everyone is singing the same tune there is a marvelous scope for each to express his individuality (simultaneously with the others who are doing the same). This personal freedom, or self-reliance, is simply and purely the way a song is sung; and it may reflect a love of individuality which characterized Plains Indian culture during its brief and tragic blooming in the nineteenth century.

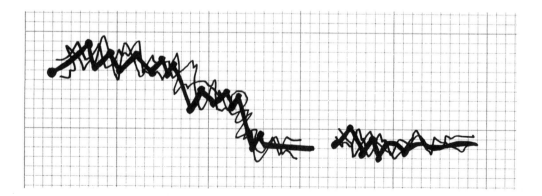

Such loose and informal togethers are found in group music-makings throughout the world. The simultaneous variations on the melody are spontaneous and unformalized, there is nothing rigid about them, they spin around the core of the melody (or rather, the *idea* of the melody since the texture may be all variation with no form of the plain, primeval, archetypal melody) like bees around a honeycomb. Village bands in eastern Europe may include several instruments doubling the melody layer with a slight tinge of heterophony, that is, with a together that is not entirely (100 percent) together, and here we may note a very interesting fact: different instruments—like people— have very different characteristics, and these differences (in fingerings, sound, techniques, easy-to- make ornamentation, etc.) can be expressed in their renditions of the same melody. Like the lion, the straw man, and the tin man walking the yellow brick road in *The Wizard of Oz*, a bagpipe, a clarinet, and a fiddle "walking" the same melody together remain preeminently themselves. Or a freer-form texture may be expressed in the style of similar instruments in a melodic ensemble as, for example, in the double-reed pipes (like the Turkish *zurnā* or Indian *shehnai*) combined with drums in folk music groups from north Africa to China. Here—as in Plains Indian singing—it is the style, the acceptable way of performing, rather than the nature of the instrument, which results in a heterophonic texture.

We might divide the world into two great zones where heterophony is an important or predomi- nant factor in communal music-making. (There was, remember, our mapping of a harmonic/poly- phonic zone also, including Malayo-Polynesia, the Caucasian area, Euro-America, and central and south Africa.) These heterophonic zones are only partially geographical; they are also stylistic and cover two different approaches to the problem. One style involving the accompaniment of a singer's voice (and melody) by an instrument predominates in a large band following melody-oriented musi- cal styles in Islamic north Africa, in the Arabic world, into Greece and the Balkans, across Iran and central Asia, and into the Far East. At one time, before the development of harmonic accompani- ments and in the days of minstrels and bands, it must have been common in Europe also. Often the instrument is played by the singer himself. In this heterophonic style his instrument—often a fiddle— weaves its line around his vocal melody: it seldom plays in absolute unison, but rather anticipates pitches or holds them (like memory), or it may fill in space during vocal pauses. The singer's instru- ment may sustain long dronelike pitches while his voice flies; or, on the contrary, the instrument— like a buzzing, darting, circling mosquito—can ornament the long held notes of the singer. Invariably, especially if the accompanying instrument is a bowed fiddle, the second heterophonic part (the in- strument's) is far more florid, busier, faster, more active, more ornamented than that of the voice; it is also more continuous. The musical relationship between accompanying instrument and the voice's melody can be extremely complex and subtle; just how it works and how far it can go to- ward independent counterpoint (two-part polyphony) depends on the unwritten laws of the ears and intuition of the musician and of the musical culture within which he creates.

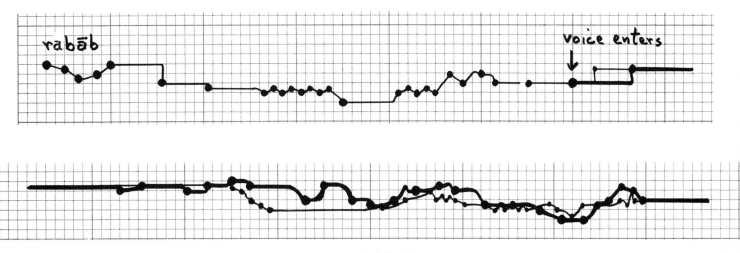

voice and *rabāb* (Syria)

A closer, less ornate style of heterophony can be seen in the music of the Peking opera, where the bowed *erh hu* fiddle (and the orchestra) plays a nonstop, breathless, continuous melody which connects with the singer's short phrases. We should note that in both of our examples the vocalist sings words also, adding an extra dimension to the musical texture.

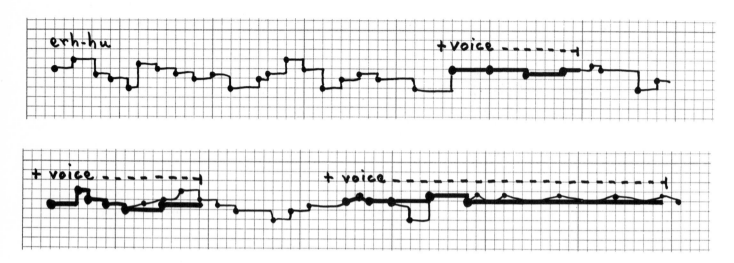

voice and *erh hu*, Peking opera (China)

The instrumental accompanist, particularly if he is playing a plucked lute—which cannot sustain sound (like the voice, or a fiddle), whose sound fades away quickly after the pluck—often scans the melody, filling the spaces between with a kind of nonstop patter. Long vocal notes may also be played in tremolo or "rhythmicized," that is, played as a rhythmic pattern resting on the same pitch.

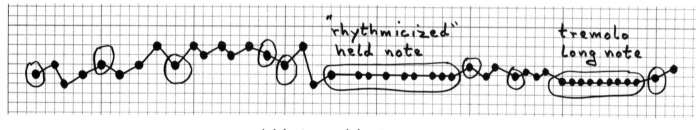

circled notes are melody notes
saz, accompanying vocal melody (Turkey)

In still another heterophonic style—found in much of the traditional music of Japan—the plucked accompanying instrument plays a simplified, straightforward version of the melody, while the voice elaborates, often in a striking syncopated "delay" which pulls against the rigid framework of the accompaniment like a rubber band stretched from a picket fence.

In the mechanics and techniques of heterophony, the other great zone (area and style) is found characteristically in the Far East, although pockets—as in almost everything else in world music—exist elsewhere (in some avant-garde music in the United States, for example). Here the relationships among the various parts are highly formalized; there are rather rigid rules about what can or cannot be done; each instrument may fit into a particular niche in the functioning of the heterophonic texture. This formal and layered heterophony is highly developed in southeast Asia, and we shall take the large *gamelan* orchestras of Java and Bali (described to an extent in the "Alones and Togethers" section) as an example.

In Java a kind of skeletal core melody is played on the *saron* metallophone. (This melody, sometimes called the "nuclear melody" by scholars, is not to be confused with the real "melody" of a piece: it is rather like the bare bones of the tune.) Other *sarons* can vary this core melody by playing repeated notes of it or by alternating its tones with other pitches according to procedural formulas. The large *bonang panembung* with its knobbed potlike gongs and the vibraphonelike *gender panembung* scan the notes of the core melody playing every four notes and every two notes respectively. The tiny *saron peking* plays the core melody at double speed anticipating its pitch changes by half a beat. The various "elaborating instruments"—the knobbed *bonang* gong sets, the vibraphonelike *gender*, the *gambang* xylophone, and the *tjelempung* plucked zither—move in and around the notes of the *saron* core melody (or of the real, "invisible" melody which is heard compositely but not "seen" in any of the single individual parts) drawing from a repertoire of possible figurations and modes of procedure. At times these parts seem like independent polyphonic improvisation, so greatly do their notes and rhythms and pitches vary from one another and from the skeletal pitches of the *saron* tune; but at all times (and this is important) their relationship is a melodic one, and it is *to a single melody*, much as all the branches of a climbing vine spread out across a brick wall yet all relate and connect to the main trunk and the roots. Finally, the *rebab* spike fiddle and the *suling* end-blown flute function in a more flexible, ear-oriented, heterophonic style in relationship to the vocal parts and the "melody" of the piece, similar in many respects to the styles in the first "heterophonic zone" (from north Africa and the Middle East, and out and across) described earlier. The female vocalist also weaves an independent vocal line, responding in a beautiful and subtle way to cues from the *rebab*.

HETEROPHONIC MELODIES IN THE JAVANESE *GAMELAN* (SHOWN IN RELATIONSHIP TO THE *SARON* MELODY)

1. "Fixed melody" instruments

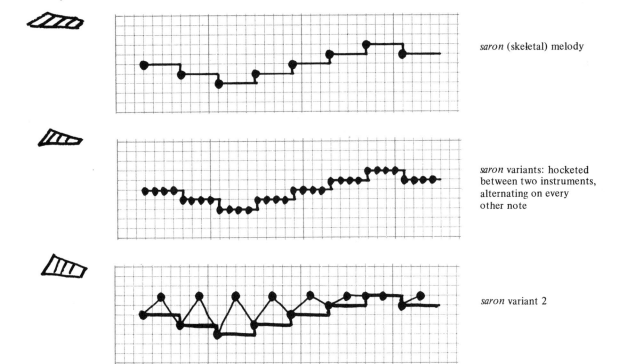

saron (skeletal) melody

saron variants: hocketed between two instruments, alternating on every other note

saron variant 2

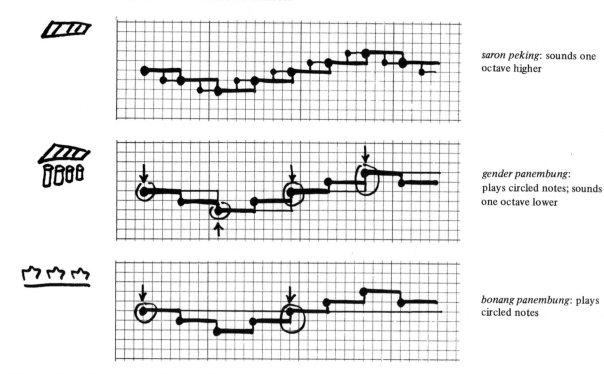

saron peking: sounds one octave higher

gender panembung: plays circled notes; sounds one octave lower

bonang panembung: plays circled notes

2. Improvising instruments (possible realizations):

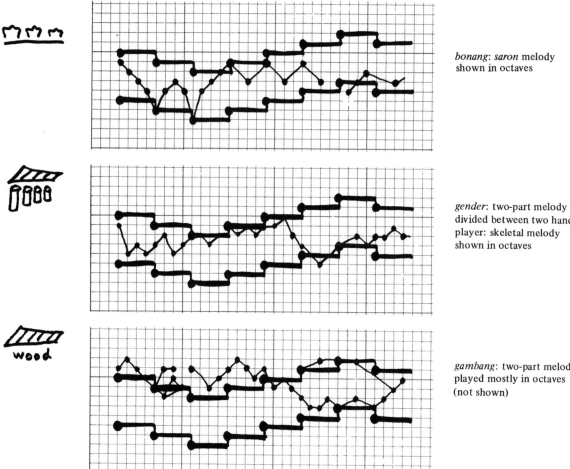

bonang: *saron* melody shown in octaves

gender: two-part melody divided between two hands of player: skeletal melody shown in octaves

gambang: two-part melody played mostly in octaves (not shown)

Sankyoku ensemble. Left to right: Ayakano Reade, *koto*; Namino Torii, *shamisen*; Shudo Yamato, *shakuhachi*.

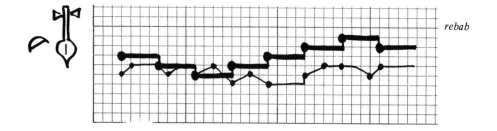

rebab

In the classical music of Thailand, the melodies of the various instruments in an ensemble all meet at the same note on key pitches of a basic core melody. These tonal meeting places are like poles, or bands of sunlight streaming through forest foliage, or islands in a musical sea. Between them—at which point everyone is in unison or octaves—each musician goes his own musical way, spinning out a semi-improvised part according to traditional procedures or the unique characteristics of his instrument.

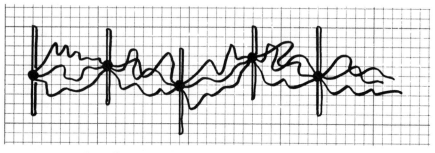

"poles" in heterophonic texture of Thai classical music

The in-between places in the texture can be quite dense and the simultaneities "dissonant" until they contract, accordionlike, to the poles. But really to "hear" this music—a problem to be met also in comprehending much of the world's heterophony and melody-based musics—we must, in a sense, "horizontalize" our ears; we must change our ingrown habits of thinking about and perceiving music vertically (that is, harmonically), and relax with the stream of melodies and the bubbling of note sequences moving through time like a cascading mountain spring. Only then can we enjoy (really) and understand (intelligently) this large segment of the earth's music.

In the _sankyoku_ ensemble of Japan the three melodic instruments—_koto, shamisen_, and _shakuhachi_—combine with the singing voice(s) of the players in an extremely sophisticated and subtle relationship that is basically heterophonic: it is an expansion of a single melodic thread. Exactly how the various parts go, how far they can move toward independent polyphony, or how they blend with and ornament the main melodic line is—like so many things Japanese—mechanically/technically elusive yet intuitively, unspokenly precise. A rightness or a wrongness, a balance of symmetry or asymmetry, can be felt—but not formalized in words or rule-book concepts. The various parts played by the instruments in the _sankyoku_ ensemble are, however, composed, written down in musical notation, and passed on according to the methods and style of a particular musical tradition. There is no improvisation. The long _koto_ zither carries the main melody (in vocal sections it follows the voice) and its part is often called the "bone." The plucked _shamisen_ lute follows with variations, at times expanding into an independent part, and is traditionally called the "flesh." The _shakuhachi_ bamboo flute also follows the melodic thread with variations; its part is the most melismatic and ornamented, and it stands out tonally because (as a wind instrument opposed to the plucked _koto_ and _shamisen_) it can sustain tones like a voice. The _shakuhachi_'s part is called the "skin." Again the characteristics of each instrument strongly influence exactly what that instrument does in the heterophonic texture; one could not, for example, play the *shakuhachi* part on the *koto*, or vice versa. At the same time—because a composition is melody-based—the various heterophonic layers can be stripped away to reveal the essential melody: the same composition could be played as a solo *koto* piece, as a duet for *koto* and *shamisen*, or arranged for the full *sankyoku* ensemble. Its setting, its texture, its rendering change, but *it* remains the same. One musician has described this phenomenon as "like an ancient temple which one day may be partially hidden by mist, on another day seen in brilliant sunlight, in the autumn covered with leaves, at dusk shrouded in the shadows of trees, or in winter clothed in snow. Yet it is always there, the same temple, and its bells ring as they have always done since ancient times."

The Geology of Music's "Earth"

We have scanned in some detail some of the ways music can be put together and we have lumped these techniques into overlapping and somewhat imprecise categories such as homophony, harmony, ostinatos, polyphony, and heterophony. Throughout these sections we have constantly touched upon what is perhaps the most important and universal of these techniques: the stacking of musical layers, each of which—like the different strata in a rock formation or in the earth's crust—have different characteristics: a different sound or density or speed or timbre or function in the musical whole.

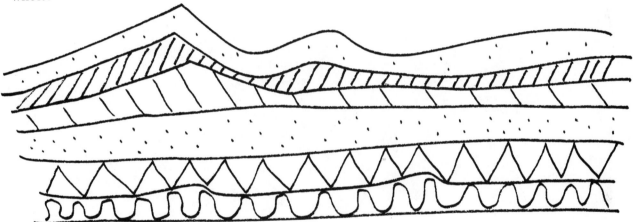

One of the most common functioning layer relationships is that of a melody with drumming (or percussion) accompaniment. It is important to note that although this two-layer relationship is clear-cut and pretty basic, the music made in it—as in the classical music of India or of Iran—is among the most complex in the world.

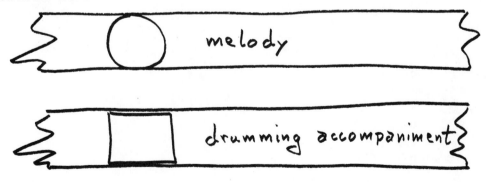

In the West the layer accompanying the melody tends to be harmonic, although a three-layer texture (melody/harmony/percussion) is extremely common in popular art forms.

Rock vocalist Tina Turner.

Each layer may, in fact, be further complicated by substrata: different musical elements working within larger musical functions and sometimes bouncing between them. In a performance by the popular rock band of Ike (b. 1933) and Tina (b. ca. 1938) Turner, for example, the main melodic line sung by a female vocalist (Tina) may be supplemented by countermelodies and short melodic spurts or fill-ins by a male vocalist (Ike), a female vocal trio (the "Ikettes"), or various instruments in the band. The harmonic layer is extremely subtle and complicated: there is rhythmic chording by the "Ikettes," ostinato patterns and chordal bursts by the trumpets and saxophones in the band, rhythmic chord changes on the guitar, and an electric bass line so strong and important that it really should have a category all to itself (the bass is really another melodic thread). The strong emphasis on rhythmic figuration and counteraccents, even in chording and melodic patterns, adds tremendously to the energy of the music and, in fact, makes the entire ensemble seem to function like an enormous percussion ensemble, capable of a variety of melody notes, chords, and timbres. It is no accident that in jazz, rock, and the entire spectrum of popular music the bass (guitar or string), chording keyboard instrument or guitar, and drum set are called the "rhythm section." The rhythmic layer, then, though beginning with the drums and other percussion instruments, filters up through the entire ensemble.

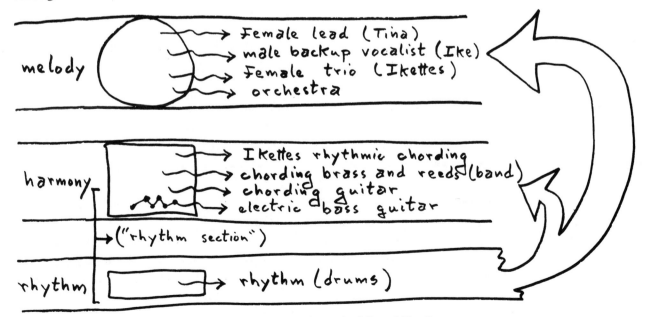

strata and substrata in the music of Ike and Tina Turner

The working out of the layer idea, sometimes quite rigidly, is extremely important (as we have seen) in the musical togethers of the larger ensembles and orchestras throughout the world. The Javanese *gamelan*, for example, might be thought of as having its instruments (and players and music) divided into six strata:

Musical layers of the large Javanese *gamelan* orchestra

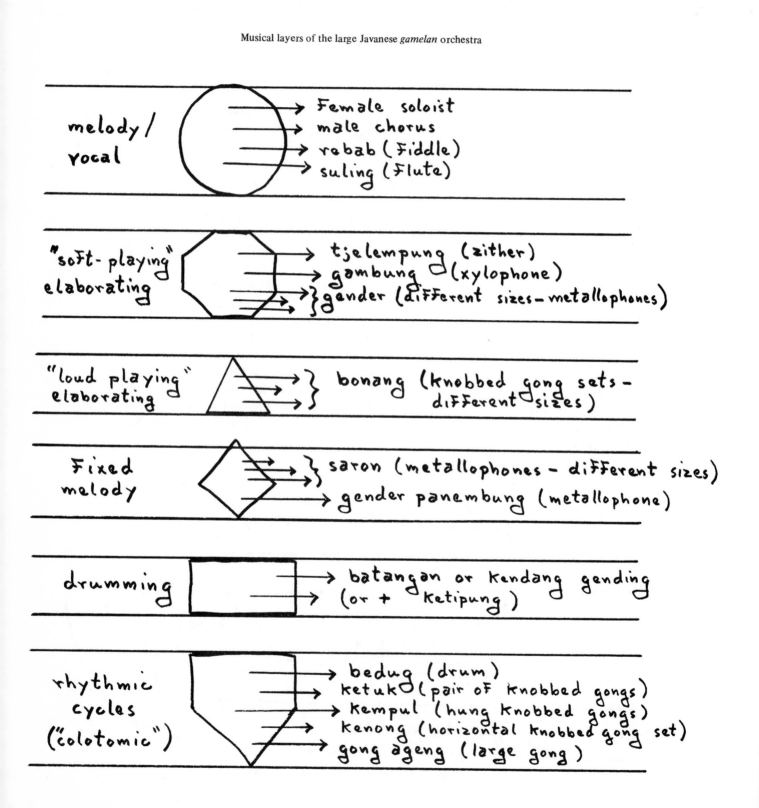

The musical happenings within each layer may (in themselves) be quite complex. This is certainly true, for example, in *gamelan* music and in the Ike and Tina Turner band, but it is also common in central and south Africa where a polyphonic chorus, interlocking xylophone parts, or stacked ostinatos may form only *one* layer in a musical texture. (The other layers could include a lead singer or instrumentalist, or a drumming section, or different types of instruments.) Western classical music tends to allow its instruments to move freely from stratum to stratum, sometimes taking the lead melody, at other times shifting into the background. In other musics musicians may stay very strictly within the functions or sound of their layer.

The stratification of music into layers is one of a number of ways musicians deal with the problem of making music together. It clarifies functions, it prevents chaos, and it may shadow a larger and deeper characteristic of the human animal: a tendency to perceive and organize (in the eyes, in the mind) a multiplicity, a *many*, as a simpler all-enclosing pattern, or *gestalt*. For example, from a distance we see not ten thousand individual trees (a many) but *a* forest or *a* woods (a simplified pattern); or from an airplane window we tend to comprehend not dozens of streets, hundreds of houses, thousands of lawnmowers, cars, people, television antennas, cats, dogs, backyard swimming pools, and abandoned Frisbees, but *a* town. Similarly, for a musician or composer, stratification allows working with larger (and potentially confusing) forces within a simplified pattern/*gestalt*. Furthermore, for the ear musician the layer idea defines his limits so that he or she can work or create freely with complete ease, within the walls of his or her allotted musical room within the structure of the entire musical castle. The putting togethers in music are, after all, the putting togethers of human beings: of *their* voices, *their* instruments, *their* ideas, *their* dreams, *their* concepts, *their* workings, *their* indistinguishable selves, *their* inner melodies.

Berliner, Paul Franklin. "The Soul of the Mbira: An Ethnography of the Mbira Among the Shona People of Rhodesia." Ph.D. dissertation. Middletown, Connecticut: Wesleyan University, 1974.

Gayle, Addison, Jr., ed. *The Black Aesthetic.* New York: Doubleday and Company, 1971.

Hodier, André. *Jazz, Its Evolution and Essence.* New York: Grove Press, 1956.

Hood, Mantle, and Susilo, Hardja. *Music of the Venerable Dark Cloud.* Los Angeles: Institute of Ethnomusicology, UCLA, 1967.

Jones, LeRoi. *Blues People.* New York: William Morrow and Company, 1963.

Kunst, Jaap. *Music in New Guinea.* Translated and corrected by Jeune Scott-Kemball. 'S-Gravenhage: Martinus Nijhoff, 1967.

Malm, William P. *Japanese Music.* Rutland, Vermont: Charles E. Tuttle, 1959.

Malm, William P. *Music Cultures of the Pacific, the Near East, and Asia.* Englewood Cliffs, New Jersey: Prentice-Hall, 1967.

McPhee, Colin. *Music in Bali.* New Haven: Yale University Press, 1966.

Morton, David. *The Traditional Music of Thailand.* Los Angeles: Institute of Ethnomusicology, UCLA, 1968.

Nettl, Bruno. *Folk and Traditional Music of the Western Continents.* Englewood Cliffs, New Jersey: Prentice-Hall, 1965.

Nketia, J. H. Kwabena. *African Music in Ghana.* Evanston, Illinois: Northwestern University Press, 1963.

Parrish, Carl. *A Treasury of Early Music.* New York: W. W. Norton, 1958.

Powne, Michael. *Ethiopian Music.* London: Oxford University Press, 1968.

Prawirohardjo, Shitalakshmi. "*Wajang Kulit Purwa.*" M. A. thesis. Middletown, Connecticut: Wesleyan University, 1972.

Sachs, Curt. *The Wellsprings of Music.* New York: McGraw-Hill Book Company, 1965.

Schuller, Gunther. *Early Jazz.* New York: Oxford University Press, 1968.

Slobin, Mark. *Kirghiz Instrumental Music.* New York: The Asian Music Society, 1969.

Sumarsam. Interviews and conversations, Wesleyan University, Middletown, Connecticut, 1973–75.

Flutist and hand-cymbal player make their music in the midst of a festival crowd, Andhra Pradesh, south India.

ALONES AND
TOGETHERS

There is a particular feeling that we all have when we are alone. The universe of our bodies and the universe of our thoughts keep us company. Sitting or standing (or walking) in isolation, we—as human animals—may have an increased awareness of our breath, our pulse, our eyes, our fingertips, our hair, our itches, throbs, bumps, nudges, tingles. We may hear our inner song. Or we may fly with our imagination into the magical labyrinth of our thoughts and feelings, introspectively, exploring, winding around mental corners, facing (suddenly) unexpected vistas, following threads of ideas and images, tying knots, making connections, zooming at will into the recollection of the past or the projection of the future like some great invisible mythical bird, conjuring the imaginary, or touching (deeply) the real. Unlike the alones of stones and sticks, our alones are extraordinarily complex. In solitude, experiencing ourselves or the world around us (seen through the telescope of our aloneness), we can have tremendous insights, feelings of intense happiness or thundering calm, peace, warmth, coziness, satisfaction, a oneness with all creation and our own inner fire. Or, at the other extreme, we can experience fear, a terrifying isolation, a disorientation, estrangement, alienation, a waking nightmare, or a Pandora's box of real or imagined gargoyles, threateningly painful, from which we cannot run because they are inside us. At times only the touch of another hand (or heart) can give us consolation or show us meaning.

Our peculiarly human aloneness can be real, that is, an actual physical (though relative) isolation—at home (usually), in the box of a car, deep in the woods, or on a mountaintop—or it may happen (more commonly) around others: we breathe, think, *are* (alone) in the physical nearness of strangers, friends, family, crowds! Except on the blackest of nights or withdrawn with closed eyes and the tentacles of our fingers and senses momentarily inert, we are never really (truly) alone. Our aloofness is never absolute. For our alone is constantly ornamented by *things*, by the objects we surround ourselves with or find ourselves in the middle of, by sounds (the distant barking of a dog, the motor of a passing car, the creaks and groans of a tree, or the melody of a bird), by heat or cold or dampness or the wind, that is, by our environment. (For the musician the most important "thing," object, or ornament to his [musical] aloneness is his instrument.) Our solitude—which appears increasingly illusory and relative the more we think about it—is also colored by our actions, by the things we make and do, and by the very processes of making and doing. Even on the hermit's tropi-

327

cal island there is the sea all around and the stars up above, neighborly birds, crabs, and insects—and work to be done.

From the world of our alones we reach out into the world of our togethers. Nature or God or Chance (fool or genius) populated our earth with fellow creatures, some of them human and, therefore, very much like us. We—humans, along with an almost limitless variety of plants, birds, animals, insects, and fishes—were also created to exist (or at least function procreatively) in pairs, male and female, a biological fact that generates not only a natural grouping in twos but much of the world's delights and headaches! As children, each of us with our parents form a unit of three, and with our brothers and sisters and relatives a larger grouping, the family. Our groupings—like the accumulative musical counting of the song "The Twelve Days of Christmas"—our togethers, expand still further through a maze of relationships with individuals, friends, shopkeepers, neighbors, associates, corporations, and they may include our town or city, region, ethnic group, race, language, religion, profession, interests and enthusiasms, country, continent, hemisphere, and world (to name only a few possibilities). Each *alone*, every one of us on earth (human or otherwise), might be thought of as existing in the middle of an ever expanding series of concentric circles that define our *togethers*, our relationships with others whose circles overlap and interrelate with our own.

Our personal world exists, then, not only in the complex that is ourselves, or in the things of our environment, but also in the adjacent worlds of others. Between these worlds the relationship can be casual, it can be intense, it may be close or distant, it may be cooperative or dominated by one or the other or even antagonistic, it may be stable—according to traditional concepts—or floating/innovative/fluctuating. It may be, in fact, anything—like fire or like ice. But whatever we do does not exist in a vacuum, it does not simply *be* (automatically, without cause or reason); and usually alones and togethers work themselves out within the respective cultural universes where we grow up and live.

In making music, as in making life, our relationships are complex and varied; and they are culturally defined (or at least influenced). There is a pleasure in singing or playing an instrument alone, with everything, the entire musical microcosm, controlled by one's own fingers and mind; and there is the equal delight of working/doing/making/inventing/creating/interacting with others, of building a communal musical macrocosm in a group, ensemble, or orchestra. For example, the Chinese scholar-musician of ancient times is often pictured sitting alone in his study, or under the branches of a pine tree on a lonely mountain ridge above fog-enshrouded valleys, quietly playing his *ch'in* zither in studied meditation, at peace with himself and the universe. In contrast, in the music of the Balinese *gamelan krawang*, fifteen, or twenty, or even forty musicians may sit among the bronze gongs and metallophones of their orchestra—sometimes joined by listening members of their families, other villagers, and an ever present conglomeration of children—to make music *together*, communally, each individual and his music fitting into the mesh of the whole, and similarly at peace within themselves and with the universe.

Besides the musical solitude or gregariousness of the musician himself (and that is really what this chapter is about), there is another extremely important factor: a collection of creatures that in the popular and classical musical worlds of the West (definitely) and elsewhere (probably) are necessary, underrated, mercurial, sometimes fickle, often problematical, hated-feared-and-loved, bowed to, fawned over, and who can sometimes spell the difference for the mere musician of stardom in the Big Apples of the world or exile in the boondocks. These are, of course, the listeners.

> Everyone has ears
> And everyone (almost—certain critics excluded)
> Has minds.
>
> No one is like
> A solitary pea in a vacuum can.

Texas songster Mance Lipscomb with young friend.

If there is a one
There is an other,
Between persons,
Within persons.

While there is definitely a pleasure in making music, and another in listening to it, these double functions cannot be separated neatly like slices of a cultural orange. Untold generations of suffering music teachers from the outer islands of Japan to the inner islands of Nebraska know what it is like to listen to budding young musicians who hammer out notes without listening to them. But beyond this level (what my guru in India, Thirugokarnam Ramachandra Iyer, distinguished as "finger music" as opposed to "musical music"), everyone involved in music is using his ears or his other senses. Even the solitary Chinese scholar-musician is playing *to* someone, to himself, to his own set of ears. In fact, every musician in the world, whether he is sitting alone or before a Woodstock-like crowd of thousands, plays first of all to and for himself.

But in many societies or performance situations on this earth there is no sharp distinction between who is a performer and who is a listener: everyone is (or can be) both, anyone can sing or dance or play at any time, adding his (or her) two-bits' worth, musically making and listening/comprehending simultaneously. Among many of the tribal groups in Africa, for example, in many of the villages of Bali, or during those (unfortunately) rare and uncharacteristic spontaneous, unstructured gatherings of American counterculture called "be-ins," for example, truly communal music-making can happen. But aside from some avant-garde improvisations or hippie freak-outs where literally anything can go, such communal music-making requires certain tacitly accepted guidelines, structures, modes of procedures, acceptable and unacceptable things to do; and, more important, it requires a certain degree of musical ability and skill on everyone's part.

It is an unfortunate fact of life on this planet that some women are more beautiful than others, that trees of the same species may grow to different heights, and that some people develop more skills and powers in music than others. Whether these musical discrepancies have to do with inborn ability, practice, luck, lineage, hard work, environment, spiritual discipline, encouragement and appreciation by others, or whatever does not concern us here; they exist, that is all. But the musicality of "talented" individuals does not exist like the solitary pea in a vacuum can of our poem, or a lonely flower on a barren hill; it has to come from somewhere (a musical culture), and eventually (even perhaps hundreds of years later) it must be appreciated by someone or it disappears like the burst of light of a match in the night, or a fallen star.

We in the West relish the myth of misunderstood solitary geniuses—like Vincent Van Gogh (1809–52) or Charles Ives—who live and create in isolation, outside the contemporary mainstream. Still, their art is less perishable than their lives, it outlives them, and we (their appreciators) catch up with them. The music of great composers like the European J. S. Bach, the Japanese Kinko Kurosawa, or the Indian Tyagaraja (1759–1847) lives on as long as it is remembered and loved and performed in the togethers of musicians and connoisseurs. Intelligent listening, appreciation, is also a skill, and an important (though often underestimated) element in music and performance. I shall never forget the first time I played in a television studio: sitting there facing lights and the impersonal faces of technicians and the machines of a technological age, I was filled with an incredible sense of isolation, of separation from the electric human contact and warmth that exists (invisibly) between performer and audience in a live concert situation. Something was missing, and even the intellectual awareness that back there somewhere behind the eye of the camera and nib of the microphone were eyes, ears, faces, and thumping hearts could not help me overcome my emotional reaction to the lack of tangible togethers.

In the classical music of India the musician is acutely aware of his audience. He encourages friends and other *rasikas* (intelligent and appreciative listeners) to sit on the front row beneath his platform where he can see their faces and gauge their responses. They, in turn, react spontaneously, visually and verbally, with shakes of the head, thrusts of the hand, tongue clicks, "ohs" and "ahs," comments (like "good, good" or "beautiful, go on!"), applause, and other culturally defined signals to encourage him, turn him on to even greater virtuosity or even more subtle expressive heights. The performer is also aware of the feedback from the audience as a whole and will modify or adjust his programming or the details of his performance accordingly. The constant interplay between Indian audience and performer bounces back and forth, accumulating energy like a bouncing electron, and generates not only increased excitement (shared by all) but superb music. This type of active musician-listener relationship is, of course, found in music situations all over the world, whether in the smiles and comments of listeners to an east African minstrel, or the shouts of crowds at Euro-American jazz and rock concerts. But there can also be a quieter, less obvious relationship: the tomblike silence (broken by embarrassed and disturbing coughs) and stony blank faces of audiences at a Western classical music concert or the strict formality of listeners at a traditional Japanese musical performance mask concentration and emotional involvement and feelings that can nevertheless (magically) be sensed by the performer. If music is a communication—and it is at least partly so—it must communicate *to* somebody; and this communication happens in a crazily mystical togetherness that involves the musicians and their instruments or voices, each other (certainly), and (ideally) the people who have taken the trouble to come and listen to them.

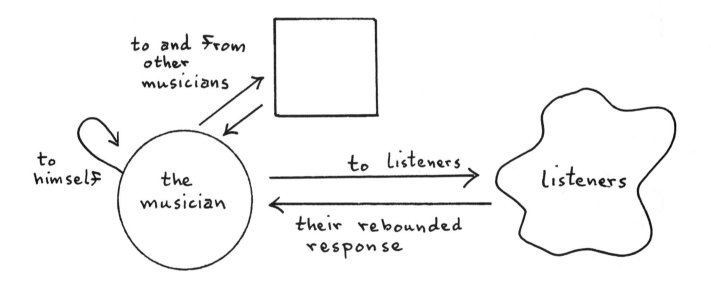

A Possible Map of Communication and Feedback in Musical Performance

This map, like all systems, is an idealized one, of course; it represents only one of perhaps hundreds of ways to look at what happens in a musical performance. And even so, it could vary depending on the situation, or from culture to culture. Most of the listeners, for example, to a player on the *tambur* (a three-stringed plucked lute) in an Afghan teahouse might be engaged in conversation or in drinking tea, hearing the music only as a background in the environment and responding little if at all. Or what happens when the performer is separated from the physical presence (and response) of his audience by a wafer-thin disk of plastic called the phonograph record, several months of time, and hundreds of thousands of miles? An Iatmul flutist on the Sepik River in New Guinea might include the spirits of ancestors existing in the set of flutes kept in the "men's house" as well as the sacred occasion during which his music is played in his togethers. A Tibetan monk might include the deity he is chanting to and for (who becomes a mystical *one* with him and his chant); a Chinese philosopher-musician might connect his harmonies with those of Nature or the Cosmos; or a classical Indian musician might include his lineage—the master musicians of his *gharana* (style, tradition)—or the spiritual quintessence of his *ragas*. The world and its musics, we must remember, is always far, far richer than anything we can say or conceptualize about it.

The Soloists

The not quite alone of a person making music begins with him/herself and a voice. The muezzin in Arabic countries, high in his minaret, sings out, sometimes in ornate melodic phrases, his call to prayer (*adhan* or *azan*) for the believers of Islam. The ballad singer of the southern highlands of the Appalachians sits on a bench on his front porch after a day's work, singing the old songs of princes and ladies, of love, and sudden tragic death, with only the crickets as his accompaniment. Across the seas in Scotland, Ireland, and England solitary singers do the same. In fact, in pockets all over the world people sing alone, without accompaniment, with the full force of musical expression focused, crystallized like a rare gem, in the beauty of a single voice, a melody, and the poetry of words. Mothers everywhere, even in the electric technology of America, sing lullabies to sleepy children; and solitary activities like spinning, grinding, weaving, hoeing, cooking, are ornamented with sung or hummed melodies. The voice, after all, is an instrument that one does not even need pockets for; it can be carried everywhere and anywhere (did the astronauts sing on the moon?), and it leaves the hands free for other activities.

The one of a music-maker can be transferred to an extension of his fingers, mind, and feelings: his musical instrument. We have examined the extraordinary relationship between the musician and his instrument, in which a thing, an object, a machination of sound, becomes an inseparable part of his musical self and perhaps also of his life. This pairing is found in almost every geographical region on earth and it cuts across every stratum of society. For example, the Bulgarian shepherd on his solitary wanderings across rock and pastureland, like shepherds-flutists everywhere, entertains himself and his flock with melodies on his end-blown flute, the *kaval*. In Japan the bamboo *shakuhachi* (an end-blown notched flute with five finger holes) has a magnificent solo tradition which emphasizes the aloneness of its sound potential, its timbre, and its unique expressive character. Scottish and Irish bagpipers excel in solo forms such as the *pibroch* theme and variations; and in the classical music of Iran soloists may weave intricate improvisations on the violin, *tār* and *setār* (plucked lutes), *santūr* zither, or *nāy* flute. A Bushman in the Kalahari Desert of south Africa may (alone or with his family group) play the musical bow, just as a boy in Java may twang his jew's-harp, or a lonely black man in Mississippi may relax with his harmonica. Many of the instruments of Asia (and their players) have extensive solo traditions and literature: the thirteen-stringed *saung* harp of Burma, the Mon *mi gyaun* and Thai *chakhe* and *grajappi* zithers, the Laotian *khaen* bamboo mouth organ, the Chinese *p'ip'a* lute, for example, not to mention the great traditions of the Far Eastern long zithers: the *cheng* and *ch'in* in China, the *kaya kum* in Korea, and the *koto* in Japan. European classical music has a similar great tradition in its music for solo keyboard instruments (piano, organ, harpsichord, clavier), for plucked strings (guitar, lute), and even for other instruments (the works of J. S. Bach for unaccompanied violin and unaccompanied cello are prime examples). To this we might add the American barrelhouse or ragtime pianist, countless accordion players, Egyptian soloists on the *qānūn* plucked zither or *'ūd* lute, and the wonderful organ grinders who caress the air for lovers in Mexican parks at night! But our catalog is from necessity incomplete because it is potentially endless: wherever there is a man and an instrument it can happen.

Our ones become hybrid alones when the musician sings with his voice while playing his instrument with his hands and fingers. This (only slightly) schizophrenic function naturally excludes instruments that require mouth and lungs to play, but with several exceptions: a player—on the jew's-harp, for example—can alternate his singing and playing; and in the Balkans *gaida* bagpipers puff their bags full of air and then proceed to sing to their own accompaniment, refilling the air bag

The Japanese *shakuhachi* has an extensive and beautiful solo literature. Artist: Shudo Yamato.

between verses of their song! Epic singers—in Yugoslavia with their bowed *gusle*, for example, or in Mongolia with their bowed *khil-khuur* horsehair fiddle—have traditionally, since the earliest of times, accompanied their tales on their harps, lyres, lutes, or fiddles. In China narrators in the *tan tz'u* tradition sang with their plucked *p'i p'a* lutes. Japanese musical history tells us of *heike-biwa*, a form of war narration to *biwa* lute accompaniment that flourished in the twelfth and thirteenth centuries, and of *gidayu-bushi* (named after its most famous singer, Gidayu Takemoto [1651–1714]) a sung narration accompanied by *biwa* or *shamisen* which flourished during the Edo period. In Africa in the upper Nile basin (Uganda, northern Zaire, Rwanda, Kenya, and Tanganyika) minstrels accompany their songs on a variety of bow harps, lyres, lutes, and zithers; and here and elsewhere in Africa the *mbira* (with its plucked metal keys), xylophones, and the guitar (adapted from Europe) are also used. A Bedouin singer on the Arabian peninsula may accompany himself with a one-stringed *rabāb* fiddle; in an American cocktail lounge it could be a piano; in Russia a *harmonika* accordion; in Latin America or Spain (in fact nowadays, everywhere) a guitar. Even fiddlers in some of the southern traditions in the United States sing along as their bows fly through reels and hoedowns. Southern bluesmen (mostly black and not to be outdone by anybody) expanded their guitar accompaniment by strapping a harmonica on a rack to be worn around the neck, and sometimes by a collection of levers and springs attached to feet, elbows, and knees, simultaneously playing bones, washboard, cymbals, and bass drum in a "one-man band." In all these forms the musician either follows on his instrument the melodies of his voice or provides an accompaniment in ostinato patterns, chords, or complex countermelodies and rhythms. His instrument may in fact—as in the performances by great singers-guitarists like Mance Lipscomb (b. ca. 1895) or Lightning Hopkins (b. 1912)—be a second voice, an alter ego, which responds/echoes/reflects in a musical dialogue with his singing: both parts like two extraordinary puppets in the hands of a single master puppeteer.

★★★★★★★★★★★★★★★★★★★ THE MINSTRELS ★★★★★★★★★★★★★★★★★★★★★

In older but not necessarily better times before entertainment was (like food) instant, easy, and (unlike food) electric, musicians alone or in small groups walked from town to town bringing their music to doorsteps and market squares in return for a few coins or a dinner. While some were bread-and-butter musicians and a few perhaps hacks, others were creative artists—composers, poets, singers, instrumentalists—of the highest caliber: European history is full of legends about the Celtic bards, the minnesingers of Germany, the troubadours in France, and others in every nation and every language; and their epics and song texts (and a few of their melodies) have survived, written down, as the foundation of literary achievement in the West. Some scholars (notably Harvard's classicist Albert B. Lord) believe that Homer must have been an epic singer, part of a great and earlier Greek oral tradition, and that he transcribed and reshaped in the *Iliad* and *Odyssey* what he and others before him, perhaps with the accompaniment of their lyres, had sung! It is important to remember that minstrels were (and are—for they still exist in many parts of the world) thorough professionals and to distinguish between them and less prestigious and skilled musical beggars.

It is impossible to gauge the excitement caused in a small rural village by the arrival of a traveling minstrel. He carries with him first of all news and gossip, stories of far-away places and wonderful things. He is the villager's tie to a larger world and to increased knowledge and understanding. Above all, he is an entertainer, and his songs and narratives, sometimes lasting long into the night, offer a temporary escape from the unchangingness of day-by-day existence. The minstrel is a carrier of cultural traditions: he may sing of gods and goddesses, mythological or historical heroes, great battles and events, moral codes—whatever is important in the racial memory of a people. But at the same time he is acutely aware of the present day: his antennas are out in all directions, and he may tie into his songs contemporary events, people that everybody knows, or grievances (suffered but not remedied) with caustic satire, burning wit, or unbounded humor. I once heard an Indian minstrel describe Krishna, a god-king incarnate and one

Naga pata singer wanders from house to house singing legends about snake deities in exchange for rice. C.P. Saraswathi, Kerala, India. The *kudam* is a one-stringed instrument similar to a washtub bass.

of the heroes of the epic *Mahabharata*, as looking up at the moon and saying, "What is this? There are *Americans* up there!" And on another occasion a comical hero explained his swift and timely arrival at a crucial battle (which took place in prehistory, before 1500 B.C.: "I came, you see, by Air-India Jumbo Jet!" The unexpected, the swift repartee, the ludicrous, are all worked into the song and narratives of the minstrel with skill and precision. And his creative freedom (and position in society) may also allow him to ridicule (usually with humor) things that the villagers may be afraid to talk about in public: a harsh landlord, bungling government officials, corrupt politicians, an absurd marriage, pompous priests, government repression, the strutting rich and educated, or even the police. Although the minstrel is a master of both verbal and musical improvisation, he may also carry on a learned tradition of beautiful songs and tales. He is at once an educator, philosopher, social commentator, humorist, artist, and entertainer, an ornament to the society in which he lives.

There are, of course, many types and strata of minstrels. Some were attached to the courts of kings or nobility or the rich, and their songs were filled with praise for the attributes (and generosity) of their hosts. In the United States in the nineteenth and early twentieth centuries the minstrel was an indispensable part of the traveling medicine show, and, sitting with his banjo on a makeshift stage on the back of a wagon, his songs and jokes and humorous monologues would precede the inevitable pitch for patent medicine by the "doctor." Hundreds of country musicians served their apprenticeships in medicine shows, men like Doc Boggs (b. 1898) who also sang and played for factory and textile mill workers as they came out of their shifts, or Uncle Dave Macon (1870–1953) who carried the traditions right up onto the stage of the Grand Ole Opry (and into modern times). The American black "songsters" and "bluesmen" were also minstrels in the true sense, playing for local dances, picnics, and barbecues, appearing on street corners and in red-light districts with their guitars and harmonicas strapped around their necks, singing of life and its pains and pleasures as it really was, and disappearing at night to another place, another town, and (often) oblivion or an early death. These men, with magical/ fanciful names like "Blind Lemon" Jefferson, "Peg Leg" Howell, "Juke Boy" Bonner, "Howling" Wolf, "Smoking" Hogg, "Black Ace," "Washboard" Sam, "T-Bone" Walker, were and are walking legends, and those who lived long or recently enough ended up enjoying the comparative stability of club jobs in big-city ghettos. The minstrel show, despite its name and importance in the history of American popular arts, belongs essentially to a different tradition: that of the professional theatrical stage, big troupes, city entertainments, vaudeville, variety shows, and the musical comedy. But the solitary minstrel, usually harassed by shopkeepers and police as a "physical obstruction" or "disturber of the peace," is appearing again on the streets of American cities, notably in San Francisco, Boston, and New York, although he is more likely to sing or play precomposed hits, or Dylan, or Bach and Mozart (even) than the creations of his own heart.

In north Africa wandering bards, with their one-stringed fiddles, sing *qasida* songs praising Mohammed or various Islamic saints, or commenting upon local events as they happen. Among the Wolof people of Gambia the *gewel* (or *griots*) are a caste of professional entertainers, and to the accompaniment of their five-string plucked *halams* they tell stories. Among the Venda of south Africa the *tshilombe* minstrels accompany their songs with the (European) guitar. In Ethiopia the *azmari* wandering minstrels fit our prototype quite well: they travel from village to village where they are received with hospitality and delight; they improvise their words to fit the occasion—weddings, eulogies, praise to the host or the beauty of the women of the area, epics of war or of the conquests of love—but their songs may also take an ironic twist and they may criticize and mock (usually with impunity) even kings and chieftains. On one occasion (in the eighteenth century) a local prince, Ras Michael, murdered some *azmari* who had ridiculed and abused him in public with their songs. Whenever he returned to the spot of their unmusi-cianly death his horse would throw him, which was taken by all to be an omen that his fortune and power were gone forever. The *azmari* minstrels—who may be, incidentally, both men and women—are masters of Amharic, the language of Ethiopia, and make full use of its subtle in-flections, expressive potential, and dramatic forcefulness for sophisticated and sometimes outrageous puns. Many of their songs have been handed down from medieval times or earlier, and they are repositories of the legends and history of the region. Their singing style varies from simple recitatives to brilliant bursts of ornate virtuosic coloratura, and their skill on the *masenqo*, a one-stringed fiddle with a triangular face, is similarly virtuosic. During the occupation of Ethi-opia by fascist Italy (1935–41) they were rallying points for nationalistic feelings—even the Italians who spoke the language could not understand the acid double meanings of their puns and imagery—and they were brutally suppressed by the conquerors.

In the Bengal region of India the Bauls are a religious community drawn from the lowest strata of society. Many are householders but others pick up their one-stringed plucked *ektār* lutes (made from a bamboo neck and a gourd resonator) and take to the road as wandering minstrels. The word *baul* means "madcap," although it may derive from the Sanskrit *vayu*, or "wind," but either meaning suggests the Bauls' crazy religious happiness, their scorn of tradi-tional social strictures, and the fact that they are inwardly and outwardly "as free as the wind." The amazing philosophy of the Bauls is summed up in their songs: in a society (India's) crammed with castes and subcastes of high and low status, full of magnificent temples, idols, and mosques and hundreds of religious cults and sects, immersed in traditions—with scriptures and festivals and rites—that go back more than four thousand years, the Bauls reject it all. They recognize no difference between one human being and another, they accept no religious path or deity as right or wrong, they place their intuitions and feelings above any rituals or scriptures.

> My body is my temple,
> Why should I worship at buildings of brick and stone?
> I am in my temple every day that I breathe,
> And my deity resides as the man of my Heart.

The beauty and wit of the poetry of the traditional songs of the Bauls are matched by the beauty of their melodies. Some songs are composed on the spot, or improvised according to the formulas or imagery of their tradition; others are passed down, learned from gurus. But there is a tendency for even the great masters, the most talented of the creators, to remain anonymous. "We follow the simple way," said one minstrel, "so that we leave no trace. See that boat going slowly across this broad river? Where are its tracks? What mark does it leave?"

Bengali intelligentsia and scholars—whose regional pride and chauvinism has nurtured a con-cern for folklore and folk arts rare in Asia—were quick to recognize the importance of the Baul tradition. Philosophers-poets such as the Nobel Prize–winning Rabindranath Tagore (1861–1941) were greatly influenced by the thought and forms of the minstrel's songs. But as always it was the literate and self-conscious "serious artist" who received worldwide recognition; it was Tagore, who translated his poems into Edwardian English, who got the prize; and the Bauls (perhaps ultimately unconcerned with it all) continue to walk the dusty roads with their *ektaras* singing their wonderful songs.

Gypsies have traditionally been traveling musicians, the combination of two violins and a small and portable (cello-sized) string bass common in eastern Europe expanding in Romania and Hungary to the small orchestras which Franz Liszt imitated (rather poorly) in his sym-

Yiddish street musicians from the film *Yiddle with His Fiddle*.

phonic *Hungarian Rhapsodies*. In western Poland up until the 1950s the duet minstrel combination of fiddle and bagpipe played regularly in markets and in city courtyards, and elsewhere combinations of violin, accordion, guitar, bass (and perhaps clarinet), and even small brass bands were also common. Mexico today retains a rich tradition of street musicians. At the (very) extended and leisurely noon hour small bands of musicians with violins and guitars may stroll into restaurants, or *marimba* bands (sometimes with drums and guitars) may set up on the sidewalks in front of the open-air cafés. In the evenings there are—besides the inevitable organ grinders—solo accordionists, violin and guitar (or accordion) duos, percussion groups, funky brass bands, or the famous *huapango* trios of native harp, violin, and small-sized guitar, or the larger *mariachi* orchestras with trumpets, violins, and all sizes of guitars which can be hired for a single song or an evening's serenading.

But despite the romance associated with minstrels and the wonderful and sometimes extraordinary traditions of their music all over the world (we have here picked only a few samples at random), one fact remains: minstrelry can be a hard and insecure life. Traveling is grueling and the income—which depends on the generosity and often questionable appreciation of strangers—uncertain. One wonders to what extent the necessities of poverty shape the lives of the "quaint" and "picturesque" singer who suddenly appears at a doorstep, on a street corner, or walking through a train. And there is the glamorous competition of the media—radio, television, movies. It is no wonder, then, that musicians prefer a regular job playing for regular patrons in a restaurant or club, at festivals, at concerts, or in the theater, or even outside of music. A Yiddish movie of the 1930s, *Yiddle with His Fiddle*, portrays the hidden dream (perhaps) of every minstrel: after hilarious but difficult wanderings in Poland, one member of the troupe (two violins, voice, clarinet, string bass) marries a rich widow in Warsaw, another her childhood sweetheart; another becomes the leader of a passenger ship dance orchestra; and the heroine—an overnight sensation on the vaudeville stage—leaves for a tour in the promised land of America!

★★★★★★★★★★★★★★★★★★★★★★★★★★

Twos and Threes

If making music alone is much like being and working alone (dealing with one's own brain and fingers, feelings, and capabilities), making music with others is like living and working with others, with *their* brains/fingers/feelings/capabilities—and, therefore, is infinitely more complex. Here is the world of *relationships*, of collective doings, controls, responses. In music these relationships may be controlled by notation (as in much Euro-American music) or by the ear (the performer's) operating within the spectrum of accepted musical procedures and practices (as in African music or rock), or by a combination of the two.

Before we look in more detail at duos, trios, chamber groups, larger ensembles, and orchestras in the music of the whole earth, we might try to map out some of the patterns of relationships which make them work in their musical togethers.

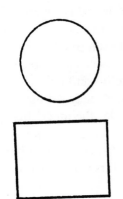

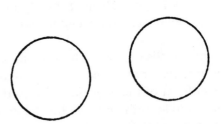

interplay of equals
(as in simultaneous melodies, group improvisation, or true contrapuntal duets or trios)

dominant-supporting
(as in melody with an accompaniment of
chords, patterns, textures, or drumming)

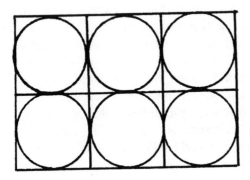

fitting into the mesh of the whole
(as in east African drumming, Webern, or the choral singing of Ituri
forest pygmies)

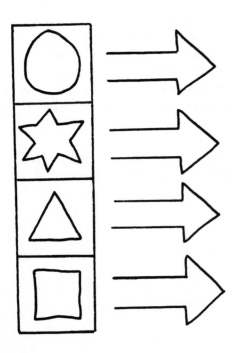

Working within different functioning musical levels (as in the music of
the Indonesian and Balinese *gamelan* and other court orchestras in Asia)

These patterns are not, of course, mutually exclusive. The mesh of drum, bell, and rattle rhythms in a Ghanaian percussion ensemble, for example, may in turn function as the background (supporting) for the master drummer (dominant) or for vocal or instrumental melodies; or in a single performance a musician may at different times (and with the speed of a chameleon changing colors) play supporting accompaniments, emerge as the dominant soloist, or engage in an "interplay of equals." Relationships can be static, but they can also be kaleidoscopic. And there may be constant feedback between musicians, an interplay of listening, picking up ideas, responding, feeding out, and re-responding like the democratic chattering in a New England town meeting.

Within and between our mapped-out patterns there can be perhaps any number of subrelationships. For instance, a group of performers may aim at a very precise melodic and rhythmic unison:

(example: choral singing of the Pueblo Indians)

or they may allow for a great deal of freedom, a flexibility of movement (sometimes called "heterophony") around a central melodic core:

(example: choral singing of Northern Plains Indians)

or certain predetermined types of ornamentation of a given melodic skeleton:

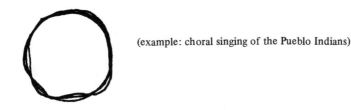

(example: *saron, bonang*, and *gender* sections of the Javanese *gamelan* orchestra)

The position of a violinist accompanying a vocalist in a performance of south Indian classical music moves constantly from the circle (in our diagram) of the melody to the box (in our diagram) of the accompaniment and the subbox of the drone.

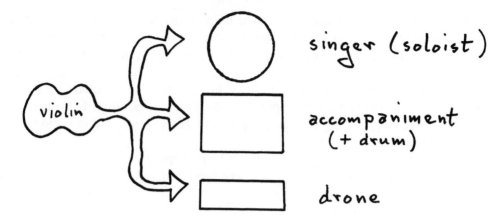

He may, for example, duplicate the soloist's melody in unison or octaves, paraphrase it, imitate fragments of it, rest on the drone notes, or come to the forefront alternating with the singer at certain permissible times. But always—even though he may be a musician of equal or superior skill—it is understood that he maintains a position subordinate (musically) to that of the soloist.

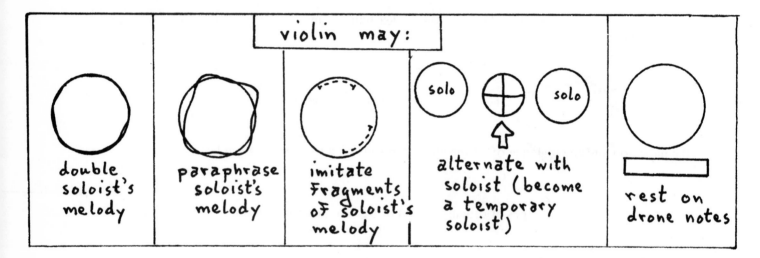

But the inner workings and relationships of musical worlds are never quite so simple as they may at first seem to be. They are full of subtle fluctuations, minute nuances, which like those in the language of words (or the language of eyes) may ultimately be of the greatest significance. Add to this the constant push-pull of the creativity of the musician (in some cultures more than in others), and we can perhaps touch upon the complexity of ingredients in the soup of a musical performance! We should remember also that these relationships and workings are—like the gears and cranks and spindles and springs of a machine—only a part of the whole: the sum of the parts adds up to the totality of the (musical) whole.

Twos

The togethers of twos in music are found all over the world. Quite often the same or similar instruments, with the same sound and capabilities, are paired (something like identical twins): in Bulgaria, for example, there are the popular combinations of two *kaba gaidi* bagpipes, or of two singers (often performing in drone-based harmonies and counterpoint); in Africa there are occasional or professional duets of pairs of xylophones, pairs of *mbiras*, pairs of flutes, or pairs of ocarinas (respectively), as well as of similar stringed instruments or paired *a cappella* voices. The grouping together into ensembles of the same or closely related instruments (as in the Chopi xylophone orchestras or the royal flute ensembles of the Bamalete, both in Africa) or sections of orchestras (as in the *sarons* or *genders* of the Javanese *gamelan* or the strings of the European symphony orchestra) is an important building-block element in making larger musical performance groups. The other principle is contrast, and this too is reflected in pairings of musical twos.

If the music of the twos of "identical twins" tends toward an interplay of equals (oo in our chart) or near unisons (o), the music of *contrasting* twos tends to be hierarchial, a dominant-supporting relationship (몸). Invariably this takes the form of a melody with an instrumental accompaniment (by the second player): the melody may be vocal or instrumental (double-reed pipes or strings or flutes are common), and the instrumental accompaniment may be on a melodic-harmonic instrument (like the accordion, mouth organ, or harp) or predominantly percussive—on a drum (like the *tabla*, the *naqqāra*, or the *duff* tambourine).

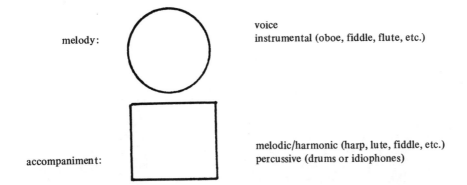

melody:
    voice
    instrumental (oboe, fiddle, flute, etc.)

accompaniment:
    melodic/harmonic (harp, lute, fiddle, etc.)
    percussive (drums or idiophones)

In Japan's classical puppet theater form, *bunraku*, the *gidayu* singer-narrator (who handles all the narration and the dialogue of all the characters) sits on a rostrum on stage left accompanied by a player on the *shamisen* plucked long lute. In China in a narrative form called *ta ku tz'u* the singer, who also plays a small flat drum with his right hand and castanets with his left hand, is accompanied by the plucked *san hsien*; while in the highly dramatic Korean *pansori* form the female vocalist is accompanied by the large hourglass-shaped drum, the *chang go*. In Iran in the *zur khanah* ("house of strength") athletes do ceremonial exercises to a singer's chanting from the classical epic *Shah Nameh* backed by the rhythmic accompaniment of a virtuoso drummer (although drummer and singer are often the same man). The combination of solo voice or instrument with drum is common in both the classical and popular musics of the Arabic/Islamic-influenced areas. For example, in Iran the voice, the *santūr* (zither), the violin, the *nāy* (end-blown flute), the *tār*, or the *setār* (plucked lutes) may be combined *en duo* with the goblet-shaped drum *dunbak*. In Egypt the *qānūn* zither (and any other melodic instrument) is paired with the set of small kettle-shaped *tabl* drums, and among the Bedouins in Syria the *nāy* flute may be combined with the *darabuka* drum. The combination of double-reed oboe with drum is also characteristic of this area, and in fact is common all along the ancient trade routes into China: for instance, in Turkey the *zurnā* pipe is accompanied by the large barrel-shaped *dhavul* drum, and in India the *shehnai* is accompanied by the *dhol* drum (not to be confused with the doldrums). In sub-Saharan Africa a single xylophone may be combined with an *mbira* or a harp lute, or a minstrel with his songs and stringed instrument, or *mbira* may be accompanied by a second player providing—besides a second voice—a rhythmic background of hand claps or of rattles, iron bells, or drum. In Mexican Indian folk music a solo flute is often combined with a miniature military drum, while in the southern mountains of the United States duos of fiddle and banjo, fiddle and guitar, or banjo and guitar were once common. Western classical music tends to combine a keyboard instrument (for the past two hundred years, the piano) with voice or a melodic instrument (like violin, flute, cello, and so on); the repertoire—including songs, *lieder*, and sonatas—is immense. There is also the possibility of piano duets, or of that once popular practice of putting two people on the same bench and having them play duets on the *same* piano. (I, incidentally, was

Two Zulu girls with *umakweyana*/musical bows, southern Africa.

Flutist, drummer, and cymbal player form a trio in stone at Konarak, Orissa, India.

always stuck with the left-hand part, which could be why I became a dissatisfied pianist and hence, probably, a composer.) Several musicians on one and the same instrument is also characteristic of the xylophone and metallophone music of Central America, Africa, and Bali (as we shall see).

Threes

Expansion into threes and consequently into larger ensembles is primarily an expansion either of functions or of numbers of players within functional groups. For example, where there is one drummer, one or two or even six more may be added; or a melody may be doubled by additional voices or instruments; or a vocal trio can become a three-part chorus. We have noted the ambivalent character of the violin accompanist in south Indian classical music—drawn simultaneously toward the melodies of the soloist and an accompanying role. In the Middle East, vocalists are often similarly backed up by an instrument, forming a trio composed of voice, accompanying instrument (in Iran it could be *'ūd, santūr, tār*, violin, or *setār*), and drummer.

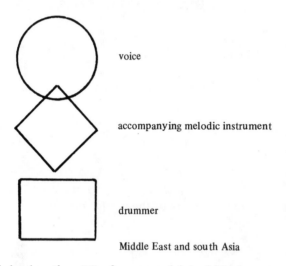

voice

accompanying melodic instrument

drummer

Middle East and south Asia

In India a soloist (on the *sitār*, for example) and his drummer (on *tabla*) are backed by a different functioning element: the background of a drone played on the *tambūrā*.

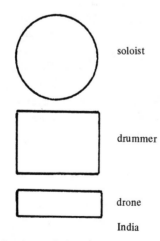

soloist

drummer

drone

India

But the functioning of three musicians together throughout the world can happen in almost any imaginable relationship, from strict melody and accompaniment to heterophony or counterpoint. Often one or more of the musicians sing as they play their instruments, further complicating (or clarifying) the texture. In Japan the *sankyoku* ensemble (literally "music for three") of traditional music is made up of the *koto* (long zither), *shamisen* (long lute), and *shakuhachi* (notched bamboo flute) and either the *koto* player or the *shamisen* player, or both, may sing as well. In Vietnam's classical music a popular trio grouping is the *ty ba* two-stringed pear-shaped lute, the *dich* flute, and the *tranh* zither, while in Sunda in Indonesia a trio may include singer, *suling* flute, and the *kachapi* plucked zither. In Africa two *mbiras* (whose players also sing) may be joined by a player on gourd rattles; among the Venda people there are trios of large *mbiras* (*mbila dzu madeza*) and of flutes (*zwitiringo*). In central Africa a three-xylophone ensemble can often be found entertaining in marketplaces, and among the Chopi people three players often play a single instrument (the *amadinda* xylophone).

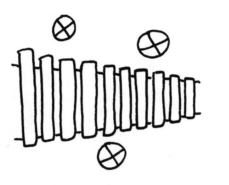

positioning of three
players around a
Chopi xylophone

In Turkish village music there is the trio of clarinet, violin, and drum; in Bulgaria a singer may be backed by two (yes *two!*) *kaba gaidi* bagpipes (one can imagine the strength of the singer's voice); in the Veracruz region of Mexico there is the beautiful combination of the *huapango* trio of violin, harp, and guitar with the violinist and guitarist also singing in an alternating dialogue or close harmonies; in the New England fiddling tradition of the United States the fiddler and his accompanist on piano (pounding out chords) may be joined by the rhythmic clacking of a player on the spoons.

All these groups of musical threes, and the many others in the world, may derive from a music-making tradition that goes back very far indeed: a relief in an Egyptian tomb dating back to the Twelfth Dynasty (2000–1800 B.C.) portrays a trio of singer, flute, and harp!

The Chamber Ensembles

When we come to fours, fives, sixes, sevens, eights, and more we run into increasingly complex problems. For example, how do so many people stay together? How do they make a music that is precise and functioning or at least on the safe side of chaos? Or secondly, where can we draw the line between a group that has a basically "chamber" or "solo" sensibility and one in which individual instruments (and/or voices) blend communally in an "orchestral" or "choral" sound? Or thirdly, how do we reconcile ensembles that have a definite, precise number of instruments/players with those ensembles where either or both (players and instruments) may be extremely flexible, varying in type, or varying in numbers—for example, from as few as nine or ten to as many as forty or more? Rather than trying to impose a scientist's geometric grid or a librarian's neat system of categories and pigeonholes onto a world of group music-making at least as liquid and shifting as the sands, waters, shells, and ocean foam of a Cape Cod beach, we shall adopt the following plan: first we shall examine the workings of some ensembles of from four to fifteen players and we shall list a few more; then we shall consider sub-Saharan Africa as a whole; then we shall discuss the wonderful phenomenon of people singing together; and, finally, we shall conclude with the great ensemble and orchestral traditions of the Orient.

Ensembles

In the classical music of India, we have seen, there are three essential functioning layers: the *soloist* (melody, *raga*), the *drummer-accompanist* (rhythm), and the *drone* background. For vocal music

Mixed ensemble including harp, lute, double pipe, and lyre. Copy of an Egyptian tomb painting, ca. 1400 B.C., by Nina M. Davies.

and sometimes for instrumental soloists also, there can be a fourth layer: a *melodic accompanist,* in north India usually a harmonium or a *sarangi* multistringed fiddle, in the south usually a violin.

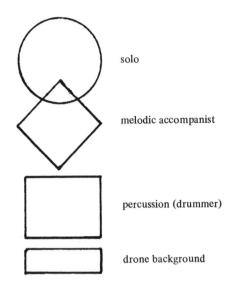

solo

melodic accompanist

percussion (drummer)

drone background

From a minimum of four players, any of these areas may be expanded: a second soloist can be added to make a featured duet (like two flutes, two voices, or contrasting instruments like the plucked *sitār* and the *shehnai* oboe); a student may back his guru up, singing or playing quietly in the background; there may be a second melodic accompanist; or there may even be still another melodic accompanist to back up the first(!). The percussion section enjoys the greatest possible expansion of all: in the south the drummer (essential) may be joined by players on the *ghatam* (a clay pot that is drummed on), the *kanjira* (tambourine), and the *morsang* (jew's-harp); and drone instruments also may be doubled—I have seen as many as three *tamburās* (plucked drone lutes) at a concert—and singers and wind players may include the free-reed *sruti-box* (with a sound something like an accordion). Thus a performance group could include as many as ten or twelve musicians, each fitting into his niche, each taking his place in a (musical) hierarchy of relationships.

But the focus is on the soloist. It is he (or she) who commands the attention of the listeners, who fills the air with the twists and spirals of virtuosic display and the main improvisations, who chooses the *ragas* and *talas* of the program, and who guides every aspect of the program—its pacing and shape —through tacit and subtle signals to the other musicians. Even the drummer, who may himself be a great virtuoso (and who functions as a kind of subking over the other percussionists, if there are any) must be careful to submit to the soloist's will, to stay in the background except when he is called upon to emerge. To do otherwise could destroy a performance. Because of this focus on the soloist and (subjectively) because of the special quality of the performance and the group's functions (an expanded four) I see Indian classical music as basically a "chamber idiom"; despite the big auditoriums and audiences of the present day, it functions best in an intimate setting.

Many of the other ensembles stretching in a cultural belt from India through Iran, Turkey, to the western and southern Mediterranean and north Africa also seem to be expansions of essentially a "chamber/soloistic" sensibility, of *the twos of melody plus drum,* or of *the three of singer, melodic accompanist, and drum.* If one instrument can play a melody, then any number of other instruments can also play the same melody in unison at octaves, adding their own timbre and perhaps also special "licks" and ornaments in what has been termed a "mild heterophony." Additional drums can be added to make a collective percussion section of rhythms and counterrhythms (and the feelings and responses of drummers) that is really cooking under the sound of the collective melody. A singer or a chorus of singers may be added on top, and a performance may be structured so that instruments may drop out (or into the background with rifflike rhythmic drone passages) while individuals play improvised solos, with everybody coming in again in *tutti* passages. Percussion instruments might include the tambourine and *darabuka* (goblet-shaped drum) and in Turkey the *naqqāra* (pair of small kettledrums); melodic instruments might be the clarinet, the *nāy* (end-blown flute), fiddles like the *kemanje* of north Africa or the *rabāb,* zithers like the *qānūn* (Egypt or Turkey) or the *santūr* (Iran to Kashmir), and plucked lutes like the *'ūd, tār, saz,* and *setār,* depending on the traditions of the area. The makeup of several ensembles picked at random is given below:

Chorus + 5 instruments (Turkey)

female chorus

3 *saz* (plucked long lutes) in different sizes
1 *darabuka* (goblet drum)
1 set *kashik* (wood spoons)

7 instruments (Turkey)

3 *saz* (different sizes)
clarinet

darabuka (goblet drum)
kashik (wood spoons)
zil (clappers)

4 instruments plus* (Egypt)

qānūn (zither)
'ūd (lute)
nāy (flute)

tabla (drum)

*doubled by additional players

Voice + 5 instruments (Egypt)

solo female vocalist

rabāb (fiddle)
argūl (double clarinet)
'ūd (lute)

tabl (drums)
tambourine

6 instruments (Algeria)

qānūn (zither)*
kemanje (fiddle)
'ūd (lute)*

darabuka (drum)
tār (tambourine)
nwakess (castanets)

In Europe and the United States where harmony (in music if not in politics) is of such great importance and classical music has nurtured a tradition of countermelody and counterpoint, group music lays great stress on these functional layers. On the other hand, a purely rhythmic layer, or a percussion underpinning—so essential in much of the music from Africa to India—may be omitted entirely.

Harmony, until the twentieth century in some forms of classical music, and more recently in jazz, is the bedrock of everything: its chord progressions and inner makeup reach through the entire musical texture like the tentacles of a (musical) octopus, to influence melody, countermelody, and counterpoint alike; everything melodic relates to it, pulls against it in tension or fits it in "harmony." Even what we consider to be fierce, independent counterpoint (simultaneous melodies), such as in

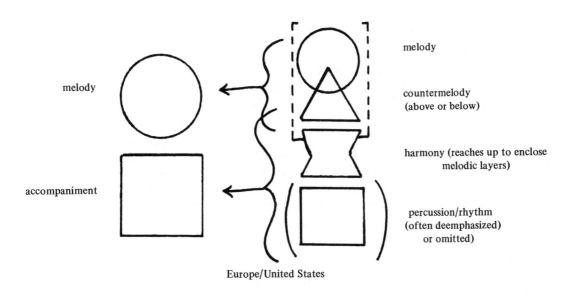

melody

accompaniment

melody

countermelody
(above or below)

harmony (reaches up to enclose
melodic layers)

percussion/rhythm
(often deemphasized)
or omitted)

Europe/United States

J. S. Bach's cantatas or in the fugues or his *Well-Tempered Clavier,* fits together in the mesh of harmonic progression and sonority.

A clear-cut dominant melody is also important in much of the music of the West, particularly in popular and folk forms, but not nearly so much as in other parts of the world. In symphonies, for example, melodies are chopped up into fragments—motifs—and tossed around in the orchestral texture; and we can enjoy music that is (at least in part) purely timbre, or sound, or a progression of lush or dissonant chords (these are subjective terms, of course), or a complex contrapuntal texture, or architectural (that is, we listen to its structure rather than its melody). Still, the basic layers of melody/accompaniment exist—and this is a very rough and imprecise estimate—in about 80 percent of the music in the total spectrum of Euro-American musical culture.

The harmonic/accompaniment layer is actually far more varied than the "oom-pah oom-pahs" we may at first associate with it: there is in this area a great deal of creative activity by ear musicians and composers alike. There is the imaginative rhythmic plunking of chords by the jazz pianist, for example, and the creative movement of bass lines in the playing of jazz and rock bass players. Chords are broken up into arpeggios which ripple along like little waterfalls, or into fragments of accompanimental melody, or into bursts of rhythm. Try focusing your attention *away* from the singer's melody in an opera by Mozart or Verdi (both real masters of creative accompaniment) and you will discover a whole musical universe of happenings and activities in the harmonic/accompaniment layer. The same might happen beneath (or *behind*) the melody in a good country and western or bluegrass ensemble, or in a fine arrangement for jazz band.

In much of the music of the West there is no rigid stratification of the musician's function in the musical texture, and he may—with a great deal of flexibility—move from a purely harmonic or subordinate accompanimental layer into the relatively more important area of counter- (or accompanying) melodies, or into the limelight of the predominant melody itself. In a Beethoven string quartet, for example, a violinist (or violist, or cellist) might sweep through the entire gambit in a few seconds. Another example: in the standard bebop jazz practice of the 1940s (still widely followed) a soloist, say on saxophone or trumpet or trombone, starts off by playing the melodic theme in unison or harmony with everyone else, then he drops out (or plays occasional accompaniment patterns) while other musicians "blow" improvised "choruses," or solos; when his time comes, he takes over, emerges from the background, plays his improvised solo—the predominant melody for the moment—and then moves into the background again, maybe to join everyone at the end for a repetition of the original (composed) melody.

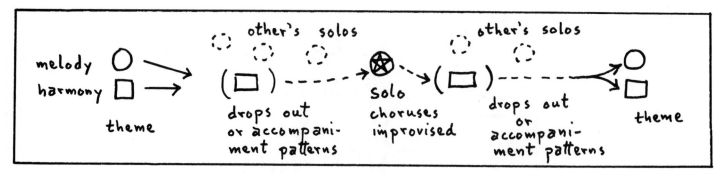

functional changes in role of player in (bebop) jazz performance

The importance of a percussion layer varies greatly in the West depending on the style of the music. Can you imagine, for example, a string quartet or a harpsichord and flute duet with a bass drum accompaniment? (It might be terrific, of course, but it just is not done.) In classical music as in the thumping of the timpani in a Haydn symphony or the crash of cymbals in Rimsky-Korsakov, percussion is usually used to back up the rhythms of the orchestra as a whole, or as an element of tone color. Works like Stravinsky's *L'Histoire du soldat* with a truly independent percussion part are rare, even in the twentieth century. Even in much popular and dance music the percussion is supposed— like the gentle swish of cymbals guiding the tiptoeing feet of foxtrotting couples—to stay unobtrusively in the background. But the emergence of Afro-American and Latin American idioms in the twentieth century has changed all that, and in jazz, rock, Latin, soul, and even in much pop music a strong, loud, driving percussion layer is an essential element of the music.

★★★★★★ SOME CHAMBER ENSEMBLES IN EURO-AMERICAN MUSIC ★★★★★★★

1. CLASSICAL MUSIC

a. Groups Standardized by Tradition

string quartet

2 violins
1 viola
1 cello

woodwind quintet

1 flute
1 oboe
1 clarinet
1 horn
1 bassoon

brass quintet

2 trumpets
1 horn
1 trombone
1 tuba

b. Iconoclastic Groups (Set by the Composer)

Mozart: Serenade No. 10 for 13 wind instruments, K. 361

2 oboes
2 clarinets
2 basset horns (tenor clarinets)
4 horns
2 bassoons
1 (string) double bass

Pierre Boulez: *Improvisation sur Mallarmé*

    1 harp
    1 tubular chimes
    1 vibraphone
    1 piano
    1 celeste
    4 percussionists (rattles, gongs,
        wood blocks, etc.)

    1 soprano

Stravinsky: *L'Histoire du soldat*

    1 speaker

    1 clarinet ⎫
    1 bassoon ⎭ (woodwind)

    1 trumpet ⎫
    1 trombone ⎭ (brass)

    1 percussion (one player on
      six drums, cymbals, and
      triangle)

    1 violin ⎫
    1 double bass ⎭ (string)

2. JAZZ: *THE COMBO*

Precise makeup varies from three players up who fill the layered
functions of melody (soloist)–(harmony)- bass-drums

Charlie Parker All Star Sextet (1947)

    1 alto saxophone ⎫
    1 trumpet   ⎬ "horns"
    1 trombone   ⎭

    1 piano   ⎫
    1 string bass   ⎬ "rhythm"
    1 drums/percussion ⎭

Ornette Coleman Quartet (ca. 1960)

    1 alto saxophone
    1 trumpet
    1 bass
    1 drums/percussion

The Galan Bogtrotters, Cummins Farm, Arkansas—a typical string band of the thirties.

Cecil Taylor Group (1960s) 7 Players

    1 trumpet
    1 alto sax
    1 alto sax/oboe/bass clarinet

    1 piano/bells

    2 string basses
    1 drums/percussion

Like the ensembles from India to the Middle East, there is great emphasis on solo and (sometimes) group improvisation. In recent years (after 1960) there has been a great deal of experimentation with instrumentation, size, and function.

3. COUNTRY MUSIC (UNITED STATES): *THE STRING BAND*

Characterized by the predominance of plucked and bowed string instruments, especially guitar, banjo, and/or fiddle, and including practically any combination drawn from the following "bank" of instruments:

    guitar (1 or more) (if 2 guitars are used, one may be a "melody-lead"
       and the other strictly harmonic)
    banjo
    violin (1 or 2)
    mandolin
    autoharp (zither)
    Dobro (slide guitar)
    steel ("Hawaiian") guitar
    string bass (recently electric bass)
    voice (singers traditionally hold—and play—a guitar, or the instrumentalists
       in the group double as singers, solo or in harmony)

The typical "bluegrass" band (the Monroe Brothers, Flatt and Scruggs, and others)

    voice(s) (the instrumentalists')
    1 mandolin
    1 banjo
    1 fiddle
    1 guitar
    1 string bass

To the twangs of this string sound other instruments can be added, depending on the style of the group:

    harmonica
    accordion
    piano (played often in "honky-tonk" style)

Although the traditional mountain musicians did not use percussion (except perhaps the occasional clacking of spoons, bones, or clogging feet)—the intensive counterrhythms and accents of banjos and guitars make percussion unnecessary—since the 1940s bands, particularly in "country and western" style, have included the standard jazz drum and cymbal ("trap") set.

4. A POTPOURRI OF OTHER GROUPS

Mariachi orchestra (Mexico)—3 to 12 or more players

> violins (2 or more)
> trumpets (2 or more)
> mandolin(s)
> guitars (often in different sizes)
> bass guitar (or string bass)

Bulgaria

> *gadulka* (fiddle)
> *tamburā* (lute)
> *kaval* (flute)
> *gaida* (bagpipe)
> *tupan* (drum)

China: *ssu-kuan* ensemble

> *san hsien* (plucked lute)
> *p'i p'a* (moon lute) or *sona* (pipe/oboe)
> *hsiao* (notched flute) or *ti tsu* (side-blown flute)
> *erh hsien* (bowed)

plus percussion:

> *ssu kuai pan*: bamboo castanets
> *hsiang-tsan*: small gong
> *my yü*: fish-shaped wood block
> *hsiao shuang*: small bells struck together

plus: medium-sized gong

Rock band (originally United States, now worldwide)

Characterized by sound of electric/amplified voice and instruments. Instrumentation eclectic, but based upon a functional core of:

> voice(s) (may be instrumentalists')

> melody—lead guitar
> chordal layer of guitar and/or keyboard
> (electric) bass
> drums/percussion

chordal layer keyboards: piano, electric piano, electric organ, or electronic music synthesizer

a few possible additions: horns (saxophones, trumpets, trombones singly or in combination, also tuba[s]), additional (electric) guitars, harmonica, electric violin, Afro-Cuban drums, tambourine

Folk *hayashi* ensemble (Japan)

Any number of players on

bamboo flutes
drums
small brass gongs

Romania/Bulgaria/eastern Europe village bands

Eclectic instrumentation depending on what or who is available, but including:

flute(s): end- or side-blown
fiddle(s): native or modeled on the European violin
oboe(s): double-reed pipes
accordion(s)
bagpipe(s)
plucked lute(s)
(zither)
drums

★★★★★★★★★★★★★★★★★★★★★★★★★

Africa

In the infinitely rich crazy-quilt pattern of musical groups and ensembles in Africa—from occasional and small togethers to royal ensembles of ten or fifteen to immense ceremonial gatherings with orchestras of between one and two hundred musicians(!)—the Ghanaian scholar J. H. Kwabena Nketia (in *The Music of Africa*) has noted several tendencies/characteristics. First, there are *spontaneous groups* of people (not in an associative relationship) who come together casually for amusement or ritually for a special occasion. Often the music that is performed by such a spontaneous group belongs to the ritual or occasion of the moment. For instance, there are work songs and hunting songs sung by the men who come together for these activities. There may also be initiation songs for girls and boys. These are learned by the children and performed together with the adults participating in the ceremony. For instance, among the Adangme in Ghana there is an elaborate puberty institution (*dipo*) for girls in which they receive several weeks of instruction about mothercraft and the customs and history of their society. Music and dance are an important part of this instruction/ritual and the girls and adult women participating become, in effect, a temporary ensemble that disbands when the ritual is over. There can also be ceremonial occasions when an entire village or tribe is involved—such as the ancestral rites of the Sambaa of Tanzania—making the potential at least for a gigantic orchestra and dance troupe, which is, like the smaller ritual musical groups, temporary.

Second, there are in many African villages *musical associations,* clubs and societies formed specifically to perform music in ensembles. Among the Nyasa of Tanzania, for example, each village has either a male or a female club, each of which specializes in a specific type or style of music; they practice regularly and seriously and compete in contests with the clubs in other villages. Then there are the *specialists and royal musicians,* the professionals. They may be attached to royal courts, nobles, or leading households and may play in set ensembles and upon prescribed sets of instruments including drums, trumpets, fiddles, or plucked harps or lutes. Other professionals may belong to craft guilds, like the male musicians among the Hausa of northern Nigeria who are tied to guilds (who may be their patrons) of butchers, blacksmiths, hunters, musicians/praise shouters (themselves), or farmers.

Fourth, there are *socio-musical groups*: social groups whose membership is selective and whose activities may include their own special ceremonies and songs. For example, the hunters' association among the Yoruba of Nigeria has its own musical form, called *ijala,* which is a chant sung at the Ogun festival (Ogun is the god of iron), at specifically musical entertainments, and at ceremonies of the life cycle connected with the hunter and his family. Finally there are the ensembles of *members of a religious cult,* whose instruments and music—like the drums and drumming patterns of many west African cults (carried to Haiti)—may be connected with specific gods.

Nketia has also looked at African musical ensembles in purely musical terms: by sound, instrumentation, and function. While there are some groups in which the texture is a complete mesh of homogeneous sound:

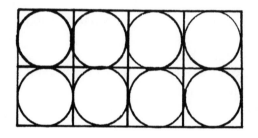

there may also be functional layers:

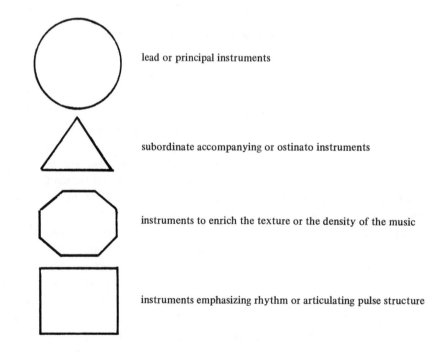

Categorized by types of instruments involved, African ensembles fall into three distinct groupings:

1. Ensembles made up completely of melodic instruments (strings, winds, or melodic idiophones—but not drums)

Drum ensemble, Bantu people, south Africa.

a. Homogeneous groups: all instruments of the same kind, like ensembles of flutes, or of trumpets, or of harps or *mbiras.*

b. Mixed groups: using melodic instruments of different kinds, like ensembles of flutes *and* trumpets, harp lutes *and* xylophones, bowed lutes (fiddles), harp lutes, *and* lyres, or any other combination.

2. Ensembles made up entirely of instruments of indefinite pitch (like drums and nonmelodic idiophones: rattles, bells, clappers, or log drums)

a. Homogeneous groups: all of the same type (like ensembles of hourglass drums, of log drums, or of gourd drums)

b. Mixed groups: varying types of drums and idiophones with different characteristics and tone colors (like ensembles consisting of a mixture of rattles, bell clappers, hourglass-shaped and barrel-shaped and footed and frame drums, and so on). It is important to remember the African aesthetic of acute awareness of the variety of sound quality (one might almost say melody) in percussion instruments!

3. Ensembles that are combinations of both melodic and percussion instruments: these are far more prevalent than groups of melodic instruments alone and may include, for example, xylophone and drum ensembles; horn, double bell, rattle, and drum ensembles; or flutes or string instruments combined with percussion

The number of players in an African ensemble can often be quite liquid: some players may quit to take a break (or go home), while bystanders might pick up an instrument—or improvise one out of a plow handle, shield, or similar resonant material—and join in. Only the royal groups or flute or trumpet ensembles, where the interlocking notes of each instrument make a specific number of players essential, are set. More often it is the instruments and their sound that are important; as long as a core of essential instruments is represented there can be any number of players, especially on the fringes. Another important fact to remember in terms of African ensembles is that they are playing by ear. An African orchestra of ten or sixteen or twenty-five musicians seems at first small, especially when compared with a European symphony orchestra of eighty to a hundred; but the European musicians are reading, they are technicians (in a sense) carrying out the directions of a composer within a very strict system of controls. One could expect nothing but chaos if he asked sixteen symphony musicians to improvise for two hours—it is simply not part of the tradition. Seen in this light, in terms of ear music and improvisation, an African ensemble of sixteen is large, and an orchestra of twenty-five is absolutely gigantic!

★★★★★★★ A SAMPLER OF AFRICAN ENSEMBLES AND ORCHESTRAS ★★★★★★★

1. Chopi *mbila* (xylophone) ensembles (southeast Africa)

Vary in size from a few players to groups of 10, 15, and even 30 musicians. Include percussion backgrounds (drums and rattles, or drum, double bell, and sticks). One orchestra of 17 instruments had the following arrangement:

8 warriors (in costume) singing
assorted rattles

17+ {
7 high-pitched *tshilandzana* xylophones with ten to fourteen keys
7 high-pitched *tshilandzana* xylophones (in a second row)
2 medium-pitched *mabinde* xylophones (ten keys)
1 low-pitched (drum sounding) *tshikulu* xylophone (one to four keys)

2. Senufo people

a. *Dyegele* xylophone ensemble

7+ | 4 xylophones
3 kettledrums
+ jangles

Orchestra is connected with *poro,* men's initiation society

b. One-string harp (*bolo-bogo*) ensemble:

11+ | 2 voices (two of the players also sing)
9 *bolo-bogo* one-string harps
+ rattles

3. Uganda: royal court ensembles

a. *Abalere ba kabaka* (flute and drum ensemble)

7 | voice plus 3 *ndere* notched flutes
4 drums

b. *Abadongo ba kabaka* (lute, flute, and lyre ensemble)

10 | 6 *ndingidi* lutes
2 *ndere* flutes
2 *endongo* lyres

c. *Entenga ba kabaka* (tuned drum band)

15 | 15 tuned drums played by six players

4. Trumpet/horn orchestras

a. Thonga *bunanga* ensemble:

12 | 10 horns (two notes each)
2 drums

Horn players dance in a circle around the drummers

b. Senufo: *gbofe* ensemble

10 | 7 wood trumpets (one to two notes each)
2 drums
1 iron bell played by one of the drummers

c. Dan *truta* ensemble:

10 | 6 ivory trumpets (two notes each)
4 drummers

5. Flute orchestras*

    a. Lango of Uganda:

5+ | sets of 5 cone-shaped end-blown flutes made of animal horn (three notes each)

    b. Chwana of the Bantu peoples

15 | sets of 15 flutes

    c. Bangwaketse at Kanye

10–23| sets of a minimum of 10 sizes of flutes with as many as 23 or more players

    d. Royal ensemble of the Bamalete people

13 | 13 flutes plus duplications
led by a *mothlabi* conductor

    e. Venda *tshikona* national dance

22 | set (*motaba*) of 19 flutes (one note each)
3 drums
led by a leader

> *Many of the flute ensembles exist in sets of different sizes and different notes of interlocking pitches—like pieces of a mosaic. Each flute may be duplicated, or doubled, ad libitum. The sets are carefully tuned; many of the flutes have adjustable tuning devices.

6. Two ensembles for accompanying dance

    a. Yogo people:

16 | 7 *mbala* wood horns
1 *kekese* basket rattle
1 *mbili* metal wrist bell
2 pod-shaped slit drums
2 small pod-shaped slit drums
2 laced (membrane) drums
1 double bell

    b. Medje people:

17+ | 4 *nabita* conical (membrane) drums
1 *nedundu* bell-shaped slit drum
2 *emandru* pod-shaped slit drums
2 *nekbokbo* small log-shaped slit drums
1 *nengbongbo* double metal bell
6 *nezeza* basket rattles
1 small hand bell

7. **Nigeria**

   a. *Iqbin* ensemble (Yoruba people)

3 | 3 footed drums of different sizes (*iya igbin, jagba, and epele*)

   b. *Dundun* or *gangan* ensemble

5 | 4 hourglass squeeze drums of different sizes (*dundun, kerikeri, gugudi, gangan, kanango*)
     | 1 *gugugu* hemispherical-shaped drum

   c. *Bata* ensemble

5 | 3 double-headed drums of truncated cone shape of large, medium, and small size (*iya-ilu, omele,* and *kudi*
     | 2 hemispherical-shaped single-headed drums of large ("male") and small ("female") sizes (*omele-ako* and *omele-abo*)

8. **Mbira ensembles (the Shona people of Rhodesia)**

In ancient times the chiefs kept large ensembles which could total from fifteen to twenty players. Special religious occasions were also celebrated with large *mbira* bands. Now the basic Shona ensemble will have from two to five *mbira* players (several of whom may also sing); they may be joined by a player on the *hosho* gourd rattle and by the hand clapping and dancing of the listeners.

9. **Ghana: high-life band**

A combination of African percussion instruments (and sometimes bamboo flute) with Afro-American jazz/pop/soul group instrumentation. One such group included:

11 musicians
| 4 drums (African)
| 1 guitar (electric)
| 1 saxophone
| 2 trumpets
| 1 vibraphone/drums
| 1 bass (string or electric)
|
| 1 flute/saxophone/drums (the leader)
|
| voices (of the leader and players)

10. **Malagasy (Madagascar) *valiha* (tube zither) groups**

Combine European and indigenous instruments. Accompany songs (sung by one or more of the performers).

Two possible combinations:

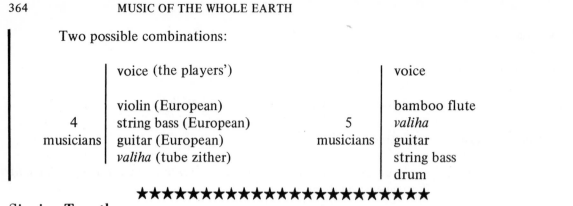

4 musicians	voice (the players')	5 musicians	voice
	violin (European)		bamboo flute
	string bass (European)		*valiha*
	guitar (European)		guitar
	valiha (tube zither)		string bass
			drum

★★★★★★★★★★★★★★★★★★★★★★★★★

Singing Together

There is something about the togethers of voices, of human instruments, pulled together into one mass of sound that—like the visual phenomena of a full starry night sky, the light show of a sunset or a dawn; or the sound of rain or the rumbling sea—touches very deep, deeply *human,* expressive roots. Perhaps buried in our collective unconscious there is the memory of our ancestors and how they sat around a fire communally singing to seal the togethers of their group or tribe or family, and also singing for Power, to and for and against the great and inexplicable and sometimes terrifying forces of the world, singing for success in the hunt, or for life—for enduring crises, sickness, changes, adulthood, birth, death—and singing (perhaps) also just for the sheer joy of singing, for happiness, and for humanness.

Choral voices somehow add magic and precision, increase the power and (for the performers) the memory of sacred texts. In Japan, Tibet, Burma, and southeast Asia choirs of monks chant the Buddhist scriptures in unison, just as in Europe for centuries the voices of Christian monks have sung the liquid melodies of Gregorian chant. In India Brahmin priests, sometimes in groups, chant the ancient Hindu *Vedas*; in the American Southwest Pueblo and Navaho sacred choirs raise their voices like one man's in sacred chants that have the sweep and breadth of mesas and skies and clouds, lightning and distant horizons.

Choirs and their music, their sound, are considered an indispensable part of Christian worship in Europe, the Americas, in fact wherever Christianity has penetrated. Congregations sing together whether in the solid strong unisons of the old German Reformation chorales, the seventeenth- and eighteenth-century sentimental harmonies and devotional texts of the Protestant hymnists, the (spoken) "lining out" and slow, highly ornamented unison grandeur of the southern American mountain style, the bouncy arrangements of Sankey, or the intense free-form style of many fundamentalist and black churches in the United States. In India Hindu devotees come together for the singing of *bhajanas* to the accompaniment of drums and cymbals, just as southern congregations (in the United States) may have their Sunday evening "hymn sings," or black congregations their gospel evenings. In sub-Saharan Africa choral singing—on the west coast, responsorial and harmonic; in central Africa, polyphonic—along with dance and instrumental music, is a part of many ceremonial functions, sacred and secular; and on the islands of the Pacific, from New Guinea eastward and northward, there has always been a similar great tradition of vocal choral music and singing together in unison or in parts and often *a cappella.*

Certain sections of the Soviet Union are also great centers for choral togethers: Georgia, the Ukraine, old "Russia," and the Caucasus. Here folk choruses sang (they still do, but now often from notation and composed arrangements) in complex harmonies and two-, three-, or more-part "ear" polyphony both for social occasions and for services in the Eastern Orthodox Church. Similar polyphonic part singing by ear is also found in Italy and Spain. In the rest of Europe and America singing by ear is often done in thirds or following simple bass movement, although much choral music is performed by note reading. In the southern United States the shaped-note notation makes possible singing (by people who "can't read music") of the wonderful and sometimes startling harmonies of native hymn settings such as those in the *Southern Harmony.* The peoples in the various tribal pockets in south and southeast Asia also sing secular and sacred choral music, *a cappella* or accompanied by

Singing in a pentecostal church, Chicago, Illinois, 1941.

instruments and (often) by dance. Their music, strikingly similar to much of the choral singing in Africa, may be harmonic or even in polyphonic drone-based parts. Singing together is also an important part of the Sufi sect of Islam, along with playing (particularly on the flute) and twirling circle dancers ("the whirling dervishes" are a subsect) a part of the ceremonial path to the experience of religious ecstasy. And in Bali, in the *ketchak* (or "monkey dance"), a chorus of (on one occasion seventy-eight) men sits in a circle around dancers and performs in a multipart rhythmic changing and chattering that imitates the sound (and the fun) of a band of monkeys!

Choral singing is also an important part of the classical music traditions associated with the courts and "high" culture in many of the earth's societies. In the Japanese *noh* theater tradition—and consequently in *kabuki*—a male chorus chants in austere unison and with rocklike gravity, commenting on the actions of the characters on the stage in front of them, much perhaps as did the choruses in the great tragic theater of Greece several thousand years ago. In Java a unison chorus often adds its voice to the music of the *gamelan* orchestra, providing a bedrock over which a female vocalist flies like a sparrow (or rather a nightingale) and around which the gongs and flutes and chimes of the orchestra weave their rich fabric of translucent textures and sonorities. In Turkey today, and to a lesser extent in Iran and in India, classical songs may be sung by unison choruses. And of course in the European tradition there are the great choral forms—the motets, cantatas, oratorios, choral symphonies, and operas with the massed voices of a chorus—both sacred and secular, and the great composers of choral music: Palestrina, Monteverdi, Gesualdo, Heinrich Schuetz, J. S. Bach, William Byrd, not to mention Mozart and Beethoven.

From the Indian ceremonials on the American high plains to the cathedrals of Europe to the jungles and savannas of Africa to the cities of Asia or the lush islands of the Pacific, man has discovered the potential of singing together, its beauty, and its power. And music is the richer for it.

The Orchestras

The idea of the orchestra—as a conception, as a fact—implies grandeur. This bigness is in part musical: instead of individual lines, the individual voices of instruments and their musicians, one hears the movement of great masses of sound; even when individual instruments sound clearly it is in relationship to a much larger group, like a tiny ray of sunlight streaming through the grandeur of a skyfull of billowing clouds, like a bird soaring out momentarily from the dark mass of the flock, like a person's position in a tribe rather than in the intimacy of his family hearth. The musical action is, as often as not, a group action, and the sound a group sound. The bigness of an orchestra is also psychological and physical. The actual music played by an orchestra is not necessarily more complex than that played by a chamber group or a soloist; often it is actually simpler. The notes in a European classical or romantic era symphony, for example—*all* of them—can be reduced to a score for piano, four hands. But the physical presence, the intangible vibrations, of a great mass of musicians sitting together and making music together, is—like the mass of crowds at a parade or ball game or concert—distinctly different. There is a visual bigness, too, in the collection of faces and hands and the many different instruments (in the Orient with colorful costumes and imposingly ornate racks and props).

There is actually no sharp dividing line between what we have called "chamber ensembles" for want of a better term and what we will call "orchestras." Clearly, many of the large groups we have listed in the previous section—particularly those in Africa—are orchestras in every conceivable sense of the word: eighty Watusi musicians playing together for a dance festival *are* an orchestra, as are fifteen to forty musicians in a Nama Hottentot flute and drum ensemble. On the other hand, many of the orchestras which we will discuss in this section, such as those of Thailand, have an intimate chamber quality. We must remember, then, that our division is geographical: we are concentrating on the great orchestral traditions of the Orient (with a bow to Europe and America); but Africa and the rest of the world too are full of orchestras.

From the earliest recorded history great orchestras have been connected with the courts of monarchs. Ancient wall reliefs on tombs and palaces show marching or sitting musicians and singers; in some cases (as in China) miniature or full-sized instruments and (in the Middle East) the unlucky

Sarons forming part of the *gamelan gong gedé*/orchestra, Bali.

musicians as well(!) were buried with royalty to entertain them in the next world (a function also of the images on the wall reliefs). An Egyptian tomb from the Fifth Dynasty (ca. 2700 B.C.) pictures musicians playing flute, clarinet, and harp along with four singers; a later relief shows a more ostentatious orchestra: seven harpists, seven flutists, and assorted singers and pipers. An image from the court of Elam (Assyria, ca. 650 B.C.) includes, besides pipes and other instruments, seven harpists with their fingers in different positions on different strings, a fact that has boggled scholars and resulted in endless (and perhaps meaningless) argument but that has also opened up the possibility that the music played by these ancient orchestras, far from being simple and monophonic, might have been harmonic or even polyphonic! Unfortunately for us the stone musicians and their instruments are silent. How fantastic it would be if they (and their music) could be magically brought to life! The Bible tells us that King David patronized an orchestra of three cymbals, eight harps, and six lyres; King Solomon consecrated the temple in Jerusalem with a massive musical force of cymbals, harps, lyres, singers (the Levites), and 120 priests playing trumpets; and a later orchestra included a chorus of a minimum of twelve singers, two to six harps, nine or more lyres, two to twelve oboes, and one pair of cymbals.

But it was in ancient China that the biggest of the big bands really flourished. During the Chou dynasty (1122–255 B.C.) the size of one's orchestra showed one's rank. High dignitaries were allowed twenty-seven—incidentally, mostly blind—musicians arranged in a half-square; lower dignitaries had to make do with only fifteen musicians who were to be arranged in a straight line. One can imagine catty wives whispering about the fact that Mr. So-and-So only had fifteen musicians in a straight line! The court of the Han dynasty in the years 58 to 75 A.D. maintained, besides a military band, no less than three orchestras: one for religious ceremonies, one for archery contests, and one for formal banquets and the pleasurable activities in the ladies' section of the palace—in all, 829 musicians and dancers. In the T'ang dynasty (618–907 A.D.) music along with all the other arts flourished to an even greater degree. There were ensembles from even the most distant provinces and beyond: from India, Tibet, and southeast Asia. A visiting orchestra of thirty-five musicians from Burma was in residence. The court retained between five hundred and seven hundred musicians. In all it must have been an extraordinarily musical atmosphere, one of the peaks in the history of world music—and we do not even have a record of the innumerable folk musicians, minstrels, and troupes who must have entertained commoners on the streets in the busy cities and trade centers of the day. Music in the court was classified into ten types—*shih pu chi*—and it is recorded that Chinese court music was performed by an orchestra using twenty-five different *kinds* of instruments (the classical European symphony orchestra used less than seventeen). The arrangement of one orchestra—with harps, flutes, lutes, mouth organs, and oboes on tiers—is given below:

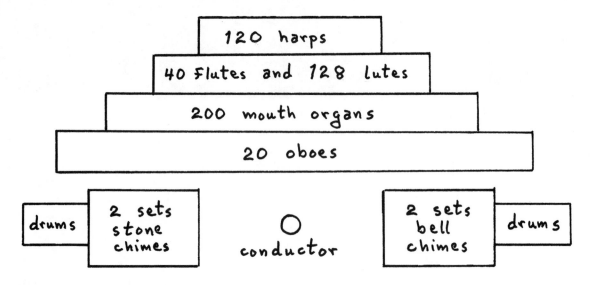

Another performance diagram shows a dance orchestra of forty-four players: twenty *ya* drums are arranged in a circle with an inscribed square containing twenty-four musicians with stamping tubes, clapper tubes, and drums.

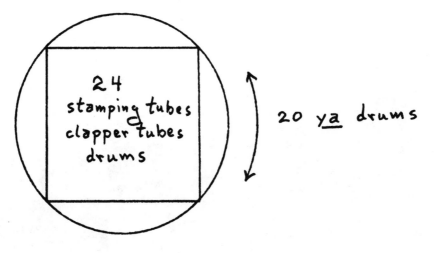

There were also all-women orchestras, chosen sometimes, it is said, more for their beauty than for their musicianship! One painting from the eighth century illustrates an ensemble of eighteen:

1 lady conductor with a clapper
1 large drum
2 harps
2 long zithers
2 lutes
2 transverse flutes   } pairs
2 oboes
2 *sheng* mouth organs
2 metallophones
2 hourglass-shaped drums

   The large orchestras of China, expensive to maintain and an expendable luxury in later, less extravagant dynasties, gradually died out, like an extinct species of musical dinosaurs that had outlived their time. But during the peak of the T'ang period influences had flooded out of China, especially into Korea and Japan. There the court orchestras survived, although with modifications, right up until the present time. In Korea there are three types of orchestra depending upon the musical repertoire: the *aak,* which performs Confucian ritual music; the *tang-ak,* which specializes in Chinese T'ang and Sung dynasty compositions; and the *hyang-ak,* which performs Korean court music. In Japan the *gagaku* (or "elegant music") orchestra modeled after T'ang sources took shape in the Nara period (533–793), flourished in the courtly life of the Heian (794–1185), and was protected by the emperors in all the succeeding centuries, through periods of turmoil and change—through modernization and through the catastrophe of World War II—like the rare and precious flower that it was, and still is.
   The music of the *gagaku* orchestra, standardized in the ninth century, is divided into two main

Korean court music ensemble, from an old postcard, showing percussion instruments, stone chimes, bell chimes, drums, long zithers.

categories: *togaku* ("music of the left") which consists of compositions from Chinese and Indian (!) sources; and *koma-gaku* ("music of the right"), which includes compositions originally from Korea and Manchuria, rearrangements of older dance pieces, and indigenous Japanese compositions (which greatly influenced the sound and style of all the music in this category). The precise instrumentation of the orchestra varies depending upon whether it is performing "music of the left" or "music of the right," and also upon whether it is doing strictly concert pieces, accompanying dance (*bugaku*) or vocal music forms (such as *saibara, roei,* or *imayo*). And the style of performance varies similarly: the same composition will sound different (stylistically) performed as an abstract concert piece or as *bugaku* dance accompaniment.

The core of the *gagaku* orchestra is in the wind instruments. The *hichiriki,* a tiny double-reed bamboo oboe with a gigantic sound, carries the main melody. Sei Shonagon, a court lady of the eleventh century, in her diary (*The Pillow Book*) compares the amazing nasal blast of the *hichiriki* to "noisy crickets in Autumn" and mentions that on one occasion it made her "hair stand on end." It is not surprising that the sound of the *hichiriki,* combined with its constant microtonal fluctuations around the thread of the melody, was often credited with supernatural powers: a thief once returned a houseful of stolen goods when the owner played on the *hichiriki*; and a drought was once ended when the *hichiriki* (played in a temple) brought billowing clouds, rain, and eventually (and unfortunately) devastating floods!

The flute section of the orchestra provides heterophonic ornamentation around the melody. Three different sizes of transverse bamboo flutes are used depending on the style of the music. The largest, *ryuteki* or *yoko-bue,* are played in the (Chinese) *to-gaku* pieces; the medium-sized *kagura-bue* are played in *kagura* style or in other Shinto ceremonies; and the smallest, the *koma-bue,* are played in the Korean and indigenous *koma-gaku* style.

The *sho* mouth organ—with seventeen reed pipes set in a cup-shaped wind chest, its sound produced by vibrating free reeds (like a harmonica's)—provides another section. The *sho* functions harmonically: its eleven possible chords (very different in sound, structure, and sequence from those of the Western music tradition) relate to the mode and basic notes of the melody.

Three types of string instruments are used in *gagaku*. All of them play stereotyped melodic patterns, occasional graces, arpeggios, bits of melody that function colotomically rather than melodically: that is, they mark off sections of time in the musical structure. The *wagon* is a six-stringed long zither, the *gaku-so* (a predecessor of the modern *koto*) is a thirteen-stringed long zither, and the *biwa* is a pear-shaped plucked lute with four strings and four frets.

The leader of the orchestra (as in many other large Oriental ensembles) is a drummer. In the (Chinese) *to-gaku* compositions he plays the two-headed cylindrical *kakko* drum, while in (Korean) *koma-gaku* pieces he plays the hourglass-shaped *san-no-tzuzumi*. He plays various stereotyped rhythmic patterns and rolls to set the tempo and mark beats and phrases. A bronze gong, the *shoko* (in three sizes depending on the style and category of the music being performed), and a suspended drum, the *taiko* (also in three sizes), mark off time units in a colotomic structure. For *bugaku* dance pieces the enormous *da daiko* drums, with their thunderous sound and imposing appearance, are played. The *shoko* gong, *taiko* drum, and (especially) the *da-daiko* drum are all suspended in highly ornate and beautiful racks, and this visual effect (supported by the elaborate and colorful traditional costumes of the musicians) is also a part of *gagaku* musical performance. A chorus may also perform with the orchestra (as in the oratorios, Masses, and choral symphonies in the West), and the leader of the chorus plays the *shakubyoshi,* two sticks that are beaten together.

The happenings in the music of *gagaku* fall into several distinct layers according to their sound and their function:

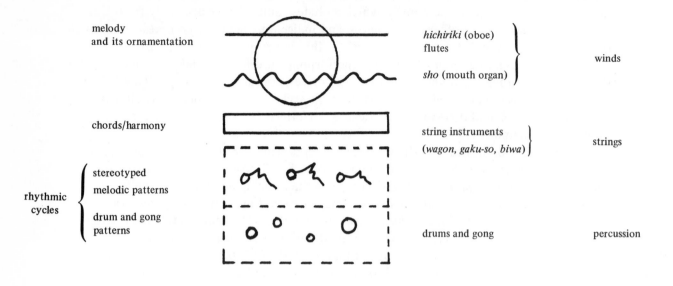

And each instrument falls rather rigidly into one of these layers in the musical texture, doing its thing within precise limitations and possibilities much as each of the different pieces on a chessboard move according to set rules and procedures. This tie-in between instruments and function is one of the chief characteristics of the great classical orchestras of the Orient—of Korea, Japan, southeast Asia, and Indonesia—and a key to the workings of their collective togethers. It contrasts sharply with the concepts of the (musical) West where (although cellos and string basses usually play bass lines, or violas harmonies and subsidiary melodies, or flutes and first violins melodies and countermelodies) each instrument can, potentially at least, be absolutely schizophrenic, playing at some time or another dominant melodies, countermelodies, chords, accompaniment patterns, melodic figuration, bass lines, and so on. Is there a connection between the strict stratification of musical layers in the Oriental orchestras and the rigidity of the human social layers found in many traditional Oriental societies? Or, similarly, do the mobility and flexibility of instruments in the layers of many of the ensembles of Western music (although under the totalitarian hand of the conductor) reflect democracy and social mobility? These are questions that we can ask but cannot readily answer; orchestras and ensembles are, after all, sometimes anachronisms, remnants of earlier times long past. But at the same time ensembles and their workings may result from the way societies and peoples relate in their togethers, and to collective and sometimes unconscious impulses and attitudes.

The variations in the instrumentation of the *gagaku* orchestra (sixteen players in its standard form) are:

To-gaku (Chinese) pieces   **Koma-gaku (Korean/indigenous) pieces**

3 *hichiriki* (oboes)   3 *hichiriki* (oboes)
3 *ryuteki* (large flutes)   changes →   3 *koma-bue* (medium-sized flutes)
3 *sho* (mouth organs)   3 *sho* (mouth organs)

2 *biwa* (lutes)
2 *gaku-so* (long zithers)   (strings usually omitted)

                                changes
1 *kakko* (drum and leader) ——————→   1 *san-no-tzuzumi* (hourglass drum and leader)

1 *shoko* (gong)   1 *shoko* (gong)
1 *taiko* (suspended drum)   1 *taiko* (suspended drum)

Bugaku (music accompanying dance)

Uses instrumentation of either
to-gaku or *koma-gaku*, depending on the style of the piece

Omits stringed instruments

May add: *da-daiko* (large drum)

Saibara, roei, imayo (vocal forms)

Use smaller ensembles drawn
from *to-gaku* or *koma-gaku*
but omit drums

The *hayashi* ensemble that sits and plays on the stage behind the beautifully masked and costumed actors in Japanese *noh* drama is actually more of a chamber group in concept than an orchestra. Yet the music of these players—a flute and two or three drummers—far from being mere incidental
or background music, is fully integrated into the structure and concept of this remarkable theatrical
form. Besides a constant interaction with the singing and actions of the actors and with the solemn
and introspective singing (*yokyoku*) of a male chorus (also sitting in the background), the *hayashi*
ensemble provides dance accompaniment (*mai*) and interludes (*gaku*). The *nohkan,* or *noh* flute,
with its distinctive sound and character has highly unusual acoustical properties: a tiny tube inserted
inside it upsets the usual acoustical properties of a wind instrument, and it overblows flat, in the regions of a major or minor seventh! The music of the *noh* flute with its many half-holed "indistinct,"
"blurred," sliding effects, its piercing sound, and breathy tone, is largely the arrangement of a large
number of stereotyped melodic patterns. The flute patterns (according to William P. Malm) signal
parts of the play, accompany dance, set the tempo, add timbre, create atmosphere for interludes,
set the pitch for the chorus, and "heighten the lyricism of certain poetic passages" in the words of
the play—altogether a multifaceted and complex functional role. Often the flute melodies seem to
have no tonal relationship to the notes and tonal centers of the chorus and actors/singers, a jarring
polytonal or—with the melodic skips of a seventh—seemingly atonal effect that increases the flute's
isolation, and hence its effectiveness.

The drums—the hourglass-shaped *ko-tzuzumi* and *o-tzuzumi* and the shallow barrel-shaped *taiko*—
with their basic sounds and strokes also play a series of stereotyped patterns (there are over two hundred) in a complex relationship with each other and with the other elements and human participants
in the drama. The drummers also shout out drum calls (*kakegoe*)! This is a practice that is unusual
in a classical music form anywhere in the world—usually musicians keep their mouths shut (unless
there is an instrument connected with them), their voices to themselves, and their signals silent or
musical. But the *kakegoe* shouts of *noh* drummers mix with the sounds of their drumming and bring
to the surface—make aurally visible—the technical structure of their patterns in a particularly Japanese way, an aesthetic honesty that is also seen, for example, in the exposure (rather than the covering) of knotholes or particularly unusual twists in the grains of wood in a house and the structural
use of these supposed "defects" in a beautiful way.

Musical elements in *noh* drama

singer/actors

chorus

hayashi
ensemble
{
nohkan (flute)

ko-tzuzumi (hourglass drum)
o-tzuzumi (larger hourglass drum)
taiko (shallow barrel drum)
}

Japanese *kabuki*—that popular and spectacular theatrical form which evolved as a major entertainment in the Edo period (1615–1868)—uses vast musical forces, some of them unique, others borrowed or synthesized from earlier art and folk idioms. The heart of *kabuki* music is *nagauta,* lyrical "long songs" with voice and *shamisen* (plucked long lute) to carry the melody, combined with the *noh hayashi* ensemble of flute and three drums. Sometimes one of the other classical bamboo transverse flutes is added to the group. While the drums may function on stereotyped rhythms much as they do in *noh* theater, the hourglass-shaped *o-tzuzumi* and *ko-tzuzumi* may also play patterns directly related to the rhythms of the *shamisen* lute. The *noh* flute and the *taiko* drum float like strange birds (or exotic fishes) outside the rest of the group, doing their own thing—unconnected tonally, melodically, thematically, rhythmically—but adding their essential color and figurations to the texture.

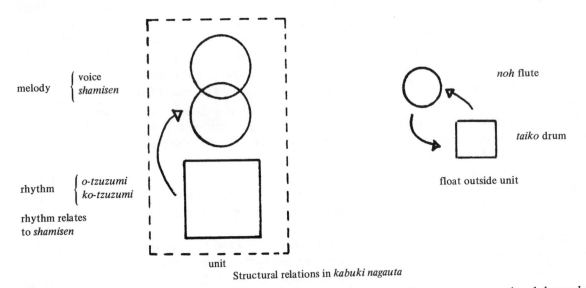

melody { voice / *shamisen*

rhythm { *o-tzuzumi* / *ko-tzuzumi*

rhythm relates
to *shamisen*

noh flute

taiko drum

float outside unit

unit

Structural relations in *kabuki nagauta*

When the *nagauta* ensemble appears on stage (on tiers in the back) it is known as the *debayashi,* and often the vocal and instrumental parts are doubled to form a chorus/orchestra of as many as eighteen or more musicians.

Kabuki also uses the twos of the *gidayu* narrator/singer and *shamisen* player combination derived from the classical puppet theater tradition—on lower stage left or in a hidden stage left alcove—whose function in the drama is to comment upon the action, set scenes, and express the unspoken thoughts of the actors. For romantic scenes the voice-*shamisen* narrative song traditions (*jorūri*) of *tokiwazu* or *kiyomoto* are drawn from; and these musicians, when they appear on stage, are placed on downstage right. The numerous musicians who appear on stage can, however, be placed anywhere depending upon the requirements of a particular scene of the play. The musicians' presence on the stage is an important part of the *kabuki* aesthetic which exploits its theatricality (as opposed to the illusion of reality), its "artificiality," through extravagant makeup, extraordinary costumes, fantastic sets and trick devices, and the highly stylized "exaggerated" movements of the actors.

But in addition to the stage musicians and their music, there is a whole other group of musicians who are invisible to the audience: the *geza-ongaku* ("offstage music") of *kabuki* who peer through a bamboo curtain from a room off downstage right! Their function in the drama is to create mood and sound effects through an elaborate system of musical stereotypes, puns, and connotative melodies. These motifs and their implications are all instantly recognized by the connoisseur much as a Wagnerite might recognize *leitmotifs,* or a Laurel and Hardy cinema fan the implications of tweeting birds after a blow on the head ("dizziness, zaniness"), a fragment of the wedding march ("marriage in mind"), a bit of the Volga boatman's song ("hard, grueling work"), or any of the other musical comedy stereotypes used by Hollywood composers of the 1930s.

The main melodic instrument in *geza* offstage music is the *shamisen* plucked lute, although instruments like the *koto, kokyu,* and *shakuhachi* are used in certain plays. The *shamisen* usually plays connotative melodies: for example, the piece *Yuki* ("snow") to indicate winter, or the boatman's song *Tsukuda* to indicate a specific river, the Sumida (Tsukida is an island at the mouth of the Sumida River in Tokyo). The *noh* flute is used backstage for plays adapted from *noh* theater and to indicate court music, while the bamboo flute may be used in combinations imitating the music of folk festivals or as a substitute for the sound of the *shakuhachi.* In addition, there is an immense battery of percussion instruments: drums, gongs, chimes, bells, clappers, castanets, scrapers, and xylophones. The most important of these is the large *o-daiko* drum—originally used as a signal drum in the watchtowers of the old *kabuki* theater compounds—which is played to open a performance and to create atmosphere through sounds, strokes, and patterns that symbolize but do not imitate) elements like wind or rain, ocean waves or darkness. Besides the three standard *noh* drums (also played onstage) there are:

okedo (drum): for folk scenes
daibyoshi (drum): for Shinto music
gaku-daiko (drum): to imitate *gagaku* large drum; for war scenes
hontsuri-gane (bell): for temple scenes and as a signal device
dora (knobbed gong): temple scenes and signals
soban (rough-surfaced gong): temple scenes and the entrance of rough characters
atari-gane (small hand gong): folk music and festival *hayashi* groups
orugoru (bell set): originally Buddhist "Sanctus" bells, indicate lightness; for example, butterflies (!)
rei (Buddhist *sutra* bell): religious services or a priest's entrance
yotsudake (bamboo castanets): goddess dances
mokkin (sixteen-keyed xylophone): for comic dances

This list is, of course, only a sampling and far from complete. The dozens of *geza* melody and percussion instruments stashed away in the back room combine kaleidoscopically in a seemingly endless variety of ways, becoming at one time a rustic folk ensemble, at another a Shinto orchestra, hinting at the sounds of *gagaku* or *noh* ensembles, paralleling the hilarious gestures of a comic pantomime, exploding into the sound effects of a great Samurai battle, or indicating the frightening calm and darkness of the dead of night.

There is still one more sound element in *kabuki:* the wood blocks (*hyoshigi*) which are clapped together by a special stagehand minutes before the curtain opens to warn the actors and audience. This clacking also accompanies the opening of the curtain and—with the player sitting on the apron of stage left—the clashes and swordplay of fight scenes and rough-style acting. Just before the curtain comes down, a sharp crack from the *hyoshigi,* like the click of a giant camera, draws the audience's attention to the actors frozen in the final tableau.

Kabuki theater performance of the Edo period, prints (triptych) by Kunisada (1786–1864).

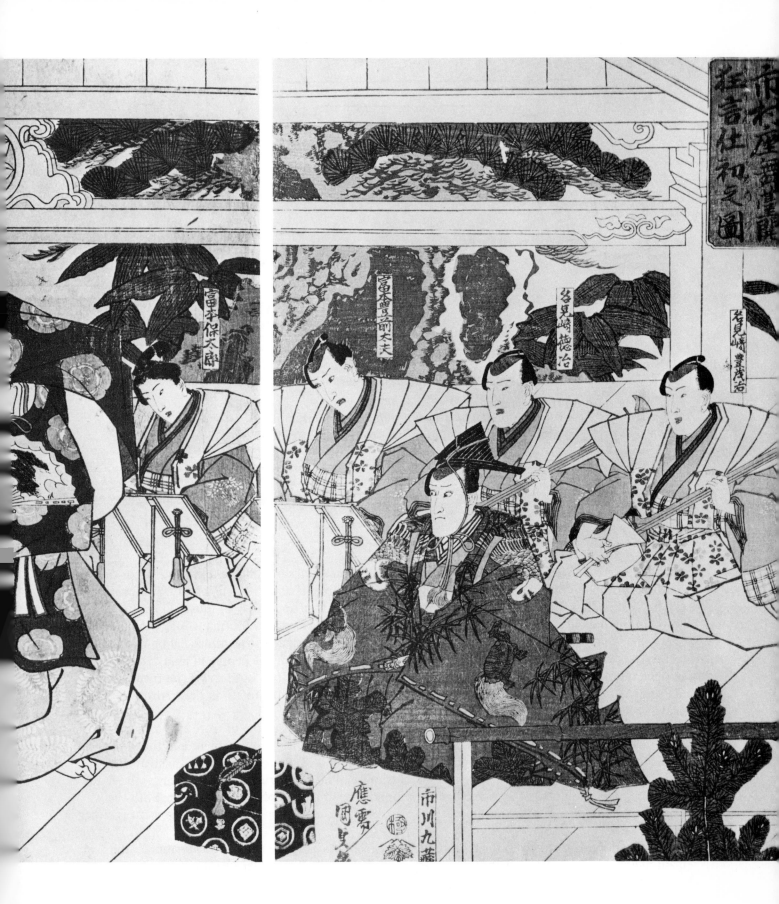

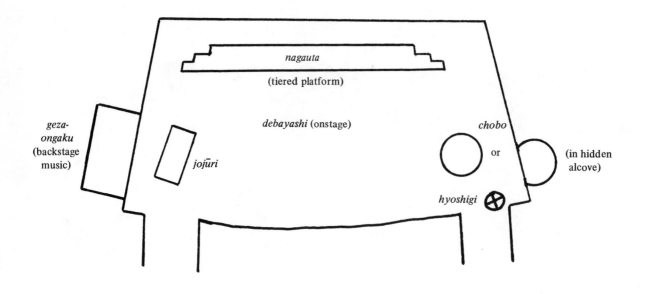

Ideal placement of musical forces in *kabuki* theater

nagauta: voice, *shamisen* plus *noh hayashi* ensemble
chobo: voice/*shamisen* narrative from puppet tradition
jojūri: voice/*shamisen* narrative
hyoshigi: wood blocks

debayashi: onstage music, placement of musicians can vary

geza-ongaku: offstage music

When one thinks of the orchestras of southeast Asia one thinks of delicate textures flitting like fireflies, of rippling xylophones, of busy ringing accompaniments and the clanging of tiny finger cymbals, of endless, breathless melodies turning with the sudden angularity of musical knees and elbows. In the old days all of the royal courts (and many of the princes) in Burma, Laos, Thailand, Cambodia, and Vietnam had orchestras. Now in the mid-twentieth century with social upheavals and cataclysmic warfare tearing apart the lives and traditional cultures of the people in many areas, it is an open question which of these musical national treasures will survive. But leaving the future (and the present) to take care of itself as we, mere musicians, must, we shall focus on the traditional classical music ensembles of Thailand.

Thai orchestras are distinguished by their timbre: the *pi phat* ensemble of from six to fourteen players is characterized by the sound of xylophones, metallophones, drums, gongs, and the *pi nai* quadruple-reed oboe; the *mahori* ensemble features the sound of plucked and bowed instruments and the flute, backed by a smaller melodic percussion section; the *khruang sai* with strings, flute, and rhythmic percussion omits the tone color of xylophones and metallophones altogether. Both the *pi phat* and *mahori* groups come in three sizes—small, medium, and large—while the *khruang sai* is either small or large.

Mantle Hood has described the texture of Thai orchestras as "polyphonic stratification": the main melody and variations upon it move along simultaneously like a river surrounded by its backwaters, inlets, and tributaries. While each of the variants in the layered texture is related to the main melody, each also has its own special characteristics (sound, figurations, and speed or density of notes happening within a given time span). Underneath this bubbling, rippling texture drums, gongs, and chimes provide a rhythmic/metric underpinning.

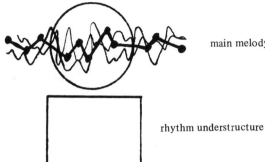

main melody and stratified variants

rhythm understructure

The Thai classical orchestras and their instrumentation in various sizes are given below.

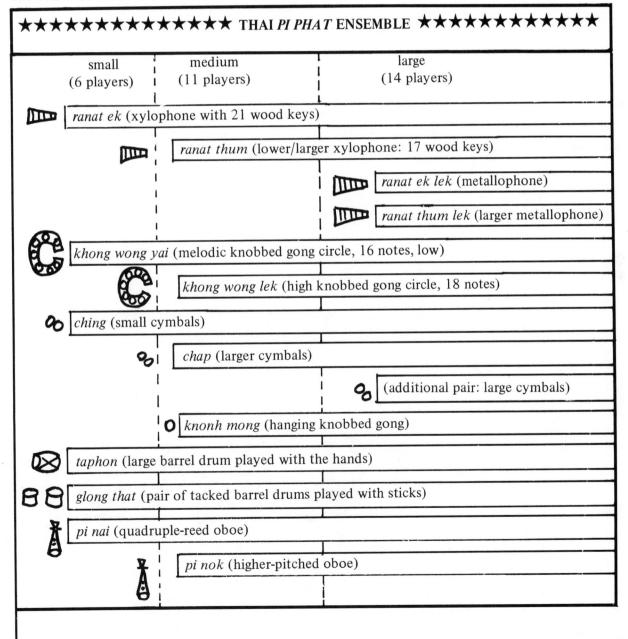

★★★★★★★★★★★★★★★★ THAI *PI PHAT* ENSEMBLE ★★★★★★★★★★★★★★★

small (6 players)	medium (11 players)	large (14 players)
ranat ek (xylophone with 21 wood keys)		
	ranat thum (lower/larger xylophone: 17 wood keys)	
		ranat ek lek (metallophone)
		ranat thum lek (larger metallophone)
khong wong yai (melodic knobbed gong circle, 16 notes, low)		
	khong wong lek (high knobbed gong circle, 18 notes)	
ching (small cymbals)		
	chap (larger cymbals)	
		(additional pair: large cymbals)
	knonh mong (hanging knobbed gong)	
taphon (large barrel drum played with the hands)		
glong that (pair of tacked barrel drums played with sticks)		
pi nai (quadruple-reed oboe)		
	pi nok (higher-pitched oboe)	

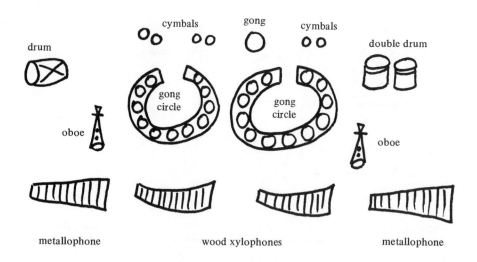

cymbals   gong   cymbals

drum   double drum

oboe   oboe

gong circle   gong circle

metallophone   wood xylophones   metallophone

Placement in the large Thai *pi phat* ensemble (14 players)

THAI *MAHORI* ENSEMBLE

Instruments:

⌢ ɸ   *jakhe*: plucked three-stringed floor zither with frets

⌢ ɸ   *khlui*: flute

⌢ ɸ   *ching*: small cymbals   + *ranat ek*: small xylophone

⮑   *chap*: larger cymbals   *khong wong lek*: small gong circle

▯   *mong*: small gong

o o   *so sam sai*: three-stringed spike fiddle

o o   *so duang*: high-register two-stringed fiddle, cylindrical body

o   *so u*: low-register two-stringed spike fiddle, half-coconut body

▯   *thon*: goblet-shaped drum

▱   *rammana*: shallow frame drum

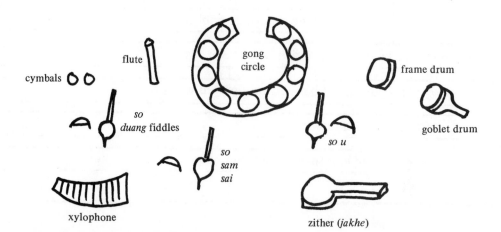

cymbals   flute   gong circle   frame drum

so duang fiddles   *so u*   goblet drum

so sam sai

xylophone   zither (*jakhe*)

Placement of instruments in small Thai *mahori* ensemble (10 players)

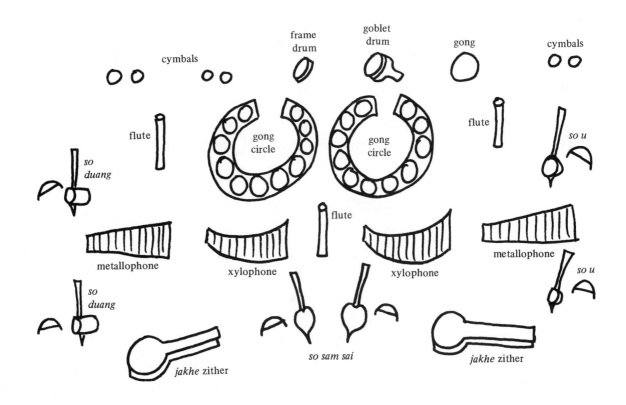

Placement in the large Thai *mahori* ensemble (23 players) (medium-sized ensemble omitted)

THAI *KHRUANG SAI* ENSEMBLE

Similar to the *mahori* ensemble, but omits wood xylophones and metallophones.

Also omits *so sam sai* spike fiddle.

Other plucked and bowed strings, cymbals, gong, and drums are same as in the *mahori* ensemble.

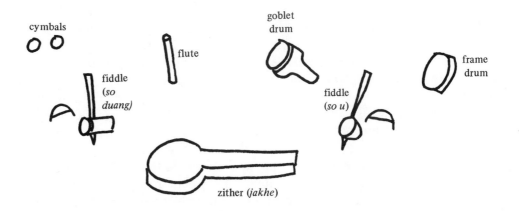

Small Thai *khruang sai* ensemble placement (7 players)

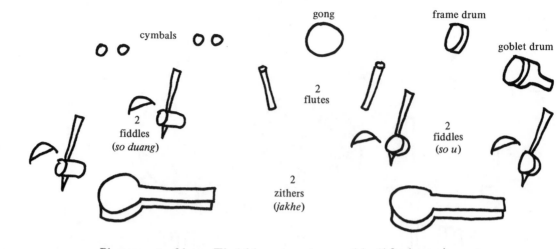

Placement of large Thai *khruang sai* ensemble (13 players)

★★★★★★★★★★★★★★★★★★★★★★★★★★★★

In the 1930s Jaap Kunst, one of the early and major figures in the field of ethnomusicology, made a musical survey of the islands of Java and Madura in Indonesia. Among other things he found over seventeen thousand *gamelan* ensembles of gongs, chimes, metallophones, and other instruments! The *gamelan* (we must remember) is not a collection of musicians who carry their instruments with them wherever they go, but a collection of instruments housed together as a unit, given a name, and owned by a village, temple, club, wealthy family, or royal court. *Gamelans* come in all shapes and sizes, from a few instruments made of bamboo, iron, or brass to village ensembles of a dozen to fifteen xylophones, metallophones, and gongs. But the large *gamelans* of the royal courts—which concern us here —may have as many as seventy-five or eighty instruments beautifully crafted and set in ornate and colorful racks and stands; and besides the metal instruments made of the finest bronze or bell metal they may include flute, zither, and the *rebab* fiddle. The massive yet delicate eloquence of such a large orchestra may be further expanded by the voices of a classically trained prima donna and a male chorus.

Like the instruments in the Japanese *gagaku* orchestra, the instruments of the *gamelan* are all tied to specific musical functions in various layers of the musical texture. One way of looking at these layers—and there are perhaps many other possibilities—is given here. The colotomic layer is the bedrock of the *gamelan*: the various gongs of different sizes and pitch mark off the rhythmic cycles of the music like a giant clockwork, repeating again and again under the evolving musical movement above them. The drums are played by the leader of the ensemble: he marks time with stereotyped patterns and signals through his drumming things like tempo, dynamics, transitions, repeats, and endings. (Sometimes subsidiary drums are included.) The fixed melody layer metallophones play rather rigidly on and around a relatively simple and unornamented core melody which must not, however (and this is important), be considered the "melody" of the piece. The real melody, according to master musicians like Bapak Sumarsam, is technically and notationally "invisible," but not aurally: it can be heard not in any single layer or instrument but in the composite sound of a number of melodic instruments played together! The next layer is the improvising one, with the gong sets of the "strong" ensemble or the metallophones, xylophone, and zither of the "soft-playing" ensemble weaving an almost polyphonic texture around the notes of the fixed melody. Improvising, we should remember, in the Asian context is no general freak-out, but rather a creative working out within a relatively strict range of possibilities and procedures. And, finally, there are the vocal tone instruments, the flute and the *rebab* spike fiddle, which relate extremely subtly to the various strata in the rest of the orchestra—particularly in the "soft-playing" improvising ensemble and to the singers: the female soloist and the male chorus.

Wesleyan University *gamelan* ensemble; Sumarsam, leader. Middletown, Connecticut.

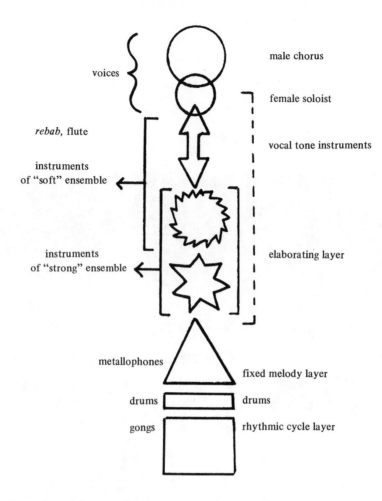

Functional layers of large Javanese court *gamelan* (orchestra)

Since most of the instruments of the *gamelan* are unfamiliar, at least by name, to most of us (who can tell a *tjelempung* from a *ketipung*?) we shall clarify our symbols, many of which we have used already in this chapter. These symbols, as you may have guessed, are stylized miniature drawings of the actual instruments, or of a key part of them. The *gamelan* instruments fall into several families:

 suspended gongs (the symbol is a cross-section "X ray"; all gongs have knobs or bosses in their center, all are tuned to specific pitches)

 gongs set potlike in a rack (also a cross-section "X ray"; smaller than the hanging gongs, they occur in tuned sets)

bonang family (up to twelve small tuned knobbed gongs placed horizontally like upside-down pots in an ornate rack)

saron family (metallophones of up to seven metal bars, or keys)

 *gender* family (metallophones of metal bars with tubular resonators under them)

 *gambang* (wood xylophone)

 rebab (two-stringed spike fiddle)

 tjelempung (plucked zither with twenty-six strings in double courses)

suling (end-blown flute)

 drums

Most of the metal instruments come in families of different sizes, and several types of drums are used. Each complete large *gamelan* is actually two *gamelans*: there is a duplicate set of instruments, one for each of the two principal scales used in Javanese music. All the instruments of one set are tuned to the five pitches of the *slendro* scale (see the section on melody); the instruments of the duplicate set are tuned to the seven pitches of the *pelog* scale. In addition, each *gamelan*—like a person marching to his own drummer—is *tuned to itself* rather than to a universal standard, giving its sound a unique quality and timbre (and perhaps the *gamelan*'s name). All the instruments, then, of a particular *gamelan* belong together like members of an inseparable family; they cannot be broken up or borrowed for another ensemble. If the instruments are a static, immobile unit, the players, the musicians, are not, and they can carry their skill, like their heads and hands, with complete mobility from a performance on one *gamelan* in one village or town to a performance on another.

★★★★★★★★★★★★★★★ THE LARGE COURT *GAMELAN* ★★★★★★★★★★★★★★★

1. Colotomic layer (repeated rhythmic cycles)

    hanging gongs

    gong ageng (largest, marks the end of a cycle and the beginning of the next)

    kempul (in sets of several different pitches, secondary emphasis)

    smaller gongs set in racks

    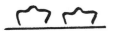 *kenong* (in a set of different pitches, for secondary emphasis)

    ketuk (used singly or in pairs to mark time units)

    engkok and *kemong* (similar to *ketuk,* used in *slendro* scale)

    kempyang (in pairs used in *pelog* scale)

     drums

    bedug (a large drum played in some compositions)

2. Drum layer

    drums (play stereotyped patterns and give signals)

played by
ensemble
leader

{ *tabangan* (two-headed barrel-shaped drum played with hands)

or

kendang gending (a larger drum) }

ketipung (a second drum played by an additional player in some compositions)

3. Fixed melody layer

saron family (bar metallophones)

   saron demung (large)

   saron barung (medium-sized)

   saron panerus or *peking* (tiny size)

   (*saron slentem* [archaic and now rarely used])

} play fixed melody,
or variations on it

gender family (bar metallophones with resonators)

   gender demung (archaic and now rarely used)

4. Elaborating layer (strong-playing ensemble)

bonang family (sets of knobbed gongs placed horizontally in a rack)

   bonang panembung (plays skeletal framework of fixed melody)

   bonang barung (medium-sized)

   bonang panerus (small)

} play improvising
melodies around
melodic core

5. Elaborating layer (soft-playing ensemble)

gender family

   gender barung (medium-sized, improvises in two-part polyphony)

   gender panerus (small, one octave higher, improvises stereotyped patterns at double speed)

gambang (wood xylophone, improvises two-part polyphony at double speed)

tjelempung (zither, improvises in two-part polyphony)

   (*siter* [one octave higher, zither, rarely used])

6. Vocal tone instruments (soft-playing ensemble)

 rebab (spike fiddle, melodic improvisation, anticipates pitches of the singers, relates to inner melodies of the rest of the *gamelan*)

suling (flute, improvises on stereotyped figures)

★★★★★★★★★★★★★★★★★★★★★★★★★★

The *gamelan* comes in four sizes (although all its instruments may be onstage for a given performance) depending upon the function, the musical purpose of the music, or the composition being played. The full orchestra is called *gamelan agen*. The middle-sized *klenengan* ensemble includes everything except the *bonang* family (4), and there may also be fewer *saron* metallophones. To play the vigorous *gending bonang* (*bonang* compositions) the *gamelan* includes the gong, drum, *saron*, and *bonang* layers but omits the instruments of the soft-playing improvising ensemble (5 and 6). Finally, the smaller, softer, more intimate *gadon* ensemble includes only the soft-playing ensemble and the drums.

FOUR SIZES OF GAMELAN ENSEMBLE				
	I. gamelan agen	II. klenengan	III. For gending bonang	IV. gadon
I. colotomic layer (gong rhythm cycles)	{ ⌣⌣	{ ⌣⌣	{ ⌣⌣	
II. drum layer	⊗	⊗	⊗	⊗
III. Fixed-melody layer (sarons)	▱▱	▱▱	▱▱	
IV. improvising/elaborating strong-playing ensemble (bonangs)	⌣⌣⌣		⌣⌣⌣	
V. & VI. improvising/elaborating soft-playing ensemble (gender, rebab, suling, tjelempung, etc.)	▱ wood	▱ wood		▱ wood

The *gamelan* orchestra in Java—like the European symphony orchestra—has a number of functions: it may give concerts, it may play at ritual or governmental ceremonials or celebrations, it may accompany the various forms of dance and dance drama (such as *wajang wong*), or it may accompany performances of the great classical shadow puppet plays, the *wayang kulit*. The instruments of the *gamelan* are treated with the greatest respect. They are kept in a special pavilion, the *pendopo*, where rehearsals and performances may take place; spirits are believed to dwell in the instruments, particularly in the large gongs, and *pujas* (religious ceremonies) are done for them on certain days and before a performance. Players remove their shoes or sandals before playing, walk bowed in a position of respect among the instruments, and never step over them. Perhaps the most amazing characteristic of the *gamelan* is the level of skill required to play the various instruments: some of them, such as the improvising *bonang, gender, gambang,* or *rebab*, require years of study and experience to master; others, such as the *ketuk* or some of the gongs, can be learned (technically) in a matter of minutes although to master the full context of the music and the repertoire, of course, takes longer. Between these two extremes are all kinds of levels of skill. A beginner in the *gamelan* can play in the ensemble almost immediately; as the years pass he can work his way up through the ranks to the more difficult instruments. Thus a master *gamelan* musician knows all the parts in a composition, and he can switch with ease from instrument to instrument, although he may specialize in a virtuoso instrument like the *gender*. And finally, although notation exists, the twenty to forty musicians in a *gamelan* basically play aurally; compositions and improvising techniques are learned by ear, and during a performance each musician, his ears alive, listens to and reacts to and interrelates with the sounds and figurations of the instruments and musicians around him. This wonderful musical together, which can put beginners and great virtuosos together in the same ensemble, with its various layers and sounds, is unique in the world. Maybe it reflects the geography of Java, or its people . . . or the moonlight.

The island of Bali, with its rice paddies, terraced hills, spectacular volcanoes, ancient Hindu temples, flowers, and clustered villages, is similar in many respects to Java, but it is also quite distinct. The *gamelans* of Bali have a brassier, "brighter" sound than those of Java—we have noted the slightly off-pitch tuning of pairs of metal instruments to achieve a vibrating, shimmering effect; and the music of the Balinese *gamelan* tends to be faster (almost double time), with jerky starts and stops, nervous, intensely syncopated, and with the bubbling, exploding hocketing of interlocking parts—this in comparison to the stately, almost "operatic" grandeur of classical music in Java.

In the 1930s a remarkable American composer, Colin McPhee (1901–64), lived in Bali, studied its music, and charted the ensembles he found there. If one-half of what he found still exists (surviving jet-age tourists, four-star hotels, and hippies) this tiny island is one of the most musical places on earth. Music was everywhere. Almost everyone—farmer, shopkeeper, villager—was a musician. Even the smallest villages and temples had *gamelans*. While we cannot in this space examine the ensembles of Bali in detail, we can at least list them, indicating the richness of performing groups in one small section of the earth.

★★★★★★★★★★★★★★ GAMELANS OF BALI ★★★★★★★★★★★★★★

1. *Gamelan gong* (twenty-five players, formerly forty): stately, used in temple ceremonies, ceremonial music, also to accompany *topeng* historical mask play and *baris* formal drill dance. Metallophones of *gender* ( ) and *saron* type ( ), a variety of gongs, with drums and clanging *chengchengs*.

2. *Gamelan gambuh* (seventeen or more players): used for dances and dance dramas with repertoire theater; more lyrical in sound, music has poetic and dramatic associations with character types or dramatic situations. Characterized by use of four large flutes (*suling gambuh*) with their rich, clarinetlike sound and the *rebab* fiddle; fewer gongs and metallophones; jingling instruments.

3. *Gamelan semar pegulingan* (eight or more players): a sweeter, more delicate chiming sound than the large *gamelan* gong, lighter, and brighter. No heavy-sounding *sarons* and fewer clashing cymbals.

4. *Gamelan pelegongan* (twenty-nine to thirty-nine or more players): used to accompany *legong* dance and dance plays of Hindu mythology and the *gambuh* theater. The peak of *gamelan* development in Bali, with a rich polyphonic orchestral style, a "shimmering spider-web" of sound, swift tempos, sudden dramatic changes of tempo, rapid figuration. Its precision requires intensive training and rehearsal.

5. *Gamelan pejogedan* (up to twelve players): a village folk ensemble used for village entertainment and to accompany the fun and laughter of the *joged* dance in which a girl dances solo and is joined by one partner after another. Ensemble includes xylophones and bamboo gongs; all instruments with bamboo resonators.

6. *Gender wayang* ensemble (four players or more): used to accompany the shadow puppet plays with stories from Hindu mythology. A quartet of *gender* ( ) for *Mahabharata* stories; joined by a percussion group to add excitement to the battle scenes of *Ramayana* stories (then the ensemble is called *gender wayang batel*).

7. *Gamelan selundeng* (seven to ten players): used for religious festivals in mountain villages, considered very sacred, kept in a special storehouse in the temple compound.

One village describes its origins as a gift from the sea god: Once in the distant past while the people were making offerings to the sea, they heard the sound of a strange and wonderful music coming from the waves. Back in the village the elders consulted and they decided to hold a special feast and ceremony (*slamatan*). The instruments of the *gamelan* appeared in the ocean and the men waded out to get them and carry them back to the village temple. For many days everyone was afraid to touch them and, in addition, no one knew how to play them. Then one day a white raven (a messenger from heaven) appeared and, sitting on a branch of a tree in the temple yard, sang and taught the villagers seven melodies.

The instruments are all rather cumbersome iron metallophones with their rough bars over wood sound boxes.

8. *Charuk* ensemble (two players): played for temple anniversaries and cremations, formerly accompanied the singing of historical/legendary narrative poems performed in a ritual context. One player plays the *charuk* bamboo xylophone, the other, two metal *sarons*.

9. *Gambang* ensemble (six players): used for *ngaben* cremation ceremonies. Four *gambang* xylophones and two *saron* metallophones; the music of this group is among the most complex forms of polyrhythmic interplay found on Bali.

10. *Gamelan luang* (thirteen or more players): the immense *gamelan gong* reduced to its essentials. Its small size gives it a distinctive lovely sound. *Luang* is said to mean "universal space, void, emptiness" which, according to McPhee, is reflected in "the serenity and timelessness of its sound and music."

11. *Gamelan angklung* (old form, twenty-two to twenty-seven players; new form, sixteen players): used in village ceremonials; light enough to be carried (strapped around the neck and shoulders of each player) on religious processions or ceremonial village expeditions to shrines. Old form: sound characterized by the tuned bamboo rattling tubes (*angklung:* see the section on musical instruments). New form: omits the *angklung* and is characterized by its four-note scales. The melodies played by the ensemble may be based on the popular

Gamelan pelegongan, Bali.

Gambang ensemble, Tabanan village, Bali.

tunes strummed on the *genggong* jew's-harp, and they have folksy, picturesque, and (sometimes) hilarious titles. Some samples:

"Fighting Cats"
"Crow Steals Eggs"
"Tree Frog Climbs the Coconut Palm"
"Burning Incense"
"Waves"
"Embracing Apes"
"Playful Butterflies"

12. *Gamelan arja* (seven to ten or more players): used to accompany the musical comedy of the popular theater (which includes spoken lines, dance, buffoonery, songs, and romance); has a soft, light timbre so that the words of the play can be understood. The sound of the ensemble is characterized by the two *guntang* bamboo one-stringed tube zithers (the players flutter the palms of their hands over the sound hole to give a throbbing, "ghostly" tone). Also includes one or two *suling* flutes, drums, and a percussion group for special effects.

13. *Gamelan gong kebyar* (twenty to fifty players): a twentieth-century development of the older *gamelan gong* (in the 1930s other *gamelans* were being melted down and recast into instruments of this newer and immensely popular form). The instrumentation and style, developed by innovative composers/musicians from north Bali, is extremely exciting and percussive and is characterized by the "explosive unison attack of the full *gamelan*," "the metallic crash of cymbals," a freedom of form, "lavish and varied orchestration," bold syncopations and intense passagework, "sudden loudness and softness" in dynamics, complicated hocketing, interlocking parts, and *chords* (!).

The instrumentation includes:

ten to twelve *gangsa barangam* and *gangsa gede* metallophones with resonators (playing melodic paraphrase/ornamental passagework and leading melodies respectively)

reong horizontal knobbed gong sets with two-and-one-half-octave range and four players on each instrument

trompong knobbed gong sets

jublag metallophones

kempur gongs

lanang and *wadon* gongs

drums (usually two drummers)

The *gamelan gong kebyar* is arranged in a large square pattern:

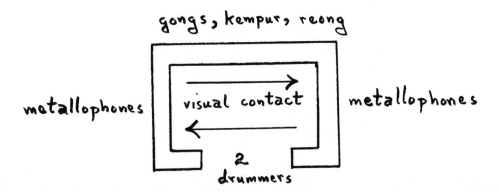

Gamelan gong kebyar, used in temple ritual, including sacred dances; for ceremonial and state occasions; and for public dance performances. I Mario, considered the creator of *kebyar* dance, teaches the interpretation in movement of the music's changing moods. Tabanan village, Bali.

The visual contact between the opposite sides of metallophones is important in performance (players watch the leading *gangsa* player's arms and mallet), and the breathtaking effect of perhaps twenty to thirty pairs of arms being raised in the air in absolute unison during sudden musical silences and then crashing down all together in equally startling musical sound is an unforgettable visual part of performance.

★★★★★★★★★★★★★★★★★★★★★★★

The West—Europe and the Americas—is another center for the development of that strange and wonderful animal, the orchestra. In the classical music tradition the various metamorphoses of this large ensemble—from the magnificent operatic accompaniments of Claudio Monteverdi (1567–1643), through the baroque period and the *concerti grossi* of Vivaldi and the suites of Bach, through the innovations of the Mannheim School (the eighteenth century's own avant garde), the classical world of Haydn and Mozart, and the grandeur and scope of Beethoven, on through the expansion and romantic outbursts of the nineteenth century (Berlioz, Tchaikovsky, Brahms, Rimsky-Korsakov, Mahler), and the more recent innovations of Stravinsky, Schoenberg, Ives, Webern, Stockhausen, and others—is a history in itself. Musical notation has contributed greatly, if not decisively, to the development of the symphony orchestra: the composer puts it all down on paper and the musicians (under the sometimes iron interpretive hand of the conductor) read. The controls are explicit down to the finest detail. The basic divisions of the modern symphony orchestra (less like functional layers than expressive timbral units) are the strings, woodwinds, brass, and percussion.

But there are other large ensembles in the West as well: there is the marching or concert band, for example, an orchestra without strings and with greatly expanded winds and percussion, whose players may number in the hundreds. There are the drum and bugle and bagpipe corps of the British Isles and the United States, or the fife and drum corps of New England. And there are innumerable orchestras in the folk and popular music traditions, some of which are ear and improvising groups (the *mariachi* orchestra of Mexico or the old-time New Orleans jazz band), while others combine reading music with improvising (Latin or Cuban orchestras or the big bands of jazz), or are basically "reading" orchestras (the Hollywood/Broadway studio orchestra or backup stage band). In all, they complete our world sampling of alones and collective togethers.

★★★★★★★★ A FINAL SAMPLER OF ORCHESTRAL TOGETHERS ★★★★★★★★

1. Tibet: monastery orchestra (12 or more players)

> 2 *rgya-glin* double-reed pipes
> 2 *rag-dung* long trumpets
> 2 *dung-dkar* conch shell trumpets
> 2 *rkang-ling* short horns
> 1 *drilbu* hand bell
> 1 *damaru* small hourglass-shaped hand drum ⎫ played by one player
> 1 *rolmo* cymbals
> 1 *silnyen* cymbals
> 1 *rgna* frame drum

2. Turkey: Janissary military band (9 or more players)

> *dawul* bass drum
> *boru* trombone
> cymbals
> *naqqāra* double kettledrum
> *zurnā* oboelike pipe
> "Turkish crescents" or clanging bell trees

Preservation Hall Jazz Band playing old-time New Orleans jazz.

The inclusion of many of these percussion instruments in the European symphony orchestra derived from a fad for things Turkish in the eighteenth century; best example: Mozart's opera *The Abduction from the Seraglio.*

3. The West Indies (particularly Trinidad): steel band (any number of players)

The basic instruments are steel "pans" (the cutoff tops and bottoms of steel industrial drums, like oil drums) which are hammered into tuned indentations, with many scales or bass notes for each pan. The steel drums are built in three or four sizes giving an entire melody-harmony range and are accompanied by assorted rattles, claves, bells, and other percussion instruments. The four basic types of "drums" in the steel band are:

> *ping pong* (soprano)
> *guitar pan* (alto)
> *cello pan* (tenor)
> *boom* (bass)

The number of tones on each pan varies from up to thirty-two on the *ping pong* to only two on the *boom.* The instrumentation can be expanded with percussion, usually the *shac-shac,* a gourd rattle filled with seeds.

4. India (Kerala region): *panchavadyam* drum and trumpet orchestra (20 to 30 or more players)

> 5 or more *thimila* hourglass-shaped long drums played with the hands
> 5 or more *suddha maddalam* double-headed cylindrical drums played with the hands
> 5 or more *kombu* curved trumpets
> 5 or more *thalam* large ringing bell-metal finger cymbals
> 1 *sangam* conch shell trumpet
> 1 *udukkai* hourglass-shaped squeeze drum played with sticks

5. United States: jazz bands and orchestras

   a. King Oliver's Creole Jazz Band (7 players)

   > 2 cornets
   > 1 trombone
   > 1 clarinet
   >
   > 1 string bass
   > (1 banjo—earlier)
   > 1 piano
   > 1 drum set

A heterophonic texture of free-swinging chordal polyphony woven around a core melody and over the rhythm section playing chords, bass line, and percussion.

   b. King Oliver's Dixie Syncopators (10 players)

   > 1 cornet (Oliver's)
   > 1 trumpet
   > 1 trombone

2 clarinets/alto saxophone
1 clarinet/tenor saxophone

1 tuba
1 banjo
1 piano
1 drum set

An expansion of the earlier group. The reeds (clarinets with the players doubling on the heavier sound of the saxophone) are a section on their own. The bass line function of the tuba was later replaced by the string bass, and the chordal four-string banjo by guitar or piano.

c. The Benny Goodman Orchestra (1937) (14 players)

3 trumpets
2 trombones

4 saxophones (various sizes)
1 clarinet (Goodman's)

1 bass
1 piano
1 guitar
1 drum set

The "big band" of the 1930s with sections of brass, reeds, and rhythm. Goodman's clarinet was featured solo.

d. The Duke Ellington Orchestra (1940) (15 players)

3 (later 5) trumpets
3 trombones (one of them a valve trombone)

2 alto saxophones (doubling on clarinet)
2 tenor saxophones
1 baritone saxophone

1 piano (Ellington's)

1 guitar
1 string bass
1 drum set

Another large band featuring not only Ellington's piano, but the solo improvisatory playing of superb soloists from every section. Players in jazz orchestras—especially in the reed section—frequently can "double" on several instruments, giving the possibility of more flexible instrumentation without increasing the number of players.

6. United States: Bob Wills and His Texas Playboys

   a. 1935 (12 players)

      1 fiddle and vocal (Wills's)
      1 vocal (male)
      1 fiddle
      1 fiddle and trombone
      1 steel guitar and standard guitar
      1 guitar and banjo
      1 guitar
      1 banjo
      1 saxophone
      1 string bass
      1 piano
      1 drum set

   b. 1941 (17 players)

      1 fiddle and vocal (Wills's)
      1 fiddle

      1 vocal (male)

      1 steel guitar
      1 fiddle and saxophone
      1 lead guitar
      1 banjo

      2 trumpets
      1 clarinet
      4 saxophones (!)

      1 piano
      1 string bass
      1 drum set

The amazing instrumentation of "western swing" orchestras which flourished in the Southwest, particularly Texas and Oklahoma, in the 1930s and 1940s was (like their style) iconoclastic and typically melting-pot American: it drew upon the earlier Texas fiddling tradition, upon Mexican ensembles with their close two- and three-part violin or trumpet harmonies, upon the Appalachian string bands (described earlier in this section), upon the blues and early jazz bands of the deep South and New Orleans, and upon the nationally popular big bands of swing. And the electric steel guitar was adapted from the earlier fad for Hawaiian music!

★★★★★★★★★★★★★★★★★★★★★★★★★

Ames, David W. "Igbo and Hausa Musicians: A Comparative Examination." *Ethnomusicology,* vol. 17, no. 2 (May 1972).
Beliaev, Viktor M. *Central Asian Music.* Translated by Mark and Greta Slobin, edited and annotated by Mark Slobin. Middletown, Connecticut: Wesleyan University Press, 1975.
Blacking, John. *How Musical Is Man?* Seattle: University of Washington Press, 1973.

Brandon, James. *Kabuki, Five Classic Plays.* Cambridge, Massachusetts: Harvard University Press, 1975.

Brandon, James R. *Theater in Southeast Asia.* Cambridge, Massachusetts: Harvard University Press, 1967.

Cadar, Usopay H. "The Role of Kulintang Music in Maranao Society." *Ethnomusicology,* vol. 17, no. 2 (May 1972).

Cage, John. *Silence.* Middletown, Connecticut: Wesleyan University Press, 1961.

Crossley-Holland, Peter, and Smith, Huston. Notes for *The Music of Tibet,* A Musical Anthology of the Orient, vol. 6. New York: Anthology Record and Tape Corporation, 1970. (A phonograph recording with extensive notes—AST 4005)

Green, Joseph. Writer, producer, director, of film: *Yiddle with His Fiddle.* New York: Globe Pictures.

Hood, Mantle, and Susilo, Hardja. *Music of the Venerable Dark Cloud.* Los Angeles: Institute of Ethnomusicology, UCLA, 1967.

Kaufmann, Walter. *Tibetan Buddhist Chant.* Bloomington: Indiana University Press.

Kirby, Percival R. *The Musical Instruments of the Native Races of South Africa.* Johannesburg: Witwatersrand University Press, 1965.

Lord, Albert B. *The Singer of Tales.* Cambridge, Massachusetts: Harvard University Press, 1960.

Malm, William P. *Japanese Music and Musical Instruments.* Rutland, Vermont: Charles E. Tuttle, 1959.

Malm, William P. *Music Cultures of the Pacific, the Near East, and Asia.* Englewood Cliffs, New Jersey: Prentice-Hall, 1967.

Malone, Bill C. *Country Music, U.S.A.* Austin: University of Texas Press, 1968.

Maquet, Jacques. *Civilizations of Black Africa.* New York: Oxford University Press, 1972.

McAllester, David P. "Indian Music in the Southwest." In McAllester, David P. *Readings in Ethnomusicology.* New York: Johnson Reprint Corporation, 1971.

McDowell, Bart. *Gypsies—Wanderers of the World.* Washington, D.C.: National Geographic Society, 1970.

McPhee, Colin. *Music in Bali.* New Haven: Yale University Press, 1966.

Morton, David. *The Traditional Music of Thailand.* Los Angeles: Institute of Ethnomusicology, UCLA, 1968.

Nettl, Bruno. *Folk and Traditional Music of the Eastern Continents.* Englewood Cliffs, New Jersey: Prentice-Hall, 1965.

Nketia, J. H. Kwabena. *African Music in Ghana.* Evanston, Illinois: Northwestern University Press, 1962.

Nketia, J. H. Kwabena. *The Music of Africa.* New York: W. W. Norton, 1974.

Oliver, Paul. *The Story of the Blues.* Chilton Book Company, 1969.

Piggot, Juliet. *Japanese Mythology.* London: Paul Hamlyn, 1969.

Powne, Michael. *Ethiopian Music.* London: Oxford University Press, 1968.

Sachs, Curt. *The Rise of Music in the Ancient World East and West.* New York: W. W. Norton, 1943.

Sen, K. M. *Hinduism.* Harmondsworth, Middlesex: Penguin Books Ltd., 1961.

Spearritt, Gordon D. "Instrumental Music of the Middle Sepik (New Guinea)." *Alumni News: Journal of the Alumni Association of the University of Queensland,* vol. 6, no. 2 (1974).

Slobin, Mark. *Music in the Culture of Northern Afghanistan.* Tucson: University of Arizona Press, 1976.

Tewari, Laxmi. "Turkish Village Music." *Asian Music,* vol. 3, no. 1 (1972). (New York: Asian Music Society)

Zonis, Ella. *Classical Persian Music.* Cambridge: Harvard University Press, 1973.

Illustration from *De Templo Musicae* by Robert Fludd (1574–1637).

10

INVISIBLE ARCHITECTURE I

"The Power of the world works in circles," said Black Elk, a holy man of the Oglala Sioux, in narrating his life story to John G. Neihardt. He explained that when the white man forced the Indians into houses—"square boxes," as he put it—it was far, far more than a simple transfer from one type of dwelling to another. A whole world, reflected in architecture and living space, was changed. The square or rectangular house, so natural and comfortable to Europeans and their immigrant descendants in America, was angular; it had corners and dark recesses, its beams and boards crisscrossed at right angles, it was geometric, logical, pragmatic, unmystical, inorganic. It was also a container, an enclosure. Cavelike, it sealed—separating and protecting—its inhabitants from the natural world thought at best to be uncomfortable and at worst, hostile. Thick walls blocked the landscape, glimpsed only through small windows; floors separated one from the heartbeat of the earth, and ceilings pushed down oppressively toward the top of the head and effectively cut off the sky. A house was connected with a stable life-style (on a farm, in a city) and perhaps also with concepts like the ownership of land. As an inert mass, a dead weight, a house had to be left behind when its inhabitants moved; it was immobile, rooted to a spot, to a specific place on the earth.

By contrast, the tepee of the Native Americans of the Great Plains was eminently movable; it could be disassembled or reassembled in a matter of hours and transported by travois, a kind of sledge made by poles attached to the backs of horses or dogs. While providing adequate shelter, the tepee did not fully separate its inhabitants from their environment: the walls (buffalo skins, and later canvas) were translucent, filling the inside with soft filtered light during the day and spilling out (like giant lanterns) the flickering light of campfires during the evenings. The floor was the earth, and in good weather the stars and the clouds could be seen through the smoke holes at the top. In the summer the bottom of the tent was rolled up to allow breezes to blow through at ground level. There was a comfortable ecological coexistence with nature—with the wind, rain, dust, snow, storms, sun, lightning, and the animals and insects of the prairie—that to us (preferring the protective enclosure of our boxes) would be absolutely disconcerting. Perhaps more important was the architectural space inside the tepee. The floor area, a slightly elliptical circle, could average eighteen or more feet

400

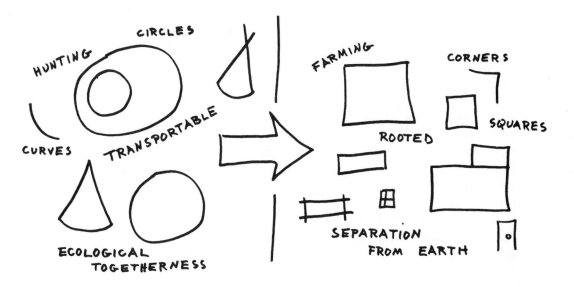

across and was not broken by cumbersome furniture; and there were no corners, a feat that created the illusion of additional spaciousness. And everything swept upward fifteen to twenty feet or more toward the apex of the poles—and perhaps beyond to the sky—creating an overhead conical space that was astounding and (like the vaults and domes of mosques and cathedrals) seemed disproportionately large.

But it was not the overhead conical space that concerned Black Elk; it was the circular pattern of its floor. For "the Power of the world works in circles." This power came to a tribe, to a people, circularly: in the form of "the sacred hoop of the nation"; and its living center, nourished by the circle of the four directions, was a flowering tree. As long as the sacred hoop remained unbroken, the people would flourish. In his greatest vision Black Elk had seen an untold number of mythical multicolored horses dancing and singing in a circle around their chief and four mystical virgins in an unearthly and powerful ceremony (the Sioux also sang and danced in a circle in their sacred rites). At a particularly transcendental moment in his vision Black Elk had seen the shape of the entire earth; it was an expansive, incomprehensible circle, "the hoop of the world," with the highest mountain at its center.

In looking at the natural, nonvisionary world, Black Elk also saw the power of the circle: wind in its greatest strength—the tornado—whirled; the sun and the moon (both round) scanned the sky in an arc; the seasons, coming back year after year, formed a circle in time and revolution; even birds built their nests with leaves and twigs arranged in a circular pattern. The Sioux—like the birds, Black Elk tells us—lived in a world of circles, real, felt, imagined. Besides the floors of their dwellings, besides the magnificent imagery and symbols (along with the rainbow, the eagle, clouds, lightning, horses, thunder, wind, seasons, directions, colors) of their mythical, psychic, ritual, and inner worlds, or perhaps in harmony with all of these, they camped with their tepees arranged in a large circle, reflecting in the microcosm of their human world the expansive encircling horizon of the Great Plains, the circular dome of the sky, and the great macrocosmic "hoop of the world." To be forced into a physical and psychological world of squares, into a foreign architectural space of boxlike huts and shacks, helped destroy the universe of the Sioux. Their "sacred hoop of the nation" was broken, and with it, their power was gone forever.

Black Elk's story, tragic in its description of the destruction of the culture and life-style of a people, illustrates the tremendous power that shapes and structures have on the life of a people. We are all surrounded by shapes and ways of seeing and doing things; somehow they seem important to us, or natural, or comfortable. We may be totally unaware of them, or take them for granted; or we may be fully conscious of them. But either way we use them and work with them, and—filtering our perspectives, marking our limits—they shape us and our lives and our livings.

The world as it is gives us shapes and shapings, and not only for our eyes: there are invisible structures happening in time, working (as we perceive and comprehend) with memory and expectation and surprise. Rain, at least in the American Southwest where I grew up, inevitably follows the warning prelude of cooling wind and black thunderheaded clouds that seem to erupt out of nowhere on hot afternoons. And as predictable as a coda to a symphony is the sudden calm and stillness afterward, the sun reflecting on raindrops hanging on desert flowers or on the scrawny branches of mesquite, while rocks—still holding the oven heat of the earlier day—transform their dampness into little mistlike clouds of steam. Is it not possible that (if we are part of the world—and we are) our bodies have photographed and cataloged such things? How many millions of mornings, and middays, and afternoons has the burning round shape of the sun etched itself on the cornea and consciousness of man? How many billions of eyes in as many years have had their vision sliced by the stark line of the horizon, cutting, separating earth (or sea) and sky? What signals have we received from our own bodies: from the mirror symmetry of its two halves (our brains, too, are divided into halves), from the balance of twos of eyes, hands, arms, legs, from the fives of our fingers (Western musical notation uses a five-line staff), or from the shape and symbolism of our sexual machinery. What have trees told us (unconsciously, consciously) about the balances of form and structure, or what have mountains said? Or the seasons, or Everyman's journey of life and death, or seeds, or other growing things, or animals? Or how has the whole crazy electricity of our body's psychological and emotional flickerings (changing abruptly, progressing, contrasting, full of tension and release, excitement and calm, action or inertia) shaped our shapings, the ways we do, make, form, perceive? And there is even a further mystery: the possibility that man has inside himself an amazing and unexplored network of patterns and form-making paraphernalia, guiding (instinctually) his mind, and hands, and eyes, and ears. Men, we know, drew mystical geometric diagrams, ground gems into multifaceted prisms, invented sound and strong structural shapes long before (by looking through microscopes and telescopes or the eye of mathematics) these things were discovered to have existed all the time in the natural world.

Balancing what may be instinctive processes in us human animals is another side: what we (exercising free will or rational or irrational criteria) have chosen, discovered, stumbled upon, invented, had hammered into our heads, or otherwise—formally or by osmosis—learned from those around and before us. Anthropologists believe, at least at the present time, that a person's culture, the hundreds of thousands of ways we do things and look at the world and which make us and our group or our society unique, are *not* racial, they are *not* part of our bloodstream, inherited like the color of our eyes, the tones of our skin, or the shape of our noses. They are, rather, the result of an interaction of the millions of bits of information fed into us and absorbed by us (stored in our memory and habits like tapes in an almost limitless computer bank) by our society and environment. This process begins from the moment (and perhaps before) each of us as individuals first opened our wonder-filled eyes on this crazy and confusing world.

So again—in dealing with structures and forms, with the way musical forces are joined together and expanded and shaped in a larger way—we, as human beings, stand as if frozen between two magnets: what is in us (instinctually, physically) because we are animals, or human beings, and what is in us (*seemingly* instinctually) as members of a particular culture or society. Black Elk's circle is certainly an archetypal image that all of us somehow carry in our unconscious; at the same time, the specific use that the Sioux made of the circle is a unique and beautiful expression of what they, as a society, had made their own.

ROOFS OF SOUND

Years ago I was working with a group of young children on a sound/music/perception project, and among the many things that we did was to try to make up our own dictionary. "What is music?" was my first question—and as any ethnomusicologist (and you readers) must know, it is an extremely rough and even controversial question. How can one put a Yakut shaman's magic formula, a Beethoven symphony, a Yugoslavian epic song, a Thai Buddhist chant, or an avant-garde Euro-American "conceptual piece" in the same bag? But my young students, wise as children usually are (and open to all types of "music"), had no such problem. One freckle-faced little lady said (simply and without hesitation):

"Music is the house that sounds live in."

This correlation between the architecture of houses—structures of wood or glass or whatever, filling up space yet creating a space inside (to be lived in), with joints and joinings and hundreds of functioning and decorative parts—with the invisible architecture of music was not only logical and imaginative; it was brilliant! For music is also a filling of space, a space that is aural, that is heard but not seen, and a shaping and building with sound elements (the wood and bricks of music) into structures that happen in time. Like houses, music has its beginnings, its limitations, its middles, and its endings. It also has its structural connectors and joints, as well as its doorways leading to familiar or unexpected musical rooms. And like houses, music may have its structural framework and its nonessential but aesthetically necessary ornamentation and decoration. And it may serve a variety of functions. Finally, just as a basic human problem, the problem of shelter is met on our globe by a variety of people in an astounding variety of ways influenced by factors as diverse as climate, materials, life necessity, or tradition, so a basic musical problem, the shaping of sound and sound ideas—is met on earth by music-making people in a similarly astounding variety of ways, and it may be influenced by the same or similar factors.

In a brilliant and ground-breaking exhibit, "Architecture without Architects," at the Museum of Modern Art in 1964 (the catalog was also published as a book), critic/architect/engineer Bernard Rudolfsky brought together examples of native architecture, town planning, and engineering from all over the world. His commentary and attitudes are not without parallels in our exploration of the earth's music. We tend to think of architecture, Dr. Rudolfsky says, either in terms of great monuments built for the state or the elite (massive temples, palaces, cathedrals, castles) or in terms of individuals—architects—to whom, as specialists, we tend to ascribe "exceptional insights into problems of living when, in truth, most of them are concerned with problems of business and prestige." In music (and we shall refer here to the traditions only of the West, although, of course, the applications are worldwide) we also have our great structural monuments—operas, Masses, oratorios, cantatas, sonatas, concertos, symphonies—which were written for the privileged few, the Church, nobility, the rich, the state, or those of us who think of ourselves as culturally or intellectually special. These "profound" and "serious" works (our culture considers Western classical music to be synonymous with "serious music" or "good music") are written by specialists—composers, geniuses, the light-beaming-down-from-heaven crowd, who (if contemporary composers are any indication) are and were really as concerned with such things as prestige and earning a living as with music.

But there is much to be learned (and appreciated), Dr. Rudolfsky asserts, from the anonymous work of builders, villagers, and village craftsmen throughout the world. For one thing, rather than trying to conquer nature or the environment, they tend to build their buildings and towns to blend harmoniously into their settings. As a particularly obvious example, we might take the stately and ancient Pueblo Indian town of Acoma in New Mexico, its adobe multistoried buildings seeming to emerge naturally from the rocks of the mesa upon which it sits, and compare it with the city of Las Vegas, which clashes with its desert environment like a junkyard of garish Day-Glo neon, plastic, and glass dumped on the shocked primeval silence of cactus and sand. Native-built musics also tend to blend with their physical or cultural surroundings, unlike the commercial electric sounds of much of today's popular music (part of the big-city environment?) or the museum-quality familiarity of the classics (nostalgia? high culture?) which through the un-miracle of the transistor radio and tape machine and phonograph system are carried—like tin cans and Baggies—into forests, wilderness areas, medieval castles, lonely beaches, mountaintops, and "less-developed countries." Indigenous architecture (like indigenous music) is born in the hands and minds of those who use it, live within it and around it, and thus it shows an uncanny sense for details of necessity: for a niche here, or a nook there, for a specially placed doorway or window, or for a hook in a rafter in a particular place. Na-

Adobe dwellings of the Pueblo Native Americans blend in naturally with their surroundings. Taos, New Mexico.

tive builders also make full use of the materials available around them. What Rudolfsky calls "non-pedigreed architecture" is eminently functional and practical, yet at the same time it displays a beautiful feeling for space and form (take, for instance, the undulating, whitewashed, vaulted ceilings and domes in many of the villages in Iran) and for decoration (like the carved pillars of Dogon dwellings in Dahomey, the woven designs of matted walls in Polynesia, the painted springtime of flowers on a Hungarian peasant's walls and ceilings, or the intricate designs of brickwork in Persia and Turkey).

Like houses and palaces, the structures of pedigreed and nonpedigreed musics around the world also show the remarkable forming and shaping abilities of men and women everywhere. Making use of available sonic materials (musical instruments, voices, timbres, melody, harmony, polyphony, heterophony, rhythm), which function like bricks, mortar, stone, wood, thatch, bamboo, reeds, or other raw materials, musicians—like carpenters, bricklayers, masons, or other craftsmen—put everything together to form structures which to us may sound ingenious or astounding (or structureless), yet which (like houses) follow the precepts, the way of doing things in their specific society. The ultimate form of a music or a piece of music, like a dwelling or a town, can be based on a kind of pragmatic necessity. It can also be decorative. And it can connect in an oddly subjective way with the geography or ecology of a region, and—perhaps most important—it can reflect the invisible attitudes, the mental and cultural environment, of a particular society: the way it feels as a group about space and shapes and movement and individuality and creation and symbols and living and time.

APPROACHINGS

Beginnings and Endings

"We shall begin at the beginning." That was the way one of my old professors, Paul Pisk, Viennese by birth and education (his eyes twinkling with excitement and wit), would introduce a new and difficult subject. And I see no reason why we should not follow his august example—but with an exception. Like the dog chasing his own tail we shall (at the beginning) also study endings. For the firsts and lasts of music have much in common. Beginnings are, after all, the first things we hear in a musical performance or a piece; they are what grab us by the scruff of the neck or gradually, subtly, pull us into the magical happenings of sounds. Endings are what we are left with, a last (and maybe lasting) impression. Together, they are the extremities of a musical island in a sea of time. And in several cultures (our own included) both are considered very important.

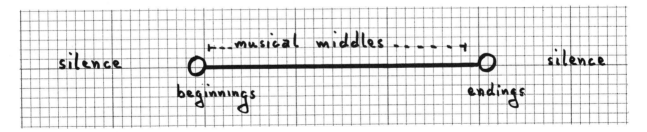

One of the most common ways of beginning is to have a special introductory section—like the front steps, door, porch, or portico of a house—which leads into the main body of the music. Western music (classical and otherwise) is full of these *introductions* and *preludes* which may be as minuscule as a few chords or a bit of melody, or as long as a full and major section. In the music of the Iraqi *maqam* there is invariably a vocal or instrumental introduction (*tahrir*) in free rhythm which sets the mood and establishes the mode and allows the principal performer to warm up his voice or fingers. This slow and unmeasured opening (with the "breath rhythms" we talked about earlier) is characteristic of musical performances in the entire Islamic-influenced area (remembering, of course, that ideas moved back and forth in *all* directions among Persia, Turkey, Arabia, central Asia, north Africa, and Saracenic Spain) and is found as far east as India, in the section called *alapana* (or *alap*) which can last anywhere from a few minutes to an hour or longer. In Java the introductory solo phrases of the *buko* played on the bowed *rebab* spiked fiddle or the *bonang* knobbed gong set (or on other solo instruments) culminates with the first striking of the large gong—its massive sound signaling the end of one time cycle and the beginning of the next—at which point all the instruments of the *gamelan* orchestra enter and the piece begins. According to some scholars, this tiny prelude not only sets the mood, but signals to the other players what the following composition will be.

Beginnings can be sharp—an everybody-on-the-downbeat sort of thing—or they can be tapered—something like a train pulling out of a station with passengers running alongside and jumping on one by one as the bogies pick up speed. In the music of the Japanese *gagaku* court orchestra (there is a serene and archaic mood-setting, tuning-up introduction, the *netori,* but nowadays it is usually omitted) the stately music begins with the melody played by a solo flute accompanied by the percussion; after several bars, usually around seven, the oboelike and shrill *hichiriki,* the chording *sho* mouth organ, and the rest of the wind instruments come in, and after them, the plucked strings. Once the *tutti*—everybody in the ensemble—are in they stay in, playing until the end of the composition. The ending, or *tomede* (coda)—we are a little ahead of ourselves here—is a kind of fizzling out: the orchestra drops to the first-chair men (one of each instrument), the tempo slows down and becomes free, like a locomotive grinding to a stop, the *sho* mouth organ thins its chords out to two or three notes, and several sharp and snapping notes of great gravity (and conclusiveness) are plucked on the now alone *so* and *biwa.*

In the Karnatic style of south India, where the playing is more by ear and less fixed, the soloist begins playing or singing a song alone, while his accompanists (usually on drum and violin) pause for a few seconds to get the feel of his tempo and to identify the piece (and sometimes also its *raga* and *tala*) before coming in to join him. This straggling type of beginning—and its relaxed informality—is found also in folk musics throughout the world. Very often it is a leader who will begin the singing or playing, with the rest of the ensemble then coming in to join him in unison or harmony (as in the *a cappella* singing styles of the Ukraine) or with a response or refrain (common in Africa). Music may also be started with shouts or drumbeats or some other signal—and here we get into an extremely important element in the shaping of music in time: the use of characteristic formulas, patterns, or signals which are part of the musical vocabulary of musicians and listeners alike (in a particular culture) and which function as landmarks with very specific meanings. There are patterns which like doorways or porticos seem to indicate "ATTENTION! NOW WE SHALL BEGIN!" or "ATTENTION! NOW WE SHALL STOP THIS" (what we are doing now musically) "AND GO INTO SOMETHING DIFFERENT" (into another musical room?). There are also patterns which signal that things are coming to an end, or that they *are* ended: "FINIS! . . . FINALIS!"

Music may also be begun with a part of the musical texture, like background chords or accompaniment patterns. In the music of the east African *mbira* the performer often begins with a gentle sequence of plucked notes meshing together in a beautiful combination at once harmonic and melodic. He saves his voice and its melodies, drawn from the total potential of the notes of his pattern on the instrument, for a later dramatic entrance. Many of the pop songs in the West also begin this way, with a chordal accompaniment or a bit of the melody played by instruments before the voice comes in. Finally, a piece or a performance may simply dispense with fancy introductions, mood setters, or special openers and—boom!—simply *start,* begin running (or walking) with the main body and texture and melody of the music flying into one's delightedly-trying-to-catch-up ears!

Whether seen pragmatically or philosophically, beginnings are the doorways to performances of a piece. They, as the first bit of information we (as listeners) receive, can and do shape our expectations, and hence our perceptions. If beginnings are treated with care, or formally, that, in itself, tells us something about the attitudes and structuring in a particular musical culture; and lackadaisical or informal beginnings (conversely) also tell us something. Either way, a somethingness has happened, we have begun, and we are riding the journey of sound shaped into music as it moves through time.

And now for the dog's tail.

Endings are like beginnings: they come in all shapes and sizes and types. The simplest ending—and one found in much of the music of the recent avant garde in the West—is simply to stop, abruptly and without fanfare. But even this honest and straightforward way of ending has its problems.

Musical doorways, like other doorways, mark transitions. Stone archway, Borobudur temple, Java.

Recently after a concert in New York I heard a dissatisfied listener scoff: "No cadence, no ending, no resolution, no point!" And in a sense—according to traditional concepts of Western aesthetics, the way we see the world and *hear* the world—he was right. We tend to demand resolutions and conclusions (in sports, at least in the United States, we hate ties and thus introduce tie breakers or extra time periods to produce a winner); and we make a big deal out of them. Music without a good and proper ending is to us like stopping in the middle of

(a sentence) (and omitting the period to boot).

Another type of ending is the fizzle. Like a dilapidated automobile clinking and clanging and sputtering and squeaking to a halt, a piece can simply effect a kind of collapse, a falling apart, with the players dropping out and slowing down or stopping at will, everything more or less informal and intentionally imprecise. Slowing down (*ritardando*) seems to indicate endings in cultures as different as Europe (and the Americas) and Indonesia (where a ritard like a sudden progressive cinematographic slow-motion effect leads to the final sounding of the great gong). Or a long-held note, particularly on the tonic or tonal center, or a held chord—both arresting the movement of musical ideas—can be heard as closings, as can extraordinary repetition—the "broken-record effect"—and the fade-out (a product of the knob turning of the electronic age). All of these are part of the repertoire of pop music techniques from Tenochtitlan to Tehran (via Nashville, Hollywood, and the Tin Pan Alleys of the earth).

But the formula ending, the stereotyped signal/pattern/sequence, is perhaps most common all over the world, at least where endings are taken seriously. In the West these include an ending or *resolution* of a melodic phrase, a return to the tonal center, and—most of all—a clichéd sequence of chords (usually ending on V–I, the dominant chord to the tonic chord). We are all familiar with the endings of classical and romantic symphonies with the chords and closing formulas being blasted away by the full orchestra and repeated like so many nails being hammered into and sealing shut the top lid of a crate. In the Orient, melodic patterns can function as special closing signals, which we call by the generic term *cadences,* but as often, endings are signaled by stereotyped patterns in the percussion, in the drums and gongs. In India complex rhythmic units (sometimes quite extended) are repeated three times to mark the end of a section, improvisation, or piece. Expanded endings, which we call *codas,* can be large and important enough to function as a section in their own right, and besides including any number of cadence formulas, signaling "STOP" as clearly as any red light on a traffic signal, they can be a kind of musical summing up (as in the music of Beethoven) of what has happened previously.

Out of a possible infinite number of endings from a bang(!) to a whisper, from cadence formulas to codas, from slowings and fadings, from lengthenings and broadenings (and fizzlings out) to sudden (out of nowhere) skiddings to a stop, we might mention just several more possibilities: (1) the ending by subtraction (with instruments and players dropping out one by one (note Haydn's *Farewell Symphony* [No. 45] or the *nokorigaku sanben* performance style of Japanese *gagaku*); (2) the ending by taking away the melody, or the voice, leaving only the accompaniment pattern or other subsidiary element; and (3) the ending by the words; that is, when the story or ballad or epic or song is over verbally, the music also may end at that point.

This last possibility—the word ending—leads us to a particularly important fact: that much of the world's music (if not all of it) is chock full of mini-beginnings and mini-endings which are happening all the time. Each musical phrase (like a sentence) has its starting and stopping, as does each verse or chorus of a song (like paragraphs) and larger musical blocks and sections (like chapters). We (in the Euro-American tradition) tend to hear these mini-endings, or cadences, with varying degrees of finality—like sentences that end with "___," or "___;" or "___?" as opposed to "___." or "___!"—and very often in our music (as in our poetry) we tend to shape them into complementary pairs:

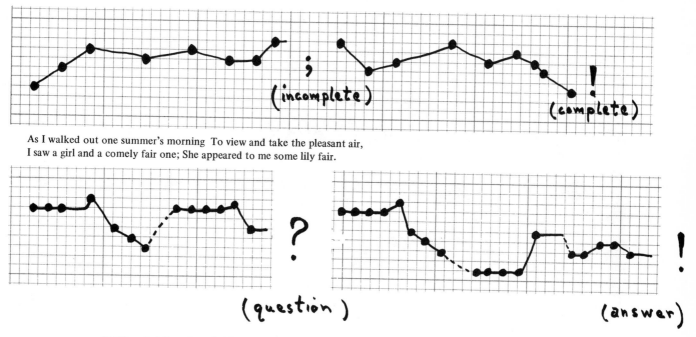

As I walked out one summer's morning To view and take the pleasant air,
I saw a girl and a comely fair one; She appeared to me some lily fair.

Rattlesnake! O rattlesnake! What makes me shake with fright?
(I) been crawling this river bottom all my life, just looking for someone to bite . . . yes, just looking for someone to bite!

This type of structuring of musical phrases (the first half of the pair incomplete, the second half ending on a full stop) has been common in practice and talked about in treatises since the Middle Ages when incomplete cadences were called *overt* and final ones were called *close*. Quite often in European folk music (although rarely in poetry) the two halves of a couplet are almost identical musically *except* in their endings, a technique also applied to dances (minuets, gavottes, reels, hornpipes) and even expanded in classical music (sections of symphonies or sonatas with a *first ending, a da capo* repetition, and, then, a *second ending*).

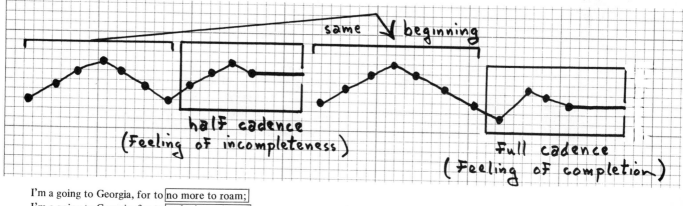

I'm a going to Georgia, for to no more to roam;
I'm a going to Georgia, for to make it my home.

Endings are (like punctuation or verbal emphasis in language) extremely important in the shapings of music on almost every level. They—if they are true cadences and not just stops—convey a feeling of rest, of closing, of psychological satisfaction, of relaxation, of pause (like sitting down or exhalation, or completion) in a variety of degrees. At one extreme they may signify a momentary stoppage leading to more activity—like the third out in the early innings of a baseball game; at the other extreme they can have the finality of the closing of a door (Beethoven and Brahms hammer their symphonies shut).

Repetition of basic patterns and elements used to make an overall design in a screen carved from a single marble slab. Jaipur, India.

★★★★★★★★★★★★★★★★★★★ **AN EXPERIMENT** ★★★★★★★★★★★★★★★★

Using a cassette machine and records, make a tape recording of the first ten or twenty seconds of a variety of music (pop, electronic, rock, blues, classical, ethnic, etc.) from one cultural area or from all over the world. Compare and catalog the types of beginnings. (Hint: there will be fewer types and less variety than one might imagine there should be.) Then do the same with endings.

★★★★★★★★★★★★★★★★★★★★★★★★★★

A Catalog of Some Openers and Closings

Start (nothing special)
Introduction }
Prelude } long/short
The bang (!)
The whimper
Chordal accompaniment
Tapered (filtering in)
Mood setting (*alapana*/*tahrir*)
Addition

Stop (nothing special)
Coda (closing section)
Stereotyped Pattern (cadences):
  melodic
  harmonic
  rhythmic
The fizzle
Slowing (ritard)
Lengthening/broadening/holding
The fade-out
Arrested motion
Subtraction
Word ends
Accompaniment (minus melody)

Devices

Music is built by using an almost infinite variety of techniques that expand and extend the timber, rocks, and bricks of musical raw materials and shape them into larger structures. Exactly what these raw materials are can vary: they can be short bits and chunks of melody (which we in the West call *motives* or *motifs*), as, for example, in the opening four notes of Beethoven's Fifth Symphony; they can be larger segments of melodies (entire *phrases*) like the *raga sancharas* of India which help give each *raga* its characteristics; or the even larger collections of phrases, such as the Persian *gusheh-ha* which serve as models for improvisation. (We shall examine some of these in detail later.) Stereotyped melodic patterns or even entire sections or songs—larger melodic units which can be shifted or arranged in toto like pieces in a jigsaw puzzle (but with a variety of possible fittings)—are a characteristic of much traditional Japanese and Chinese music. Basic building tools can also be rhythms (used, like melody, as motivic bits, long units, or stereotyped patterns), or, in fact, almost anything that we can hear and comprehend. But the important thing is that they are the beginning, they are what is started with, the given, and the structuring is done using them—and therefore it is influenced by them. Size and rigidity have a lot to do with it. For instance, there is a world of difference between building a house with mud bricks and building a house with prefabricated walls. But before we go on to specific techniques, maybe we should examine some of the factors that underlie them.

★★★★★★★★★★★★★★★★★★★★ **INTERLUDE** ★★★★★★★★★★★★★★★★★★★★

We, as people (or perhaps we should/could also say: we, as people, plants, and animals), tend to experience our livings as a push-pull between opposites—or, at the very least, differing psychological gravitational poles. These opposites or poles are by nature magically relative rather than absolute; and they can be extremely subjective, not only among people but within the same person, their changes depending on the situation or the hour from day to day or minute to minute.

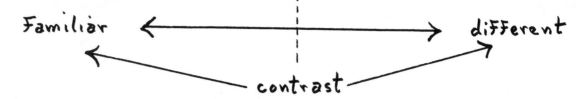

To begin with, there is the experiential comfort of the *familiar* (house, faces, landscape, food, language, thought patterns, and on to infinity) and opposing this, the *different*. The relationship between these two poles is one of *contrast*.

Each of us has his or her familiar ground which is bounded on all sides by a fluctuating threshold of the different. If someone comes up to us and says, "Hello!" we feel comfortable and we know how to react, perhaps instantly and spontaneously; if he says, "Buon Giorno," there is certainly a difference and we might be taken aback for a moment, but we might adjust and even enjoy the experience for the sake of variety and surprise; but if a stranger or a friend told us, " வணக்கம் " (which means the same thing) we might not only regard it as linguistically strange but as an outright act of hostility!

As we move through time (as we do in life *and* in music) we project what will happen next through our experience and perception of the present and the past; that is, we have *expectations*. These expectations are based on what we consider to be *probabilities*. At the same time (our experience has told us) we must allow for the possibility of impossibilities, for the *surprising* and the *unexpected* (not to speak of the *illogical* or *random*). We drive along a road at night, able to see less than thirty yards ahead of us, and we assume that the road will continue to be there and that the town on the map will be there after a certain number of miles. Yet there is the possibility, however faint, that there will be a detour, or that the road is blocked or washed out, or that the town has ceased to exist, or even that the map is outdated and therefore wrong. Or that unexpected scenery will emerge.

There can also be a movement backward through time, into the past, into the previous. Our rememberings can conjure up snapshots, events, faces, feelings, and contemporize them (it is *now* that we remember them). They can come back to haunt us like ghosts. And they are, after all, what have shaped us and the present—or at least led up to it. Besides *memory* there is the *return*. Our beginnings and our journeys (physical/mental/emotional) and consequent wanderings can lead us far afield, but we can and do constantly refer to what has come before, and we can—like the perennial mythic hero after the completion of his quest (and unlike Thomas Wolfe)—return home again. The return (to the old, to the familiar, to the previous, to the comfortable) is never a mere exact repetition even when it appears to be so, because the very concept of the return includes the contrasts and experiences of the journey. To come home we must have been away.

If we enjoy *unity* (a sameness, similarity, cohesiveness in people, ideas, experiences, things) we also enjoy *variety* (the changing, differing, contrasting). But what precisely comprises the terra firma of unity and variety in living or art or music is a problem that has caused more intellectual wars among scholars and critics than you and I have fingers and toes! And it is a question that is especially pertinent to our study of world music. How often have we heard the living music of a people (from the classical traditions of Europe to those of the Bushmen of south Africa) dismissed with a wave of the hand and the comment, "It's boring!"?

We as people moving and acting in the play of the world tend to do more things repetitiously than we perhaps realize. To begin with, there are the motor responses of our bodies—breathing and heart-beating, for example. Walking is a repetition of leg movement; eating or washing dishes or grinding corn or weeding or planting or screwing in screws on an automobile assembly line are pretty much repetitions of the same act or motion of the hands and arms over and over again. Then there are the larger repetitions of our lives: maybe the way we shave or bathe or get dressed; there are the routines of our days, the goings to work and the comings home. Then

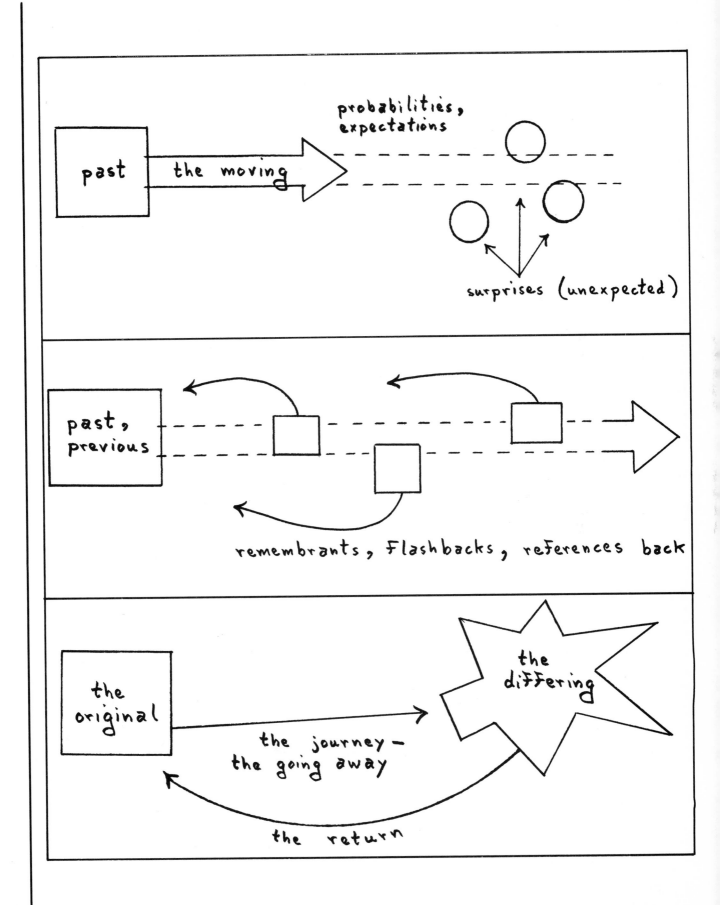

there are the repetitions of our minds, our habits and responses and stubbornly unchanging re-
actions. There is something very human about the principle of *repetition*, and people who
deal with it directly (weavers moving the shuttle of a hand loom, potters working their wheels,
sorcerers repeating a magic formula, people relaxing by walking, jogging, or controlled breathing) tune into it and get something very satisfying out of it. But except on machines exact repetition is an impossibility, and either by accident or intention (a balancing pole, a human instinct
for change) minute differences can happen—that is, there can be *varied repetition*. Larger
changes give us varying degrees of *variation*, and, if the umbilical cord is broken, a whole
world of contrast, difference, variety.

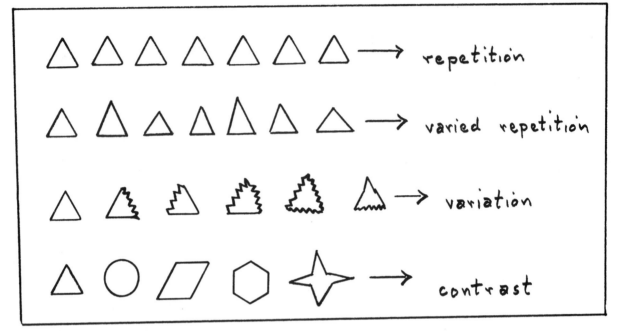

All of which brings us back to the question of sameness and boredom. Unity and variety, we
must remember, are actually and perceptibly extremely viable members of a family of viables
and about as tangible as a puff of smoke on a windy day. A little bubble in a straight line, for
example, running across this page represents a noticeable change of great (relative) significance.
The same bubble as part of a jagged erratic line would be absolutely unnoticeable.

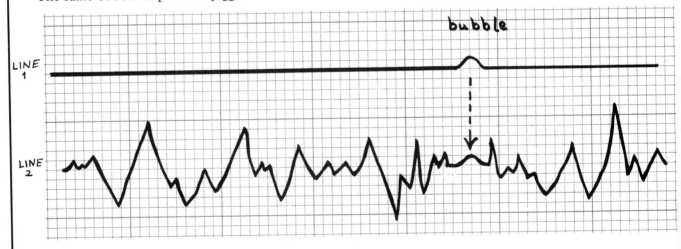

This is an important image to remember when we talk about shapings in music. Once a group
of people and I who were particularly outspoken about a particularly outrageous policy of our

government in Asia were invited by the consulate (in Madras, India) to view a film of the president of the United States—who shall go unnamed—delivering what was described as "a major new statement of Asian policy." The film was about twenty-five minutes long. Except for two slow zoom-ins there was absolutely no movement by the camera (a technique used by avant-garde film-makers but avoided by most professionals who regard twenty *seconds* of one image a lengthy shot and twenty-five *minutes,* of course, unthinkable). The president's face was frozen, uneasy, sullen, expressionless. His speech was a predictable repetition of past statements and frayed clichés. Needless to say, after about a minute any normal human being (excluding little old ladies from the Daughters of the American Revolution, the feeble-minded, or half-soused American Legionaires) would be bored by this film as we, admittedly not a sympathetic crowd, were. But after about sixteen or seventeen minutes of an unmoving visual image (one began to notice the flecks of dust projected from the camera lens dancing on the screen), and mixed with the steady verbal drone and clichés of the rhetoric, a fly, which had somehow evaded the Oval Office's elaborate human and electronic security systems and seemed attracted by the smell of hair oil, started buzzing around the president's head. After a few seconds the mischievous fly swooped down and landed on the *very tip of the nose of the president of the United States,* a feat that, despite the frantic swats of the Great Man's hand, the fly managed to repeat several times! The whole incident lasted perhaps less than twenty seconds, but the point is that within the twenty-five-minute aesthetic time scale of the film and its texture of sameness, the hilarious Fly-on-the-Nose Incident was the high point. It was like our bubble on the long straight line.

The unity/variety polar axis—admittedly with highly irregular and subjective parameters—reflects other concepts that seem to oppose each other like Heaven and Hell, Sin and Pleasure, in the cosmology of a Jesus-freaks' commune. There is the opposition of *tension* and *relaxation*, for example, with its seemingly infinite number of parallels in our bodies, minds, hearts, nervous systems, seeings, beings, and livings. In Western aesthetics, and not only in music, the tension/relaxation principle is considered such a basic theorem that what is amazing is not that it *can* be applied to and found in other civilizations (and their music)—which it can be, and is—but that there are places (and musics) where it does *not* seem to apply. And we must make note of this fact. And remember it.

Finally, there is *simplicity* and *complexity*, the opposition between what is clear, lucid, transparent, straightforward, easy and that which is dense, entangled, intricate, difficult. In music we can apply these terms in a purely technical way; we can say, for example, that the choral polyphony of the Ituri forest pygmies is more complex in texture than an English folk song, or that the rhythms found in Brahms are more simple than those found in the classical music of India—but again we must be careful: everything is in flux, and our perceptions (the words) are relative. Rather than to draw broad comparisons across cultural boundaries, it is far more useful to examine the simplicity or complexity of a piece of music within its own borders, within itself or its cultural context. The nineteenth-century Danish philosopher and theologian Søren Kierkegaard has given us a further useful and related tool: the opposing ideas (not originated by him, of course, although he brilliantly expounded them) of the *Apollonian* and *Dionysian*. The Apollonian is the clear, the balanced, the logical. It is restrained, cool, proportionate, relatively unemotional, classical; it is Mozart; it is ice. The Dionysian, by contrast, is what is fiery and unabashedly emotional. It is unrestrained, hot, complex, disproportionate, asymmetrical rather than symmetrical; it is the romantic and (at least in Kierkegaard's mind) Beethoven. It is illogical and unpredictable, full of happy violence and sharp contrasts. If a Saturday afternoon tea with music (like Dvorak's *Humoresque,* maybe) at a women's club in Scarsdale is Apollonian, a Saturday night rock show at the Apollo Theater (no pun intended) in Harlem is Dionysian. In terms of musical structure, pieces and performances that are carefully balanced, with clear-cut and elegant sections, control, and restraint—and perhaps also fairly precise musical notation—might be called Apollonian. The classical *sankyoku* music of Japan is a good example. Forms that are loose and open-ended, perhaps also with a tendency toward improvisational possibilities and a great deal of freedom for the individual performer, might be termed Dionysian. The music of the Native Americans of the Great Plains could be an example.

And rather than go on indefinitely, we shall stop.

★★★★★★★★★★★★★★★★★★★★★★★★★

One way of extending musical ideas while achieving a balance of unity and variety is through a technique with the somewhat antiseptic name of *isorhythm*. This technique, which was developed into a fine art in the Eurpoean Middle Ages, permeates the music of the West, folk, pop, and classical: it is simply the repetition of a rhythmic unit or phrase (more or less precisely) at different pitches of a melody. For instance, the popular old southern hymn "Whispering Hope" is based predominantly on the following rhythm (and its variant, the last two notes merged into one):

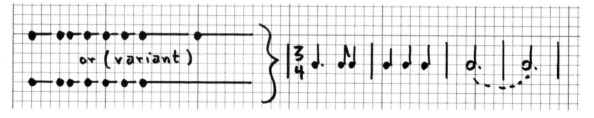

Different pitches occur with each repetition of the rhythmic phrase, and together they make up the melody.

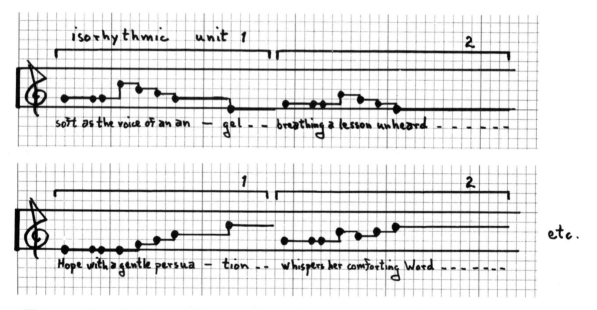

The opposite technique—which to my knowledge does not have a name—is the repetition of a few notes of melody (or, rather, a group of pitches) to variations in rhythm. In the improvisatory music of both India and Persia, for example, musicians will spin out variants on the same limited group of notes (usually within a limited range), nudging a note here, looking another (expressively) there, or flying around and in and through them, ornaments flitting off like sparks. When finishing with one pitch area or note grouping, they will (like a musical prospector panning for gold) move on to new ground.

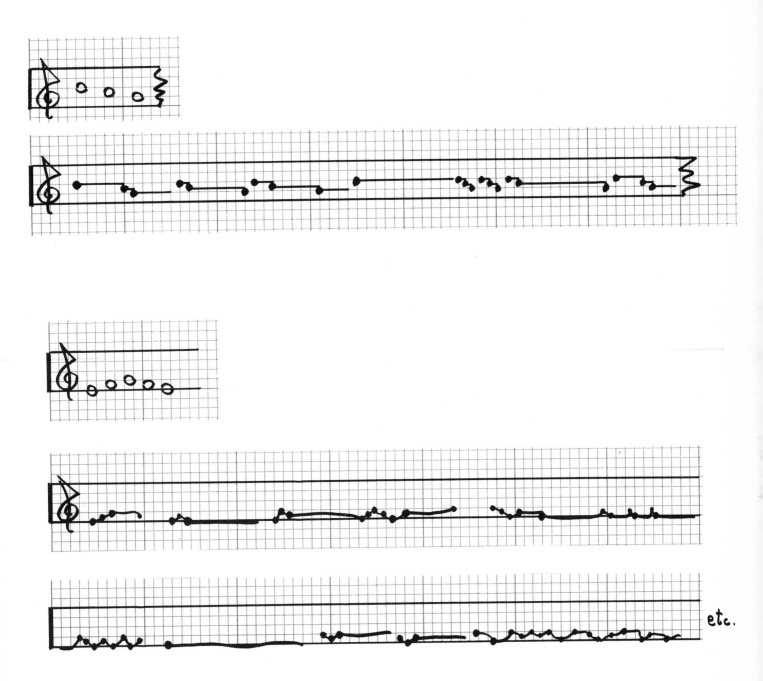

Perhaps the most common way of extending basic musical building blocks is through *repetition* pure and simple. Usually we tend to connect repetition with so-called primitive musical cultures, like the Botokudos of eastern Brazil who have lengthy songs made up of only two notes alternated in the same rhythm, or the people on the island of Lifou in southwestern Polynesia. But recently the avant garde in the "advanced" industrial nations—Europe, the Americas, Japan—often using the most recent and sophisticated electronic gadgetry, has explored repetitive techniques and made new and exciting music with them. To some scholars a short musical phrase repeated and repeated and repeated and repeated (and repeated) has an intoxicating effect; it is a "potent narcotic," or a stimulus, and seems to induce—or at least have a subtle affinity for—magic and trance. As likely and as important is the fact that repetition is something we instinctively, aesthetically, enjoy: African and Polynesian art forms, for example, are full of repeated motifs, zigzags or incisions, lines or patterns. Much of the music, too, from the same (but by no means limited to) Pacific and sub-Saharan areas uses the technique of repetition, but usually with a creative looseness and flexibility that we might better call *varied repetition.* For example, a performance in Africa lasting maybe half an hour to forty-five minutes might be made up of a couple of phrases (short, and eight to sixteen beats long) repeated (as a unit) over and over again. But if we tune into the wavelength of the performance we will notice that the repetitions are never the same in a machinelike way; a voice may anticipate its entrance in one place, another singer may hang over or drag behind a little bit, a drummer may add a new skip to his beat, or an individual in a sudden burst of enthusiasm or inspiration may add a shout or a warble or a new touch of melody or harmony. The effect is much like the subtle changes of light and shadow in a window during the day (the window and its glass remaining the same) or the color changes in a minutely moving kaleidoscope.

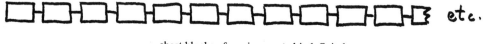

short blocks of music repeated indefinitely
(but with subtle internal changes)

★★★★★★★★★★★★★★★★★★★★★★★★★★

One way of labeling blocks of musical shapes as they are strung out in time is by assigning letters to them. The above example could also be charted:

A___A___A___A___A___A___A___A___ etc.

If there are variations in a repetition (but it—the music—still retains its recognizable face), prime numbers are added to the letters:

A___A^1___A^2___A^3___ etc.

Differing, contrasting sections are labeled with other letters (usually B, C, D, and so on, although actually any letters would do). Therefore a map of a musical form written A___B___A^1___ gives us an instant visual image: a first section (or phrase)—A___—followed by a contrasting section (or phrase)—B___—followed by a return to the first section/phrase, but with variation—A^1___.

★★★★★★★★★★★★★★★★★★★★★★★★★★

We in the Euro-American tradition tend to be just a little bit snobbish about repetition as a legitimate music-building technique, although we have buildings built of bricks, skyscrapers with hundreds of identical windows, printed fabrics or quilts with repetitive flowers or designs, serial modern art, and jobs where we repeat the same operations hour after hour, day after day. But we do in actuality have many forms of repetition in our music, although we may not always be so aware of it. Many of our hymns and pop and folk songs repeat entire phrases (perhaps with different endings). The German folk song "Ach du lieber Augustine," for example, is built from four phrases, three of which are virtually identical! And the third phrase is made up of two halves, the second of which is a repeat of the first!

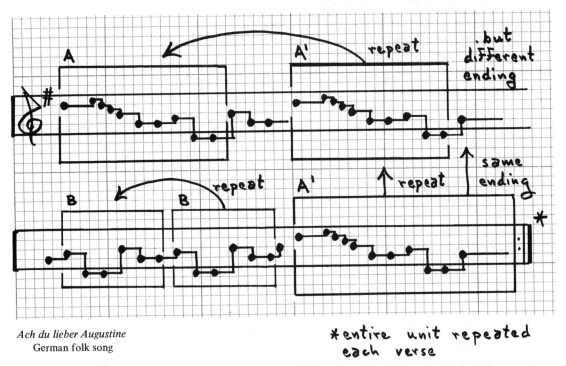

Ach du lieber Augustine
German folk song

*entire unit repeated each verse

In the West actually there have been no qualms about repeating large sections of compositions (or their entirety). A European or American folk song—and indeed folk songs almost the world over —can repeat a chunk of the musical verse or stanza or chorus three, four, five, ten, maybe twenty times, as long as there are words to be sung. Classical and dance music are full of repeats and *da capos, del signos,* and *recapitulations* (repetitions of previous material and sections which, like memory and returns from journeys, come after musical others). Or contrasts.

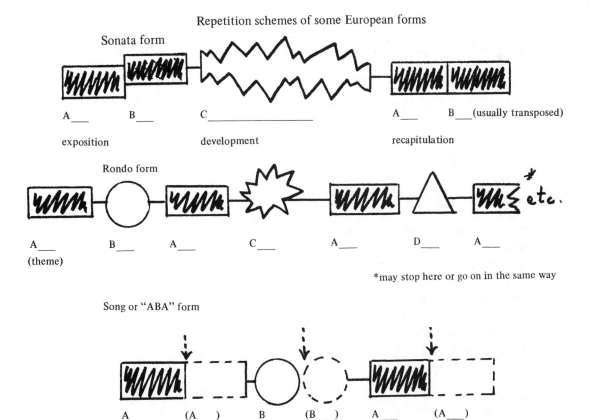

Repetition schemes of some European forms

Sonata form

A___   B___   C_____   A___   B___(usually transposed)

exposition   development   recapitulation

Rondo form

A___   B___   A___   C___   A___   D___   A___
(theme)

*may stop here or go on in the same way

Song or "ABA" form

A___   (A___)   B___   (B___)   A___   (A___)

(return or *da capo*)

(dotted-line repeats of sections optional)

One way of varying a repeated element, whether a tiny motif, a phrase (think of a phrase as being the size of a sentence), or larger blocks and sections (paragraphs, chapters), is through transposition to higher or lower pitch levels—a process not at all dissimilar to a shopkeeper's arranging units (like oranges, apples, strawberries, bananas) higher and lower in his store window in various patterns. Again we meet with a balance between unity and variety: the repetition of a musical unit provides unity, while its shifting to a higher or lower pitch level adds an element of freshness, hence variety. The unit can be changed slightly in its transposition; its intervals can flex, expand, or contract (often to fit different areas in the scale underlying the music), but as long as it retains a more or less recognizable shape (in melody and rhythm) it can be heard and tied conceptually to what has come before. *Transposed repetition* is found in music throughout the world—not only in European classical music, but in the folk songs (consistently) of eastern Europe, in the whole Mediterranean-Turkey-Iran-central Asia-India cultural belt, in the music for the Indonesian *gamelan* and of China, Korea, and Japan. If transposed repetitions happen in a string—one after another like beads on a necklace or steps on a staircase—the effect is called a *sequence*.

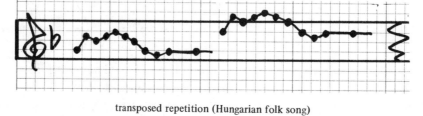

transposed repetition (Hungarian folk song)

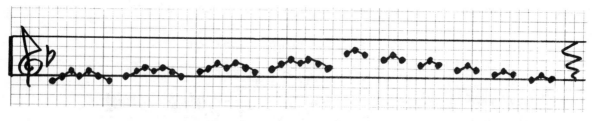

two strings of sequences (India: *raga nathabhairavi*)

Largers

All of which leads us to the larger putting together of music. Just as the method and approach to construction of a dwelling will influence whether it ends up as a yurt or a tepee or a Bedouin tent, a log cabin or a hogan, the procedures in the invisible architecture of music—the ways of thinking about and using basic structural units—greatly influence its shape and sound. There is the way—we could almost say the *tao*—of *development,* for example. In music, development is taking basic ideas (motifs, rhythms, melodies, harmonies, and so on) and working with them, molding them, reshaping them, transforming them, expanding them, cutting them down (and up), gluing them back together again, doing all sorts of things with them *in an organic and logical manner.* In the classical music of the West, development technique is what the craft of composition is all about (or at least it was until recently). The word *organic* is an important one, for it implies that there is a continuation, that one thing leads to the next like the branches and stems of a tree, or the flowing of a river. And the working out and building are usually logical (though they may be instinctive): the composer or musician (writing or improvising) formulates and develops his ideas in the same way that a philosopher, essayist, or author develops his; the only difference is that the musical architect thinks in sound, he structures aural objects rather than words, his concepts and workings and brilliance (and surprises) are heard, not seen.

★★★★★★★★★★★★★ DIVERSION 1: IRAN ★★★★★★★★★★★★★

Another approach to shaping music is what we might call *the Way of building on a model.* The classical music of Persia is perhaps the best example, although the system is also used in classical music of the Middle East and India, and it might even apply to some forms in the United States (the blues). The Persian musician, while knowing and using all the tricks of the trade of developmental technique, starts with far more than a few basic motifs or themes. He bases his improvisatory art on a *radif* (literally, "row"), a basic repertoire containing as many as 250 *gusheh-ha* (or melody types) illustrating the various characteristics of the modes of Persian music. There are many "books of the *radif,*" and each tradition or each great teacher has compiled his own, although recently the government has published an "official" version. The mode, or *dastgah,* of Persian music (we should remember) is far more than a scale; more correctly, *dastgah* is translated as "an apparatus, a mechanism, scheme, or organization." Ella Zonis has pointed out that there are *dastgah* for weaving the patterns of rugs (*dastgah-e golichi*), for government projects, and for the electronics of radios, and she has suggested the beautiful image of looking upon a musical *dastgah* not as a mode, but as "a loom for weaving music." The seven subsidiary "looms" are called *naghmeh,* or "melody." Each *dastgah* has an expressive aura around it. For example, *shur,* the most popular *dastgah* (its scale is similar to the Western minor natural scale with the second degree a quarter-tone flat), has been called "spicy and clever." Its mood is one of seriousness; it "embodies the spirit of the Iranian people." It is noble, mystic, a counselor, "like an older person speaking"; it is "lovely scenery"—gardens, flowers, rivers.

Now, the *gusheh* is a melody type, which in a limited (usually) four- to five-note range embodies many of the expressive and technical characteirstics of the parent *dastgah* mode "apparatus." Each *gusheh* will have (besides its range or pitch area) melodic configurations, a hierarchy of notes (stressed, for stopping, or important in terms of frequency), a melodic shape, motifs and cadence formulas, certain ornaments, and perhaps also rhythms, a tempo, and extramusical associations. It is like the essence or extract of the *dastgah,* or a refinement and condensation of its essential elements. As a student, the Persian musician studies and memorizes numerous *gusheh-ha*; but as a performer he does not perform them: rather, they serve as models for his improvisation, he embellishes and elaborates them, adding repetitions, extensions, ornaments, joining together short fragments to make longer patterns much as a Persian rug weaver elaborates and extends his basic motifs (the learned, the given) to spread across the entire surface of his rug. Traditional musicians (and singers) keep their improvisations very close to the framework of the *gusheh* they have chosen to use from the *radif* repertoire, although recently less traditional musicians (usually instrumentalists) improvise more freely.

The process of playing the *radif* (playing traditional classical Persian music) is called "going to its corners." A series of *gusheh-ha* (each in a limited range, remember) is chosen and arranged usually in an ascending order. Each ends with a *farud,* or "descent," which is simply an ending or cadence formula. There is, then, a gradual exploration of fresh tonal areas—a process also seen (and heard) and experienced in the improvised *raga alapana* of India.

Tār/lute, played by Houshang Zarif, Music of Iran ensemble.

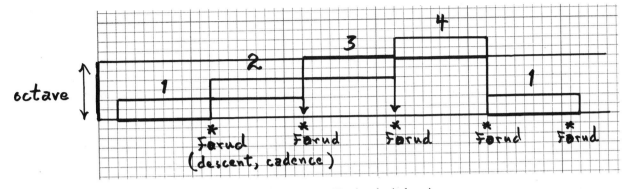

range areas in a performance of Persian classical music

The performance of a *dastgah* is, as Bruno Nettl has pointed out, "a highly sophisticated structure" with a sequence of *gusheh-ha* used in a distinctive way to form an organic whole. There are themes, developments, variations, episodes, tension and relaxation, higher and lower points of interest making up a large number of interacting parts, which are, however, shaped by the performer into a single, complex form. The pitch level and dynamics help to underscore the overall shape; familiar motifs serve as "landmarks."

Nettl further sees in a typical performance a constant movement from the familiar to the unfamiliar (the new), and back again (a return), with the basic psychological tension and relaxation cycle that this—like all journeys and returns—implies. We could map this tendency as a kind of arclike movement.

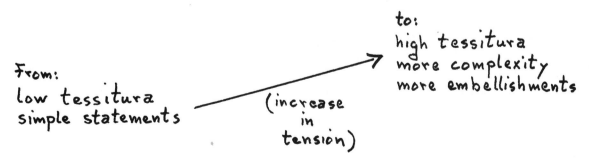

There is also movement from a low to a high tessitura (or average pitch range) and from simple musical statements to more complex and embellished ones, creating a gradual increase in emotional tension (or excitement) throughout the performance.

The musical world of each *gusheh*, of each section, as well as the macrocosm of the performance of the *dastgah* as a whole, according to Nettl, falls into four shapes.

1. 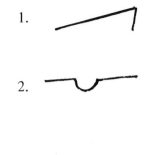 all *gusheh-ha* treated in the same way, all sections the same length (averaging about one minute each), in an ascending order, with a corresponding increase in tension.

2. symmetrical, with one *gusheh* (usually the *daramad*—the first and principal *gusheh*) dominating the performance and occurring at both the beginning and the end, with one to three shorter sections in the middle.

3. emphasis on the beginning *gusheh-ha,* with a tapering off to the end, perhaps connected with radio performances (and the limitation of time).

4. like number 3 (tapered) but doubled: two main *gusheh-ha* with a tapering off after each.

The larger performance is made up of a number of sections. In those called *daramad,* the basic ideas of the *gusheh* are developed in a free rhapsodic style. In the *tekke-ha* ("pieces"), which are composed and standard, there is metric regularity (a beat and a time signature). The *tekke-ha* have a significant difference from what we call compositions in the West: although they have identity in their melodic shapes and rhythms, the exact notes (pitches) of their melodies are *not* fixed, and each can be played in any of the twelve *dastgah* modes. They are something like precise recipes for very specific and recognizable foods—bread, biscuits, pancakes, muffins—for which the ingredients and type of flour (sourdough, buckwheat, whole wheat, bleached white, soy flour) can vary. As Aunt Jemima said (in perhaps her greatest poem), "A pancake is a pancake is a pancake."

While there is actually nothing rigid and fixed about a performance, three possibilities are given below. If the performance is a vocal one the element of poetry is also a factor.

1.

Introduction (*chahar mezrab*)		unmeasured or rhythm 1
Gusheh I:	poetry (sung, of course)	rhythm 2
	tahrir (trill) unmeasured	
Gusheh II:	poetry	rhythm 2
	instrumental interlude	
Gusheh III:	poetry (voice)	rhythm 2
	longer instrumental interlude	rhythm 3
Gusheh IV:	poetry (voice)	rhythm 2
	tahrir (trill)	unmeasured
	instrumental conclusion	rhythm 4

2.

Moqadameh (introduction) slow, stately	unmeasured
First *daramad*	unmeasured
Second *daramad*	unmeasured

Third *daramad*	unmeasured
Fourth *daramad*	unmeasured
*Kereshmeh ("nod" or "wink," a *tekke* [piece] with strong rhythmic patterns)	measured (with a beat)
Gushehe-ye rohab	unmeasured
*Kereshmeh (repeated)	measured
Fifth *daramad*	unmeasured
*Kereshmeh (repeated)	measured
*Avaz ("song," often a well-known melody)	unmeasured
*Chahar mezrab (a virtuoso piece, or rather style, using ostinato patterns and fast passagework)	measured
*Naghmeh (melody, with much repetition)	* = *tekke-ha*
*Hazine ("sad")	(compositions)

From the first selections written in the opening *gusheh* of *shur* (*dastgah*/mode)
in the *Ma'ruffi radif*.

3.

(voice accompanied by *santūr*—hammer zither)

Gusheh I:	*daramad* 1	(*santūr*)	(begins in *shur*—*dastgah*/mode)
	daramad 1	(voice)	
	daramad 1	(*santūr*)	
Gusheh II:	*daramad* 2	(voice)	
	daramad 2	(*santūr*)	
Gusheh III:	*salmak*	(voice)	(six verses of poetry preceded by an intro-
	salmak	(*santūr*)	duction)
Gusheh IV:	*shahnaz*	(voice)	
	shannaz	(*santūr*)	
	shahnaz	(voice)	
	shahnaz	(*santūr*)	
	shahnaz	(voice)	
	shahnaz	(*santūr*)	
Gusheh V:	*razavi*	(voice)	(*forud*/cadence returns to *shur*)
Gusheh VI:	*daramad* 2	(voice)	

Generally a performance in its totality follows the shapes already described. If it is a vocal performance there is an alternation between the voice (shadowed and imitated by the accompanying instrument) and solo sections by the instrumentalist (on the *santūr* zither, Western violin, *tār* plucked lute, *kamanchay* Iranian fiddle, or *nāy* flute). Each couplet of the poetry is set to one *gusheh* (melody type). There may also be an alternation between sections set in free or unmeasured rhythm, and those that are measured, that have a definite beat and metrical feeling and include the drum, usually the goblet-shaped *tombak*. In a long performance there are eight to ten sections. Toward the end the soloist shows increasing virtuosity with more and more elaborate melismas; and at the two-thirds point (in the length of the performance) the instrumentalist(s) and drummer may plan an extended solo.

Iranian classical music may be divided into three broad categories:

1. The music of the *radif* (which we have described), improvisations based on the models of the *gusheh-ha*, on the free rhapsodic *daramad-ha*, and the metric *tekke-ha*.
2. Compositions
3. Suites

The most popular composed form is the *tasnif*, or ballad. Although dating back to earlier periods (Rudaki, who lived in the tenth century, was a famous harpist and *tasnif* singer of legendary skill), this form is still used today. The words may be old or new poetry, often of a topical and satirical nature. The music may be composed in one of the *dastgah*/modes, or—in recent times—in the major and minor scales of the Western tradition. Just as in popular music and jazz in the United States, individual singers are expected to embellish the song, the *tasnif*, with their own touch, their special nuances and expression (or *halat*). A *tasnif* may be preceded by a composed instrumental introduction and by a kind of interlude or ritornello that is repeated between verses. And in the twentieth century harmonizations have also been introduced. Other composed forms are the *pish-daramad*, an introduction/overture that can precede the improvised singing of a *daramad*, and the *reng*, a dance form in triple meter (threes) and with galloping dotted (♪♫ ♪♫) rhythms.

The Persian suites are collections of pieces or movements put together from various sources. Usually all the movements are in the same *dastgah*/mode. A typical suite might have the following four sections:

1. *Pish-daramad* (overture)
2. *Avaz* (sung poetry from the classical tradition of the *radif*)
3. *Tasnif* (ballad)
4. *Reng* (dance piece)

The suite called *Taruna* has the following format:

1. Orchestral introduction to the *tasnif*
2. Verses of the *tasnif* (ballad) with orchestral ritornelli between them
3. Orchestral conclusion to the *tasnif* (or repeat of 1)
4. Part of the classical tradition of the *radif* with instrumental solos between singing of *avaz*
5. Repeat of orchestral introduction to the *tasnif* or a part of the *tasnif*

Both these forms combine composed pieces or sections with sections of improvisation, a beautiful balance between the creativity of the performer and the earlier work of the composer, a coordination between the musical past and the touch of the present moment through the loom of a great tradition.

★★★★★★★★★★★★★★★★★★★★★★★★

Besides the way of structuring music by the principles of repetition, development, or expanding a model, there is what we might call building by the arrangement of parts. This technique, common in the Far East, begins with raw material of musical chunks or fragments which can be put together or arranged in a certain order according to the ear of the composer and the criteria of the tradition. The Japanese art of *ikebana* (flower arranging) or the Euro-American modern art techniques of collage and assemblage are part of a similar methodology. I think especially (in this connection) of one of my childhood heroes, the German Dadaist Kurt Schwitters (1887–1948), who besides creating extraordinary poems and objects ("I am a painter and I nail my paintings together") recycled used and discarded trolley tickets, shoelaces, cigar bands, envelopes, cheese wrappers, feathers, bits of wire, dishcloths, pieces of wood, buttons, string, newspaper, tin can tops, lace, and indescribable fragments of junk into expressively delicate assemblages, into works of art! In Chinese opera in a technique called *ban ch'iang,* arias are put together using preexisting stereotyped melodies. These melody fragments are, however, subject to extensive variation depending on the dramatic situation. Opposed to this pastiche technique is *lian ch'ü,* where composers or singers select the music to fit a particular operatic situation or mood from a standard repertoire of *complete* pieces, not unlike J. S. Bach's well-known habit of necessity: the borrowing of choral movements and arias from earlier works for inclusion in toto in his later cantatas and passions.

In traditional Japanese music, stereotyped patterns (and their arrangement in the process of composition) play an extremely important role. We have noted, for example, that the plucked string instruments in the ancient *gagaku* court orchestra play standardized patterns and arpeggios. In an early form called *heike-biwa* (a war narration) the singer, accompanying himself on the moon-shaped *biwa* plucked lute, fitted his singing of heroic poetry to stereotyped melody fragments drawn from what might be called "a library of pieces of melody." A written notation gave the singer only the text and the name of the pattern, and he had to interpret the pattern (memorized during his apprenticeship) according to the style of his guild and the requirements of a particular performance. The music of *noh* theater is also based on stereotyped patterns. The drums, for example, play series of standardized rhythmic patterns peppered with the shouts of the players which signal and control the progression of beats. There are over 200 rhythmic patterns, which must be played in certain prescribed orders and which relate to specific situations. The *noh* flute and the singers work with stereotyped melodic patterns (in themselves made up of a smaller, more common "shared" raw material of tiny motifs and turns of phrase) which connect with certain scenes or structural sections in the drama. For example, in the fourth *dan*/section of the play, at a point called the *kuri,* the emotional tension is supposed to reach its highest intensity; the singers touch their highest notes and they sing melodic fragments that occur only here. These stereotyped melodic patterns (which are, incidentally, like the other patterns, the same for every drama in the repertoire) thus are connected in the minds of performers and listeners alike with this crucial and tense moment in the progression of the play.

The music of *kabuki* theater is also (as we saw in the "Alones and Togethers" section) built up by the arrangement of materials from an immense collection of stock melodies, rhythmic/melodic fragments, signals, and sound effects. The structuring of these elements, like an immense, interlocking picture puzzle (invisible and put together in time), is determined largely by the dramatic nuances, moods, settings, remembrances, thoughts, and actions of the play and its characters. *Kabuki* makes extensive use of musical styles from other traditions, from *noh,* for example, or the *gidayu-bushi* music of the classical *bunraku* puppet plays, with its singer/narrator accompanied by a *shamisen* (plucked lute) player. In the narrative, or *jojūri,* style of the puppet theater the singer/narrator also works from (you guessed it!) stereotyped patterns which he has learned by rote and which he uses in performance almost like conditioned responses. This is an extremely important point, and a technique that touches upon what we call (somewhat inaccurately) *improvisation.* The musical, dance, and theater traditions of India—an area I know fairly well—might serve as a typical example, although many oral traditions throughout the world might serve equally well. In India a student or an apprentice (called a *sishya*) is literally programmed over a period of perhaps fifteen to twenty years through formal study procedures and osmosis (watching, hearing, or both), with a vast repertoire of patterns. If he is a dancer, the patterns may be hand movements (*mudras*)—each with very specific meanings like nouns and verbs, or eye movements, arm, foot, leg and body movements; if he is an actor or a story-teller he absorbs key phrases, similes, images, examples, ways of stringing things together or creating episodes as well as the particular manner of speaking of gods or men, villains or heroes; if he is a musician he is "programmed" with melodic formulas and ornaments and subtle details of playing certain *raga*/modes, or with rhythmic patterns, improvisatory tricks of the trade, or other procedures. In performance, then, the dancer, actor, or musician *appears* to improvise, but it is an improvisation that grows out of a specific repertoire of stereotyped patterns that he has absorbed and memorized—through intensive, almost unimaginable discipline— and that have become almost second nature to him. This is a way of working with and making music that we in the West seem to find particularly foreign. We tend to think of ear music as either the exact memorization of a piece (usually from notation) or as a completely-by-ear instinctive freak-out, rather than as the result of years of discipline and absorbing very formal and specific patterns, which then (like the words and structures of our language) occur almost automatically in performance. It is only with extreme naïveté (and gullibility) on our part that we can accept the claims of the American jazz musician or avant-garde composer who spends several weeks in Africa or Asia, or several months toying with a *gamelan* orchestra, and then emerges in all seriousness as a self-proclaimed expert.

★★★★★★★★★★★★★★★ DIVERSION 2: JAPAN ★★★★★★★★★★★★★★★

The use of stereotyped patterns (melodic and rhythmic)—almost like pieces of mosaic—that can be put together freely in Japanese music to form larger structures may relate to a larger aspect in a uniquely Japanese approach to life and art. According to the ethnomusicologist William P. Malm, the Japanese are an island people; nestled between the sea and mountains good land is scarce; living and working space is at a premium; therefore, the Japanese have always been aware of the necessity for working and living with a limited number of materials within precisely prescribed limits. This characteristic world view might also be seen as carrying over into the traditional arts—painting, poetry, calligraphy, music, the theater, pottery, flower arranging, as well as into forms like the *chado*/tea ceremony: at all times the artist or practitioner is creating or doing within a carefully prescribed range. Just as the farmer works within the borders, terraces, and rice paddies of his lands and farms them intensively and with care; just as the painter uses a limited number of strokes, colors, and images; so the Japanese composer or musician works within the "territory" of his available patterns.

In the larger architectural shapings of Japanese music perhaps the most important force is the aesthetic principle called *jo-ha-kyu. Jo* is usually translated as meaning "the introduction"; *ha* is "the scattering"; *kyu* is "the rushing to the end"—and the usual image or simile given is that of a stream, at first with its waters in a placid pool, then spreading out and beginning to flow around dispersed rocks and in rivulets, and finally rushing downstream in torrents, rapids, and waterfalls. The three-part *jo-ha-kyu* principle is supposed to work on every level of the microcosm and macrocosm of Japanese music, in each phrase, within a section or song, and, finally, in shaping a complete performance that may take from ten or fifteen minutes to several hours. The structure of a *noh* theater performance is an excellent example.

Noh drama in its theoretical/ideal form (we must remember that forms in any culture almost anywhere in the world are idealized models and have many variants) consists of five *dan* (or sections) separated into two acts. There are four *dan*/sections in the first act, and one *dan* in the last act; there may be a comic play or musical interlude between acts. The *jo-ha-kyu* principle is superimposed on this structure.

The musicians in *noh* are on the stage and include the *hayashi* ensemble of flute and drums and the male chorus. Most of the actors are elaborately costumed and masked, and they are divided into a hierarchy beginning with the *shite* (the principal actor), around whom the play revolves, and followed by the *waki* (secondary actor) and lesser roles. Of great importance is a long ramp on stage right down which the actors make a long and dramatic entrance.

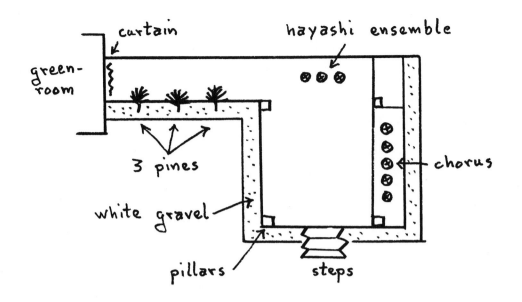

design of the *noh* stage (*Nōgaku-dō*)

In the music of *noh* the flute provides dance accompaniments, creates moods, and marks off sections of the play. The drums play stereotyped rhythmic patterns which control and signal the progression of beats. The chorus provides a stately and imposing commentary on and background for the action. The actors themselves sing, often in a kind of heightened speech similar to *sprechstimme*; they also dance. The idealized shaping of a drama is as follows:

ACT I

I. *Jo* (introduction)

First *dan*/section

    Shidai: introductory music, portrays character of secondary actor

    Waki (secondary actor) appears, sets scene, and prepares for appearance of main actor

II. *Ha* (exposition, scattering)

Second *dan* (section)

    Shidai: introductory music

    Issei: first song (in upper and middle singing register)

    Michiyuki: the entrance of the *shite* (principal actor) via covered ramp to the stage, accompanied by either *sageuta* (shorter song in low range) or *ageuta* (longer song in higher range)

    (This *dan* may also include *sashi*—heightened speech/recitative)

Third *dan*

Mondo (question and answer between the two principal actors in recitative style; commentary by chorus)

May also be

Kudoki: section for tender and feminine scenes

Fourth *dan*

Kuri: basic emotional tension of the plot is revealed; has the highest musical note

Kuse: a dance showing the full spirit of the principal character; the music here is governed by strict sets of rules

Rongi: exchanges between the two actors either in song or heightened speech

Nakairi: choral song

(*NAKAIRI*): (INTERLUDE)

Kyogen (comic play) or *hauashi*/musical interlude

Machiutai ("waiting song"): transition into last act of the drama

ACT II

III. *Kyu* (denouement, rushing to the end)

Fifth *dan*

Issei: first song

Mondo: dialogue

(Usually the *shite*/main actor appears in a new role, often a supernatural being)

Mai: a dance (the high point of the act)

Waka: a short poem

Kiri: a final commentary by the chorus

The stories of *noh* drama are divided into five categories. There are the *waki noh* (god or celebratory) plays in which the main actor is always a god, demigod, or god's messenger; the *shura mono* (ghost) plays, usually about the ghost of a dead warrior; the *katsura mono* (woman or wig) plays about beautiful women; the *zatsu noh* plays about miscellaneous subjects, the most common being *kyojo mono* (mad woman) plays about deranged women; and, finally, the *kichiku mono* (demon) plays about devils and demons. The plots of the some 240 stories in the *noh* repertoire are each based usually on a single episode, which may or may not have the sharp conflicts and contrasts we connect with high drama; the emphasis is rather on the subtle imagery of the poetry, on the expressive force of the performance, and on the evocation of a particular mood. For example, the plot of the god play *Takasago* is as follows:

Noh theater performance, Japan.

Bunraku performance. Note the *gidayu*/chanter-narrator and *shamisen* player at right, accompanying the action of nearly life-size puppets worked by manipulators robed in black. Japan.

A priest makes a pilgrimage to a beautiful bay. There he hears the wind swishing through the pine trees and the sound of the waves beating against the shore. In the distance the soft tones of an evening bell float through the mist on a mountaintop. An old couple appear and they sweep up leaves and purify the sand on the shore. They quote ancient poems about the wedding of pines (pines are symbolic of eternal life) at Sumiyoshi and Takasago.

The old man explains that the hearts of a married couple should always be together, even when they are separated. He goes on to talk of the seasons and all living things. Then he announces that he and his wife are the spirits of the pines. They board a boat and disappear into the mist of the bay.

In the second act the god of Sumiyoshi (where there is a beautiful grove of pines) appears and dances, announcing prosperity and long life for mankind.

The flutist in *noh* theater plays mostly in the *mai* dance accompaniments and in the *gaku,* or *hayashi* interludes, and uses a way of structuring his musical ideas that Malm calls a "typical Japanese variation technique." After a short introductory phrase, a basic melodic line (*ji*) is played and repeated two or three times. In various later *dan*/sections, this basic melody is repeated, but with subtle pitch variations and melismas. New melodic material may then be interpolated between the repeats of the *ji,* and then this new material may be varied (along with the original melody) in later sections.

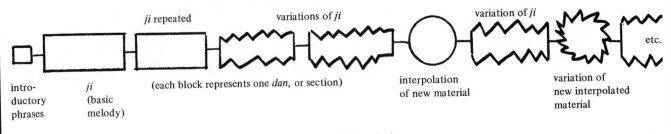

variation technique in *noh* flute playing

The musical workings in the classical puppet play form *bunraku,* like those in *noh,* also support and follow the psychological buildup and shape of the drama. On one level there is the interplay and alternation of introductions, scene-setting, narrative, commentary, dialogue, and songs, all performed by the *gidayu* singer in a format that resembles narrative forms and storytellings with music all over the world. There are also musical interludes played on the *shamisen.* The two musicians sit in full view of the audience on a rostrum on stage left, while on the stage the large, ornately costumed puppets are manipulated by men dressed in black standing behind them. The movements of the puppets are extremely lifelike and subtle, with nods of the head, arm and body movements, apparent breathing, and gestures; and as many as three or four men might be required to manipulate (manually) a single puppet!

The form of the *bunraku* drama usually has five parts, but it is musically subdivided into eight sections:

1. *Oki*: setting the scene and mood
2. *Michiyuki*: introduction of the characters
3. *Kudoki*: lyric section (often the lamenting of the heroine)
4. *Monogatari*: the story progresses to the crucial point
5. *Uta*: song ⎫
6. *Odori*: dance ⎭   the musical high points
7. *Miarawashi*: the problems come to a dramatic head
8. *Chirashi*: the solution (usually tragic)

The stories of the *bunraku* puppet theater tradition are extremely important in Japanese cultural history, and many of them have been adapted for the *kabuki* stage or (in recent times) metamorphosed into novels, short stories, and the cinema.

The structures in the music for the *shakuhachi* bamboo flute, although like those of almost all Japanese music based on stereotyped patterns and the aesthetic principle of *jo-ha-kyu,* are more problematical. First of all, the characteristic melodies of the *shakuhachi,* particularly in the *honkyoku* (or old, original music) repertoire, are inherently connected with the special characteristics of the instrument itself. Although the *shakuhachi* has only five finger holes, each hole theoretically has three levels of highness in pitch (*kari*) and three levels of lowness (*meri*) depending on fingering and blowing techniques. But the variety of pitches possible within the extremities of the range of the instrument is actually infinite. There is therefore a great subtlety in the bending and coloring of pitches. Execution of the attacks (beginnings), middles, and endings of each tone and each breath phrase are also important, as are the controls and fluctuation of timbre: swells, breathiness, overblown tones, overtones, and so on. The form of *shakuhachi* music gives the impression of being almost "formless"—that is, it seems improvisatory, free, and episodic. But according to Malm, underneath a music that gives the illusion of the natural, as "free as the wind in the pines," there is a "covert discipline of form." This is an approach to art that is also wonderfully Japanese. It can also be seen in other art forms: as, for example, in the seemingly effortless and spontaneous brush strokes of a master in painting or calligraphy which mask years of discipline and practice, also a "covert discipline of form."

Shakuhachi music, as Malm hears it, tends toward an alternation of one basic melodic idea with sections of new music. The returns of ideas—of musical motifs and fragments—are, however, inexact and subtly varied.

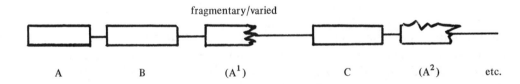

There is a static, tranquil quality in the flow of the music, but there is also a tendency for pieces or sections to begin in a low register, and then to build up to a climax—often with quite angular melodic leaps—before returning to quieter music.

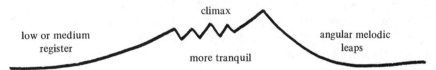

Of particular interest structurally is the beautiful *shakuhachi* duet *Shike no Tone* ("Deer Calling to Each Other in the Distance") by Kinko Kurosawa (1710–71). This piece, making use of many imitations of natural sounds in stylized patterns, is supposed to represent the calling of a buck and doe to each other in the forest. At first the phrases of each flute (answering each other back and forth) are musically divergent and their sound is distant and vague. But as the piece progresses, mirroring the movement of the deer toward each other through the stillness of the deep mountain forest, the phrases become more and more alike; they get shorter, closer, and then begin to overlap, finally merging into one exquisite unison melody!

1

2

But ultimately the form of *shakuhachi* music is deceptively elusive; it is like the wind, or the mist, or water, rather than solid and tangible like rocks, trees, or mountains; it seems to slip through the fingers, evading words and concepts and mappings. It can be felt by the heart and bones, but not grabbed by the hand or mind. That, after all, is its character.

The generic term for the music of the beautiful thirteen-stringed long zither, the *koto,* is *sokyoku. Koto* music (or *sokyoku*) occurs in a number of general types: there is music with singing, there are purely instrumental pieces; there is a solo literature, and duets; and there are arrangements and compositions for chamber music combinations with other instruments (like the trio "*sankyoku* ensemble" of *koto, shamisen*, and *shakuhachi*). The oldest genre, called *kumiuta,* is vocal music made up of a set of several poems. The singing of each poem is called a *dan,* literally "a step," a term that in the architecture of Japanese music also means "section." Each *dan* (poem/"step"/section) has a fixed length: in the older days 64 beats long or 120 beats long, depending on the style. More recently—since about the middle of the eighteenth century—*kumiuta* song sets have had shorter *dans*.

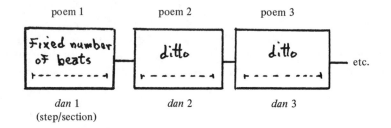

kumiuta koto music

Shirabemono is the main type of purely instrumental *koto* music. This is primarily a variation form: a basic theme is presented in the first *dan*/section; then, in later *dan,* this theme is treated with variations, while new musical material is interpolated between its phrases. The interpolated sections may also then be varied; they can be quite extensive, and they may also relate to each other. The variation technique seen in building the form of *shirabemono koto* music is similar to (but much longer and more complex than) that of *noh* flute playing (note our graph, page 432). The famous classical piece *Rokudan* ("six sections") ascribed to Yatshuhashi-Kengyo (1614–85) is perhaps the best example of this form.

The *jiuta* (or *tegotomono*) style is a hybrid, combining as it does characteristics of the two previous genres: a cycle or set of songs is separated by extended, and often virtuoso, instrumental interludes. The simplest form of *jiuta* style may have only three sections: *maeuta* (fore-song), *tegoto* (instrumental interlude), and *atouta* (after-song); but larger structures lasting up to twenty minutes or more and with a variety of song/interlude arrangements are also common. Here are several possibilities:

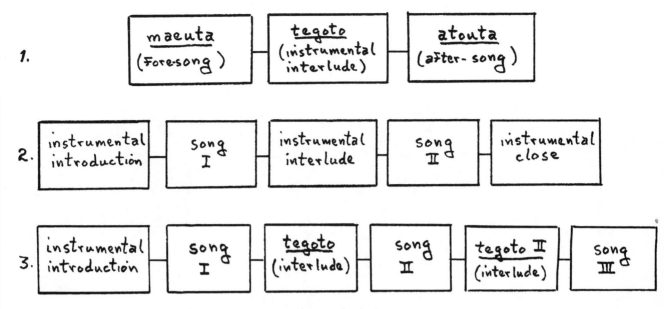

three structurings of *jiuta sokyoku* music

In *kabuki* theater the most important lyrical forms of music are the "long songs," or *nagauta*, for voice, the *shamisen* plucked lute, and assorted instruments. An important feature of *nagauta* is the use of certain stereotyped melodies (cataloged as the forty-eight *ozatsuma-te*) which form the basic accompaniment for sections, particularly introductions, cadences, and recitatives. These patterns are recognized by musicians and connoisseurs and function as signals, much as certain chords, textures, or motifs signal openings, changes, endings, or beginnings of new sections in the classical music of the West. The standard *nagauta* form is interrelated with *kabuki* dancing and the events on the stage. It has six sections, and like so much Japanese music it follows the aesthetic principle of *jo-ha-kyu*/introduction-scattering-rushing to the end.

Jo　{ 1. *Oki*: introduction, sets the scene
　　　{ 2. *Michiyuki*: entrance of the actor on the stage (often via a long ramp);
　　　　　 music portrays the character's personality and manner of entrance
　　　　　 (walking, running, etc.)

Ha　{ 3. *Kudoki*: dance section for female impersonators, soft in style
　　　{ 4. *Odoriji*: a lively contrast, exploits the *taiko* drum

Kyu　{ 5. *Chirashi*: literally "a scattering"; more free, and pointing to the con-
　　　　　 clusion
　　　　{ 6. *Dangiri*: the finale; the actors group in the final tableau (*mie*), familiar
　　　　　 cadences signal the end

Finally, there is in Japanese music (when there are words) an almost mystical connection between words and music. The forming of the general musical mood and movement is a reflection of the poem, and sometimes even a word or a turn of phrase may find its echo in a sudden turning of sound. It often seems that the music reaches behind the words, expressing what may be implied but is left unsaid—like the hidden emotions of a court lady thinking of a lost love, like the smell of the seasons, or the invisible path of a bird in the sky.

★★★★★★★★★★★★★★★★★★★★★★★★★

Kabuki theater performance: scene from "Musume Dojoki." Notice the ensemble of on-stage musicians in background. Japan.

The stereotyped patterns and formulas that lie under the constructive processes in much of the music of the earth are by no means all there is. Making music is much, much more than a mere painting by numbers or a putting together of a crossword puzzle. There is first of all the human factor. The creative performer, though he may be "programmed" with what Mark Slobin has called "the construction kit handed him by the musical tradition," adds his own creative spark, that special something that brings the music to life. In a sense he "recycles" what he has learned and absorbed and infuses it with a freshness of approach and an expressive immediacy. At this point we might also reevaluate our attitudes about what improvisation actually is.

Grove's Dictionary of Music and Musicians says that improvisation is "the primitive act of music-making, existing from the moment that the untutored individual obeys the impulse to relieve his feelings by bursting into song. Among all primitive peoples, therefore, musical composition consists of extemporization subsequently memorized. . . ."

As amazing as it is to realize that this statement was written in the twentieth century and in a respected dictionary, it does exhibit many of the prejudices that we who exist in an overwhelmingly literate society (with even our music written down) hold. We have seen how "the construction kit" which underlies improvisation in Iran and India, for example, is dizzyingly complex, and that performance—far from being "a primitive act of music-making"—is highly disciplined, elaborate, and part of a high classical tradition. The condescending picture of "untutored individuals obeying the impulse of their feelings to burst into song" (presumably like children, monkeys, or birds) is equally obnoxious. Many improvising musicians have undergone dozens of years of study and apprenticeship; and there is in every society the Invisible School of the Cultural Tradition where the "construction kit" of music is learned (like language) thoroughly and flawlessly. To say that anybody "obeys the impulse to relieve his feelings by bursting . . ." etc. to make music is not only a gross oversimplification (one can burst into tears to relieve feelings, or shout, or sneeze, or cry), but a misreading of the basic magical impulses that cause men and women all over the globe to make music.

In the final analysis the differences between improvised music and written-down music are not as great as we might at first think. Improvising musicians and composers alike inherit or learn the "construction kit of their musical tradition." Both add the spark of their individual creativity. But the differences are really just a matter of time (in the process of making). The theorists of classical Indian music have thought about these distinctions and separated music into *manodharma sangita* ("imagined music") and *kalpita sangita* ("arranged, made, fashioned, formed music"). Both approaches to music use the same vocabulary; but in *manodharma sangita,* or improvisation, the emphasis is on the performance and its "heat"; the musician must make his decisions instantaneously, spontaneously, and as a result there is an "edge," a freshness, an immediacy resulting from the simultaneity of creation and performance in the same electric moment. In *kalpita sangita* the composer has time to think about and polish his ideas at his leisure. What is lost in freshness and spontaneity is made up for in the craftsmanship of the final (musical) product. Creation and performance may be separated by years, and performance is actually an expressive re-creation, with the musician following the "map" of the composer. On the surface it would seem that composition allows more for development of consciously thought-out, rational processes and structures; but the analysis of recordings of improvised music by master musicians from around the world (from American jazz to the classical systems of Egypt or Iran or India) has shown an amazing capacity of the human brain to think and shape—spontaneously, instinctively, subconsciously—in a rational way! We (particularly in the West) also tend to think of improvisation as more free and less controlled than written-down music, and this is true to an extent within our culture. But the moment we look outside our ethnocentric box to the East, or the Mideast, this criterion, like so many others that we hold, simply does not apply. The truth is that a composer sitting at a desk or at a piano and a performer improvising with his voice or horn or pipe or 'ūd are basically doing the same thing: they are creating, working with, and shaping musical materials, adding to it a spark of life, their own personalities, their fingerprints.

Image: The raw materials of music are like the bride of Frankenstein lying on the table in the laboratory of the mad professor's castle. Lightning flashes from the sky, into the laboratory's electrical system, and she blinks to life, twitching/walking/moving. The creator/composer/musician/improviser does the same thing to the inert and rigid mass of the materials/processes/forms of his musical tradition. He is the lightning, the catalyst, that brings them to life.

VARIATION

In our excursions into the invisible architecture of the music of Iran and Japan we have touched upon another of the world's techniques for infusing new life into the familiar: that of *variation.* Precisely what constitutes the borderline between a variation and something entirely new and original is subjective and somewhat fuzzy. (This is a problem which the patent office must have to face every day.) But basically, variation must retain a recognizable face of some kind; there must be a thread (obvious or hidden) that provides the unity, the familiar, which is then subjected to the processes of variation. If a series of identical television sets on a factory assembly line represent *repetition,* and if a television set compared with, say, an electric steak knife represents *contrast,* then a conglomerate of different makes, models, and sizes of television sets in a store window might be viewed as *variations on a theme*: each is different, yet each has a screen, control knobs or buttons, an antenna, a plug or batteries, and similar internal workings—in short, all the things that make a television set a television set.

Once when I was a little boy and my eyes were full of wonder (they still are) my family went to a performance of a small tent circus. Before the main show in the big/little top, we were persuaded by the colorful incantations of the barker to step into the sideshow where wonderful things (we were assured) awaited us. It was only after some time that we noticed that Zorbo the Fire Eater had earlier—on another platform in the tent—been Mandrake the Magician, and that Sophia, Mandrake's lovely assistant, was in reality no other than Leela, the Courageous Snake Lady of an earlier incarnation. But the metamorphosis was by no means over, and, with quick changes in costume and makeup, Zorbo alias Mandrake reappeared as Igor the Russian Sword Swallower and Knife Thrower while the beautiful Sophia alias Leela became the lascivious Natasha squirming between the ring of knives that pinned her (breathlessly) to the target! In all about six performers appeared in about fifteen sideshow acts, each remaining the same person, yet each undergoing a series of transformations in names/personalities/costumes/roles. In other words, *variations on a theme*—the theme being themselves as individual people. The same transitory existence was shown by the circus performers in the little/big top, and I would swear (although I could not prove it) that the ringmaster who was at times a minor acrobat, the wild animal trainer, and the assistant to the exquisite lady high on the trapeze was NONE OTHER THAN Mandrake/alias Igor/alias Zorbo; AND (hold your hats) that the lady on the high trapeze herself was none other than (yes) the lovely Sophia/Leela/Natasha!

Variation can happen on every layer and level of a musical texture from tiny motifs, to the molding of phrases, to entire sections. In much of the singing of sub-Saharan Africa—with call-and-response formats or the repetition of relatively small units—the variation can be subtle or sudden, unpredictable or carefully planned, or even accidental—that is, an "ear variation" worked into the texture spontaneously by the performers. In drumming in Ghana an individual musician may have a choice of several possible variations of the rhythmic ostinato he is playing, but his choice is limited. In south India the *sangati*/variation is tied in to the musical phrase, and only one part of the phrase (the beginning, middle, or end) is given variation treatment. The *sangati*/variations spin out progressively, beginning with little nudges or ornaments to notes here and there in the original theme and getting increasingly complex as the cycle of the phrase (repeating, varying) turns round and round, finally culminating in florid runs and virtuoso passages.

While variation techniques exist—informally and unconsciously (as in folk music of the American Appalachians) or formally and consciously (as in the music of the Indonesian *gamelan* orchestra)—all over the world, as a larger architectural form the variation (or *theme and variations*) is important in the Euro-American classical tradition and is found in compositions from William Byrd (1543–1623) —the famous *Fitzwilliam Virginal Book,* a manuscript compiled about 1620, has dozens of sets of variations—to Haydn, Mozart, Brahms, Hindemith, and Webern. The theme is usually treated as a block unit and is followed by the other block units of the variations strung out in time like so many sausages. Each block treats the theme with a certain type of variation, and the entire set gets increasingly complex or ornate until the end, where there may be a simple repetition of the original theme. In the West themes are varied with almost the entire repertoire of tools available to the composer: the theme may be covered with figurations (like frosting on a cake), it may be surrounded by countermelodies or contrapuntal workings, it may be treated to a variety of timbres, orchestration, textures, harmonies, settings, moods, rhythms, meters, tempos; it can roar like a lion or squeak like a mouse; it can, in fact, have as many faces as Zorbo the Fire Eater or the beautiful Natasha.

Variation as an overall form is particularly strong in the Far East. We have noted the *danmono* variation genre of *koto* music in Japan. In Korea there is the big solo instrumental variation form called *sanjo,* which—particularly when performed on the twelve-stringed *kaya kum* long zither—is strong, jazzy, intense, powerful, and filled with snaps of the string, intense vibrato, and accents that make it, in the eyes of one observer, the musical equivalent of the favorite (hot and spicy) Korean food *gimchī.* The repertoire for the *ch'in* long zither in China also includes variation forms.

BRAIN GRIDS

While music may be structured instinctively, unconsciously (seemingly), automatically, and without effort or thought, it may also be structured using extremely cerebral processes and procedures. This is not to say that the brain is not working in making all types of music, but only that it works in different layers, on different levels, and in different and perhaps infinite numbers of ways. Rational processes tend to appear more in musical systems that have become self-conscious, that is, that have an elaborate theory and philosophy surrounding them. And this tendency toward the cerebral may also reflect a particular world view of a culture at a particular time in its history. The United States in the mid-twentieth century is an excellent example. Inheriting a musical system from Europe (including instruments and innovations) the people of the United States afford tremendous prestige to the rational sciences: to medicine, physics, mathematics, engineering, research (in any field), electronics, and so on. One might say that in a sense Americans "believe" in technology—as a medieval peasant might have believed in God—surrounded as they are with machines and computers and other products of man's invention and reason. Artists and composers since the 1950s have been particularly concerned with rational systems, with mathematical relationships, number theory, proportions, and a kind of working out of things on a logical grid. (There has also been an opposing tendency, a reaction, to chance and the totally irrational—but that is another story.) John Cage (b. 1912), for example, has structured music through architectural systems based on star charts, the *I Ching* (an extraordinary ancient Chinese text on the art of divining), and the sequence of stops on a New York subway!

Cerebral devices have always been a part of the classical music of the West, particularly in contrapuntal writing. Johannes Ockeghem (1430?–95), a great composer of the so-called Netherlands School, used *canons* (a form with the second part following, or "imitating," the first, something like a complicated round) that were built from:

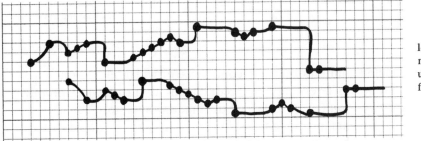

lower melody
mirrors the
upper (it also
follows it in canon)

1. *Mirror inversion*: the melody appears upside down, in reflection

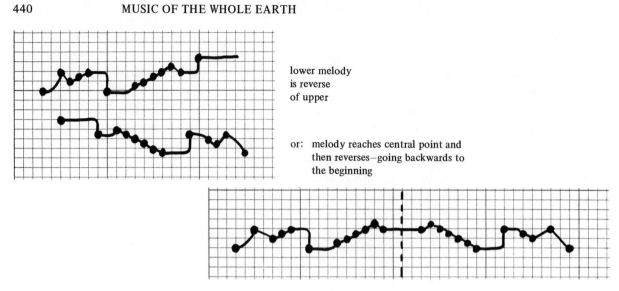

lower melody
is reverse
of upper

or: melody reaches central point and
      then reverses—going backwards to
      the beginning

2. *Retrogrades*: the notes of the melody (or music) run backwards note for note,
     like a movie projected in reverse; also called *cancrizans* ("crab")

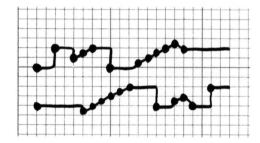

lower melody = upper melody *but*
backwards and upside down

3. *Retrograde inversions*: backwards and upside down!

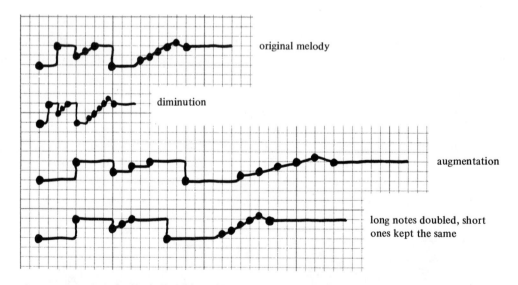

original melody

diminution

augmentation

long notes doubled, short
ones kept the same

4. *Mensuration canons*: melodic imitations, the second voice of which moves on
     the same melody but at a different rate of speed, commonly in *augmentation*
     (twice as slow) or *diminution* (twice as fast), but sometimes in more complex
     mathematical ratios (for example, long notes in one melody may be held pro-
     portionately longer than those in the other—the short notes remain the same
     —get it?)

All these techniques are stock-in-trade for the Western composer; J. S. Bach used them in works like *The Musical Offering* and *Art of the Fugue* (more rigidly) and in his keyboard and choral pieces (more freely). In the twentieth century the twelve-tone system developed by Arnold Schoenberg uses these and many other rational processes to generate permutations from a basic twelve-pitch series. His student Anton Webern combined the twelve-tone system with the ancient medieval techniques of canon, applying almost all of Ockeghem's devices not only to the inner workings of his compositions, but to entire movements and pieces as well. Postwar composers have carried this mathematical and eminently logical way of building music even further.

★★★★★★★★★★★★★★★★★★★★★★★

Jon Gibson (b. 1940) is a young American performer/composer whose work and associations touch upon much that is happening in the new music scene of the 1970s. As a virtuoso wind and keyboard player (flute, saxophone, clarinet, organ) he has performed with almost every avant-garde group or composer of note; he can both read music of the most complex kind and (as we used to say in Texas about musicians who really got "cooking") improvise "like a barrel of mosquitoes in a windstorm." As a composer—and we have chosen him from dozens of extraordinarily interesting contemporary composers for this reason—he has fluctuated between two structural extremes: on one hand, an intuitive, free, and almost improvisatory approach to music; on the other, the setting up of a more or less rigid system which is then carried out automatically, strictly, in a machinelike process of logic and inevitability.

In *Visitations (4)* (1973), in what Gibson calls "a sixteen-track multitextured environmental soundscape," diverse sounds ranging from wood flutes, bells, *maracas,* bowed and struck cymbals, and synthesizer to bird calls (slowed down to one-eighth speed), "vocal drumming" (percussive throat sounds played at half-speed), running water in a brook, and ocean waves were recorded separately on sixteen tracks, or layers. Then they were combined in various ways "by a process of intuition and trial and error." Each of the sixteen tracks of shaped and ordered sound (although they occur simultaneously) could be considered a complete piece in itself. The resulting music has been compared by composer/critic Tom Johnson of the *Village Voice* to "a dense fog of sound" in which the ear picks out blurred and distant images (flute, waves, a knocking, swells, whooshing, bells) which appear and disappear, and which finally, at the end, reveal their true and clear sound identity (*as* ocean waves, *as* bells, etc.) "as if the fog had finally lifted." Johnson goes on to note that "there are no rhythmic motifs, no quotations or references to musical styles or forms, and no manipulation of melodic ideas or pitch systems." The listener must focus his ears on one of the many elements happening simultaneously, and when he does, he hears "sounds and not ideas" (musical ideas in the conventional sense).

Structurally it is almost impossible to map out *Visitations (4)*; we know how it was made and what the original sounds were (the composer tells us), yet there are no clear-cut sections or climaxes or contrasts or grindings to an inevitable end. The sounds simply drift by in a kind of "dynamic staticism" that—as an extension of our perception, our experience of hearing—parallels the visual effect of objects drifting past us on a fog-filled, slow-moving river. This tranquil, *Zen*-like piece, despite its avoidance of what we might hear as clichés and form-building signals, is extremely successful and aesthetically satisfying to hear, a reflection of the rightness of the composer's intuition and improvisatory (by ear) processes.

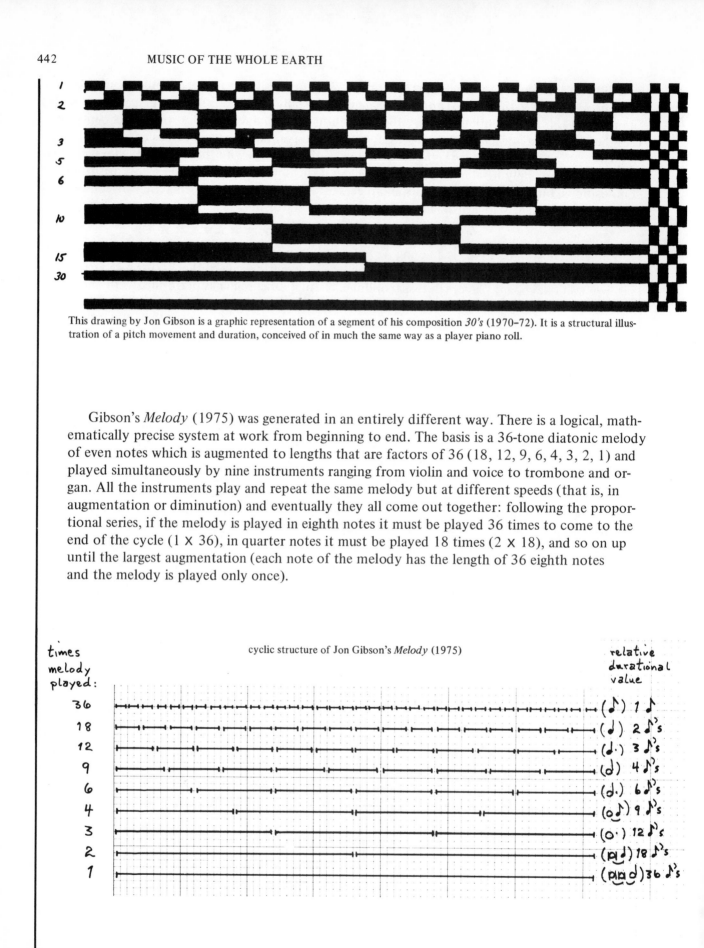

This drawing by Jon Gibson is a graphic representation of a segment of his composition *30's* (1970–72). It is a structural illustration of a pitch movement and duration, conceived of in much the same way as a player piano roll.

Gibson's *Melody* (1975) was generated in an entirely different way. There is a logical, mathematically precise system at work from beginning to end. The basis is a 36-tone diatonic melody of even notes which is augmented to lengths that are factors of 36 (18, 12, 9, 6, 4, 3, 2, 1) and played simultaneously by nine instruments ranging from violin and voice to trombone and organ. All the instruments play and repeat the same melody but at different speeds (that is, in augmentation or diminution) and eventually they all come out together: following the proportional series, if the melody is played in eighth notes it must be played 36 times to come to the end of the cycle (1 × 36), in quarter notes it must be played 18 times (2 × 18), and so on up until the largest augmentation (each note of the melody has the length of 36 eighth notes and the melody is played only once).

times
melody
played:

cyclic structure of Jon Gibson's *Melody* (1975)

relative
durational
value

The harmonies formed by the many speeds of the melody being played together are accidental (what Stravinsky called "pandiatonic"), and they seem to move, though in reality this is an illusion. The sound, perhaps because of the diatonic nature of the melody and the many layers of rhythm, is strangely reminiscent of medieval Church music. After the cycle is played through once, one instrument to a layer, Gibson superimposes another calculated process. Through two more cycles of the structural format, the instruments begin hopping from one layer to another, at first slowly, and then with increasing frequency, until they are switching parts every eighth note. How they hop and when is determined by a mathematical chart related to the original 36–18–12–9–6–4–2–1 series.

★★★★★★★★★★★★★★★★★★★★★★★★★★★

The use of rational/cerebral processes in structuring music does not necessarily mean that making music is reduced to a purely mechanical process which, once set up, seems to click away by itself, something like the springs and gears of clockworks. There is no doubt that there is a kind of Apollonian abstract beauty in a system, and to many people in music this is enough: the system itself and its relationships, no matter how arcane or how hidden, is all the justification needed—the resulting music will automatically have logic, unity, order, and consistency. And beauty. But as often as not there is and has to be *a mystical something more.* Rational systems can be used badly, or brilliantly; Ockeghem, J. S. Bach, Webern, and Cage (to name only a few) have used them brilliantly. But the system is invariably tempered with what we might call a creative spark, a something else, a human touch (maybe "genius" is a good word to use here), breathing life and expression and emotion into the music. It is almost as if flowers could grow in a computer, or minstrels and soul bands sing higher mathematics; it is as if Ma Rainey had married Albert Einstein.

Consciously rational processes, as tools and as ways of putting entire pieces together, are by no means limited to the music of the West. The music of the Javanese *gamelan,* Hardja Susilo and Mantle Hood have noted, uses all kinds of compositional devices, among them augmentation, diminution, inversion, and retrograde! John Blacking has shown that in a certain Venda children's song, *Potilo* (the Venda are a south African people), *the structure is determined by the number of fingers on the hand,* since the song is a counting song. There are ten little three-note phrases, and on the second beat of each a finger is grasped, beginning with the little finger on the left hand and working across. On the second beat of the tenth phrase there is a big clap. Blacking also notes that children's pieces on the *mbira* are often determined by the structure—the placement of keys and tuning—of the instrument itself. Put in another way: *the instrument becomes the system.* Another specific example is the classical Thai piece *The Waves Beat Against the Shore,* written by King Rama VII in 1931, which contains echoing sections (musically representing the waves) that become progressively shorter, following the precise mathematical formula of 4–2–1.

But it is in the classical music of India that one finds perhaps (though I am prejudiced) the most amazing collection of rational elements, even more so in that these elements coexist with and are assimilated into a musical texture of great emotional and expressive and creative freedom. Complex rhythmic closing patterns, for example, called *mora*—well thought out, rationalized, in advance—are tacked onto the most spontaneous improvisations. In the southern form called *pallavi,* the performer takes a theme and then puts it through a series of augmentations and diminutions which pull against the *tala*/time cycle and must be repeated a certain number of times to come out again on the right beat, a cerebral operation similar to the Jon Gibson example (page 442), although in the Indian form the different speeds of the melody are performed one after another, not simultaneously. The great composer Muthuswamy Dikshitar (1776–1835), who was also a renowned Sanskrit scholar and astrologer, wrote music that was so full of intellectual complexities that much remains to be discovered even to this day. Among his techniques (shared to a lesser extent in the music of other Indian performers and composers) were:

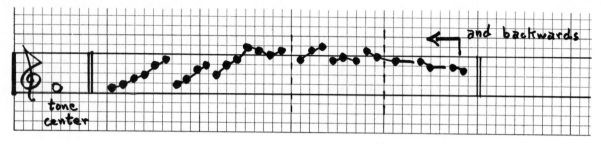

Kamalam bhajare (Kalyani ragam, adi tala)

1. *Viloma krama* (the same as *cancrizans*/retrograde): a melody going along one
   way and then reversing itself

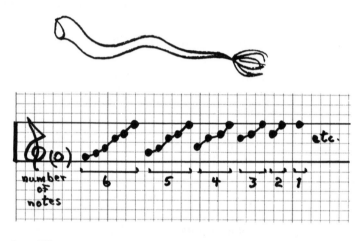

2. *Gopuchcha* ("cow's tail"): the notes of the melody are sequentially subtracted,
   forming phrases of regularly diminishing magnitude, tapering off to the end
   like a cow's tail!

(from improvisation of B. Rajam   the same technique in words, the poetry of songs:
Iyer in *Mohanam raga, adi tala*)   *srira sapade*
                                                                ra sapade
                                                                sapade
                                                                pade

(*Sri Varalakshmi namastubhyam Sriragarupaka Fala*)

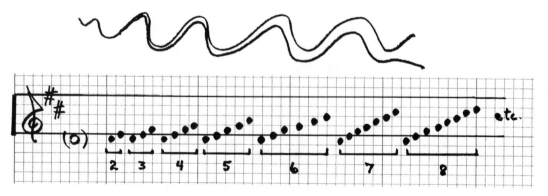

3. *Srotovaha* ("river's source"): just as a river gets larger and larger, so phrases
   grow longer and longer in a kind of additive technique

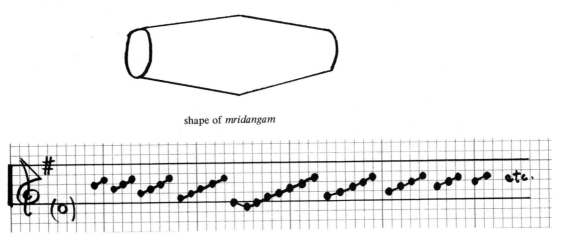

shape of *mridangam*

4. *Mridangam* (so called from the barrel shape of the drum): phrases get longer, reach
    a central point, and then get shorter

There is also a similar technique called *damaru yati* (from the hourglass shape of the *damaru*/drum).

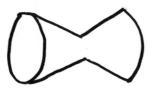

shape of *damaru*

And regular phrases of the same magnitude (although the norm in music of Europe and America) are
so unusual in Indian music that they are regarded as a special technique called *sama yati* (or "sameness")! Another highly prized device (*svarakshara*) is to wed the syllables of the poetry to the names
of the notes in a kind of musical/literary punning.

sa ri ga ma pa da ni sa

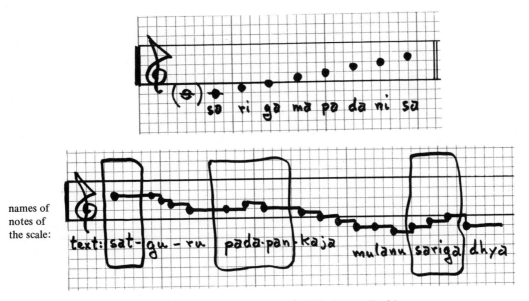

names of
notes of
the scale:

text: sat-gu-ru pada-pan-kaja mulanu sariga dhya

incidence of *svarakshara* circled (*Sadguru pada: Bilahari raga, adi tala*)

This device was also used in European classical music (using either the note names "A–B–C–D–E–F–G" or the syllables "do–re–mi–fa–sol–la–si–do"), most notably in the numerous compositions based on the motif B–A–C–H (H is used in Germany for the note B natural; "B" is B flat) and in Alban Berg's deriving of a tone row–like set of notes from the names of himself, Arnold Schoenberg, and Anton Webern which he then used as the central motive of his *Chamber Concerto*.

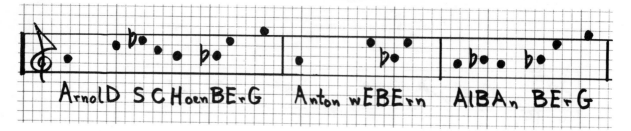

SHAPINGS

Just as the architecture of a house may be characterized by any number of elements (basic materials, roof, windows, environments, skeletal structure, colors, texture), so music may be formed by almost anything that we (listeners, musicians, composers) notice and mark as significant. Tones/melodic workings and rhythm (to a lesser degree) are habitually assigned automatic importance in the Euro-American tradition; but the invisible structure of music can also be shaped by—to name only a few elements—harmonies, simultaneities, orchestral sound, texture, movement, speed/tempo, relative complexity/simplicity, mode (*raga, maqam*, etc.), tonality, mathematics, time (clock or otherwise), number or type of performers, range, tessitura, space (musical or physical), words, lyrics, stage action, ceremonial order, religion, work to be done, magic, a thing being described or a "program," chance, process (as, for example, set up on a computer), timbre, instrumentation, concepts, and extramusical events. For example, in the musical sound world of the circus the acts in the ring determine and shape much of the music: the long snare-drum roll signifies danger and tensely accompanies, say, flips and spinnings and twists on the high trapeze or a particularly precarious balancing act; honks and slides and beeps and pops echo the antics of clowns as they move through their hilarious routine; and stirring, galloping march music may change abruptly to the exotic sounds of the Middle East as the elephants (in the center ring) switch from one action to a proboscidean belly dance! Music may also be shaped by the energy or tiredness of the performers: musicians at the point of exhaustion (like at an all-night wedding or ceremony) may be stumbling along on clichés and time-marking patterns, until they are joined by a fresh batch of replacements who immediately bring in new life, and the music explodes in a burst of highly creative energy. Avant-garde composers in the West have used physical exhaustion as a shaping element in music, as well as the musician's capabilities: the speed at which he can play a group of notes, or the length he can hold a tone.

We can graph (remembering that the ingredients may be any combination of the above elements) or symbolize many of the shapings in music. For example, music may be

sectional:

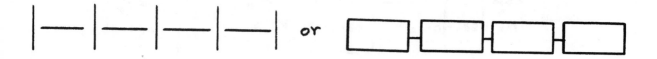

or *continuous:*

It can be *directional,* and build to a peak:

or it may map out *nondirectionally,* in a series of plateaus:

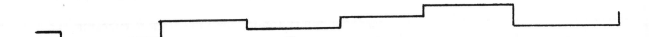

A piece of music or a performance may be *self-contained*; it may be composed and have a set beginning and an end:

or it may be *open-ended*—that is, it may have no set length or duration; it may be performed ad lib, with repetitions or creative improvisations continuing as long as is necessary:

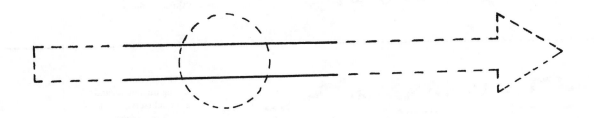

Music may be made up of a *repetition* of elements, or of *varied repetition, variation, alternation, contrasts,* and *returns*:

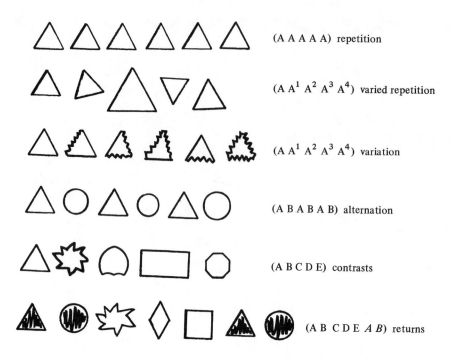

(A A A A A) repetition

(A A¹ A² A³ A⁴) varied repetition

(A A¹ A² A³ A⁴) variation

(A B A B A B) alternation

(A B C D E) contrasts

(A B C D E *A B*) returns

There can be *development*, the *arrangement of stereotyped patterns*, or the *building on a model*:

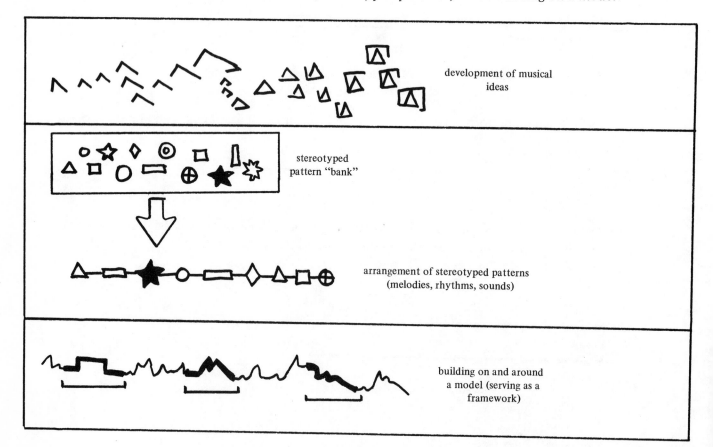

development of musical ideas

stereotyped pattern "bank"

arrangement of stereotyped patterns (melodies, rhythms, sounds)

building on and around a model (serving as a framework)

There can also be *no contrast, subtle contrast and change, gradual contrast,* or *sudden contrasts* (remembering the relativity of all things):

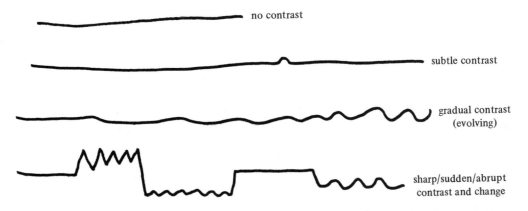

Finally, there is the microcosm and in-between-cosm and macrocosm of the piece or performance as a whole: each little moment has its shape, its gesture; these combine (like rivulets into a larger stream) into phrases or larger entities, which in turn form larger shapings: sections, units, bigger chunks of time, everything culminating in the shape of the whole:

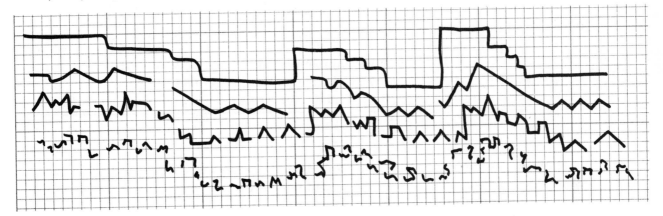

Sometimes these smaller shapings reflect the shaping tendencies of the whole, sometimes they do not. In the music of Europe and America there is a strong inclination to follow the *exposition-development-(climax)-resolution* (⌐) format on many levels. Similarly, in Japan it is believed that the *jo*/introduction-*ha*/scattering-*kyu*/rushing to the end principle works in every level of a traditional piece or performance, as it does in all art and, indeed in nature and in life itself.

★★★★★★★★★★★★★★ DIVERSION 3: FORM IN ISLAM ★★★★★★★★★★★★★★

The architecture of music, we have noted again and again, seems to have connections with the shapings and symbols of a particular culture as a whole. These relationships can be quite complex, they are seldom simpleminded or obvious, and they may in fact be hidden. To make matters even more difficult, no single culture or society today is simple (if it ever was); there may be dozens of subcultures in each, many of them unique and diametrically opposed to each other. If we are aware of the shape of the whole cloth, we must also be aware of the intricacy and diversity of its internal designs.

The so-called music of Islam is a case in point, because within this conceptual bag we lump (uncomfortably) Morocco, Tunisia, Algeria, Egypt, many countries bordering the southern Sahara, Jordan, Syria, Lebanon, Iraq, Saudi Arabia (not to mention Yemen, Muscat, Oman,

Qatar, Kuwait, and the Trucial States), Turkey, Iran, Afghanistan, and many southern Asian states in the Soviet Union, each with many layers in the tapestry of its own culture. At the same time, there are certain similarities that seem to stretch across such diverse areas of geography and peoples—in religion, art, architecture, language, literature, aesthetics (often combining with local elements in a unique flowering). It is these similarities which concern us here.

The *muwashshah* is a form of vocal music (which seems to date from developments in Islamic Spain as early as 900 A.D.) found today in north Africa and the Arab Near East. Performed by a chorus, or a chorus alternating with a soloist, and accompanied by instruments, the *muwashshah* is based on a repeated rhythmic pattern or mode (*iqa*); it is monophonic, strophic (that is, in verses), and has a repeated refrain. The name of this form derives from the noun *wushah* (a sash, scarf, or belt worn diagonally from shoulder to waist and usually studded with alternating patterns of jewels); the prefix *mu* designates the object of the action, in this case, "that which has been beautified." *Muwashshah* is also thought to carry the meaning of "encircling": just as the jeweled sash encircles the body, the highly ornamented melody of the refrain encircles each strophe.

Each verse of poetry in *muwashshah* form falls into three sections:

I. *dawr* ("turn, circle") or *badaniyyah* ("body") music of the opening *juz* (strophe) A or A A¹	II. *khanah* ("inn," or "square of a chessboard") or *silsilah* ("chain, series") either entirely new (B), or new plus a return to the refrain (B A¹) B or B A¹	III. *qaflah* ("key," or "closing") or *ruju* ("return") or *ghita* ("cover") new poetry set to a repeat of the music of part I A or A¹

This entire process forms a kind of self-contained box, a unit which—like the melody of an Anglo-Celtic ballad—is repeated for each verse of poetry. It can happen only once (one verse) or it may be repeated again and again, depending on the number of verses sung at a performance.

There may also be optional additions, a fourth and fifth section:

IV. new *khanah* or *silsilah* C or C A¹	V. *qaflah* A or A A¹

The musical format for a verse of *muwashshah* is:

$$\begin{array}{ccccc} & & & \text{optional} & \\ A & B & A & \left(C \qquad A \right) \\ \text{or AA}^1 & -\text{or BA}^1 & -\text{or AA}^1 & -\left(\text{or CA}^1 -\text{or AA}^1\right) \end{array}$$

Islam, as a religion, according to scholar Lois Ibsen al Faruqi, "is dominated by a unique preoccupation with . . . the concept of *tawhid,*" or the "oneness and utter transcendence," the "singularness," "uniqueness," and "other-than-nature/human-ness" of God. Following this religious precept there is, then, in Islamic art an avoidance of figural and literal representation (of religious symbols other than the words of the Koran, of man, animals, nature, or God) and an opposing emphasis of denaturalization and stylization. Nature is further transfigured (or disguised) by the use of symmetry and repetition. The Islamic artist, following this aesthetic, tends toward a certain abstract quality in his designs, with an elaborate use of the arabesque. These and other qualities, according to al Faruqi, can be seen in rugs, in brass engraving, in architecture and stucco and brickwork, in painting, literature, and in music, particularly in *muwashshah.*

Qualities in Islamic Art (and the vocal form of *muwashshah*)

1. *Abstraction*: the music does not shadow the words or the mood of the poetry. Everything is denaturalized, stylized.

2. *Lack of individuality*: a suppression of individuality and specific character. The poetry may be about love, but the love is indefinite, abstract. There is no musical variance in volume, range, or tempo.

3. *Nondevelopmental character*: the overall form is not an unwrapping or evolution. It is a succession of parts, all of which are equal. There is a lack of progression, a lack of climax and finality (though there are many centers of tension). Each section is self-contained, and each can end the performance; there can be as few as one or as many as twenty. The successive parts thus do not evolve "organically."

4. *Repetition (takarrur)* and *symmetry (tanasuq)*: similar to the working out of motifs in Islamic visual arts. There are exact or sequencelike repetitions of sections (strophe and refrain), whole phrases, and smaller themes and motifs. Symmetry is found in poetic rhyme patterns and the ordering of phrases.

5. *Arabesque (tawriq,* "foliation"): the complex arrangement (in art) of geometric figures, calligraphy (the words from the Koran), stylized (denaturalized) flowers and other elements. The arabesque has several characteristics:

    conjunct (mutawasil) arabesque: "the connected," an unending succession representing an "infinite pattern."

    disjunct (munfasil) arabesque: "the divided," a series of self-contained units (like in *muwashshah* form), each complete, yet woven with others to create a larger pattern. Seen in rugs, in the episodes in literature (*The Arabian Nights*), room groupings around central courts in Islamic architecture. Any one unit may be the "thought center" (or aural or visual focus), the starting or ending point for perception.

    intricate movement: there is an intricate, darting quality in the music, a moving around in small melodic intervals and microtonal inflections, with a few long notes, just as every square inch of a table or screen or a stucco facade might be covered with patterns of tiny flowers. Visual movement.

    outpouring (dafgah): a kind of "periodic launch" at the end of an arabesque when the pattern is grasped and understood and "the spectator feels an emotional release in this success and the completion of the unit."

★★★★★★★★★★★★★★★★★★★★★★★★★

Elaborate abstract ornamentation and calligraphy completely cover the surface of an Islamic prayer niche. Isfahan, Iran.

11

INVISIBLE
ARCHITECTURE II

The large overall form of a piece or performance of music, that is, its external architecture, might be seen as happening in a number of ways. There can be an organic whole, a large-scale, overall blueprint that is followed from beginning to end; there may be a stringing out in time of short units, repeated or varied, like beads on a string; there can be a succession of relatively longer but different sections, movements, or pieces: a suite, medley, etc.; there can be the setting up of strata or plateaus, which, with occasional shifts to other levels, is more or less continuous. The music might evolve like a growing plant; it might have distinct sections, with their own mini-beginnings and mini-endings, musical joints, elbows, connectors, and transitions. It might be fixed, that is, composed and notated; or it may allow for considerable variation by the performer; or the piece itself might be improvised (following, of course, the rules and procedures of the tradition). In a sense large-scale form might be compared to a settlement or a village: everyone might live in one giant-sized longhouse (as do the Iban tribesmen in Borneo); there might be a series of gradated houses, depending on wealth, status, or prestige, but forming an organic whole; a village might be made up of innumerable repetitions of basically identical houses, or variations on a theme; the town might be planned, it might be walled (that is, with marked limits), or it might filter out into the countryside.

William P. Malm has classified form according to four main types: *iterative* (one small formula repeated), *reverting* (a return after a digression), *strophic* (repeats of a larger formal unit like a verse), and *progressive* (developing organically from one idea to the next). He notes, however, that these terms apply only to "simple music" and that larger structures are infinitely more complex. Rather than trying to put together a logical sequence of the larger forms and workings in world music we shall pick out at random a few ideas, techniques, and concepts that seem important and that can then be applied to the music of specific cultures.

453

A PRIMER OF TECHNIQUES/CONCEPTS/WORKINGS/FORMS

Iterative

A small chunk of music (or a larger one) is repeated. The repetitions may be varied (slightly)—admittedly a subjective and highly relative term (one tribe's identical twins might be another tribe's second cousins). This technique is characteristic of both the so-called primitive and the so-called avant garde.

Although usually applied to the repetition of short (two- to three-second) phrases of music, this concept applied to larger units (phrases, verses, sections, movements) is one of the most important in the earth's music. It encloses many of the following forms. The exact number of repetitions may be random, or determined by time, the magic of numbers (*mantras* in India are chanted 108, 1,008, etc., times), ceremony, custom, or words.

Iterative/Variation

A large part of the unit remains the same and is repeated; over and above the scaffolding of this sameness, variations occur.

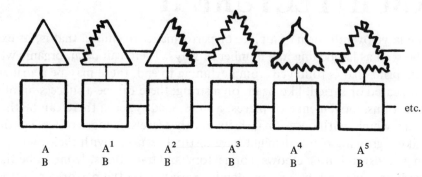

This is one of the most beautiful concepts in world music, and it balances the unity of a recurring pattern (sameness, familiarity) with the variety and spontaneity (change, contrast) of the new and evolving. Some examples: blues form (United States) where a recurring twelve- or sixteen-bar sequence of chords repeats as a unit under the verbal/musical invention of the soloist; Shona *mbira* music (Rhodesia) where a block of melodic/harmonic music (often forty-eight beats long) is repeated throughout a piece on the instrument, while the singer weaves out variations; Ravel's *Bolero*, where the only changes in basic repetitions of a melody and its harmony and rhythm are in orchestration, texture, and dynamics.

Much of the music of the New England fiddling tradition is based on two-part strophic songs, each half of which may be interchangeable. Fiddler Bob Christopher at New England Fiddle Contest, Hartford, Connecticut.

Variation

A working with and a changing—often getting increasingly complex—of the basic block of music is variation. The element varied can be as short as a phrase, or it may be a complete melody, or it can be as long as a multipart section. The important thing is that variation *is* the main form, and not just a technique used in another form.

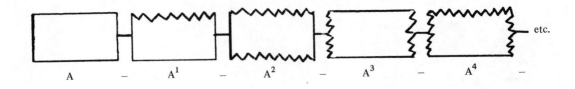

Variation form is important in the classical traditions of Euro-America, the Far East (China, Japan, Korea), and southeast Asia.

Strophic

Strophic music (derived from the Greek *strophe,* "a turning") is organized into neat, blocklike units, roughly corresponding to a verse in poetry, which are then repeated. Strophic songs may be built from two, three, four, or more musical phrases, usually of equal length. The entire unit may be repeated as a block, while the words (if there are any) continue to change and progress, telling a story or developing an idea. Almost all European/American folk and pop music (not to mention hymns) is strophic, and this form is characteristic also of much of the vocal music of Africa.

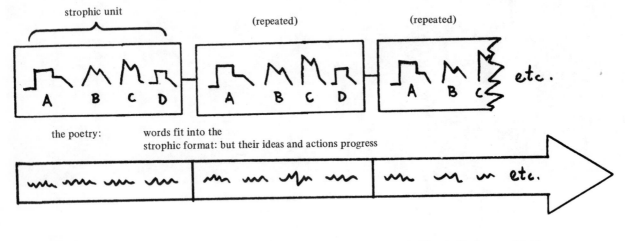

1. Come all you fair and
       tender girls,
   Take warning my friend;
   And learn the ways
       of this wide world,
   That upon your lives
       depend.

2. When I was in my
       sixteenth year,
   Sweet Willie courted
       me;
   He said if I'd run
       away with him,
   His lawful wife
       I'd be.

3. My mind had so combined
       with his,
   That I could not
       well say no;
   My mind being bent on
       rambling around
   That with him I
       did go.

   etc.

Anglo-Celtic folk song
(Kentucky)

Strophic song may consist of verses or stanzas only (as in the preceding example); or it may be made up of verses leading up to a chorus or refrain, that is, basically, with a two-part alternating internal structure. The words of progressive verses (and occasionally—especially if it is improvised—the music also) tend to vary and change, while the words (and music) of the repeated refrain remain the same.

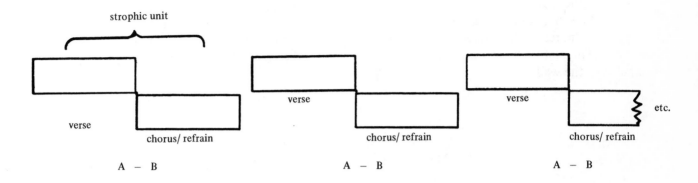

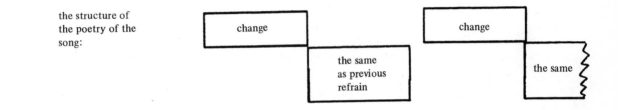

Examples of Strophic Song with Chorus

(verse 1)

When Louis came home to
   the flat
He hung up his coat and his hat,
He gazed all around, but
   no wifey he found,
So he said, "Where can Flossie
   be at?"

A note on the table he spied,
He read it just once, then
   he cried,
It ran, "Louis, dear it's too
   slow for me here,
So I think I will go for
   a ride."

(chorus)

"Meet me in St. Louis, Louis,
   Meet me at the fair,
   Don't tell me the lights are shining
   Any place but there.

We will dance the Hoochie Koochie,
I will be your tootsie wootsie,
If you meet me in St. Louis, Louis,
Meet me at the fair."

(verse 2)

The dresses that hung in
  the hall
Were gone, she had taken
  them all.
She took all his rings and
  the rest of his things;
The picture he missed from
  the wall.

"What! moving?" the janitor said,
"Your rent is paid three months
  ahead."
"What good is the flat?" said
  poor Louis, "read that."
And the janitor smiled as
  he read:

(chorus)

"Meet me in St. Louis, Louis
Meet me at the fair,
Don't tell me the lights are shining
Any place but there.

We will dance the Hoochie Koochie,
You will be my tootsie wootsie,
If you meet me in St. Louis, Louis,
Meet me at the Fair."

etc.

(Andrew B. Sterling &
Kerry Mills)

For Judy Garland aficionados only: the "somewhere over the rainbow" section of the song is the chorus; the part about the star is the verse.

As in almost all the forms we are mapping out, the possibilities for variance and permutation in strophic form are almost infinite: a short refrain passage can be incorporated into the verse, there can be internal musical rhymes (repeats) not necessarily coinciding with those of the words, verse and refrain may be built on the same music, and so on.

Alternating

There is a seesawlike alternation between one section of the music and another or others. This back-and-forth structural plan may pit one (or more) familiar and recurring elements against the ever new and contrasting; or it may be a simple alternation, as in the strophic verse/chorus format of America's Tin Pan Alley, or as in certain Plains Indian songs.

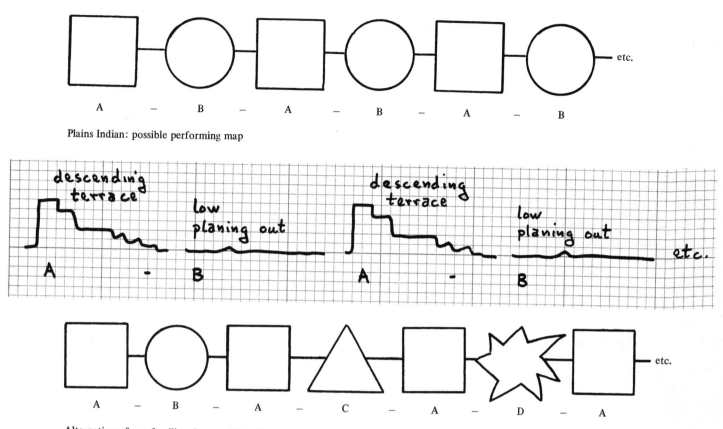

Plains Indian: possible performing map

Alternation of one familiar element (A) with evolving new (B, C, D, etc.)

The last example above with a theme or motto or chorus alternating with contrasting sections is familiar in the West as *rondo* form, and it is also found elsewhere (in India, for example). Both types of alternations are found in the call-and-response and antiphonal formats.

Call-and-Response or Responsorial

Correctly speaking, these are not forms of music but ways of performing: a leader (or chanter) sings (calls) out a phrase, and one or more followers, often in chorus, respond; and on they go in regular alternation until the end of the piece or performance.

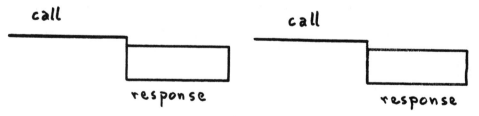

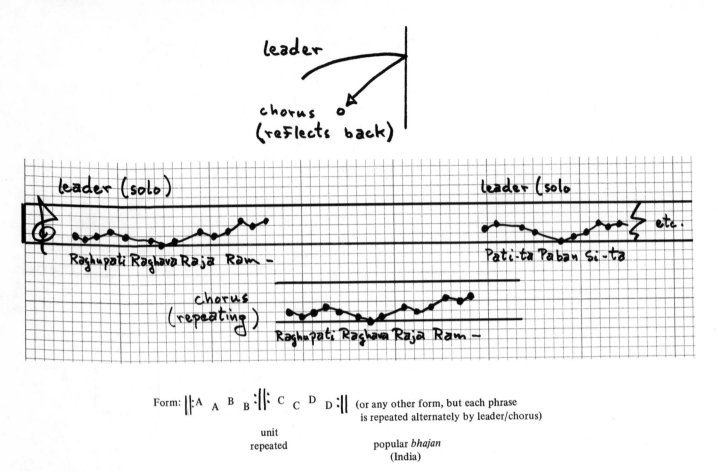

Form: ‖:A A B B :‖: C C D D :‖ (or any other form, but each phrase
                                            is repeated alternately by leader/chorus)

            unit
          repeated   popular *bhajan*
                                              (India)

Musically, a number of things can happen. The chorus (or responder[s]) can reflect back the melody of the leader(s) like a ball bouncing off a wall, in essence repeating it. The melody can have any form, but often it is strophic. This is the form of the religious *bhajana* group singing of hymns in India. A similar technique is the archaic practice of the *lining out* of Christian hymns in the rural Appalachian hills and mountains. A leader (half speaking, half singing) chants out the words of each line (quickly), followed immediately by the extremely slow and stately singing of the line with its melody by the congregation.

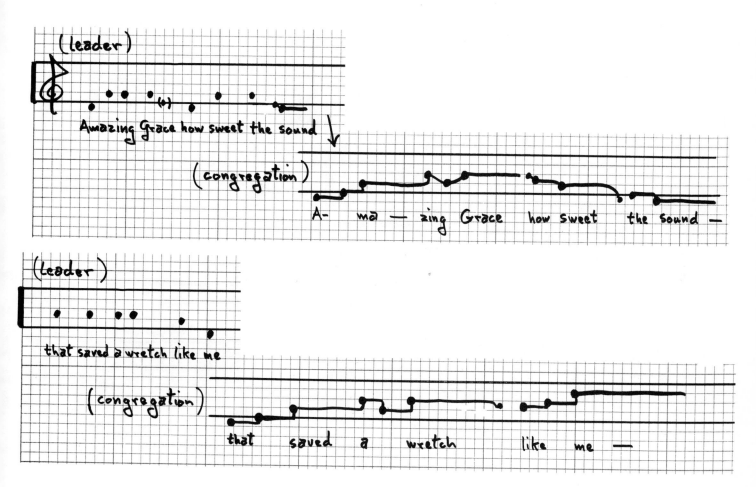

In effect the leader feeds out to the congregation—many of whom, in the old days, at least, could not read—the words of the hymn phrase by phrase.

Call-and-response structure (or performance practice) is one of the major characteristics of the vocal music of sub-Saharan Africa, and it has carried over into Afro-American forms from work songs to spirituals, gospel, soul, and jazz. It is also found, dating from the earliest times, in the liturgical traditions of the Church—deriving possibly from earlier practices in the Middle East. In Africa, besides the reflecting back of the leader's musical ideas by a chorus (imitating, repeating), the leader/chanter may sing his own tune, often improvising new words and melody to the extent of his imagination while the chorus responds in a stock repeated refrain, ostinato, or melodic/harmonic fragment.

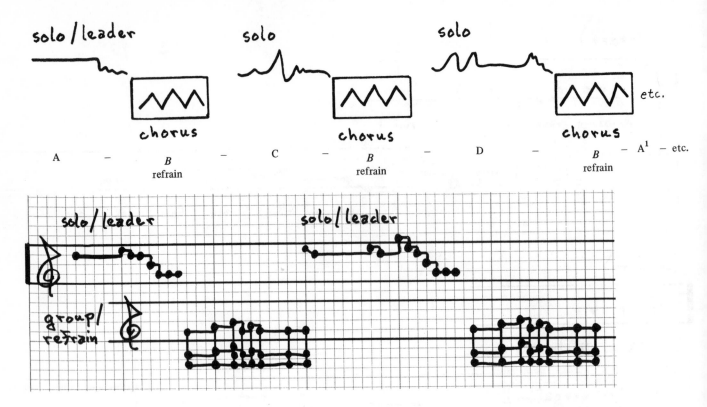

There are numerous possible variants of these patterns, and it is to the credit of the imagination of the music-making people of the world that they have discovered most of them: for example, the leader's part and the choral response may overlap; there may be two refrains which are performed alternately; the chorus may pick up on the last bit of the solo/leader's melody (and then go into their response/refrain); each call-and-response unit may be repeated; or considerable variation may be introduced into the refrain.

The call-and-response format is in fact an extraordinary invention. It balances the unity and togetherness of a group/choral/response/refrain with the individuality and alones and variety (often improvised) of the soloist/caller/chanter/leader. It is ideal for the coordination of group work or action under the eye of a leader or foreman: work gangs on the railroad used to sing in this way, the rhythm of the music guiding the rhythm of their action—hammering or laying in rails; in the days of sailing ships, chanteys with their "heave hos" signaled and coordinated the pulling of the ropes to raise or lower the sails or cargo. I once turned on my television set to hear (with utter surprise) an almost classic work song call-and-response music performance. The singers were white and black, in fact from a mixture of ethnic groups; they were male and American. The location was Arkansas. And the performance itself—basic training for the United States Army with the recruits marching and jogging and responding in song to the incantations (and calls *and* singing) of their drill sergeant!

Antiphony

This is the alternation of (usually) two (but sometimes more) *equal* groups. Whereas call and response implies a special social/musical relationship—a leader/chanter/foreman/drill sergeant/superior performer/priest/soloist/preacher/caller who is no doubt the boss and to whom the group/chorus/choir/ensemble/recruits/workers/chain gang/tribe respond; antiphony is more democratic, like a dialogue between equals. Almost any musical form can be performed antiphonally. One chorus or group may, for example, sing half of an idea or phrase, while the other answers and completes it.

Parallel lines of antiphonal Abhuj Maria dancers represent the groupings of different sonic materials in the musical texture. Madhya Pradesh, India.

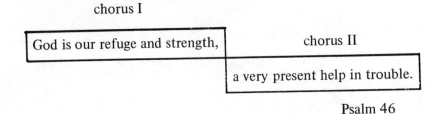

Psalm 46

Antiphonal psalmody, either with the phrases split (as in the above example) or with alternate verses sung in turn by the two choruses, dates from the earliest days of the Christian Church. A similar technique is found in the singing of the Yemenite (Jewish) liturgy: two male choruses sing alternate halves of each verse; the first half-verse, however, is sung by a soloist, and the last verse is sung in unison by everyone.

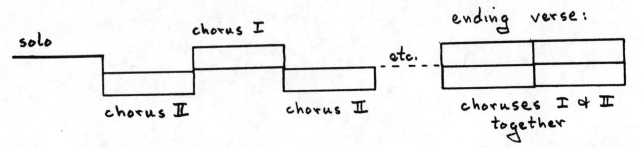

The idea of space is extremely important in antiphony. Many churches and cathedrals place the two choirs on opposite sides of the nave or in opposite balconies, a linear spatial separation that is also found in tribal Asia and Africa where opposing lines of dancers/singers also sing antiphonally in alternation.

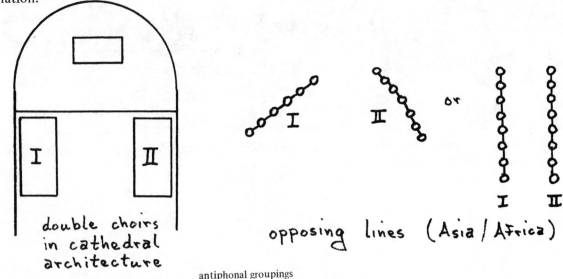

antiphonal groupings

It was in the flourishing civilization of sixteenth-century Venice that antiphonal music reached a peak (at least in the West). Composers such as Giovanni Gabrieli (ca. 1557–1612), who was choirmaster at the Cathedral of Saint Mark, wrote works for two, three, four, and even five choruses intermingled with instruments of diverse timbres, which would answer each other antiphonally, alternate with solo voices, and join together for massive, sonorous climaxes. St. Mark's Square—175 meters long and 82 meters at its widest point—provided an imposing setting for processions and for working with musical space; while in the cathedral itself two separate choirs (*cori spezzati,* or "divided choirs") and two separate pipe organs were placed on opposite sides of the church. Later composers have also used antiphony, particularly in choral works: for example, Heinrich Schuetz (1585–1672), who had studied with Gabrieli in Venice; J. S. Bach in his cantatas and passions; and in the twilight of the romantic era (and its fondness for bigness and grandeur), Gustav Mahler and Arnold Schoenberg.

We should perhaps make the distinction between an antiphonal musical relationship and the antiphony of spatial location. Both (music and space) may happen together—as for example, among the Asura tribals of Bihar state in India where women form two different groups, each with its sonic character (drums for one, cymbals for the other), sing alternating phrases of the music and dance shoulder to shoulder in two separate lines. Or the pure idea of space may be the thing. The American genius Charles Ives conceived (in his *Universe Symphony*) of choirs and instrumental groups of violins and other strings, trumpets, trombones, flutes—everything, in a variety of combinations—placed on the crags and mountaintops and valleys of a (presumably) New England location. Unfortunately he never completed this project, but the idea itself, as a conception, has a certain transcendental beauty about it. In the postwar era of serial writing, electronic music experimentation, and the (then) "international style," composers such as Karlheinz Stockhausen (in his *Gruppen* for three orchestras) wrote for multiple musical forces. The mappings for the placement of musicians in the gigantic orchestras of ancient China seem to indicate at least a feeling for antiphonal space—although we do not really know, of course, how the music was actually performed or what it sounded like. Similarly, today in Japan the multiple performing groups of *kabuki* theater, although they do not make antiphonal music in the strict sense, are spaced ingeniously in different areas of the stage or off to the side.

★★★★★★★★★★★★★★ **DIVERSION 4: SOUTH INDIA** ★★★★★★★★★★★★★★

There are a number of forms used for composed pieces in the classical (karnatic) musical tradition of south India. Each piece is written in a *raga*/mode-mood-expressive complex, and in a *tala*/time cycle. It is important to remember several factors. First, a piece, though composed by one composer at some point in history, is passed along from teacher to pupil aurally (mouth to ear). Thus over the years different ways of performing a piece develop—according to the strands of different traditions—and form and content can vary considerably (though the piece remains recognizable). Second, a performer's attitude toward a composed piece can be highly creative and dynamic; there is a great deal of flexibility in performance; and variations or ornamental touches may be added, or sections may be cut short or condensed. Third, a piece may serve as a framework and point of reference for the performer's improvisations. Finally, a composition in south Indian music is always a song, that is, a melody with words. (Instrumentalists—on flute, *veena,* or violin—in effect play "songs without words.") Everything else in a performance (besides the central core of the melody)—the texture, the melodic accompaniment, and the drumming or other percussion—is improvised according to the rules and procedures of the tradition.

Varnam

The *varnam* is a concert etude. Advanced students work with this form to acquire technique, to become familiar with the "personality" of a *raga* (shown briefly, in a nutshell), and to follow models for improvisation. The *varnam* is also performed as the opening piece at concerts and, in a slightly altered form—with more words and extended variations—as a major selection in the *bharatanatyam* classical dance recital.

The *varnam* has two main *angas* (literally, "limbs"), or sections:
1. *Purvanga*/first section

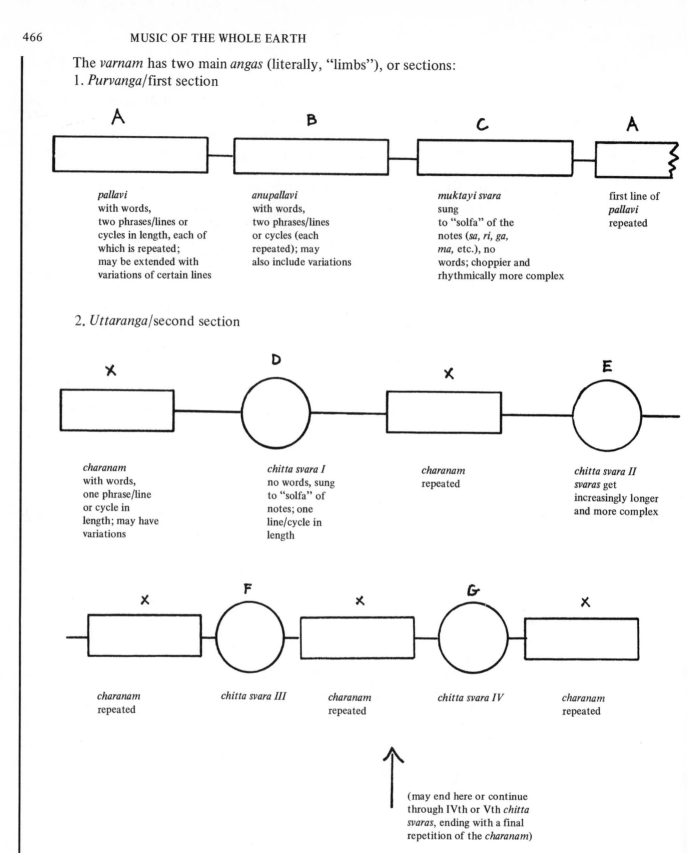

A

pallavi
with words,
two phrases/lines or
cycles in length, each of
which is repeated;
may be extended with
variations of certain lines

B

anupallavi
with words,
two phrases/lines
or cycles (each
repeated); may
also include variations

C

muktayi svara
sung
to "solfa" of the
notes (*sa, ri, ga,
ma,* etc.), no
words; choppier and
rhythmically more complex

A

first line of
pallavi
repeated

2. *Uttaranga*/second section

X

charanam
with words,
one phrase/line
or cycle in
length; may have
variations

D

chitta svara I
no words, sung
to "solfa" of
notes; one
line/cycle in
length

X

charanam
repeated

E

chitta svara II
svaras get
increasingly longer
and more complex

X

charanam
repeated

F

chitta svara III

X

charanam
repeated

G

chitta svara IV

X

charanam
repeated

(may end here or continue
through IVth or Vth *chitta
svaras*, ending with a final
repetition of the *charanam*)

The first section has three more or less equal subsections (A___ B___ C___) with a partial repetition of the opening phrase (A___) to round it out at the end. The second half is a rondolike alternation of a theme (the *charanam*) with increasingly complex contrasting sections (the *svaras*), a format that parallels the procedure for improvising around a central theme.

There are a number of ways of treating a *varnam* in performance. The *purvanga*/first section may be done at a comfortable speed and then—like the shifting of gears in a car—the *uttaranga*/second section may be performed at a faster tempo. Or (hold onto your hats) each section may be subjected to double time (everything twice as fast) or a series of gradually increasing speeds which move and pull against the constancy of the beat and the tempo! For example: All notes in the piece originally sung as equivalent to

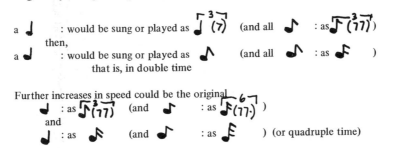

All this while the beat and the tempo keep clunking away with clocklike regularity!

Kriti

The *kriti,* which means "a creation" or "that which is made," is the principal concert form; and (like the sonata form of Western classical music) it is extremely elastic and exists in seemingly infinite variety. The *kriti* in its idealistic form has three *angas*/sections:

1. *pallavi* (literally,   2. *anupallavi* (literally,   3. *charanam* (literally,
   "to blossom")   "after the *pallavi*")   "a foot")

⊢- - -⊣ ⊢- - -⊣   ⊢- - -⊣ ⊢- - -⊣   ⊢- - -⊣ ⊢- - -⊣

|–––| = one cycle, 8 beats, if *kriti* is in *adi tala*

The first two sections (*pallavi* and *anupallavi*) each have two separate phrases—melodic ideas that last for the length of one *tala*/cycle in the longer *talas* (for example, in *adi tala* of eight beats each melodic phrase would be eight beats in length). Each phrase is performed twice. The last section (*charanam*), however, can have any number of phrases.

In addition, there are "decorative" *anga*/sections:

> *chitta svara*: a section with words or without (singers would sing the names of the notes here), choppier, rhythmically more complex, and often full of mathematical cerebral workings; put in after the *anupallavi* (just as in the *varnam* form); and
>
> *sangati*: variations on a single phrase which are usually spun out in groups of increasing complexity. Key phrases in both *pallavi* or *anupallavi* may be chosen for variation.
>
> Both decorative *angas*/sections are often composed by different musicians than the original composer of the *kriti*.

In performance certain sections are repeated, and there is a returning several times to the first phrase of the *pallavi* or its variation. In general, after the third section (*charanam*) there is a recapitulation to some place within the *anupallavi*, giving an A___B___A___ shape to the piece as a whole. A typical *kriti* could be mapped out as follows:

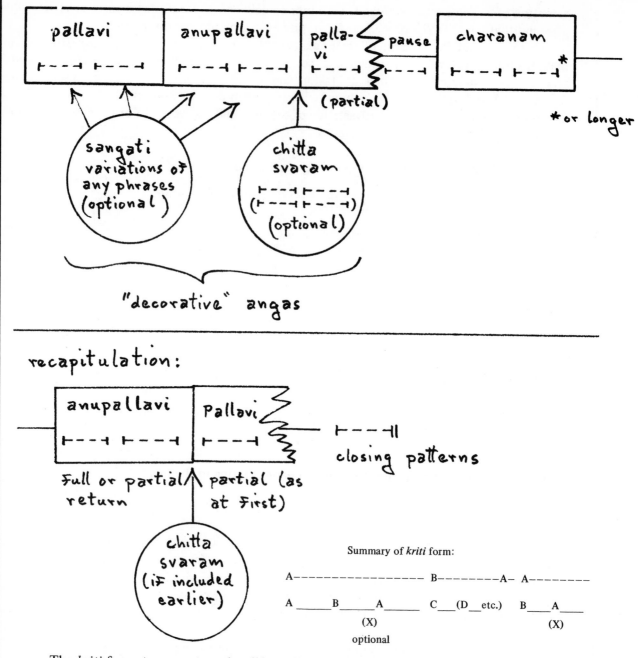

"decorative" angas

recapitulation:

closing patterns

Full or partial
return

partial (as
at first)

chitta
svaram
(if included
earlier)

Summary of *kriti* form:

A—————————————— B———————A— A————————

A_____B_____A_____   C___(D__etc.)   B___A___
    (X)   (X)
optional

The *kriti* format permeates other "forms" of south Indian music, many of which are chiefly distinguished by their tempo or the character of their lyrics rather than by their musical structure. Another common structure, especially for lighter pieces and classical dance compositions like the *tillana* and *svarajati,* is the alternation of a *pallavi* phrase with a string of *charanams* creating a rondolike overall shaping:

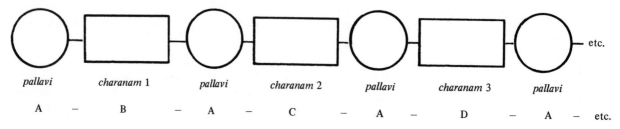

The *kriti* may be performed alone, for its own intrinsic beauty, or it may also be used as a basis, a kind of central pillar, around which elaborate improvisations are spun.

Suites and Larger Forms

Many of the great composers of south Indian music have written songs that fit together in a larger unit such as a group, set, song cycle, or suite. Often the words (always religious in nature) revolve around a particular theme; there may be a relationship also between the *ragas* and *talas* used. Individual *kritis* from these song sets are regularly performed at concerts, but the entire set is usually done only on special festival occasions. The *Pancharatnam* ("five jewels") by the great composer Tyagaraja is the most famous group; it is performed every year at festivals commemorating his *samadhi,* or death/enlightenment. Each of the five *kritis* is in one of the *pancha ghana ragas,* a series of five *ragas* of very strong and auspicious character often improvised upon as a set. Other song sets include the *pancha linga sthala* ("five holy places of the *lingam*" [the *lingam* is a shaped stone symbolizing the god Siva]) *kritis* by Muthuswamy Dikshitar which celebrate five ancient Siva temples, each connected with one of the five elements, fire, earth, water, air, and ether. The *nava graha* ("nine planets") *kritis*, also by Dikshitar, describe the sun, the moon, Mars, Mercury, Jupiter, Venus, Saturn, and the two (invisible) "shadow planets," Rahu and Ketu, and are filled with astrological references.

Another large form is the music drama, or opera: a dramatic performance using classical songs, dance, recitative, narration, pantomime, and (sometimes) dialogue. Usually only the songs are fully composed; for narration and recitative a *raga*/mode is indicated and the stage manager/head singer/narrator (all the same person) improvises the melody as he reads the text. Melattur Venkatarama Sastri, who lived in the eighteenth century, was the greatest composer of operas. He wrote in a form called *bhagavata mela natakam.* In recent years dance dramas have been extremely popular; like the operas, they always have religious/mythological themes. One delightful form is the *kuravanji natakam,* in which at some point a gypsy woman appears to read the heroine's palm and to predict a happy ending to the invariable *affaire de coeur.* There is also a nearly extinct folk opera form, *theru koothu natakam,* or "street drama." Musical-dramatic works in India (we have mentioned only a fraction of the forms and styles) often last all night, although city performances are usually no more than a couple of hours.

Another larger structure in classical music is *harikatha kalakshepam,* a religious/musical discourse by a single performer (and his accompanists on instruments and drums) which combines story-telling, narration, sermonlike commentary, dialogue, sung recitative, and songs. There is no set format, and the skillful performer, called the *bhagavatar,* puts the components together according to the needs of the moment. The songs are drawn from the classical or religious music tradition.

Manodharma Sangita (Improvisation)

South Indian music is divided into two categories: *kalpita sangita,* or composed pieces; and *manodharma sangita,* or improvisation. There are four principal types of improvisation.

1. *Alapana* is the gradual unfolding of the characteristics of a *raga.* It is in free rhythm and may be fairly long (usually fifteen to twenty minutes) or condensed into a nutshell. Tradition tells of great performers who have sung *alapana* for up to eight hours, and one singer ("Todi" Sitaramayya) is said to have sung his favorite *raga*—which gave him his nickname—for eight days running!

   A typical *alapana* begins with the *a'kshiptika,* where the first manifestation of the *raga* takes place, usually in the lower register, with a predominance of longer, slower notes. Important phrases and ornaments in the *raga* are explored in all their subtlety. Then comes the *raga vardhani* section in four stages: there

Yakshagana theater performance. Mythological and social themes are enacted in all-night productions using dialogue, songs, and music. Mysore, India.

is a gradual movement of range from the low to the middle to the highest octave, the artist brings out more unusual phrases (and a bit more of his own creativity), and there is a gradual quickening of intricate movement and virtuoso display, culminating in *brigas*—fast-note phrases and runs that sweep across the full range of the voice or instrument. Then there is a brief concluding passage in the lower register again.

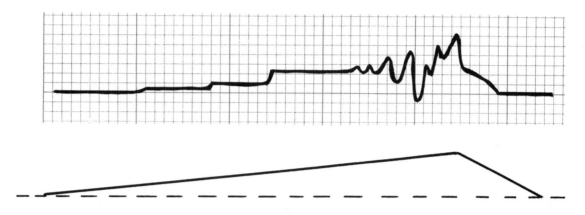

Alapana usually follows the exposition-development-building to a climax-resolution format (familiar to and preferred in the West), but on a much slower time scale.

2. *Tanam* or *madhyamakala* is the working with fast note groups in various permutations. It is highly rhythmic and choppy, full of the uneven sharp accents inherent in groupings of elevens, fives, sevens, thirteens, or other uneven combinations of notes. There is, however, no *tala*. *Tanam* may follow the same gradual buildup (from lower to highest octaves) as *alapana*; or it may—if extended and played in the old style—seem to lack such a progression, giving the impression of directionlessness and an automatic, rigid working around ideas.

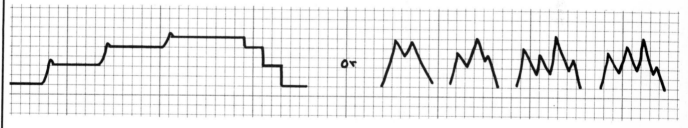

terraced structure   no overall (building) shape

Tanam is frequently played (especially on the seven-stringed *veena* lute) in *raga malika,* that is, a "garland of *ragas*"—usually the five *ragas* that constitute a kind of *raga* set: the *pancha ghana ragas.* Each *raga* is explored in turn. Theoretical books give various names to certain types of *tanam* playing or singing, such as "the peacock," "the elephant," or "the *chakra*/wheel"; and certain great *veena* players of the past are said to have imitated the cries of wild animals, or the roar of thunder, or the torrents of rain falling in the monsoon season.

3. *Niraval,* or "filling up," is an improvised variation of a line or phrase of a *kriti*/composition. The words of the phrases are kept the same, the poetic idea of the text is dwelled upon—almost as if it were put on ice—while the performer

spins out variation after variation (of increasing complexity) on the melody. *Niraval* must fit into the *tala*/time cycles of the piece.

4. *Svara kalpana* ("imagined notes") can be inserted almost anywhere in a *kriti*/composition (often right after performance of *niraval*), or it may be performed after the piece is completely sung through or played. It is in the *tala* of the piece. The *kalpana svara* improvisations (which in vocal music are sung to the "solfa" names of the notes) are woven around the *idam* (literally, "place"), which is a melodic phrase taken from the composition. The improvisations begin as only three or four notes (before returning to the *idam*/theme); but they get progressively longer and more complex. Often highly rational rhythmic formulas (previously thought out and precomposed) are tacked onto the end of freewheeling improvisations. Set to any pitches within the *raga*, these pull polyrhythmically against the beat of the *tala*/time cycle until they resolve on the first note of the *idam*/theme fragment.

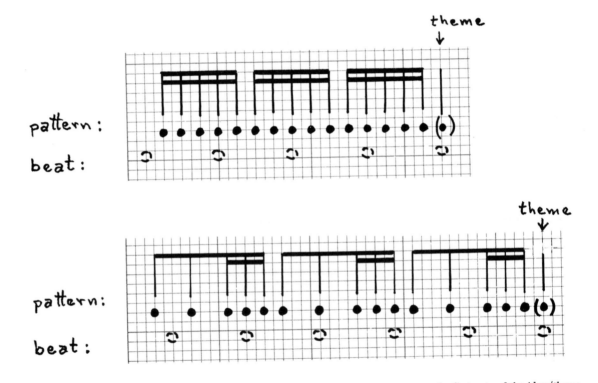

two possible rational ending patterns, and one way they can work against the beat to meet the first note of the *idam*/theme beat to meet the first note of the *idam*/theme

Kalpana svara, after having been increased to improvisations of considerable length, may then undergo a process of shortening, in which a kind of improvised question and answer between soloist and accompanist, two soloists, or soloist and drummer in alternation get closer and closer together until they are alternating on every beat or even half-beat. Everything is then brought to a close with a *mora,* an extended and complex closing pattern, which crowns the improvisations and brings the music back to a final occurrence of the *idam*/theme or the finishing out of the *kriti*/composition.

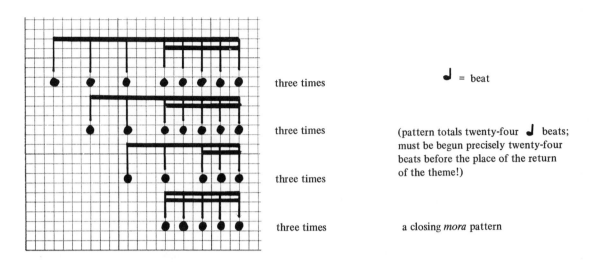

three times

three times

three times

three times

$\textbf{\textit{♩}}$ = beat

(pattern totals twenty-four ♩ beats; must be begun precisely twenty-four beats before the place of the return of the theme!)

a closing *mora* pattern

Not every composition will be wrapped in such elaborate improvisations. A *kriti,* for example, may be performed alone, preceded by an *alapana* only, or preceded by an *alapana* and followed by *kalpana svaras.* But at least several times in a concert a *kriti* will be given full or nearly full treatment. All parts of the improvised performance surrounding a composition are in the *raga* and *tala* of the *kriti*/composition. (There may be a temporary diversion to other *ragas* in the *tanam* section, if it is performed.) The drummer begins playing at the beginning of the *kriti* (and its *tala*/time cycle) and continues to the end. He is silent during the initial *alapana* (and *tanam*) improvisations.

We might map out a typical performance and include a rough imaginary (and subjective) graph of the psychological shapings based on factors like relative melodic and harmonic complexity, tessitura, and the slowness or fastness of the musical happenings:

Performance plan of a *kriti* with improvisations

. . . . . : improvised (but often using precomposed formulas)
_____ : composed

raga (same as in *kriti*)   (may have *raga malika*: other *ragas*)
. . . .   (. . . . .)

alapana _____   *tanam* _____

(accompanist's *alapana*)

(no *tala*/time cycles)

tala ⟶

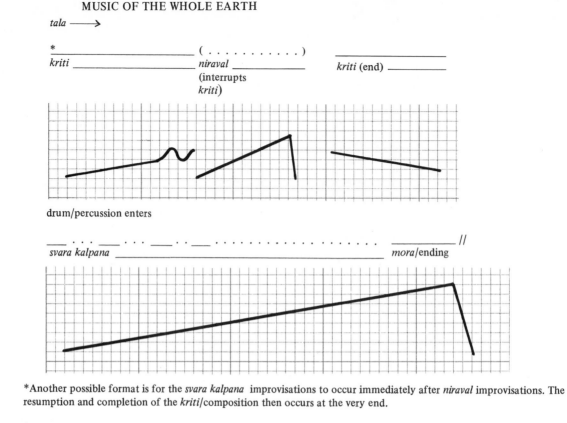

*
kriti _____ (. . . . .)   _____
kriti _____ *niraval* _____   *kriti* (end) _____
                        (interrupts
                        kriti)

drum/percussion enters

___ . . . ___ ___ . . ___ . . _ . . . . _____ //
svara kalpana _____ *mora*/ending

*Another possible format is for the *svara kalpana* improvisations to occur immediately after *niraval* improvisations. The resumption and completion of the *kriti*/composition then occurs at the very end.

*_____ (. . . . .) . . . . _ . . . . . _ . . . . . (etc.) _____ //
kriti   *niraval*   *kalpana svara*   completion
(beginning)   of *kriti*

Ragam, Tanam, Pallavi

Ragam, tanam, pallavi is a complex three-sectioned improvisatory structure, a really heavy-weight form in south Indian music that allows the master musician to display the full range of his virtuosity and creative powers. Though there is a lot of planning in a *pallavi* performance the only really fixed element is a single line of music (the *pallavi* theme), usually coinciding with one full cycle of the *tala,* which is then subjected to variations and permutations before becoming the *idam*/place, the stable and solid rock in an ocean of improvisation, a point of reference to which the artist returns again and again. The blueprint for a *ragam, tanam, pallavi* performance is as follows:

1. *Ragam*: an exposition of the essence of the *raga* in an extended *alapana.* (No *tala* here.)

2. *Tanam*: an exploration of the (same) *raga* in *tanam* rhythmic permutations and virtuosic display.

3. *Pallavi*: set in the principal *raga* and in *tala*; accompanied by drums/percussion.

   a. Enunciation and repetition of the *pallavi* theme three or four times (so that listeners and accompanists become familiar with it).

   b. *Sangati*: variations on the theme.

   c. *Anuloma* and *pratiloma*: *Anuloma* is the permutation of the speed of the theme through progressive mathematical proportions (the underlying *tala* cycle remains the same). Sometimes the theme must be repeated several times (or through several *tala* cycles) before it comes out again on the right beat. *Pratiloma* is the changing of the speeds of the *tala* and its beats moving against the constancy of the original *pallavi* theme.

d. *Tisram*: a shifting of the subdivisions of the beat from multiples of four to multiples of three. Occasionally the beat is also subdivided into fives and sevens.

e. *Niraval*: improvised variations on the theme; the same as in a *kriti*.

f. *Kalpana svara*: improvisation—just as in a *kriti*—using the *pallavi* theme as the *idam*/place of return.

g. *Raga malika*: improvisation (and occasionally the theme also) moving through a series of different *ragas,* finally returning again to the original (and principal) *raga.*

h. *Tala malika*: moving through a "garland" or series of different *tala*/time cycles, finally returning to the original.

The performance usually ends with an elaborate closing pattern formula and a final statement of the *pallavi* theme. Or a solo for the drummer or percussion (*tani avartanam*) may be inserted at this point.

South Indian classical music (and that of the north, which uses related but different forms) represents a beautiful fusion between the fixed, the preexistent, and the creative imagination of the performer riding the edge of time from moment to moment. The preexistent elements are not only compositions and blueprints for procedure, but models and formulas that are absorbed into the very process of improvisation. They are what constitute the musician's ground—his territory, country, sound environment, tradition. Over it (and within it) he must fly.

★★★★★★★★★★★★★★★★★★★★★★★★★★

Continuances and Returns

A piece or performance of music, as we keep emphasizing, is like a journey: it begins somewhere, it moves—through time and across the country of musical ideas and happenings—and at some place it stops. This journey might be progressive, a movement from one place to another, away from the point of origin and ending at a distant spot. Humanly, externally and internally, physically or intellectually, we have all made in our lives at some time or another one-way journeys of this sort. We move from one city to another, to new places and friends and life-styles; or our minds grow and change. History, nature, and time, despite their cycles and recurrences, seem to move inexorably from a past into an evolving and unfolding future. And the real world has (at least at the present) no one like the fictional hero of H. G. Wells who can get into his Time Machine and travel forward or backward at will. Our own physical lives are perhaps the best examples of progressive movement: we are born, we are children, we grow old, and we die; and—despite our denials and temporary delusions, face-lifts, little liver pills, rejuvenation powders, magical Madison Avenue face creams, girdles and retainers, youthful fashions, queen bee's royal jelly, fallen-arch pads, regularity tablets, four-star vacation packages, and myths of magic formulas discovered in (1) Florida, (2) Tibet, (3) southern California, or (4) by the Incas, Rosicrucians, Theosophists, Druids, ancient Egyptians, or Bulgarians—these are facts that we must live with and (ultimately) die with.

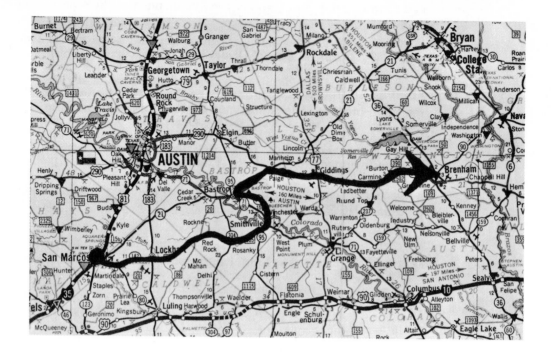

Nonreturning forms in world music come in a variety of shapes and sizes, and with a variety of internal workings. In Europe, east and west, strophic songs and dances are often built from progressive changing phrases:

although the unit as a whole, the verse, may then be repeated ad infinitum. The popular dances of the sixteenth and seventeenth centuries (gavotte, allemande, gigue, etc.) were built on a two-part format, with each half repeating, as were many songs from the classical music of later periods.

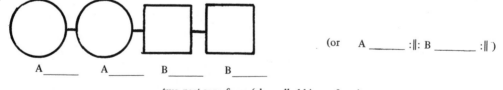

two-part song form (also called binary form)

On a much larger scale the collection of separate pieces and movements in a medley, suite, sonata, or symphony—each (usually) with its different melodies, themes, and characteristics—is a progressive nonreturning format.

★★★★★★★★ EUROPEAN/AMERICAN LARGER PROGRESSING FORMATS ★★★★★★★★

SEVENTEENTH-CENTURY ENGLISH CONCERT DANCE SUITE

1. Allemande: moderately fast; 2/4 time; origin, Germany
2. Courante: moderate; 6/4 time; origin, France
3. Sarabande: slow and stately; 3/2 or 3/4 time; origin, Spain
4. Gigue: fast "jig"; usually 12/8 time; origin, England

PIANO SONATA (THREE MOVEMENTS)

Mozart, K. 332:

1. Allegro: fast; sonata-allegro form: AB–C–AB
2. Adagio: slow; two-part (binary) form: AB
3. Allegro assai: fast; sonata-allegro form

The first movement in a classical piano sonata is usually fast in tempo (allegro) and in sonata-allegro form; the second movement is either slow (adagio, andante, etc.) or a moderately paced dance movement (minuet and trio, rondeau en polonaise, etc.); the final movement is fast again (allegro, allegretto, vivace, presto) and can be in sonata-allegro form, or theme and variations, or rondo.

Exceptions to this format abound. Example: Beethoven's op. 27, no. 2 ("Moonlight Sonata"):

1. Adagio sostenuto: slow
2. Allegretto: medium fast
3. Presto agitato: fast

SYMPHONY (FOUR MOVEMENTS)

Haydn/Mozart

1. Allegro: fast, but with slow introduction; sonata-allegro form
2. Andante or adagio: slow; in ABA or condensed sonata-allegro form
3. Minuet and trio: moderate tempo; *da capo* repeat of the minuet after the trio making an
    ABA format (later composers like Beethoven substituted a faster movement—a scherzo—
    here)
4. Finale: very fast; allegro or presto; and in rondo (ABACADA), sonata-rondo, or sonata-
    allegro form

MEDLEY (A SEQUENCE OF ANY NUMBER OF DIFFERENT TUNES)

Football halftime show played by marching band on the theme "South of the Border":

1. Introductory fanfare
2. Marching to formation: "South of the Border"
3. "Brazil" (samba)
4. "Green Eyes" (rumba)
5. "Tea for Two" (cha-cha-cha)
6. "Tequila" (mambo)
7. "Kiss of Fire" (tango)
8. "Brave Bulls" (paso doble)

Appropriate formations accompany each selection in the medley; for example, a winking eye for "Green Eyes," a teacup for "Tea for Two," and so on. Main selections are separated by fill-ins or drumming while the band changes to a new formation/design on the field.

Other basically progressive (nonreturning) forms in the West can include (but not always) the cantata, oratorio, opera, fantasia, tone poem, and perhaps also the overall performance of a concert (four to six compositions played in sequence with none repeated).

★★★★★★★★★★★★★★★★★★★★★★★★★

In the non-Western world—both in terms of large-scale, overall form and in terms of smaller internal construction (*within* stanzas or other sections)—one-way progressive forms also abound. For example, the careful, slow exposition of *raga* and *maqam* (in India or the Middle East respectively) moves progressively and directionally from beginning to end, though there may be some repetition of motifs and phrases. Extended suites—collections of movements and pieces played in sequence—are found in classical music traditions as diverse as those of Egypt, Turkey, Iran, Thailand, Indonesia, and China. There are also the great religious song cycles, such as those of the Navaho in the American Southwest, which fit a progressive overall scheme, coinciding with the specific parts or times of a ceremony.

The musical journey with returns can happen in a number of ways. First of all, the departures can be like a series of excursions, a leaving and a coming back, or a moving out and around and back to a central pole much like goslings or baby chickens (back in the days when there were farmyards and animals were allowed to run free) moved out to explore the (for them) new world only to return from time to time to the reassurance of their mothers' wings. Or like a delivery van making its rounds, but periodically returning to the central warehouse to fill up on goods.

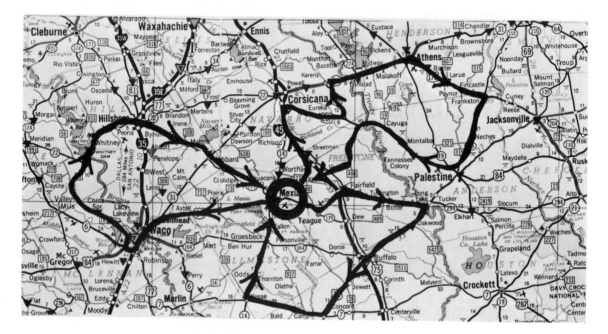

Music using this pattern (such as the *kriti*/composition form of Indian music, or improvisations returning to a central theme) might have formats like this:

$$A\ B\ C\ A\ D\ E\ A\ F\ G\ H\ A \ldots \text{etc. or } A\ B\ C\ D\ B\ E\ F\ B \ldots \text{etc.}$$

$$\text{or}$$

$$A\ B\ A\ C\ B\ A\ D\ C\ B\ A\ E\ D\ C\ B\ A\ F\ E\ D\ C\ B\ A \ldots \text{etc.}$$

(an accumulative song form example: "The Twelve Days of Christmas")

In these cases the return is not such a big thing: the home or base theme or section returned to is commonplace; it is touched again and again as a point of reference; it has the stability and recognizability of the familiar, like the face of a friend in a crowd.

But what we might term the major return is a gargantuan event, like a four-generation reunion or a homecoming from an extended journey. Musically or otherwise it is a time for fireworks and a celebration. The departure and the absence which have preceded it are of greater magnitude—maybe the distance, and the time, and the danger are also relatively greater; and the return, even before it happens, generates excitement and anticipation.

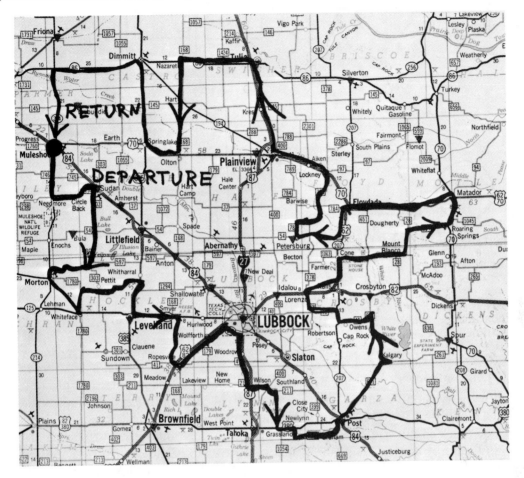

It is important to note the differences between a Real Return and musical references, recurrences, repetitions, alternations, and hints of memory. A Real Return is a (BANG!) Return (it may have firecrackers); but it may also, like March, come in like a lamb. The recapitulations in the *kriti* form of south Indian music, for example, sometimes happen so smoothly, so subtly, and are so brilliantly connected to the previous contrasting section that they seem to appear magically out of nowhere! The European composer Franz Joseph Haydn, a master carpenter of tones and structure if there ever was one, delighted in *false returns*: apparent recapitulations which would then gently disintegrate and lead to new material.

The most straightforward architectural return shape is the statement–contrast–da capo format known in the West as *ternary, ABA,* or *three-part song form*. (*Da capo* means "back to the head," that is, a repetition of or return to the first section.) Innumerable European slow movements in sonatas and symphonies, innumerable operatic arias, and innumerable songs, lieder, and piano pieces are in three-part form. The minuet is a good example.

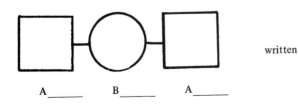

written

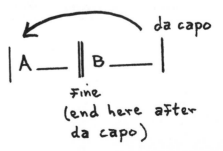

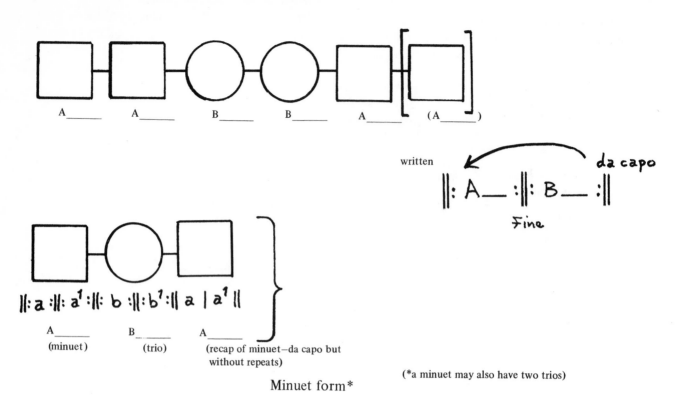

A ___ A ___ B ___ B ___ A ___ [(A ___)]

written

‖: A __ :‖: B __ :‖

da capo

Fine

A ___   B ___   A ___
(minuet)   (trio)   (recap of minuet—da capo but
                             without repeats)

Minuet form*

(*a minuet may also have two trios)

A return can be exact; or it may be abridged or modified. In the Western classical music tradition —at least until the twentieth century—musical returns, called *recapitulations,* were considered to be as essential to musical forms as roasted chestnuts to a cool autumn day in New England. One of my teachers (back in my student days) once played through one of my struggling attempts at composition (a kind of musical soup full of bits of Stravinsky, Schoenberg, Ives, Webern, and Varèse) and remarked incredulously, "What! no recapitulation?!?"—which was something like saying, "What! no pants?!?" to a confirmed nudist who had wandered by accident into a bicentennial meeting of the Daughters of the American Revolution.

Sonata form or *sonata-allegro form* is the structure par excellence of European art music from the classical period (beginning around 1750) through the romantic nineteenth century and into the twentieth. After an optional introduction, there is a first section (or theme or melody group), then a second and contrasting section (or theme or melody group) in a related key, usually the dominant. Then there is a development section with modulation and (sometimes) a working out of the motifs of the previously stated two themes, and, finally, a recapitulation of the original two sections/themes/melody groups and a return to the original tonal center/key. An optional coda can close out the form.

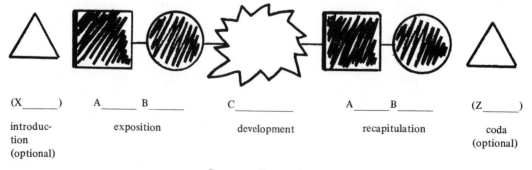

(X ___)   A ___ B ___   C ___   A ___ B ___   (Z ___)

introduc-   exposition   development   recapitulation   coda
tion   (optional)
(optional)

Sonata-allegro form

Our perception of this form—found in the symphonies and sonatas and concertos (where a *cadenza* is added for the soloist) of all the great masters—with emphasis on the importance of the return/recapitulation, however, may be distorted: contemporary performance practice ignores the repeat signs (notated by the composers) that would indicate that the sonata-allegro form might just be an overgrown binary structure. A Haydn or Mozart or Beethoven symphonic first movement—with repeats—might take this shape:

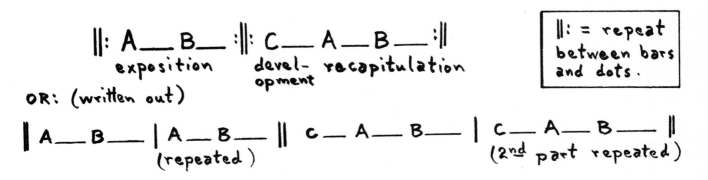

The sonata format is very similar to the structure of phrases in a famous melody for the Japanese *gagaku* orchestra, *Etenraku,* dating from T'ang dynasty China (618–907 A.D.). In this case each section is repeated, and then the entire piece is repeated before ending on the *tomede,* a coda in which the instruments more or less fizzle out.

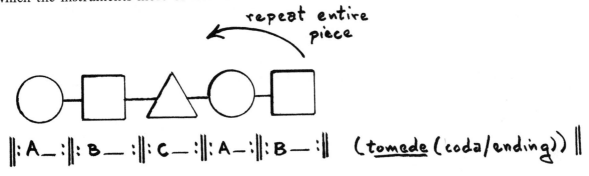

Etenraku piece for Japanese *gagaku* ceremonial court orchestra

THE ORGANIC VINE VERSUS THE STRING OF BOXES

The architecture of music can connect and develop in time and the mind's space in two ways. One way—like our drawings of formal plans—is in terms of *sections*: blocks of musical ideas that happen in a sequence like rooms in a house, each with its little beginning and end, connected by a variety of musical elbows and joints, transitions and passageways.

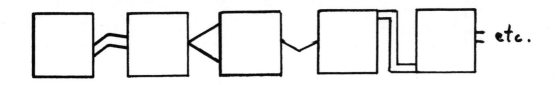

sectional structure

Strophic songs in Africa and in Europe (east and west) with the unit of their verses (and choruses) fit this concept nicely. So does the music of Stravinsky, Mozart, and Haydn. Japanese classical music, especially for *koto* and/or the *sankyoku* ensemble, uses the sectionalization of the *dan*/
"step," and the format for the *gamelan* music of both Java and Bali fits into block units controlled by the cycles of the gigantic gong. Traditional jazz (up until the innovations of the 1960s)
occurs in the boxlike units of solos and choruses, in the same way that an underlying harmonic
sequence (repeated ad lib) forms the framework for music as diverse as the blues (United States)
and the repertoire for the *mbira* (Rhodesia/Africa).

★★★★★★★★★★★★★★★★ DIVERSION 5: TIBET ★★★★★★★★★★★★★★★★

THE STRUCTURE OF TWO RELIGIOUS CHANTS

Performers: chorus of Buddhist monks (chanting), monastery orchestra (double-reed *shawms*
—like large conical oboes—two long trumpets, two conch-shell trumpets, two short horns,
hand bell, hand drum, two pairs of cymbals, and frame drum)

1. *Guru Drakmar Gin-beb Daang-yang* (service chant asking the blessing of Guru Drakmar)

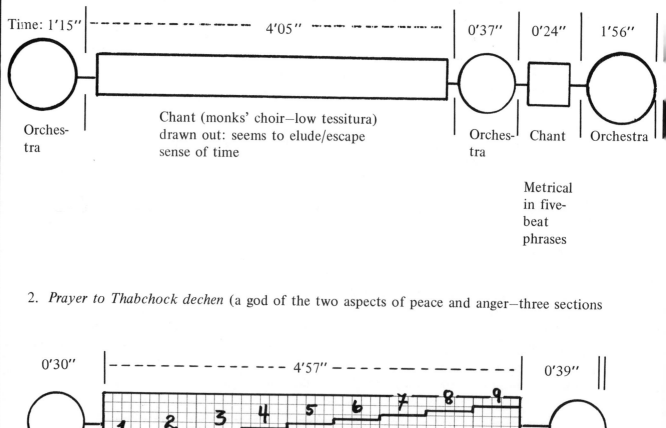

2. *Prayer to Thabchock dechen* (a god of the two aspects of peace and anger—three sections

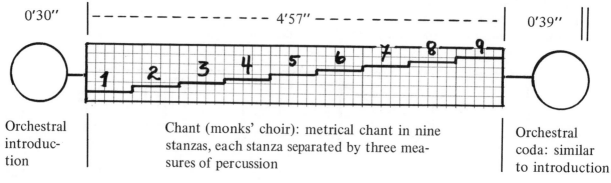

Procession of Tibetan musicians playing trumpets and cymbals at Jumbesi monastery during a spring fertility ceremony. Solu Khumbu, Nepal.

Tibetan long trumpets played before high lamas at Thami monastery, Solu Khumbu, Nepal.

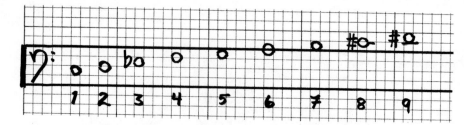

Each stanza of the chant is sung at a successively higher pitch, following this sequence of tones.

Total vocal range of chanting:

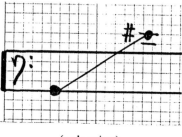

(male voices)

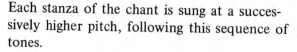

Opposed to the boxlike sectional approach (imagine this: a freight train with boxcars, flat tops, oil cars, coal cars of different colors and markings strung out behind the engine) is the musical architecture of *fluidity*: an organic, continuous, plantlike structure each "part" of which (if there are parts) seems to emerge from the previous, subtly, indistinguishably. The organic approach—besides the analogy to plants in general and vines in particular—might also be compared to water: it flows.

organically connected structure

The exquisite solo repertoire for the Japanese *shakuhachi* bamboo flute, especially the "original pieces" (*honkyoku*) composed by early masters, abounds in organic shapings. *Shakuhachi* music—in form and in sound—has been compared to water, smoke, mist, wind. The *taqsim* based on the *maqam*/mode in Arabic countries, an unmeasured *gusheh* based on the Persian *dastgah*/mode, or an *alap* based on the *raga* concept in Hindustani music also develops organically, one idea leading to the next, without a sharp, boxlike separation between sections (if there are sections). In the West much of the "serious" music of recent years, electronic or otherwise, flows from beginning to end, often through gradual permutations and changes of sound.

A third approach is the building up of continuous levels and the occasional shifting to plateaus. In certain styles of west African drumming, for example, a rhythmic-melodic texture will be set up through the superimposition of many relatively short units. Once set up, it is there—like a pot bubbling and cooking—but apparently unchanging, going around in circles. However, in this rhythmic-melodic texture minute changes do occur; and although the music *seems* to be going nowhere, there is—and this is very important—an accumulation in time. This accumulation, like water building up behind a dam, is both psychological (for both listener and performer) and purely—abstractly—musical; and it is an important factor in the perception of the shape of this music.

small
unit

layer is set up - continuous -
apparently unchanging

but

a psychological/musical accumulation effect
(which may level out after some time)

like water behind
a dam

On the surface an uninformed and unintelligent listener/critic will criticize, say, a performance of African drumming or xylophone playing (or an avant-garde electronic piece in New York, or piping and drumming in rural Turkey) because the music is static, repetitive, nondirectional, and therefore "boring." But this is a basic misunderstanding of the importance of time in what we have called "continuous level" music. You cannot listen to it in chunks and fragments—even though what is happening in a "now" is essentially the same as the "then" of five or ten minutes earlier. Or the "will be" of six minutes hence. *The factor of time* (whether of twenty or forty-five minutes or two or three hours)—*and the accumulation of musical elements in time—is absolutely essential to the musical structure.*

The great expressive power of west and south African drumming grows in part from the blocks of time during which it happens. One might say the same for all-night *wayang kulit* Javanese shadow puppet play accompanied by *gamelan* orchestra, or a three-hour-long Bhutanese Buddhist ceremony of chant with instrumental interludes. Or the avant-garde music of a Steve Reich or Philip Glass. That the time factor is an essential element is notoriously misunderstood by our European and American record companies (there have been a few exceptions in recent years, however): performances of epic singing, drumming and "primitive" music (especially), and other extended forms are chopped up and faded out to two- or three- or four-minute "samples." This practice is doubly unfortunate because most of our knowledge of the ethnic musics of the world, at least in terms of their sound and actual performance, must come from phonograph recordings. In a sense, if we hear three minutes of a three-*hour* performance, we are not hearing it at all! One can imagine visitors from

Itinerant epic singer from Montenegro accompanying himself on the beautifully carved *gusle*/fiddle. He is singing the "Ballad of John Kennedy." Macedonia, Yugoslavia.

another solar system coming to planet earth, settling in Carnegie Hall, and then making "definitive" recordings of the Great Masters of European Civilization first by omitting an essential structural element—like harmony—and then making a sampler: thirty-six seconds of Bach's *St. Matthew Passion,* one minute of Mozart's *Don Giovanni,* two minutes of Wagner's *Ring* cycle, twenty-three and one-half seconds of Beethoven's Ninth Symphony, and three-quarters of a second of Webern's *Five Pieces* for orchestra!

Music that builds up to levels or textures and is then "set"—continues more or less in a predominantly repetitive manner that "accumulates" in time—often works on the principle of plateaus. At a certain point or a signal from a master drummer or leader, the musicians plug into a different texture/level which then continues until the next shift to another plateau.

musical texture—shifting plateaus

Much of the xylophone and drum ensemble music of central Africa might be looked at in this way. And some contemporary music in the West from Stravinsky's *Le Sacre du printemps* (1913) to the recent avant garde also is built on the plateau principle.

SUITES

A *suite* is a number of things constituting a set, series, complement, or sequence. There are, for example, suites of rooms in hotels, or suites of matching furniture for a bedroom or living room. In music a suite is a series of pieces, each complete in itself, which are arranged in a certain order and played in sequence. Western classical music distinguishes between a *movement* (of a symphony, sonata, or concerto) which is "heavier, more ponderous, and more serious," and a *piece in a suite* which is "lighter and incidental"—that is to say, "less prestigious." These distinctions need not apply—outside the West—in our exploration of world music: we shall call any series of pieces combined into a set for performance a suite.

European music has suites of dances, of pieces drawn from incidental music for plays (like Grieg's *Peer Gynt Suite*) or ballets (like Tchaikovsky's *Nutcracker Suite*), of descriptive music, of random collections of pieces, and of pieces conceived as a unit. In American jazz, dance, and cocktail (club) music the selections played in a "set"—that is, one sitting (between which the musicians take a break)—might be considered a suite. In New England fiddling contests the standard set is three pieces: a reel, a waltz, and a jig (all of which have to have been written at least fifty years ago). Indian music, we have seen, has suites of songs (or song cycles) which go together around a certain theme, such as temples dedicated to a certain deity, the planets, the elements, or related *raga*/modes. American Indian music, particularly among the Zuni, Pueblo, Apache, and Navaho of the Southwest, also has song sets, usually connected with ritual observances. In the repertoire of the Chinese *nan-kuan* ensemble chamber music compositions for instruments alone (*ta-p'u*) are arranged in sets (*t'ao*), among them *A Hundred Birds Returning to Their Nests* (in six parts), *Scenery of the Four Seasons* (eight sections), and *Eight Handsome Horses* (eight sections). Suites are also common in both mainland and island southeast Asia, and we might as well explore a few of the musical structures in this area.

★ ★ ★ ★ ★ ★ ★ ★ ★ ★ ★ ★ **DIVERSION 6: THAILAND, JAVA** ★ ★ ★ ★ ★ ★ ★ ★ ★ ★ ★ ★

Thailand

The classical music of Thailand is played by ensembles like the *pi phat* (xylophones, metal-lophones, drums, cymbals, gong, double-reed pipe), the *mahori* (smaller sizes of the melodic percussion instruments plus bamboo flute and plucked and bowed strings), or the *khruang sai* (strings, flute, and rhythmic percussion). The musical workings are built around the central core/strand of a melody in a "horizontal complex"—as scholar David Morton puts it—or heter-ophony. The main melody occurs at the same time variations of itself happen, much like "an idea viewed simultaneously from several viewpoints." Each melodic line is influenced by the character of the instrument that plays it, and although the musical texture may seem at first chaotic to an outsider, the underlying structure is actually very orderly and logical.

The pitches in Thai music tend to be nearly equidistant; there are main pitches (giving a pentatonic effect) and others which may be "nonfunctional" or passing or decorative; there is modulation or *metabole*: a changing to different tonal levels. There are three tempos or speeds, each of which is distinguished by a rhythmic pattern on the *ching* hand cymbals and gong:

slow: *phleng cha* ("slow song"), *prop kai*, or *sam chan*

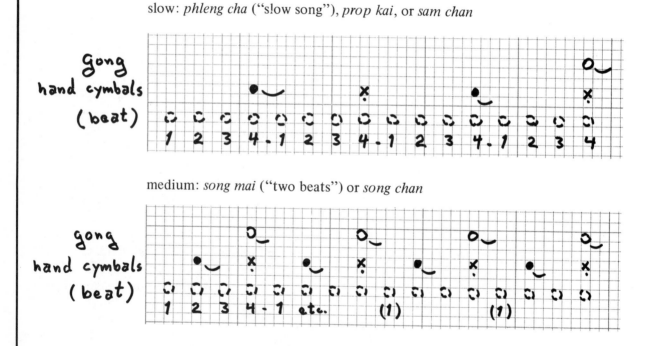

medium: *song mai* ("two beats") or *song chan*

fast: *phleng reo* ("fast song") or *chan dio*

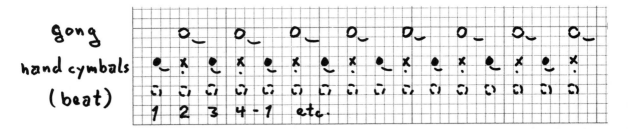

The many melodic layers of the ensemble—some instruments playing in faster and shorter note values—all relate to the basic tempo set by the *ching*/hand cymbal pattern.

1. The *ruang*, or old suite, is a medley of compositions. The ideal set is of three, following the tempo changes of slow-medium-fast and ending with a coda (*la*) which is always the same, regardless of the compositions played before it.

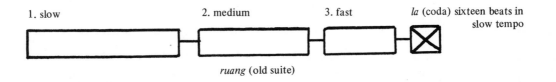

ruang (old suite)

In the old days the *ruang*/suite provided continuous music before a Thai Buddhist ceremony; a performance, lasting several hours, began in the middle of the afternoon, and the final piece ideally would start about the time the monks arrived (between 5 and 6 o'clock). When the monks were seated and ready to start the ceremony with prayers, the orchestra would rush to the ending of the suite and finish with the slow *la*/coda.

2. The *thao*, "a set of something in graduated sizes," is a variation form. The composer selects an existing short piece—usually sixteen measures of 2/4 meter—and puts the *song chan* hand cymbal pattern to it for the "middle version." Then, working according to certain principles, he expands it to twice its original length: the *sam chan*, or "extended version." Finally, he contracts the piece to half its original length: the *chan dio*, or "short version." The three variations are then arranged in this order: extended–middle–short–slow, medium, fast.

In building the extended version the composer keeps important phrases of the original melody and then fills in between them. For the shortened version he cuts out less essential material, that is, he contracts the original.

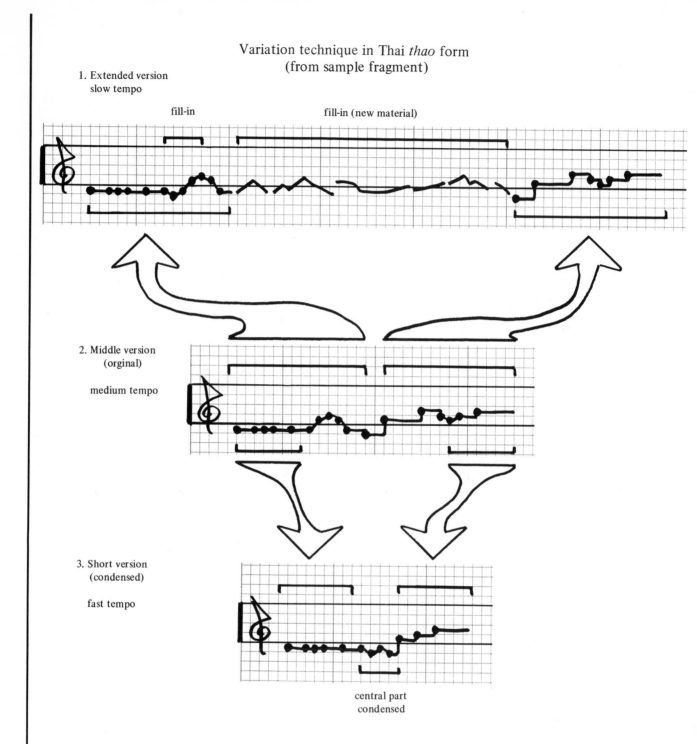

Variation technique in Thai *thao* form
(from sample fragment)

1. Extended version
   slow tempo

fill-in   fill-in (new material)

2. Middle version
   (orginal)

   medium tempo

3. Short version
   (condensed)

   fast tempo

central part
condensed

There is also a virtuoso form of *sam chan* (the "extended version") which is enlarged by inserting developmental passages alternating between xylophone and the gong circle. These sections follow a pattern of decreasing phrase length—such as measures of eight, four, two, one, and one-half—ending on a trill. In the piece *Khlun Krathop Fang* (*The Waves Beat Against the Shore*), written in an extended version based on an earlier composition by King Rama VII in 1931, the decreasing phrase lengths represent first the large swell of the waves dashing against rocks, then undercurrents that blend with the waves above, and finally little wavelets chasing each other to the shore.

Java

The musical structure for the *gamelan* orchestra of Java is based on a number of inter-related factors. The large court *gamelans* used for classical concert music, dance, and the *wayang kulit* shadow puppet plays (we remember) are made up of instruments, mostly idiophones, grouped into functional layers or families, each of which has its role to play in the stratified texture of the music.

1. The *colotomic layer* (various sizes of hung or horizontally racked knobbed gongs) provides a rhythmic scaffolding which repeats under the development of the other musical happenings above it. The end of a cycle (and the beginning of the next) is marked by the massive sound of the large *gong ageng*. These gong cycles—and the number of beats and distribution of subsidiary accents between the strokes of the large gong—are the basic units of the musical structure. A gong cycle may vary from as few as four beats to as many as 64, 128, or 256 beats to a single cycle.

Several gong cycles in Javanese music

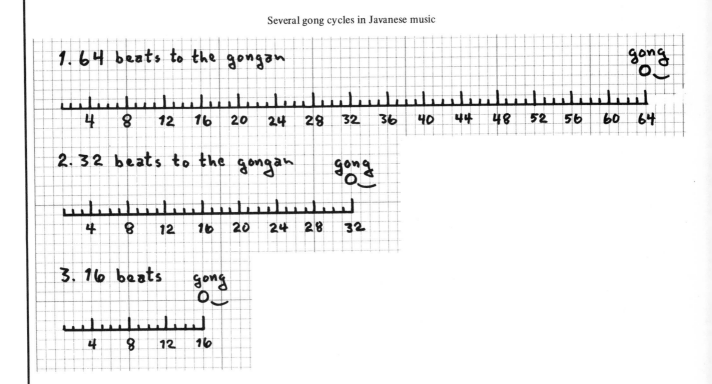

2. The *drum layer*—primarily the playing of the *kendang* by the leader of the ensemble—signals tempo/speed, the dynamics of loudness and softness, and transitions into new sections or movements. Tempo is extremely important in the formal workings of *gamelan* music, and accelerandos or ritardandos as well as a kind of "settling down" to a steady pace mark sections of the performance. Just as in Thai classical music, in slow tempos the elaborating instruments have more space between beats to fill in their lacelike texture of patterns and phrases (not "improvised" in the strict sense, but drawn from a repertoire of possibilities). In faster tempos there is less "space" between beats (and the notes of the skeletal melody) and, consequently, less ornate elaboration.

space between beats for elaborating passagework

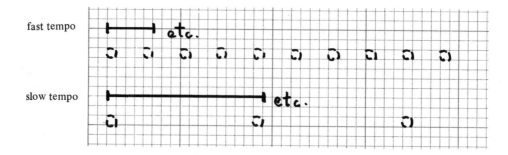

fast tempo

slow tempo

3. The *fixed melody* instruments play the skeletal melody that is the basis for the composition. As pointed out by two scholars-musicians, Sumarsam and Vincent McDermott, one cannot always tell the actual shape of a skeletal melody on a single instrument because the melody often literally "runs off the edge of the instrument"—that is, certain notes or phrases go higher or lower than the range of an instrument (such as the *saron* metallophone), those notes must be transposed back into the range of the instrument.

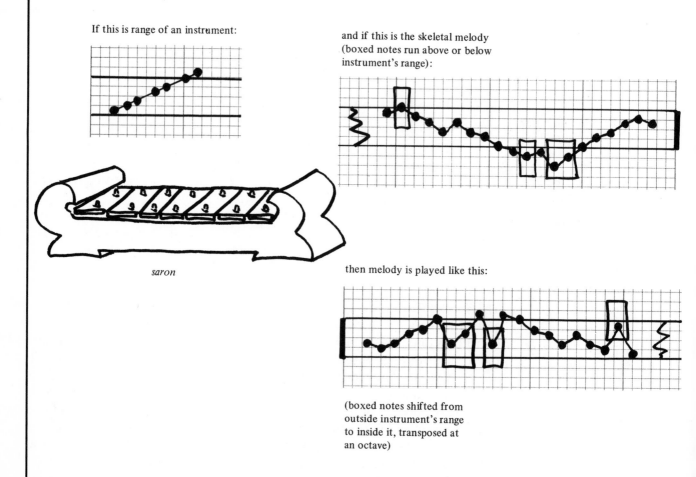

If this is range of an instrument:

saron

and if this is the skeletal melody (boxed notes run above or below instrument's range):

then melody is played like this:

(boxed notes shifted from outside instrument's range to inside it, transposed at an octave)

4. The *elaborating instruments* layer forms a heterophonic ornamentation around the fixed (skeletal) melody. The players choose what they play in a particular situation from hundreds of (memorized) stereotyped patterns; these patterns and the procedures for putting them together are more fixed than improvised. The elaborating is both melodic and harmonic/contrapuntal. The space for passagework depends on the tempo (see 2), and there is a kind of shifting of gears as slower tempos allow a bubbling texture of elaboration (more space) and faster tempos restrict to a simpler, more austere elaboration (fewer notes, less space).

There is a further subdivision into instruments of the "strong-playing ensemble" (*bonangs*—knobbed gong sets—of various sizes) and those of the "soft-playing ensemble" (*gender*/metallophone, *gambang*/xylophone, *tjelempung*/zither, and the *rebab*/fiddle and *suling*/flute).

5. The *vocal tone instruments and voices* relate to the other melodic layers in a variety of ways: improvising, anticipating ornaments or pitches, or following stereotyped patterns or composed melodies. Besides the *suling*/flute and *rebab*/fiddle there are one or more female singers (*pesinden*) and a male chorus (*gerong*).

The word *gending* is the generic term for a musical composition in the Javanese language, but it is also (like the word *sonata* in European usage) used to describe a particular musical form. There are many types and sizes and varieties of *gending* in Javanese classical music; and many of these occur—with specific functions and fairly definite expressive nuances—in the structure of the *wayang kulit*/shadow puppet plays.

Wayang kulit—with the master *dalang*/story-teller/philosopher/poet/singer and his ornate collections of beautiful shadow puppets backed by the full classical *gamelan* orchestra and singers—is, in the words of scholar James R. Brandon, "one of the world's most complex and refined dramatic and theater forms, having developed through an unbroken succession of artists, generation by generation, for more than a thousand years. Its classic dramatic repertoire . . . constitutes the fullest artistic expression we possess of traditional Javanese culture." And it is not only revered, but extremely popular as well. If there were to be an equivalent in the West one would have to imagine an art form combining the symphony orchestra, grand opera, Shakespeare's plays, poetry from John Donne to e. e. cummings, topical comedy, slapstick, and the popularity of a hit movie or baseball—all of this enjoyed by an audience that ran the full spectrum of society from the educated elite and the so-called beautiful people to garbage collectors or migrant workers!

A performance, traditionally lasting all night, is divided into three main sections, each of which is marked by a *patet*/musical mode, a time scheme, certain characters, and a development of the story line. Symbolically, a performance and its sections represent the span of human life from creation (birth) to death and *moksha* (release, enlightenment).

1. *Patet nem*: from 9 P.M. to midnight (creation, infancy), the basic story unfolds, preliminary conflicts between the forces of Good and Evil, with the forces of Evil (*kiwa*, "the left") dominating at the end of the section.
2. *Patet sanga*: from midnight to about 3 A.M. (the growth of a person and adult involvement in life), entrance of the clowns, gradual ascendency of the Good, the virtuosic "flower battle" and other more frequent conflicts; forces balanced at end of section.
3. *Patet manjura*: from 3 A.M. to dawn (the wisdom and maturity of old age, a philosophical readiness for *moksha*/enlightenment), the crucial battles with the forces of Good winning out in the end over those of Evil, resolutions, restoration of the balance of the world.

Shadow puppets dramatize the great epics of Java in *wayang kulit*.

The music for the *wayang kulit*/shadow puppet play—all of it in the five-tone *slendro* tuning—corresponds to the *patet*/mode of each of the three parts of the play. Thus in section 1 only compositions (and improvisations) in *patet nem* are played; in section 2 all melodies are in *patet sanga*; and in the final section everything is in *patet manjura*. The tonal centers for each of these modes is progressively higher, and this general rise in pitch, particularly at the junctions between one part of the play and the next, creates a growing sense of tension and excitement.

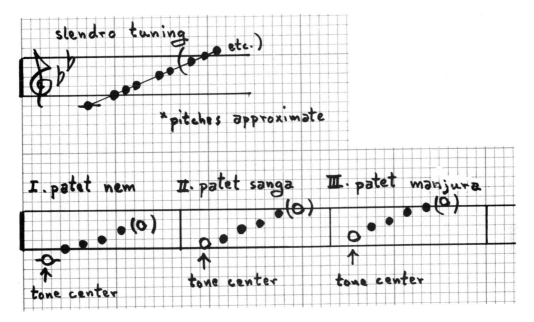

The changes from one mode to the next—after nearly three hours of music in the earlier mode—are among the most beautiful moments in the music of *wayang kulit*.

The internal structuring of the performance is entirely under the control of the *dalang*/ puppeteer who draws upon his experience, creativity, and knowledge of the thousand-year-old tradition. There are *djedjer*, or "major audience scenes," shorter and less weighty scenes (*adegan*), and *perang* ("battle scenes"), all ornamented with description and poetry, dialogue, jokes, songs, or virtuosic movement of the leather shadow puppets. Specific compositions are connected with each type of action or scene, or with locations (the woods, a palace, the sea), or with specific characters or character types. For example, there may be a number of pieces identified as "battle music." Before a certain battle—like the great decisive battle in the last part of the play (*perang amuk-amukan*)—the *dalang*/puppeteer will signal the musicians in the *gamelan* which "battle piece" he wants played by working a pun or allusion or the name of the piece into the dialogue or narration. Then that specific battle music will be played as the puppets battle to the death on the screen. (Incidentally, the English expression *running amuck*— "to rush out recklessly in a murderous frenzy and attack everyone met"—is related linguistically to the crucial *amuk-amukan* battle of the shadow play; both are from a Malay source.)

Besides the compositions with specific connotations of action/scene/location/character there are what might be called "general purpose pieces" which occur many times during the course of a play: *ajak-ajakan* (accompanies entrances and exits), *srepegan* (accompanies faster exits and entrances, and slower, more showy battles in the early and middle parts of the play), *sampak* (accompanies excited exits and entrances in the latter part of the play and the loudest, fastest battles).

A *gending*/composition thus opens every major scene and closes it as the puppets make their exits; it sets moods or signals a change of mood within the scene itself. During the *dalang*'s recited descriptions there is a quiet, semi-improvised (working with set patterns) background, called *sirepan*, played on the gender metallophone with resonators. There are also mood songs of great emotional power sung by the *dalang* himself. Called *suluk*, these mood songs come in three categories:

1. *Patetan*: used for description or where the emotional content is slight. Accompanied by four instruments drawn from the *gamelan* ensemble—*rebab* fiddle, *suling* flute, *gender* metallophone, *gambang* xylophone—and gongs, as well as by the *dalang*'s tapping metal plates (*tjempala*), played, incidentally, with his feet.
2. *Sendon*: used for scenes of great emotion or pathos. Accompanied by the same instruments minus the *rebab* fiddle (which is considered too close in sound to the human voice, and thus distracting in this context).
3. *Ada-ada*: the simplest and fastest of the three forms of *suluk*, used for more violent emotions (anger, exasperation).

The *patalon* or *talu*—an overture played by the *gamelan*—opens every *wayang* performance. Not only is this overture important for setting the mood and the stage, but it has a practical purpose: in the villages and towns in Java people (in the old days before watches or clocks) would hear the gentle sounds of the *gamelan* drifting through the night air, recognize that they announced the beginning of a performance, and then follow the invisible road of sound to the place where the *wayang* performance was being held. In addition, the *patalon*/overture is a kind of sampler of all the forms and structures of compositions used in a play beginning with those having long gong cycles and working down to shorter ones (often the progression is from cycles of sixty-four beats to thirty-two, sixteen, eight, four, and/or less). Like the *wayang* performance in its evening's entirety, the *patalon*/overture in its fixed pieces and set order (lasting about half an hour) symbolizes the life of mankind from birth to *moksha*/release, heaven.

Sequence of Compositions/Forms in One *Patalon*/Overture to *Wayang Kulit* Shadow Puppet Play

1. *Gending* (*tjutjurbawuk*, birth, and *pareanom*, young manhood). A long form often having 64 beats to a gong cycle, but it may have as many as 128 or 256 beats to a cycle. Usually a soft composition. (Analyzed in detail later.)
2. *Ladrang* (*srikaton*, growth of personality). A smaller form, usually of 32 beats to a gong cycle.
3. *Ketawang* (*suksmailang*, preparation to go to heaven, face the soul's departure). An even smaller form: 16 beat cycles to the gong.
4. *Ajak-ajakan* (selection of the good deeds from the bad ones). Irregular phrases. Small gong every four beats. (Used in the play for entrances and exits.) Faster tempo; rhythmically complicated.
5. *Slepegan* (last-minute preparation to go to *moksha*). Fast *kempul* small gong sounds every two beats. (Used in the play for fights, quicker exit/entrances.)
6. *Sampak* (the struggle to face death's agonies, and the soul's leaving the body). *Kempul* gong sounds every beat. Fast. (Used in the play for violent fights.)
7. *Suwuk* (the peace of *moksha* after death). A gradual slowing down to a tranquil, beautiful ending.

(The *dalang* then begins the *wayang kulit* performance.)

Gending form is one of the principal structures in Javanese *gamelan* music. It is the first (and largest) piece in the *patalon*/overture and is also found in concert and dance performances. It has at least two large sections—the *merong* and the *minggah*—and a number of subsections:

Buka: a brief introduction which may be performed by the *rebab* fiddle, voice, *gender* or *bonang* metallophones, or drum, leading up to the first stroke of the large gong, at which point the full *gamelan* ensemble begins playing.

1. *Merong*
   a. *Ompak* (first section)
   b. *Ngelik* ("to go up"): uses higher pitches than the first section. The chorus may sing in this part.
2. *Minggah*
   Can happen in a number of ways: the *minggah* can be a variation or expansion of the melody or theme of the first (*merong*) section; the drum plays different patterns; the elaborating instruments adjust to the new setting and fill in the melody. There can be:
   a. *minggah tjiblon*, which is happy and lively (the name refers—according to Shitalakshmi Prawirohardjo—to "boys and girls frolicking in the water and the act of producing different sounds by splashing water with the hands");
   b. *minggah kendang*, which is "beautiful, solemn, and dignified"; or
   c. *minggah ladrang*, a complete shorter composition (*ladrang*) in the same mode which is assimilated into the piece.
   Any of the above possibilities can constitute the first part of the *minggah* (also called the *ompak*); and there can also then be a *ngelik* or "higher section":
   a. *ompak* (comprised of any of the above)
   b. *ngelik* (higher pitches)
   To lengthen the form, several smaller forms—smaller compositions—(other than a *gending* or, if used previously, a *ladrang*) may be tacked onto the end. These are called:
3. Additional pieces/sections
   a. *kaladjengaken*
   b. *dados*
   Any of the sections can be repeated ad lib at the drummer *gamelan*-leader's discretion. There can also be transitions (alternate endings) which lead from one section to the next. Finally, the *gending* is brought to a close by a *suwuk* cadential ending.

A Typical *Gending* Form

Buka (introduction on the *rebab*/fiddle)

1. *Merong*
   a. *Ompak*
   b. *Ngelik* (higher version)
   Composition: *gending gambir sawit* in *slendro* scale, *patet sanga*

2. *Minggah*
   a. *Minggah tjiblon*
   b. *Ompak*
   c. *Ngelik* (higher version)
   (*Minggah ladrang*) composition: *ladrang gondjang-gandjing* in same mode

3. Additions
   a. *Kaladjengaken* — Composition: *ajak-ajakan* in same mode
   b. *Dados* — Composition: *slepegan* in same mode.

Suwuk (ending)

★★★★★★★★★★★★★★★★★★★★★★★★★★

Ensemble of musicians from Tunisia playing pipes and drums.

The countries in the Islamic/Arabic/Mediterranean complex are renowned not only for their sweets (for the stomach), but for their classical and popular suites (for the ear). Like Moslem calligraphy with its intricate balances and traceries of intersecting lines, these multimovement sets display a subtlety of design and architecture, as well as internal workings full of relationships and a sense of order. Melodic and modal ideas (from the *maqam* or its equivalent—such as the *makom* in Tadjikstan and Uzbekistan or the *dastgya* of Azerbaijan) are presented, worked with and around, developed, contrasted with other sections, and put through (sometimes) set changes of mood and tempo. Usually instrumental solos and orchestral pieces are interspersed with unison choral songs or solo sung recitations of classical poetry. There may be an introductory solo improvisation (called a *taqsim*) which sets the basic mode, mood, and the melodic phrases which will occur in the pieces in the suite to follow. In north Africa and Egypt all the principal sections are in the same *maqam*/ mode, although there can be modulations (to different modes) within one section for contrast. These subsections, called *khana*, are differentiated (according to William P. Malm) both by "the change of mode and by the particular rhythmic patterns they employ." North African and Egyptian suites may have as many as eight or ten sections.

Besides the suites found in southeast Asia (described in Diversion 6 in this section), dance suites (called *ngodo*) with numerous movements, lasting sometimes several hours, are found in the repertoire for the large xylophone (*timbila*) orchestras of the Chopi people in Mozambique. Extended multimovement sets are also found among other peoples and orchestral traditions in sub-Saharan Africa. The high civilizations of pre-Columbian America might also have had suites: there is a fifteenth-century record that Inca Pachacuti ordered a collection of narrative songs about the deeds of earlier rulers.

Finally, we should note the connection between sets of pieces—suites—and dancing, a worldwide connection that stretches from Asia and central and south Africa to the village musics of eastern Europe, the British Isles, and the ballrooms and Fillmore Auditoriums (east and west) of the United States. Who says that the demands of the foot—or body (for contrast, excitement, amusement, or rest)—cannot determine the architectural shape of music for the ear?

TALES AND SHADOWS

In the year 586 B.C. at the Pythian games at Delphi there was a music festival at which the famous piper Sakadas performed (on his *aulos* double oboe) an instrumental concert piece (*nomos*) describing the great contest between Apollo and the dragon. The five movements, as described by musicologist Curt Sachs, were:

1. a prelude
2. the first onset
3. the contest itself
4. the triumph following Apollo's victory
5. the death of the dragon, with a sharp harmonic when the monster breathed his last breath

The idea, therefore, that music—besides its potency as a magical force, a power, a curative, an abstraction, or simply a thing to be enjoyed in itself—can also paint a picture or tell a story is not a new one. Sakadas's composition, the ancient historians tell us, was a sensation and was remembered and talked about for several hundreds years afterward. And now, twenty-five hundred years later, precisely how or why tones can create visual or mental images is still something of a mystery, although there are a number of scientific and unscientific clues to help us untangle this perceptual knot. First of all, there is *the law of sound-alikes*: similar sounds are identified with each other. This rule-of-thumb was especially evident in the early days (1950s and 1960s) of electronic music and *musique concrète* (music made from electronic manipulation of nonelectronic sounds) when stunned listeners walked (or rather staggered) out of concert halls convinced they had heard *not* the abstract sonic materials intended by the composers, but fire sirens, radio static, belches, explosions, screams, running water, internal combustion engines, and bubbles! If a composer or a musician wants to imitate the actual sound of a galloping horse, a machine gun, a creaking door, or thunder on his instrument or instruments these are fairly simple things to do.

Second, there is what we might call *the law of imaginary alikes*: for example, we tend to think of sound with increasingly faster vibrations as going "up" or "higher," and sound with slower vibrations as being "down" or "lower." Music that "ascends" in this way can thus be made to describe any ascent—a cannon ball, a rocket, a sunrise, a soul on its way to heaven; and similarly, "descending" patterns of music can represent the fall of a missile, a hero, or torrents of rain. Or a "galloping" rhythm—like the theme from Rossini's *William Tell Overture* which several generations of radio listeners in the United States heard as the Lone Ranger riding his dashing horse Silver across the prairies followed by his faithful Indian companion Tonto—can seem to depict galloping horses, even though the similarity in sound is rather opaque. Such connections are partially culturally defined.

Third, there is *the inscrutable law of association*: we tend to associate a certain type of music or a specific piece with the certain thing, situation, or action it is usually associated with. For example, we in the United States with a predictable Pavlovian, instantaneous reaction associate snare drums and a march theme with the military, taps played on the bugle with death or the end of a day, the sound of bagpipes with Ireland or Scotland, a single phrase from Mendelssohn's *Wedding March* with marriage or the thought or marriage, Offenbach's famous *opéra comique* "can-can" with the city of Paris, or the tune of "Jingle Bells" with Christmas and snowflakes. All such associations, of course, are entirely determined by the cultural complex and time and place in which we live.

Fourth, there is the (more ponderous/complicated/intentional/high art) *law of the symbol*. Like words in a language, certain musical sounds or themes or phrases or textures or modes can be assigned specific meanings. The listener must learn (consciously or through absorption) this musical language in the same way that he has learned the meanings and implications of "house," "tree," "I love you," or "Help!" Specific art forms or composers or pieces might each have their own special vocabulary and syntax. The *geza* offstage music in the *kabuki* musical theater tradition of Japan is an excellent example, and it combines all of our somewhat whimsical laws (sound-alikes, imaginary alikes, associations, symbols) into a complex and beautiful sound language that undershadows the progressive action, moods, and scenes of the drama.

The operas and concert music of Schumann, Berlioz, Liszt, Wagner, Richard Strauss, and other romantic era composers in Europe (with musical *leitmotifs* representing specific characters, emotions, concepts) are also a working with a systematic symbolic tonal language, as are the stereotyped patterns of Peking opera, or the classification of *gending*/compositions used at specific places in the performance of Javanese *wayang kulit* shadow puppet plays. The expressive complex surrounding the *maqam*/mode in Arabic countries, the *dastgah*/"apparatus" in Persia, or the *raga*/mode in India (mood, character, time of day or night, season, flavor, power) is a similar systematization.

Finally, there is *the puzzle of the human being*, of his own mind's consciousness and the way it perceives, symbolizes, transfers, puts things together. Recent experiments coupled with the unscientific private investigations of the counterculture of the 1960s in "mind-expanding" and "consciousness-raising" drugs (from LSD to the relatively mild peyote) indicate the possibility that there might be a perceptual threshold where sounds and visual images meet. The exact how, or why, or if of this exciting possibility is not known—it may, in fact, be an illusion (but one that is experienced as real). Whatever the case, it could help explain why musicians and listeners all over the world in widely diverse cultures and spanning at least several thousand years have "seen" images, colors, emotions, and stories in the "pure mathematical abstraction" of musical thought.

The European tradition has a long and checkered history in working with and thinking about extramusical elements. First of all, there is the problem of *mood*. From the times of the ancient Greek concept of musical ethos (emotional power of melodies according to their scale) there has been no doubt that music plugs into human emotions deeply, significantly, profoundly, in some way. But whether without the suggestions of the stage (opera, drama, dance, cinema) or of words (poetry, lyrics) music can express—at least in Western culture—*specific* moods is an open question, and one that is debated, defended, or debunked according to the credo of the times. At the same time there are certain conventions that almost every music student in the West has been exposed to at some time or another. Among them:

Major scales (or major keys): "happy"
Minor scales (or minor keys): "sad"
Consonance: "restful," "peaceful," "placid"
Dissonance: "agitation," "stress"
Tempo: slow (lento, adagio): "mournful," "melancholy"
          fast (allegro, vivace): "joyous," "vivacious"
and so on.

Expression of a mood or the evocation of a situation in a piece of music is certainly one of the major genres of Western music from the Renaissance and the great keyboard works of Elizabethan England to pieces like Debussy's *Afternoon of a Faun* or Charles Ives's *Three Places in New England* of more recent years.

Then there is *tone painting* and *program music*: the integration of realistic sounds (who could forget the "cannons" and the "church bells" of Tchaikovsky's *1812 Overture*) or the actual following of a story line. Entirely in the tradition of the Greek Sakadas, Johann Kuhnau (a German, 1660–1722) wrote a sonata based on the fight between David and Goliath, and I remember as a child listening to my mother play on the piano (at my insistence) a work called *The Charge of the Light Brigade* (a depiction of a tragic episode in the Crimean War). Both Monteverdi (in his operas) and J. S. Bach (in his cantatas) were masters of tone painting and programmatic elements. The descent of Orpheus into hell and darkness in Monteverdi's *L'Orfeo* and the subsequent ascent into the world of the living and light are brilliant examples, as are the various devices found in Bach's Cantata No. 4 (*Christ Lag in Todesbanden*): words like "life," "joyful," or "hallelujah" are expanded with ornamental melismatic passages, while "death" is treated with chromaticism and descending patterns, most notably in a gigantic octave-and-a-half drop at the "dissonant" interval of a tritone in a solo passage for bass voice—a representation of the depths of the grave if there ever was one!

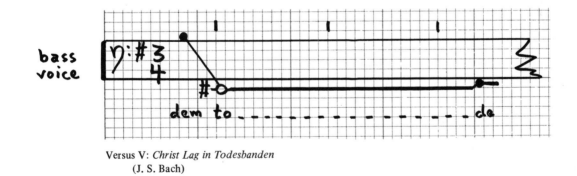

Versus V: *Christ Lag in Todesbanden*
(J. S. Bach)

But it was in the nineteenth century that programmatic elements in music predominated. To the romantic temperament the distinctions between poetry and painting and literature and musically organized sound and life disappeared in a kind of highly charged emotional and expressive never-never land. Hector Berlioz (1803–69), for example, in his *Symphonie fantastique* wrote an elaborate program (in words) which describes "the situation that evokes the particular mood and expressive character of each" movement including an *idée fixe* (obsessive image of the hero's beloved), a "march to the gallows," and references to Goethe's *Faust* and De Quincey's *Confessions of an English Opium Eater*. The *symphonic poems* or "tone poems" of Franz Liszt (1811–86)—most of them written between 1848 and 1858—were even more programmatic in that (as the scholar Donald Jay

Grout has stated) "content and form are suggested in or analogous to some picture, statue, drama, poem, scene, personality, thought, impression, or other object not identifiable by the music alone." Later composers like Richard Strauss (1864–1949) of *Till Eulenspiegel* fame boasted that they could describe specific nonmusical events in music, even "the drawing of a line by a pencil on a piece of paper." Strauss's *Don Quixote* includes representations of the baa-ing of sheep and of episodes like the famous tilting with a windmill.

Programmatic music in the West might be thought of as existing in several types and layers. There is music that follows a precise story line; music attached to generalized emotions or ideas, that is, "philosophized"; music meant to describe a particular scene, that is, to "paint" a picture; and music meant to evoke a mood. In all forms, one must be clued in (by words) to be able to understand the programmatic content. Structurally, nonmusical ideas can be superimposed on purely musical forms (like the sonata, symphony, or rondo), or the literary and pictorial ideas themselves may influence and shape the development of the musical happenings. More often there is a combination of abstract, purely musical structures with the nonmusical. A musical "thunderstorm," for example (of which there are many), may begin with birds singing, shepherds piping, and the calm before the storm, followed by "thunder" (the bass drum), "lightning" ("flashes" in the brass and woodwinds and cymbals), and "torrents of rain" (usually downward sweeping passages in the violins), and then a return to the calm after the storm—in abstract terms a classic ternary or A—B—A format.

While it may be difficult for us, from the perspective of the late twentieth century, to reconstruct the tendency of nineteenth-century romanticists to hear or "see" a story in almost everything musical, or to appreciate the great intellectual battles between those (like Liszt) who thought of music pictorially and those (like Brahms) whose approach was toward abstraction (with purely musical ideas and forms), we are left with a significant repertoire of programmatic pieces. It is probably best to approach them and enjoy them on their own terms.

The traditional musical complex of China is another area of the world where programmatic and mood pieces are of great importance. *The Great Ambuscade*, for example, written by the composer Han Tse around 581 A.D. for the *p'i p'a* moon-shaped lute describes an epic battle between the kingdoms of Chu and Han. The structure of the piece, very definitely influenced by the story line and filled with musical pictographs, sound imitations, and tone painting, falls into eighteen sections:

1. The massing of troops
2. The lineup
3. Drumbeats
4. The signals
5. The artillary barrage
6. Bugle calls to open the gate
7. Calling the generals
8. Taking the battle stations
9. The dispatch
10. The ambush
11. The skirmish
12. The cannonade
13. Shouts
14. The charge
15. The siege
16. The call to retreat
17. The Chu army routed
18. The suicide of the Chu marshal (!)

Other Chinese compositions stress the importance of a background story surrounding its origin and expressive or pictorial purpose. *The Elegant Orchid*, for example, ascribed to Confucius and supposedly written about 550 B.C., has the following story:

Confucius had traveled far and wide in the provinces, but he had been singularly unsuccessful in converting others to the ideas of his philosophy. On the way home he came to a lonely valley where he saw exquisite orchids growing among the more ordinary wildflowers and rough grass. He mused upon the similarity between this scene and his own plight: he (a great scholar, an orchid) was not accepted by princes and other royalty, and he was forced to speak to commoners (wildflowers and grass). He noted the parallels between man and nature, and the harmonies of his composition symbolized the rare fragrance and nobility of orchids.

Other programmatic works touch upon a uniquely Chinese poetic perception of the beauties of nature. The flute composition *Three Variations on the Peach Blossom* attributed to the Chin period scholar Huan I (and later transcribed for *ch'in*) has ten parts:

1. Evening moon over the mountains
2. First variation: calling the moon (the tones penetrate into the wide mist)
3. Second variation: entering the clouds (the tones penetrate into the clouds)
4. The Blue Bird calls the soul
5. Third variation: trying to pass the Heng River (the tones imitate a sigh)
6. Tones of a jade flute
7. Plaques of jade hit by a cool breeze
8. Tones of an iron flute
9. Peach blossoms dancing in the wind
10. Infinite longing

There are also compositions that symbolize a Taoist mystical journey, in which (according to Van Gulik) "the ethereal tones of the *ch'in*" zither played by the scholar-musician "loosen the soul . . . from its earthly bonds and enable him [the player] to travel to the mystic heights where the immortals dwell." *Traveling to the Palace of Wide Coolness*, found in an early Ming handbook, has the following sections (the traveler ascending to the clouds, feasting with the Immortals, and then returning to earth):

1. Treading the cloud ladder
2. Ascending into pure emptiness
3. Feasting in the Pavilion of the Wide (Coolness)
4. Cutting the cinnamon (used in preparing the elixir of immortality)
5. Dancing in rainbow garments
6. Dancing with the Blue Phoenix (in the middle of this section there are several heavy chords, explained by the remark that this is the sound of the Jade Hare pounding the elixir of immortality—according to popular Chinese belief, the hare lives on the moon)
7. Asking for longevity
8. Returning in the cloud chariot (including some high notes which are explained as "the sounds of laughing and talking of the Moon Goddess")

More recent pieces in the very, very long history of Chinese music continue this love of the programmatic, the descriptive, the evocative, and even the unabashedly sentimental. *The Court of the Phoenix*, which features the *sona* oboe accompanied by other instruments, is filled with realistic imitations of bird calls. *Moonlight on the Springtime River* and *Winter Ravens Sporting Over the Water*, folk tunes from the fifteenth and tenth centuries respectively, are evocative by their titles alone although each has a short program to describe it. Today, even the pragmatic revolutionary concepts of Mao Tse-tung and the addition of military march music, Russian-like choral works and epic symphonies, and commemorative pieces have not changed this romantic tendency toward the picturesque, although the acceptable subject matter varies. Recent compositions include *The Red Guards of Hung Lake, The Ming Tombs Reservoir,* and *Gifts for Chairman Mao*!

Programmatic pieces are also found in Japan, Korea, and southeast Asia—and, as in China or in Europe, they may vary from the explicit (like the *shakuhachi* duet describing the calls of two deer in the woods), to mood settings, or symbolism, such as man's life cycle as seen in the structure of the *wayang kulit* shadow puppet play in Java and its *gamelan* instrumental overture. Folk musical traditions the world over also have innumerable pieces shaped by extramusical elements, stories, or descriptions. Harmonica players, for example, in the country and backwoods style of the American South and Appalachians frequently play programmatic "fox hunts" or "coon hunts" complete with the yelping of the dogs, the running of the chase, and the pitiful (and hilarious) squeaks and growls of the cornered animal. Similarly, fiddlers (and harmonica players, too) love to imitate trains with puffs of (musical) steam, a gradual accelerating, the clicking of the wheels against the rails, shrill whistles, and a final squeaking of the brakes. The popular country fiddling warhorse *Orange Blossom Special* by Ervin Rouse, who first recorded it in 1939, is a composed version derived from this tradition.

Word-based musical architecture might also be connected with forms that include actual words (spoken or sung), story lines, action, pantomime, dance, happenings, or events. Here we might categorize songs and song cycles, cantatas, oratorios, ballets, dance performances, opera, musical theater, the theater, cinema, and similar multimedia genres found throughout the world—like Japan's *kabuki* theater or the *wayang kulit* shadow puppet plays of Java and Bali. The words/story/mood quite often influence the structure of the music in these forms in a multitude of ways. Or these influences may be superimposed on the substructure of purely musical (abstract) shaping principles; that is, they may be like ornaments, colors, materials, textures, built over a basic architectural blueprint for a house, adding beauty and a more specific expressiveness (and individuality) to the mundane functional framework underneath.

THE RITUAL WORLD

On this crazy and complicated earth of ours music can be and is shaped by anything. Musician's hands and minds—like working with clay or mud or thatch or brick or wood—mold forms out of abstract musical materials using the methods of their various traditions, innovations, rational processes, or instincts. Or music may be shaped by words (a piece may end when the words are finished), instruments, things, or physical exhaustion or energy, by star charts, by stories or clock time. Music-that-goes-with-something-else can be shaped by that something else. And one of the most common something elses is ritual.

Ritualistic practices, invariably embodying music of some sort, are found all over the world. While it is easy to picture the sonorous chanting accompanying a Tibetan Buddhist ceremony, the drum beating and singing of an Eskimo shaman's journey to unseen worlds, the strong choral songs resonating in the sacred circular space of a Pueblo Indian *kiva*, the drums and drum patterns evoking gods and possession in Haiti or west Africa, or the chanting and polyphonic singing of a Roman Catholic Mass, not all ritual situations are religious. There are, for example, political rituals, such as the terrifying ceremonial gatherings involving millions of participants staged by Goebbels for Hitler in Nazi Germany of the 1930s and 1940s. Or on a less grandiose level there is the comic ritual pomposity of the American political convention. Or parades, and speeches, and celebrations. Or in sports, there is American football with its high priests (superstars) and symbolic vestal virgins (cheerleaders and spangled, baton-twirling majorettes), its ritualized sequence of events—from the toss of the coin to the final gun—all this with musical happenings integrated into the shape of the whole from the initial "Star Spangled Banner" and alma maters to raucous fight songs and the formations and marching display of the halftime show. There is also a strong ritual element in the presentation of outdoor rock and folk festivals, and their resemblance to large religious gatherings and festivals in Africa and Asia is hardly coincidental. It may be merely human.

Music may actually be shaped by ceremonial events, but more often chunks or pieces of music

Navaho men participating in all-night singing during the puberty ceremony *kinaaldá*. Frank Mitchell, main singer, is seated in the west, with his male helpers to his right. Chinle, Arizona.

are fitted into the order or events sequentially—that is, in their given place and time. Norman Hall, a versatile pianist who has studied the phenomenon of "society orchestras" on the east coast, has noted the great care that goes into shaping the musical numbers in a debutante or charity ball. The favorite songs of important guests are researched, the timing of entrance music is planned—sometimes down to the second!—and the band leader (baton in one hand, stopwatch in the other) carefully gauges the tempos and sequence of selections (foxtrot, rumba, and so on) to the progressive moods and responses of his audience as the evening wears on. The age of the party-goers is another factor (most of the "beautiful people" prefer the songs they grew up with, up to when they left college); and special musical requests must also be absorbed—but smoothly—into the planned format.

But it is in religious ceremonials since the most ancient of times that ritual-shaped musical structures have reached their highest and most beautiful expression. In China and Korea there was music for Confucian rituals and throughout the Far East for the Buddhist services. There are ritual musical plays and dance dramas—such as *chhau* in eastern tribal India or the masked "lama dances" of the Himalayas—in which participants represent or are mystically transformed into the gods themselves. Among the Native Americans there are numerous musical rites, such as the great healing ceremonies of the Navaho people, with extended cycles of powerful songs and procedures and sand paintings combined to set the sufferer in harmony with the universe. The tribes of the High Plains have their Sun Dance, and its music, as do the False Face healing societies of the Seneca and Iroquois. The Mass of the Roman (Catholic/Christian) Church is another excellent example.

Mass comes from the Latin of the closing words of the Roman service: *Ite missa est* ("Go, [the congregation] is dismissed"). In the Low Mass the words are spoken by the priest in a low voice, but in the High Mass the service is recited and sung using Gregorian chant or chant plus polyphonic music. Besides those parts that are chanted by the priest alone and those that are sung or carried forward by the choir, there are two further divisions: the words of the *Proprium missae* (Proper of the Mass) change according to the season or to the dates for special feasts (such as saints' days) or commemorations, while the words of the *Ordinarium missae* are nonvariable. The great polyphonic settings of the Mass such as Bach's Mass in B Minor or Beethoven's *Missa Solemnis* are always of the six unchanging sections—Kyrie, Gloria, Credo, Sanctus, Benedictus, Agnus Dei—of the Ordinary. The Mass itself is a mystical commemoration or reenactment of the Last Supper of Christ; the ritual core is the consecration of the bread and the wine (as body and blood of the Deity) and the partaking of these by the priest and faithful. Everything else in the liturgy is a leading up to or a conclusion after these central acts.

The priest—who is the ceremonial practitioner—and the choir relate in a responsorial (call-and-response) way; antiphony in both chanting and more elaborate polyphonic settings (of the Ordinary) sung by the choir split into two groups is also part of the musical tradition of Church performance. There is no improvisation in words or the ordering of elements; there is, however, a choice of music for chants (from collections such as the *Liber Usualis*) or more elaborate choral settings. Formerly there was strict rigidity about the music canonically approved for the Ordinary, but in recent years the Church has opened the way to a variety of indigenous styles and there have been "folk Masses" as well as settings in *ragas* (India) or utilizing African techniques (*Missa Luba* is a famous example).

★★★★★★★★★★★★★ **THE STRUCTURE OF THE MASS** ★★★★★★★★★★★★★

	Musical	Non- or Less Musical
Ordinary	Proper	

Kyrie
Gloria

Introit (verse of a psalm
  with antiphon)

Collects (prayers)
Epistle (for the day read)

Gradual
Alleluia
(Tract replaces Alleluia
  in penitential seasons)

Gospel (for the day read)

Credo

Offertory (here the bread and wine are
  prepared)

Prayers and Preface

Sanctus
Benedictus

Canon (prayer of consecration)

Agnus Dei

Communion

Partaking of the Sacrament

Postcommunion Prayers

Ite missa est or
Benedicamus Domino (dismissal)

★★★★★★★★★★★★★★★★★★★★★★★★★

★★★★★★★★ *KINAALDÁ*: A NAVAHO PUBERTY CEREMONY ★★★★★★★★★★

Long ago in the days before time, fog appeared at the top of a sacred mountain, and in four days it had covered everything down to the base. The mischievous and curious Coyote went to take a look, and there, in a lake near the peak, he found a baby floating in the water. He tried to pick it up but could not. Then he came back and told Hogan God, who also failed.

Then Talking God went and got the baby and brought her down. She was Changing Woman (who might also be White Shell Woman and Turquoise Woman), and in four days she reached puberty and all the Holy People (who traveled on sunbeams, rainbows, and lightning) came to her *kinaaldá* and sang songs for her. The beautiful Changing Woman was impregnated by the Sun and soon gave birth to twin Hero Sons (slayers of monsters and ideals of young manhood). Later she and the other Holy People instructed the Earth People (ancestors of the Navaho) how to live and build hogans and grow corn. And she taught them the sacred lore and the ceremonials and how to keep in harmony with all the forces of the universe.

Today, when a girl reaches her first menstruation, she also celebrates a *kinaaldá*, for happiness, joy, and hope, and in remembrance of the original rite of passage celebrated by Changing Woman and the Holy People.

The Navaho call their life cycle "a walk through time," and for girls (as in many other places in the world) puberty is the crucial passage from childhood into adult womanhood, eventual marriage, and childbearing. The *kinaaldá* ceremony invokes a positive blessing, ensures health and well-being, and protects the girl from potential misfortune. It is also educational. How a girl acts during the ceremony may also be a portent for how she will be, look, and act in the future.

To traditional Navaho people, the world is a dangerous place to live in. A balance of forces and harmony—between the individual and the universe—must be maintained at all times; and to cease to do so might cause bad fortune, illness, or even premature death. Ceremonials help to maintain or restore this harmony. If an individual is mentally or physically sick or troubled, he or she may be treated with one of several curing ceremonies, categorized according to the nature of his problem: Enemyway, Red Antway, Shootingway, Beautyway, Lifeway, Mountaintopway, Evilway, or Moving Upway are several possibilities. Other ceremonials are prophylactic—they prevent trouble before it happens—and "for good hope." These are drawn from the Blessingway ceremonial. Changing Woman is the chief deity, and the *kinaaldá*/puberty rite belongs under this category.

The *kinaaldá* is a typical Navaho ceremony in that it uses songs, prayers, taboos, purification, symbolic observances, and a final night of singing. It does not, however, utilize sand painting or masks. A male ceremonial practitioner or Singer, aided by others in attendance and the family and relatives of the girl, is in charge of the happenings. The actual ceremony is four nights in length (part of five days) with a period afterward of four days during which the girl is to remain "quiet and thoughtful."

The Music

As many as seventy-five (!) songs might be used in a single *kinaaldá*, and they are drawn from the Blessingway ceremonial repertoire. They might be "fixed"—specific songs or sets of songs that occur at specific places in the ceremony—or "free"—songs chosen and sung by anybody during a period on the last night when the leader relinquishes his leadership for several hours. The songs are sung unaccompanied in a style described by Charlotte Johnson Frisbie as "characterized by nasality, vibrato, a tense, rigorous manner, medium to high pitch level which rises during the night, occasional indefiniteness of certain note pitches, a few ornaments, sharp emphasis, and much individual variation." Although there is a lead singer, other singers in the group may not know a song equally well, or they may be singing another version of it. This creates, as David McAllester notes, "the impression of a group of individualists who tune their differences to each other at the moment of singing in a dynamic creative way." One cannot speak of a variant since there is no "original" melody to be varied.

Melodies are restricted in range, and their limited tonal systems emphasize what we call the major triad. There are a variety of contours and movement by both steps and skips, with skips of thirds, fourths, and fifths common.

Navaho *kinaaldá* ceremony: *kinaaldá* girl Marie Shirley blesses the *'alkaan*/ritual corn cake with cornmeal after the batter has been poured into the cornhusk-lined baking pit. Chinle, Arizona.

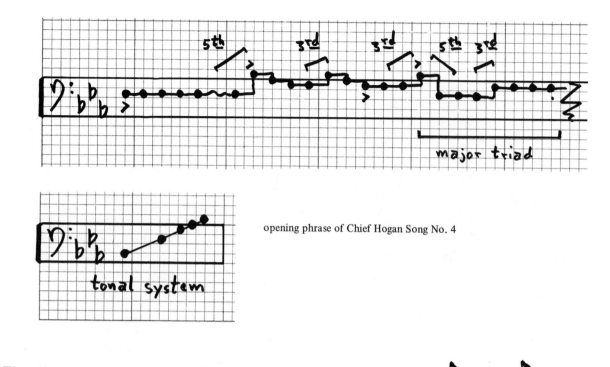

tonal system

opening phrase of Chief Hogan Song No. 4

The phrases are short and repetitive; the tempos are very fast (from M.M. ♪ = 138 to ♪ = 184). The rhythm is mostly in ♩ and ♪ but it is extremely fluid: there is a seemingly unpredictable subtle shift from accented units of two (♫) to those of three (♪♫), and the steady metronomic pulsation is constantly being interrupted by breaks and subtle pauses. There are both closing and opening formulas.

The structures of Navaho ceremonial songs vary, but several may be noted as "typical" (with all the reservations that this word implies). McAllester has mapped out one such form:

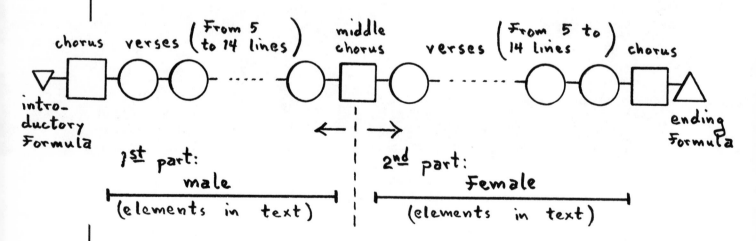

The duality and balance of male and female elements in the text of the song is an important characteristic. Either the sexes alternate with each verse, or (as in our example above) the song as a whole is split into male and female halves.

Each line or verse often ends with musical and verbal material taken from the chorus, which recurs something like a refrain:

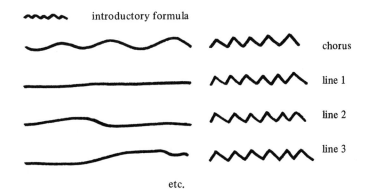

This way of working can also be seen in the texts:

Chíih Song

heye neye yana   (introductory formula)

    The red ocher of old age,   (chorus)
        with the red ocher she nears you,
    The red ocher of old age,
        with the red ocher she nears you,
    The red ocher of old age,
        with the red ocher she nears you   (lines ↓)

Now the child of Changing Woman, with the red ocher she nears you.
In the center of the turquoise house, with the red ocher she nears you.
On the even turquoise floor covering, with the red ocher she nears you.
On the smooth floor covering of jewels, with the red ocher she nears you.
       . . . etc.

Sung language differs greatly from spoken Navaho, which in itself is one of the most complicated languages on earth. For example, Frisbie notes fourteen ways from *yaitinana* to *etiye* and *wotai*—to sing a single word: *'atiin* ("road")! There is extensive use of vocables which one great singer has termed "links" and "stretchers." Far from being mere "nonsense syllables" (a misnomer), vocables have a distinct musical function: they do link and stretch the meaningful words of the text to help them fill out the (primarily syllabic) musical space. Seeming vocables may also be archaic Navaho words whose meanings have long been forgotten, or they may represent the special calls and speech of the gods.

The Ceremony

The structure for a *kinaaldá* in Navaho society is not entirely fixed. There are variations from area to area and from one Singer to the next. At the same time there are certain things that must be done, certain rules that must be followed. This attitude reflects a strong characteristic shown in many aspects of Navaho life (and in music): a beautiful balance between traditional formalism and individual creativity.

The *kinaaldá* charted out here was celebrated for Marie Shirley in Chinle, Arizona, June 19 to 23, 1963. The ceremonial practitioner was Frank Mitchell. The total time for the ceremony was about four and a half days.

A NAVAHO *KINAALDÁ*/PUBERTY CEREMONY

I. First day (begun in the afternoon)

   1. Comb hair of girl   (No music, but in some areas "Combing Songs" or
                                      "Fixing Up Songs" are sung here)

   2. Dress up girl

      Brushing the girl's hair is an act of ritual purification. Her hair is tied up in a pony tail, and she is dressed to resemble Changing Woman. It is believed that dressing in turquoise, silver jewelry, and with belts and sashes will bring wealth, success, and blessings.

   3. Mold girl inside hogan

      In molding, the girl lies down on several blankets and her body is pressed and massaged. It is believed that at the time of *kinaaldá* her body is malleable and that she can be made to have a more shapely figure and posture.

   4. Girl lifts people

      Lifting others—especially children—will help them grow taller, it is believed.

   5. First run   (No music, but in some areas "Racing Songs" are
                                      sung here)

      Racing, that is, a run by the girl, is a very important part of the ceremony. The girl must race three times a day (at daybreak, noon, and sunset). Since the *kinaaldá* was begun in the afternoon she only runs twice on the first day. Each race is to become progressively longer, but the distances are at the girl's discretion. Others may join her to "share in her blessedness." Special shouts accompany the run.
        Racing is thought to increase endurance, fortitude, strength, and bravery. It increases energy and the chances for a long and happy life.

   6. Second run (at sunset)

   7. Corn grinding (by girl, and other women)

      The corn is being ground for a large ritual *'alkaan* cake which will be baked outside in a pit as an offering to the Sun. Grinding helps make the girl industrious; it also passes the time. "Unofficial" Corn Grinding Songs may be sung by the participants.

  (At the end of each day the girl puts her jewelry in a basket and sleeps in a sacred spot within the hogan.)

II. Second day

   1. Dawn run (by the girl)
   (She and others do chores during the day, or visit.)
   2. Corn grinding
   3. Noon run (by the girl)
   4. Corn grinding
   (plus an afternoon nap)
   5. Sunset run (by the girl and others)

  (Sleep, same as first day)

III. Third day
    1. Dawn run
    2. Corn grinding and chores, girl cleans hogan
    3. Noon run
    4. Sunset run (with others)
    5. Sleep

Although the ceremony has begun, the first three days are rather informal. People talk, visit, cook, do chores, and make preparations for the fourth day—*Bijí*, or "Special Day." Up until now there has been no music although in some areas there may be some.

IV. Fourth day: *Bijí* (Special Day)
    1. Dawn run (by the girl and others)
    2. Chop wood; boil water
    3. Digging a pit
        A circular pit about a foot deep and a little less than five feet in diameter is scooped out of the earth to bake the *'alkaan* cake in.
    4. Butcher sheep
    5. Start fire (in pit)
    6. Everyone changes clothes (into their "Sunday best")
    7. Breakfast (mutton and tea)
    8. Boiling water (for the cake)
    9. Noon run (by girl and fourteen others)
        The racing time is longer, lasting now for around forty minutes.
    10. Mixing of the batter for the *'alkaan* cake
        Powder symbolizing mirage and corn pollen (a ritual substance of importance in all Navaho religious practices) are first mixed into the cornmeal. Then the batter is prepared with boiling water, cornmeal, and sugar.
    11. Wood chopped (by men)
    12. Lunch
    13. Many people arrive
        Afternoon activities include further preparation of the *'alkaan* batter, wood chopping, last-minute purchase of essential materials. Cornhusks are torn, soaked, and prepared to serve as a bed for the cake in the pit.
    14. Pouring the batter into the pit
        The fire is removed from the pit, the pit is lined with cornhusks, and the batter—carried in procession from the hogan—is poured into the pit with blessings and prayers. It is covered, and coals are raked over it.
    15. Sunset run (by girl and others)
    16. Supper

V. Fourth night
Musically, this is the most important night of the *kinaaldá*; there will be an all-night sing, and songs will also accompany the next morning's events. Everyone is expected to stay up all night.
    1. Hogan is prepared (for the ceremony)
        A blanket is hung on the door, a place is prepared for the girl, a mound of sand is placed in the center under the smoke hole, a pail of water is brought in.
    2. Goods to be blessed are brought in
        Items—including two ceremonial baskets, buckskin, and pollen pouches—are placed on a blanket.
    3. The ceremonial practitioner and other singers enter

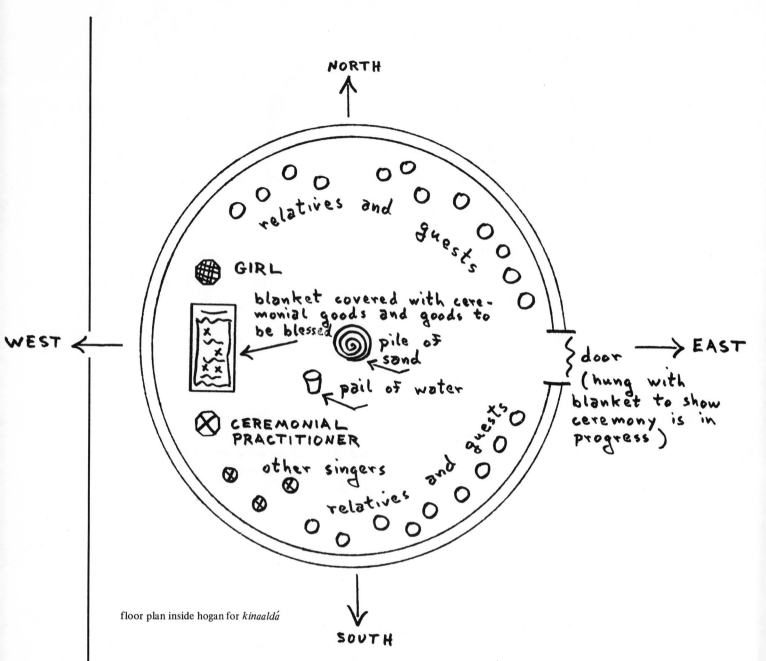

floor plan inside hogan for *kinaaldá*

4. Hogan blessing
   Pollen touched to beams in four directions and scattered.
5. Girl circles fire
6. People bless themselves with pollen

A. Fixed singing
   The singing begins with Hogan Songs. These are believed to be ancient, dating back to the original mythical *kinaaldá* of Changing Woman, Talking God, and the other Holy People. There are two sets, used on different occasions:
   1. Chief Hogan Songs are sung for a girl's first *kinaaldá*, or first menstruation. The words have to do with the building of the original conical-shaped hogan, the

placing of its beams, and its furniture and care. A cycle of fourteen songs (in Frank Mitchell's performance). Three related sets go with the Chief Hogan Songs. These describe the original inhabitants of the earth, the appointing of their chiefs, their garments, and their instructions (wisdom).

  a. 8 songs (4 selected)
  b. 8 songs (4)
  c. 5 songs (3)

In Frank Mitchell's ceremony a total of 11 songs (4, 4, and 3) were selected from the related sets and sung after the Chief Hogan Song cycle:

  14 Chief Hogan Songs
  11 songs from related sets
  ————
  25 songs

 2. Talking God Hogan Songs are sung for the second *kinaaldá*, or menses. Talking God is one of the chief Navaho deities. The 25 songs in the cycle are subdivided in the following way:

  12 Songs of Talking God (the ceremonial hogan, the trail toward it, and so on)
  12 Songs of White Shell Woman's home in the West
   1 "long song" (describing the beautiful house and its surroundings)
  ————
  25 songs

B. Free singing

The second group of songs consists of "free songs" chosen and sung by any of the participants. At this point in the ceremony the ceremonial practitioner relinquishes his control and vocal leadership (although he continues as a kind of master of ceremonies). The songs may be any of those connected with the Blessingway ceremonial complex (of which *kinaaldá* is a part); either song sets or individual songs may be sung. Possible kinds include: Mountain, Horse, Bead, Sheep, Soft Fabrics, Jewels, Journey, Earth, and Corn Songs, Songs Pertaining to Bad Dreams, and the Songs of the Grasshopper, Women, Talking God, Hogan God, and the Water Men.

In one *kinaaldá* the following free songs were sung:

  8 Songs Pertaining to the Pairs
  2 Songs of Old Age
  2 Songs Pertaining to the Pairs
  8 Songs for Administering the Pollen
(food break)

Fixed song: Twelve Word Song

Inserted into the middle of the free singing by the ceremonial practitioner, the Twelve Word Song is believed to bring special blessings and to cancel the effects of previous (ceremonial) mistakes. It is accompanied by the rite of passing of corn pollen.

The title refers to the use of twelve word/images in the text which are alternated with one or more refrains.

The Plan for Frank Mitchell's Twelve Word Song No. 1

Refrain I (sung after first, thrid, fifth, seventh, ninth, eleventh lines):
    (In blessedness, now he has come upon long life,
    In blessedness, now he has come upon everlasting beauty,
    Blessedness is before, blessedness is behind,
    It is blessed, it is said.

    He came upon it, he came upon blessedness.)

Refrain II (sung after alternating lines):
    (*The same as the first, but changing the order of the words "before" and "behind."*)

Lines:

Now he has come upon (1.) Earth	_____ (7.) Talking God
_____ (2.) Sky Darkness	_____ (8.) Hogan God
_____ (3.) Mountain Woman	_____ (9.) White Corn
_____ (4.) Water Woman	_____ (10.) Yellow Corn
_____ (5.) Darkness	_____ (11.) Corn Pollen Boy
_____ (6.) Dawn	_____ (12.) Corn Beetle Girl

Closing verse:
    Blessedness is behind, blessedness is before,
    Blessedness is below, blessedness is above,
    Blessedness is extended all around, as far as the horizons, it is said.

———————————

(Corn pollen passed)

Continuation of the Free Singing
    1 Placing of the Earth Song
    5 Songs of the Picking Up of Changing Woman
    5 Corn Beetle Songs
    1 Horse Song

VI. Fifth day
    When it is decided that dawn has come, the ceremonial practitioner reestablishes his leadership and control of the ceremony and its songs. All the songs to follow are fixed.

A. Fixed Songs
    1. Girl's hair (and jewelry) are washed
        The purification rite is accompanied by Dawn Songs (or Washing Songs). Musically they are faster in tempo. There are four songs to a set, and each song has four verses, one for each of four deities:

        Dawn Boy (the east)
        Sunbeam Girl (the south)
        Evening Twilight Boy (the west)
        Dipper Girl (the north)

    2. Final run (by the girl and others)
        Sung in the fastest of tempos, the four Racing Songs are timed to the aural signals (the special shouts) of those running. The texts, among the most beautiful in Navaho

poetry, deal with the idea of motion (as the girl runs), with her clothes and jewelry, the wind rushing past her body, symbolic colors, dawn, animals, and the singing of birds.

(During the running, *dleesh*/white clay is prepared in one of the ceremonial baskets for painting the girl.)

3. Second Twelve Word Song

   One of the most solemn moments of the ritual, the singing of the second Twelve Word Song—with its special blessing and power—is followed by passing the corn pollen; all bless themselves.

4. Blessing with corn pollen

   Then everyone goes outside where the *'alkaan*, a sweet cake of corn meal, has been cooking all night in its earthen pit lined with cornhusks.

5. Removing and distributing cake

   The *'alkaan* is cut, first from the east, then from the west, and distributed. Later its center is buried in the pit.

6. Meal (fry bread, corn mush, and *'alkaan*)

7. Combing girl's hair

   Two Combing Songs accompany the fixing up of the girl (combing is a ritual act of purification). The texts describe dressing and decorating.

8. Painting of the girl

   The girl is painted with the *dleesh* (white clay) prepared earlier on her soles, knees, chest, back, shoulders, hands, and cheeks. The ceremonial practitioner smears his cheeks and hair with the sacred *dleesh,* and then the others are painted on their cheeks. An upward dab is believed to help children grow tall.

A White Clay Song is sung during the girl's painting.

   This is the last of the music for the ceremony. Approximately seventy to seventy-five songs—in sets or alone—have been sung.

Ordering of Songs in *Kinaaldá* (Final Night)

Fixed songs (led by ceremonial practitioner)
   25 Talking God Hogan Songs   (11:00 P.M.–12:50 A.M.)

Free songs (led by others)
   8 Songs (Pertaining to Pairs)
   2 Songs (of Old Age)   (12:50–2:10 A.M.)
   2 Songs (Pertaining to Pairs)
   8 Songs (for Administering the Pollen)

Fixed song
   1 Twelve Word Song   (2:10–2:14 A.M.)

Free songs
   1 Placing of the Earth Song
   5 Songs (of the Picking Up of Changing Woman)   (2:15–3:34 A.M.)
   5 Corn Beetle Songs
   1 Horse Song

Fixed songs
   4 Dawn (or Washing) Songs   (3:35–3:55 A.M.)
   4 Racing Songs   (3:55–4:35 A.M.)
   1 Twelve Word Song   (4:37–4:45 A.M.)
   2 Combing Songs   (6:40–6:45 A.M.)
   1 White Clay Song   (6:47–6:50 A.M.)

---

9. Final Molding
   Just as on the first day, the girl is pressed and molded as she lies on blankets and
   skins.
10. Girl (representing Changing Woman) returns guests' blankets and other goods
11. Girl returns to hogan
    The public ceremony completed, the girl remains quiet and thoughtful for another
    four days.

★★★★★★★★★★★★★★★★★★★★★★★

THE CONCEPTUAL/THE FLOATING-IN-TIME

In conceptual music an initial idea or group of ideas is the important factor. A process is started, a situation is set up, and then the music happens, goes on from there, in a sense shaping itself—like a leaf that is placed in a stream (the leaf, the stream, the place decided) and watched floating (where and how it flows is up to the leaf, or nature, or circumstance, or chance).

An American composer, La Monte Young, has written a piece stipulating that a butterfly is to be let loose and watched until it flies away (the end of the piece). The inimitable avant-garde Korean composer Nam June Paik has directed in one of his "Danger Musics" (dedicated to Dick Higgins) that the performer climb into the vagina of a (live) whale! Whimsical or not, much of the earth's music might be better understood if it is approached from this angle: that of a concept/situation/process set up and then allowed to work itself out. At a Turkish wedding celebration the musicians—pipers and drummers—may be hired and directed to play all afternoon or night. What they play or how or in what order or shape may not be important. Only the situation—music at a wedding—is. A Hindu ascetic may chant a *mantra* (a phrase or sound of great religious power) 108,000 times. What is important is the *mantra*, its pronunciation and sound, and the number of repetitions. Beyond that the performance shapes itself. A similar approach might be applied to extended west African drumming performances, or even to a rock festival.

The work of Alvin Lucier (b. 1931 in the United States) combines—in different pieces—the mechanics of the latest sophisticated electronic gadgetry with musical instruments, the human voice, the voices of animals (like whales or dolphins), or electronically generated sound. In his *The Queen of the South* he uses the Chladni principle of sound in vibrating media: the vibrations of sound can be made visible through a transference of the vibrations to any responsive material (such as sand, iron filings, or water). The visible patterns can be changed through different sounds or combinations of sounds. The title of Lucier's composition refers to the mystical personality in alchemy also known as *Sapientia Dei*. She is connected with the south wind (in the writings of the Church Fathers an allegory for the Holy Ghost) and the process of sublimation in Arabic alchemy. The complete score is given below.

★★★★★★★★★★★★ **THE QUEEN OF THE SOUTH (1972)** ★★★★★★★★★★★★

For players, responsive surfaces, strewn material and closed-circuit television monitor systems.

Commissioned by and dedicated to Gerald Shapiro and the New Music Ensemble, Providence, Rhode Island.

Sing, speak or play electronic or acoustic musical instruments in such a way as to activate metal plates, drumheads, sheets of glass or any wood, copper, steel, glass, cardboard, earthenware or other responsive surfaces upon which are strewn quartz sand, silver salt, iron filings, lycopodium, granulated sugar, pearled barley or grains of other kinds or other similar materials suitable for making visible the effects of sound.

Surfaces may be excited by making sounds through nearby loudspeakers, directly-coupled audio transducers or directly on or very near the vibrating media themselves.

Alvin Lucier working on his composition *Queen of the South*. Grains of wheat, scattered on a sheet of plexiglass, move into changing patterns caused by sonic vibrations from the speakers under the plexiglass.

As the strewn material responds to the disturbances caused by the musical sounds in the vibrating media, observe, while playing, continuous variations of concentric radial patterns in round surfaces, parallel diagonal patterns in rectangular surfaces, increases in the number of elements with increases in frequency, whole movements or migrations with increases in amplitude, interference phenomena, visible beats and imperfectly formed patterns caused by the peculiarities of both the musical sounds and the vibrating media.

Make musical activity either to discover in real time the visual images characteristic of the identity of the performing ensemble with respect to the time and place of the performance, or make pre-determined patterns including lattices, networks, labyrinths, flows, currents, rotations, bridges, streams, beams, heaps, eddies, dunes, honeycombs, imbrications, cells, textures, turbulences, vortices, layers, figure-eights, lemniscates, spirals, rings, rivulets, trees, branches, pools, dendrites, bushes, balls, pigeon eggs, quadratoids, tetragons, pentagons, hexagons, flowers, hollows, ramparts, figurines, walls, peaks, pillars, columns, volutes, annuli, fissures, plates, rams' horns, crypts, spicules, worms, webs, clouds, storms, spherules, zebras, plumes, embryos, rills, buttes, mesas, grooves, fountains, swastikas, mandalas, crowns, crosses, scapulas, beads, madallions, topologies of near or far environs, plaids, tweeds, road signs, floor plans, tapestries, diamonds, stars of David, gardens, corals, sunbursts, faces, angels' wings, fans, berms, gullies, washes, mosses, daisies, weaves, signs of the zodiac, almonds, clock faces, calendars, moons, planets, mirrors, demons, gems, stigmatas, sanctuaries, playing fields, wheels, whales, palms, ferns, cypresses, blindfolds, ladders, urns, Adams and Eves, cisterns, sepulchres, tongues, dragons, toads, eagles, swans, fishes, dishes, plumes, rooms, tombs, hosts, hats, animal tracks, fossils, footprints, rugs, bones and ghosts.

From time to time, apply fire and ice to the vibrating surfaces to change their temperature environment and thereby alter their characteristics.

Make liquid versions using water, glycerine, mercury, plasma, heated raolin paste or other viscous liquids to bring about hydrodynamic phenomena including frequency-dependent site locations, constant directions of eddy-rotations, amplitude dependent rotation speeds, the creation of Lissajous figures and anti-gravitation effects which occur if sounds remain constant and the vibrating media are tilted or held vertically.

Take sounds from the vibrating media by contact, vibration or air microphones in order to discover and amplify changes in the original sounds due to the physical characteristics of the media through which they travel and for purposes of single or multi-channeled playback during performance or recording on electromagnetic tape.

Use closed-circuit television monitor systems in fixed closeup positions with rear-screen projectors to verticalize and enlarge for the players and audience the visual images made by the players' sounds on the material-strewn surfaces.

All musical considerations including pitch, timbre, lengths of sounds, texture, density, attack, decay and continuity are determined only by the real-time decisions necessary to the image-making processes.

Thanks to E. F. P. Chladni (1756–1827) and Hans Jenny (1904–).

Alvin Lucier
January 19, 1972
Middletown, Connecticut

★★★★★★★★★★★★★★★★★★★★★★★★

THE SOUND OF ONE HAND CLAPPING

One *Zen koan*—a terse aphorism meant to spark a sudden burst of realization, a perception of what life and the universe really are all about—asks the question, "What is the Sound of One Hand Clapping?"

In trying to chart the invisible architecture of music, we, also, have faced a similarly stunning question. (How does one pinch smoke? Or mark moving water? How do you grab time? Or hold sound with the eye or the palm of the hand? Or the mind?) But music is—everywhere on earth, in every culture—put together in some way. Like a house it has its basic raw building materials, its methods of construction, its joints, elbows, connectors, doorways, rooms, endings, and overall plan. And like a cluster of houses in a village or town, music can be combined and built up into larger structures. Somewhere in the background—perceiving, feeling, shaping, working—is the musical human animal. And behind him the shaping forces of the society he lives in, his spot in place, in environment, and in time.

And behind that, ultimately, the universe. The sound of one hand clapping.

---

al Faruqi, Lois Ibsen. "Muwashshah: A Vocal Form in Islamic Culture." *Ethnomusicology*, vol. 19, no. 1 (January 1975).

Berliner, Paul. "The Soul of the Mbira. An Anthology of the Mbira Among the Shona People of Rhodesia." Ph.D. dissertation. Middletown, Connecticut: Wesleyan University, 1974.

_____. *Best of All*. Dayton, Tennessee: R. E. Winsett Music Company, 1951.

Binion, W. T., Jr. *The High School Marching Band*. West Nyack, New York: Parker Publishing Company, 1973.

Blacking, John. *How Musical Is Man*? Seattle: University of Washington Press, 1973.

Brandon, James R. *On Thrones of Gold*. Cambridge, Massachusetts: Harvard University Press, 1970.

Crossley-Holland, Peter, and Smith, Huston. Notes for *The Music of Tibet*, A Musical Anthology of the Orient, vol. 6. New York: Anthology Record and Tape Corporation, 1970. (A phonograph recording with extensive notes—AST 4005)

Deva, B. C. *An Introduction to Indian Music*. New Delhi: Director Publications Division, Ministry of Information and Broadcasting, Government of India, 1973.

Forrest, Wayne. Interview, 1975.

Frisbie, Charlotte Johnson. *Kinaaldá: A Study of a Navaho Girl's Puberty Ceremony*. Middletown, Connecticut: Wesleyan University Press, 1967.

Grout, Donald J. *A History of Western Music*. New York: W. W. Norton, 1973.

Hall, Norman. Talk and personal communication, 1973.

Hane, Mikiso. *Japan: A Historical Survey*. New York: Charles Scribner's Sons, 1972.

Hood, Mantle, and Susilo, Hardja. *Music of the Venerable Dark Cloud*. Los Angeles: Institute of Ethnomusicology, UCLA, 1967.

Johnson, Tom. "Jon Gibson: 36-Tone Logic." Review in *The Village Voice*. New York: The Village Voice, May 26, 1975.

Kluckhorn, Clyde, and Leighton, Dorothea. *The Navaho*. Garden City: Doubleday and Company, 1962. (Doubleday Anchor: American Museum of Natural History)

Kojiro, Yuichiro. *Forms in Japan*. Translated by Kenneth Yasuda, photographs by Yukio Futagawa. Honolulu: East-West Center Press, 1965.

Laubin, Reginald, and Laubin, Gladys. *The Indian Tipi*. Norman, Oklahoma: The University of Oklahoma Press, 1957.

Lucier, Alvin. Personal communication, 1970–75.

Malm, William P. *Japanese Music and Musical Instruments*. Rutland, Vermont: Charles E. Tuttle, 1959.

Malm, William P. *Music Cultures of the Pacific, the Near East, and Asia*. Englewood Cliffs, New Jersey: Prentice-Hall, 1967.

Maruoka, Daiji, and Yoshokoshi, Tatsuo. *Noh*. Osaka: Hoikusha Publication Company, 1970.

McDermott, Vincent, and Sumarsam. "Central Javanese Music: The Patet of Laras Slendro and the Gender Barung." *Ethnomusicology*, vol. 19, no. 2 (May 1975).

McPhee, Colin. *Music in Bali*. New Haven: Yale University Press, 1966.

Merriam, Alan P. "African Music." In William R. Bascom and Melville Herskovits, *Continuity and Change in African Cultures*. Chicago: The University of Chicago Press, 1959. (Phoenix Books)

Merriam, Alan P. *Ethnomusicology of the Flathead Indians*. Chicago: Aldine Publishing Company, 1967. (No. 44 in Viking Fund Publications in Anthropology, edited by Sol Tax)

Morton, David. *The Traditional Music of Thailand*. Los Angeles: Institute of Ethnomusicology, UCLA, 1968.

Neihardt, John. *Black Elk Speaks*. Lincoln: University of Nebraska Press, 1961.

Nettl, Bruno. "Aspects of Form in the Instrumental Performance of the Persian Avaz." *Ethnomusicology*, vol. 18, no. 3 (September 1974).

Nettl, Bruno. *Folk and Traditional Music of the Western Continents*. Englewood Cliffs, New Jersey: Prentice-Hall, 1965.

Nketia, J. H. Kwabena. *The Music of Africa*. New York: W. W. Norton, 1974.

Prawirohardjo, Shitalakshmi. "Wajang Kulit Purwa." M.A. thesis. Middletown, Connecticut: Wesleyan University, 1972.

Richter, Hans. *Dada: Art and Anti-art*. New York: McGraw-Hill Book Company, n.d.

Rothenberg, Jerome. *Technicians of the Sacred*. Garden City, New York: Doubleday and Company, 1969.

Rudolfsky, Bernard. *Architecture Without Architects*. Garden City, New York: Doubleday and Company, 1964.

Sachs, Curt. *The Rise of Music in the Ancient World East and West*. New York: W. W. Norton, 1943.

Sachs, Curt. *The Wellsprings of Music*. New York: McGraw-Hill Book Company, 1965.

Sambamoorthy, P. *South Indian Music*, Books III and IV. Madras: Indian Music Publishing Company, 1964.

Sanger, Penelope, and Sorrell, Niel. "Music in Umeda Village, New Guinea." *Ethnomusicology*, vol. 19, no. 1 (January 1975).

Sharp, Cecil J. *English Folksongs from the Southern Appalachians*. London: Oxford University Press, 1932.

———. *Shelter*. Bolinas, California: Shelter Publications, 1973. (Distributed by Random House)

Singer, Alice. "The Metrical Structure of Macedonian Dance." *Ethnomusicology*, vol. 18, no. 3 (September 1974).

Singer, Milton. "The Great Tradition of Hinduism in the City of Madras." In Leslie, Charles, ed., *Anthropology of Folk Religion*. New York: Random House, 1960.

Slobin, Mark. Unpublished paper, 1973.

Tsuge, Gen'ichi. Classroom lectures and conversations, Wesleyan University, 1971–74.

Williams, Christopher. *Craftsmen of Necessity*. New York: Random House, 1974.

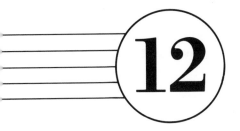

AFTERWARD: PAUSE.
AND BEGIN AGAIN.

Many, many words ago we began a journey, an exploration that took us in our mind's eye and in our ear's thoughts to the far corners of the musical earth. From the beginning it has been an impossible task: a true book on world music would be composed of hundreds of volumes, filling entire sections of libraries, disappearing into time. Even a wall full of recordings could not touch what is or has been, somewhere, here, or there. A complete study of the music of even one tribe or one segment of a musical culture would of necessity be encyclopedic in proportion. Still, we have tried; and we have had to pick and choose and simplify and eliminate in the process. Much of the music of the world has been passed over in this book—this is no reflection on its beauty or value or complexity—but I hope that in the process of examining some of the musical systems and instruments and cultures of the world we have developed at least some of the tools necessary for exploring the rest of them.

Since our journey has been a partial one, reflecting also my own personal interests and available materials, we must realize that our conception, our picture of the earth's music is like the pre-Columbian maps of the earth: flat and with few lands, indistinct in places and perhaps fanciful, full of blank spots, and with monsters and dragons at the extremities. Still, a poor map is better than none at all.

It is easy to forget—reading words, dealing with words describing music, living in a word-dominated culture—that the core of this book is not on the page. As the Little Prince remarked in Saint-Exupéry's wonderful story, "What is essential is invisible." To this we can add, invisible, but not inaudible. For the core of our book is in the music itself. And in the musicians who make it. To really understand the music of the whole earth is to listen to it, and to enjoy it, and perhaps (if one is lucky) to travel to where a particular musical style is practiced and to experience it in its natural environment. It is hoped that you, the reader, can go on to add your own experiences and perceptions to those we have described or outlined.

Finally, we should take note that our book, our explorations of music as a thing in itself—the makings, doings, and workings of it—are really only at a halfway point on our journey. For music is also a thread of the whole cloth, a tiny but beautiful part of the total fabric of life in a particular culture. Ultimately everything may relate, or seem to relate: the way people scratch their noses, or dress or walk, or paint, or create; what they value and what the cherish; how they think, and form,

523

and see; the way they catalog relatives or view history; what work they do or want to or where they live, and how, in what environment and life-style. Religion is a factor, too, and language. And many other things. This complex and amazing web of interlockings (including also lives and livings, our feelings and humanness) might be looked upon as being like a tree with its roots and trunk and limbs and bark and branches flowing through time and the seasons, and with music as one of its flowers. Why should we not enjoy the fragrance of such rare (and variegated) and beautiful flowers? Or at least try?

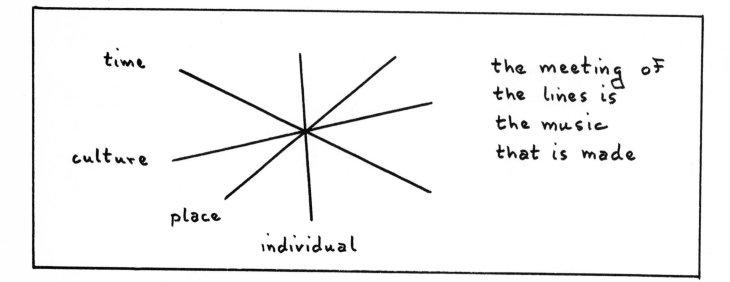

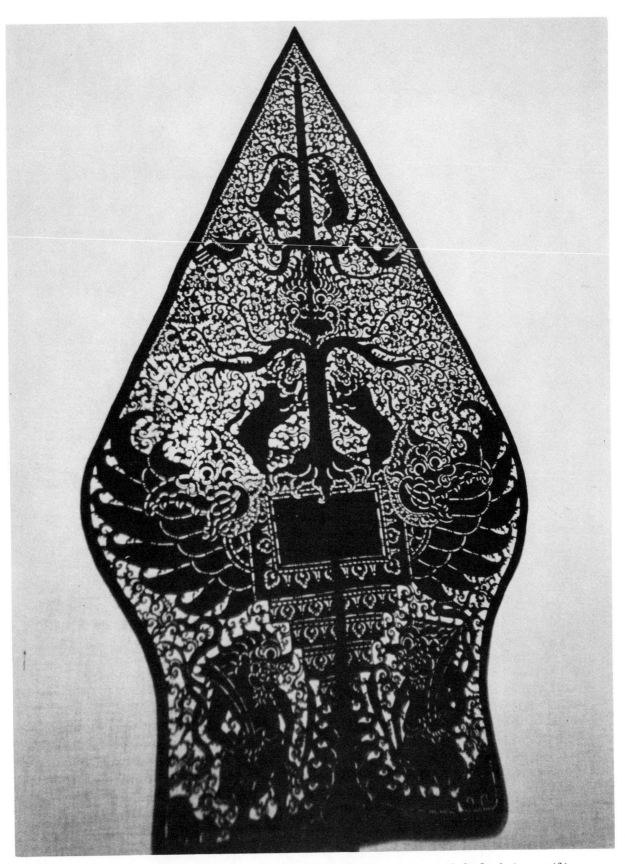

Kayon, Javanese shadow puppet with numerous and important functions in *wayang kulit*. Its design motif is the Tree of Life.

INDEX

INDEX

tion of, 334, 427; heterophonic music of, 319-21; *honkyoku* repertoire of, 433; *insenpō* and *yosenpō* traditional scales in music of, 199, 206-7; instrument design in, 59; introductions and endings in music of, 406, 408, 428-32, 481; *jiuta* or *tegotomono* style in music of, 434-35; *jo-ha-kyu* principle in music of, 249, 428-32, 433, 435, 449; *kabuki* theater of, 183, 224, 233, 261, 366, 374-78, 427, 433, 435-36, 465, 500, 504; *kumiuta* vocal music of, 434; Meiji Restoration in, 36; musical forms of, 456; musical system of, 188, 233; musicians of, xii, 9, 29; myth of origin of music of, 8; *noh* theater of, 84, 171, 205-6, 233, 243, 249, 261, 268, 366, 373-74, 427-32; nuclear tones of *noh* tonal system of, 205-6; *ozatsuma-te* of, 435; poetry and *jo-ha-kyu* of, 249; polyphonic music of, 311; preservation of ancient music forms of, 42; programmatic music of, 504; *ryo*/male and *ritsu*/female scales in music of, 204-5; *sankyoku* ensemble of, 239-40, 268, 319-21, 346-47, 415, 434-36, 482; stereotyped patterns in music of, 406, 408, 427, 428-35; timbre in music of, 259-61, 268; tonal system in music of, 204-7, 246; transposed repetition in music of, 420; Western culture transferred to, 36-37, 41; words and music in, 435

Java, xiii, 4, 64, 94, 136, 143; aerophones of, 112; "automatic" harmony in music of, 295; cadential patterns in music of, 224; choral singing in, 366; drums of, 107, 110; *gamelan* orchestras of, *see gamelan* orchestras; *gending* of, 493, 497; gongs of, 251; idiophones of, 95, 159; Indian influence on, 28; introductions in music of, 405-6; *pelog*/scale of, 213, 215; *slendro*/scale of, 213, 215-16, 495, 497; tonal system in music of, 213-16, 218; tuning system in music of, 194, 213; *wayang kulit* puppet play of, *see wayang kulit* classical shadow puppet play; Western culture in, 37

jazz, 4, 13, 87, 100, 183, 194, 219, 232, 273; beat in, 165; call-and-response format in, 461; chords in, 292, 302, 311, 350; combos, 353-55; harmonic/accompaniment layer in, 351-52; heterophony in, 314; improvisation in, 186, 311, 355, 437; instruments, 61, 311, 352; ostinato and, 285, 286-87; polyphony in, 311; scat singing of, 261; "set" in, 487; structure of, 482; syncopation in, 227; timbre of, 261, 268

jazz bands, 393-94, 395-96, 397
Jefferson, "Blind Lemon," 336
Jewish music, 222, 338-39, 464
jew's-harp, 12-13, 62, 77, 85, 86, 87, 98-100, 107, 121, 332; romantic associations with, 49, 100, 254
jingles, 97-98
joged (Balinese dance), 389
Johnson, Tom, 441

kaba gaidi (Bulgarian bagpipes), 342, 347
kabuki theater. *See* Japan, *kabuki* theater of
kachapi (Javanese zither), 143, 347
kagura-bue (Japanese flutes), 371
kajrak (Uzbek idiophone), 91
kakegoe (Japanese drum calls), 373
kakko (Chinese drum), 371

Kamaiura Indians of Amazon, flutes of, 46
kamanchay (Iranian fiddle), 208, 425
kāmanja (Arabic lute), 131, 134, 141
K'ang-hsi, Emperor of China, 88
kanjira (Indian tambourine), 349
kantele (Finnish zither), 144
kanun (Lebanese zither), 60
Kasai, Basongye people of, 47
kashik (Turkish wooden spoons), 350
kathakali (Indian dance form), 110
kaval (Balkan flute), 71, 111, 332, 356
kaya kum (Korean zither), 128, 143, 259, 313, 332, 439
kazoo, 111, 259
kemanje (African fiddle), 350
kempul (Javanese gongs), 91, 159, 176, 251, 297, 385
kendang (Javanese drum), 491
kenong (Indonesian gong), 176
Kenya: bow harp of, 127, 129; Kamba people of, 46
kerar (Ethiopian lyre), 129
ketipung (Indonesian drum), 384, 386
kettledrums, 49, 74, 102, 103
ketuk (Javanese instrument), 388
khaen (Cambodian mouth organ), 60, 83, 119, 235, 237, 257, 266, 295, 332; chords of, 295; drones and, 281
khalam (Senegalese lute), 132
khil-khuur (Mongolian lute), 57, 134, 136, 334
khlui (Thai flute), 259
khong vong yai (Thai gongs), 107
Kierkegaard, Søren, 415
kihembe ngoma (African drum), 74
kissar (African lyre), 73, 130
kithara (Greek lyre), 9, 74, 129
kiyak (Kirghiz lute), 136
Kniffen, Fred Bowerman, 15-17
kobuz (Kazakh fiddle), 134
kobza (Romanian lute), 133
koma-bue (Japanese and Korean flute), 371
kombu (Indian trumpet), 43
Kojiki (Japanese literary work), 8
konkovka (Slovakian flute), 69-70
kora (African "harp" lute), 137
Koran, 450
Klangfarbenmelodie, 254
komung go (Korean zither), 313
Korea, 28, 30, 100, 111, 259, 370; *aak* orchestras of, 266, 369; aerophones of, 115; *chang go*/hourglass-shaped drum of, 73, 76, 343; chordophones in, 128, 143; heterophonic music of, 311; *hyang-ak* orchestras of, 176, 268, 369; *japka* ballads of, 261; *koma-gaku* instrumentation in music of, 371, 372; musical forms of, 456; *p'ansori* ensemble of, 313, 343; polyphonic music of, 311, programmatic music of, 504; ritual music of, 506; *sanjo*/variation in music of, 439, singing in, 233; *t'ang-ak* orchestras of, 266, 369; transposed repetition in music of, 420
koto (Japanese zither), 13, 57, 59, 77, 143, 144, 206, 319-21, 332, 371; bridge of, 137; construction of, 154-55; *danawase* and *dangaeshi* polyphonic styles for, 311; finger picks for, 139; in *kabuki* theater, 375; range of, 189; in *sankyoku* ensemble, 346-47,